BRICs & THE GLOBAL TRANSFORMATION

Considerations on the BRICs Summit of Think Tanks in Brasilia

Edited by **Li Yang**

社会科学文献出版社
SOCIAL SCIENCES ACADEMIC PRESS (CHINA)

Contents

Innovation and Perspectives of BRICs' Cooperation

Media Reports

Preface

The world economy is entering a post-crisis period after the impact of the global financial crisis. The problem for this period is that the variety of factors which brought about the crisis has not yet been effectively addressed. Among them, there are global imbalances and North-South imbalances. The former is characterized by the imbalance between economies on consumption and savings, while the later by the inequalities between developed and developing countries on resources possession and international voice, as well as the manner and outcome of the international financial system. In addition, as the old problems remain unsolved, some new problems have been created by the anti-crisis measures. As long as these questions are not effectively settled, the global economy could hardly access recovery.

In this context, the financial problems have become the serious consideration in pulling the world economy out of its slump. This crisis is actually the general outbreak of all the contradictions accumulated in the over-development of the financial sectors in the previous period. The so-called over-development is that the financial sector has been out of its starting point of servicing the real economy and accessed into a realm of self-expansion. Instead of being solved at the roots, these problems are temporarily concealed in a harmful way. The lack of financial regulation which is exposed by crisis is still seeking radical solutions. The financial factors that caused this crisis have yet to be eliminated, such as the gradually ineffective monetary policies, the governance crisis of financial institutions, unfair international monetary system and increasing gap between the real economy and financial sectors. In addition, the high debt ratio or excessive leverage is to be effectively controlled.

Therefore, in the post-crisis period, it is required by the overall recovery to seriously address the above problems and make the necessary innovation and reform in financial sectors. For example, the financial regulation should be promoted from the micro-to macro-level in order to prevent relatively radical policies and realize the principles of prudence with a combination of macroeconomic balance and stability. It is a good path to the stable macro economy. However, in a globalized world, it is hard to perform financial innovation and reform without global cooperation and policy coordination; it is similarly difficult to establish an effective, healthy global financial system without the collaboration between nations.

The post-crisis period will be an era in transformation as well. As the major emerging economies, BRICs countries, by throwing influences to the changes of the world structure after the global financial crisis, are attracting more and more attentions. I thus believe that we have large potentials in financial cooperation. We could work closely on the financial supervision and coordinate our positions in the reform of international financial system.

The global financial crisis, which evolved from the U.S. subprime crisis, has shocked the world economy in the once-in-a-century scale and consequence. Despite that the worst part of the financial crisis is behind us, the world economic recovery remains quite slow, and even fragile. BRICs countries confront the common challenges of getting rid of the shadow of the financial crisis and speeding up the process of economic recovery. Based on the actual circumstances, BRICs governments respectively implemented economic stimulus packages, which have proved to be effective, especially in relieving the economic impacts of the crisis to a certain extent. In the past year, Chinese government has taken measures in the following four aspects: first, substantially increasing financial input, including launching a structured tax cut; second, implementing the industrial restructuring and rejuvenation program on a large scale; third, actively encouraging innovation in science and technology; fourth, drastically raising the level of social security. With these measures, China's economy grew by 8.7% in 2009. Being generally optimistic about BRICs countries' economic situation in 2010, the international financial institutions regard them as one of the important factors in steering the world economy out of the crisis. In this regard, broader and deeper post-crisis intra-BRICs cooperation would benefit our own economic resilience and the worldwide recovery. BRICs countries are thus facing a rare historical opportunity for cooperation.

Along with that, BRICs countries also meet with the requirements for expanding and advancing cooperation. The strong complementariness in our endowments and economic structures has formed a sound foundation for collaboration. During the ascending phase of world economic cycle before the crisis, intra-BRICs trade increased rapidly by an average of 73.8% annually, from USD 35.9 billion to USD 168.5 billion between 2003 and 2008, which is over 3 times of the growth of global trade in the corresponding period. Notwithstanding its declining by 15% in 2009 due to the crisis, the trade among our four economies has displayed unique vitality in comparison with that in the world. China replaced U.S. as Brazil's largest trading partner, while Brazil-India trade kept growing. It reveals that BRICs countries, in spite of certain competition resulted from the similar growth stage, are in the occasion to explore potentiality, adjust structure, reduce frictions and create facilitation in our bilateral trade. However, we should recognize that there's still room for trade cooperation left by our uneven developments. I believe that, in the current circumstance, BRICs countries should seize the opportunity to make further coordination in trade policies, so as to improve international trade environment and create conditions for a complete worldwide recovery.

In the post-crisis period, we will also find the essential and irreplaceable impact of FDI on the world economic recovery, which make it an import field to expand intra-BRICs cooperation. As FDI recipients, BRICs countries have been favored by global investors in recent years. In 2008, FDI draw by the four economies reached USD 265.2 billion, increasing its global share from 10% in 2005 to 16%. The financial crisis has changed the direction of international capital, emerging markets and developing countries have surpassed developed countries in FDI inflows. China attracted a total FDI of USD 90 billion in 2009 and became the second largest recipient, while Russia being the fourth one. In its annual *World Investment Prospects Survey 2009-2011*, UNCTAD points out that BRICs countries tends to be FDI's major destination during the crisis. Nevertheless, we notice that intra-BRICs FDI remains limited and is lagging behind other modes for economic and trade cooperation. In this way, larger mutual investment could make more space for deepening intra-BRICs cooperation. To this end, the four nations can make a difference through improving the domestic investment environment, strengthening their attraction efforts for mutual investment, providing the correspondingly appropriate enabling conditions and etc.

The potential of intra-BRICs cooperation lies as well in the science and technology innovation. In financial crisis, the four countries have been seeking a breakthrough for science and technology innovation. In doing so, they tried to find a positive and effective way for industrial upgrading, economic stimulating, and crisis curbing. Chinese government has a basic observation on the long-term economic development and crisis management. That is to develop new technology and newly emerging industries, such as New Energy, key technology for Sensor Network and The Internet of Things, Micro-Electronics and Photoelectrons, Life Sciences and Earth, Marine and Space Sciences. Any of these industries will bring about great effects in its development, and thus become our essential way out in post-crisis period. As a result, Chinese government sped up the process of 16 major national science and technology projects, which were launched in the *National Mid-Term and Long-Term Science and Technology Development Plan (2006–2020)*, while announcing the 4-trillion-yuan (USD 585 billion) stimulus package. Once success has been achieved, any of these cutting-edge projects would create business opportunities.

Meanwhile, the other three BRICs are striving for breakthrough on the basis of their own strengths. For example, the S&T priority is on nanotechnology and nuclear technology in Russia, on clean energy technology as ethanol and biodiesel in Brazil, and on information industry in India. Thus, there is great potential to strengthen intra-BRICs cooperation with each nation exploiting its particular advantages for mutual benefit and development.

Climate change, which is the major challenge facing human society, offers not only a new project for BRICs think-tank, but also another platform for intra-BRICs cooperation. After the Copenhagen Climate Summit, the low-carbon economy has become a hot concept, and even a real industry in some countries. We stand by the low-carbon economy itself, but firmly against its utilization in restricting economic development of developing countries, for which we should maintain the necessary vigilance. However, leaving the other factors behind, the concept of low-carbon economy, in an economic perspective, provide a new way of thinking for development and technology innovation and an occasion for economic restructuring. In this way, we should boost the green economy, low carbon economy and recycling economy, develop and promote the climate-friendly technologies and foster greater harmony between economy and environment. In this field, Brazil has accumulated a wealthy of experiences and is in the international leading position. Except for coordination in our standpoints on the major issues, BRICs countries should further expand cooperation in energy saving and emission reduction through specific technological exchange on clean energy, forest conservation, energy efficiency and so on.

The global financial crisis brings about not only tough challenge to BRICs countries, but also great potential and opportunity for expanding and deepening our cooperation. Although there's obvious difference in our national situation, we face the common tasks to rehabilitate our economy into the normal track of sustainable development, and to create a pleasant place for living and working for our people. We also have common post-crisis interest, which is to strive for a bigger say for developing countries through the reform in global financial system. All these are the foundation for closer intra-BRICs cooperation and the direction for our endeavor. In advancing our cooperation, we should adhere to the principles of seeking common ground while reserving differences, strengthening unity and cooperation, safeguarding the common interest of developing countries and pursuing the maximization of the interest of developing countries.

In exploring the mechanism for deepening post-crisis cooperation, we, BRICs think-tanks, can play significant roles with our researches and efforts. The first two BRICs think-tank dialogues have demonstrated their advisory functions in selecting cooperation areas. Such dialogue has become an important mechanism for the academic community to discuss in depth bilateral collaboration, to exchange views on major international issues, and to make positive policy proposals to the high-level meetings. I believe that, in intensifying cooperation of our four countries, think-tanks will shoulder greater responsibilities and missions, which set forth stricter requirements to our colleagues here. To perform better as the platform for Brain Trust, BRICs think-tanks should closer routine academic exchanges and carry out more targeted collaborative research. As one of the important think-tanks in Asia and even the world, Chinese Academy of Social Sciences is willing to strengthen contacts and cooperation with all the relevant institutions from the other three BRICs. We should exchange our research results in order to offer timely and effective suggestions for BRICs summit and the intensified cooperation and sustainable development in our four nations.

Li Yang
Vice-President
Chinese Academy of Social Sciences

BRICs and the Financial Crisis

Crisis as an Exam for the BRICs

Vladimir M. Davydov[*]

The BRICs as an interacting community of the new centers of the world economy and international politics is a historically recent phenomenon. But over the four years it passed a long way from the start of regular political consultations on the level of Ministers of foreign affairs to the start of an annual summit. The process of intensive "quadrilogue" presents a tendency to diversification covering ever more wide range of problems dealing with the national interests of the four group members and the interests of the international community in general.

Meanwhile the analytical and scientific perception of the BRICs phenomenon presents a contradictory picture. On the one hand, it showed capacity of foreseeing (analyses by Goldman Sachs); on the other hand, it frequently lags behind the practice. Recognizing the presence of extraordinary market and industry potential in each of the four countries, some do not see a sufficiently wide basis for coincidence of the national interests; they do not see quite high rates of growth of the commercial and economic relations between the four members, what objectively does create a platform for cooperative interaction. Such interpretations shall be associated with the following two reasons. First, it's the West-centric inertia of the contemporary global development perception. Second, it's the aspiration of certain circles in traditional centers of the global economy and politics to impede the rapprochement of the four countries and to sow the seeds of distrust between them.

---

* Vladimir M. Davydov, member of the division office of the social sciences of the Russian Academy of Science (RAC), Director of the Institute for the Latin American Researches of the RAC, member of the research council of the Ministry of Foreign Affairs of the Russian Federation.

In academic community the investigation of the BRICs phenomenon till now was mainly individual and country-based passing to the genre of international comparisons. But taking into account the existing practice of interaction between the four members and probable perspective of its enrichment, the researcher's aim is to determine the possibilities of their joint potential realization, interaction effect within the group of four and its aggregate influence on the global development process. From this point of view, it's difficult to overestimate the importance of the present academic forum taking place in parallel with the II BRICs summit that has a chance to become a regular event.

Recognizing the relevance of the above mentioned task we involuntarily refer to the consequences of the present global economic crisis. Economic crisis which is still present brings a new quality to the global range of problems of development and highlights in a new way the role of the BRICs. It's some kind of litmus test and a difficult exam. The prism of the present crisis allows to understanding better the new imperatives of the global development and how the BRICs countries could react to them, what could be their strategy in changing circumstances, logic of joint activity at the world arena.

Peculiarities of the present crisis

Analyzing the present crisis we should be aware of the fact that it has a strongly marked extraordinary nature. It is prominent in the line of cyclic drops of the second half of the XX century (refer to the figwre 1,2).

For the first time over the three decades the stronghold of the contemporary capitalism which is the USA economy became epicenter of crisis.

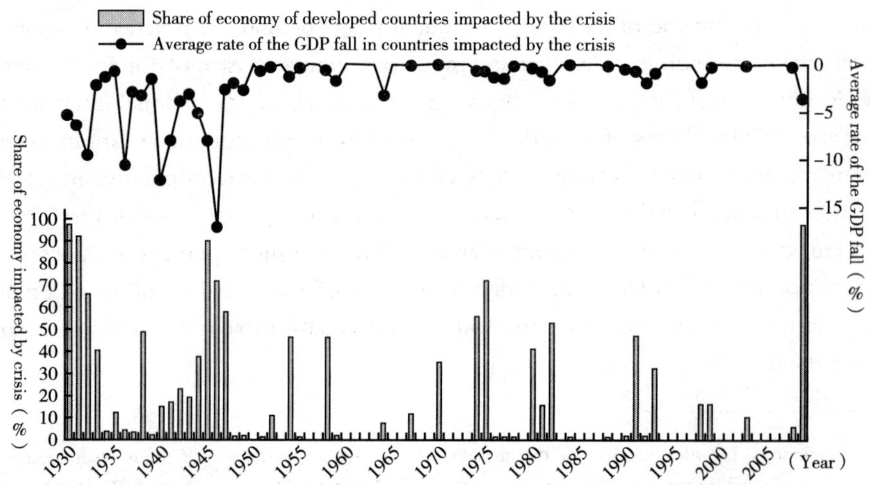

Figure 1 Long-term trend of crisis impacts on development economics

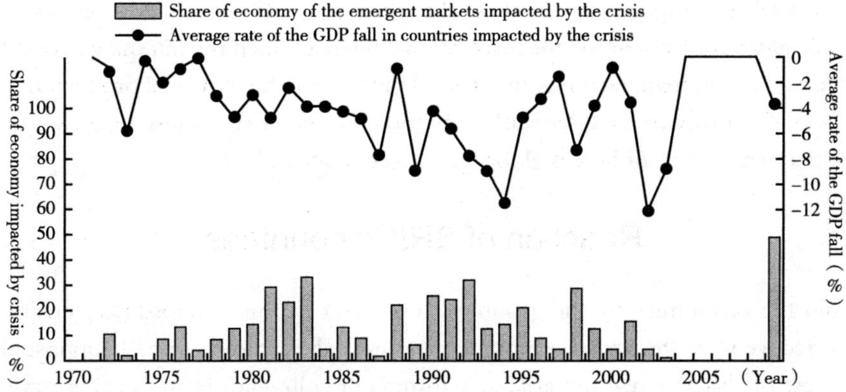

Figure 2 Long-term trend of crisis impacts on emergent markets

The present crisis holds the records in what refers to the depth of recession of the global economy, to the rate of spread and coverage of the national markets of the countries of the world.

The extraordinary nature of the crisis gave enough arguments for those who compare it with the Great Depression of the years 30s of the past century. Nevertheless, comparing parameters of these two crises we are obliged to affirm that the present one doesn't beat the records of the Great Depression in what refers to the depth of recession and its duration (taking into consideration a modest growth since the second half of the 2009). But, apparently, it beats the records in rate of spread and coverage.

The last fact leads us to the effect of globalization that transformed the mechanism of reproduction in the global economy and in national economy systems. Globalization created new risks of break out of the market power in conditions when regulation on the national and international levels was based mainly on the "pre-globalization" standards.

We can affirm that the extraordinary nature of the present crisis consequences is determined exactly by this circumstance. Apparently what is meant here is the first crisis of the globalization era, a crisis that revealed so noticeably the contradictions and risks accumulated with the beginning of the globalization process based on the technological results of the "microelectronic" revolution.

The situation was undoubtedly aggravated by the neoliberal deregulation in pre-crisis period and the state's deviation from the economic and social responsibility.

The existing national and international regulators couldn't control the dramatically accelerating processes of overaccumulation of the financial instruments (first of all derivatives) and effect of overindebtness in traditional centers of the global economy – masses of households, corporate sector and separate states. The giant sector of the offshore business became even less controllable. This is not surprising that failure in one link (at the USA mortgage market) along the whole chain of interconnection destabilized the whole globalized system of the international finances, then the international trade and then the real sector, manufacturing in the key branches of the industrial production. That's why we find it difficult to agree with definition of the crisis as just financial one. We believe that what is meant here is global general economic crisis.

Reaction of BRICs countries

How did the economies of the group of four react to this extraordinary crisis? How much effective were the anti-recessionary measures taken in each case? I suppose that in the process of discussion at our academic forum our colleagues from Brazil, Russia, India and China will give their opinions based on direct knowledge of the concrete situations in each of these countries.

My task here is to give a brief preliminary characteristic of the experience of the countries of the group with an aim to compare and come to general conclusions in what refers to the lessons of the crisis, the general imperatives of the economic policy and the forthcoming agenda of interaction in the BRICs format. I'll be grateful to the colleagues for the criticism and correctives in my interpretation.

First of all, I'll mention that in general the BRICs economies bear the misfortunes of the crisis better than an average of the global economy. However the countries of the group showed different level of soundness during the crisis. Let's present some considerations according to the order of letters in the BRICs abbreviation.

So, let's start with Brazil. As it was specified in The Economist magazine (London), Brazil was one of the last countries to enter the crisis and was one of the first ones to start recovering from it.[①] The growth of the GDP here over the 2009 practically didn't overpass the fatal zero mark staying at the minimal positive value (0.3% by some estimates, or 0.6% by other ones).

Relative soundness of the Brazilian economy after the first shocks of the crisis was ensured, in our opinion, by the least (as compared to the zone of highly developed economies) involvement in speculative financial turnover and high share of the real economy, as well as stability of the credit and banking system and preservation of the national control in its regulation.

Furthermore, an important role was played by an effective use of the pre-crisis period of *fat cows*, firstly, to transmit the external debt in a regulated channel, and then on the basis of accumulation of significant liquidity reserves to enter the category of net creditor. Second, the country managed to eliminate the old defect of the Brazilian economy achieving self-

① "Brazil Takes off," *The Economist 2010*, London, 14-20.11.2009, p.5.

sufficiency in provision with raw hydrocarbons. Third, Brazil considerably advanced in diversification of foreign trade, substantially widening the segment of relations with the most dynamic markets (including those within the BRICs). Finally, considerable results were achieved by the realization of the large-scale social programs that contributed to the reduction of poverty area and therefore to consolidation of domestic market.

Special attention should be paid to realization of the PAC (Plan to accelerate Growth program) for the 2007-2010 period aimed mainly at modernization of infrastructure. Financial resources mobilized for this program (280 million US dollars) allowed significant advancement in modernization of transport, power system management and communications as well as expansion of house building. Thereby significant support to the business activity was ensured and, respectively, the functioning of the internal market was enhanced by the time of the crisis.

A constructive role in recovery from crisis was played by the state banks that still possess high share in the credit and banking system of the country. A share of the state banks in total volume of credit activities increased from 34% (12% of the GDP) in June of 2008 to 41% (18.5% of the GDP) in September 2009[①]. The state banks activity stimulated recuperation of the private lending by the end of the last year.

Estimates of the Brazilian GDP growth for the year 2010 fluctuate between 3-5% predicting sustainable recovery of the economy. Foreign and national businesses have already supported that, accumulating direct and portfolio investments in the Brazilian economy.

Naturally, the Brazilian case is far from the ideal situation. The Brazilian economy has quite a lot of obstacles, among them extreme social polarization and preservation of a wide zone of poverty. Enhancement of the investment climate is impeded by the high crime rate. Expenses for research and development (R&D) were increased in the country, but their level is obviously insufficient for adoption of the model of innovation development. To confirm the status of one of the global economy new leaders Brazil will need to widen the accumulation of productive investments that should increase general dynamics of the economic growth.

Reaction to crisis in Russia seems to be less successful, although the Russian economy had considerably higher growth rates and considerable accumulation of foreign exchange reserves during the pre-crisis period. Naturally, in this case the economic growth was favored by the high pricing environment of energy products on the world market, as well as domestic political stability ensured during the last decade.

Drastic recession in the main centers of the global economy was especially harmful for Russia due to the narrow specialization of its export on oil and gas, as well as to the

---

① CEPAL, Balance Preliminar de las Económicas de América Latina y el Caribe – 2009, Santiago de Chile, 12.12.2009, Brasil, p.1.

fact that minimization of the external public debt was accompanied by excessive increase of the external corporate debt. The last fact could be explained by low availability and expensiveness of the long-term credit money (and vice versa their excess offer at the foreign market), lack of due control of the foreign loans of corporate sector by the national regulators.

Resources accumulated during the pre-crisis period gave opportunity to mobilize large amounts to overcome the liquidity shortage. As the Head of the Russian government V. Putin said, by the spring of the 2009 resources directed for recovery from the crisis equaled to 12% of the GDP. It's important to note that government has chosen to successively support the most vulnerable parts of population. While adjusting the state budget for the years 2009-2010 the main articles of the social expenditures remained in their initial amounts, some of them were increased. That naturally restrained the effect in other areas in short term perspective.

Among the programs launched were partial etatization of distressed assets of the strategically important companies, support of the cities with extremely narrow specialization of economy that allow to prevent catastrophic spread of unemployment. Some measures, although insufficient, for support of the small and medium business (taxes exemptions and enlarged access to credit financing) were also taken in the 2009. The results of the measures taken became notable since the middle of the 2009. Drop in production in some industries was arrested. The unemployment growth stopped by the end of the year; it began to reduce gradually by the beginning of the 2010.

Meanwhile those who criticize the anti-recessionary measures reasonably note that their realization was accompanied by sensible delay and considerable expenses. In the process of "pumping" liquidity in the banking sector, no strict limits were set for special-purpose use of the credit means provided by the government. As result they were used for financial and exchange transactions, and leak of the capital took place. Bureaucratic vertical in anti-recessionary measures implementation was late several months.

Nevertheless, resuming we can affirm today that positive tendencies dominate. Learning lessons from the grave crisis the government of the state adopted a policy aimed at modernization of economy, diversification of exports, successive transition to innovation-based development. It's an absolutely necessary strategic change.

The traditional orientation of the Indian economic policy (founded yet by J. Nehru), directed towards the auto sufficiency of the country, revealed itself in the anti -crisis policies of nowadays. The state support of the banking system was realized rather narrowly, whereupon the volumes of micro credits were widened. The internal consumption was stimulated by the tax regulations. Considerable investments were directed to the infrastructure area. Meanwhile this area (including its transport and energy branches) is still a weak and a vulnerable point of the Indian economy. There are some reasons to foresee by the 2010 to the previous GNP growth rates, though the long-term dynamics is impossible without the modernization of the infrastructure.

The recent decision about the free secondary education -is a great step forward in the accumulation of the "human capital" directed towards the surmounting of social backwardness. Though hard for the state budget, this decision in the long term will change the situation on the labor market. But in the short term it will aggravate the budget deficit, which is nowadays the highest among the BRICs (evaluated as 6.4% of the GNP for 2010).

China's economy was previewed to maintain the stability of income on the maximum level for the crisis period (about 86%). The results of the 2009 affirmed that. Surely, the situation was smoothed by the avalanchine currency reserves of more than 2 trillion dollars and the grown up internal market. But for China this indicator is not fully satisfactory. Its demographic and social imperatives do demand higher development dynamics. Its slow down will undoubtedly sharpen the internal contradictions and disproportions in the economics as well as in the Chinese society.

Meanwhile, the image of China as one the most powerful locomotives of the modern economy is getting even stronger. The Brazilians not without reason think, that the exports to China is its strongest anti-crisis reserve. Indeed, in 2009 the PRC overshadowed the USA as the leading importer of the Brazilian goods. Meanwhile in other directions there were noted severe limitations.

The anti-crisis policy in China was limited by the following main actions: directed financial support of the strategic enterprises; transfer from the "hard" to the "soft" financial and credit policy; from the practices of slow raising of the national currency course to its binding by the dollar course (with a view to maintain exports); development of the inner consumption, including the special prices for the long-term goods; broadening of the social security scales (among the country people); return to export stimulation policy through the mechanism of taxation.

The colossal financial reserves, accumulated by this country by the beginning of the crisis permitted to destiny a sum up to half billion dollars to maintain the real sector of economy. A special attention was paid to the projects of infrastructure, which became an additional impulse to the accelerated modernization of the transport and energy systems began even before the crisis. In sum, the volume of the anti-crisis measures, taken by the beginning of the last year is evaluated as 13% of the GNP.

The existing political system helped the state to operatively direct its decisions for the fulfillment on the local level. The "power vertical" in China provides for the "transmittance" of its decisions not only at the upper and medium level of governance, but also at the level of the economic agents. It ties up not only big, but, practically, all medium private sector enterprises. Surely, one shouldn't overvalue the Chinese "vertical". But one needs to recognize: during the world economy crisis the government did much to strengthen the economy discipline. It could mobilize the reserves of the internal market, the preferential development of which was planned still in the decisions of the XVII Congress of the Communist Party of China.

Some lessons of the crisis and interaction among the BRICs countries

With all the positive or negative features, which revealed themselves during the crisis, we can state, that the BRICs' do remain the part of the world economy, which can seriously contribute to its dynamics. The overall imput of the BRICs in the world GNP growth in 2008 was more than 52% (see table 1).

Table 1 Contribution to the dynamics of world economy

	Share in world GDP	Share in the increase of world GDP		Share in world GDP	Share in the increase of world GDP
USA	20.7	2.7	Brazil	2.8	4.6
Japan	6.2	-1.5	Russia	3.3	5.8
Euro zone	15.6	3.9	India	4.9	11.0
EU(27)	21.9	7.6	China	11.3	31.1
BRICs	22.3	52.5			

Source: Estimated basing on IMF and WB statistics. Год планеты. Ежегодник. Выпуск 2009. Гл. ред. В.Г. Барановский. М., 2009, с. 302.

If we compare the forecasts about the dynamics of the GNP of the world economy leading centers, we will see that in the "peak" of the crisis -in 2009 and in the period after it (2010 -2011) the BRICs have a good chance to continue as the main "donors" of the world economy growth, more to that -to enhance their contribution.

Table 2 Estimations and forecasts of increase (decrease) of GDP

	2009	2010	2011
USA	-2.4	3.1	2.9
Japan	-5.7	1.7	1.6
Euro zone	-3.8	1.2	1.4
BRICs			
Brazil	0.3	5.0	4.5
Russia	-7.0	3.5(5.0*)	4.3
India	5.5	7.7	8.0
China	8.2	9.6	8.1

* WB estimations.

Source: The Economist Intelligence Unit – The Economist. London. 28.11.2009, p.97; 27.03.2010, p.97.

During the last years the mutual trade between the BRICs proves the objective character of the need of cooperation between the "four". In the last decade (until 2008) the mutual trade growth rates as a rule were significantly higher than the medium world ones and the rates of the BRICs trade with the traditional centers of the world economy.

More to that, one should pay attention that in 2009 the indicators of the mutual trade between the "four" showed major stability compared with the general world conjuncture. One could definitely say that this sector of the world trade resulted the most durable in the atmosphere of the crisis.

In general, within the BRICs we have the reduction of the commodity export values at 20.4%. The general world indicator is 23, the EU (27 countries) -21.3%, Japan -25.7%.

In Brazil the exports to the BRICs zone even grew absolutely from 22.2 billion dollars in 2008 to 26.5 billion in 2009. As a result, the share of BRICs in the Brazilian exports grew from 11.2% to 17.3%.

Russia, which experienced a significant fall of its exports (mainly by the value of it), nonetheless augmented the share of sales in with the BRICs destination -from 6.0 % (2008) to 7.9 % (2009). The share of the BRICs in the Russian of trade turnover rose from 9.5 to 11%.

Somehow this indicator lowered for India from 8% to 7%. But in case trade with Russia the situation is the opposite the volume of Russian exports rose in 2009 by 13.5%. And the Indian exports to Russia stayed at the 2008 level.

The situation of 2009 in China is different. After the stable raise of the commerce volumes to the BRICs zone during the pre-crisis period (up to 2008), there was observed a significant fall approximately to 26.5%. Nevertheless, the conjuncture of the first months of 2010 shows, that the commercial activity in the BRICs direction has a recovery tendency.

Surely, every BRICs country draws its own lessons from the crisis. We'd like to pay attention to the conclusions, which are common to all of them, which refer to three levels of analysis. The first one deals with the problems of the national development, the second with the relations within the BRICs, the third one with the coordinated positions on the reconstruction of the international regulatory mechanisms in the world economy. Precisely in this respect we'll try to expose some ideas.

The crisis with all the evidence strengthens the organizational work of the state in the processes of the economic development, industrial modernization and the process of innovation. It presupposes the determination of the strategic perspectives of the development and creation of the beneficial conditions for the business activities, though not replacing the business in the spheres, where it can effect significantly. All the BRICs countries do possess the prerequisites of such approach in the traditions of their economic policies and in their social psychology.

Special significance here acquires the economic security mechanism and the ability of the preventive anticyclic actions. The problem is not in the accumulation of vast international reserves, but in the ability to use of them in a productive and rational way.

Besides, also critical is the capability to control the involvement of the national economy and its financial sector to the transnational speculative interchange. The lessons of the crisis are significant enough in this sense. The future perspective of the development does not provide any guarantee of non revision of those ups and downs. The long statistical rows directly point up to that historic regularity, to the probability of the cyclic fall up to the end of the next decade. The corrections, made in the economic policy and in the mechanism of the state regulation still do not make us believe that this can prevent the transformation of the next ordinary crisis into extraordinary.

In all the four cases the first place is occupied by several key issues, without which it's impossible to maintain high standards of the economic growth for a long time and to provide a progressive modernization. We speak about the primordial development of the infrastructure, the backwardness of which in all the four cases has become one of the strongest obstacles, that places in question the possibility of high dynamics of economical growth in a long term.

One of the main imperatives – the increase of efforts and means with a view of limiting the levels of poverty and income disproportions (social and territorial). Without this the BRICs won't make active the potentially enormous reserve of its inner markets for a long time and in so doing to elevate their stability during next cyclic ups and downs (especially extraordinary ones).

The BRICs countries enter in the innovative époque with the different histories and different prerequisites. The aim of Russia -to stop the erosion of the R&D sphere (having a great heritage), to re-establish the intermediate locks in the chain, which connects the fundamental science and the sphere of production, to construct a system for effective incentives in the enterprises.

In other cases the task of the "four" can be exposed in other way. China has seriously moved forward in the imitation phase of the innovation cycle and does a lot to "construct" the higher stages. But, still, it demands long time and significant work. In India and Brazil there have been created the minimum prerequisites for the deployment of the innovative process in some perspective directions, though the lack of resources, qualified cadres and institutional incentives still limit the leap forward. So there is a need of concentrated efforts along all the innovative chain, but, specially in the upper "stages" of the R&D.

Since the launch of the consultative mechanism of the BRICs on the diplomatic level, the political "quadrilogue" has begun, it seems, to take the upper hand of the economic cooperation, which up today was being realized on the bilateral level.

Though one must recognize that recently there took place four-lateral consultations on several economic issues (finance, energy, agriculture). For the first time there takes place the businessmen meeting during this very summit in Brasilia. But, it's evident that the future must be connected with the mutual realization of the big scale projects (not necessarily with the participation of all, "triangles" also permitted). The areas of common interest could be the aerospace sphere, the sphere of the traditional and non-traditional energy, the resolution of the food problem.

The trade between the "four" has already proved its growing significance for the BRICs. Its possible growing in the perspective is a great reserves for the stability of the four economics (especially during the extraordinary falls). This must be surely counted for in the trade and economic policy of the BRICs. Still there is no talk about any of the integration programs. As it seems, there hasn't yet formed the necessary objective prerequisites for that. But we can't exclude the appearance of the necessity to elaborate the four sided programs of the branch cooperation.

The coordinated position of the BRICs on the correction of the deficiencies in the world economics and financial architecture has already demonstrated itself in the G20 summit in Pittsburgh. There was made a first step towards the redistribution of voices and capital in the key world financial institutions. But it is obvious that the process is still in its beginnings. The world community, the G20 (as its economically most ponderous part) still lack the comprehensive receipts of the world mechanisms reconstruction. There exist much talking about this, but still there is a lack of a political will to make serious changes and also the principal actors seem technically not to be ready for them.

I don't think that we can speak about the sui generis "world economic government" with more proportional representation. Still in the agenda is the improvement of the existing institutions with critical approach to their experience or using them as the raw materials for the building of new architecture. The process of the restructuring has already begun on the regional level. The EC actively discusses the perspective of the European IMF, some experiments in this direction are also taking place in Latin America on subregional level. The BRICs undertake preventive measures to safeguard themselves from the dollar fluctuations, diversifying their financial actives and transferring part of their payments to the national currencies.

In these conditions the BRICs as a sui generis coalition of the ascending economies, not only interested in the world economic stability, but possessing a unique potential, is capable to play an historic role in the movement of the world community towards a mechanism of global regulation, adaptable to the needs of the XXIst century, in minimization of the transitional period risks and elaboration of a flexible formula of the world economy stable development.

BRICs' Cooperation Potential in the Post–Crisis Era

Li Xiangyang[*]

The international financial crisis hasn't finished, there are many risks in the recovery, especially rising risks from the Greece debt crisis and its spreading to whole Europe economy. However, we have to pay close attention to the prospect of long-term economic growth and global governance, as there will be great changes in the post-crisis era. To some extent, BRICs' role in the global economy will depend on their cooperation. Compared with the pre-crisis era, BRICs' cooperation potentials will rise in the future.

Timing of stimulus exit and coordination of BRICs' economic policies

For BRICs, the first challenge reflects, in large part, a differing pace of recovery across countries and regions. The recovery is led by the emerging economies, especially by BRICs (see Figure 1). Now, most of the emerging economies have gotten out the recession, but the recovery in developed economies has many uncertainties, and the sovereignty debt crisis in Greece is spreading to EU economy and global economy. Recently we have witness the great fluctuation in the international financial market. The difference in the recovery pace has brought a dilemma for BRICs' policy-makers. If the exit is too early, the recovery may come to a premature end; if the exit is too late, domestic inflation may be out of control.

While global economic recovery has not firm foundation, most of BRICs economies have emerged too hot signs, such as rising inflation (expectation) and asset-price bubble. Because of Greece crisis, the Euro exchange rate has depreciated greatly. As a result,

* Li Xiangyang , professor and the Director General of the Institute of Asia-Pacific Studies, Chinese Academy of Social Sciences.

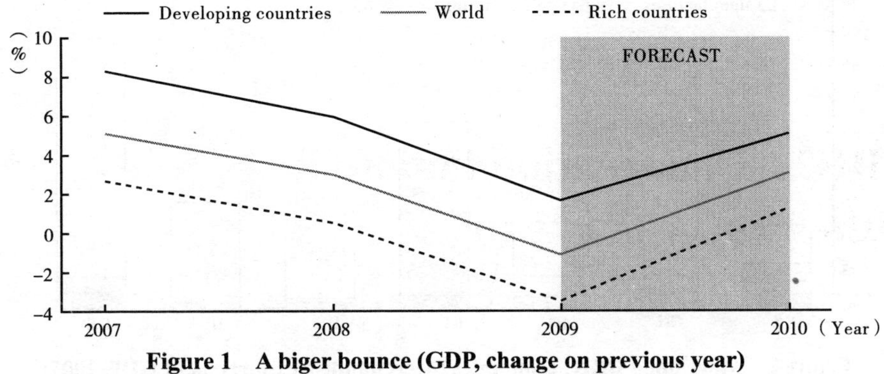

Figure 1 A biger bounce (GDP, change on previous year)

Source: IMF

BRICs economy will face new pressures from currency appreciation and hot-money inflow, which lead to deterioration of inflation and asset-price bubble.

The stimulus exit has become a challenge for the BRICs policy-makers. For one thing, to prevent the over-heating economies, it is imperative for most of BRICs to return to normal macroeconomic policy. In fact, Brazil and India have begun to raise their interest rate, and China increased its reserve rate. For another, the risks of recovery from developed economies have forced BRICs to take a wait-and-see policy.

In the short term, it is necessary to coordinate their timing of stimulus exit between BRICs, and between them and developed countries in the G20 forum. Otherwise, as the recovery leader, BRICs economies may get in the double-dip recession.

Global rebalancing pressure and BRICs' economic adjustment

In past twenty years, the rapid growth of BRICs economies, to larger extent, has stemmed from their open models, for example, BRICs' export dependence ratio is larger than their developed counterparts (Germany is a exception) (see Figure 2), and they have been the largest host of FDI in the developing countries. Meanwhile, the U.S. economy has acted as an engine of global consumption demands. For most of BRICs economies, especially for China, the U.S. market has been their major export destination. However, great changes will take place in the U.S. demand structure. This is, U.S. is set to shift away from private consumption and debt towards export and saving, which results in global rebalancing. At same time, EU and Japan economies are expected to make similar adjustment. At least during a transition, it is not realistic to expect consumer demand of major developed economies to regain its pre-crisis growth pace. To restore sustained global growth, the sources of global expansion therefore will need to shift.

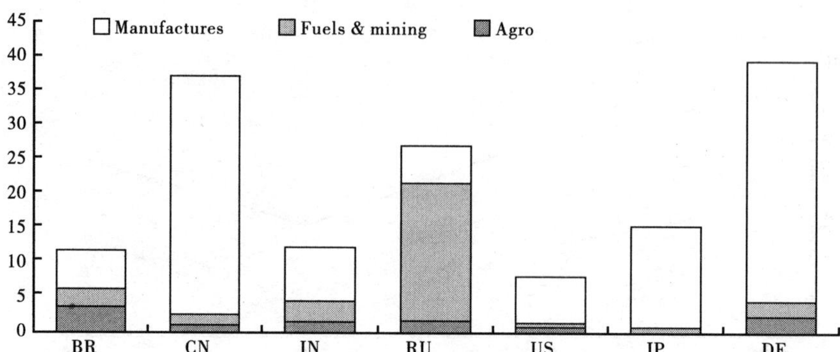

Figure 2 More open BRIC economies (Merchandise exports % of GDP, 2007)

Source: WTO.

Given the adjustment of consumption demand in the major developed countries, it is very important for BRICs and other export-led economies to fill the demand gap left by developed economies. But by GDP and consumption expenditure, BRICs couldn't undertake the task in the short term (see Figure 3 and Figuer 4).

In the long term, due to rapid economic growth, BRICs have great potential of domestic consumption. In China, government has begun to adjust its economic development pattern from the export-driven model to the consumption-driven model. This is called transformation of economic development pattern. During the international financial crisis, its stimulus policy has pulled domestic consumption demand, such as China has become the largest car market in 2009 (see Figure 5). In India, the re-industrialization strategy will bring about similar outcome. If BRICs make success of the adjustment, they will continue to act as the engine of global economic growth as before (see Figure 6).

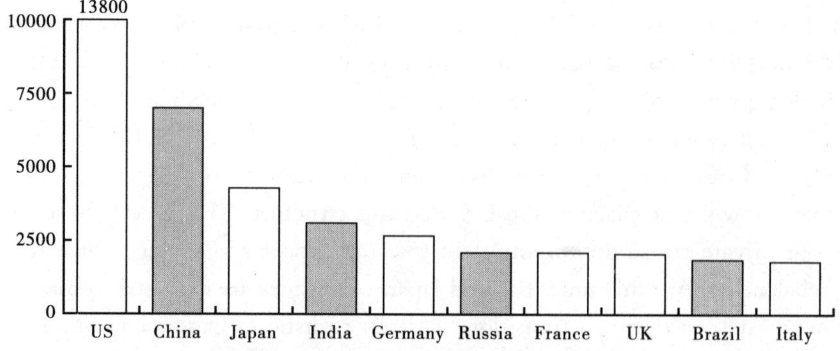

Figure 3 The size of BRIC economies (GDP at PPP exchange rates, USD bn, 2007)

Source: IMF.

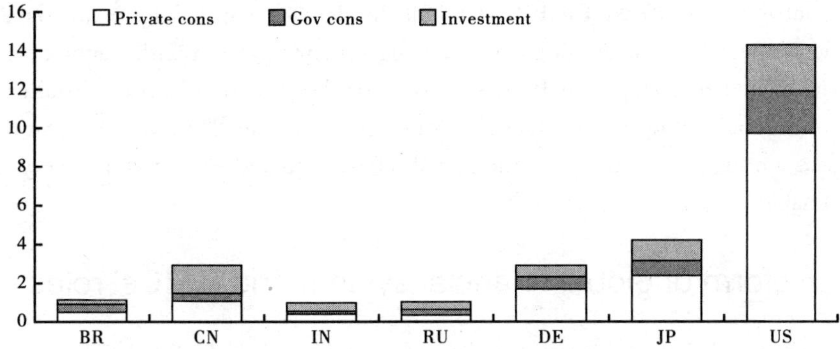

Figure 4 Expenditure, current USD bn, 2007

Source: IMF.

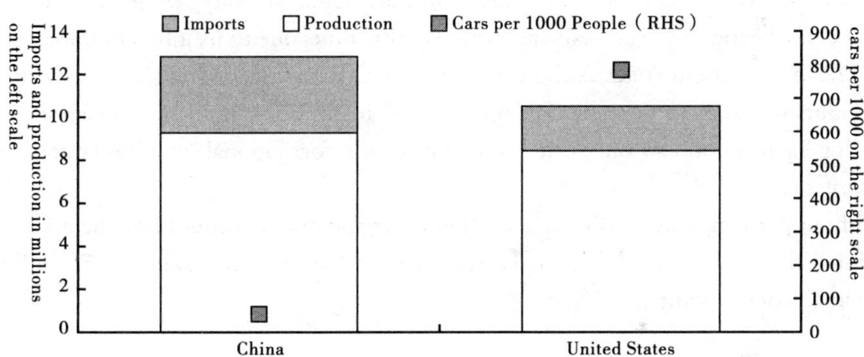

Figure 5 China overtakes the U.S. in car production and import

Source: U.S. census, Chinese statistics authorities.

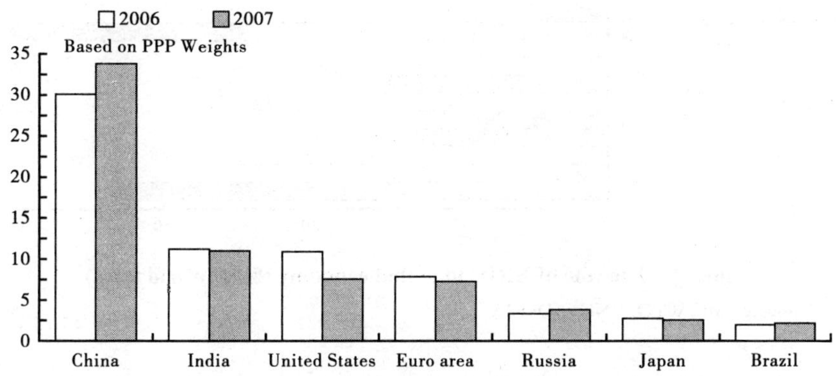

Figure 6 Contrbution to real GDP growth

Source: IMF (2008) World Economic Outlook.

Of course, it is not easy for BRICs to fill the demand gap left by major developed countries, especially to keep global rebalancing synchronization with major developed countries. Need to note, both BRICs and major developed countries should realize that global rebalancing is a gradual and long-term process. Without cooperation and consensus among major countries, the global rebalancing and economic recovery will be unsustainable.

Reform of global financial system and BRICs' roles

The international financial crisis has showed that necessity of global financial system reform. In macroeconomic level, the international monetary system based on the U.S. dollar has inherent contradiction: as the issuer of world currency, the U.S. hasn't taken responsibility for currency stability (and world economic stability), which resulted in an over-indebted economy and financial crisis. At same time, due to its inherent imperfection, the SDR in IMF couldn't act as the world currency. In microeconomic level, we can trace the origins of crisis to deregulation on financial institutions, market, derivatives, credit rationing agencies and so on. So it is imperative to reform global financial system in the post-crisis era.

Without participation of BRICs and other emerging market economies, the adjustment of global financial system won't make real progress, as they are taking more and more share in global economy (see Figure 7).

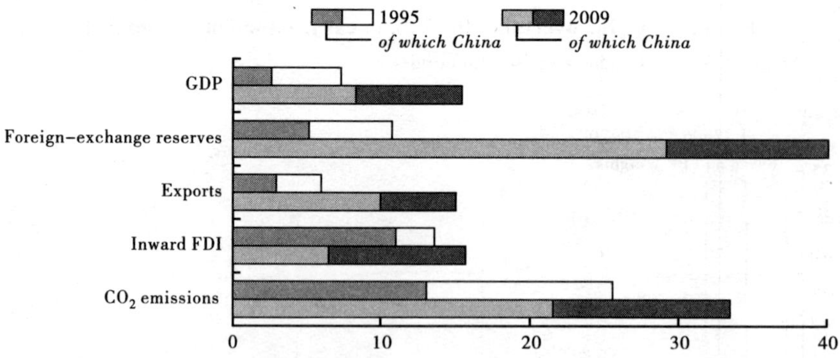

Figure 7 The role of BRIC in global economy (% of world total)

Source: IMF; WTO; UNCTAD; EIA.

In macroeconomic level, the direction of international monetary system reform is to play the role of SDR as world currency in the long term, and to extend share of emerging market economies (especially BRICs) in SDR and IMF in the short term. Recently, there are some progresses in this field, but we have a long way to go. BRICs' roles don't match with their share in global economy. Moreover, the stability of international monetary system depends on fiscal balance of major economies. Unfortunately, the fiscal challenges ahead are formidable in major developed economies (see Table 1). IMF projections indicate that government debt in developed economies will reach nearly 120 percent of GDP by 2014. This is a potential threat for stability of future international monetary system.

Table 1 Countires ranked* by sustainability of debt position

	% of GDP, 2010, forecast		GDP growth less cost of finance♀, %	Sovereign debt, years to maturity♁
	Primary budget balance, cyclically adjusted§	Net debt§		
Greece	-4.6	94.6	-3.2	7.7
Ireland	-7.0	38.0	-5.1	6.8
Britain	-6.7	59.0	-1.5	13.7
Japan	-5.9	104.6	0.1	5.4
Portugal	-2.7	62.6	-2.3	6.5
Spain	-4.3	41.6	-3.0	6.7
France	-3.8	60.7	-0.7	6.9
United States	-7.0	65.2	1.4	4.8
Poland	-5.3	32.4	-0.7	5.2
Italy	2.2	100.8	-1.0	7.2
Hungary	4.2	62.1	-3.5	3.3
Belgium	1.3	85.4	-0.6	5.6
Netherlands	-1.4	36.5	-0.6	5.4
Austria	-0.9	42.9	-0.6	7.0
Germany	-1.2	54.7	-0.5	5.8
Czech Republic	-1.9	5.3	0.0	6.4
Norway	-7.8	-143.6	2.4	4.9
Canada	-2.7	32.6	2.0	5.2
Denmark	-1.4	1.6	0.1	7.9
Australia	-0.7	-1.3	0.2	5.0
Switzerland	0.4	11.0	0.5	6.7
Finland	-0.9	-46.4	0.9	4.3
Sweden	-0.3	-13.1	1.5	6.4

* Based on the sum of the countries' rank for the first three debt measures

§ General government

♀ Forecast average nominal GDP growth for 2010-2011 less latest yield on government bonds of average maturity

♁ Weighted average

Sources: Bloomberg; EIU; DECD; The Economies.

In microeconomic level, to make financial institutions better equipped catastrophe, economists, bankers and government officers have made much different proposals to improve the financial supervision, such as In December 2009, under instruction from the G20, the Basel club of bank supervisors published new proposals on capital and liquidity "buffers". These could be in force by the end of 2012. In the United States, after the "Volcker Rules" (or "Volcker Plan" including to end the mentality of too big to fail, Overhauling capital requirements and Improving macroprudential regulation) has been put off, a weaker financial-reform bill has been passed in the U.S. Senate on May 20, 2010. The legislation is intended to prevent a repeat of the 2008 crisis, but also reshapes the role of numerous federal agencies and vastly empowers the Federal Reserve in an attempt to predict and contain future debacles. Despite the biggest overhaul of the financial system since the Great Depression, some of the most important reforms are outside its purview, such as toughened-up capital and liquidity standards for banks. Moreover, for both the Basel proposal and the financial-reform bill, their implementation will depend on international cooperation. More importantly, the precondition is that the reform shouldn' t harm developed countries' international competitive advantage in financial sector. So BRICs have to actively participate in the rules-making in order to avoid an outcome: as developed countries got ill, developing countries will take medicine!

New protectionism and how to promote the Doha Round negotiation

During the financial crisis, protectionism measures increased evidently. A study of World Bank shows that newly-initiated trade remedy investigations (and new-imposed trade remedies) are related with economic cycle (see Figure 8). Meanwhile, some new-type protectionism measures emerged in the economic stimulus policies, for example, buy

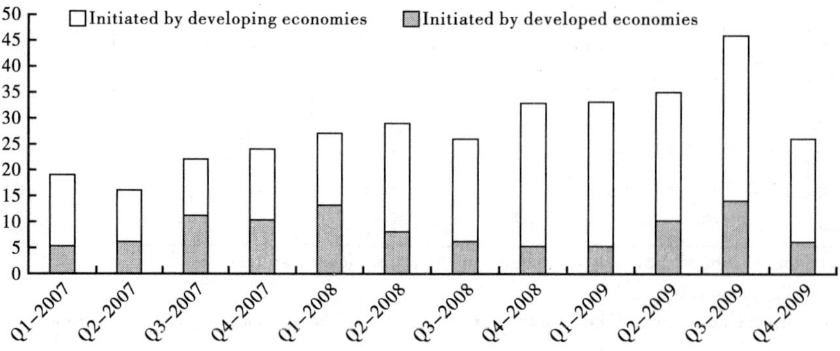

Figure 8 Newly-initiated trade remedy investigations, 1Q 2007-4Q 2009

Source: *Global Antidumping Database.*

American procurement rules, financial protectionism, investment protectionism, and so on. Though these new-type protectionism measures don't transgress current norms of WTO, they evidently are inconsistent with discriminatory principle of WTO. Thus, G20, G77 and other international organizations have recently called for ending Doha Round trade talks to prevent future global financial crisis and protect development gains.

In the new Doha Round negotiation, it is question of whether all members reach a consensus on new multilateral trade rules. Launched in 2001, the Doha Round of world trade talks has been deadlocked in the past eight years due to differences between developed and developing countries over access to agricultural and non-agricultural markets. After the international financial crisis, they seem not to narrow the differences, but to widen the differences. First, more and more developing countries haven't accept the Anglo-Saxon model and idea ("Washington Consensus") any longer. Second, as developed countries and developing countries face different challenges, the former tends to relate the climate change and the intellectual property protection with new rules. As Mr. Lamy, the secretary of WTO, said in the Trade Ministers' meeting in Bali in 2007, "Climate First, Trade Second". The latter is willing to promote the market access and constraint on new protectionism. Third, some developed countries, for instance, the U.S. and France, have proposed carbon tariff bill, which may become a new-type protectionism measure, and harm trade interest of developing countries.

As the representative of developing countries, BRICs should not only narrow the difference of both sides, but also prevent developed countries from harming the interest of developing countries.

Global climate change rules and transition of economic growth pattern in BRICs

In the past-crisis era, there two important preconditions for global sustainable growth, one is global rebalancing in demand side, another is emissions reduction or low carbon economy in supply side. The emissions reduction is new challenge for BRICs (Russia is exception, as member of the Kyoto protocol), and will affect their economic growth pattern and industrialization process, once global rules of emissions reduction (or global climate change rules) begin to be in force.

Without question, it is very necessary for all countries to reduce greenhouse-gas emissions. However, the distribution of costs and return from emissions reduction isn't equal among all participators. In the cap-and-trade (or emission-trading system, ETS), for some countries, emissions reduction may be an asset, but for other countries, it may be a liability. This is where the problems start. For BRICs, the challenge from the emissions reduction is much larger than its opportunity. .

First, compared with developed countries, BRICs' industrialization is in the early phase. Fossil fuels are the most important source of energy, and economy is composed of the energy intensive industries. So carbon intensity in BRICs far exceeds in developed countries (see Table 2).

Table 2 Carbon intensity by sector (2004) (Direct plus indirect)

Unit: tons per million US dollar

	EU27+EFTA	US	Japan	Brazil	China	India	Russia	World
Agriculture	74	141	76	129	350	301	307	168
All Energy	541	1096	433	186	2800	1749	1333	928
All Manufacturing	62	159	79	168	681	518	848	187
Energy Intensive	107	272	140	286	1163	888	1193	330
Other	42	111	51	107	459	354	568	122
Other Industries	46	69	46	89	561	287	381	132
Service	46	94	40	101	340	231	409	92
Total	74	153	70	149	772	535	767	187

Source: Mattoo,A. et al (2009a) Reconciling Climate Change and Trade Policy. *Policy Research Working Paper, No.5123.*

Second, relatively speaking, BRICs have comparative disadvantage in the emissions reduction, such as carbon capture and storage (CCS) (or carbon sequestration), the clear energy technology (wind power, fuel cells, lighting, solar PV, electric car, et al). As a result, the emissions reduction may is a liability.

Third, without redistribution, BRICs and other emerging economies may become major cost-taker from the emission reduction (see Figure 9).

Fourth, based on carbon leakage mechanism, developed countries may make new constraint on import from developing countries by carbon tariff or higher fuel-efficiency standards.

On the contrary, after the international financial crisis, it's an urgent need for major developed countries to find a new industry (as engine) to promote sustainable growth, because financial industry couldn't restore in the short term, and most of manufacture have transferred to developing countries by FDI and outsourcing. Clear energy or low carbon economy is an ideal candidate. As an emerging industry, its products have competitive advantage over fossil fuels, and its product market is all over the world. Only global climate change rules can satisfy both needs. For one thing, the rules will change price relations between clear energy and fossil fuels. For another, unlike the Kyoto protocol, new rules will cover all countries. So developed countries will be winner of new rules.

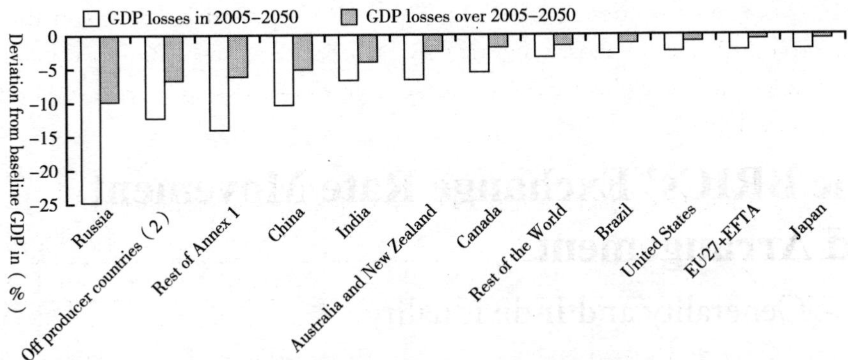

Figure 9 Costs of abatement without redistribution (Regional costs from stabilising long-run greenhouse gas concentration at 550 ppm, GDP losses relative to baseline[1])

1. This scenario assumes the implementation of a world carbon tax, or equivalently of a world permit trading system with full auctioning. "GDP losses in 2050" denotes the cost as a per cent of GDP in 2050 relative to baseline. "GDP losses over 2005-2050" denotes the gap (in per cent) between the (undiscounted) sum of annual GDPs over 2005-2050 in the 550 ppm scenario and the corresponding sum in the baseline scenario.

2. The region includes the Middle East, Algeria-Libya-Egypt, Indonesia, and Venezuela.

Source: OECD ENV-Linkages model.

In the negotiation on climate change, BRICs have to insist that new rules be base on "common but different responsibility" principle. Only fair rules can clear energy or low carbon economy become precondition of sustainable growth in the post-crisis era. Otherwise, global de-carbonization will inhibit developing country industrialization.

In sum, cooperation between BRICs will contribute to safeguard the interest of developing countries, and to improve current global governance.

The BRICs' Exchange Rate Movement and Arrangement

— Generality and Individuality

Huang Wei[*]

November 2001, in paper *Building Better Global Economic BRICs*, Goldman Sachs firstly proposed the concept BRICs: Brazil, Russia, India and China. And in Oct 2003, Goldman Sachs published another paper *Dreaming with BRICs: The Path to 2050*. The paper predicted that by 2025 BRICs could account for over half the size of the G6. And only the US and Japan may be still among the six largest economies in the US dollar terms in 2050, while BRICs will pass other current G6 countries – British, Germany, French, and Italy. From academic perspective, there are some issues in Goldman Sachs's study. However, the bold conclusion with logical analysis framework (Population Prediction, Capital Accumulation, and Productivity Increase Model) has attracted widespread interest in business and academic field. Jim O'Neill, the paper's author, indicated that the prediction is just an estimation for BRICs future development potential, based on BRICs economic balance ability, the stable inner and external macroeconomic environment (including stable pricing), the system construction corresponding to economic development. However, due to vast land and huge population of BRICs with rapid GDP growth, BRICs will bring huge influence for future world economy.

In the prediction, Goldman Sachs specially indicated that the BRICs' exchange rate will have outstanding appreciation and the one thirds of GDP growth would come from the currency revaluation. The average currency value would increase 2.5% per year. Chinese RMB will be doubled in the next ten years. However, global financial environment has changed a lot since 2007. Developing countries have suffered less than developed

* Huang Wei, research associate professor, the Institute of World Economics and Politics, Chinese Academy of Social Sciences.

countries in the financial crisis. But BRICs still have to face the contraction as well, because of the economic globalization.

Although Brazil, Russia, India and China are the world's largest emerging economies, most of these countries had suffered serious financial crisis, as showed in table 1. Although in the table India has not showed any trouble, the country suffered "Rupee crisis" in 1990s as well. The balance-of-payments (BOP) crisis threatened the country's international credibility and pushed it to the brink of default. Foreign exchange reserve was short of demand[①], while rupee sharply depreciated from 17.5 rupee: 1 $ in 1991 to 45 rupee: 1 $ in 1992. The financial crises are not only related with national situation, but also highly related with the management of domestic and foreign price and the degree of capital control.

Table 1 Countries and Debt-Crisis episodes

	Number of Crises	Years in Crisis (Year)	Crisis episodes (entry-exit)
Brazil	3	16	1983-1995,1998-2000,2001-2002
China	0	0	
India	0	0	
Russia	1	3	1998-2001

Sources: IMF; Standard & Poor's; World Bank; and authors' calculations.

A country is defined to be in a debt-crisis if it is classified as being in default by Standard & Poor's or receives a non-concessional IMF loan in excess of 100 percent of quota.

Pre-crisis Exchange rate arrangement in BRICs

In the last 20 years before global crisis, the four countries have a same character: They all experienced a relative long term nominal depreciation followed with another long term nominal appreciation against the US dollar, and the turning point is around 2002, as showed in figure 1. Nominal exchange rate of two different currencies is decided not only by host country's domestic economic and policy, but also by the situation of the US dollar. February 2002 is the watershed of strong dollar and weak dollar. As displayed in figure 2, the US dollar index had fallen since then, and the falling trend continued until March 2008.

① India had $1.2 billion foreign exchange reserves in January 1991, but depleted by half by June. Monetary authority had to secure an emergency loan of $2.2 billion from international monetary fund by pledging 67 tons of India's gold reserves as collateral: 47 tons of gold to the Bank of England and 20 tons of gold to the Union Bank of Switzerland.

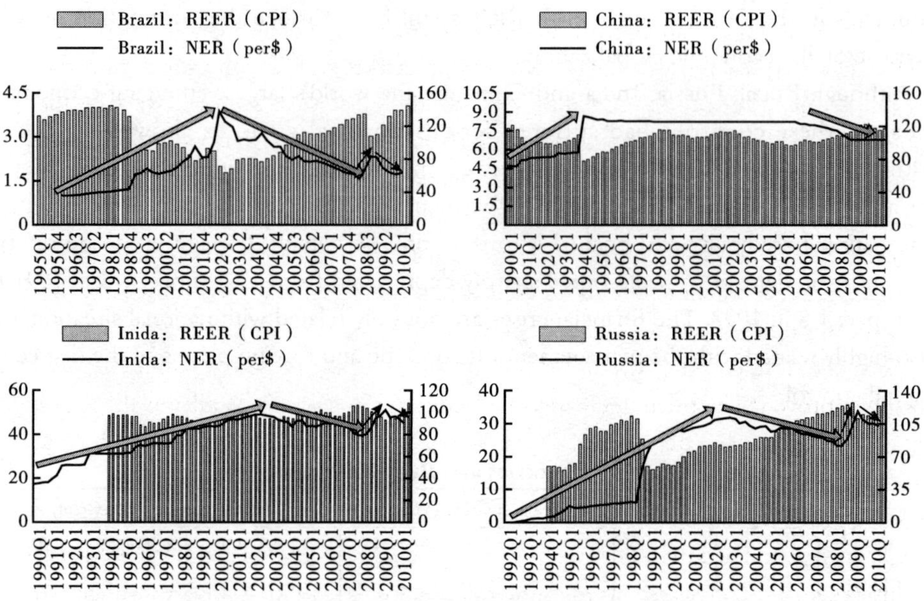

Figure 1 Nominal and Real Exchange rate of BRICs

NER (Nominal exchange rate) REER (Real effective exchange rate).
Left arrow represents depreciation; while the right one represents appreciation.
Data source: IMF, BIS.

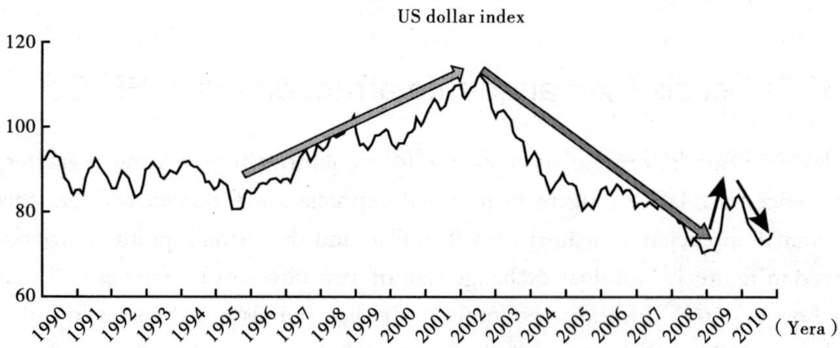

Figure 2 The trend of US dollar index

Data source: FRB.

Because of difference national condition and degree of openness, each country's turning point, period and the amplitude of fluctuation have a little bit different. In the early 1990s, the long term nominal currency depreciated trend had first showed in China and India, and then followed by Russia and Brazil. With the development in emerging market economies, in the early of this century, currencies in BRICs against the US dollar had changed to appreciation trend until the breakout of global financial crisis. Although BRICs all are typical representative of emerging market with a high growth rate, they had very different historical and social experience, therefore case analysis could be the best choice. In the third of the article, we analyze each country's exchange rate arrangement and the potential driving force behind the fluctuation of exchange rate.

Although nominal exchange rate volatilities in four countries are more consistent, the trends of real exchange rate are significantly different, because the changes in domestic price levels are quite different within countries. In comparison, China and India's real exchange rate and domestic inflation was relatively stable, without lasting significant up and down.

Since the 21st century, Brazil's domestic price level control capabilities have been greatly improved. The price fluctuation has reduced significantly. Similar as the movement of nominal exchange rate, the real exchange rate in Brazil fell to the bottom in 2002, and recovered to the same level as that of the end of last century in 2010.

Comparing with other three countries, the volatility of the domestic price level in Russia is greater. The inflation remained at double-digit annual rate, as illustrated in Figure 3. Russia's financial crisis occurred in the third quarter of 1998. Ruble's exchange rate was 6.2 rubles to the dollar at the end of June 1998, and jumped to 20 rubles to the dollar by the end of 1998. The devaluation process continued. The price of the dollar was 24 rubles at March 1999, and then reached the acme of 28 ruble in December. Nominal exchange rate devalued 4 times, while the consumer price index was barely doubled. Since there was only a negligible change in the world price level, Russia's real exchange rate devalued about 50 percent at this period. The sharp depreciation of ruble's real exchange rate improved the competitiveness of Russian products in international market. With the stabilization of domestic economy, in the first ten years of 21st century, the ruble's real effective exchange rate maintained a gradual appreciation trend.

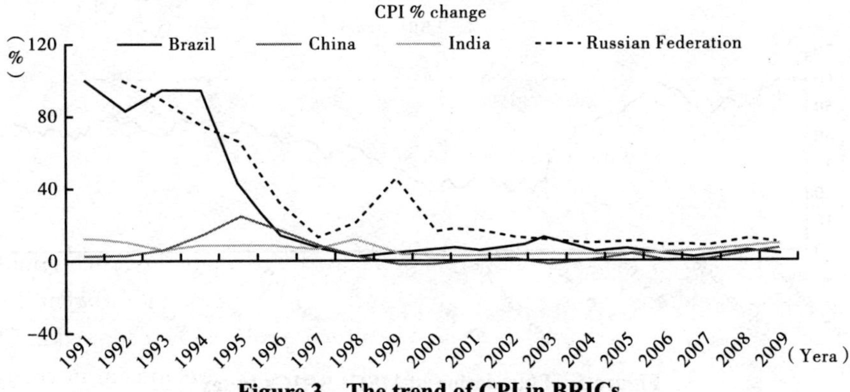

Figure 3 The trend of CPI in BRICs

Data source: IMF.

Post-crisis Exchange rate arrangement in BRICs

In 2007 to 2008, when sub-prime mortgages collapsed in United States, many believed BRICs countries could be isolated from the global financial turmoil. However, with the financial crash in most developed countries at the end of 2008, foreign investors fled the BRICs. There is a sharp falling in 2008 both in the national foreign exchange reserve and the MSCI BRICs index, which represents overall equity performance of the four stock markets, as displayed in figure 4 and figure 5. Because the fall is so unusual, authorities in Russia and Brazil even shut stock market temporarily to prevent further losses. However, because of strong domestic consumer demand, high level of foreign exchange reserve and large trade surplus, it is reason to believe that BRICs would recover faster than other countries.

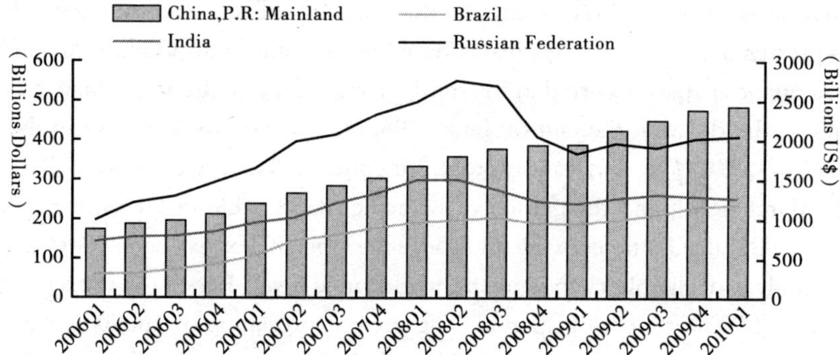

Figure 4 Change in BRICs' foreign exchange reserve

China refers right axis, while other countries refer left.
Data source: IMF.

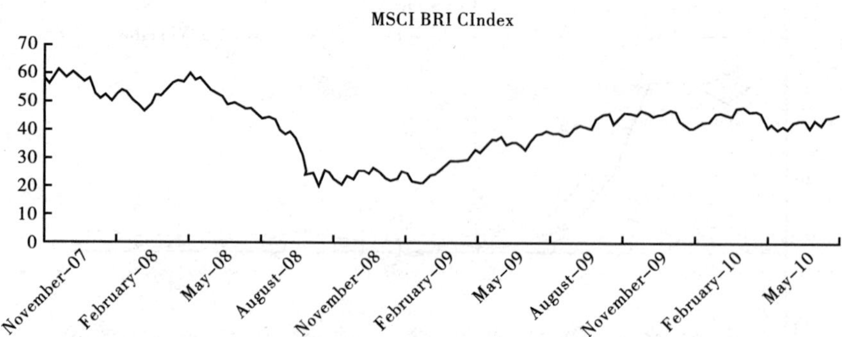

Figure 5 Fluctuation of MSCI BRICs Index

Data source: IMF.

Since the global financial crisis, except China, the other three countries showed a second round of appreciation after devaluation, and the watershed is the 4th quarter of 2008. (see figure 1) In financial markets turmoil, the risk appetite of international investors has been significantly reduced. International capital was seeking safe haven. The dollar regained safe-haven status. International capital began to chase dollars assets and withdrew from developing countries. Since March 2008, the US dollar shows a rising trend after a 6-year decline. A strong US dollar makes exchange-rate depreciation in countries with floating or managed floating exchange rate system. This phenomenon occurs not only in emerging countries, also exists in developed countries. As the crisis has slowed down and economy recovers, the US dollar has re-entered the depreciation path since March 2009. After the crisis, India is the first depreciating country, followed by Russia and Brazil. But in Q1 of 2009, the money of these three countries starts the appreciation almost at the same time. Unlike other countries, China's RMB was pegged to the dollar during the crisis, therefore the movement of RMB against the dollar was relatively stable.

From the fundamental characteristics above, an undisputed fact is that, at least so far, the US dollar as an international currency, its rise and fall in large part determines the trend of exchange rate changes of emerging countries. For emerging countries, a difficult puzzle is how to gradually avoid the impaction from a long-term weak US Dollar without hurting their own economic development.

Case analysis of BRICs' Exchange rate arrangement

China

Since 1980s, the China's exchange rate system could be roughly divided into three phases.

1981-1984: China entered the period of taking economic construction as central task. To solve the high cost of swap in export sector, the exchange rate was replaced by dual exchange rate. In January 1981, the monetary authority of China cut the value of the Yuan by half in trade transactions by introducing an internal settlement rate of 2.8 Yuan to the dollar while the official rate remained 1.5. Since then, the official rate had been gradually depreciated and closed to the internal settlement rate.

1985-1993: In the early of 1985, the internal settlement rate was abolished. All transactions no matter trade or non-trade were to be handled at the unified official exchange rate. In order to change the BOP deficit appeared 1984, government implemented export-oriented policy. Authorities gradually devalued RMB for improving the competitiveness of export products and reducing import demand. The nominal exchange rate of RMB was significantly declined from 2.8 Yuan to the dollar in the early of 1985 to 8.7 Yuan to the dollar in 1994.

1994-2004: In 1994, authorities officially announced adopting a managed floating exchange regime. Actually, after short period of appreciation of nominal exchange rate, the RMB was de facto fixed to the US dollar since 1995. During that time, China achieved rapid and stable development of the national economy. The scale of trade surplus had expanded year by year. For maintaining a stable exchange rate, the People's Bank of China had to make a large scale of intervention in market, with soaring reserves to more than 30% of GDP by the end of 2004. The RMB has faced increasing appreciation pressure since 2003.

2005-2007: In July 2005, authorities announced a new exchange rate system with reference to a basket of currencies, with numerical weights unannounced, allowing a movement of up to +/- 0.3% within any given day. The announcement opened the appreciating channel again. The RMB against the US dollar was increased 2.1 percent in value at the time. In less than three years, the RMB had appreciated more than 26%. However, in some studies, the de facto regime of China remained a peg to a basket with almost all weight on the dollar. (Frankel and Wei, 2007)

2008-2009: Since global financial crisis happened in 2007, the floating range of RMB exchange rate was narrowed between 2008 and 2009 in line with China and world economic interests. The RMB exchange rate remained basically stable against the US dollar at 6.83 Yuan to the dollar in the crisis, while a number of other currencies had an obviously volatility against the US dollar. The stable exchange rate helped China to deal with the change of external demand and mitigate the shocks of the financial crisis.

The major events and characteristics of evolution of China's exchange rate system since 1980s are listed below.

Table 2 Historical perspective of China's Exchange rate regime

Time	Change
1980	The State Council issued a decree prohibiting the use of foreign exchange for making payments within China.
1981	1) A dual exchange rate structure was adopted. Internal settlement rate ($ 1=¥ 2.8)was adopted in trade-related transaction under the foreign exchange allotment quota, however other transactions still were handled by official rate ($1 = ¥ 1.5). 2) An experimental trading system for foreign exchange has been established by the Bank of China.
1985	The internal settlement rate was abolished, and the dual exchange rates were unified into a single rate. Chinese residents were granted to hold foreign exchange and have foreign exchange accounts to deposit and withdraw in foreign exchange.
1986	The exchange rate was frequent adjustment and put under a "controlled floating" based on balance of payments and the rates of competitors. Shanghai International Trust And Investment Corporation was authorized to handle exchange business.
1991	The management of the exchange rate was altered to a procedure under which the rate would be adjusted frequently in light of certain indicators including development in international exchange markets, relative price performance, and trends in export production costs. At the end of 1991, the rate is $1= ¥ 5.43.

Continue Table 2

Time	Change
1994	The official rate and swap market rate is unified. Currency swap centers are replaced by the China Foreign Exchange Trade System (CFETS) in Shanghai (an integrated electronic system for interbank foreign exchange trading). The exchange rate is kept stable but is allowed to slowly appreciate 4% from 1994-1997. (from $ 1 = ¥ 8.7 to $ 1 = ¥ 8.28)
2005	The RMB exchange rate regime was reformed by moving into a managed floating exchange rate regime based on market supply and demand with reference to a basket of currencies on July 21, 2005. At the end of 2005, the rate became 8.07 Yuan to the dollar, and then gradually appreciated more than 15 percent to 6.83 Yuan to the dollar at the end of 2008.
2010	In June, The People's Bank of China announced that China will proceed further with reform of the RMB exchange rate regime and to enhance the RMB exchange rate flexibility.

Source: the People's Bank of China, IMF.

Comparing to the other three countries, China's exchange rate regime is still in the process of reform. The arrangement of exchange rate and the openness of capital account would be the major projects in external financial construction in near future. From historical perspective, China's economy is more stable, nevertheless it does not mean the future path is smooth as well.

India

The period after independence in 1947 was followed by a pegging exchange rate regime where India rupee was fixed to pound sterling because of the historical natural link with Britain. With the breakdown of Bretton Woods system in the early 1970s and the declining share of the Britain in India's trade, the India Rupee was delinked from pound sterling to a weighted basket of currencies of India's major trading partners. From 1975 to 1979, the exchange rate of rupee was officially determined by the Reserve Bank within a nominal band of +/-5percent of the weighted basket of currencies of India's major trading partners. As Dr. C. Rangarajan said in 1993, "The exchange rate regime of this period can be best characterized as an adjustable nominal peg with a band, with the nominal exchange rate being the operating variable to achieve the intermediate target of a medium-term equilibrium path of the real effective exchange rate".

India had a sharply deteriorating current account position in the late 1980s. The current account deficit was jumped 3 to 4 times in that decade. The deficit rose from approximately $ 2 billion in 1980 - 1984 to over $7 billion in both 1988 and 1990. Given this deteriorating trend, it is not surprising that India experienced a balance of payments crisis in 1990-1991. India entered into the 1990s with a burden of high current account deficit, about 3.2 percent of GDP in 1990.

Unsustainable constant account deficit was leading to a crisis, because of the tightening of access to short-term credit. India's foreign currency assets sharply shrank from $ 3.1 billion in August 1990 to $ 975 million (even less than one month of imports) on July

1991. In 1991, because of the increasing trade deficit and external debt①, India rupee faced depreciating pressure. India's government launched economic restructuring reform "Liberalization, privatization and internationalization" to deal with the severe domestic economic crisis and deteriorated international debt. Besides the adoption of a market determined uniform exchange rate in 1993 (as showed in table 3), Reserve Bank of India took measures to broaden and deepen the foreign exchange market involving institutional changes, relaxation of operating limits in financial area, and reducing government intervention to financial institutions.

Table 3 Historical perspective of India's Exchange rate regime

Year	Change
1931	The Indian Rupee was formally pegged to the Pound Sterling at the prevailing rate of Re. 1= 1sh 6d (or £ 1 = Rs. 13.33). A de facto sterling standard for the rupee was established.
1961	Full current account convertibility was restored to sterling in February. The dollar pool arrangement within the sterling area began and this weakened the sterling area link.
1966	The rupee was devalued by 36.5 per cent on June 6 against the sterling i.e. £ 1 = Rs. 13.33 to Rs. 21.00. The corresponding devaluation with respect to the US dollar was from $ 1= Rs. 4.7619 to Rs. 7.50 and the gold parity from Re. 1= 0.186621 gm to 0.118489 gm.
1967	Sterling was devalued in November from $ 2.80 to $ 2.40 (14.3 per cent) and consequently the rupee-sterling parity changed to £ 1 = Rs. 18.00, with the US dollar and gold parity remaining unchanged since 1966.
1971	The Bretton Woods system broke down in August. The rupee was pegged to the US dollar at $ 1= Rs. 7.50 but re-pegged to the pound sterling at £ 1 = Rs. 18.9677 in December, with a margin of 2.25 per cent on either side.
1972	The pound sterling was floated on June 23. India's pound-rupee parity was revalued on June 26 to £ 1 = Rs. 18.95. The Reserve Bank temporarily suspended the purchase of US dollars between June 24 and October 9. Rupee was revalued to £ 1 = Rs. 18.80 on July 4 due to the depreciation of the pound against US dollar.
1975	The rupee was pegged to an undisclosed currency basket on September 25 with the prevailing margin of 2.25 per cent on either side. The rupee sterling rate served as the intervention fixed at the time at £ 1 = Rs. 18.3084.
1979	The margin around the basket related parity was broadened to 5 per cent on January 30, thus giving a 10 percent band.
1991	The rupee was devalued by 17-18 percent through rupee-sterling rate, from £ 1 = Rs 34.36 to Rs. 37.19 on July 1 and further to Rs. 41.56 on July 3. The rupee depreciated against the US dollar from $ 1= Rs. 21.2 to Rs. 25.8.
1992	The Liberalized Exchange Rate Management System (LERMS) was introduced under which 40 per cent of the proceeds under exports and inward remittances are purchased at the official rate of exchange by the Reserve Bank for official use. The remainder of the receipts and other payments are converted at the market rate of exchange. Permissible receipts and payments on capital account are transacted at market rates (except in the case of official transactions like the IMF). The US dollar became the intervention currency with effect from March 4.
1993	Market related exchange rate introduced from March 1.

Source: RBI Annual Reports, EXIM Bank, 1993.

① Government of India borrowed heavily during the 1980S to finance the current account-deficit which kept on rising steadily. Total external debt (EDT) outstanding (as reported in World Bank's World Debt Tables) increased from $ 20.6 billion in 1980 to $ 71.6 billion in 1991 — a 248 percent increase as against a GDP real growth of 71 percent during the period.

In 1996, the Expert Group on Foreign Exchange Markets proposed a roadmap for foreign exchange markets reforms in India. The Reserve Bank decided to put government debt service payment (civil) through the market for ensuring that the exchange rate of rupee fully reflected the demand and supply situation. Cash reserve requirements on inter-bank borrowings were removed. In order to provide greater operational flexibility, banks were given freedom to fix their own open exchange position limit. With an aim towards providing hedging facilities to residents involved in foreign exchange transaction, monetary authority permitted banks to enter into a forward contract, foreign currency option contract, foreign currency-rupee swap, interest rate swap/currency swap/coupon swap/foreign currency option/forward rate agreement(FRA) contract with authorized dealers.

India's present exchange rate regime is managing volatility with no fixed rate target, and allowing the exchange rate movements decided by the underlying demand and supply conditions over a period in an orderly way. Nowadays there are three targets in India's exchange rate managing policy: 1) maintain healthy environment in the foreign exchange market by providing foreign exchange as considered necessary from time to time, and to prevent the emergence of speculative activities; 2) help maintain an adequate foreign exchange reserves; 3) help eliminate market constraints with a view to facilitating the development of healthy foreign exchange market. In IMF study of 20 selected developing and industrial countries, India's exchange rate policy has been described as "ideal" for Asia.

In India's experience, there is considerable merit in careful calibration of the pace and sequencing of external sector reforms. It should be recognized that reversal of any step in liberalization is very difficult since markets tend to react very negatively to reverse. Under floating exchange rate regime, exchange guarantees, both direct and indirect, should be avoided as much as possible. Economic entities should be encouraged to use hedging instruments for managing the risks in exchange rate movements. On the other side, we should be clear that capital flows prefer short-term debt flows. Therefore, direct investment should be given priority over portfolio investment.

Brazil

Since beginning of the 1980s, Brazilian economy has had a low and volatile growth while with a relative high inflation (until June 1994). Between 1991 and 2006, the average GDP growth was 2.1percent, contrasting with economic growth of 7.1percent in 1940s-1980s, that was during the period of import substitution industrialization (ISI). Brazil's investment rate has been low and stable for years because of the external vulnerability caused by the financing needs of balance of payments (at least until 2002), and the very high real interest rates (around 11percent in 1999-2006 on average).

At the beginning of the 1990s, Brazil implemented different currency strategies: from

1990 to 1994 economic policy was based in a crawling peg exchange rate regime with nominal diary devaluations and a policy of high real interest rates, which generated both high trade balance surplus and the attraction of capital flows, at the costs of a very high inflation. In 1994-1999 period Brazil embarked on a successful economic stabilization program, the Real Plan①, and adopted the US dollar as nominal anchor (1 Real= 1 $). Inflation, which had reached an annual level of nearly 5,000 percent at the end of 1993, fell sharply, reaching a low of 2.5percent in 1998.

Between 1994 and 1998, the real was set to a crawling peg permitted the currency to gradually depreciate at a controlled rate against the dollar. From 1996 to 1998, the central bank of Brazil used its foreign exchange reserve to prevent the currency from drastically devaluation. The reserves dropped by $24 billion or 40percent at that period. While the IMF provided $41.5 billion loan in 1998 to help Brazil defend its currency, the central bank decided to devalue the real by 8percent in January 1999, and in the end of January the real devalued 66 percent against the US dollar. With the large amount of foreign capital flight and lasting trade deficit, foreign exchange reserve sharply declined. Brazil's monetary authority had to shift from an essentially fixed exchange rate regime to a floating regime in January 1999.

Actually, in 1997 Brazil government realized the market pressure of depreciation on the real, and used $7.5 billion in reserve to defend the real's crawling peg. Current account deficit, stalled GDP growth and soaring public debt were the origin of the pressure. The East Asian financial crisis showed that even countries with strong economic growth and sound fiscal situation are subject to the speculative attack. Brazilian government had reason to believe there would be an attack on the real. However, with a pegged exchange rate regime and nearly $100 billion in public debt, the central bank of Brazil could do little to improve its situation. Pegged regime with free international capital mobility means less effective on the monetary policy such as over interest rate, while fiscal policy was not feasible because of the huge amount of public debt and a budget limitation. Therefore, we need to understand the publicly recognizing the real's overvaluation by the central bank of Brazil after getting the IMF loan in 1999. On the one hand this is a signal to the market that bank is acting transparently, in the other hand the following sudden devaluation of real damaged Brazil's credibility.

Russia

Russia became independent at the end of 1991, when the Soviet Union dissolved into 15 independent states. The Central Bank of the Russian Federation (CBRF), the government of Moscow and the association of Russian Banks established an independent

---

① Real Plan, use currency "Real" replacing the old currency "Cruzado", rate of new to old is 1 Real=2750 Cruzado.

joint stock company "Moscow Interbank Currency Exchange" (MICEX) for organizing interbank trading in currency and other financial instruments in January 1992. Since then the CBRF has used the exchange rate of the ruble, set at the MICEX, to set the official exchange rate of the ruble against foreign currencies.

Russia implemented the transition to a market economy under the suggestion of America economist Jeffrey Sachs and the leadership of Premier and reform economist Yegor Gaydar. The country resolutely carried out the total liberalization of prices in the beginning of 1992 and the ruble began to be internal convertibility and traded at current market rates. However, because civilian industry lack of competitiveness in Russia, as soon as the price liberalization began, prices started to rise sharply. Consumer prices shot up 25 times by the end of 1992, meanwhile the purchasing power of ruble declined sharply. Ruble's exchange rate declined from 100 rubles to the dollar in January 1992 to 415 rubles to the dollar at the end of the year. The ruble's depreciation was milder compared with the magnitude of the rise of prices, therefore foreign goods could be purchased cheap. The policy of stabilizing the ruble's exchange rate at a high level had its largest impact on its main objective of slowing down price inflation. However the policy of overvalued ruble at that time also had negative impacts: Export industries lost international competitiveness, while low price of import products harmed the sector that competes with foreign products. Economic recession and hyperinflation induced by radical reform greatly stimulated the domestic dollar demand. Ruble depreciated accompanied with capital flight. In July 1995 the ruble stood at 4553 to the dollar.

The corridor system that was introduced on July 1995 was instrumental by CBRF and government in stabilizing the ruble exchange rate. The corridor system is designed to limit the ruble's fluctuations within a narrow range by limiting its upper and lower limits[①]. The corridor system was subsequently extended until early 1998.

Because of financial crisis broke out, the policy of raising interest rates reached its limit. But Russia government and monetary authority strengthened the policy of stabilizing the ruble's exchange rate. In the beginning of 1998, the Russian monetary authority fixed the ruble's exchange rate at 6.2 rubles (6.1 rubles to the dollar from 1999) to the dollar with a margin of 15percent on either side for stabilizing domestic price. The new system was similar to the previous corridor system in that the ruble's fluctuation is limited within a certain range, while it is more fixed in nature than the corridor system since the central rate is fixed. At the same time, the government implemented redenomination of the currency. The ruble was devalued to one 1000th, which means 1000 old rubles has effectively become new 1 ruble.

---

① Under the system, Ruble would be allowed to move between first 4300-4900 Rubles to the Dollar, and then changed to between 4550-5100 Rubles to the Dollar in January 1996.

The sharply decrease in oil price and the breakout of Asian currency crisis, the situation of ruble was getting worse. The wave of ruble selling in August 1998 developed into a currency crisis. The momentum of ruble selling was stronger and the government was unable to hold on to the lower end of the exchange rate. On September 9, the Russian government had to abandon the target zone. From that day, the ruble shifted to a floating exchange rate system (managed floating).

Given the history of BRICs' currency system, it obvious that a fixed exchange rate was not the only cause of Brazil and Russia's economic woes, nor is a floating rate can fix all of the problems. Inflation could be the primary reason that Brazil and Russia adopted a crawling peg (corridor system) in the first place.

Conclusion

Between 2002 and 2007, annual real GDP growth averaged 10.4 percent in China, 7.9 percent in India, 6.9 percent in Russia and 3.7 percent in Brazil. Fast growth, strong economic foundations and large populations have made BRICs into the world's most promising markets. Although BRICs countries have suffered from the global financial crisis, large trade surpluses and foreign exchange reserves make them more resilient to the crisis.

BRICs exchange-rate and exchange rate systems have both common characters and differences. The financial crises in some BRICs' countries' history prove the importance of handling well the Rhythm and relationships between opening and development. China and India's cases show how is correct to implement a gradual and careful management of policies oriented towards the reduction of external vulnerability. Because of the impact of historical national financial crisis, Brazil, India and Russia had to turn to floating management in exchange rate in open financial market. Compared with other three countries, China falls behind in financial openness. Of course, it also helped us to avoid the consequences of blind and rapid opening of capital market in the wrong time. History is a textbook. China is similar with other three countries in economic development, model, and scale. So the experience and lessons in managing exchange rate of these countries are good references to China.

BRICs and Trade

Trade Linkages of BRICs in the World Economy

Zhang Yuyan, Tian Feng[*]

BRICs – Brazil, China, India and Russia – have been playing increasingly important roles in the world stage in the recent decades. Each of the four member countries is now an important player in the global goods trade field. (see Table 1, Table 2 and Figure 1). BRICs countries recorded a combined US$1.8 trillion worth of exports in 2009, accounting for 14 percent of the world's total. BRICs imported a total of US$1.6 trillion worth of goods in 2009, accounting for 12.5 percent of the world's entire value. By country, China's exports totaled US$1.2 trillion in 2009, accounting for 9.6 percent of the world's total, and its imports amounted to US$1 trillion, accounting for 8 percent of the world's total. China is now the world's biggest exporter of goods and the second largest importer of goods, with either its exports or imports two times the total size of foreign trade in Brazil, India and Russia. The other three BRICs countries – Brazil, Indian and Russia – are all among the world's top 30 trading powers. BRICs countries' relatively swift economic recovery and growth in the wake of the global financial crisis put themselves under increasing spotlight, further lifting their status in the global economic governance landscape. The heads of state from the four countries held their first summit in Yekaterinburg, Russia on June 16, 2009. However, some key questions related to the development of BRICs have not been inadequately resolved yet. They include: what is the current state of BRICs' trade linkages in the world economy? What kind of significant changes has brought about to such linkages if compared with that in the past? What kind of impact such changes are likely to have on their economic growth prospects? And what are the prospects of the internal trade within BRICs block?

---

* Zhang Yuyan, professor and Director General of the Institute of World Economics and Politics, Chinese Academy of Social Sciences; Tian Feng, research associate fellow, Institute of World Economics and Politics, Chinese Academy of Social Sciences.

Table 1 BRICs: merchandise trade (export), 2009

Unit: Billion dollars and percentage

	Value	Annual % change				Rank	Share
	2009	2005-2009	2007	2008	2009	2009	2009
Brazil	153	7	17	23	-23	24	1.2
China	1202	12	26	17	-16	1	9.6
India	155	12	23	30	-20	22	1.2
Russia	304	6	17	33	-36	13	2.4
World	12147	4	16	15	-23		

Note: 1. The Value calculated under world does not exclude the internal trade in the EU block.

2.To keep in consistency with the data from WTO, the amount of world value does include significant re-exports or imports for re-exports that is 12,461 trillion US dollars.

3. EU is not treated as single block when calculating rank.

Source: WTO website.

Table 2 BRICs: merchandise trade (import), 2009

Unit: Billion dollars and percentage

	Value	Annual % change				Rank	Share
	2009	2005-2009	2007	2008	2009	2009	2009
Brazil	134	15	32	44	-25	26	1.1
China	1006	11	21	18	-11	2	8
India	244	14	29	40	-24	15	1.9
Russia	192	11	36	31	-34	17	1.5
World	12385	4	15	16	-24		

Note: 1. The Value calculated under world does not exclude the internal trade in the EU block.

2.To keep in consistency with the data from WTO, the amount of world value does include significant re-exports or imports for re-exports that is 12,461 trillion US dollars.

3. EU is not treated as single block when calculating rank.

Source: WTO website.

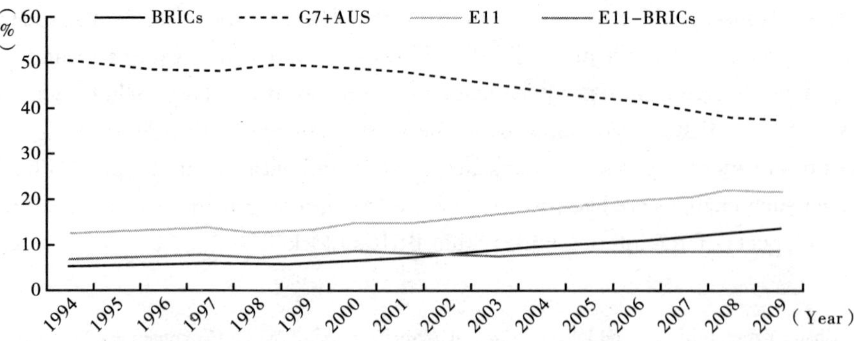

Figure 1 BRICs: merchandise trade/world total merchandise trade (1994- 2009)

Source: WTO website.

To address the above-mentioned questions, we tentatively conducted some preliminary studies. First, we analyzed the specific channels through which global financial crisis are affecting economic growth in BRICs countries through international trade. And based on this study, we raised our views on the notion of "decoupling" (emerging economies, BRICs countries included, can manage to grow on its own lastingly no matter what happens in the developed countries). Secondly, we examined the changes in the number of merchandise BRICs exported to different markets and further explored what possible significance such changes will bring to economic growth in each of the BRICs countries. In the third section, we systematically examined BRICs countries' trade balance situation with the world, other representative countries and representative groups of countries, revealing each member country's evolving comparative advantages behind the changing trade balance situations and what impact such changes are having on their economic growth. In order to fully understand and analyze what impact the trade linkages in the world economy are having on BRICs countries, we in the forth section calculated competitive complementarities index and competitive stress index BRICs countries have with some designated countries or specified groups of nations. And the fifth section is our conclusion.

In order to facilitate this study and comparison, this paper is inclined to focus on the trade relations between BRICs and other three representative groups of countries when analyzing BRICs' trade linkages in the world economy. These three representative groups of countries are: BRICs itself, which is referred to "BRICs" hereinafter; emerging economies, represented by E11 in the paper and the major developed countries, represented by G7+AUS in the article.① E11 refers to the 11 developing countries inside the G20 group, and G7+AUS refers to those developed countries inside the G20 excluding EU. In addition, we also analyze trade linkages between BRICs countries and some major developed countries such as America, Japan and Germany so as to present a clearer and more comprehensive picture to the readers. In order to reflect the latest developments and unless otherwise stated, the individual country's trade figure we use in this article are from year of 2009. Due to data availability, India's sub-trade figures is from 2008 but its total trade value figures is still from 2009.

---

① E11 refers to Argentina, Brazil, China, India, Indonesia, South Korea, Mexico, Russia, Saudi Arabia, South Africa and Turkey. G7+AUS refers to the United States, Japan, Germany, Britain, France, Italy, Canda (G7) and Australia. For detailed discussion about that, please see Zhang Yuyan and Tian Feng, "The Definition of Emerging Economies and Their Status in the World Economy Landscape ", *International Economic Review*, forthcoming.

Global financial crisis transmission and BRICs' trade linkages

The notion of "decoupling" has been a hot topic in the world economic arena before the outbreak of the global financial crisis. The supporter of decoupling basically holds that emerging economies, BRICs countries included, can manage to grow on its own no matter what happens in the developed countries. Some trade figures lend supports to the theory. Figure 2 shows that BRICs states' exports to developed countries (G7+AUS) have generally been in decline until 2007 when the subprime crisis turned into a global financial crisis. Only Russia's exports to G7 countries and Australia roughly maintained the same level as it did in 2000. In a stark contrast to their declining reliance on developed countries, BRICs countries' exports to emerging economies (including BRICs, E11 and E11-BRICs) have increased significantly. For Brazil, the importance of emerging economies has already been at par with or even exceeded that of developed countries.

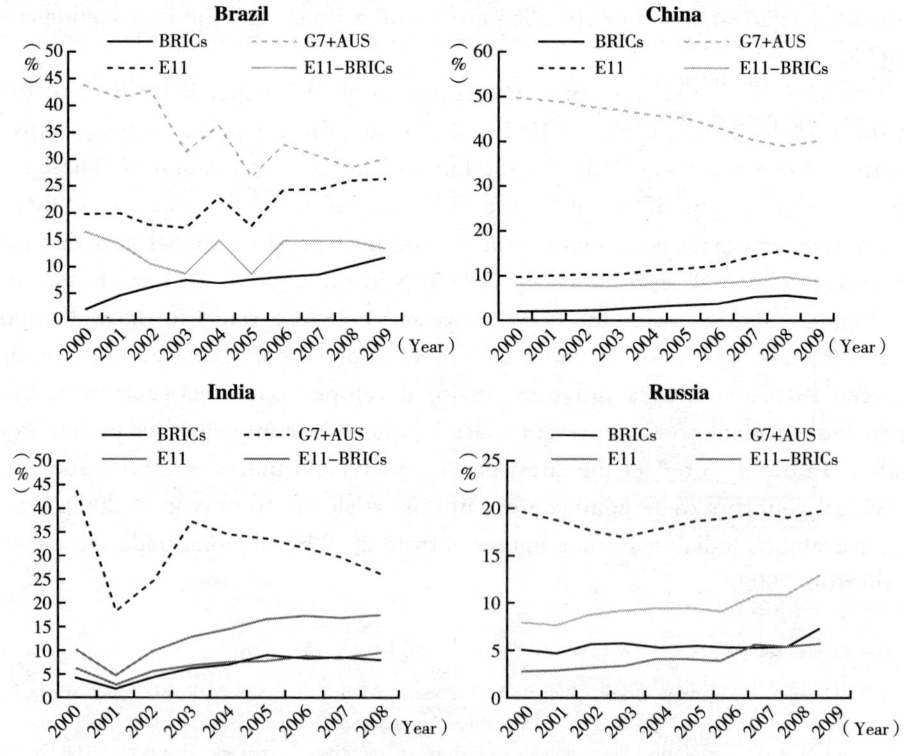

Figure 2 BRICs: export/total export (2000-2009)

Source: UN COMTRADE; Authors' calculation.

The outbreak of the global financial crisis has, to some extent, cast some doubt over the "decoupling" theory. A series of empirical studies have shown that international trade is one of the major channels through which crisis contagion spreads across borders (Eichengreen and Rose, 1999; Glick and Rose, 1999; Forbes and Chinn, 2003).① (Exports in Brazil, China, India and Russia tumbled 23 percent, 16 percent, 20 percent and 36 percent year-on-year in 2009 (see Table 1 and Table 2). It is apparent that the economic recession and imports scale-back in the developed countries have seriously affected BRICs' exports, then how did this occur?

However, although the importance of developed countries to the BRICs (based on percentage of export in their total export volume) is declining, G7 and Australia are still the most important exports market for them (see Figure 2). In 2007, 31.8 percent of Brazil's exports ended up in G7 and Australia, while the figure for China, India and Russia was 40.5 percent, 29.4 percent and 20.6 percent respectively. At the same time, the internal trade among the BRICs only accounted for 10 percent of Brazil's exports, the figure for China, India and Russia was 5 percent, 8 percent and 5 percent respectively. The exports bounded for E11 countries accounted for 25 percent, 14 percent, 17 percent and 11 percent of Brazil, China, India and Russia's exports respectively. And if we judge the importance of developed countries to BRICs' exports by using the export/GDP methodology, the importance held largely steady for Brazil, China and India during the 2000 to 2007 period, and it only dropped slightly for Russia.

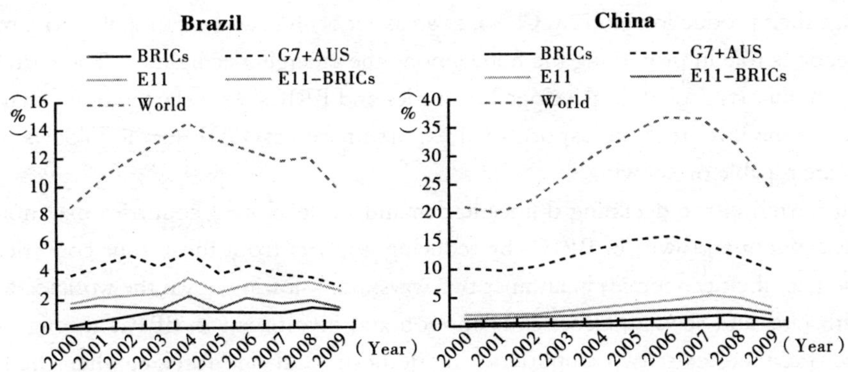

① Eichengreen, Barry and Andrew Rose, 1999, "Contagious Currency Crises: Channels of Conveyance," in Takatoshi Ito and Anne Krueger (eds.), *Changes in Exchange Rates in Rapidly Developing Economies*, University of Chicago Press, Chicago. Glick, Reuven and Andrew Rose, 1999, "Contagion and Trade: Why Are Currency Crises Regional?" *Journal of International Money and Finance,* Vol 18, August, pp. 603-617. Forbes, Kristin and Menzie Chinn, 2003, "A Decomposition of Global Linkages in Financial Markets Over Time," NBER Working Paper No. 9555, NBER, Cambridge, MA, March.

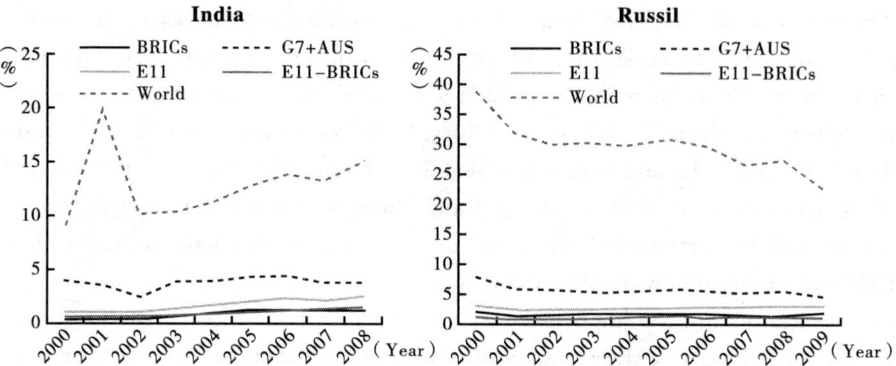

Figure 3 BRICs: export/GDP (2000-2009)

Source: UN COMTRADE; Authors' calculation.

The crisis contagion is also closely correlated to trade structure. Although figures show that trade between BRICs countries and G7 and Australia, trade among BRICs countries and trade between BRICs nations and E11 countries all expanded markedly in terms of value during the same period, the drivers behind their growth may vary considerably. The trade growth between G7 and Australia and BRICs may have reflected the former group's demand for product variety against the backdrop of a gigantic domestic market. While the trade growth among BRICs and with E11 countries may have reflected the improved vertical divisions of labor of production enterprises have been able to achieve after they arrange their production globally. China, as an assembly hub and exports platform, made a tremendous role in promoting the trade among the emerging economies. The correlation between imports growth in developed countries and BRICs' exports, therefore, may have exceeded the level that the export/total export or export/GDP methodologies we are using are capable of showing.

Furthermore, the declining domestic demand in developed countries may not only affect economic growth in BRICs by reducing imports from those four countries, but also impact their economies in another two ways: first, slowing down the world economic growth rate; and second, affect consumption and investment in BRICs through trade. Therefore, there exist two amplifiers, one domestic and one foreign, when the global financial crisis is spreading through the international trade. In the international amplifier front, each economic recession occurred in the United State between 1948 and 2006 was accompanied by a significant drop in its imports growth rate accordingly. For example, America's GDP growth rate decreased 2.9 percentage points in 2001, its imports growth rate slumped 14.6 percentage points at the same time. Meanwhile, 74 out of the world's 130 economies saw both their GDP expansion rate and US-bound exports growth rate decline. Moreover, the more their US-bound exports growth rate dropped, the steeper their GDP expansion rate declined. It indicates that America's economic recession will not only cause its imports growth rate to decrease, it will also drag down the GDP growth rate at those exporting countries. Imports decline in the United States will cause some exporting countries' GDP growth to slow down, which will in turn cause those countries themselves to curb imports as their income shrinks, resulting in a chain of reaction that will amplify the impact the America's imports slowdown has on the world trade and global economic growth rate. Eventually, it will amplify the impact the global financial crisis has on trade and economic growth at BRICs.

Export diversification and BRICs' trade linkage

Our analysis in the proceeding section has shown that BRICs' exports value to the three groups of countries and the world as a whole all expanded significantly in 2000 to 2009 period. In the international trade theory, export growth can be divided into extensive margin and intensive margin growth. Extensive margin growth indicates an increase in the range of product varieties exported to existing or new markets, while intensive margin growth means more exports of the same varieties to the same markets. In this section, we try to examine BRICs' trade linkage in the world economy through the extensive margin approach that is relatively rarely used in researches.① The specific approach is as follows: based on the HS96 six-digit, we analyze the items of BRICs' exports and their changes between 1999 and 2009.②

Figure 4 shows the following characteristics demonstrated by the product items BRICs exported in 2009: (1) Brazil exported 4,209 product items in 2009, China had 4,569 items, Russia boasted 4,036 items while India exported 4,829 product items in 2008; (2) The number of product items BRICs nations exported to developed countries far exceeded that recorded in trade between themselves. Considering data availability and importance, we selected America, Japan, Germany and G7+AUS as a group to record the number of product items each BRICs country exported. We found that we could draw the same conclusion mentioned above either by calculating it country by country or calculating it by treating BRICs and G7+AUS as two groups. The only exception may be China, which exported almost the same number of product items to Brazil, India, Russia, America, Japan and Germany in 2009. And the number of its export product items to other BRICs countries and G7+AUS has only 458 in difference based on HS 96 six-digit.

① It should be noted that there are still quite a few researchers who have done important studies in this area and we will mention them in the later paragraph.

② Limited by the availability of the data, we used data recorded in 1999 and 2008 when we analyzed India's exporting merchandise varieties.

The changes in the number of merchandise BRICs countries exported to their trading partners during the 1999-2009 period are as follow: (1) BRICs countries saw the number of their exporting merchandise only increase slightly, or even decline in some countries. This phenomenon might have been caused by the following two factors: first, the four BRICs countries had already exported a considerable number of merchandise in 1999, which, to some extent, may have limited the room for further increase; secondly, the global financial crisis might have affected the number of BRICs countries' exporting merchandise.① (2) Each of the BRICs countries saw the number of merchandise it exported to other three members increase markedly, and the number of China's exporting merchandise and the number of products other three member countries exported to China, in particular, showed the most dramatic increase. In breakdown, the number of merchandise Brazil exported to China, India and Russia rose by 750, 637 and 385 respectively during the decade. The number of product items China exported to Brazil, India and Russia increased by 1470, 1615 and 1555 respectively. The number of merchandise India exported to Brazil, China and Russia increased by 1117, 1611 and 558, respectively, during the period. And the number of merchandise Russia exported to Brazil, China and India rose by 193, 186 and 481 respectively between 1999 and 2009. (3) Each of the BRICs countries saw the number of merchandise it exported to America, Japan, Germany and other developed economies increased moderately, with growth rate generally lower than that recorded in their trade with other BRICs members. China best exemplifies this phenomenon. (4) If comparing the changes in the number of merchandise Brazil, China, India and Russia each exported to BRICs, G7+AUS and the world as whole, it showed the biggest increase in BRICs-bound exports, followed by G7+AUS and the world, which even reported decline in some cases.

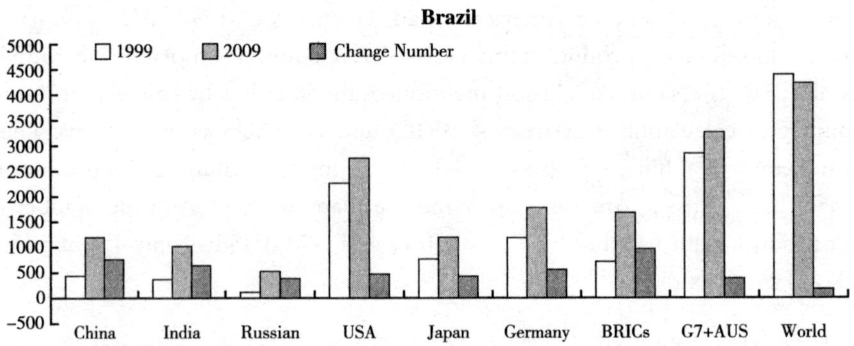

① Despite this deficiency, we still used 2009 data in our research in order to show the latest developments.

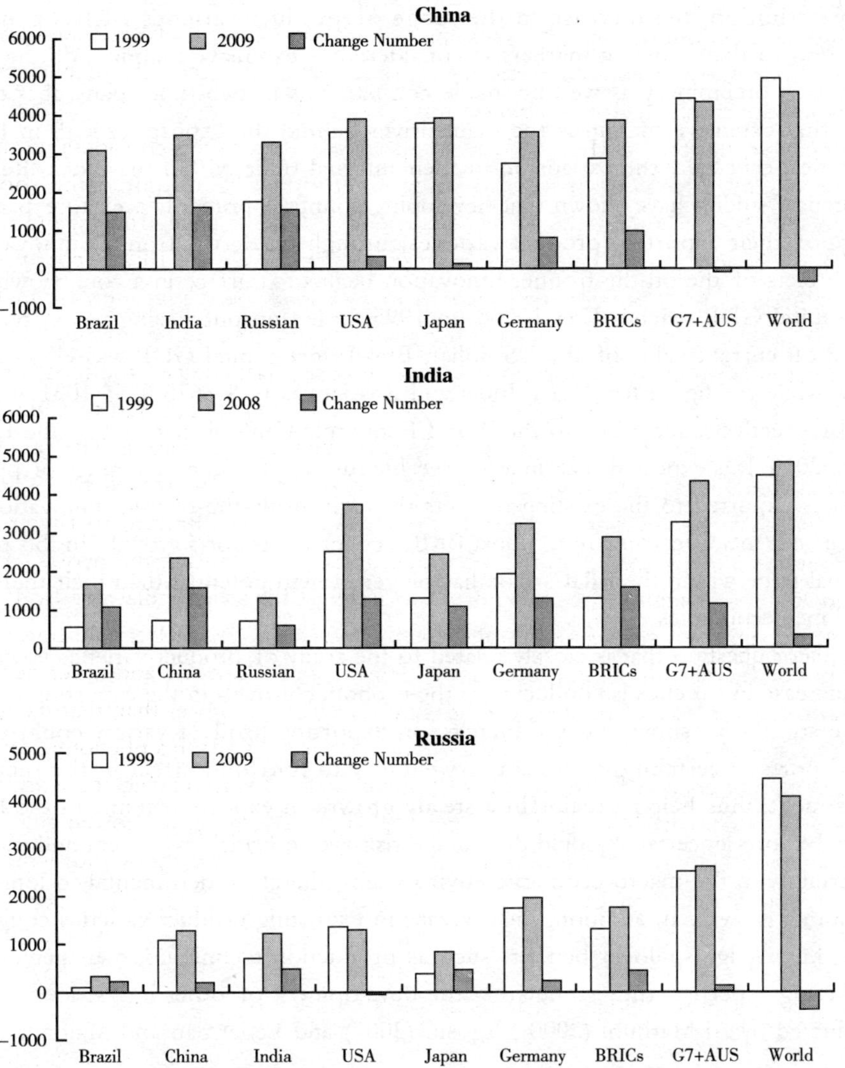

Figure 4 BRICs: export diversification (1999-2009)

Note: 1. Calculations are based on HS96 code system.

2. Limited by availability of data, we used data recorded in 1999 and 2008 when analyzing India's exporting merchandise varieties.

3. When tallying the changes in the number of merchandise varieties exported by BRICs and G7+AUS when they are considered as two groups, we omit the products that may cause double calculations because of the internal trade. For example, if China exported animal grease to Brazil in 1999 but not to Russia and it exported the merchandise to both Brazil and Russia in 2009, then we say the number of merchandise China exported to Russia increased by one during 1999-2009 period, but the number of merchandise China exported to BRICs did not increase.

Source: UN COMTRADE; Authors' calculation.

By definition, the increase in the range of product varieties BRICs countries exported to their existing markets is considered as extensive margin. Although our analysis is preliminary as we only made comparisons in two time spans, it is crystal clear that extensive margin is the main driver behind the exports growth in BRICs countries, especially the expansion in their internal trade within the block. Relevant theoretical studies have shown that developing countries primarily seek to expand the range of their exporting product varieties through inside-the-frontier innovation.[①] The effects of the on-the-frontier innovation begins to surface in a country when its per capital GDP reaches US$ 10000 (in 1995, based on purchasing power parity).[②] Based on current value of the US dollar, Brazil's per capital GDP was US$ 8220 in 2009, while the figure for China, India and Russia was US$ 3678, US$ 1031 and US$ 8694 respectively, according to the World Economic Outlook released by the IMF in April, 2010. It is expected that, in a foreseeable future, expanding the range of product varieties exported to the existing markets through inside-the-frontier innovation will remain as a major instrument to boost BRICs countries' exports growth. In this regard, internal trade within the BRICs bloc has bigger growth potential than their trade with developed economies.

A major question that is closely related to the study of product varieties is whether the increase in varieties is conducive to the economic growth in the exporting country. Some studies 5[③] show that the increase in exporting product variety could reduce the exports uncertainty in the country, similar to portfolio effect in the securities investment, thus helping maintain a steady growth in exports revenue in the longer term. Exports uncertainty could discourage risk-averse firms' investment and raise the uncertainty in the macro economic environment, therefore detrimental to long-term economic growth. In addition, the increase in exporting product varieties could also bring knowledge spillover benefits such as production techniques, management and marketing expertise, thus stimulating the development of other industries.[④] Studies conducted by Al-Marhubi (2000), Agosin (2007) and Lederman and Maloney (2007)

---

① It means technology proliferation.

② It means inventions and creations. Refer to Klinger, B., and D. Lederman, 2006, "Diversification, Innovation, and Imitation inside the Global Technological Frontier," Research Policy Working Paper 3872, World Bank, Washington, D.C.

③ Hesse, Heiko, 2008, "Export diversification and Economic Growth", *Working Paper* No.21, World Bank, Washington, D.C. Ghosh, A. R., and J. Ostry, 1994, "Export Instability and the External Balance in Developing Countries." *IMF Staff Papers* 41: 214-35, Bleaney, M., and D. Greenaway, 2001, "The Impact of Terms of Trade and Real Exchange Volatility on Investment and Growth in Sub-Saharan Africa," *Journal of Development Economics* 65: 491-500.

④ Amin Guitierrez de Pineres, S., and M. J. Ferrantino, 2000, *Export Dynamics and Economic Growth in Latin America*, Burlington, Vermont: Ashgate Publishing Ltd.

all collaborated this findings.[①] The increase in the exporting product varieties in the internal trade within BRICs block is of positive significance to every member country's economic growth.

Trade balance, change in comparative advantage and BRICs' trade linkages

In the post-crisis era, the attention is shifting to how to keep the world economy growing in a sustainable and balanced pattern. Trade balance is not only one of the focus issues in the bilateral trade relations, it is also increasingly becoming a highly politically sensitive subject. In this section, we will examine and systematically analyze the trade balance between BRICs countries and the world economy as whole, and between them and some representative groups of countries, in a bid to show the corresponding changes in their comparative advantages behind the changes in their trade balances, and what kind of impact such changes may have on economic growth in BRICs.

Table 3 BRICs: trade balance (2009)

Unit: million US$

	Brazil	China	India	Russia
		BRICs		
Brazil	0.0	-14162.5	2080.8	-2515.6
China	4279.7	0.0	-18346.1	-6760.1
India	1224.1	15952.3	0.0	3294.1
Russian	1456.5	-3769.2	-3236.9	0.0
		E11-BRICs		
Argentina	1503.8	-823.1	-211.0	-953.5
Indonesia	163.1	1056.8	-3786.2	-357.5
Mexico	-107.5	8417.1	-1083.4	88.0
Korea	-2196.2	-48871.8	-4103.7	609.0
Saudi Arabia	355.4	-14642.4	-17647.3	305.1
South Africa	826.5	-1327.7	-3073.7	-124.6
Turkey	210.5	6588.0	-276.8	7045.2

① Al-Marhubi, F, 2000, "Export Diversification And Growth: An Empirical Investigation." Applied Economics Letters 7: 559–62. Agosin, M. R, 2007, "Export Diversification and Growth in Emerging Economies," *Working Paper No. 233*. Departamento de Economía, Universidad de Chile. Lederman, D., and W. F. Maloney, 2007, "Trade Structure and Growth." In *Natural Resources: Neither Curse Nor Destiny*, D. Lederman and W.F. Maloney, eds. Palo Alto: Stanford University Press.

Continue Table 3

	Brazil	China	India	Russia
		G7+AUS		
Australia	-351.5	-18793.2	-8243.6	-530.8
Canada	110.8	5648.9	-903.5	-604.4
France	-676.0	8580.6	-3026.0	-1169.0
Germany	-3690.7	-5844.5	-4844.6	-9273.6
Italy	-647.4	9223.3	-400.7	12434.1
Japan	-1097.9	-33026.6	-3734.4	-246.2
United Kingdom	1318.5	23400.0	398.4	3346.7
USA	-4469.2	143539.9	-2179.3	-1019.4
		GROUPS		
BRICs	6960.3	-1979.4	-19502.2	-5981.6
E11	7715.9	-51582.6	-49684.3	630.0
E11-BRICs	755.6	-49603.2	-30182.1	6611.6
G7+AUS	-9503.4	132728.4	-22933.7	2937.4
World	25347.4	196091.5	-133851.2	124357.1

Note: 1. The seed data – individual country's import and export figures – used to form this Table are sourced from UN's COMTRADE database, but due to difference each reporter has in their statistics, the trade figures may show disparity. For example, when Brazil is a reporter to the COMTRADE database, it reported a US$4.28 billion trade surplus with China, but when China is reporter, it reported a US$14.16 billion trade deficit with Brazil.

2. Limited by availability of data, we used 2008 data when tallying India's trade balance figures.

Source: UN COMTRADE; Authors' calculation.

Table 3 shows that three BRICs countries have trade surplus except India. Brazil recorded US$ 25.3 billion trade surplus in 2009, nearly one third of which came from its trade with other BRICs countries. The South American country registered a US$ 4.28 billion, US$ 1.22 billion and US$ 1.46 billion trade surplus with China, India and Russia, respectively, in 2009. China reported nearly US$ 200 billion trade surplus in 2009, nearly two thirds of which was generated from its trade with the major developed countries such as G7+AUS. China recorded trade deficit with each of all the E11 and BRICs countries. In particular, countries included in the E11 group but were not members of the BRICs are the major trade deficit source for China. Russia recorded a staggering US$ 124.36 billion trade surplus in 2009, of which US$ 2.93 billion came from its trade with G7+AUS, US$ 6.6 billion from non-BRICs E11 countries. Other three BRICs countries contributed US$ 6 billion trade surplus to Russia. India booked a trade deficit of US$ 133.85 billion in 2008, making it the only BRICs country that recorded a deficit. Other three BRICs countries contributed US$ 19.5 billion to India's trade deficit.

Our analysis of BRICs' trade balance in 2009 is helpful for us to grasp the latest development in the field, but as we stated before, 2009 was a special year because of the global financial crisis, which may have had significant impacts on BRICs' trade balance as their exports and imports had been affected by the changes in internal and external macroeconomic environments. In order to present an outlook, we need to find out what are the structural factors that have caused the changes in BRICs countries' trade balance. We are now, based on HS96 Two-digit, conducting a more thorough analysis by combining it with a research into their situation in 2000.

Firstly, we assume that a country's surplus/deficit recorded for all specific merchandise should move in a way that is in proportion with its overall trade balance situation if its comparative advantage does not change. Otherwise, it can be roughly said that a specific merchandise' comparative advantage has changed. For instance, if China's trade surplus in 2009 was three times that in 2000 while the trade surplus generated from garment sector in 2009 was four times that in 2000, then we might draw conclusion that China's comparative advantage in its garment industry strengthened during the period. Based on such assumption, we calculated BRICs countries' trade surplus/deficit recorded in their trade with the word and among themselves in 2000 and 2009 separately. And we draw a scatter plot showing changes of each specific country's trade balance during the period. For those products that are moving astray from the main curve, we conclude that these products' comparative edges may have altered during the set period. For details see Figure 5.

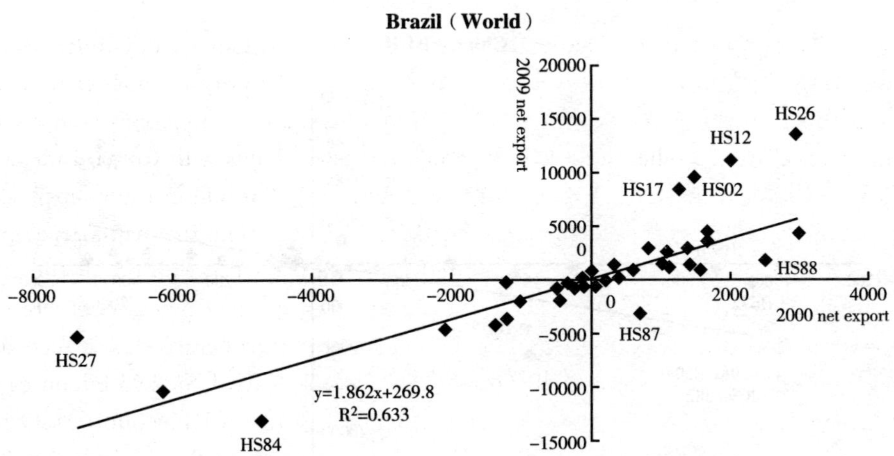

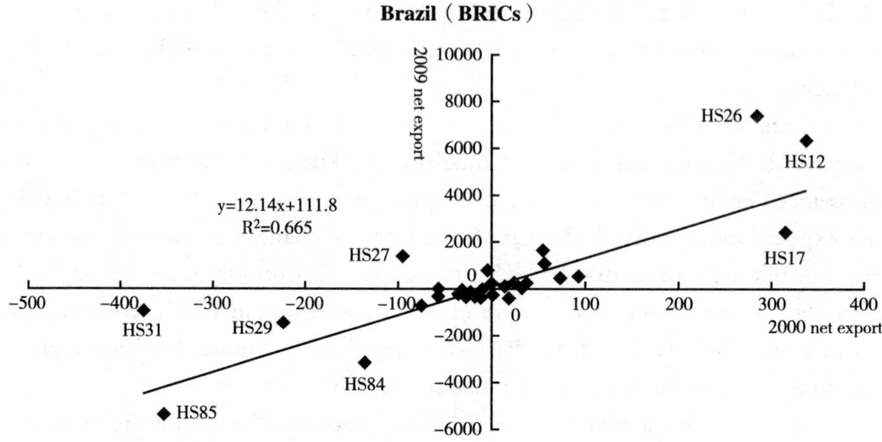
Brazil (BRICs)
2009 net export
10000
8000
6000
4000
2000
0
-2000
-4000
-6000
y=12.14x+111.8
R²=0.665
HS26
HS12
HS17
HS27
HS31
HS29
HS84
HS85
-500
-400
-300
-200
-100
0
100
200
300
400
2000 net export

Chian (World)

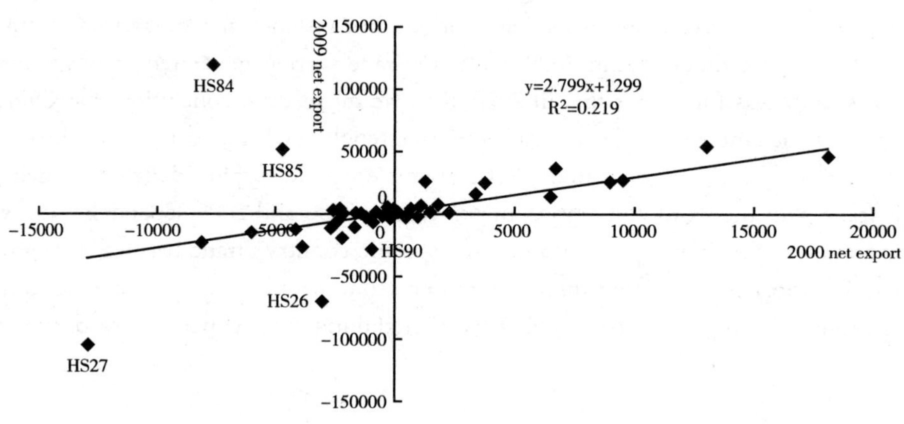
2009 net export
150000
100000
50000
0
-50000
-100000
-150000
y=2.799x+1299
R²=0.219
HS84
HS85
HS90
HS26
HS27
-15000
-10000
-5000
0
5000
10000
15000
20000
2000 net export

China (BRICs)

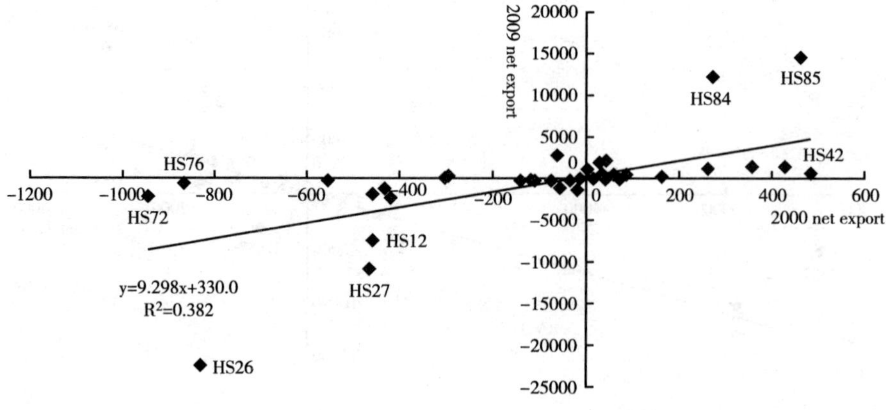
2009 net export
20000
15000
10000
5000
0
-5000
-10000
-15000
-20000
-25000
HS85
HS84
HS42
HS76
HS72
HS12
HS27
HS26
y=9.298x+330.0
R²=0.382
-1200
-1000
-800
-600
-400
-200
0
200
400
600
2000 net export

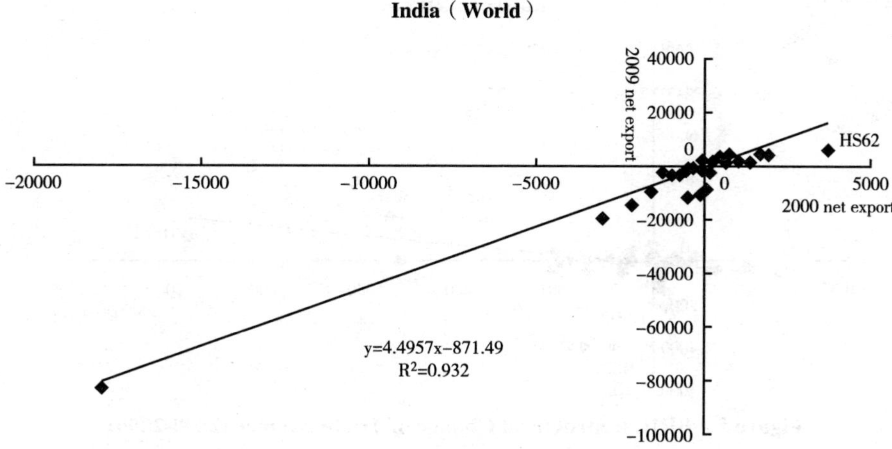
India（World）
2009 net export
40000
20000
0
–20000
–40000
–60000
–80000
–100000
–20000
–15000
–10000
–5000
0
5000
2000 net export
HS62
y=4.4957x–871.49
R2=0.932

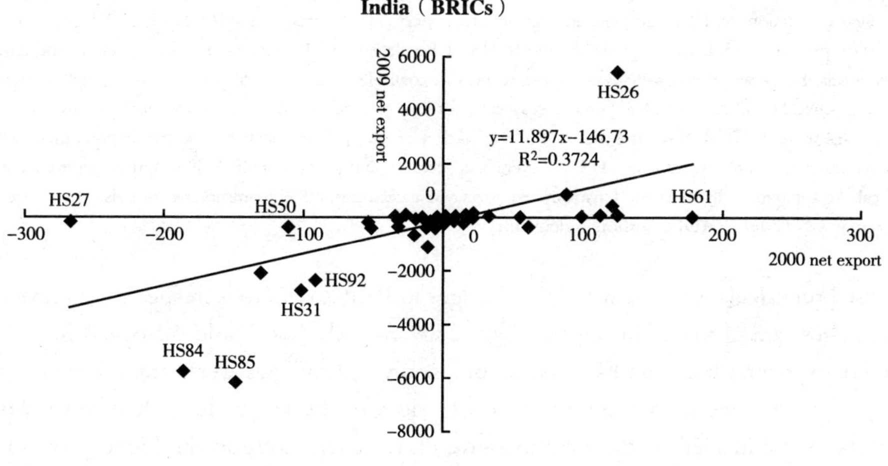
India（BRICs）
2009 net export
6000
4000
2000
0
–2000
–4000
–6000
–8000
–300
–200
–100
0
100
200
300
2000 net export
HS26
y=11.897x–146.73
R2=0.3724
HS27
HS50
HS61
HS92
HS31
HS84
HS85

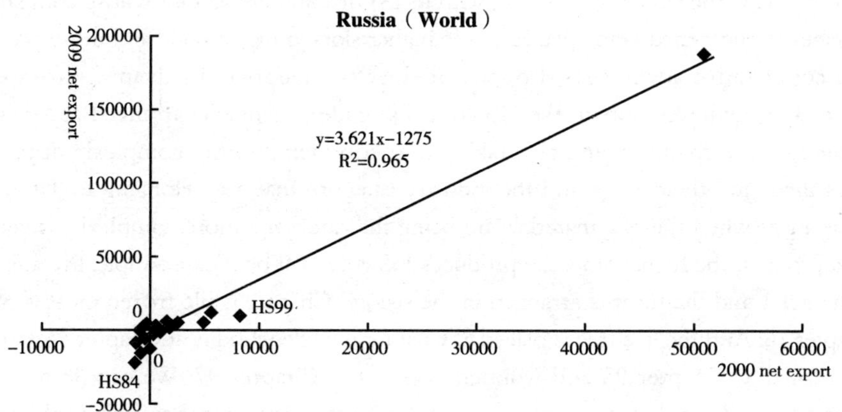
Russia（World）
2009 net export
200000
150000
100000
50000
0
–50000
–10000
0
10000
20000
30000
40000
50000
60000
2000 net export
y=3.621x–1275
R2=0.965
HS99
HS84

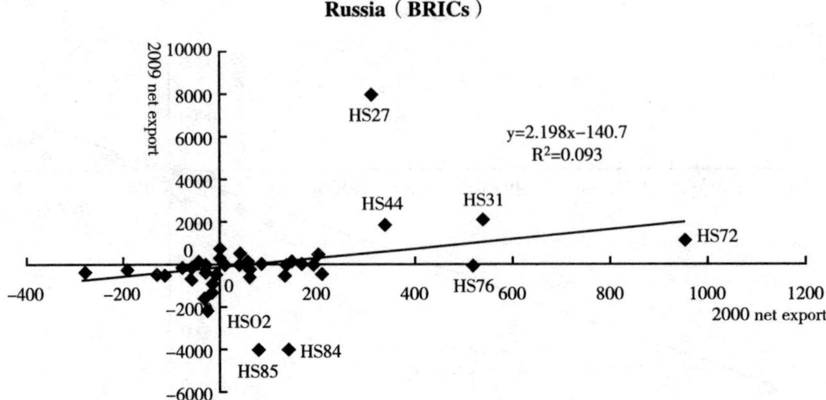

Figure 5 BRICs: Structural Change of Trade Balance (2000-2009)

Unit: Million US$

Note: HS02 Meat and edible meat offal; HS12 Oil seed, oleagic fruits, grain, seed, fruit, etc, nes; HS17 Sugars and sugar confectionery; HS17 Sugars and sugar confectionery; HS26 Ores, slag and ash; HS27 Mineral fuels, oils, distillation products, etc; HS29 Organic chemicals; HS 31 Fertilizers; HS 42 Articles of leather, animal gut, harness, travel goods; HS44 Wood and articles of wood, wood charcoal; HS 50 Silk; HS 61 Articles of apparel, accessories, knit or crochet; HS 62 Articles of apparel, accessories, not knit or crochet; HS 72 Iron and steel; HS 76 Aluminium and articles thereof; HS84 Nuclear reactors, boilers, machinery, etc; HS 85 Electrical, electronic equipment; HS 87 Vehicles other than railway, tramway; HS 88 Aircraft, spacecraft, and parts thereof; HS90 Optical, photo, technical, medical, etc apparatus; HS 92 Musical instruments, parts and accessories; HS99 Commodities not elsewhere specified.

Source: UN COMTRADE; Authors' calculation.

Based on calculations, we listed the changes in BRICs countries' respective comparative advantages taking place during the 2000-2009 periods (see Table 4). Brazil, India and Russia's exporting merchandise whose comparative advantages were strengthened during the past decade were basically in the lower slots in the HS code , while those whose advantages diminished or their comparative disadvantage were in the higher slots in HS code. For China, the situation reversed, with its exporting merchandise whose comparative advantages strengthened being placed in the higher slots in ht HS code and those products whose comparative advantages dropped or their comparative disadvantage rose being positioned in the lower slots in the HS code. HS code is generally arranged according to the origin of merchandise, and also taking into consideration the complexity it takes to process them and their usage and the industry category that are belonging to. Under the circumstances when the raw materials are being the same, the more complexity it takes to make a product, the higher slots the product's HS code will be. Fox example, live animal is the Chapter 1 and the meat is arranged in the second Chapter while frozen meat is placed at Chapter 16. And the live tree is placed at Chapter 6 while wood is at Chapter 44, wooden toy is placed at Chapter 95 and wooden crafts is at Chapter 97. We can draw a basic conclusion that China's comparative advantages in the area of processing sophisticated products improved, while other three BRICs member countries saw their comparative advantages enhanced in some agricultural and mineral products categories, indicating that the trade complementarity between China and the other three BRICs countries in increasing and the competition among the other three countries is intensifying.

Table 4 BRICs: change of comparative advantage (2000-2009)

Unit: Million US$

	Brazil		China		India		Russia	
	World	BRICs	World	BRICs	World	BRICs	World	BRICs
HS02	+							–
HS12	+	+	–					
HS17	+	–						
HS26	+	+	–	–		+		
HS27	+	+	–	–		+		+
HS29		+						
HS31		+				–		+
HS42			–					
HS44								+
HS50						+		
HS61						–		
HS62					–			
HS72			+					–
HS76			+					–
HS84	–	–	+	+		–	–	–
HS85		–	+	+		–		–
HS87	–							
HS88	–							
HS90				–				
HS92						–		
HS99							–	

Note: HS02 Meat and edible meat offal; HS12 Oil seed, oleagic fruits, grain, seed, fruit, etc, nes; HS17 Sugars and sugar confectionery; HS17 Sugars and sugar confectionery; HS26 Ores, slag and ash; HS27 Mineral fuels, oils, distillation products, etc; HS29 Organic chemicals; HS 31 Fertilizers; HS 42 Articles of leather, animal gut, harness, travel goods; HS44 Wood and articles of wood, wood charcoal; HS 50 Silk; HS 61 Articles of apparel, accessories, knit or crochet; HS 62 Articles of apparel, accessories, not knit or crochet; HS 72 Iron and steel; HS 76 Aluminium and articles thereof; HS84 Nuclear reactors, boilers, machinery, etc; HS 85 Electrical, electronic equipment; HS 87 Vehicles other than railway, tramway; HS 88 Aircraft, spacecraft, and parts thereof; HS90 Optical, photo, technical, medical, etc apparatus; HS 92 Musical instruments, parts and accessories; HS99 Commodities not elsewhere specified.

Source: UN COMTRADE; Authors' calculation.

It is noteworthy that Brazil, India and Russia's comparative advantages mentioned in chapter 26 and 27 have all increased. Both chapters discussed mineral resources, with chapter 26 dwelling on mineral sand, mineral slag and mineral ash, and chapter 27 talking about mineral fuel, mineral oil and its distilled products. The three countries' increased comparative advantage in those areas is mainly reflected in the internal trade within BRICs block. This phenomenon bags a question: will the augmented comparative advantage in the resource products jeopardize their long-term economic growth?

The term "resource curse" refers to a phenomenon where an abundance of natural resource will depress the economic growth, noting that nations with rich endowments of natural resources often dramatically underperform economically relative to what one would expect. The term Dutch Disease originated in 1960s, when a large natural gas discovery was made in Netherlands, The rapid development of the resource industry as a result of the gas discovery, however, depressed Dutch's agriculture and other industrial sectors and also flagged the growth of its export-oriented sectors. Since then the term "Dutch Disease" purportedly refers to an economic situation in a country where an extremely booming resource-based sector leads to decline in other industries.

Recent studies and research, however, show that the "resource curse" is not necessarily true. Lederman and Maloney (2007)[①] pointed out its deficiency in their studies. World Bank (2002) studies find that abundant resource could stimulate technological advancement and produce new knowledge.[②] And the experiences of Australia and Canada also demonstrate that countries endowed with abundant natural resources could also realize industry varieties and economic diversity. We, therefore, should conduct in-depth analysis and research on the preconditions and mechanism under which the development of the resource industry can spur the economic growth, laying a foundation for BRICs' further co-prosperity and cooperation.

Competitive complementarities, competitive stress and BRICs' trade linkages

In this section, we are going to adopt in our research the Competitive Complementarities Index and Competitive Stress Index proposed by Fan Gang, Guan Zhixiong and Yao

① Lederman, D., and W. F. Maloney eds., 2007, "Trade Structure and Growth," in *Natural Resources: Neither Curse Nor Destiny*, Palo Alto: Stanford University Press.

② World Bank, 2002, "From Natural Resources to the Knowledge Economy: Trade and Job Quality," *Latin American and Caribbean Studies*, World Bank, Washington D.C.

Zhizhong in 2006.[①] CCI, which is set between 0 and 1, is used to determine whether a designated country or a group of country shares more competition or complementarities. The bigger the number is, the fierce competition between two countries is. CSI, which is also set between 0 and 1, is used to gauge one country's competitive stress on its trading partners The bigger the number is, the more competition stress its trading partners feel. CCI is calculated by tallying the proportion of the overlapping parts of trade one specific country and its trading partners exported to a designated market among their combined exports volume. CSI is calculated by tallying the proportion of overlapping parts of trade one specific country and its trading partners exported to a designated market among its total exports. Based on HS code system, we also calculate competitive stress and competitive complementarities in the trade relations between each of the BRICs countries' with other three members and between BRICs countries with E11 and G7 + AUS and the world respectively.

BRICs countries generally have more competition with emerging economies that they do with the major developed countries. The value of CCI that Brazil, China, India and Russia recorded with other BRICs member countries, or with E11 nations are bigger than that with G7+AUS. China is an exception. China's CCI with G7+AUS was 0.286 in 2009, which is higher than the 0.178 it recorded with BRICs but still lower than the 0.367 it recorded with E11. However, in terms of the developing trend, the speed with which BRICs countries is having more competition with major developed countries is much faster than that with emerging economies. China, in particular, had far more competition with major developed nations in 2009 than that between other three BRICs countries and developed economies.

On the other hand, when Brazil, India and Russia saw their competition with other BRICs member states and major developed countries increase considerably, their competition with China dropped by varying degrees.

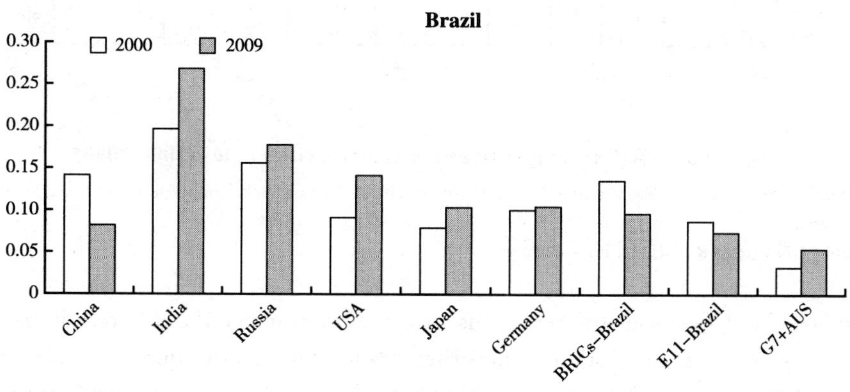

① Fan Gang, Guan Zhixiong and Yao Zhizhong, " Analysis of the International Trade Pattern: Technology Distribution," at *Economic Research*, Issue 8, 2006.

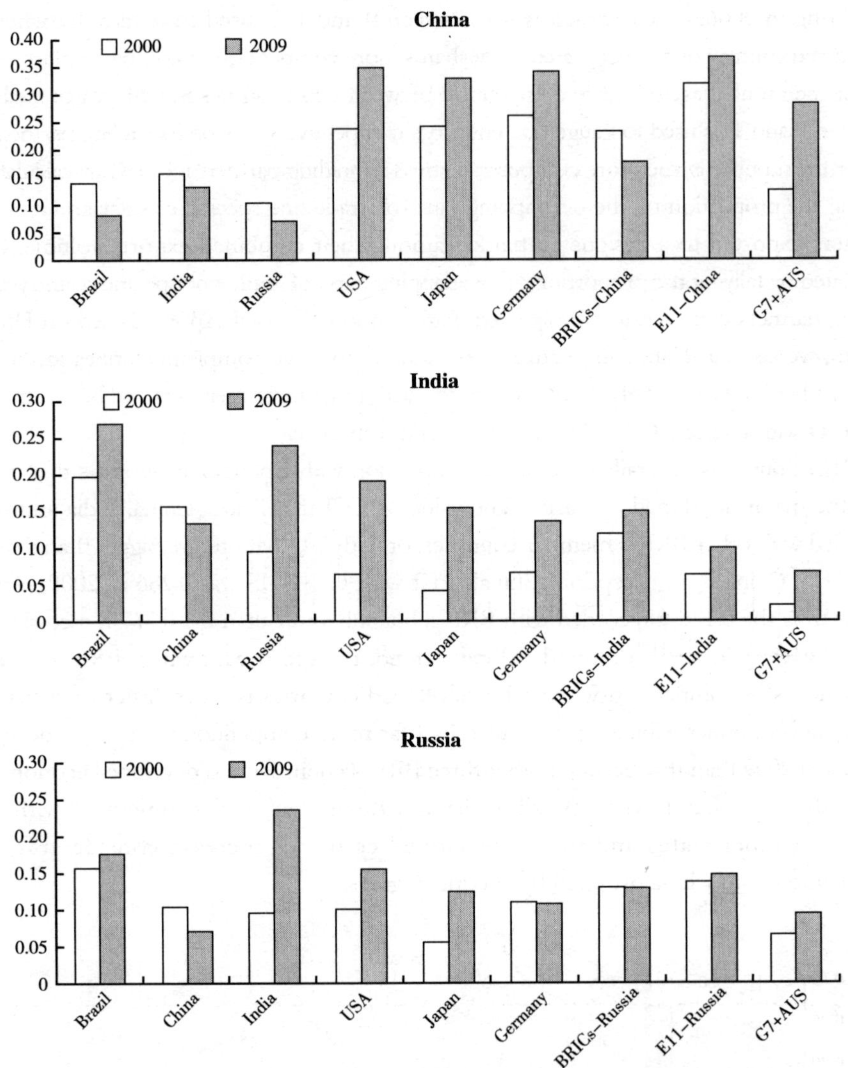

Figure 6 BRICs: competitive complementarities index (2000-2009)

Note: Due to data availability, we used 2008 data for Argentina, India, South Korea and Japan and 2007 data for Saudi Arabia.

Source: UN COMTRADE; Authors' calculation.

One of the deficiencies of the CCI is that it can not gauge the different impact two economies exert on each others when their trade scale is not equal. For example, if country A and country B both export garment of the same quality to the world market at the same time, and country A exports US$ 10 billion worth of garment while country exports US$2 billion worth of garment; it is obvious that country A exerts far more competitive stress on country B in the areas of garment than country B does to country A. In order to make up for this deficiency, we also calculate the CSI.

The study (see Figure 7) show that the competition stress China detects from other BRICs member countries, America, Japan, Germany and emerging economies and that from the major developed countries dropped significantly during 2000-2009 period. India is another way around. Except for China, the competition stress India feels from other countries and groups of countries all increased. Brazil's situation is similar to China. The South American country feels increasing competition stress from India and Russia while feels decreasing stress level from China. Russia see the competition stress from emerging economies (either individual country or as a whole) increase while feels reduced stress from America, Germany and G7+AUS.

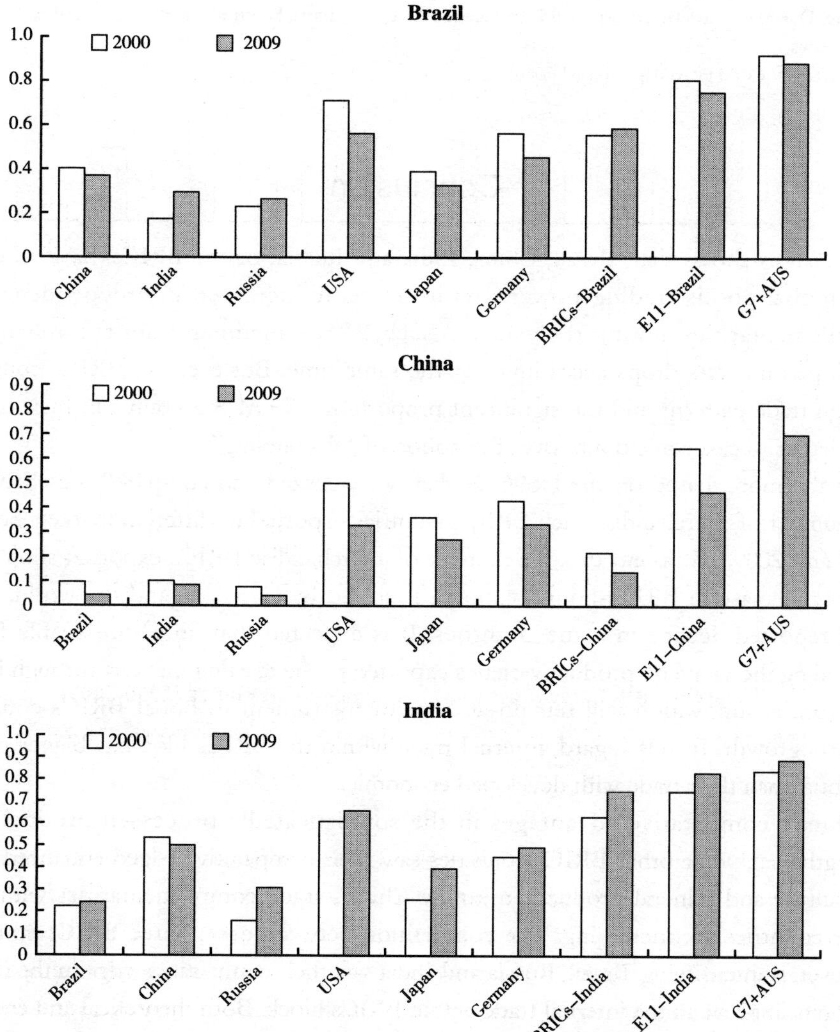

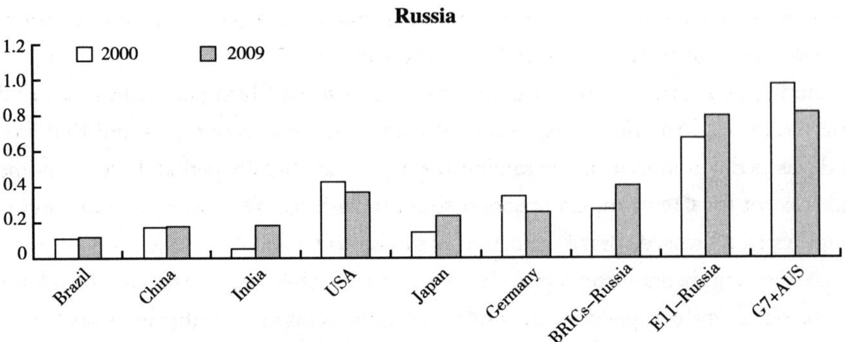

Figure7 BRICs: competitive stress index (2000-2009)

Note: Due to data availability, we used 2008 data for Argentina, India, South Korea and Japan and 2007 data for Saudi Arabia.

Source: UN COMTRADE; Authors' calculation.

Conclusion

Our analysis shows that, Brazil, China, India and Russia, or the BRICs, have all grown into global goods trading powers, with markedly increased interdependency and complementarities among themselves. Each BRICs member country's reliance on developed markets drops accordingly at the same time. But even so, BRICs countries' foreign trade patterns and the significant proportion G7+AUS accounts in their exports have led us to cast some doubt over the notion of "decoupling".

Furthermore, based on the HS96 six-digit we analyzed and compared the changes in the number of merchandise each BRICs countries exported to different markets between 1999 and 2009. We found that the number of merchandise BRICs exported showed the biggest increase in BRICs-bound exports, followed by G7+AUS and the world, which even reported decline in some countries. It is expected that, in a foreseeable future, expanding the range of product varieties exported to the existing markets through inside-the-frontier innovation will remain as a major instrument to boost BRICs countries' exports growth. In this regard, internal trade within the BRICs bloc has bigger growth potential than their trade with developed economies.

China's comparative advantages in the sophisticatedly processed products area strengthened, while other BRICs countries saw their comparative edged enhanced in the agriculture and mineral products, meaning China's trade complementarities with other three countries are increasing. The competition between other three BRICs countries, however, is intensifying. Brazil, Russia and India saw their comparative edge in the mineral products improve in the internal trade within BRICs block. Both theoretical and empirical studies have shown that the "resource curse" is not necessarily applicable to every country. We should conduct in-depth analysis and research on the preconditions and mechanism under which the development of the resource industry can spur the economic growth, laying a foundation for BRICs' further co-prosperity and cooperation.

Our studies into competitive complementarities and competitive stress between BRICs member country and their main trading partners show that BRICs have more competition with emerging economies than they have with major developed countries. However, in terms of the developing trend, the speed with which BRICs countries is having more competition with major developed countries is much faster than that with emerging economies. In addition, the competition stress generated from their internal trade is far smaller than what BRICs member states feel from the single external stress source.

We have the very reasons to be optimistic about the future prospects of the development of the internal trade within BRICs block and we hold that such development will help their economic growth. It should be noted, however, that a series of challenges, ranging from the gloomy world economic growth outlook, stalled Doha Round, the rising worldwide protectionism, ineffective policy coordination to the lack of consensus on the global economic governance mechanism, are expected to bring uncertainties to the further advancement of the internal trade within BRICs block. BRICs countries should gradually push forward cooperation in the trade area and strengthen their coordination in some major issues under the global economic governance platform G20.

The Geography of Brazilian External Trade: Right Option for a BRICs?

Renato Baumann[*]

Introduction

Words can make a difference sometimes. The five-letter BRICs acronym increased the focus on a specific set of countries. Brazil, in particular, is considered in a different way as it used to be: it has become for several analysts not only 'another developing economy', but rather one of the candidates to play a major role in the international scenario in the near future.

This change of perspective is not only a matter of semantics. Recent economic performance and macroeconomic indicators of these economies contribute to a more careful consideration of their possibilities. Large domestic market makes it more likely to obtain 'growth-led exports' rather than 'export-led growth', which implies a pro-active role in international relations.

It is no coincidence that in recent years Brazil has been invited to participate (even with a less-than-expected role) in meetings of the group of richest countries, in meetings of several groups of countries concerned with the multilateral negotiations at the World Trade Organization, at the same time that former Brazilian authorities often take part in selected groups of experts dealing with the intended reforms of the international financial system. Brazilian delegates often play an active role in the debates within multilateral agencies, aiming at contributing to change the 'political economy' of the decision-making

* Renato Baumann, UN/ECLAC and Universidade de Brasília. The views expressed here are my own, and do not necessarily correspond to the official position of these two institutions. I thank Ricardo Bielschowsky and Carlos Mussi for comments on a preliminary version.

process in these agencies.

This adds up to the peculiar characteristic of the country having been a founding member of the most important multilateral institutions, and traditionally having its diplomatic action concerned with the respect to the agreed rules and disciplines in each of these organisms.

From a Brazilian perspective, these movements have reinforced a desire to become a permanent member of the UN Security Council, as well as an aspiration to participate in a more active position at the meetings of the G7 (to be expanded to a possible G10, for that matter).

It is expected that a successful country in the set of 'BRICs' shall have a productive capacity corresponding to its economic potential, a relatively stable economy and a high profile in the international scenario. These are the conditions that qualify these countries to participate at the high-level forums.

The Brazilian economy gets most of its dynamism (80%) from domestic demand (especially consumption, as the investment ratio to GDP accounts for only 20%). The weight of external demand has increased in recent years, and trade policy puts emphasis on regional trade, as one major source of dynamism for exports with higher value-added and higher technological content.

This emphasis has been the object of some fierce criticism. To start with, Latin America and the Caribbean account for only 6% of the World's Gross Domestic Product①. Its potential for absorbing Brazilian products is, hence, limited.

The regional market is also rather vulnerable to variations in the terms of trade: recent drop in the price of commodities (most of the region's exports) have strongly affected Brazilian exports of manufactures to the region②. This reduction in export revenue has stimulated some countries in the region to raise trade barriers, and several analysts expect this movement to gain momentum in the coming months, if there is no positive change in the international scenario③.

Half of total industrial exports from Brazil depend on subsidiaries of transnational companies. This means that the degrees of freedom for the authorities in re-designing the geographical orientation of trade flows is subject to internal decisions in those firms and to their control over sales channels. This imposes some limits for the country to explore the markets for products with high value-added and high technological content in industrialized countries. The regional market can, therefore, provide some space for improving the export structure.

---

① According to the World Bank Development Indicators Online.

② The increase in Brazilian manufactured exports to Latin America in the fourth quarter of 2008 was only 1/3 of the corresponding figure in 2007.

③ Including more pro-active policies adopted by Brazil to foster economic activity in neighboring countries.

The argument in favor of intensifying regional trade is based mainly on its contribution to the country's negotiating capacity in international forums[①] and the 'quality' of trade flows, allowing for a significant share of industrialized exports with higher technological content. Critics would stress that the regional emphasis diverts efforts that could promote exports to larger, more promising markets, where fierce competition could stimulate the degree of sophistication of the export bill.

This discussion mixes the geographical orientation of trade flows with the sector concentration of incentives to export. In the 1980s some American economists[②] worried about competition by Asian countries have developed several models providing a rationale for what was called 'strategic export policy'. In essence, the idea was to provide incentives to domestic firms in some sectors so as to provide them a competitive edge over foreign-owned competitors.

The analysis that follows differs from this approach in that it does not necessarily aim at biasing trade policy towards any specific sector. Instead, the argument concentrates on the identification of gains that could accrue from trade relation with neighboring partners. It is based on the assumption that the political will favoring regional integration will help to overcome recent protectionist trends. It is argued that there is a case for caring about regional trade, but also that there are a number of obstacles to further pursuing this option.

After a brief presentation of the major characteristics of recent economic indicators (next Section) the text shows (Section III) specific aspects of the relationship of Brazil and the main international agencies (its multilateral approach), as an indication that the multilateral dimension has always been present in the Brazilian perspective. The fourth Section discusses the regional option as a tool for improving the technological content of exports. The argument put forward here is that this option is to some extent inevitable, in view of geographical determinants and in face of the several regional groupings in other regions, but it presents a number of difficulties, discussed in Section V. Last Section presents some final remarks.

Recent trade trends

Brazilian economy presents a trade performance equaled by few other developing economies. Exports have systematically surpassed imports in the last three decades. In the 34 years from 1974 to 2008 in only 12 a trade deficit obtained: from 1974 to 1979, and more recently between 1995 and 2000.

---

① See, for instance, the statement by the Foreign Affairs Minister in Amorim (2008).

② See, in this regard, Helpman/Krugman (1989) and Krugman (1990).

External prices do play a role as an explanatory factor. In 1974-1980 the dependence of Brazilian economy upon oil imports was a binding constraint, at a moment when oil prices reached by then record levels. This (plus strong import repression) explains why export growth was far more intense than imports in terms of volume and yet trade deficits obtained. The same is true for 1995-2000, as illustrated by Table 1. As a matter of fact it was only between 1991 and 1995 and more recently, after 2005, that the growth of imports surpassed exports in volume.

Table 1 Brazil–trade growth in volume (1975 – 2007) (yearly average)

Unit: %

	Export	Import		Export	Import
1975-1980	7.3	-0.0	1996-2000	8.1	3.7
1981-1985	6.1	-0.1	2001-2005	13.1	1.3
1986-1990	5.9	2.2	2006-2007	1.4	19.8
1991-1995	6.9	28.9	1975-2007	6.6	5.3

Source: FUNCEX.

Export performance – a more than fivefold increase in value between 1990 and 2007 (from US$ 31 billion to US$ 160 billion) – was accompanied by the intensification of trade relations with other Latin American and Caribbean countries, as shown in Table 2. Relative weight of exports to the region has more than doubled between 1990 and 2006, and remained constant in recent years, when total export value boomed.

Table 2 Brazil - relative importance (% of total exports) of exports to Latin America & the Caribbean (1985 – 2006)

	1985	1990	1995	2000	2006
Latin America & Caribbean	9.2	11.4	22.5	24.6	25.5
of which: South America	7.8	8.6	20.4	20.1	19.4

Source: ECLAC/BADECEL.

Efforts to stimulate regional trade are often justified on the grounds that the regional market allows for: i) developing dynamic comparative advantages, since most of the exports are industrialized products; ii) these comparative advantages stem not only from the higher value-added of the export bill, but also from the easier market access for technologically more elaborated products; iii) a 'learning process' in the exporting activity, allowing domestic producers to acquire expertise by exploiting initially less sophisticated markets and qualifying themselves to subsequently face more demanding consumers in industrial economies; iv) geopolitical arguments that stress the higher negotiating capacity in international forums of joint positions held by neighboring countries.

As Table 3 shows, exports to Latin America and the Caribbean have a higher share of industrialized products than exports to other regions. For instance, in 1990 most① of total Brazilian exports to other Latin American & Caribbean countries were industrialized products. The same picturing obtains, sixteen years later. As is well known, this corresponds to the typical Latin American standard of industrial exports being concentrated in the US and other Latin American countries. As the degree of technological intensity is considered, exports of products of medium and high technology are more intense in trade with Latin America and the Caribbean than with any other market. Presence of these products in regional trade is almost twice as high as their participation in total exports.

This is a totally different pattern than that observed in exports to Europe or to Asia, where primary products are dominant.

The scenario Table 3 indicates is one where Brazilian producers and traders exploit the regional market so as to take advantage of the comparatively higher degree of industrialization and the more intense R&D activity in Brazil (as discussed in following sections) to exploit neighboring markets. A good deal of these trade flows takes place on the basis of preferential access condition②.

Table 3 Percentage of selected products of brazilian exports to specific markets (1990 – 2006)

Industrialized Products – Low Technology								
	Latin America* & Caribbean(33)	USA	European** Union (27)	Asia-*** Pacific (16)	China	Japan	Others	World
1990	14.0	20.6	10.7	23.5	17.3	5.3	14.0	14.7
2000	16.8	16.2	9.0	11.6	4.5	3.3	5.7	12.1
2006	11.6	13.9	8.6	9.6	5.5	2.4	3.9	9.2
Industrialized Products - Medium Technology								
	Latin America* & Caribbean(33)	USA	European** Union (27)	Asia-*** Pacific (16)	China	Japan	Others	World
1990	48.3	28.7	16.1	39.3	28.9	18.1	19.6	25.7
2000	44.9	26.6	14.8	26.8	9.0	8.0	12.8	25.1
2006	46.9	32.0	17.5	18.9	7.8	10.1	14.5	26.4

① As indicated by 14.0% of low technology products, 48.3% of medium technology products and 8.5% of high technology products.

② See, in this regard CEPAL (2006): in 2005 2/3 of regional trade took place under preferential agreements.

Continue Table 3

	Industrialized Products - High Technology							
	Latin America* & Caribbean(33)	USA	European** Union (27)	Asia-*** Pacific (16)	China	Japan	Others	World
1990	8.5	7.7	2.9	1.8	0.3	0.9	1.7	4.3
2000	12.6	22.3	9.2	2.6	5.1	10.6	5.4	12.5
2006	12.3	11.0	5.0	4.0	1.4	0.4	5.5	7.7

* Antigua & Barbuda, Argentina, Bahamas, Barbados, Belize, Bolivia, Chile, Colombia, Costa Rica, Cuba, Dominica, Ecuador, El Salvador, Granada, Guatemala, Guyana, Haiti, Honduras, Jamaica, Mexico, Nicaragua, Panama, Paraguay, Peru, Venezuela, Dominican Republic, St.Kitts&Nevis, St.Vincent & Grenadines, St.Lucia, Surinam, Trinidad &Tobago, Brazil, Uruguay.

** Germany, Austria, Belgium, Cyprus, Denmark, Slovakia, Slovenia, Spain, Estonia, Finland, France, Greece, Hungary, Ireland, Italy, Leetonia, Lithuania, Luxemburg, Malta, Netherlands, Poland, Portugal, United Kingdom, Czech Republic, Rumania, Sweden, Bulgaria.

*** Australia, Brunei Darussalam, Cambodia, Philippines, Hong Kong, India, Indonesia, Lao, Malaysia, Myanmar, New Zealand, Korea, Singapore, Thailand, Vietnam, Thailand.

Source: CEPAL, 2008.

From the mid-1980s to about year 2000 a number of factors have affected Brazilian export dynamism. High domestic inflation (until 1995), reduction of incentives to exports, less investment stemming in part from the process of adaptation of firms to a new scenario with less presence of the State and higher import competition, lower real exchange rate and other elements all have contributed to a sharp reduction in the Brazilian presence in the international market: from a maximum of 1.49% in 1984 the participation of Brazilian exports fell to only 0.85% in 1999 (Figure 1).

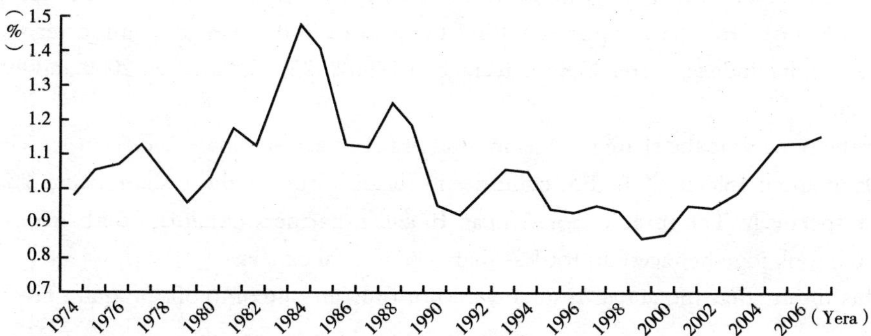

Figure 1 Brazil-share of world exports (1974-2007)

Source: Ipeadata.

Since 2000 change in the exchange rate regime with significant devaluation, plus the understanding that some more active trade policy is needed, so as to avoid the negative effects of external shocks (as experienced in the second half of the 1990s), coupled to the benefit of higher commodity prices, have led to more pro-active trade policies and a higher profile in the international trade scenario, but the share of Brazilian products in total world exports still remains below the 1.2% level.

This of course means that there are 98.8% of the international markets as potential opportunities to improve Brazilian export share, and a number of recent trade measures reflect this perception. On the import side, in recent years there have been renewed concerns regarding the inflow of products, in particular of Asian origin.

Both movements (bigger exports and imports) influence Brazilian positions in international negotiations: it is convenient that a country searching for new markets stick to the basic WTO rules, so as to avoid new barriers. At the same time, intense import growth often leads to the initiation of legal procedures against accusation of dumping practices.

A good deal of the efforts to foster exports in recent years has been concentrated in regional markets, as well as exploiting new, non-traditional markets in Asia, Africa and Eastern Europe. Diversification of the geographical destination of exports has become a central issue in trade policy: in 2000 the ten major Brazilian trade partners corresponded to some 70.4% of total exports, whereas in 2006 the ten major partners imported only 59.2% of total Brazilian exports.

The share of the US as a destination for Brazilian exports has fallen from 24% in 2000 to 15% in 2007[①]. This is not to say, however, that there has been a withdrawal from the US market, since in volume terms Brazilian exports to the US presented the following indexes[②]: 43.0 on average in 1990-1995, 54.8 in 1991-2000 and 94.0 in 2001-2007[③].

A similar result obtains for exports to the European Union. In 2000 the EU absorbed some 28% of Brazilian exports, falling to 24% in 2007. Yet in volume terms the corresponding indexes were: 43.8 on average in 1990-1995, 53.7 in 1996-2000 and 89.1 in 2001-2007.

At the same time the share of Asia in total Brazilian exports increased from 15% in the 1990s to about 18% in 2007. For countries in Eastern Europe those shares were 3% and 4%, respectively. The three major African Brazilian partners (Angola, South Africa and Nigeria) took together account for less than 3% of total exports[④].

This means that the actual results were not only an outcome of the quite favorable

---

① CEPAL (2008).

② 2006=100. Data from FUNCEX.

③ Data from FUNCEX.

④ Trade with other BRICs is also rather limited: in 2007 only Russia (2.3%) and China (6.7%) absorbed significant shares of total Brazilian exports.

evolution of export prices in this period①, but rather the noticeable increase in the share of the regional market was an actual gain in a period of overall good export performance with market diversification.

Brazilian economy has become more intensely related to the international market also in relation to capital flows. The gross inflow of foreign direct investment ranged between US$1.0 and 3.0 billion a year between 1980 and 1995. Since then the amount has increased systematically, reaching fairly high levels in 2000 (US$ 40 billion) and 2007 (US$ 50 billion). In recent years Brazil ranked second among developing economies in attracting FDI, being surpassed only by China.

Brazilian gross foreign direct investment abroad was marginal (averaging less than US$ 800 million per year) until 1994. In more recent years it has shown quite impressive amounts, although with sharp variation in yearly figures.

Gross inflow of portfolio investment has also been remarkable. Until 1993 the typical yearly figure would be less than US$ 25 billion (taking into account the non-resident resources invested in stock exchange, fixed interest rate bonds and other investments), largely affected by legal restrictions on non-resident investors. The annual figure increased very sharply in recent years, up to a total of US$ 210 billion in 2007.

What these figures indicate is that the Brazilian economy has become more exposed to the international markets for goods, services and capital. The intensity of the changes and the magnitude of the flows are not irrelevant. As a consequence, they have led to an intensification of the traditional Brazilian approach to multilateral institutions, centered on a) the concern with the application of institutional rules and b) the worry with differential treatment to developing economies, as briefly discussed in the next Section.

Multilateral approach

Brazil was among the 23 founders of GATT in 1947. Why a developing economy has joined what was originally seen as a 'rich boys' club', is an issue in itself. In any case, this early adhesion is symptomatic of one of the characteristics of Brazilian diplomacy: having frontiers with nine other countries and no significant conflict a good deal of Brazilian diplomatic activity has concentrated over time on economic issues. From the perspective of a weaker player in the international market it is important to preserve the existence and efficiency of disciplinary rules and supervision. Among other initiatives, Brazil has been one of the active defenders of the ´special and different` treatment that the WTO

① Export prices increased on average 2.3% in 1009-1995, fell on average by 3.1% between 1996 and 2000, and then increased at a yearly rate of 6.1% from 2001 to 2007.

provides to developing countries[①].

This explains in part the pro-active role Brazil has played at the GATT and more recently at the WTO. Since the creation of the WTO in 1994 Brazil has a high profile in numbers of dispute cases: 24 cases as complainant, 14 cases as respondent and 49 cases as third part. Overall the outcome has been positive to the country, with mostly favorable decisions.

If at previous negotiating rounds Brazil and other developing economies typically presented a low profile, benefiting from the negotiations among other members on the grounds of the MFN clause, since the Uruguay Round and particularly in the process of trying to foster a Doha Round Brazil is without doubt one of the developing economies ranking among the major players, participating in a number of countries groups, from the Group of Cairns to the several Gs (G77, G20, G4, etc).

The higher exposure in trade and the parallel initiatives that this brings about in different forums have, of course, stimulated Brazilian policy-makers for quite some time now to try to make part of the group of the most important nations in the international scenario. This has led to the by now recurrent and long standing candidacy to become a permanent member of the UN Security Council, as well as to frequent signaling of Brazilian desire to be invited to the meetings of the G7, the group of the richest countries.

Improved economic conditions, better access to the international capital market and changes in investment priorities have also led to changes in the relations with multilateral agencies in charge of providing foreign exchange liquidity (IMF) and long-term capital (World Bank).

Brazil was one of the signatories of the Bretton Woods Agreement, in 1944, and as such its relation with the IMF and the World Bank goes back to the very beginning of the operations of these institutions. The first operation with the Fund dates from 1954, when the Fund provided support for a loan by the US Ex-Im Bank. The first loan dates from 1958.

Relations with the Fund have not always been friendly, as in the 1959 bilateral conflict. In the 1980s Brazil signed a set of six Letters of Intentions with the Fund, and most of the commitments were not achieved. The next decade was also one of difficult relations. In 1994 the Fund decided not to give support to the Real Plan, on the basis of considering the fiscal adjustment not sufficient to sustain low inflation levels, as well as

---

① The GATT has since its very beginning accepted that developing economies present specific economic problems. This has led to Article XVIII of the GATT and the idea gained momentum in the 1950s-1960s. Part IV of the General Agreement – dealing with Trade and Development – was a political achievement by developing countries. Later on, the adoption of an Enabling Clause reinforced the GSP mechanism. Brazilian diplomacy was very active in fostering these instruments.

revealing skepticism with regard to the exchange rate policy.

International shocks hit Brazilian economy hard in the second half of the 1990s. In November, 1998 Brazil signed an agreement with the IMF, the World Bank, the IDB and a few countries, in order to stabilize the public debt ratio to GDP. In 2001 and again in 2002 and 2003 new agreements were signed. In 2005 Brazil decided to stop renewing the credit lines with the Fund and actually returned the amount of credit available from the several agreements which had not been used.

A member country can have access to resources in a given proportion to the quotas the country deposits at the Fund. In four occasions, however (1992, 1998, 2001 and 2002), Fund loans to Brazil were well above its quotas (respectively 103%, 600%, 400% and 902%). No other Latin American country has ever drawn such high percentage in relation to its quota as Brazil did in 2002.

Relations with the World Bank also come a long way. The first loan (US$ 75 million) dates from 1949 (energy) and from then on the Bank has played a major role in financing the country's infrastructure. During the 1950s Bank loans to Brazil were concentrated in infrastructure projects, especially energy and transportation. In the 1960s while energy remained as the most important absorber of the Bank funds, agriculture and manufacturing industry also captured a good deal of resources. This diversification was intensified even further in the 1970s.

The most significant changes took place from the 1980s onwards, when the Bank changed its policy, giving increasing emphasis to foster governance and finance policies, apart from projects, with an increasing concern with poverty, environment and gender issues. At the same time Brazilian government reduced its public investments in infrastructure and productive activities.

Be it for the changes in the approaches both from the viewpoint of the Bank and Brazilian government or for other elements, the fact is that the net inflow of resources from both the Bank and the IMF became negative for many years.

The experience with these multilateral agencies, plus the increased access to international market both for sovereign and private debt since the 1990s, and even more so in the 2000s have led the country to adopt a more cautious approach. As a matter of fact Brazilian authorities have often argued in favor of changes in the way the IMF deals with liquidity crises, by demanding the creation of additional credit lines and a more preventive role by the Fund. Brazil has also often emphasized the need for changing the political economy of the institution, by increasing the share of developing economies in the decision process.

Increased possibilities to access international capital markets actually stimulated domestic efforts to adjust regulation and norms so as to facilitate Brazilian firms to benefit from these improved credit conditions. A number of Brazilian firms have been able to take advantage of this liquidity to finance themselves by issuing ADRs at increasing proportions: total transactions in 2004 were worth US$ 434 million; in 2008 that amount had increased almost fivefold, reaching US$ 1.9 billion[①].

Brazil is also one of the founders of the Inter-American Development Bank, has often relied on its resources for the financing of infrastructure projects and – since the mid-1990s – also for projects in social areas, environment and public sector governance. As similar to the IMF and the World Bank, however, in recent years the net inflow of resources from IDB became negative, calling for an adaptation of bilateral relations.

The country has recently increased its share in the capital of CAF (Corporación Andina de Fomento), a regional institution that mobilizes resources from international markets to Latin America, in order to provide multiple banking services to both public and private agents. Many of the projects financed by CAF aim at fostering regional integration. This is one of the reasons why Brazil has adopted a higher profile as a stockholder.

Last but not least, Brazilian external policy has put increasing emphasis in the support the country can provide to other developing economies, the so-called South-South cooperation[②]. This is a process where the basic criteria are still being gradually defined. In any case, it can be said that there are two broad patterns: a) cooperation with closer neighbors (Mercosur partners in particular) reflect the efforts to overcome difficulties in the integration process, with joint action in areas such as sanitary policies, technical norms, institutional strengthening, consumer rights and others; b) cooperation with third countries, comprising a broad range of subjects.

Cooperation with non-Mercosur countries include actions in labor training, basic education, prevention of AIDS, transfer of agricultural technology, exchange of experiences in the combat to hunger and poverty, and other subjects. The countries with which Brazil sustains cooperation programs comprise Portuguese speaking countries in Africa, East Timor, other South American countries, Haiti and others. Apart from a genuine support to populations dependent upon external help South-South cooperation is also a means for the country to maintain a higher profile in the international scenario.

At the same time that Brazilian external policy maintained an active role in the international setting, with an increasingly higher profile (as expected from a major player), however, it has clearly given priority to intensifying regional ties. This, of course, corresponds to favorable expectations with regard to the gains from regional markets, as discussed in the next Section.

---

① See www.cvm.gov.br for data.

② For detailed information see www.abc.gov.br.

Is the regional option a mistake?

External political commitments notwithstanding, the important question from the strict viewpoint of the Brazilian economy is whether the regional market is able to provide dynamism to domestic producers and exporters, as well as to improve the technological content of domestic production.

Regional trade in primary products is by and large determined by commodity prices determined elsewhere. It is a matter of specific negotiation if bilateral trade can provide these products at lower costs than in the international markets.

Trade in services is still rather limited in scope and importance, so the argument with regard to the regional market is largely concentrated in manufactured goods. The question is, therefore, whether the regional option can be a tool to provide sustained manufactured exports and market for technologically high-level products. Latin America and the Caribbean account for 6% of the World's Gross Domestic Product)[①]. Concentrating efforts in a market with comparatively limited potential as this might be seen as a myopic bet.

The answer depends on: a) the income level and pattern of demand of the other countries in the region; b) the comparative advantage of Brazilian products versus local production in those countries, as well as in comparison to competing imports from third countries into those markets; and c) local consumer's preferences for Brazilian products.

The pattern of demand that has allowed for Brazilian exports to other Latin American countries in recent years has clearly benefited from the wealth effects stemming from terms of trade effects[②], from labor market improvement (increase in formal employment and higher wages[③]) and social policies. This has helped to enlarge the medium class in the region and as a consequence broadened the regional market for manufactured goods, especially vehicles and other durable consumer goods.

Lower export prices are likely to affect income and thus reduce regional trade. This is one of the major threats (apart from protectionism) that might affect regional demand for Brazilian manufactures. Acceptance of traditional Brazilian brands and preferential access to markets might contribute to sustain a certain level of export activity. And as discussed later, there are specific mechanisms that could be adopted so as to maintain regional trade

① In constant dollars (base year – 2000). Figures from the World Bank (World Development Indicators Online).

② Latin American countries as a whole have benefited from terms of trade gains equivalent to 1% of GDP in the present decade (CEPAL (2008)).

③ CEPAL 2008a.

when liquidity of foreign currencies is limited.

Also, agents matter. Transnational subsidiaries are important players, for they account for half of total industrial exports and for most of the exports of products with medium to high-technology. Their policy so far has been to use Brazil as an export platform to the regional market①. This is an outcome of the internal policies of these firms but also a reflection of the still limited competitiveness of Brazilian production. There is hardly a significant indication of these companies planning to move their plants to other countries in the region②. If anything, the movement in recent years has been towards concentrating activities in Brazil.

Furthermore, exporting to the regional market has proved to be an important issue for small and medium firms: regional trade flows show a higher presence of these firms than total exports. There are, hence, additional arguments favoring the regional option, on the grounds of domestic distributive effects.

Most of the R&D activity in the region takes place in Brazil. Its domestic market allows for large-scale production, at unmatched dimensions in the region. Brazil also presents a more varied set of sector policy instruments than most countries in the region.

These peculiarities are indicative that Brazilian producers are more likely to benefit from gains from scale and technical progress than their local competitors in neighboring countries. This shall provide comparative advantage in an extensive spectrum of products for quite some time.

Sustaining or improving market share for Brazilian products will depend on at least three elements: i) competitiveness of Brazilian brands; ii) differentiated access to markets provided by cost differentials and trade preferences; iii) lack of repudiation to Brazilian products on political grounds. Performance of specific brands is a microeconomic issue that depends on the performance by each firm. More relevant to the present argument are the other two elements.

Most regional trade takes place on the basis of preferential trade agreements. Yet, preferential margins in the region are still rather limited and there is a long way to go in order to make regional trade really free from barriers. This is a pressing issue, as a means to deal with increasing competition of imports from third countries③, as a step towards fully benefiting from regional integration, and as an instrument to protect regional trade

① See, in this regard, Baumann/Galrão (2002).

② Except, perhaps, a few investors in Chile, taking advantage of the bilateral preference agreements signed between that country and several others, such as the US, European Union and some Asian countries.

③ As illustrated, for instance, by the recent Brazilian market-share in Argentina: imports from Brazil fell from 36% in 2005 to 31% in 2008; at the same time Chinese products tripled their share, from 4% to 12% (CNI (2008)).

from trade diversion imposed by the multiplicity of preferential agreements signed between other Latin American countries and some industrialized competitors.

This is, of course, a very sensitive issue. Given the disparities in size and potential competitiveness among countries, further concessions can only be achieved if economic agents identify clear gains in this process. Systematic trade imbalances, investment diversion favoring the larger partners and job creation at a slower pace than expected tend to act as a centrifugal force on regional integration exercises. It is by now generally accepted that at least within Mercosur the smaller members have little motives to celebrate[①].

As Venable (2008) suggests, the way to go with lack of factor price equalization, trade diversion penalizing the smaller economies and re-location of firms increasing the income gap among countries is "to extend both the width and the depth of economic integration". This calls for more active measures to reduce disparities.

The argument here is not to think in terms of Brazil becoming a 'regional hegemon'. Instead, emphasis shall be given to the fact that the sustainability of a regional integration process depends on the specific conditions that allows all the participants to benefit from the specific concessions they make.

To what extent can one expect that exploring the regional market instead of, say, that of industrialized countries, might affect the technology intensity of the export products?

By and large most of the dynamism for manufacturing and hence the margin to absorb gains from scale and the stimuli to improve the technological content of Brazilian production is provided by the domestic market. Export coefficients in most sectors account for about one-fifth of output.

Considering the share that is actually exported, it is an empirical issue to determine whether there are differences between the products that go to regional markets and those shipped to OECD countries. The concern with regional trade harming technological incorporation would only make sense if the differences were significant, with sophisticated products being destined to high-income markets. In any case, changing this scenario is not only a matter for domestic policy, as trade in most of the medium and high technology products corresponds to market strategies by subsidiaries.

In summary, there are potential gains stemming from the regional market, which should not be disregarded by policy-makers. Absorbing these gains (and even more, making them sustainable over time) is not a trivial matter, though. There are a number of obstacles to intensifying regional trade, as shown in the next Section.

---

① For instance, Baumann/Mussi (2006) shows some indicators that the gains have not been evenly distributed among the four founding members of Mercosur.

The challenges involved in the regional option

Emphasis in the economic and political relations with other Latin American countries and even more so with South American neighbors is one strong characteristic of recent Brazilian external policy. Approximation with neighboring countries has intensified since the mid-1980s, and gradually gained momentum in the diplomatic agenda.

The basic skepticism with regard to the emphasis on regional trade has to do with the relatively low share of regional trade when compared to other regions. Intra-regional trade among Asian countries corresponds to some 35% of total exports, whereas in Western Europe that figure surpasses 60%. In Latin America as a whole, intra-regional exports are close to 20% of total exports.

This raises the question as to what could be a reasonable level of importance for regional trade, given the actual conditions of the economies and a number of other determining elements. Is a 20% share of regional trade on total exports a reasonable level? Is there an ideal, alternative figure? There is probably no immediate answer to these questions, and it goes beyond the purposes of this paper to discuss whether the regional market is able to provide a significant dynamism to Brazilian manufacturing sector, both in terms of production growth and in reducing its technological gap.

Be that as it may, it is argued here that however justifiable in terms of the geographical proximity and potential achievements, the regional option is not free from difficulties, demanding far more decisive action than has been recorded so far. The argument is presented in taxonomic form, as five challenges involved in the intensification of regional relations.

Challenge # 1: Dealing with different actors

One basic characteristic of Brazilian economic and political diplomacy has been to preserve its characteristic of a global player in the international scenario. The expression 'global player' applied to a Brazilian perspective means not only that the country cares about sustaining and improving trade flows with most other countries in the world, diversifying both the commodity structure of its trade flows and the geographical destination of its exports. It also means that the country maintains positive diplomatic relationship with every country, with no conflict or interruption of bilateral relations.

Clearly the United States and Western Europe are the traditional partners in terms of economic and political matters. Long-standing ties in terms of trade relation as well as investment flows, the sheer importance of these markets and the weight of these economies in the international scenario all make it inevitable that most of the economic and political relations be related to these countries.

Asia is the new economic frontier, given the dynamism of the largest economies in that continent and the close (and increasing) links among Asian countries.

Africa is an important potential partner, given the historical roots that link Brazil to most countries in Western Africa, the still low share of Brazilian products in the regional market, the high proportion of African-descendents population in Brazilian society (which in principle might help create specific economic links, based on affinity of interests) and the economic potential of some African economies, such as South Africa.

Eastern Europe is seen as a promising potential market, in view of the still low participation of Brazilian products in those markets. Trade with transitional economies has increased, even though from very low levels.

But Brazilian diplomacy has for quite some time now looked for a more intense relationship with other Latin American economies, South Americans in particular. This region has concentrated a good deal of Brazilian diplomatic efforts in recent years.

A systematic and sustainable approximation with other South American partners is a challenge in itself. Not only there are significant natural barriers to a more intense economic relationship, such as the Amazon jungle and the Andean Mountains, all of which call for heavy infrastructure projects to facilitate transportation, as there are also cultural, institutional and sociological peculiarities that differentiate Brazil and Spanish-speaking America. In any case, lack of bilateral conflicts in more than a century is an important asset in fostering proximity with neighboring countries.

The economic and geographical distance among the different economies is also decisive. Brazil has 190 million inhabitants; the next largest population in South America is Colombia's, with 46 million inhabitants, the third Argentina's, with 39 million inhabitants, and these are followed by much smaller countries.

The argument in favor of a more intense relationship on a regional basis follows from the several aspects already listed in previous Sections but also to the fact that South America is a very rich continent in terms of natural resources (Brazilian iron, soy and sugar, Argentina's wheat and beef, Venezuela's oil, Bolivia's natural gas, Chile's copper, Surinam's bauxite, etc), so that there are large potential gains stemming from the systematic exploitation of these results. Furthermore, South America has the largest tropical forest with the highest biodiversity of the world, as well as the largest reserve of non-salt water.

An indication of the increasing interest in South America is that Brazilian exports to the region increased 17% between 1995 and 2000, and 140% between 2000 and 2006, when it corresponded to some 19% of total exports.

Brazilian economy accounts for approximately half of the total production value of South America (60% of total manufacturing value and about half of the agricultural production). This differential has a number of implications, ranging from the better supply conditions – which have led to recurrent trade surpluses with neighboring countries – to more intense R&D activities: 80% of R&D activities in South America take place in Brazil, and this is likely to lead over time to higher competitiveness vis-à-vis other countries in the region.

In the last decade or so there has been an increasing disequilibrium of the regional trade balance in technologically advanced products, favoring Brazil. As a consequence, intraregional trade is comparatively more dynamic for Brazil in medium and high-technology products than its trade with other regions, as shown in Table 3.

Regional capital flows are still limited, but FDI flows from Brazilian firms have been active in the acquisition of firms from neighboring countries, in as varied sectors as cement, financial services, steel, food, auto parts, gas, textiles and footwear.

The way to deal with these discrepancies is to pursue joint programmes leading to more intense productive complementarities among countries, as well as joint research activities. In recent years there have been a few initiatives in these directions. Mercosur's FOCEM (Fund for Structural Convergence and Institutional Strengthening) is only one example. Far more intense action is needed in this regard.

Regional infrastructure constraints among South American countries are to be dealt with by a number of projects related to the so-called Infrastructure Initiative in South America. These should help overcome the strong existing limitations in energy supply, transportation, and communication.

Physical barriers are a major characteristic and a binding constraint to integration among South American countries. Difficulties go beyond the inadequate infrastructure in transportation and communication. Several countries face serious difficulties in energy supply, and even though a number of proposals have been put forward this remains a major constraint to growth. The Amazon region – a political web comprising nine countries and nine Brazilian states – correspond to a large share of the regions' territory (60% of Brazilian territory), has clear comparative advantages in a number of areas, but the efficient, sustainable and systematic exploitation of its potential remains undetermined.

Inadequate infrastructure and difference in supply potential are only part of the difficulties conditioning Latin American regional trade. Limited trade preference margins among neighboring countries and the multiplicity of agreements both within the region as well as with countries elsewhere further contribute to a rather complex scenario.

Challenge # 2: Regionalism in a world of preferential trade agreements

Due to several factors – not least the disenchantment with multilateral negotiations after the failure of the Seattle meeting, in preparation for the Doha Round of the

WTO – the number of bilateral and plurilateral agreements has boomed in recent years. They establish trade preferences but often comprise also disciplines regulating issues that are often not directly related to trade issues. Property rights, government procurement policies, competition policies, environmental issues, labor policies and others are often part of the commitments required for the signing of these agreements.

Latin American and Caribbean countries are no exception and in fact have been quite active in participating in this new wave of agreements. An increasing number of countries have negotiated agreements with countries in other regions as well as with neighboring partners. The parallelism between the several integration initiatives and a number of extra-regional agreements might affect the outcome of regional integration schemes. Table 4 illustrates the situation in Latin America and the Caribbean.

Apart from the potential risks in terms of trade diversion implicit in this web of agreements, this increasing simultaneity of agreements brings about costs of several kinds. They imply higher administrative costs, as custom officials have to deal with different tariff rates for any given product, according to their geographic origin. Simultaneous agreements raise the risk of having to adopt more ambitious norms than those already agreed at the WTO level, and even more so if negotiations take place between countries of markedly different economic sizes: developing countries are more vulnerable to interest groups in industrialized countries. The mushrooming of preferential agreements might also negatively affect the very existence and operational capacity of the WTO, by weakening its role as a ruler of international trade.

Table 4 Variable geometry in Latin America and the caribbean (2006)

	Signed Agreements	Present Negotiations
Intra-Regional	LAIA, MERCOSUR, ANCOM, CACM, CARICOM, NAFTA, ALBA, UNASUR, SACN, ACS MERCOSUR-Chile; MERCOSUR-Bolivia MERCOSUR-Peru; MERCOSUR-Colombia, Ecuador, Venezuela Venezuela-CARICOM; Chile-Bolivia; Colombia-CARICOM; Chile-Colombia; Bolivia-Mexico; Chile-Ecuador; Colombia-Venezuela; Chile-Peru; Costa Rica-Mexico; CACM-Dom.Rep.; CACM-Chile; Costa Rica-Trinidad&Tobago; Costa Rica-CARICOM; Nicaragua-Mexico; Mexico-Guatemala, El Salvador, Honduras CARICOM-Dom.Rep. Chile-Bolivia; Chile-Venezuela; Chile-Colombia; Chile-Mexico; Chile-C.America; Chile-Cuba Mexico-Venezuela, Colombia; Mexico-Costa Rica; Mexico-Uruguay; Mexico-Panama	CARICOM – MERCOSUR CAN – Guatemala, El Salvador, Honduras Mexico - MERCOSUR

Continue Table 4

	Signed Agreements	Present Negotiations
Extra-Regional	Chile – Canada, USA, EU, EFTA Mexico – USA, Canada, EFTA, UE, Japan CAFTA-Dom. Rep-CACM Dom.Rep.-USA; Ecuador - USA Costa Rica – Canada Chile-S.Korea; Chile-New Zealand, Singapore, Brunei MERCOSUR – India; MERCOSUR-Israel; MERCOSUR-SACU Peru – Canada; Peru – USA; Colombia - USA	Ecuador – USA MERCOSUR– European Union CACM – European Union CARICOM – European Union CARICOM – Canada Chile-China; Peru – Thailand MERCOSUR– Persian Gulf Countries Brazil-Morocco; Brazil - Egypt

Source: adapted from ECLAC (2006), p. 84.

Even if the different agreements were conceived as 'building blocks', it is by now conceded that one major problem is the relatively slow pace comprised in the chronograms of tariff reduction in the various agreements. A good deal of barriers remains and are likely to be in operation even within several years from now.

There are (at least) two other reasons that support the argument for promoting faster convergence of these schemes: i) tariff preferences correspond to an increasing share of trade in Latin American and Caribbean countries (over two-thirds of total trade by Latin American and Caribbean countries are done on the basis of some type of intra- or extra-regional preferential market access); ii) regional integration schemes favor the exports of products with higher value-added.

In summary, the option for more intense regional ties might be seen as inevitable. Nevertheless, lack of clarity with regard to what can be expected from Latin American regional trade often leads to the perception that this is a goal too difficult to be reached, even though the goal itself is not clearly specified. As a consequence, the negotiation processes to drop remaining barriers becomes increasingly complexes.

Furthermore, if some decades ago this option was rather undisputed as a tool to promote industrialization, today what can be expected from a more intense integration process is less defined, from the perspective of an economy with the characteristics of the Brazilian economy. Given the differences in size and productive potential among Latin American countries this makes the objectives for regional integration less clear and as a consequence affects the whole negotiating process.

Challenge # 3: Where exactly are we going?

The idea of creating a common market to facilitate industrialization in the region – by means of enlarging the domestic markets and therefore allowing for gains from productive plants of larger scale – has been present in the reasoning about regional integration by some think tanks such as ECLAC since the late 1940s.

In the 1950s and 1960s the perspective of recurrent balance of payments disequilibria, reducing the access to imported capital goods, required for making viable the priority given to industrialization, reinforced the demand for regional integration. Trade preferences should be granted gradually, so as not to disturb the (limited) access to capital goods. Moreover, those preferences should be granted to the highest possible number of countries in the region, with differential treatment given to smaller economies.

The 1970s were a period of very low interest in regional integration in Latin America. Difficulties comprised the payment constraints following the first oil shock, limitations imposed by the decision process in LAFTA[①] and – not less important – the fact that several countries in the region had military governments, not prone to make concessions that affect national sovereignty.

The second oil crisis plus the debt crisis imposed a shortage of foreign currencies to most Latin American countries. Reduced trade performance, coupled to idle capacity in some countries and excess demand in others led to regional integration gaining momentum in the political agenda of the region since the mid-1980s.

In this new era regional integration was seen as not only a means to widen domestic markets and allowing for scale gains, but it also proved a way out of crises: regional trade makes it possible in the short run to use installed capacity, and clearing schedules adopted by central banks in the region allowed for regional trade with less need of scarce foreign currencies. Furthermore, in the long run what makes integration sustainable is not the unlimited elimination of trade barriers, but rather the efforts to complement productive structures, so integration exercises should be seen as also a tool for the creation of common economic spaces. Lastly, because the renewed interest in regional integration took place at the same time that most economies adopted more liberal trade policies as a means to fight inflation, not only the integration processes should be designed in such a way to be compatible with multilateral opening, but exports to neighboring countries should be seen as a 'learning process', by which producers could gain experience that would later make them able to try and explore more sophisticated markets (ECLAC 1984; CEPAL 1985).

The 1990s – the 'decade of reforms' in Latin America – added new arguments. The economic reasoning in the 90s stressed competitiveness, in the same way as it emphasized multilateral opening. There are benefits stemming from regional integration in that it allows for the reduction of unproductive rents related to lack of competitiveness, affects expectations of domestic and foreign investors, reduces transaction costs, increases productive efficiency, therefore contributing to price stability and facilitating the absorption of technical progress by stimulating less vertical productive processes, sub-contracting of smaller firms and the employment of qualified

① Latin American Free Trade Area.

workers. The liberalization of regional trade should also provide support to intra-industry specialization, given that the products traded within the region tend to be more technology-intensive than the exports to the rest of the world. According to the new thinking, the benefits of integration go even further, by affecting positively the economic and institutional environment: joint infrastructure projects, as well as joint initiatives in areas such as education and development of capital markets have widespread effects (ECLAC 1994).

There were, hence, in the 1950s, 1960s, 1980s and 1990s clearly identifiable arguments in favor of policies stimulating regional integration. In the years 2000s, however, new overall conditions impose a challenge in trying to identify clear arguments for integration.

The outcome of trade concessions is affected by the international movement of capital; hence trade liberalization cannot be thought of independently of the policies towards the capital account. This is particularly relevant in a context such as the Latin American, where there has been little if any macroeconomic coordination.

Regional negotiations (the regional agenda) should go beyond the trade dimension: there is an increasing need to deal, for instance, with financing infrastructure items, such as energy, environmental policies and water supply, not to speak of measures to improve financial cooperation. This can be a major constraint when a given regional agreement is formed by countries with very different economic conditions.

The record of regional integration in Latin America in the years 2000s show relatively slow progress, when compared to other regions. This is due in part to the fact that regional integration takes place in parallel to an increasing number of extra-regional preferential agreements. It is also due to the fact that the domestic political environment in several countries is not compatible with the concessions required to foster integration processes.

High mobility of international capital, in a context where most countries have opened both their trade and capital accounts, is a major element affecting bilateral exchange rates, therefore determining trade flows and output growth, and hence also the expectations of potential investors.

The weakening of the WTO, in parallel to the mushrooming of bilateral and plurilateral agreements, imposes a challenge to regional preferences in that they increase the probability of trade diversion, negatively affecting regional trade. As a consequence, it reduces the margin for exploiting the potential these regional agreements might provide as a tool to foster economic development via changes in the productive structure.

Furthermore, the emergence of new actors in the international scenario (such as some Asian countries), in parallel to the weakening of some industrialized economies, raises the perspective of a new 'polycentrism' in international economic and political relations. This increases the list of 'natural candidates' that Latin American countries should look for in their selection of potential partners for bilateral agreements. To the extent that recent agreements involve themes that go beyond purely trade subjects, the approximation with different partners at the same time might have damaging effects on a given group of countries participating in the same regional initiative.

Lastly, agreements negotiated by each country individually with third parties might deal with one same subject in different ways, leading to different rules than those prevailing within the regional agreements.

It is, therefore, less clear in the present decade, as compared to previous periods, what each country or group of countries can expect from regional preferential agreements.

Volatility of capital flows is indeed a matter for concern. In a situation where it has become clear that supervision at the financial centers are not as efficient as one would have thought and expected it to be, and even more, in a context where new players (such as sovereign funds) are having an increasingly important role, this poses a challenge to macroeconomic policies in developing economies and seems to be an argument for monetary coordination, eventually with the formation of common funds to provide liquidity in emergency situations.

Challenge # 4: The much needed monetary cooperation

Monetary and financial cooperation in the region has two basic characteristics. It is quite limited, in view of what is needed and in comparison to the experience in other regions. It is also strongly influenced by the concerns with fostering regional integration, that is, the various initiatives aim at improving the financing of large and much needed infrastructure projects, or at building a mechanism to deal with foreign exchange shortages, or even to build a regional capital market.

These are all noble objectives in themselves. When taken jointly, however, they make the actual direction to follow less clear, both with regard to the instruments as well as in relation to the priorities.

In the last 25 years Latin American countries have looked for the support by the IMF in situations of liquidity crises, with a much higher intensity than, say, Asian developing economies. This obtained both in terms of number of operations (84 operations by Latin America countries between 1984 and 2007, more than twice the 35 operations by Asian countries) and in terms of their total value (DES 26 billion in Asia in 1984-2007, as compared to DES 66 billion in Latin America). As it turned out, Asian countries have focused and acted more on the basis of building up regional mechanisms to deal with external shocks (pool of reserves, regional bond markets, joint surveillance mechanisms and other initiatives), whereas in Latin America one might identify some type of 'moral hazard' that has postponed more decisive action towards regional solutions for the crises[①].

This is not to say that in Latin America there has been a total accommodation. As a matter of fact, there are at least two remarkably positive experiences, in providing a mechanism to foster regional trade and in dealing with the provision of liquidity.

The Agreement on Payment and Reciprocal Credit was signed by the Central Banks of LAIA member countries in 1965. By 1989 this mechanism was used to facilitate not less than 90% of total regional trade. Between 1966 and 2004 (when its conditions changed and the mechanism became virtually non-existent) this instrument made possible that almost ¼ of total regional trade took place without foreign currency transfers among Central Banks. This is one type of 'swap' of foreign currencies that took place well before the Asian so-called Chiang Mai Initiative (put in place in 2000).

In 1978 the Latin American Reserve Fund was created among Andean countries. This fund played an important role in providing foreign exchange to member countries during the external debt crisis. Again, this anticipated by 22 years the Chiang Mai Initiative.

Be that as it may, the perception in Latin America of the importance of some kind of monetary and financial coordination in order to foster regional integration is still conditioned by the traditional approach to monetary cooperation as a last stage of regional integration.

This understanding has been increasingly questioned by facts, as coordination can be an important tool to promote the very process of integration in its different stages. And lack of coordination might impair integration processes, whenever external shocks are dealt with by uncoordinated devaluation by individual countries.

Recently Brazil and Argentina have adopted an alternative mechanism, by allowing bilateral trade to be financed in local currencies. It is still too early to know the actual outcome of this facility, but it seems reasonable to expect that the implicit reduction of transaction costs will stimulate bilateral trade, especially by small and medium firms.

Theory would suggest that the higher the weight of trade with neighboring countries the higher the interest in promoting macroeconomic convergence, because the impact of bilateral disequilibria would be more intense. Latin American regional trade still accounts for a limited share of total external trade. One of the reasons for that is the difference in productive potential, as already mentioned.

In order to deal with these differences Brazil and other South American countries have tried to foster complementary productive projects, for this would help improve supply conditions in smaller economies and allow for the absorption of gains from larger productive scale, which, on its turn, helps improve competitiveness. This calls for the need of creating some mechanism–such as a regional capital market, and/or improved access

① Baumann/Mussi (2008).

to external financing sources-to provide low cost long-term capital to finance investment projects.

At the same time, turbulence caused by external shocks can be damaging if there is a regional contagion. It is, therefore, to the interest of all countries in the region to count with some mechanism for the provision of foreign currencies to deal with unpredicted shocks. Latin American countries (and, for that matter, most developing economies) have built relatively large reserves of foreign exchange in recent years, profiting from the favorable external conditions and based on the lessons from the mid-1990s crises. Provided that there is no efficient universal mechanism most countries have looked for some type of 'self-insurance'.

The problem is that high level of reserves means high fiscal costs. The Asian and the Andean experiences are, in this sense, rather suggestive that an adequate level of reserves can be obtained at lower costs if there are mechanisms for the pooling of reserves.

The regional agenda should therefore comprise the resumption of demand-inducing mechanisms to foster regional trade, such as the Reciprocal Credit Agreement, as well as the increase of the existing preferences for trade among LA countries, at the same time that it should provide instruments to deal with external shocks, such as joint liquidity provisions (swap mechanisms and pooling of reserves).

Challenge # 5: What about the effects of the crisis?

The present situation of low economic activity and restrained liquidity imposes new challenges for regional trade. Previous sections have shown the increasing risks of trade diversion stemming from the various preferential trade agreements and parallel weakening of the WTO. Low economic activity is likely to reduce the stimulus to negotiate new preferential agreements. If anything, it is more likely that political pressure will go on the opposite direction, with increasing resistance to grant any concession, so as to preserve domestic jobs.

As far as the effects on multilateral negotiations are concerned the trend is less predictable. There can be pressures to foster negotiations as a means to open additional markets for exports. But there might be instead – at least for some time – a movement towards the reduction of preferences, if domestic producers are allowed an active lobbying capacity, with the consequent resistance to resume the Doha Round.

In any case, it is not realistic to expect that - in a context of reduced production and increasing unemployment, with a difficult dialogue to resume multilateral negotiations at the WTO - we are not going to see some trade distortions, be it in terms of new open or disguised barriers or subsidies to specific sectors.

Such circumstances might provide additional arguments in favor of intensifying economic relations on a regional basis. The experience of the early 1980s is suggestive in that sense: when Latin American countries lacked hard currencies they have been able to sustain the rhythm of activity and trade flows by intensifying regional trade. It should be no surprise if Latin American governments would signal in favor of the regional market as a mechanism to compensate for the less dynamic external demand.

Recent example of Asia is also remarkable: the relatively high share of regional on total exports reflects complementarities of productive structures for goods aimed mostly at the US and European markets. Recession in these markets led to impressive reduction of activity in Asia. This is a very different situation from Latin America, where regional trade has a good deal of final goods for domestic consumption. Productive complementarities to jointly explore third markets seem to be a necessary condition to overcome disparities among countries and hence allow for deepening integration. But it should not replace the need for reducing trade barriers, so as to improve the conditions for exploring the peculiarities of the regional market.

In summary, the regional option is not a sufficient condition. It should be seen as a complementary measure to a 'global trader' perspective. Yet it goes in the right direction, and not only for political or diplomatic reasons. From the strict economic viewpoint there are important dynamic gains that can accrue from closer trade relations with neighboring countries, even with the discrepancies among the economies of these countries. The necessary condition for that is to overcome such discrepancies and turn the whole process into a positive sum game.

Final remarks

Policy-makers in economies with large potential domestic markets face a natural difficulty in dealing with the stimuli to domestic economic development and at the same time providing the conditions for an efficient relation with the rest of the world. It is comparatively 'easier' for small countries to opt for a full adhesion to international markets.

Brazil has gradually increased its degree of exposure to international flows of goods, services and capital. Notwithstanding considerations about the depth, pace and sequencing of this opening, this article has discussed some of the basic characteristics of this process.

Emphasis in closer regional links is likely to remain an important issue in the Brazilian international agenda. Be it for the specificities of the recent conjuncture or for the structural trend to look for deeper and more substantive productive relations with neighboring countries, it is very unlikely to see this issue as downgraded as it was back in the 1970s.

Such a process depends on joint action by the government and private actors. The involvement of these agents requires positive expectations with regard to what can be achieved.

These expectations are, nevertheless, not as clear today as one would have expected. What level of relative importance can or should regional trade achieve, in relation to total exports? How efficient is regional trade in stimulating medium/high technology products in comparison to trade with other regions? How sensitive to the business cycle is regional trade as compared to other markets? To what extent is regional trade dependent on terms of trade gains by neighboring countries? Will the recent pace hold in the present scenario of lower commodity prices? What institutional arrangements are required to help deepen regional trade? To what extent has regional trade led to convergent interests, so as to provide positive outcomes in international negotiations? To what extent the emphasis in regional markets affects potential gains stemming from closer relations with other, wealthier partners?

The option for intensifying regional trade links is a reasonable one and perhaps even inevitable, taking into account the experience elsewhere, but the actual regional conditions raise a number of questions that have to do both with further empirical assessment and to more specific identification of expectations with regard to probable achievements. This article has shown that the road to reach significant progress in this direction is not flat and requires more clear signaling to economic agents, strong political will and a good deal of specific measures. But it has also suggested that it might provide positive results.

The policy suggestions that the analysis presented leads to are, first and foremost, to broaden regional trade preferences. Secondly, to adopt measures that might allow for joint exploration of third markets, such as complementary investment programs. Both measures should contribute to improve the positive perception from the agents in neighboring countries, with regard to the benefits of regional integration, a pre-condition for its sustainability. Third, to create mechanisms that stimulate transnational subsidiaries operating in Brazil to speed up the technological content of the export bill; overcoming infrastructure limitations and fostering human qualification are necessary conditions for that. Fourth, in times of reduced availability of foreign currencies, past experience has proved the importance of mechanisms to allow for the financing of regional trade; it is in moments when resources are scarce that the good will to create such mechanisms favors initiatives in that direction.

BRICs and Investment

Prospect for Direct Investment among the BRICs Countries

Liu Youfa[*]

Analysis on the prospect of direct investment among the BRICs countries

Under the chemistry of the international crisis, the "BRICs", originally a pure academic terminology has now become a new modality of cooperation among the emerging great powers, which composes a new cooperative model for countries from different regions, with different political systems, with different development modalities and with different civilizations. Brazil, Russia, China and India (BRICs) all belong to the emerging great powers, all implement modalities of economic and social development with their national characteristics, all enjoy comparative advantages in relevant industries and technologies with their national characteristics, and are all posed for rapid economic growth. Ever since the eruption of the international financial crisis, the four countries have been playing an ever increasing role in international affairs.

More importantly, common international concerns have converted the four countries into an ad hoc political group, common economic development stages have propelled them to formulate the similar development theories, and the common development strategies have prompted more and more areas for cooperation, especially in direct investment. Simply said, during the post financial crisis, further cooperation among the BRICs countries will facilitate the steam that would help to boost the collective influence of the four countries, increase the collective economic weight, and convert their geographical economic powers into geo-political influence, in order to contribute to the global peace, development and cooperation.

---

* Liu Youfa, the Vice President of the China Institute of International Studies.

Common international strategies have turned the BRICs countries into a political club

From the perspective of modern international relations, no other international factors have ever exerted such an impact as the 2008 international financial crisis that literally ushered the BRICs countries into the center stage of the international affairs, and empowered them to be the important participants as well as decision makers vis-à-vis the relevant international issues, and become the important promoters for the construction of the new global order. Meanwhile, the financial crisis also provided the political and economic bedrocks for the four countries to promote closer economic cooperation, especially with regard to the intra-BRICs investment.

The reasons are self-evident. Nearly all the developed countries became the victims of the international financial crisis, and the recipients of the international rescue. Meanwhile, the BRICs countries, except Russia successfully withstood the impacts of the crisis, realized their economic recovery and maintained the momentum of growth. According to the World Bank statistics, the four countries contributed more than 50% of the global economic growth, thus becoming the rare bright spots of world economy during the crisis year.

During the crisis, the "BRICs", as a new political force, actively participated in and promoted the international rescue and crisis management efforts. One the one hand, leaders from the four countries timely coordinated their crisis management policies, in an effort to avoid the drastic contraction of the mutual trade, and ensure stable economic and trade relations through mutual investment. On the other hand, the four countries fully utilized the relevant international summits, jointly pushed for the resolution of important international issues, during which voices from the BRICs received prompt attention or responses from the relevant attendees in particular, and the international community at large. In the field multilateral diplomacy, leaders from the four countries coordinated their policy stands, jointly put forward proposals on the reform of the existing international game rules, in order for the developing countries, especially the BRICs to seek a level plain business field.

From the future perspective, against the backdrop of the globalization, mutual investment will be a key to make the intra-BRICs trade sustainable, a sure road map for furthering the said economic relations, as well as an important platform for the BRICs countries to fully utilize their natural resource endowments and realize the "spill over effects" through international economic cooperation. During the post crisis era, the BRICs countries will have to continue to jointly push for the international community to reform the game rules vis-à-vis international finance, continue to overhaul the existing international financial institutions, when they wish to maintain the momentum of economic growth, and to bring up their comparative advantages during the pending low-carbon economy. More importantly, the four countries will have to follow the trend of the times, and fully tap into the political advantage of the "BRICs", exert collective influence to push for the construction of new international order, put forward joint principles, propose joint agendas, protect and promote common interests, and further elevate the statuses and positions of the four countries in the international affairs.

On the analysis of all the existing international cooperation mechanisms, the four countries have every reason to further strengthen economic and trade cooperation, especially in the area of mutual investment, in order to facilitate the economic foundation for the already cordial intra-BRICs political cooperation. As a matter of fact, the on-going financial crisis has laid the solid political and economic foundation for the BRICs to further boost the above said cooperation. The reasons are simple. Closer cooperation among the BRICs countries will help boost the collective influence of the four countries, to promote their economic growth, to transform their economic power into the respective geopolitical influence, which would, in turn, contribute to the global peace, security and development.

Common challenges have transformed the BRICs into an interest party

From the perspective of micro economy, when the dusts of the crisis are settling down, the problematic transaction means prevalent in the international financial field prior to the crisis are still in effect, the toxic financial derivative products are still being traded in even larger scales and volumes. Those who actually caused the on-going crisis are still roaming at large. The proposed reform of the financial system being carried out by the developed countries is too soft to effectively prevent the similar financial risks. Consequently, the problematic system that brought about the global financial crisis is still in function, as if nothing has happened.

On the above analysis, the BRICs will continue to face both the lingering impacts from the crisis, new international situation and new problems resultant from the said crisis. From the perspective of international fame rules, the "BRICs", as late-comers of the industrialization, will surely have to endure the strategic containment from the traditional major powers, to overcome the barriers of the existing international economic system, and face the challenges from the international game rules. Therefore, it will be the natural choice by the leaders of the four countries to further their cooperation, in order to bring into full play of their comparative advantages, and realize the comprehensive advantages for development.

From the macro economic perspective, the "BRICs" countries all stand for multi-polarization in the international relations, respect the diversity of development modalities, promote equal cooperative partnership, and to promote win-win economic and trade relations. During the post financial crisis era, the four countries have formed broad common interests and concerns in the international affairs.

Firstly, they have to coordinate policy stands and strengthen cooperation accordingly, in an effort to effectively manage the financial crisis, expedite the economic recovery and seek early opportunity of economic development during the post crisis.

Secondly, they have to balance their economic relations with both the developed countries and the other developing countries. While pursuing the cooperation and competition with the developed countries, the four countries will have to give special attention to their long term cooperation with other developing countries, in order to secure more opportunities of development.

Thirdly, they have to join hands, in order to effectively push for the reform of the international political and economic systems, and promote the formation of the new world order. The four countries will have to chart out a scientific road map that will be conducive both to the reform of the international political and economic systems and the creation of the new international order.

Fourthly, the BRICs will have to prevent the possible resurgence of international trade protectionism. They will have to build up their "tool boxes" that would be effective to ward off the said trade and investment protectionism, in order to create an international environment that is a precondition for their common goals of development.

Fifthly, they have to coordinate policy stands vis-à-vis field diplomacy. During the post crisis era, world economy will encounter many new problems and challenges. The four countries will have to jointly search for solutions to the international issues i.e. climate change, environment protection and nuclear proliferation. And, they have to put forward joint agendas and protect their common interests.

Similar economic development stages and strategies have prompted the BRICs to form cooperative partnership

On the analysis of the existing economic and trade cooperation mechanisms, inter-state economic and trade relations usually start with trade, to be followed up by closer cooperation in investment, which will further be assisted by cooperation in science and technology.

From the perspective of development status, the "BRICs" countries have basically built up their economic structures with their national characteristics, and formulated their industrial advantages that are in line with their national endowments, through industrialization, transformation of economic modality, economic reform and opening up to the outside world. For example, the four countries have been very competitive in the areas of energies, natural resources and capital respectively, which, in turn, form the mutual complementarities in terms of economic cooperation, and provide steam for win-win business opportunities, especially in the field of direct investment.

More importantly, the BRICs countries are all encountering the same task of further elevating the level of economic development, and further improving people's living standards. And, they hold the same or similar policy stands on international issues, and attach importance to expanding and deepening mutually beneficial cooperation, all of which will form the necessary political foundation for the four countries to carry out further cooperation in the relevant fields, especially in direct investment.

There is no doubt that the "BRICs", as emerging great powers, still suffer from the following symptoms of the duel economic structure: Firstly, it is the low productivity. The four countries all lag behind the developed countries in terms of productivity, even though they each enjoy great potentials in the relevant industries, natural resources or human capital, etc. They still have to import high end industrial products from the developed countries.

Secondly, it is the duel economic structure. The said duel nature is not only evident among the different industries, between the urban and rural areas, but is also easily seen among different social groups and different regions across the country. History has repeatedly demonstrated that the above mentioned disparities would be the political problems that would induce the loss of steam of national development, as well as the economic bedrocks that would cause the social disorder and even the change of hands of the state power.

Thirdly, it is the backwardness of the industrial structure. Off all the industrial structures of the four countries, the primary industries still hold the bulk of the total national products, while the manufactory industries, especially the service industry still takes up the less dominant market shares. This is an important benchmark to differentiate a developed country from a developing one.

Last but not least, the four countries are all in disadvantageous position in the international economic relations. Therefore, they all have to settle for the second best when they come to international trade and investment. As a result, the relevant countries may keep expanding the scales of their external economy, but not the economic interest resultant from the above development.

From the perspective of national development strategies, upon entering the 21st century, the "BRICs" countries have expedited their pace of national rejuvenation or national development. As the "BRICs" have launched their historical process of institutionalization, the four countries will further deepen the intra-BRICs cooperation and quicken its tempo, in order for the member states to fully tap into their comparative advantages, and realize the comprehensive benefits of the cooperative development.

However, as the BRICs are all latecomers in terms of industrialization and globalization, they lack the contingent of transnational corporations to serve as the media of mutual direct investment. Companies and enterprises of the member states are following somewhat different market rules, abide by somewhat different corporate cultures, lack of understanding of the business environment of the other member states, and are still to acquire practical experience vis-à-vis market entry. On the above analysis, the effective promotion of the intra-BRICs investment will rely mainly on the political will and guidance of the leaders of the courtiers concerned, depend much on the governmental policy support, in order for the member states to benefit from the comprehensive economic weight resultant from the enlarged intra-BRICs investment, and achieve the "spill-over effects" of the above said economic development.

From the perspective of intra-BRICs trade, as the four countries further move forward with economic and trade cooperation, they will certainly boost the economic complementarities and mutual dependency rate. According to the trade statistics from the relevant authorities of the United Nations, the four countries have increased their exports to the other three states. In 2000, Brazil registered 3.1%, Russia 6.4%, India 4.2% and China 2.0%. By 2008, those figures rose to 11.2%, 6.1%, 7.9% and 5.8% respectively.

According to the trade figures from the World Trade Organization, between 2003 and 2008, the exports from the four countries grew at an average annual rate of more than 20%, during which China scored the best. In 2003, the export of China registered only 5.9%. However, by 2008, that figure grew up to an impressive 9.1%. In 2008, the exports from the four countries constituted 14.5% of the total global trade, with imports taking up 11.9%.

From the perspective of the intra-BRICs investment, the four countries now collectively occupy a land area that is 40% of the global land surface, support 42% of the global population, and contribute to 14% of the global GDP, and own more than three quarters of the global foreign currency reserves. In 2009, the four countries contributed more than half of the annual global GDP growth. According to some expert projections, the four countries are producing an ever growing middle class that is to surpass that of the developed economies in Europe, America and Asia. The above scenario will form a formidable consuming market to attract foreign direct investment. Simply put, the rapid growth of the rich and well-to-do people of the said countries will provide a strong market support for the four countries, in terms of attracting the FDI, elevating the structure of the relevant industries, and transforming the patterns of their economic growth.

From the perspective of science and technology, it constitutes the life line for any country to realize its sustainable economic development. During the post financial crisis era, what the countries across the world are to embrace is the low carbon economy that has the benchmark of high end technology, thus constituting the latest stage of the world economy. Against the above background, whether individual countries will be able to grasp the historical opportunity to seek a favorable status, and reap the intended policy goals, will largely depend on the capacity of the countries concerned, in terms of technology research and development.

Based on the experience of the existing regional integration mechanisms, science and technology composes the key for the member states to maintain sustainable economic development, an effective means to elevate international competitiveness, and an important means to build up and maintain the momentum of regional integration and the economic growth. And, it is the key for the member states to keep investing in scientific research and development, and in establishing and fortifying a dynamic system that would support the national scientific and technical creation.

During the post financial crisis era, development of the world economy will, first of all, dwell on a new round of readjustment of industrial structures, characterized in low-carbon economy, and dominant in international competition vis-à-vis the R&D on alternative energies and clean energies. It is a sad fact that developed countries have mostly managed to build up their competitive advantages, thus occupying advantageous positions in the pending competition in the relevant fields. Therefore, the "BRICs" will have to form an institution that is dedicated to the R&D in industry-specific sciences and technologies, in an effort to harvest the benefits from the collective endeavor during the post financial era. This is simply a to-be or not to-be choice.

Policy proposals for direct investment among the BRICs countries

The biggest lesson that the BRICs should learn from the 2008 international financial crisis is that any sustainable economic development will not only need the invisible hand of the market, but also the visible hand of the government. This principle also applies to the pending intra-BRICs investment, in order for the member states to fully benefit from the potentials of the expended investment cooperation. It is true that the pending low carbon economy is around the corner, in the wake of the international financial crisis. Therefore, the BRICs countries, as the emerging great powers, have every reason to actively coordinate their policies and strategies, further promote economic and trade relations, especially in direct investment, and chart out a collective blue plan for sustainable development, on the basis of comprehensive national strength, and in accordance with the principle of equality, mutual complementarities and mutual benefits.

Bring into full play of the government role in promoting mutual investment

In short, expansion of direct investment among the BRICs countries will depend much on the guidance of the relevant governments, on the specific policy support, on the comprehensive information service as well as the strong industrial oversight and management.

Firstly, it is the institution building. The BRICs leaders should institutionalize the summit mechanism, in order for them to reach political consensus on issues of common concerns, formulate political decisions on things of common interests, and resolve major problems, in order to cement the on-going political integration among the four countries.

Secondly, it is the annual ministerial meeting mechanism. The four countries should establish the mechanism of annual ministerial meetings, which would facilitate opportunities for the ministers of the member states to carry out the political resolutions by the BRICs leaders, evaluate the progress of intra-BRICs trade and investment over the past year, conduct regular policy coordination, and expedite the intra-BRICs investment, in order for each and every member country to extend its production chains, in line with the comparative advantages of their national industries, and benefit from the pending economic integration.

Thirdly, it is the trade and investment mechanism. The four governments should negotiate and sign the investment promotion agreement at their early convenience, in order to effectively reduce the business risks of the enterprises when they decide to extend their business operations into the other three countries, and in order for them to fully tap into the potentials of the enlarged market.

Fourthly, it is the investment promotion mechanism. The four countries should create a tangible investment and trade promotion system, in accordance with the said agreement, which would facilitate attractive conditions for the enterprises of the member states to develop markets in the other countries.

Last but not least, it is the information service mechanism. The four countries should establish a comprehensive information system, which would be in capacity to collect, process and disseminate all the information about the status of the economic and social development, economic structure, industrial policies, market accesses, business opportunities, and project tenders, etc.

Establish the BRICs R&D mechanism and promote economic development

Science and technology have become the critical factors for the sustainable development for any country, which has much to do with foreign direct investment. Against the backdrop of the low carbon economy, the BRICs countries have to ride along with the curve of the world economy, and take stock from their collective strength, and form an alliance in the above regard. The four countries should abide by the following principle: Jointly seek breakthroughs in key technologies, joint research and development, internationalize technology transfer, mutual benefit.

Firstly, it is the joint R&D mechanism. The BRICs countries should establish a dynamic mechanism of joint research and development, which is consisted of the professionals and think tank experts, in order for them to probe into the globalization and its experience and lessons, identify the problems vis-à-vis the institutionalization of the BRICs, its future trend, and search for policy proposals, so that the leader and ministers from the four countries could seek reference.

Secondly, it is the R&D fund. The four countries should establish a high-tech R&D fund which would provide critical capital support for the BRICs enterprises and institutions in their efforts to research and develop new technologies or up grade existing technologies.

Thirdly, it is the technology promotion mechanism. The four countries should establish a dynamic technology promotion mechanism, in order to help member countries to elevate their industrial capacities, and fully realize both the economic and social benefits of the relevant technological inventions and renovations.

Fourthly, it is the technology transfer mechanism. The four countries should establish a BRICs technology transfer mechanism, which would help to extend the life expectancy of the relevant technologies, and provide technical support for other developing countries in their efforts to realize their sustainable economic development.

Last but not least, it is the personnel exchange mechanism. The four countries should create a personnel exchange mechanism for the engineers and scientists among the BRICs countries, in order to provide fresh human capital support for the respective countries to build up their own contingent of engineers and scientists.

Establish a BRICs financial mechanism and further promote investment

Finance is the most critical sector within modern economy and constitutes the core industry for any country to realize its sustainable economic and social development. Therefore, financial cooperation will provide a sound institutional protection for promoting direct investment among the said countries.

Firstly, it is the policy coordination mechanism. The BRICs countries should further strengthen the financial policy coordination among the central banks, in order to boost the relevant financial information, provide better service to their enterprises, and jointly fence off the relevant financial risks.

Secondly, it is the financial consortium. The four countries should establish a financial consortium, in order to provide adequate funding for major projects among the member countries, and beef up the capacity of their commercial banks in their respective commercial operations in the member states.

Thirdly, it is the development bank. The four countries should establish a BRICs development bank, which would provide adequate cash flows for their enterprises and companies. At the same time, it would provide financial services for the local governments of the four countries, in their efforts to carry out cooperative projects within the sister city framework.

Fourthly, it is the project cooperation mechanism. The four countries should design and carry out major joint projects among the four countries, in order to bring into full play of the comparative advantages of the member states, to further promote mutual investment, and to up-grade the infrastructure of the BRICs countries.

Last but not least, it is the money swap mechanism. The four countries should further expand their existing money swap deals, in order to provide effective cushions for the enterprises of the member states, in terms of operational costs and the exchange rate risks when carry out their investment plans into other member states.

Further open markets and promote trade–related investment

As is known, international trade has been the main engine for both the world economy and international investment. Therefore, during the post financial crisis era, the BRICs countries will have to double their efforts in the above regard, in order to bring into full play of the comparative advantages of the respective countries, maintain the momentum of development and, above all, to fortify the market foundation for more investment within the four countries.

Firstly, it is the policy coordination mechanism. The future BRICs summits and ministerial meetings should iron out and adjust principles that would guide the trade flow among the member states, and provide policy guidance for the trade related investment among the member states.

Secondly, it is the oversight and self-management mechanism. The four governments should help their national companies to form business councils or chamber of commerce at the residing countries, empower them to be vehicles of self management and oversight on their business activities, in order create the business standards and business ethic code, to effectively promote the quality of their products and services, and build up or maintain the images of the respective countries.

Thirdly, it is expo mechanism. The four countries should establish the "BRICs" expo mechanism within which new project proposals would receive more potential competitors, new products would enjoy more platforms for marketing, and the new industrial technologies would find more potential customers.

Fourthly, it is the trade remedial mechanism. The four countries should establish a BRICs trade remedial mechanism, in order to provide lubricsants to the trade and investment.

Last but not least, it is the industrial park mechanism. The four countries should create or better utilize the existing export processing zones and high-tech industrial parks that would attract more FDI from the member countries.

The Internationalization of Chinese Firms

Luciana Acioly, Maria Abadia S. Alves,
Rodrigo Pimentel F. Leão, Zhou Zhiwei (translator)[*]

Introduction

The aim of this paper is to describe in summary the recent process of internationalization of Chinese firms, the characteristics and the principal policies formulated to support this process. It also deals with the presentation of preliminary result of the research "Internationalization of Brazilian Firms" still in progress under the DICOD.

The classical theories of productive internationalization aren't able to explain fully this process in China.[①] In this country, the internationalization is strongly controlled by the state and only from the recent political and institutional changes can be better understood. Since 2002, with the institution of the policy "Go Global", the Chinese state began offering a series of incentives to those firms internationalized, besides facilitating the administrative procedures for making investments. The observation of the general characteristics of Chinese investment abroad also allows argue that the motivations to internationalizing go beyond the purely commercial nature, through the issue of sustainability of the balance of payments and even geopolitical objectives.

---

* Luciana Acioly, researcher of IPEA in Department of Development and Cooperation (Dicod); Maria Abadia S. Alves, Fellow in Department of Development and Cooperation of IPEA, Postdoctoral candidate in public policies and government by EAESP-FGV; Rodrigo Pimentel F. Leão, Fellow in Department of Development and Cooperation of IPEA, Master Candidate in economic development by IE/UNICAMP. Zhou Zhiwei, research associate fellow, the Institute of Latin American Studies, Chinese Academy of Social Sciences.

① See Moraes et. All. (2007).

The international trends of foreign direct investment

Between the 1980s and 2000, the world economy underwent several transformations that can be observed by the rate of economic growth in various countries, as shown in Table 1. In the first decade (1980-1989), showed an expansion of the global economy by about 3%, especially in the Asian countries and USA. In the following decade, the developing countries of Asia were those with the highest rate of growth, and China is the principal representative (average of 10%). Among the developed countries, only USA achieved a reasonable level of GDP growth (average of 3.1%), Japan and the European Union were virtually stagnant, especially the first country. Finally, in the current decade, the Latin America and Caribbean, besides Asia, is that lead the world economic growth, the latter group of countries, the great protagonist.

Table 1 Average growth rate of GDP in the world and selected counties and regions (1980-2007)

Unit: %

	1980-1989	1990-1999	2000-2007
World	3.02	2.72	3.19
European Union	2.28	2.18	2.09
United States	3.10	3.13	2.52
Japan	3.71	1.50	1.74
China	9.75	9.99	10.11
South Asia	5.55	5.32	6.79
East Asia & the Pacific	7.71	8.21	8.82
Latin America & Caribbean	1.80	2.94	3.52

Source: World Bank database.

This means that the movement of expansion since the decade before 2007 was driven particularly by the developing countries, namely until 2007, South Asia grew 6.8%, East Asia and the Pacific grew 8.8%, Latin America and Caribbean at 3.5%. It is in this context that have been configured the movements of outgoing and incoming of foreign direct investment (FDI), in which the developing countries have been gaining more weight and importance.

Specifically concerning the internationalization of production through FDI, shows a significant growth since the mid-1980s, with only two retractions during periods of global economic slowdown that occurred between 1991-1993 and 2001-2003, from US$230 billion in 1990 to US$1.8 trillion in 2007.[1] The transnational companies' agents of this process gave the movement some characteristics different from those observed between the postwar and early 1980, as a redirection of FDI mainly to the services sector and the prevalence of mergers and acquisitions (including the mega-agreements between companies above US$1 billion) on the new investment project (Greenfield investment). Geographically, the FDI inflows in the 1980s focused almost entirely in the United States, Japan and the European Community, until then. The resumption of foreign investments, after the recession of 1991-1992, began to incorporate in a large number of the developing countries, and the growing presence of developing countries as executors of FDI in the world since 2000.

Factors such as the sustained growth of the five largest economies in the world, the emergence of the dynamic Asian hub, the expansion of liberalization of the capital account, the volatility in exchange and interest rate associated with the development of securities markets, changed the direction and the forms undertaken by international capital flows and, consequently, the investment and location strategies of the great transnational enterprises. The international financial changes ensures a cross flow of investments in profitable assets, without which it would become difficult to explain the volume reached by transnational mergers and acquisitions (engine of the grow of FDI) during almost the entire period. [2]The new financing instruments, to provide an overall mass of global loan funds, ensured the great operations between companies. Moreover, the rise of Asia as a manufacturing center, with the high growth rates, led to a reconfiguration of world production and showed the results of different options of insertion of developing countries in the process of globalization over the past decades.

The direct investment of developing: countries: the emergence of Asia

Over the past three years, the Transnational Corporations (TNCs) accounted, on average, respectively 10%, 16% and 12% of assets abroad, sales and employment of all corporations in the world, giving them a key role in restructuring the world economy. Although this list is composed mostly by companies of developed countries, more recently, some companies of developing countries now appear in the list of 100 largest non-financial TNCs in the world (classified by the value of their assets abroad about the value of total assets, the methodology of UNCTAD).

---

① *Annual Report of UNCTAD (2008).*

② Acioly, L.(2004). Brasil, China e Índia: O Investimento Direto Externo nos anos 90. Tese de Doutoramento, IE: UNICAMP. Campinas, São Paulo.

According to UNCTAD data, among the 10 largest transnational corporations from developing countries in 2006 (by foreign assets), nine are of Asian origin, five from China (including Hong Kong) and South Korea, namely: *Hutchison Whampoa Ltd., Samsung Eletronics Co., Hyundai Motor Company, China International Trust and Investment Corporation (CITIC) Group and Jardine Matheson Holdings.* A participation of Latin America can be considered smaller, compared to Asia, as only six companies of the region appear in the list of top 30, especially Mexico and Brazil that have five companies in this list: Cemex S.A., Company Vale do Rio Doce, Petrobrás, América Movil and Telefonos of Mexico. In this list, we can find a sectoral diversification in the top 10 companies, ie, there is no domination of any specific sector, however it should be noted that two companies, both South Korean, are of consumer electronics.

From the viewpoint of sales abroad, there are differences between the firms analyzed. In this case, among the 10 largest TNCs, seven are Asian (all Chinese or South Korean) and three Latin-American (two Brazilian and one Mexican), and the predominant sectors are consumer electronics, non-metallic mineral and petroleum.

Taking into consideration the factors explained above and the Table 2, it is clear that China, South Korea, Brazil and Mexico have been the leading countries of the internationalization process of companies, in Asia and Latin America, respectively.

Table 2 The largest transnational corporations in selected countries in 2006(by foreign assets)

Unit: US$ 1000

Corporation	Country	Sector	Foreign Assets	Total Assets
Samsung Eletronics Co., Ltd.	South Korea	Electrical and Electronic Equipment	27,011	87,111
Hyundai Motor Company	South Korea	Electrical and Electronic Equipment	19,581	76,064
Hutchison Whampoa Limited	China	Diversified	70,679	87,146
CITIC Group	China	Diversified	17,623	117,355
Cemex S. A.	Mexico	Non-metallic mineral	24,411	29,749
America Movil	Mexico	Telecommunication	8,701	29,473
CVRD	Brazil	Mining	14,974	60,954
Petrobras	Brazil	Oil	10,454	98,680

Source: UNCTAD, 2008.

This process of further internationalization of the enterprises in developing countries through the FDI can be seen from those three "waves" of FDI.①

① GAMMELTOFT, P.(2007), Emerging Multinationals: Outward FDI from the BRICs Countries Copenhagen Business School. Disponível em http://www.inderscience.com/research/index.php?action=record&rec_id=16184&prevQuery=&ps=10&m=or (acesso em 01-04-2009). http://www.fmprc.gov.cn/zflt/eng/zyzl/hywj/t280369.htm

Decade of 1960 and 1980

The biggest presence was of those Latin-American companies (Argentina, Mexico, Colombia and Venezuela) and some Asian (Singapore, Malaysia, Philippines, Hong Kong, South Korea and India). The main motivation for the internationalization was the need to overcome trade barriers, and the main activities were related to the extractive industries, the civil engineering and construction. The neighboring countries were the main destination of these investments.

From mid-1980s to 1990s

The Asian companies (Hong Kong, Singapore, South Korea and Taiwan) take a leadership position in this movement, whose main motivation was to develop the new markets. Most of the investments occurred in segments of greater technological sophistication (IT, electronics, automobile), sought to export, not just the internal market of those recipient countries.

Recent period

Greater geographic diversification with the resurgence of Latin America and the inclusion of Russia and South Africa. The major investors are: Hong Kong, Taiwan, Singapore, Brazil, South Africa, China, South Korea, Malaysia, Argentina, Russia, Chile and Mexico. The destination of these investments is global, even for developed countries, although still dominant regional. The main reasons were related to increase the market power, especially in natural resources, and to increase the price of assets.

The chinese direct investment: a characterization

The consolidation of China's position as a major executor of FDI occurs in the third wave described above. The flows of Chinese direct investment in the world multiplied by almost 30 times between 1990 and 2007. The amount invested by this country rose from US$44 million in 1982 to US$830 million in 1990, amounting in 2007 to about US$22.5 billion (Table 3). The acceleration of this growth was higher from 2003 to 2004, when a series of policy changes, to encourage the internationalization and the simplification of procedures, has been implemented.[①] Thereafter, the investments made by China supplanted the investments abroad of other Asian developing countries, like South Korea and Singapore, and in 2007, according to UNCTAD's data, show that China was the second largest among developing countries and regions, after Hong Kong. In terms of stock, however, China accounted for only 0.6% (US$75 billion) of the world FDI stock in 2006.

① *Annual Report of UNCTAD(2008).*

Table 3 Foreign Direct Investment (FDI) in China in recent 25 years

	1982-1989 (average)	1990-2000 (average)	2001	2002	2003	2004	2005	2006	2007
Total (US$ million)	4.53	21.95	68.85	25.18	28.55	54.98	122.61	211.60	224.69
% of Asian developing countries	9.5	8.1	13.9	6.8	12.7	6.1	15.4	15	11.5
% of developing countries	7.2	5.9	8.3	5.1	6.3	4.6	10.4	10	8.9

Source: UNCTAD, 2008.

In terms of the direct investment accumulated, the shows that the Chinese investment abroad, compared to other BRICs countries and South Africa, occupies the second position behind Russia between 2000 and 2007. In the 1990s, its leadership was undisputed.

This performance of China is related to the aggressiveness of internationalization of their companies, which supported by the incentive policies. The Table 4 shows the five largest Chinese TNCs (excluding Hong Kong companies) by volume of foreign assets in 2006 which represent the core of this process of internationalization. About these companies, it is noteworthy that all are state owned. In relation to the sectors that they serve, there exists some diversification: two are oil companies, one operates predominantly in the financial sector, one acts in the sector of transportation, and another in the sector of civil construction.

Table 4 China: major transnational corporations and their positions within the developing countries in 2006 (by volume of assets abroad by US$ million and the workforce)

Foreign Assets	Assets		Sales		Job		Subsidiaries	
Corporation/Rank	Abroad	%(total)	Abroad	%(total)	Abroad	%(total)	Abroad	%(total)
CITIC Group/7	17623	15.02	2482	24.54	18305	17.05	12	10.71
COSCO Group/13	10397	55.57	8777	55.77	4432	6.37	245	25.87
CSCEC/19	6998	43.78	4483	24.17	25000	21.01	23	32.86
CNPC/21	6374	3.56	3036	2.65	22000	1.88	5	7.69
Sinochem Co./26	5326	59.86	19374	82.11	220	1.05	31	19.25

Source: UNCTAD, 2008.

Among these companies noted in the table, the most internationalized is the CITIC Group, founded in 1979 and became the largest transnational corporation in China. Currently, it has 44 financial subsidiaries abroad, and the main markets are Hong Kong, USA, Canada, Australia and New Zealand. The company also has representative offices in Tokyo, Frankfurt and New York. The main sector of the company's operation is financial, aiming to sponsor the development of the industry and the service industries.

According to UNCTAD, the company had US$17 billion of assets abroad (15% of total company assets). In terms of international sales, the company is the one presenting the lowest value at US$2 billion, about 25% of total sales. The jobs created abroad are also significant: about 18,000 (17% of total).

The second largest conglomerate with volume of assets abroad in 2006 is the China Ocean Shipping Group Company (COSCO) which operates in the field of maritime transport and related activities. Founded on February 16, 1993, the COSCO Group incorporated three other major companies: *China Ocean Shipping Agency, China Marine Bunker Supply Company and China Road Transportation Company.* In addition, the Group is consisted of 8 subsidiaries that operate more than 600 ships in 1100 ports of 150 countries. The principal markets where the company operates are Asia and Europe, especially Germany, Singapore and Thailand.

The same data from UNCTAD show that the COSCO had US$10 billion of their foreign assets in 2006, which meant 55% of the total. The overseas sales were US$8 billion (also 55% of total). The total overseas jobs were only 4,000, just 6% of the workforce employed by company. That is, although the COSCO focus its activities abroad, has much of its workforce in China itself.

At the position below the COSCO comes the China State Construction Engineering Corporation (CSCEC). The company, established in 1982, acts mainly in planning, projects development, design and management of the civil construction sector. According to the newspaper Engineering News-Record (ENR), the Chinese giant was placed in 2002 the 16th among the world's largest contractors. The main countries where the conglomerate involved are concentrated in Asia and Africa, namely, Singapore, South Korea, Namibia, Philippines, Thailand, Botswana, Algeria and Hong Kong.

Despite being a ranking below the CITIC and the COSCO, the company had in 2006 a significant amount of assets in foreign markets: more than US$ 6 billion, which represented 43% of its total assets. The sales and the jobs abroad were lower in percentage terms (in relation to total foreign assets), but still significant: 24% (US$ 4 billion sales) and 21% (25,000 employees), respectively.

In the same classification of UNCTAD, the fourth was the most internationalized company China National Petroleum Corporation (CNPC). The state oil company, founded in 1988 and operates in the foreign market since 1993, conducts the exploration and production of oil and gas, as well as the transportation of fuels. As a leading global provider of the services of oil, engineering and construction, the CNPC is specialized in all fields of exploration, development, refining, chemical, geophysical, drilling, production of tests and engineering of the sector. Not coincidentally, those countries where the company has subsidiaries are major oil producer, located mainly in the Middle East, Africa and Asia. Among all firms demonstrated in Table 4, the CNPC is the one with the lowest percentage of assets, sales and jobs abroad. In all items, this percentage does not exceed 5%, i.e. the concentration of activities and employment generation is in China. Still, it is interesting to note that the company has US$6 billion of assets and 22,000 jobs abroad.

In the fifth and last position is the Sinochem. The Chinese state company that operates in the petroleum and chemical industry in 2006 had US$5 billion of foreign assets, about 60% of its total assets. The overseas sales totaled US$19 billion and 82% of its overall sales and the volume of jobs created in the international market was negligible, about 1% of the total.

In short, we can describe some trends in the internationalization process of Chinese companies: first, the companies employ little abroad, that is, the workforce is concentrated predominantly in China. Second, the sales abroad have already assumed significant proportions in the turnover of these companies, since at least 1/4 of their total sales are made abroad (except for CNPC).Finally, these Chinese giants focus their activities in the sector of infrastructure and oil, a fact which testifies to the strategic roles that they perform for the development of Chinese economy and its position in foreign markets. In the case of oil, for example, the high investment of Chinese state is related to the need for natural resources and energy that the country demands to maintain the current pace of development.

Thus, in terms of the sectoral characteristics, the relative scarcity of natural resources in the Chinese territory has made investments in these resources become a logical option, as indicated above. In recent years, China has engaged in an aggressive overseas investment policy, like Resource Seeking (oriented to natural resources), led by large state-owned enterprises in these sectors. The Box 1 brings some majors recent investments made by Chinese companies in these sectors. Furthermore, it shows the main sectors of the Chinese FDI.

Box 1 Examples of Chinese FDI in natural resouces

- The *China National Petroleum Corporation* (CNPC), *China Petroleum & Chemical Corporation* (SINOPEC), *China National Offshore Oil Corporation* (CNOOC) and other Chinese companies invested in 139 projects in 30 countries, with over US$7 billion.

- The *China Minmetals Corporation* (CMC) bought 25% of *Chili GABY Copper Mine*. The initial investment was US$550 million and could reach US$ 2 billion. The CMC invests in iron in Brazil, and uranium in Australia.

- At the beginning of decade of 90, the *China's Capital Steel Corporation* bought 98.4% of *Peru's Iron Ore Corporation*. The *Bao Steel Corporation* entered into cooperation with Vale do Rio Doce of Brazil in 2001, and with the Australian *Hamersley Iron Ore Co. Ltd* (subsidiary of Rio Tinto) in 2002. the *Wu Steel, Tang Steel, Ma Steel* and *Sha Steel* signed a *joint venture* with *Australia's Brokenhill Biliton Corp*. The objective of these investments was to ensure the supply of iron ore. The Chinese steelmakers produced 400 million tons of steel in 2006, over 30% of the global consumption.

Source: Yang and Teng (2007).

Among the sectors where China invests abroad, the service sector, especially finance, was the main target of these investments, reaching 45.4% of the total investments in 2006. The manufacturing sector is what has been receiving a smaller flow of Chinese investment, accounting in 2006 for just 5% of the total. The Box 2 shows some important investments made in this sector.

Table 5 China:Sectoral distribution of FDI flows between 2003 and 2006 (US$ million)

Sectors	2003	2004	2005	2006
First Sector	1460(51.1%)	2089(38.0%)	1781(14.6%)	8725(49.5%)
Agriculture, Forestry, Livestock and Pascal	80(2.8%)	289(5.3%)	105(0.9%)	185(1.0%)
Mining and oil	1380(48.3%)	1800(32.7%)	1675(13.7%)	8540(48.4%)
Second Sector	620(21.7%)	756(13.7%)	2280(18.6%)	907(5.0%)
Third Sector	775(27.1%)	2654(48.3%)	8200(66.9%)	8003(45.4%)
Financial and credit services	280(9.8%)	749(13.6%)	4942(40.3%)	4522(25.6%)
Wholesale and Retail	360(12.6%)	800(14.5%)	2260(18.4%)	1114(6.3%)
Transport and Storage	80(2.8%)	829(15.1%)	577(4.7%)	1377(7.8%)
Others	55(1.9%)	276(5.0%)	422(3.4%)	991(5.6%)
Total	2854(100%)	5498(100%)	12261(100%)	17634(100%)

Source: OECD, 2008.

Box 2 Examples of Chinese FDI in the secondary sector

- The Trade Area at the Russian border town of Ussuriysk received 60 Chinese companies in the manufacturing sector of leather (shoes, bags, jackets) and electronic material.
- In November of 2004, the *Shanghai Automobile Group* (SAG) bought 48.9% of *Ssang Yong Motor Company*, the fourth largest automaker in South Korea at a price of half a billion dollars. This was the first overseas purchase of an automobile company by China. In 2005, the SAG bought the *Rover's IP* (to manufacture two models of cars).
- In 2003-2004, the TCL (electronic) merged with the giant Thomson (TV) operation of 450 millions Euros. The TCL also has established a joint venture with the France's *Alcatel* (mobile phones) to enter the European market. In 2004 -2005 *Lenovo* invested 1.75 billion Euros in buying the PC operation of the IBM.
- In 2005, another Chinese giant of electronic industry *Haier* failed in its attempt to merge with the *American Metec.*
- The biggest manufacturer of telecommunications equipment *Huawei* has aggressively expanded its operations in the developing countries in recent years.

Source: Yang and Teng (2007).

For forms of entry in the foreign markets, the most common methods of investment abroad of Chinese companies are by establishing subsidiaries and joint venture, although recently there is a growing use of mergers and acquisitions as form of entry in other countries. The flow of Chinese FDI through mergers and acquisitions rose from US$

60 million in 1990 to over US$ 15 billion in 2006, falling to US$ 4.5 billion in 2007.① Its presence in the international investments through such operations, compared to other BRICs countries and South Africa, has been growing, but not dominant.

These operations are used especially in the areas of technology, communication and natural resources, becoming an option to obtain technology, brands and distribution networks, characterizing investment as the type of motivation of Strategic Asset Seeking (oriented to seek strategic assets) and Market Seeking (oriented to exploit the internal market).

From the standpoint of the geographical distribution of Chinese FDI by 2006, more than 5,000 Chinese investors in the world, held about 10,000 projects, involving more than 170 countries. Although this large number of countries seems to indicate diversity of the location of investment, these flows are highly concentrated in some countries. Between 2003 and 2006, over 80% of the foreign investments were made in Hong Kong and in tax havens like the Virgin Islands and Cayman Islands, used to form holding companies and also financial investments. In more detailed form, we observe some trends and characteristics of the Chinese investments.②

• Asia and the Middle East are the main hosts of Chinese investments, receiving approximately 60% of the volume of these investments. This is attributed to the historical relations between the countries and the availability of oil in the Middle East and some regions of Asia.

• In Asia, most of Chinese investment is directed to the countries comprising the Association of Southeast Asian Nations (ASEAN 12) (20% to 30%). In these countries, China has invested in the sectors of commodities and natural resources, such as rubber, palm oil, petroleum, gas and agribusiness in Thailand, Cambodia, Malaysia, Indonesia, Philippines, Vietnam and Singapore.

• China is the biggest investor in Gulf. The investments concentrated in fields of petroleum and gas.

• In South Asia, the investments are concentrated in Pakistan. China is investing 80% of capital (€ 250 million) and technology for the construction of the third deep-water port, and also is investing in Haier Economic Zone where they will be assembled electronic products. Likewise, the plans are underway for the construction of a railroad, such as an alternative route to the Strait of Malacca.

• In Latin America, the primary concern has been the access to the natural resources (oil, copper and iron), and also increasing the market for Chinese products. At the moment,

① *Annual Report of OECD (2008).*

② ANG, M. E TENG, S.(2007), "China Overseas Direct Investment," *EAI Background Brief n. 340.* Singapore: East Asian Institute. National University of Singapore.

there exist real space for the growth of economic relations between Latin America and China, which now have been evolving slowly, because they were being stalled by the manner that Chinese companies like to use abroad, especially in the construction sector. In Africa, for example, the Chinese groups often take their manpower to work on some projects, the method that would be difficult to be replicated in Latin America. The increased presence of Chinese goods in the domestic market has generated tensions from local businesses. The large number of proposed anti-dumping actions against China, the evidence of this hostility.①

• The Chinese investments in Africa are increasing significantly in recent years, as we shall see. Africa surpassed the United States, becoming the third largest recipient of Chinese investments. On this continent, the investments are concentrated in oil exploration, mining and infrastructure (hereafter, we will explore in somewhat more detail the Sino-African relation).

The Chinese direct investment in Africa deserves some considerations, because it has seen a huge growth in recent years. According to OECD figures, in the second half of the 1990s, the investment was estimated at US$107 million per year, and in the period 2003-2006 the average annual investment had more than tripled, reaching US$2.6 billion.

Despite the strong growth, China is still one of the lowest foreign investors in Africa, accounting in 2006 for less than 1% of the stock of foreign investments on the continent. According to UNCTAD, the main holders of foreign investment in Africa, in terms of stock, are the United Kingdom, the United States and France, with respectively 16.6%, 9.2% and 7.7% of total foreign investments.

However, despite the low participation, there is an expectation that it will increase gradually in the coming years. Moreover, China is the major developing country to invest in Africa, and among Asian countries, China surpasses Japan and Korea in investment in this continent.

The characteristics of Chinese investments in Africa show that there are approximately 800 companies installed and 100 of these are state owned, accounting for major investments, especially in the field of exploitation of natural resources. The private companies usually operate in the manufacturing and service sectors with fewer investments.②

The major infrastructure projects are also being operated by the Chinese. These projects are intended to facilitate the performance of Chinese companies themselves, both installed on the continent, and based in China but exporting to Africa. The Chinese investments are geographically scattered across Africa, totaling 48 countries. The five

① http://noticias.uol.com.br/midiaglobal/fintimes/2007/12/21/ult579u2329.jhtm

② *Annual Report of OECD (2008).*

countries with the largest stock of Chinese investment were Algeria, Nigeria, South Africa, Sudan and Zambia. China also has invested in countries where human rights abuse, corruption and repressive regimes, where other countries have avoided investing or even withdrawn in recent years.

Box 3 The strategic relationship between China and Africa

The growing Chinese interest with regard to productive investments in Africa is related to the increasing demand for energy and natural resources in China, and the abundance of these resources in Africa may explain, in part, the Chinese interest in the continent. However, the geopolitical motivations should also be incorporated into the analysis, exemplifying a new motivation for Chinese investments overseas. As already mentioned, this possibility has also been suggested to understand the expansion of Chinese investments in Latin America.

In the 1950s, under the bipolar order established after the World War Ⅱ, the objective of China was to increase the number of its allies. When the country's relations with the USSR were shaken in the 1960s, this strategy became clearer when China declared its fight "against the hegemony of the superpowers." During this period, the Chinese government began to support a number of liberation movements in many African countries and a series of contacts and conferences strengthened the relations between China and several countries of this continent. In 1950, Beijing had diplomatic relations with 5 African countries. In the late 1960s, this number had risen to 19.

This strengthening of ties with Africa had very clear goals, according to de Oliveira Amauri Porto (2007): block the establishment of diplomatic relations with Taiwan and accumulate supports at the UN General Assembly. When in 1971 the General Assembly withdrew the representation of Taipei at the UN in favor of Beijing, a third of votes were cast by the African countries.

In the 1970s, the Sino-African relationship was marked by ambiguity: firstly, China continued supporting, even arming the national liberation movements, like the territories under Portuguese colonization. On the other hand, openly helped the operations of France or of the USA, since they tended to neutralize or restrain the Soviet penetration in Africa. Nevertheless, China continued to expand its diplomatic presence in Africa, at the end of the decade, 44 African countries maintained formal relations with China.

In the 1980s and 1990s, Africa was away from the focus of Chinese foreign policy. Only in recent years, especially from the year 2000, which is again intensified the political relationship between China and the continent. This year is symbolic because it was when was held the first "Summit of the Forum on China Africa Co-operation (FOCAC), which laid the foundations of current cooperation between China and Africa. In November 2006 came the third Summit which was released a package of aids to Africa, and was established a series of goals that gave rise to the "Beijing Action Plan (2007-2009)."

Some of the proposals* included the launch of a line of preferential credit of US$5 billion, the establishment of a fund also worth US$5 billion to support Chinese investments in the continent, a commitment to opening the Chinese market to African exportations, a series of infrastructure projects, cancellation of official debt of some countries with China, and establishment of three to five areas of cooperation in Africa.

* See the link:http://www.fmprc.gov.cn/zflt/eng/zyzl/hywj/t280369.htm.

Source: Oliveira (2007).

The relationship established in Africa shows that this goes beyond the commercial interests of China. The abundance of natural resources and the great possibilities for building infrastructure, and the opportunities related to the African consumer market, are allied to the geopolitical interests of China. Although Africa is not the number one priority of Chinese diplomacy, the African continent since the beginning exerted a strong attraction to the PRC as a source of raw materials, a market for exports and a political arena.[①]

The process of internationalization of chinese enterprises and major policy measures

The process of internationalization of Chinese enterprises comprised five stages. In the beginning, between 1979 and 1983, the need was to ensure supplies of raw materials for the manufacturing industry, being the main motivation found by the Chinese government to encourage their enterprises.

In this period there was no regulation on the internationalization of Chinese enterprises. The state-owned enterprises were practically the only ones to invest abroad and each proposal was reviewed individually by the State Council, which was the only authority responsible for approving the projects.

From the mid 1980s until early 1990, the Chinese government began to allow private companies seek permission to establish subsidiaries in other countries, occurring also a movement to standardize the procedures for authorization, with the release of certain rules and procedures to be followed by companies wishing to invest abroad. Some cases of internationalization of Chinese enterprises in this period occurred in a movement of return (round-tripping) in which the companies were installed in the United States or the Virgin Islands, and then returned to China with the status of foreign companies and thus receive the same advantages offered to foreign companies, as lower interest rates.[②]

Between 1993 and 1998, there was a relative backsliding in the movement for greater liberalization of investments abroad. This occurred as a result of losses in applications in the real estate sector in Hong Kong and also with speculation in the stock market. So some arrangements were made to ensure the priority for productive investments and not merely speculative. For this purpose, the agencies were created that would examine the investment projects larger than US$1 million before they were submitted to the Ministry of Foreign Trade and Economic Cooperation (MOFTEC). The MOFTEC also issued new regulations and requirements to be followed by companies wishing to invest abroad.

From the late 1990s until 2002, there was a process more effective of incentive to the internationalization of the Chinese enterprises, with the launch of the document "Suggestions on Encouraging Enterprises to Develop Business in Overseas Processing and Assembling the Supplied Materials", which made clear the priority for productive

① OLIVEIRA, A. P.(2007), A Política Africana da China.(Disponível em http://www.casadasafricas.org.br/site/img/upload/674760.pdf). Acesso em 25-03-2009.

② YANG, M. E TENG, S.(2007), "China Overseas Direct Investment," *EAI Background Brief n. 340*, Singapore: East Asian Institute, National University of Singapore.

investments. The State Council also began providing financial and technical assistance to companies that they used in their production internationalization of raw materials and Chinese machinery. Some sectors such as textiles, machinery and electrical equipment, were especially encouraged to internationalize.

From that period to the present, the guidelines for the internationalization of Chinese enterprises are given by the decisions taken at the 16th Communist Party Congress, at the program "Go Global" with the aim of increasing Chinese investments abroad. In this sense, a landmark document was released in 2004: "Decision of the State Council on Reforming the Investment System"①, indicating the change of stance of the Chinese government regarding the foreign investments. This document has such objectives, for example, recasting the system of examination and approval of projects to ensure the right of companies to make their own decisions of investment, expanding the channels of financing for projects of internationalization, and simplifying and regulating the procedures for the examination and approval of investment projects, etc.

A brief review of just some of the objectives listed in this document, as summarized above, allows clearly identify this new position of the Chinese government on internationalization of their domestic firms. The unfolding of the general guidelines put in this document will be treated in the following items.

Control of capital, formation of the sovereign fund and the internationalization of chinese enterprises

It should be noted that by the end of the 90s, Chinese investments abroad were severely restricted by SAFE (State Administration of Foreign Exchange), with the aim of conserving foreign exchange reserves of the country. However, the capital controls exercised by the SAFE, has undergone significant transformations in recent years, especially from the moment when China's reserves skyrocketed.

With the increase of the reserves, there had a first attempt of liberalization of projects of processing or assembling of the products overseas in 1999. In this case the investments should be in commodities and equipment and non-cash, while allowing the use of letters of credit without the use of security deposit. There was a need, however, refer to the remittance of profits directly to China. In 2002, SAFE released the foreign investments from 14 Chinese provinces and cities. From this year, the obligation to remit profits immediately to China, ended at least for the companies based in these 14 provinces and cities. The investors, therefore, could reinvest their profits abroad. In 2005, the decentralized units of SAFE were also authorized to liberalize the investments that amount up to US$10 million. In the same year, the benefits restricted to only the 14

① http://en.edrc.gov.cn/policyrelease/t20060207_58851.htm

provinces and cities were extended to the whole country.

In 2006, a circular was released by the SAFE, with the objective of detailing the procedures related to the control of capital.

The increase of China's reserves also allowed the formation of a large sovereign fund in the country that has important impacts on Chinese investment abroad. These funds are created with reserves of the countries, but these reserves are managed separately. It is a form of investment used in most of the time, in order to acquire shares in foreign companies, and to realize its strategic and financial goals. They are higher-risk investments with high-returns. According to UNCTAD, among the largest sovereign wealth funds stand out to Dubai, Norway, Qatar, Singapore and China. Currently there exist over 40 funds with a total of over US$3 trillion.

The sovereign wealth funds are not a new phenomenon on the world stage, existing since the 1950s, especially in countries exporting natural resources, especially oil. However, previously, they were limited to purchase debt securities from developed countries, and currently most resources of the funds are invested in the more profitable fields, like buying real estate, gold and stocks of large companies.

The Chinese fund was created in 2007 with 200 billion dollars, and has acted very aggressively in the purchase of various assets. For example, in 2007, were used US$3 billion of the fund to buy nearly 10% of the shares of the *Blackstone Private Equity Fund*, one of the most aggressive companies of the United States, owner of the companies like the Hilton hotel chain and the *Deutsche Telekom*. For some analysts, the motivation of this great purchase, via the sovereign wealth fund, not only is financial, but also introduce a strategic direction with increasing Chinese participation in the western companies.

Incentives policy for internationalization and simplification of procedures

Consonant with the aim of encouraging the foreign investment, the Chinese government has implemented a series of measures to facilitate "going global" of the domestic investors, promoting changes in the administrative procedures, funding or directing the investors. Moreover, the Chinese government also seeks to influence or facilitate the investment abroad on the side of the country receiving the investment, either through bilateral contracts that seek to establish some compromise in the country that will host the Chinese investment, either through strengthening diplomatic relations with other countries.

Regarding simplification of the procedures of analysis to project approval, the regulation of Chinese FDI is still in the process of formation and adaptation. Besides the Council of State, three other agencies exercise control over the internationalization of Chinese enterprises: the DRC (National Development and Reform Commission), the MOFCOM (Ministry of Commerce of the People's Republic of China - former MOFTEC) and the SAFE. However, "These three institutions are locked in a constant battle to retain and grow their influence, any opposing efforts to consolidate the ODI regulation regime in the People's Republic".①

Despite this dispute, in recent years these three agencies have sought solutions to facilitate the procedures and approval of investments abroad. From October 2004, two documents were launched with the objective of simplifying the procedures. The first was the "Interim Measures for the Approval of the Overseas Investment Projects" issued by the National Development and Reform Commission of China "and the second was the" Provisions on the Examination and Approval of Investment to Run Enterprises Abroad ", released by the MOFCOM.

Among the changes, three can be considered major. The first was the decentralization of the approval procedures. From the release of these documents, the local authorities could also approve investments of up to US$ 30 million (this ceiling was previously only US$ 1 million). Furthermore, there was a simplification of the bureaucratic procedures. Previously the investment project should be accompanied by a technical and economic-financial report. Since then, only one application, available on the Internet is now required to enter in the authorization to invest abroad. Other documents and regulations also became available via the Internet.

Fiscal and financial incentives

The Chinese foreign investment projects can be ranked according to their priority. In the preferred investment group include:

1. Projects covering the lack of domestic resources;

2. Industrial and infrastructure projects that can stimulate domestic exports, generation of employment and technology;

3. Research and development projects;

4. Projects of mergers and acquisitions that will increase the competitiveness of the Chinese enterprises in foreign markets.

These projects have broad financial support from the Chinese government through lines of credit with interest rates below the prevailing market. Two public banks excel at subsidized financing, although other public banks also provide credit to foreign investment: the China Development Bank (CDB) and the China Export and Import Bank (Exim Bank).

Among these banks, the Exim Bank has a role even more important. From 2004 the NDCR signed an agreement with the bank in which for the projects of foreign

---

① MULCAHY, N.(2007), "Chinese Regulation of Outwards Direct Investmen," *Memorandum*, Arnall Golden Gregory LLP, 18 September, National of Statistics of China, p.3.

investment, the interest rates should have agreed a discount of at least 2% compared to the current rate, and provide other facilities to finance the investment. The difference between the market rate and subsidized rate would be covered by the Ministry of Finance of China.

In addition to subsidized public financing, the OECD report (2008) also mentions the existence of special funds, created in the country aiming to encourage the Chinese investments abroad. These funds would provide loans and direct subsidies to favored investors.

Providing information and guidance and other support

The MOFCOM has also sought to guide investors. In 2004, the ministry launched a guide for the companies wishing to invest abroad involving 67 countries, identifying a number of the promising sectors in these countries, highlighting mainly the sectors of agriculture, mining, industry and service. Moreover, the government maintains a database on investment environment in various countries that can be consulted by the enterpriser. The information ranges from those related to the business environment in the country to issues related to culture and politics.

The Chinese government is also concerned about the competitiveness of its domestic firms in foreign markets, to the extent that, according to a report in 2005, approximately 70% of mergers involving Chinese companies resulted in decline in stock price. Other data indicate that approximately 30% of the foreign investments abroad had losses, 40% broken and only 30% proved profitable.

In an attempt to increase the competitiveness of its enterprises, the Chinese government created the Council Research and Development Centre and the China's Academy of Social Sciences, and other institutions devoted to the study of issues related to the competitiveness and the industrial policy.

The Chinese government also encourages the enterprises to invest collectively in the same industrial parks or Export Processing Zones, which has been built in Vietnam, Cambodia, Pakistan and Russia.

International agreements

Finally we should complement the role of international agreements (International Investment Agreements - IIA) in internationalization of the Chinese companies. These treaties generally have any provisions relating to investment promotion and legal protection of investments and foreign investors.

Although, in general, these agreements still have a limited potential to leverage new investments, these have been used increasingly by China as an additional tool to encourage the internationalization of their companies.

The bilateral agreement between China and Kuwait determines the areas where investments will be most beneficial for both countries:

"Article 2

Promotion and Protection of Investments

[...]

The Contracting States shall periodically consult between themselves concerning investment opportunities within e territory and maritime zones of each other in various sectors of the economy to determine where investments from one Contracting State into the other may be most beneficial in the interest of both Contracting States, and accord them appropriate facilities, incentives and other forms of encouragement to such an extent and on such terms and conditions as shall, from time to time, be determined by agreement between the Contracting States here to.

In the same agreement, was also foreseen the possibility of obtaining tax exemptions for the foreign investments made between the two countries:

With respect to Article 2: Investors of either Contracting State shall be entitled to apply to the competent authorities in the host State for the appropriate facilities, incentives and other forms of encouragement (including inter alia, tax relief) to such an extent and on such terms and conditions as shall, from time to time, be determined by the law send regulations of the host State or by agreement between the Contracting States thereto as the case may be.

The agreement between China and Korea predicts the occurrence of periodic meetings between the two countries to establish specific recommendations for the reception of foreign investment coming from the two countries:

Article 14

In order to facilitate the implementation of the present Agreement, the Contracting Parties agree to set up a Joint Committee composed of the representatives of the Contracting Parties. 2. The functions of the Joint Committee shall include, in particular: (a) reviewing the implementation of the Agreement and the matters related to investment between the two States;

(b) holding consultations on the operation and the matters related to the operation of the present Agreement in connection with the development of legal systems or of policies of either or both of the two States with respect to the receiving of foreign investment;

(c) making appropriate recommendations to the Governments of both States. The Joint Committee shall meet alternately in Seoul and Beijing at the request of either Contracting Party.

The agreement between China and Cote d'Ivoire states established that both countries should organize meetings to discuss the promotion of investments:

Article 13

Consultations

The representatives of the Contracting Parties shall hold meetings from time to time for the purpose of:

(a) reviewing the implementation of this Agreement;

(b) exchanging legal information and investment opportunities;

(c) resolving disputes arising out of investments;

(d) forwarding proposals on promotion of investment;

(e) studying other issues in connection with investment.

We draw attention, like UNCTAD, to the fact that 9 of the 14 bilateral international treaties signed by China, involving African countries: Benin, Djibouti, Equatorial Guinea, Madagascar, Namibia, Seychelles, Tunisia and Uganda, demonstrating a great relationship with Africa. Perhaps the most unstable political conditions of that continent explain the need to establish more formal contracts that have a minimum guarantee for the Chinese.

Conclusion

The article concludes on the process of internationalization of Chinese enterprises should be raised the following points:

1. The existence of a consensus that it is necessary to internationalize the companies, given its multiplier effects and the chain-reacting of this process on the economy (scale of production, competitiveness, remittances of interests and dividends to the country, etc.).

2. The existence of strategies for production expanding depending on the objectives of the industrial policy of the country, along with the concern about the viability of the balance of payments, without which any policy of modernization in non-convertible currency countries tends to lose strength.

3. The role of the government policies in support of the internationalization when designed in a coordinated way (which does not mean absence of conflicts). In this direction, the institutionalization set up to support the initiatives is critical.

4. The role of banks, especially the banks in channeling credit, not only in terms of volume, but fit the profile of industry and the area of destination for investment (to be detailed in our study).

5. The perception that the game of wealth is global and therefore, The Internationalization of Chinese Firms has an important role in the redesign of the world production and the country's political position on the world stage.

More specifically, it can be noted that:

6. The major Chinese companies investing abroad have already an asset size and sales abroad significant, but the job creation has not yet been transferred to the outside at the same pace, i.e. the workforce of these companies is still concentrated in China itself.

7. From the standpoint of geographical distribution of most Chinese investments are directed to Asia and the Middle East, because they are regions of greater dynamism.

8. In the context of policies to support the internationalization, the actions seem complementary, which can be inferred by the convergence of the policies on finance, fiscal and financial incentives, provision of information and guidance to companies, and the implementation of international agreements for priority areas.

BRICs and Environment

In Pursuit of More Brilliant Future for Our World–Environmental Issues and BRICs

Wu Enyuan[*]

Human environment is currently confronted with radical challenge as global climate change triggered frequent occurrence of extreme weather and climate issues. Over the past five decades, environmental problems has become increasingly prominent as represented by wider range of extreme temperature changes, ozone depletion, loss of biodiversity, overspread of acid rain, land desertification, water and air pollution, destruction of forest vegetation, pollution of persistent organic pollutants (POPs), etc.. In recent years, the issue of climate change, environment, and greenhouse gas emission has become hotter issues of global concern.

In 2007, the United Nations Intergovernmental Panel on Climate Change (UNIPCC) launched a report titled "*Climate Change 2007: the Physical Science Basis*" which dedicated to an analysis of the cause of greenhouse gas emission, changes in atmospheric greenhouse gas concentrations and ultimate cause of climate change. This analytical effort concluded that greenhouse effect, as the result of increased greenhouse gas concentrations of the greenhouse effect, has been the major cause of global warming as demonstrated by the rise in global average temperature through observation. Global climate change will trigger melting glaciers, rising sea levels, ecosystem degradation, frequent natural disasters, etc.. These severe consequences are expected to pose a threat to the security of agriculture, of food supply, of water resource, of energy, of ecosystem and of public health; and thus undermine the survival and development of human society. The *National Assessment Report on Climate Change*, co-released by Ministry of Science and technology of China, China

* Wu Enyuan, professor and the Director General of the Institute of Russian, East European & Central Asian Studies, Chinese Academy of Social Sciences.

Meteorological Administration, Chinese Academy of Sciences, etc., holds that the pace of climate change will further accelerate in China. According to this report, China's average temperature will rise by 2-3 centigrade over the next 50-80 years; and China's coastal sea level will rise by 0.01-0.06 meters by 2030. Such changes are expected to enhance the likelihood of flood in many coastal areas and pose grave impact upon agriculture production. Extreme weather, e.g., typhoons and floods will significant increase following these changes.

In pursuit of objectives for sky to turn bluer, water cleaner, environment more graceful and human life happier, preserving the earth and our homeland has become the consensus of the of the world, including people in BRICs countries. Ancient Chinese proverb "It takes more than one cold day for the river to freeze three feet deep" vividly disclosed the cause of current human environment change. Relevant research results indicate that current problems inclusive of climate change were, to a large extent, a result from the process of industrialization in developed countries over the past 150 years. Therefore, developed countries ought to undertake the legally binding obligation for the amelioration of world environment. The effective coordination of each country's stance towards environmental preservation is dependent upon developed countries' recognition of their historical responsibility. Definitely Newly Industrialized Countries should also undertake corresponding duties and obligations owing to their rapid growth. Nowadays, Brazil is known as World Resource Base, and Russia World Gas Station, India World Office, and China World Factory.

Over the past three decades, China has launched remarkable efforts into environmental preservation in response to climate change. Chinese Government has established an integral system for environmental preservation through the perfection of relevant taxation and price system by stipulating a series of laws and regulations. The government attaches importance to both energy conservation and the vigorous promotion of renewable energy. China has achieved highest growth rate in terms of the application of clean energy inclusive of wind and solar energy. In addition, the growth rate of renewable energy reached 51% with average annual growth rate of 14.7% in China. China's renewable energy consumption totaled an equivalent of 250 million tons of standard coal in 2008. This year, 30.5 million families in rural area have access to biogas–an equivalent of the reduction of over 49 million tons of carbon dioxide emission. China ranks first place in terms of installed capacity of hydropower, nuclear power construction scale, collector area of solar water heater as well as PV capacity. Forestation area in China, totaled 54 million hectares, is the widest in the world. In a word, China has fulfilled its responsibility by conducting practical actions in either energy conservation or environmental preservation.

Having overtaken the United States as the world's biggest emitter of carbon dioxide,

China is under the pressure of emission reduction from the international community. The international efforts to reduce greenhouse gas emission have significantly narrowed the margin for world non-renewable energy consumption. The modernization pattern sustained by high level of energy and resources consumption once adopted by developed countries is by no means feasible for developing countries. China's heavy industry-dominated process of industrialization poses an inevitable demand for energy and resources at its accelerating phase of industrialization and urbanization. China's economic and social development with sustainable nature has been placed under radical threat of energy security, under bottleneck of resources, and under severe environmental constraint. Thus the Eleventh Five Year Plan has established a compulsory targeting constraint for energy conservation and emission reduction in 2010. China's *National Assessment Report on Climate Change 2007* explicitly stipulated the low-carbon path of economic development. However, special difficulties exist in significant reduction in emission in short run as China currently remains at the key phase of industrialization, urbanization and rapid modernization, and as China's structure of energy consumption is still coal-dominated. In despite of such facts, environmental preservation in response to climate change has been an important strategic mission at all times. Carbon dioxide emission intensity per unit of GDP dropped by 46% over the 1990-2005 period. China proposed a further cut in carbon dioxide emission per unit of GDP by 40%-45% as compared to the 2005 level, surplus to the requirement of Bali Road Map. During this period, arduous efforts are necessary for such a significant cut in carbon dioxide emission.

The 2009 United Nations Climate Change Conference, commonly known as the Copenhagen Summit, is both the largest and highest-ranked international climate conference since the initiation of climate change negotiations in 1990s. We are pleased to note that Russia, India and Brazil have stretched their sincere wish for environmental preservation through reduction in emission. Russia scheduled to cut 20%-30% by 2020 as compared to the 1990 level; India decided to cut 20%-25% by 2020 compared to the 2005 level; Brazil scheduled to cut 36.1%-38.9% by 2020 compared to expected level.

BRICs countries share similar missions and demands regarding the simultaneous targets of economic growth and energy conservation for environmental preservation. This bloc of countries either needs to upgrade their mode of production or undertakes historical mission of environmental preservation. Without active participation of BRICs countries, any proposal for environmental preservation is obviously meaningless and the effectiveness of actions for greenhouse gas reduction will be compromised. As representatives of Newly Industrialized Economies and leaders of developing countries, the four countries are possessed of 42% share of world population and 15% share of aggregate GDP in the world. The views and stances of BRICs countries about way of living and mode of development in the future ought to be highly respected.

Kyoto Protocol is the first binding cooperation agreement signed by the international community in response to climate change. It is known that this Protocol has explicitly stipulated the emission reduction targets for developed countries at the first commitment period by 2012. However, emission targets for many developed countries elevated rather than cut considering the actual implementation. It is advisable for the international community to urge the developed countries to honor their commitments by means of designing effective institutional arrangements under the framework of the Convention. Such commitments are inclusive of providing adequate financial support, accelerating the transfer of climate-friendly technology, and preserving the environment in response to climate change through the cooperation of the international community. It is advisable to adhere to the principle of "common but differentiated responsibilities" — the core and foundation for international cooperation in response to climate change. The meeting of BRICs foreign ministers at Yekaterinburg maintains that permanent sustainable growth can only be realized under a just global economic system, and with each country's benefit adequately considered.

The consolidation of mutual cooperation among BRICs countries has been equipped with favorable condition as both bilateral relations and political trust among BRICs are increasingly strengthening; as economic and trade relations increasingly intimate; and as the mechanism for mutual cooperation is continually perfecting. We are firmly convinced that the sphere of cooperation among BRICs countries is immense in environmental conservation. In the post-war era, particularly following the end of Cold War, Western countries are used to make the world accept schemes produced via the negotiation inside of their circle. Such behavior reoccurred at Copenhagen Summit but effectively resisted with the awareness of solidarity among developed countries resurging. BRICs countries, the four BASIC countries, and Group of 77 are exceptionally objected to the mode "developed countries to stipulate, for developing countries to comply with". BRICs countries have played an essential role being the representative of emerging economies and leaders of developing countries. Copenhagen Summit indicates the increasing voice of emerging developing countries in international arena.

Environmental Crisis–Human Dimension

Nikolai Mikhailov[*]

"There is enough on earth for everybody's need, but not enough for anybody's greed."
Mahatma Gandhi

Imagine there is a frog which is sitting in a pan full of water on a burning gas stove. The water is warming up and soon will start boiling. The frog is warming up accordingly but is unable to feel any discomfort. The question is: "What should happen or what should be the force to make the frog jump out of the water before its too late?" Let me suggest the answer: the frog does not have a chance to escape unless there is a noticeable threat coming from outside or a superior order to evacuate. The problem is that we do not consider global warming to be a decisive threat like for example an asteroid colliding with our planet on a given day and time simply because no one can give us the exact deadline and there is still no global government which will give us orders. Let's hope the extraterrestrials will help.

In other words we don't believe something really bad will happen, we don't believe we will die. Now getting from frogs to humans and assuming that we are more sensitive and sensible than frogs let us see what we can and should be doing in the wake of the global catastrophe.

When faced with a change in our environment, we have just three choices: move or migrate, adapt or degenerate, and perish. In the wake of a disturbance, such as draught, famine, epidemics or any other natural disaster, animals including humans always react in one of these three ways. Two of the choices offer survival and if these options are not

* Nikolai Mikhailov, Professor of the Russkiy Mir Foundation of Russia.

available an individual, tribe and finally mankind will face death and extinction. At the current rate of resource use, pollution output, and overpopulation it is very unlikely that the planet Earth will continue to exist in its current state for much longer.

In case of chronic disturbances such as resource depletion or pollution humans normally would move to a better habitat. First they move within the country and if it does not help they cross the country borders in order to leave polluted area for a better environment. Clearly environmental migrations will grow but it is also clear that tensions resulting from massive migrations will grow in proportion. When we amount to 9-10 billion in just 40 years there will be very little place to take refuge and the receiving party will offer no welcome kits.

Human biology makes it possible to adapt to quite a range of changing conditions; however, such flexibility has its limits. If we go beyond those limits we loose biological sustainability and face extinction. Those who are unable or unwilling to move, have no other choice but adapt, weaken and finally degenerate. One may argue that humans have been migrating and adapting to new conditions thru centuries. There is much difference though between adaptation to different natural conditions and adaptation to unnatural conditions such as polluted soil, water and air. In current conditions created by technogenic civilization our resources for adaptation to a new unfriendly environment rapidly decrease.

The essence of environmental problems in the modern world lies in growing contradictions between the human productive activity and the stability of the global environment and its numerous ecosystems. Human wealth basically comes from agriculture, manufacturing, and mineral resources. Everything in our complex modern society is built around the exploitation and use of mineral resources and ever growing consumption, be it energy, automobiles, food, pesticides or plastic bags. But only recently did we realize that practically every economic activity produces the destructive effect on the environment.

The harms include deaths from disease, droughts, floods, heat and intense storms and damage to cities and villages from rising oceans, adverse impacts on agriculture, first social and then political and military disputes. In the event of a cataclysmic disturbance, acute or chronic, it is unlikely that the global population will be able to cooperate. It is likely that primal instincts will take over and cause a rift among humans in which case there would be fighting instead of cooperation.

Challenges

The most intensive impact on the environment started in the last quarter of the XIX century but only recently did we come to an understanding that such a development presents a threat to our biological existence. Only recently did we realize that every global problem of the modern world, be it energy, food or demography is finally an environmental problem which applies to all of us.

What other important discoveries did we make? We also realized that there must be limits of growth and that those limits arise mainly due to depletion of natural resources. As a result the developed countries responded by turning over to other countries' resources thus generating the continuing "resource wars". It all started with colonial conquest and continued through the second half of the XX century when there were 73 military conflicts and wars, almost all driven by greed to control resources of oil, diamonds, copper, cacao, coca, and even bananas. It should be no surprise if new and even greater resource wars will take place.

By far more vital and dramatic discovery, however, was the understanding that there exist limits of our existence. It took us some twenty years since the end of the WWII to realize that mankind is no longer immortal. And only recently did we realize that if we maintain the same pace of economic development the global environment may react in such a way that mankind would not be able to outlive the first quarter of the current millennium.

Who has contributed the most to overconsumption and pollution? The more developed nations with 23 percent of the population, who use about 66 percent of the Earth's resources or the less developed nations whose populations will double again in 30 years, who will run out of food and water first, and whose pollution due to coal burning, lack of emission controls, misuse of pesticides, and toxic waste from under-regulated industries, will only worsen with the increase of population?

There is no need to prove that a human population of 6 billion is not sustainable. The world population has doubled in the last forty years. The present global population is about 30% more than the Earth's biological capacity to sustain present standards of living, but growth may not even stabilize at the projected 10 billion by the year 2050. The animal population is not sustainable either – no living community can indefinitely sustain a loss of 70,000 species a year. As our population grows, the number of extinctions will increase. Our population might become stable at 12 billion but that does not mean the rest of the living community would be stable.

If we ask the developed countries to cope with natural, biosphere-friendly cycles they will have to reduce their overall consumption by ten-fold and the U.S., by fifty-fold. It is evident however that there will be no immediate response. The world needs to immediately reduce by 1/2 its carbon dioxide emissions, yet United Nations' member countries have only agreed to reduce it by 5% by 2012.

For quite a while we have been doing our best creating an economy whose output is inflated by drawing down the earth's natural capital. The challenge is to deflate the global economic bubble before it bursts when it will affect the entire world. To avoid this, urgent action must be taken to reduce energy and water consumption, stabilize emissions to a sustainable level and address population stability, particularly in developing countries.

It is probably for the first time since the Noah Flood that mankind is facing a truly global threat. Since then never in the history of mankind there were anything similar to such numerous and impending threats to its existence as today. The whole world has entered the critical phase in its history and it's time to ask the fundamental question about the cause of it.

Anthropocentrism vs. Ecocentrism

The modern economic development has its foundation on the anthropocentric concept of human domination of nature which proclaims the man to be the main driving force and the owner of the planet. It all started since the so-called Renaissance when nascent "humanists" decided to put man in the center of the universe and proclaimed him as the Lord displacing the Creator. The key question here was how man and nature correlate. In line with the thrust of scientific development of his time, Francis Bacon advocated scientific methodology to manipulate nature for human benefit. The experimental method of the sixteenth century was reinforced by the mechanical philosophy of Rene Descartes, who saw that through method we could "render ourselves the masters and possessors of nature". Thus Nature was degraded and put at the service of Man. This concept created the basis for the technocratic thought and finally technocratic ideology which has the objective to dominate over nature and transform it in every imaginable way. The industrial revolution was in fact the media which helped to reform and finally change the traditional concept about Man's place and role in the world.

The traditional view of the world, and especially of man's status within it, was cast into doubt during the modern era as a result of at least two scientific revolutions: the theory of evolution in the nineteenth century, and the emergence of biotechnology in the twentieth. The evolutionary approach challenged the notion that species are eternal by reasoning that all biological species including man -evolve and change their forms over time.

Moral and ethical norms were overshadowed by economic and financial interest. In fact Man has got full authority to do anything while pursuing these interests without limits. At the same time this concept made it possible to ignore the remnants of traditional moral concepts and aspects in social and environmental practices. The universe and the being received a simplistic explanation, with the centric position being occupied by the evolution theory with its quantitative transformations.

Classical science, which is still very dominant, has developed into a dualist paradigm in which the scientific observer is separate and distinct from his or her observations. This has contributed to a conception of the world consisting of independent material objects, each having independent properties, with the behavior of the whole explainable by the behavior of its constituent parts. This science represents the source of absolute truths on which to base decisions and is often regarded as the most respectable way to know nature.

Nature is viewed as separate from humanity, machine-like and reducible to basic components, which can be known objectively and predicted. Nature is also perceived as an inanimate warehouse for all kinds of resources and semi-products which should be appropriated by Man according to his will. All that remains of man's essential nature is his ability to fashion his own form. Because of this, the nature of man ceases to be a constant and eternal truth becomes fluid. The freedom given to man does not manifest itself in a need to fulfill a certain role in the world, as is required of other creatures, but rather in the ability to construct himself according to his own choices.

It is largely accepted that humans are the center of all value. Accordingly, anthropocentrists would argue that since all value originates from humans, non-human entities and objects have value only in relation to humans. A further understanding of anthropocentrism defines value as the satisfaction of human preference. This type of aggressive anthropocentric approach is the real philosophical cause of the environmental crisis.

Three most significant and pressing factors contributing to the environmental crisis are the ever increasing human population, the energy crisis, and the abuse and pollution of the earth's natural systems. These and other factors contributing to the environmental crisis can be directly linked to scientific, anthropocentric views of the world. The perception that value is located in, and emanates from, humanity has resulted in understanding human life as an ultimate value, superior to all other beings. This has driven innovators in medicine and technology to ever improve our medical and material conditions, in an attempt to preserve human life, resulting in more people being born and living longer. In achieving this aim, they have indirectly contributed to increasing the human population. Perceptions of superiority, coupled with developing technologies have resulted in a social outlook that generally does not rest content with the basic necessities of life. Demands for more medical and social aid, more entertainment and more comfort translate into demands for improved standards of living. Increasing population numbers, together with the material demands of modern society, place ever increasing demands on energy supplies. While wanting a better life is not a bad thing, given the population explosion the current energy crisis is inevitable, which brings a whole host of environmental implications in tow.

We normally perceive science as a tool that can be used to provide the ecological insights needed to save the Earth and its natural values. Instead, billions of dollars are spent each year on applied research in biotechnology, chemistry, the military, industrial agriculture and the like. Every day we hear appeals to "massive mobilization of resources to develop the innovative technologies and support the deployment and use of all the best technologies and expertise".

The anthropocentric strategy designed to transform certain elements of the environment without taking into account the complexity of the environmental system as a whole produced changes in quite a number of factors which have already reduced the overall quality of the system and require additional efforts, energy and resources to neutralize those negative factors. Many present efforts to guard and maintain human progress, to meet human needs and to realize human ambitions are simply unsustainable -in both the rich and poor nations. As a matter of fact our achievements will always bring contradicting results: while pursuing the short-term goals we will always get a by-product which we did not expect. These consequences are rather contrary to what we tried to achieve and may easily cross out the positive results.

This human-centered research increases short-term profits and competitiveness and improves industrial output, defense capability, health, comforts and food production. At the same time we learn daily of the collapse of fisheries; the depletion of soils; the contamination of groundwater, freshwater and soils; the death of lakes; the destruction of Earth's ozone shield; the slow poisoning of entire landscapes by chemicals produced through research; the acceleration of deforestation; the extinction of thousands of species; global warming; the increasing misery of people in impoverished countries; the dramatic increase in ecological refugees fleeing ravaged lands.

With the full knowledge of influential governments and corporations, millions of species, natural ecosystems that have sustained life on Earth for several billion years are being weakened, degraded or eliminated. Novel chemicals such as hormones and pesticides are being deliberately added to the human food supply. Genetically modified foods are widely used in food production without public consent. In short, while the Earth and its inhabitants are in big trouble, our governments and captains of industry continue to finance the very kinds of research that contribute to deepening of the environmental crisis.

Leaving environmental problems in the hands of science would, therefore, effectively result in a narrow understanding of the problem, and hence a limited and short-sighted solution. In this light, science should not be viewed as the ultimate source of hope for the future, and clearly should not be given full responsibility for addressing the environmental crisis. That is why the concept of sustainable development produced by modern economic science may be accepted just as a technical transitional response but not as an overall solution.

The new model for science needs to be ecological -not economic and exploitive. At stake is not only the Earth, most of its more complex and beautiful life forms and ecosystems but also the quality of humanity's existence on this beautiful planet. The guiding principles that should set the priorities for today's science are these: the intended research should provide a more sympathetic understanding of fundamental values of nature; it should provide people with an understanding that we all, from bacteria to humans, are responsible for the stability of the planetary ecosphere.

What other threats do we have in store for us? Rationalistic and destructive approach to nature so noticeable in modern science and technological trends produces another effect: while we cripple nature and environment we also cripple our own nature what leads directly to man's enslavement. It is not an exaggeration. After enslaving nature man enslaves another man and finally himself. Indeed, the technocratic media first separates us from nature but at the same time ties us up to it even stronger creating new needs until it cultivates the mega-need to satisfy every need by means of a technical mediator.

While submerging into hostile, artificial environment humans are losing their natural qualities. With the decrease of physical labor and increase of intellectual labor humans get weaker, new diseases, birth defects, addictions and phobias appear. Our senses as well as our immune system deteriorate; stress, insomnia, depression, and different allergies overwhelm us. If we look at growing numbers of people in the developed countries who can no longer live without constant medical support it will be only possible to call such life "artificial". In other words we are converting ourselves in weird creatures whose physical abilities are no longer needed since there is always a robot around.

Humans cannot stop changing nature around them but they must stop changing it in an irresponsible way without considering environmental laws. That is why another commonly accepted option for dealing with the crisis at hand is that of environmental policy, legislation, and regulation, which can curb the effects of environmental pollution and improve the quality of the environment. Unfortunately individual governments largely have been reluctant to formulate such policies. It would be politically suicidal for the government to include such policy recommendations because they would eventually contradict the competing political programs dedicated to increasing GDP and the prosperity of the individual voter. Clearly then, placing the burden of responsibility on either science or government policy will do little to correct the situation as long as the values which motivate our actions remain unchanged.

The point is that we all contribute to the crisis this way or the other, and we are thus all responsible for what happens to the world around us. Accepting responsibility entails not only an acknowledgement that our individual actions contribute to the environmental crisis, but also that we are accountable for our actions.

If the risks of climate change are to be averted we must change and change radically -in our allocation and deployment of our resources, economic, human and institutional -in our mindsets and our behavior. The crucial challenge of our time is civilization redesign -the environmental crisis therefore has an anthropological dimension. This implies that we will need to re-evaluate our cultural and social models turning away from a culture based on consumption and possessions. The environmental imperative calls to redefine the very meaning of the individual and collective human behavior.

Innovation and Perspectives of BRICs' Cooperation

Comparison of Government Functions of BRICs in "National Innovation System"

—From the degree of homoplasy and embeddedness

Zhong Huibo, Zheng Bingwen[*]

Abstract: in this paper, the authors apply a lot of data to analyze and compare the features of government functions of BRICs in the national innovation system from the perspective of investment, policy and existing problem, and consider that, on one hand, the coordination of government policies of BRICs plays a key role in establishing national innovation system and evolving national innovation capacity. However, at the same time, the innovation policies of the BRIC are growingly converging and gradually getting close to the best international practice; on the other hand, the innovation system of BRICs lack of some embeddedness, and an efficient national innovation system can be established only the innovation policy is considered from the perspective of specific economic and social conditions and overall development.

Keyword: BRICs; national innovation system; technology innovation; knowledge economy; government function

Introduction

Since the 1990's, national innovation system (NIS) has draw more attentions of the whole world. It is generally considered that the so called national innovation system refers to the mechanism network among the private enterprises, public enterprises,

* Zhong Huibo, associate professor and postdoctor of the College of Humanities, Beijing Institute of Technology; Zheng Bingwen, director and researcher of the Institute of Latin American Studies, CASS.

universities and governmental institutions that produce mutual reaction on the application and development of science and technology in the territory of one country; the reaction of these institutions under the mechanism network aims to promote the occurrence, diffusion and sustaining of technology innovation; the reaction method can be technical, commercial, legal, social and financial①. In the national innovation system of a country, due to the high uncertainty, high risk, high complementation and quasi-public goods, etc. of the innovation and its process②, it is far from automatically adjusting the social resource allocation used for innovation to the best level only depending on market mechanism③, the leading role of the government must be given play to solve "market failure"④. For BRICs, which are all developing countries, it is the key strategic measure to consciously realize the forging ahead strategy through the forced and seductive system led by the government and technology evolution. Therefore, government intervention becomes the primary driving force for the evolution of national innovation system.

The evolution of national innovation system is affected by the technology and economic development scale and level, industrial structure feature, technical path dependence, etc. of a country, with distinct regional embeddedness. The government function in the national innovation system is decided by its policy system, economic system and social economic development stage, and the roles of different governments in the innovation system are different.

In this paper, the authors try to compare and analyze the government functions of BRICs in the national innovation system from three aspects: first, to compare the construction situation of national innovation system directly invested by the governments of the four countries; second, to compare the policies and measures taken by the governments of the four countries in the construction of national innovation system; third, to compare the problem and improvement direction of the relationships between the governments of the four countries and their national innovation system.

---

① Zheng Bingwen: *Knowledge Economy and National Innovation System*, Economy & Management Press, 1998.

② Zhong Huibo, Lian Jianhui: "Contemporary Venturing Enterprise: Comprehensive Pricing Mechanism of Innovation Knowledge," *Study in Science of Science*, Vol.6, 2005.

③ Of course, the importance function of government is not limited by resource allocation optimization, and is more reflected in the core of promoting the learning and creating of NIS, that is, the main function of government is reflected in resource (especially knowledge) creation instead of only resource allocation. See Jia Genliang: "Essence of Innovation System and East Asia Mode," *Nankai Journal*, Vo1.5, 2001.

④ Zheng Bingwen: *Knowledge Economy and National Innovation System*, Economy & Management Press, 1998.

Comparison of national innovation system investment mechanism of BRICs' governments

The direct investment of the government can provide capital reserve and talent and public hardware supporting condition to the technology innovation, guide the direction of industrial technology innovation, and mobilize the growth of enterprise technology innovation input. It can be said that the investment mechanism is the most direct approach for the government to affect the national innovation system. Generally the government investment includes the R&D fund for technology innovation, especially the support on the basic scientific research and source innovation, invested public hardware condition required for establishing innovation, and education investment for cultivating innovation talent, etc. Owing to different development histories and social and economic foundations, the direct investment of the governments of BRICs in national innovation system have their own characteristics.

From the perspective of government expenditure in R&D fund, the comparison of 2002 and 2007 (see table 1) shows that if the total amount of government expenditure in R&D fund is calculated according to purchasing power of USD, Chinese government expenditure in R&D fund will be the highest, reaching 20.14 billion USD in 2007. Followed by India, reaching 18.75 billion USD in the same year. There is a large difference between Russia, Brazil and China, India, respectively 6.89 billion USD and 3.68 billion USD; on the growth rate of government expenditure in R&D fund, the annual growth rate from 2002 to 2007 was the highest in India, reaching 18.5%, followed by China, reaching 15.6%, the annual growth rate in Russia was 15.2%, close to China, and the annual growth rate in Brazil was the lowest, only 9.5%; on the proportion of government R&D fund in the total expenditure, China presented an obviously falling tendency, 28.7% in 2002, 19.2% in 2007. The situation in Russia is contrary, presenting a rising tendency, 24.5% in 2002, 29.3% in 2007. The figure in Brazil and India basically kept unchanged, respectively 21% and 75%. The change of these data indicates that: first, both Chinese government and Indian government are increasing the input in R&D, especially the Indian government, although its total amount of expenditure in R&D fund is less than China, its annual average growth rate is 3 percentage points higher than China, the annual average GDP growth and total financial revenue of Indian were less than China, however, the difference between Indian and China in the total amount of government expenditure in R&D fund was less than 1.4 billion USD, which indicates that the Indian government increases input in R&D fund. Brazil and Russia are increasing input in R&D fund, however, the degree is far less than India and China; second, the R&D fund expenditure structure in China has become rational, the rapid growth of enterprise R&D expenditure makes Chinese government increase the R&D expenditure with the annual average growth rate of 15.6%, however, the proportion of government R&D expenditure in the total expenditure was reduced by nearly 10 percentage points in the 5 years; third, except for the government in India, the efforts of other innovation bodies in innovation are not effectively activated, and the R&D fund mainly depends on the unilateral expenditure of the government; fourth, in Brazil, in despite of government, or enterprise, college, etc., the innovation efforts of their innovation bodies are weak in BRIC, which is reflected in the low growth rate of government expenditure in R&D fund and unchanged R&D expenditure structure; fifth, the increase of government expenditure in R&D fund in Russia fails to mobilize the innovation activeness of enterprise, college, etc., which makes the proportion of government expenditure in R&D fund in total proportion increase by nearly 5 percentage points from 2002 to 2005.

Table 1 Comparison of government expenditure in R&D fund in BRIC from 2002 to 2007

Country	Total amount of R&D expenditure (unit: 100 million USD)		Proportion of government expenditure in R&D (%)		Total amount of government R&D expenditure (unit: 100 million USD)		Proportion of R&D expenditure in GDP (%)	
	2002	2007	2002	2007	2002	2007	2002	2007
Brazil	121	173	20.6	21.3	24.9	36.8	0.9	1.0
China	394	1049	28.7	19.2	113.1	201.4	1.1	1.5
India	129	248	75.6	75.3	97.5	187.5	0.7	0.8
Russia	160	235	24.5	29.3	39.2	68.9	1.2	1.1

Data source: GERD, Researchers' data and related indicators: UNESCO Institute for Statistics (UIS) estimations, May 2009.

From the perspective of innovation talent training, the comparison of 2002 and 2007 (see table 2) shows that: on the total number of researchers, the advantage of China is extremely obvious, reaching 1.42 million in 2007, accounting for 1/5 of the total number of researchers in the world, 3 times more than that in Russia, 9 times more than that in India and 12 times more than that in Brazil. Brazil has the fewest researchers, only 118,300 in 2007, accounting for 1.7% of the total number of researchers in the world; on the increase of researcher, China has the highest annual average growth from 2002 to 2007, reaching 15.12%, followed by Brazil, 12.95%, the annual growth rate of India is 8.8%, while the annual growth of Russia is -1%; on the proportion in total number of researchers in the world, the proportion of China was increased from 14% in 2002 to 20.1% in 2007, with the increase of 6.1%, the proportion of Brazil had little increase, India basically remained the same, while the proportion of Russia was reduced from 8.5% in 2002 to 6.6% in 2007, with the decrease of nearly 2 percentage points; on the number of researchers per 1 million of population, Russia had the highest number, 3291.8 in 2007, followed by China, with the largest population base, 1071.3 in 2007, 7.9 times more than India, 1.7 times more than Brazil; on the per capital scientific research fund, if it is calculated according to the purchasing power of USD, India and Brazil had the highest, 150 thousand USD in 2007, 2 times more than China, 3 times more than Russia; on per capital scientific fund increase, from 2002 to 2007, the researcher fund in Brazil presented a negative growth status of annual average 2.6%, the researcher fund in Russia, China and India were respectively increased at the speed of 10.8%, 10.3% and 8.8%. To sum up, we can believe that, first, Chinese government has prominent achievements in training innovation talent, and the indicators as number of researcher, growth rate and number of researcher per 1 million of population are good; second, Indian government and Brazil government achieve certain progress in innovation talent training, however, the result is not prominent; third, Russia government is backward in training innovation talent, the total number of researcher, proportion in the number of researchers in the world, number of researcher per 1 million of population, etc. in 2007 were lower than that in 2002.

Table 2 Comparison of number of researchers and expenditure in BRIC from in 2002 and 2007

Country	Total number of researchers (unit: 10 thousand)		Proportion in total number of researchers in the world (%)		Number of researchers per 1 million of population		Expenditure in every R&D personnel (unit: 10 thousand USD)	
	2002	2007	2002	2007	2002	2007	2002	2007
Brazil	7.18	11.83	1.2	1.7	400.7	624.8	16.85	14.62
China	81.05	142.34	14	20.1	629.1	1071.3	4.87	7.37
India	11.59	15.48	2.3	2.2	110.8	136.5	11.13	16.02
Russia	49.19	46.91	8.5	6.6	3365.8	3291.8	3.25	5.01

Data source: UNESCO, Human Development Report 2009.

From the perspective of government's support on education development (see table 3): on the basic education, Chinese government inputs a lot and has promoted 9-year compulsory education policy since 1986. As the most populous country, the adult literacy rate in China has reached 90.9%, only little lower than Russia in BRICs, however, 30% higher than India, whose adult literacy rate is only 61%; on higher education, the enrollment rate of higher education in Russia has prominent advantages, reaching 68.2% in 2004, higher than the sum of China, India and Brazil. The continuous supply of high-quality research talent is also the main reason why the number of researchers per 1 million of population in Russia is far higher than the other three countries. Since the Mid 1990's, Chinese government has begun to increase the input in higher education, and the enrollment rate of higher education in China has reached 19.1% since 2004, in which the engineering students account for 40%. India has begun to set technology and management university since 1950's, which provides a lot of talents for the development of its software industry and communication technology industry. Although India government is committed to developing higher education, in 2004, there was still a gap between India and China in the enrollment rate of higher education, only 11.8%. Obviously, the relatively lower enrollment rate of higher education will become a barrier for the continuous and rapid development of knowledge intensive service industry in India. Although the development of higher education in Brazil is slow, the enrollment rate of higher education is still little higher than China and India; on the educational hardware infrastructure and education quality, according to the survey data of World Bank in 2006, China does the best in school Internet facility, with the score of 4. On science and mathematics education quality, India does the best, with the score of 5.7, 2 times more than Brazil. On personnel training intensity, Russia has the lowest score, only 2.9, and the score of the other three countries is about 4. On the education quality of Business College, the score of India is 6, 2 points higher than Brazil that ranks the second, which may be related to the background that English is used as the official language of India. The phenomenon worth noting is that the proportion of financial education expenditure in GDP in 2005 in China was 2.2%, 1% lower than India, whose figure is 3.2%, the figure of Russia and Brazil were respectively 3.8% and 4%. Considering that lack of government's education investment will affect the human resource and international competition strength of a country, China has increased the investment in education field in the past few years. According to the statistics, the financial education expenditure in China in 2009 has accounted for 3.59% of GDP, 0.26 percentage points more than 3.33% in 2008①.

Table 3 Comparison of relevant data of governmental support on education development in BRICs

Indicator	Brazil	Russia	India	China
Literacy rate (%, population above 15, 2006)	88.6	99.4	61.00	90.9
Average educated age (2000)	4.88	10.03	5.06	6.35
Secondary education enrollment rate (%, 2004)	102.00	92.90	53.50	72.50
Higher education enrollment rate (%, 2004)	22.30	68.20	11.80	19.10
School Internet access situation (1-7, 2006)	3.60	3.80	3.80	4.00

① The Ministry of Education, National Bureau of Statistics, the Ministry of Finance: Announcement on Statistics of Execution Situation of National Education Funds in 2009, China Education Daily, December 7, 2010.

Continue Table 3

Indicator	Brazil	Russia	India	China
Proportion of financial education expenditure in GDP (%, 2005)	4.0	3.8	3.2	2.2
Science and mathematics education quality (1-7, 2006)	2.90	4.50	5.70	4.10
Personnel training intensity (1-7, 2006)	4.20	2.90	4.80	3.40
Business college quality (1-7, 2006)	4.10	3.60	6.00	3.40
Talent loss (1-7, 2006)	3.90	3.50	3.70	3.80

Data source: WB website: www.worldbank.org, relevant indicator score is summarized in the form of seven-mark system according to "best", "worst".

From the perspective of governmental support on developing public hardware facility, whereas the knowledge communication, diffusion and use are the core functions of NIS, information and communication infrastructure is one of the main aspects of government investment in NIS hardware facility construction. Compared to the other three countries (see table 4), the information and communication infrastructure construction in China is the most efficient and modern. Compared to India with the same population scale, except for few indicators as proportion of information and communication expenditure in GDP and per capital Internet service expenditure, etc., the rest indicators of India are lower than 1/3 of China. The overall situation of Russia is better than Brazil, however, Russia had the lowest proportion of information and communication expenditure in GDP in 2005 in the four countries, less than 1/2 of Brazil that ranks the first. It is worth mentioning that another significant measure for supporting NIS hardware infrastructure construction is that the governments of BRICs vigorously promote the development of technology incubation center and hi-tech park. China established Beijing hi-tech industrial trial area in 1988, and provides this area with 18 preferential policies as tax reduction and exemption, etc. By 1999, China has established 54 hi-tech industrial parks[①]. Indian government invested 6 billion rupee in establishing the first software technology park in Bangalore in 1991, the export of this technology park in 2008 has reached 15 billion USD, and the software export accounts for 20% of global market share[②]. The first technology park in Russia was founded in Tomsk in 1990, by the end of 2005[③], there have been nearly a hundred of technology parks in Russia. Most technology parks are established

① Lv Ping., 2010, "The Role of The State In National System of Innovation-China Case Study ," IDRC Seminer: Comparative Study of the National Innovation Systems of BRIC Countries, Rio de Janeiro, Brazil.

② Zhou Chuxing, etc.: "Enlightenment and Recommendation of Indian Software Industry Survey," *Bulletin of Foreign Economic and Trade Cooperation Bureau of Jiaxing*, Vol.9, 2009.

③ Gong Huiping: "New Development of National Innovation System in Russia," *The World Sci/ Tech Economic Outlook*, Vol.12, 2006.

nearby colleges in Brazil, and the technology park established by St. Paul University has become the largest "silicon valley" park in Latin America①.

Table 4 Comparison of information and communication infrastructure of BRIC

Indicator	Brazil	Russia	India	China
Quantity of telephone owned per 1,000 persons (2004)	587.10	773.10	84.50	499.40
Quantity of telephone line owned per 1,000 persons (2004)	230.40	255.80	40.70	241.10
Quantity of mobile phone owned per 1,000 persons (2004)	356.70	517.30	43.80	258.30
Quantity of computer owned per 1,000 persons (2004)	105.20	132.20	12.10	40.90
Proportion of household TV ownership (%, 2004)	90.00	98.00	37.00	91.00
Quantity of newspaper owned per 1,000 persons (2000)	46.00	—	60.00	59.00
Network bandwidth (byte/person, 2004)	149.30	99.90	11.40	57.40
Quantity of Internet used per 1,000 persons (2004)	119.60	111.20	32.40	72.50
Per capital Internet service expenditure (USD/month, 2003)	28.00	10.00	8.70	10.10
Proportion of information and communication expenditure in GDP (%, 2005)	7.82	3.58	5.91	5.28

Data source: WB website, www.worldbank.org.

Comparison of BRICs' Governments Policies and Measures on NIS

Similarities of BRICs' governments policies and measures on NIS

Incentive policy is adopted to promote innovation effort of main body

BRICs' governments all adopt a series of policies and measures for encouraging the enterprises and research institutes to conduct innovation activities, including providing the technology-oriented enterprises with tax preference, interest subsidy and financing support, providing the research project closely related to the future of the country with capital subsidy, providing the commercialization of innovation result with financial and tax support, supporting innovation-oriented product through government purchase, etc. For example, Indian government established technology development commission in 1996 to be responsible for raising capitals, supporting commercialization of R&D project, and developing preferential policies as tax reduction and exemption, customs tariff exemption, financial support and subsidy, government reward, etc. that support the technology activities of enterprises; Russia established "foundation for promoting

① Yu Zhaoxing, Chu Han: "Discussion on the Cause for Scientific and Technological Progress in Brazil," *Latin American Studies*, Vol. 3, 2006.

development of technology small enterprises" in 1994 as the small enterprise technology supporting institution, which subsidizes the technology development of small enterprises through extra-budgetary funds; Brazil promulgated Law on Technology Progress in 1984 to regulate that 50% of the income tax can be reduced and exempted if 5% of the enterprise output is used for technology investment. Since 1990, Brazil government has issued a series of laws on encouraging the enterprise technology innovation①; Chinese government promulgated Law on Promoting the Transformation of Scientific and Technological Achievements and Regulation on National Awards for Science and Technology respectively in 1996 and 1999 to encourage the innovation activities of main body. In 2007, 13 ministries and commissions jointly issued Several Policies on Supporting Innovation of Medium and Small Enterprises, which especially proposes relevant financial and tax supporting policies for medium and small enterprises.

Committed to improving the innovation environment

First, the governments of the four countries are committed in establishing and maintaining market environment, and protecting innovation income. To encourage and protect knowledge innovation, Brazil introduced patent law in 1997, and issued new Industrial Property Code, and promulgated Law on Application Research and Knowledge Transfer in 1998. In 2000, Brazil established "new millennium research institute plan" and "technology center: innovation and promotion" plan, which aims to follow up the international cutting-edge technology, promote international exchange and cooperation, promote commercialization of technology achievements, cultivate technology talent, create good technology innovation environment; to adapt to the change of market environment, improve the market environment that supports innovation, since 1990's, India has revised Patent Law for many times, and promulgated Copyright Law, Trademark Law, Appearance Design Law, etc.; since Mid and later 1990, Russia has focused on constantly modifying relevant intellectual property right laws, and strengthened the legal protection of knowledge property transfer. In 1995, Russia proposed copyright law amendment, modified State Secret Law in 1997, proposed patent law modification in 1998, proposed the amendment draft of patent law, trademark law, computer software and database protection law, integrated circuit topological graph protection law and copyright law in 2000, implemented co-owned technology transfer law in 2009; while China promulgated Trademark Law, the first law related to the protection of intellectual property right in 1982, and issued Patent Law (1984), Technical Contract Law (1987), Copyright Law (1999), Regulations on Computer Software Protection (1991), Technology Progress Law (1993), Law on Promoting the Transformation of Scientific and

① Yu Zhaoxing, Chu Han: "Discussion on the Cause for Scientific and Technological Progress in Brazil," *Latin American Studies*, Vol. 3, 2006.

Technological Achievements (1996), etc.

Second, the governments of the four countries are committed to encouraging the organic combination of production, learning and research, promoting the innovation environment construction for innovation result commercialization. The current innovation system reform of Russia is characterized in establishing the intensive and continuous relationship of industry and research institution, with the reform direction of encouraging the industry and technology to establish better cooperation, support the mobility of researchers, and partnership of public and private departments①; since 1990, Indian government has attached importance to strengthening the cooperation of production, learning and research. In 1992, the government subsidized India University of Technology to establish "innovation and technology transfer foundation" to establish relationship between institutions of higher learning and enterprises. The Ministry of Science and Technology of India directly establishes the state-owned enterprise "India National Research Development Corporation (NRDC)" to transfer the technology achievements of national research development laboratory to the industrial department. 2003 technology policy of Indian government proposes to establish autonomous technology transfer organization as the auxiliary organization of universities and national laboratories to promote the transfer from knowledge to industry, and encourage the scientists and technical experts to transfer the knowledge produced to the industry, and become the party that receives economic return; in 2004, Brazil government promulgated Technology Innovation Law to encourage the organic combination of industry, learning and research, and establish a harmonious strategic partnership to make the scientific research institutions and institutions of higher learning participate in the whole course of innovation, so as to cultivate the independent innovation capacity of enterprises, strengthen development originality, improve competitiveness, change the passive phase that the technology achievements commercialization is lagged, and promote the sustainable socio-economic development; in 1996, Chinese government promulgated Law on Promoting the Transformation of Scientific and Technological Achievements, which becomes the representative law to promote the cooperation of innovation bodies, and makes clear regulations on the organization of result commercialization and responsibilities and duties of relevant parties. China also vigorously develops technology enterprise incubator, technology consulting institution and productivity promotion center and other technical service agency that promotes commercialization of technology achievements, and make them become the important channels to transfer, spread technology achievements and effectively allocate technology resources.

---

① Liu Xielin, Duan Xiaohua: "National Innovation System in Transformation in Russia," *Study in Science of Science*, Vol. 3, 2003.

Third, governments of the four countries actively explore the development of technology finance, and provides the innovation system with financial supporting subsystem. In 1986, Indian government decided to appropriate 0.1 billion rupee every year to establish the first venture capital fund in India. According to the statistics, in 2006, Indian venture capital invested in 94 projects, with the involved amount of 50.5 billion rupee, accounting for 7.06% of the market share of private equity in India[①]. Brazil has proposed the idea of establishing venture capital fund early in 1970's, however, due to the influence of repeated fluctuation of economic output in the same period, Brazil formally established venture capital fund in 1986, which develops rapidly under the support of government, and the scale of venture capital in Brazil has reached 0.65 billion USD by 2005[②]. Restricted by the limitation of financial budget and insufficient driving force for investing in high risk project, Russia established the first venture capital fund in 2000. In August 2006, Russian government decided to appropriate 15 billion ruble (about 0.5 billion USD) to formally establish the national venture capital fund, with the main investment field of just the hi-tech project and medium and small enterprise innovation that the non-governmental venture capital funds are not willing to involve[③]. It is worth mentioning that although Russian government has begun to attach great importance to the construction of venture financing platform since 2000, and Russia has had more than 40 venture funds investing in innovation project by 2009, the direct investment of venture fund in the hi-tech project is less than 1% of its total investment amount in Russia[④]. Chinese government has issued a series policies on developing technology financial service, such as Decision of the Central Committee of the Communist Party of China on Technology System Reform in 1985, which proposes to support the development of hi-tech industry in the form of venture capital for the first time, Several Opinions on Establishing Chinese Venture Capital Mechanism (1999), Several Regulations on Foreign Investment in Venturing Investment Enterprise (2001), Several Opinions on Promoting Reform and Opening up and Stable Development of Capital Market (2004), Interim Measures for Venturing Investment Management (2005) and other technology finance

① Sunil Mani., 2010 "Financing of Industrial Innovations in India, How Effective are Tax Incentives For R&D?" IDRC Seminer: Comparative Study of the National Innovation Systems of BRIC Countries, Rio de Janeiro, Brazil.

② Luiz Martins de Melo and Márcia Siqueira Rapini., 2010, "Innovation, Finance and Funding The National System of Innovation: The Brazilian Case," IDRC Seminer: Comparative Study of the National Innovation Systems of BRIC Countries, Rio de Janeiro, Brazil.

③ Gong Huiping: "New Development of National Innovation System in Russia," *The World Sci/ Tech Economic Outlook*, Vol.12, 2006.

④ Preliminary., 2010, "Innovation, Finance and Funding The National System of Innovation," IDRC Seminer: Comparative Study of the National Innovation Systems of BRIC Countries, Rio de Janeiro, Brazil.

policies that support venture capital investment in hi-tech industry. Corresponding to the great support of the government, Chinese venture capital industry develops rapidly, the annual average growth of asset scale is 48% from 2006 to 2009. By September 2010, there have been 571 registered venturing investment enterprises in China, with the asset scale of RMB 107.4 billion[①].

The technology development direction is guided on the level of national strategy

Brazil promoted "new millennium research institute plan" and "technology center: innovation and promotion" plan in 2000 to follow up the international cutting-edge technology, promote international exchange and cooperation, and create good technology innovation environment. In 2002, the Ministry of Science and Technology of Brazil issued technology innovation green book, held national technology innovation conference to confirm the technology development guideline and strategic planning in 10 years. Technology Innovation White Book issued in 2002 explicitly proposed to promote the technology innovation in key fields as biological technology, aerospace, health, etc., which lays a foundation for Brazil to promulgate technology innovation policy. In 2005, the third national technology conference was held to promulgate 10-year strategic plan for technology innovation and overall planning for national technology innovation, so as to reinforce and expand national technology innovation system, and make technology innovation promote harmonious social development. In 2007, Brazil government issued "2007-2010 technology and innovation action plan", proposed to reinforce and expand national technology innovation system, promote the innovation in the strategic fields as energy, biology, aerospace, national defence, public security, etc. Through developing technology development plan, guiding innovation direction and integrating technology resources, Brazil has preliminary formed the technology innovation policy system[②].

Russian government attaches great importance to guiding and planning technology innovation direction, approved 2010 Basic Development Direction of Innovation System Policy of Russian Federation in 2005, which conducts medium term planning of the construction of NIS. In 2008, Russian government issued "economic and social development strategy before 2020", which explicitly proposes to give priority to developing technology, and realize national strategy to transform serious dependence on natural resource export to innovation driven type of social and economic development form. In 2009, the Ministry of Science and Science and academy of sciences of Russia promoted three editions of "long-term technology development prediction" report, to predict the

① Department of Finance of NDRC, Venture Capital Investment Committee of the Investment Association of China: Report on Development of Chinese Venture Capital Investment Industry, Financial Press, 2010.

② Lu Lifeng, Li Zhaoyou: "Evolution and Enlightenment of Technology Innovation Policy in Brazil," *Technology and Innovation Management,* Vol.3, 2010.

technology development before 2030. In addition, Russian government also focuses on give play to the technology strength, actively lead the international cooperation in significant technology tackling project, such as advocating the establishment of international disaster early warning aerospace and aviation system, appealing to develop "traffic rules" in space, participating in the new generation of laser research project in Europe, etc.

Indian government inputs a lot of labors and materials in predicting the national technology development direction. In 2003, Indian government established national technology information prediction assessment commission composed of 20 governmental departments, published 2020 India—New Millennium Vision to comprehensively assess the strengths and weaknesses of India in technology field, evaluate and define the technology capacity and technology innovation direction for Indian to depend on so as to become one of the four major economic entities in the world, support the technology field included in the scope, with profound influence on the overall technology innovation direction.

Chinese government always keeps developing the strategic planning on promoting national technology development. In 1980's, the Ministry of Science and Technology has organized and implemented Technology Innovation Program, spark program, torch program, national key technology tackling project, hi-tech research development plan (863 program), etc. In 1990's, the Ministry of Science and Technology and other governmental departments have promoted the development strategy of developing the country through science and education, the tenth five-year program "talent, patent, technical standard", knowledge innovation plan, etc. the representative event in the 21st century is that the improvement of independent innovation was explicitly proposed as national strategy and National Medium and Long-term Science and Technology Development Planning Outline (2006-2020) was issued at the national technology conference in 2006, which explicitly defines the key field and prior theme, significant project, cutting-edge technology, etc. of medium and long-term national science and technology development.

In general, the governments of BRICs construct the policy system of NIS from incentive mechanism, environment mechanism and guiding mechanism, therefore, the NIS policy structures of the four countries are similar. However, in despite of the developing countries, the four countries have large difference in economic development stage, economic structure, resource endowment, political system, technology foundation, marketization degree, historical and cultural background, etc. therefore, the four countries focus on different policy objective, mode, approach and direction, and there may be large difference in the implementation effect of the same policy in different countries.

Differences in BRICs' government policies and measures on NIS

Different policy focuses

An important characteristic of NIS of Brazil is the unbalanced socio-economic structure, which is reflected in the income distribution structure①. According to the statistics, from 2003 to 2006, the annual Gini coefficient of Brazil was more than 0.55②, at the edge of wide gap in income. The highly intensive income distribution structure affects the mode of demand and consumption, and affects the production structure and demand on innovation③. Therefore, relevant policies that change the socio-economic structure become the important components of NIS policy measure of Brazil.

The prominent characteristics of NIS of India are the absolute leading position of the government in the construction of NIS. The government bears most R&D expenditure, for example, the fund provided by Indian government in 2007 accounted for 75.3% of R&D expenditure of this country. At the same time, most of the R&D activities are centralized in the research institution set by the government. For example, in 2005, in 230,000 researchers, 159,000 researchers (69%) were from the government research institutions④. therefore, the recent Indian innovation policies focus on changing the unilateral leading position of the government, encouraging enterprises and other main bodies to participate in the innovation activities, promote the exchange and interaction of production, learning and research⑤.

Russia is characterized in inheriting the technology foundation and technology management system of former Soviet Union, therefore, the policy measure of NIS of Russian government focuses on changing the planned economic form in NIS, realizing the flexible system structure transformation of national R&D system from centralized control structure to free market economic environment.

The focus of Chinese NIS policy is closely related to the national strategic with the center of economic construction, with the resource and environmental restriction caused by the continuous economic growth since the reform and opening up, China is in the key period for transforming economic growth method, and the current Chinese NIS policy mainly focuses on improving the enterprise innovation capacity, especially the independent innovation capacity, depending on technology to realize revival of

① Rodrigue, O., 2007. Furtado e a Renovação da Agenda do Desenvolvimento. In Celso Furtado e o Século XXI. Sabóia, J.; Carvalho, F. (org.). Barueri, SP: Manole; Rio de Janeiro: Instituto de Economia da Universidade Federal do Rio de Janeiro.

② IBGE (2008). Estatística do Cadastro Central de Empresas 2006. Fundação Instituto Brasileiro de Geografia e Estatística (IBGE). Rio de Janeiro.

③ Cassiolato, J.; Lastres, H., 2008, "Discussing Innovation and Development: Converging Points Between the Latin American School and the Innovation Systems perspective?" GLOBELICS Working Paper Series No. 08-02. The Global Network for Economics of Learning, Innovation, and Competence Building System.

④ Zhang Junfang: "Historical Evolution of National Innovation System in India," *China Youth Science and Technology*, Vol.7, 2007.

⑤ V.V.Krishna., 2010, "Role of The State In The Evolution of The National Innovation System In India," IDRC Seminer: Comparative Study of the National Innovation Systems of BRIC Countries, Rio de Janeiro, Brazil.

nationhood and constructing innovation country.

Different technology foundations and policy objectives

BRICs have different technology foundations and policy objectives: Russia starts from "ownership", so as to realize the wealth effect of technology①, China starts from "key breakthrough", so as to realize innovation national strategy, India starts from "self-dependence", so as to improve its global competitiveness, and Brazil starts from "technology introduction", so as to realize independent innovation.

Russia inherits the advanced science and technology foundation of former Soviet Union, and this foundation is still leading in many technology fields in the world. At the same time, Russia is still one of the countries with the largest proportion of researchers in 1 million people. However, Russia fails to effectively transform its world-level science capacity into social wealth. In 2007, the hi-tech product export of Russia only accounted for 0.3% of the total global export, the output value of innovation product only accounted for 5.5% of GDP of Russian②. Therefore, to effectively transform the science capacity into wealth has always been the objective of NIS reform of Russia since 1990's.

When the technology resource is relatively rare, China takes planned technology system to input centralized and limited technology resource in the scientific research project with significant meaning to long-term economic and social development, which plays an important role in the prominent breakthrough of Chinese technology force. In 1998, China proposed the national policy to realize revival of nationhood through technology, in 2005, China proposed the significant strategy to construct innovation country, and further proposed the national strategy of independent innovation in 2006.

Indian government is always focusing on the industrial development and industrial technology foundation, focusing on basic research and development, and promoting the technology policy of independent government-led R&D, which achieves certain effect and forms a complete technology system. Since the economic system reform in 1991, without giving up the independent technology policy, India has attached more importance to the global technology cooperation and improving the global competitiveness of economy and enterprise with the economy being merged in the global economic system. In 2003, 20 governmental departments of India jointly issued 2020 India-New Millennium Vision, which evaluates and defines the technology capacity and technology innovation direction

---

① Albergin: *Prediction on Development Prospect of Russia—the Best Proposal in 2015*, Social Sciences Academic Press, 2001.

② Tatiana Kuznetsova., 2010, "The Role of The State In National System of Innovation In Russia," IDRC Seminer: Comparative Study of the National Innovation Systems of BRIC Countries, Rio de Janeiro, Brazil.

that India shall depend on for becoming one of the four major economic entities in the world, and becomes the policy objective of NIS of India.

Brazil once realized industrialization and created "Brazil Miracle" through introducing foreign capital and technology. However, in this process, the technology capacities of local enterprises were still backward and lacked of international competitiveness. In 1990' s, Brazil government began to attach importance to independent innovation, and issued a series of technology innovation policies, with the short-term policy objective of reducing the dependence on external technology, medium and long-term objective of realizing technology breakthrough in key field, and improving the international competitiveness of Brazil[①].

Different policy routes

From the focus in the support of R&D, Brazil, India and Russia focus on basic research, while China focuses on application research. According to the statistics, 75%-80% of R&D expenditure of Brazil government are used in basic research[②], 18% of R&D expenditure of Indian government are used in basic research[③], 13.1% of R&D expenditure of Russian government are used in basic research[④], while the proportion of basic research expenditure in the total R&D expenditure in China is only 5.2%[⑤]. From the policy transmission mechanism, Brazil, India and Russia focus on promoting the construction of NIS through providing R&D project and hi-tech enterprises with capital subsidy and financial tax incentive, and focuses on direct innovation supply; China also attaches importance to direct subsidy and financial tax incentive to promote the innovation effort of main body, however, at the same time, China is committed to multi-channel to increase innovation supply, including vigorous development of basic education and higher education to improve quality of the national and the ability to absorb innovation knowledge, and increase the quantity of researchers and improve R&D capacity, actively merge into the globalization process and share the technology overflow of international trade and international investment.

---

① Priscila Koeller and José Luis Gordon., 2010, " The Role of The State In National System of Innovation In Brazil," IDRC Seminer: Comparative Study of the National Innovation Systems of BRIC Countries, Rio de Janeiro, Brazil.

② Li Mingde: "Development of Science and Technology System and R&D System of Brazil," *Latin American Studies*, Vol.3, 2004.

③ Zhang Ruishan: "Enlightenment of Scientific Research Institution Layout of India on China," *South Asian Studies Quarterly*, Vol.3, 2006.

④ Center for S&T Statistic Analysis of the Ministry of Science and Technology: "International Comparison of Characteristics of Chinese R&D Expenditure," *S&T Statistic Report*, Vol.22, 2008.

⑤ Center for S&T Statistic Analysis of the Ministry of Science and Technology: "International Comparison of Characteristics of Chinese R&D Expenditure," *S&T Statistic Report, Vol.22, 2008.*

Problems of the governments of BRICs and NIS

Common problems in BRICs

Over-focus on the R&D and technical factor of innovation

It is true that it is impossible for the innovation system without science and technology system or technology accumulation to create the satisfactory innovation capacity. However, the innovation capacity does not only lie in the improvement of technical level, but also in the transfer, diffusion and application of new technology in production department, and the latter is the key point for an economic entity to obtain continuous high-speed economic growth and international competitiveness. The governments of BRICs over-emphasize on the R&D and technology factor of innovation, neglect the social, system and market factor of commercialization of new achievements, which obstructs the comprehensive coordination and evolution of NIS.

For example, since 1990's, the NIS policy of Brazil has had three purposes: to inspire the enterprises and research institutions to conduct innovation activities, to sponsor basic research and to promote the cooperation of enterprises and research institutions. these innovation policies that focus on R&D have the following problems: first, the policy that focuses on technology innovation and gives priority to supporting R&D neglects other importance decisive factors of innovation activity, especially the unbalanced economic and social development in Brazil, while the latter is just the source for the contradictoriness and fragility of NIS of Brazil[①]; second, the focus on the establishment of direct partnership between enterprises and research institutions makes it more difficult for the agency service institution and other entities to participate in the innovation process[②]; third, the technology-led innovation policy deems innovation as a simple linear process, while technology R&D is the source of this process, "technology R&D—manufacturing—marketing—user"[③]. This innovation system that over-focuses on the technology supply neglects the influence of consumers, enterprises and other interest related parties on the technology development, and also the market demand, which greatly reduces the commercialization rate of innovation.

For example, until 1990's, the science and technology policy in India has focused

① Song Xia: "Deep Cause for Influencing the Competitiveness of Brazil: Contradictoriness and Fragility of National Innovation System," *Latin American Studies*, Vol.6, 2008.

② Priscila Koeller and José Luis Gordon., 2010," The Role of The State In National System of Innovation In Brazil," IDRC Seminer: Comparative Study of the National Innovation Systems of BRIC Countries, Rio de Janeiro, Brazil.

③ Paul Trott: *Innovation Management and New Product Development,* China Renmin University Press, 2005.

on technology supply, as a result, a huge science and technology system is established, including a series of "grand science" department and hi-tech accumulation in a number of fields, however, these technology capacities are not effectively utilized. As what Rosenberg said, India represents a coexistence of low salary and developed science and technology infrastructure…there are still a lot of works to do in the relationship between various public departments and private institutions on the way of innovation[①]. After the Mid 1990's, Indian government began to gradually concern the demander of innovation, however, the effect was not satisfactory. A main problem in current innovation system of India is the lack of innovative ecological system of venture capital and agency mechanism to promote the transfer and commercialization of public research achievement.

Compared to Brazil and India, the tendency of Russian government in unilaterally leading the innovation supply is more obvious, 61.9% of the R&D fund are provided by the government, 73% of the research institutions are attached to the government, 78% of the researchers work in the research institution of the government, and 86% of the R&D fixed assets belong to public assets[②]. The result of the combination of government-led technology innovation-oriented innovation policy that lacks of effective supervision mechanism and the economic growth form promoted by natural resource export is the coexistence of low resource service efficiency of R&D department and insufficient innovation demand of commercial department, which is also the key problem that NIS of Russia shall solve.

China also has the problem of over-concerning the innovation supply, a lot of innovation policies has focused on the restructuring of scientific research institution and improving the innovation capacity of industrial enterprise since 1998[③], the long-term existing state of separating economy, science and technology, education and industrial department has not been effectively solved yet.

Various policies lack of effective integration

Undoubtedly, the government must consider the overall development of the whole country when developing the innovation system policy. Therefore, the design of innovation system must consider the specific historical, economic and social development environment, innovation support and the effective integration of education policy, macroeconomic policy and social development policy, etc. in the environment subsystem.

---

① Rosenberg, N., 1990, *Inside the Black Box: Technology and Economics*, Cambridge: Cambridge University Press.

② V.V.Krishna., 2010, " Role of The State In The Evolution of The National Innovation System In India", IDRC Seminer: Comparative Study of the National Innovation Systems of BRIC Countries, Rio de Janeiro, Brazil.

③ Lv Ping., 2010, " The Role of The State In National System of Innovation-China Case Study ," IDRC Seminer: Comparative Study of the National Innovation Systems of BRIC Countries, Rio de Janeiro, Brazil.

For example, the innovation policy and education policy in Brazil are obviously separated. Driven by the technology supply-led innovation policy, Brazil owns advanced higher education talent training system and research system. However, the middle school and primary school education is lagged, the overall national quality is low, which results in the serous lack of qualified, skilled human resource that can absorb innovation knowledge in the enterprises①. According to the survey, 44.9% of the industrial enterprises lack of qualified labor, and this situation is more serious in service enterprise, 60.3% of the telecommunication enterprises, 67.6% of the information service industry lack of qualified labor②. As a result, the enterprises have to spend a lot of energies and money on making up the insufficient basic education of most employees, and are incapable to train high skill talent or conduct innovation activity. The lack of effective integration of technology policy and education policy means that the innovation system of Brazil loses a lot of opportunities for development and evolution③.

Russian innovation policy lacks of effective integration, which makes the reform of governmental R&D department seriously lagged behind other economic departments. The market-oriented reform started in 1990's involved all aspects of economic system of Russia, however, the effect of the market-oriented reform in scientific research system field is slight. In 2007, only 3.3% of the organizations and enterprises in Russian economy are state-owned, however, the proportion of research institution reaches more than 70%④. The fund system and supervision rule of most research institutions still remain the form of planned economy, as a result, the technology system of Russia has a trend of contradiction in which the continuously growing governmental R&D input and obviously lagged development of technology department coexist, and low-efficient use of a lot of technology resources.

The problem of India in this aspect is reflected in the lack of innovation ecological system that the venture capital investment and various agencies can participate in and can promote technology transfer and commercialization, in addition, the national laboratory and university research institution master most scientific research funds, and the technology capacity cannot be effectively utilized. At the same time, India has not made

① Song Xia: "Deep Cause for Influencing the Competitiveness of Brazil: Contradictoriness and Fragility of National Innovation System, "*Latin American Studies*, Vol.6, 2008.

② PINTEC., 2007, Pesquisa Industrial de Inovação Tecnológica 2003-2005. Instituto Brasileiro de Geografia e Estatística – IBGE. Rio de Janeiro.

③ Priscila Koeller and José Luis Gordon., 2010, "The Role of The State In National System of Innovation In Brazil," IDRC Seminer: Comparative Study of the National Innovation Systems of BRIC Countries, Rio de Janeiro, Brazil.

④ V.V.Krishna., 2010, "Role of The State In The Evolution of The National Innovation System In India," IDRC Seminer: Comparative Study of the National Innovation Systems of BRIC Countries, Rio de Janeiro, Brazil.

systematical arrangement on the NIS policy yet, the technology and innovation policies are designed according to the department (such as aviation, atomic energy, biological pharmacy, computer software, etc.) and problem orientation (such as climate change, disaster recovery management, etc.), various policies and innovation main bodies lack of the mechanism of coordination and network integration, far from being a complete system[①].

For China, due to the different duties and objectives of the governmental departments, different departments are separate in the innovation management process, and lack of effective coordination mechanism, which greatly limits the improvement of Chinese innovation capacity[②].

Individual problems in BRICs

Brazil

Since the Mid 1980's, Brazil government has issued a series of policies and measures on the establishment and improvement of NIS, however, the execution effect is not satisfactory. According to the assessment of the world economic forum, the rank of comprehensive competitiveness of Brazil is at the lower-middle position. Although the economy in Brazil keeps growing in recent years, the rank is still unsatisfactory. In 2006, the international competitiveness of Brazil ranked No.62 in the world, fell to No.72 in 2007, ranked No.64 in 2008, and No.56 in 2009[③].

The root of aforesaid problems lies in the contradictoriness and fragility of NIS of Brazil, which makes the advanced science and technology resource of Brazil fail to transform into productivity and competitiveness in the reality[④]. The specific manifestation includes:

First, the continuous economic growth and serious gap between the rich and the poor coexist, which makes the development and distribution of knowledge and innovation seriously unbalanced, and makes Brazil knowledge innovation present the characteristics of coexistence of elite science and "proper technology" that meets the employment requirement of the poor, and it is hard for the created new knowledge to enter the production application due to insufficient effective requirement.

---

① V.V.Krishna., 2010, "Role of The State In The Evolution of The National Innovation System In India," IDRC Seminer: Comparative Study of the National Innovation Systems of BRIC Countries, Rio de Janeiro, Brazil.

② Lv Ping., 2010, "The Role of The State In National System of Innovation-China Case Study ," IDRC Seminer: Comparative Study of the National Innovation Systems of BRIC Countries, Rio de Janeiro, Brazil.

③ http://www.weforum.org.

④ Song Xia: "Deep Cause for Influencing the Competitiveness of Brazil: Contradictoriness and Fragility of National Innovation System," *Latin American Studies*, Vol.6, 2008.

Second, the technology progress of Brazil develops rapidly, however, the development of innovation capacity is very unbalanced, the innovation behavior is only limited in new fields, and the technology development strategy fails to benefit most industries to the greatest extent. On one hand, Brazil lacks of a culture of intellectual property right protection, registration and application of patent, as Carlos Vogt, the chairman of FAPESP, says, there is "culture barrier" in the innovation system of Brazil. According to the report of world intellectual property right organization, about 600,000 patents were registered in the world in 2005, 6.6% more than 2004, while the intellectual property right department of Brazil received 16,100 patent applications, 2,349 registered patents in 2005, the quantity of registered patents was 13.8% less than 2004, and 90% of the registered patents were from foreign enterprises①; on the other hand, the historically formed independent scientific research mode makes Brazil lack of an innovation mechanism to apply science and technology achievements in the economic and social field. In 2004, the newly issued Innovation Law in Brazil encouraged the joint innovation of university and enterprise, which was greatly opposed by the science groups, who considered that the university under the market pressure would damage the balance of knowledge development, such innovation only pursued the industrial benefit and ignored the requirement of social development related to the common people, which was easy to result in the privatization of public resource; third, Brazil emphasizes on the higher education and ignores the basic education, makes it difficult to find technician with sufficient education level, which affects local enterprises to master the advanced production technology, and brings long-term harm to the innovation.

Third, the knowledge and innovation are over-centralized in the "theory" research in universities and public research institutions, the national medium and small enterprises (small and mini-enterprises account for 90% of Brazil enterprises) as the economic entity lack of innovation driving force and innovation capital. The statistic data of applied economics research institute of Brazil in 2007 showed that the technology input of national enterprises was less than 0.6% of their all incomes, and less than 19% of the enterprises utilized the governmental innovation supporting fund②.

Of course most of these problems are the result of historical deposit, and cannot be solved in one day. Since entering the 21st century, Brazil government has realized and begun to solve these problems, such as Innovation Law in 2004, "innovation action plan" in 2007, etc. aim at encouraging enterprise innovation, promoting new mechanism that combines production, learning and research, expanding and reinforcing NIS. It is

---

① http://www.wipo.int/portal.

② Priscila Koeller and José Luis Gordon., 2010, "The Role of The State In National System of Innovation In Brazil," IDRC Seminer: Comparative Study of the National Innovation Systems of BRIC Countries, Rio de Janeiro, Brazil.

obvious that except for the current measure, if the unfair distribution system, irrational education system and traditional innovation "culture barrier" are not completely reformed, the contradictoriness and fragility of NIS of Brazil will not be fundamentally solved. It can be said that the separation of macroeconomic policy, education policy and social development policy and innovation policy is the main barrier for Brazil NIS to get result.

Russia

Russian government has done a lot in establishing and improving NIS, and the latest innovation policy document of Russia shows that Russia is gradually getting close to the international convention[①]. However, the execution effect is slight. On one hand, the natural resource export dependent economic growth mode of Russia has no fundamental change, according to the statistics, the proportion of fuel product export of Russia in the past few years in the total export kept high, this indicator in 2004 was 59.9%, reached 61% in 2005, further increased to 67.8% in 2006, 67.7% in 2007, basically as same as 2006, and increased to 73% in 2008[②]. At present, 30% of GDP, 50%-60% of national budget income and 60% of foreign exchange income are from the export of resource product[③]; on the other hand, the phase of insufficient enterprise innovation requirement has no fundamental change. In 2007, the enterprises took charge of only 10.6% of the R&D projects in Russia, and only 5.5% of the innovation results were from enterprises[④]. There are three deep causes:

First, on the verge of strange circle of resource course. The rich natural resource makes the risk for Russian enterprises to invest in researching and developing innovation higher than the risk to invest in mining industry, and the profit is less, the enterprises have no interest in innovation activity. In another word, under the condition of owning a lot of natural resources and the income from exporting natural resource is far higher than the income from innovation, the policy to encourage innovation naturally has no response. It can be said that the economic growth form singly driven by oil gas and natural resource is the key problem for NIS of Russia to solve, and also the cause for the slight result of NIS of Russia. Therefore, only the macroeconomic structure changes can the enterprises be expected to play the role of center in R&D and innovation, can the

① Tatiana Kuznetsova., 2010, "The Role of The State In National System of Innovation In Russia," IDRC Seminer: Comparative Study of the National Innovation Systems of BRIC Countries, Rio de Janeiro, Brazil.

② Zheng Xinli: *International Economic Analysis and Prospect,* Social Sciences Academic Press, 2010.

③ Euro-Asian Social Development Research Institute, Development Research Center, the State Council: Euro-Asian Situation and Prospect (2009).

④ Tatiana Kuznetsova., 2010, "The Role of The State In National System of Innovation In Russia," IDRC Seminer: Comparative Study of the National Innovation Systems of BRIC Countries, Rio de Janeiro, Brazil.

problem of insufficient innovation requirement of commercial department be expected to fundamentally solve.

Second, lack of market regulation mechanism. In the economic transformation, Russia has not established a complete or basic market mechanism, and the endogenetic and exogenetic regulation function of enterprises under the market system are hard to form. In the typical case, the ownership system reform with the core of privatization makes the enterprises and technology organizations of Russia have a clear property relation, however, most of the industrial enterprises of Russia have no powerful R&D capacity, and the scientific research organizations with powerful R&D capacity are not enterprises originally. In the situation of lack of or slight function of factor market and capital market, the organizations of two systems have no channel to closely unite the organizations. In another word, in the situation of incomplete market mechanism, the reform of ownership system may not promote the innovation capacity of enterprises, but becomes the short-term barrier for improving innovation capacity. Therefore, the industrial enterprises in Russia have not become the due important force in the innovation[①].

Third, ineffective public administration coordination. The technology management system of Russia has complex level, the department segment is divided, lacks of effective coordination mechanism, which greatly reduces the service efficiency of R&D resource. Longitudinally the technology management system of Russia is divided into legislative body, management department and activity body; there is also work division inside the hierarchy, such as education and science committee set in the State Duma, which is divided into education committee and science committee. Horizontally, the same level has institutions mutually restricting each other, such as the administrative scope of the State Duma and Federation Committee includes the committee of science and technology problem. Owing to the complex technology system design, the cross-department coordination institutions are increased, for example, "crass-department technology policy coordination committee" has the representatives in civil and military department, and also the representatives of federation organ, local and academic and science management department. Such situation with a number of departments and division affects the decision-making efficiency, and also cause a great barrier to the development and utilization of new technology. In May 2009, Russian President Dmitry Medvedev held "economic modernization and technology innovation committee" meeting and severely criticized the ineffective work of technology department, for it made the economic structure regulation difficult, the innovation activeness of enterprises halted, and scientific

---

① Zhang Yinsheng, Bao Ou: "Progress of Science and Technology Innovation System Reform in Russia," *Comparative Economic and Social Systems*, Vol.3, 2005.

research fund embezzled①.

Finally, lack of entrepreneur spirit. Besides the problems in economic environment and system, the cultural factor that lacks of entrepreneur spirit also restricts the evolution of NIS of Russia.

To sum up, besides certain problems in micro-level, the NIS of Russia also has a lot of problems in macro-system level, which is the fundamental point to solve problem to some extent.

India

The characteristics of Indian NIS can be summarized as government-led, technology-led and self-dependence-led, such mode can centralize resources to realize the technology breakthrough in key field and specific national strategic objective, with significant meaning to the construction of national technology system and innovation capacity, however, it also has its own problem.

First, over-emphasize on government leading and centralization. The innovation decision-making of India over-emphasizes on the leading role of government, which inhibits the "grass root innovation" of a lot of enterprises to meet the market requirement, and unfavorable for forming the innovative society full of creativity, and will cause waste of innovation resource for the governmental subsidy lacks of effective supervision means.

Second, over-focus on national defence technology. Many research projects led by the governmental research institutions focus on national defence technology, space technology and atomic technology, ignore the civil science and technology closely related to the economic development and people's lives, the association of technology progress and economic development is not close enough, the improvement of technology capacity is separated from the industrial demand, and a lot of technology achievements are laid aside.

Third, over-emphasize on self-dependence. The innovation policy tends to neglect the absorption of global knowledge due to over-emphasizing on self-dependence, the survey result of 2006 Indian enterprise observation report of World Bank shows that to most Indian enterprises, the acquisition of global new knowledge is more favorable for improving labor productivity than domestic knowledge created.

Besides the aforesaid problems, Indian NIS also faces other challenges, such as: the proportion of R&D expenditure in GDP is low, less than 1% in 2007, lowest in BRIC; low higher education enrollment rate, lack of research university and innovation culture; lack of efficient supervision mechanism for hi-tech department to execute innovation policy, etc.

---

① Dong Yue: "Future Science and Technology: Road of Rise for Russia, India and Brazil," *Economic Information Daily*, June 2, 2010.

China

Since the reform and opening-up, Chinese government has taken a series of measures on all levels to promote the construction of NIS, such as developing policy, implementing technology planning, direct investment or sponsoring R&D, tax incentive, public purchase, technology reward and technology resource allocation including management element, etc. These measures play an extremely important role in creating a good technology progress and innovation environment system. However, generally speaking, the gap between progress achieved by NIS and Chinese economic and social development requirement still exists, and there is still a series of problems and difficulties to solve.

First, the innovation capacity as the main body is still weak. First, enterprise is not the main force of commercialization of scientific and technological achievements, most enterprises lack of technology innovation capacity, participate in market competition in virtue of cost advantage, focus on equipment introduction, neglect digestion, absorption and innovation. For example, Chinese hi-tech enterprises as Lenovo, Huawei, etc. draw attention in international market, however, less than 1% of Chinese enterprises apply for 1 and more patent, and only 0.03% of the enterprises own independent intellectual property right[①]; second, Chinese scientific research institutions lack of original innovation capacity, supporting condition of technology development, with low efficiency of technology resource integration and utilization; third, as the important platform for talent training and innovation, the potential of university is not given full play, the mechanism and system for utilizing university technology resource are to be improved; finally, the force of agency that serves innovation is weak, and cannot meet the requirement on integrating and spreading innovation element and giving full play to the innovation network function.

Second, the environment condition for commercialization of scientific and technological achievements is to be improved. The market environment that supports the industrialization of independent innovation result still has many defects, which is mainly reflected in: first, the laws and regulations on promoting industrialization of scientific and technological achievements are not improved; second, the intellectual property right lacks of protection, the infringement of intellectual property right is serious, and the difficulty in obtaining high return from independent innovation is increased; second, lack of financial system that supports the industrialization of scientific and technological innovation achievements; finally, the marketization of independent innovation achievement lacks of guidance and cultivation in early period, the low-efficient government purchase measure cannot provide sufficient support to the industrialization

---

① Liu WeiLing., 2005, "High Tide," *China Daily*, 12/12/2005, page9, http://www.chinadaily.com.cn/english/doc/2005-12/12/content_502577.htm.

of independent innovation achievement.

Third, the innovation mechanism is not improved. First, the open, interactive, competitive and cooperative mechanism is not formed, the innovation element is separate, lacks of cooperation, the mobility efficiency of knowledge and information is low; second, the interactive mechanism of production, learning and research is to be improved, the university, research institution and enterprise lack of relation and cooperation; third, the technology investment mechanism fails to meet the innovation requirement, in recent years, although the governmental scientific research expenditure keeps growing, the increase is lower than the increase of total financial expenditure in the same period, and the use of governmental scientific research expenditure also lacks of effective supervision mechanism. At the same time, lack of effective mechanism that guides and encourages various social resources to invest in innovation; finally, the leading role of market mechanism in guiding and promoting innovation is not given full play.

Fourth, the innovation culture fails to meet the development requirement. First, part of universities and scientific research institutions remain the form of administrative management, and the academic democracy is insufficient; second, the insufficient cooperation spirit obstructs the exchange and cooperation between innovation bodies, and increases the innovation difficulty; third, the phenomenon of being eager for quick success and instant benefits is serious; finally, the competition consciousness and innovation spirit are to be strengthened. Due to long-term planned economic system and scientific research system and incentive mechanism, the researchers lack of competition driving force and entrepreneur spirit and courage.

Homoplasy and embeddedness: two brief conclusions

From the analysis and comparison of the functions of the governments of BRICs in NIS on investment, policy and existing problems, we can come to the following two conclusions:

The construction of NIS in BRICs has the tendency of homoplasy

The government function and policy coordination play a crucial role in the establishment and evolution of national innovation system and national innovation capacity, however, the policies and measures of the governments of the four countries become increasingly similar. Although the history, system and economic and social environment vary a lot in BRICs, and the intensity, direction, objective, path, etc. of the policies and measures of the governments of the four countries have different focuses in the establishment and improvement of respective national innovation system, the policies and measures adopted are largely identical but with minor differences. For example, to strengthen the governmental R&D input, improve legal system environment, develop national innovation strategic planning, support the construction of innovation basic platform, encourage enterprise to become innovation body, cultivate technology innovation talent, promote cooperation of production, learning and research, etc.; the role of the governments of the four countries in the construction of NIS is mostly centralized in creating good environment and appropriate mechanism for innovation activity, solving market failure, guiding the effective allocation of innovation resource, promoting and encouraging the mutual function of innovation elements, monitoring and assessing the establishment process of NIS, etc.

In general, the policies of BRICs in constructing NIS become increasingly similar, and get close to the best international practice. Of course, the factor to weigh the government function in NIS is neither the quantity of issued policies, nor the quantity of technological achievements produced, but the final function and effect in the economical and social development.

The current situation that the construction of NIS in BRICs lacks of embeddedness

Innovation has regional embeddedness, and the establishment of NIS has profound economic, social, historical and cultural background characteristics. As Deacon says, innovation is a social process of embedding sociality and institution, and the increase of technology supply will not automatically bring the development of economic society[①]. Although the NIS aims at promoting the occurrence, diffusion and sustaining of technology innovation, besides the consideration of technology supply (directly acting on innovation as R&D policy, etc.), the focus of government in establishing NIS must be considered from macro-social and economic condition and historical and cultural background (indirectly acting on innovation as development policy, etc.), the integration of social development policy and innovation policy must be considered, and how to break the strange circle of "resource curse" to solve specific development problem must be considered.

In another word, the innovation policy must consider the actuality of the country so as to act on economic and social development, instead of copying the prescription of developed countries. Only the innovation policy is considered from the degree of overall economic and social development and systematical and embedded degree can it be possible to establish an efficient NIS. At the same time, the establishment process of NIS is also the process of evolution of social and economic structure and differentiation strategy and establishment of national competition advantage.

---

① Dicken, P. 1998, *Global Shift*, 3rd edition, New York: The Guilford Press.

BRICs: Cooperation Perspectives in the International Security Sphere

Boris F. Martynov[*]

The imperatives of cooperation between the BRIC countries in the security sphere, which are revealed on the inter-state, regional and global level, suggest possibilities in all the range of the modern notions about security and have their own specific features. These are a special, respectful attitude towards the international law and a special, "civilizational" perception by the BRICs of many of the current international problems. It seems to be clear today, that the successful resolution of those problems based on the methods, which came to us from the époque of the "balances of forces" is no longer possible. The modern world is short of innovations, which can come only from those countries-civilizations, which earlier stood apart from the "big" policy, which completely discredited itself in the XXth century.

But even before the moment, when the new world actors could positively influence the tissue of the world order, their own security may be jeopardized, which would put in doubt the perspectives of their ascension. The possible threats to their security could be internal, connected with the natural problems of rapid growth, as well as external, conditioned by the ill will of others. So, the reiteration by the BRICs of their basic security rights in the economic, political, cultural, environmental and informational affairs seems to us completely natural in the present stage of their development.

By all means, the security threats for different BRICs are not equal. The security of Russia and China -nuclear powers and permanent members of the Security Council, and also of nuclear India, seem to be "guaranteed" by their very status. But this is not completely so. Today, security threats have mostly nonmilitary character and concentrate

* Boris F. Martynov, professor of the Moscow State Institute of International Relations.

mainly within the state borders. The fall of the Soviet Union -the nuclear super-power, is evidence to this.

Russia and other multi-national BRICs -China and India have similar security problems: aggressive nationalism, xenophobia, separatism and political extremism, terrorism, corruption and narcotraffic. To deal with those problems Russia and China created in 2001, together with Kazakhstan, Uzbekistan, Tajikistan and Kirgizstan, the "Shanghai organization for cooperation" (ShOS). India also showed its interest towards ShOS, and became its observant member. In the same year of 2001 the ShOS members signed a special Anti-terrorist and anti-separatist convention. Later, they created a special Anti-terrorist committee, whose task is to supervise collective measures, such as interchange of information and experience, collective maneuvers, measures of financial control, etc.

Notwithstanding the mentioned, one often hears the opinion, that, from the point of view of the security, Brazil, a far-off country, is not of such importance for Russia as near-off China and India within the same BRICs paradigm. On our point of view this is a short-sighted position, which contradicts some important modern tendencies. First, we can't omit the existence of problems, though nowadays not very pronounced, but which can be quickly aggravated already by the 20-th of the present century. Second, we mustn' t ignore the process of globalization, which not only accelerates the flaws of peoples, goods and information, but also makes common the problems of seemingly distant nations. And, at last, it's evident enough, that any treaties and conventions, concluded in the security sphere will never be binding in the situation, when the international law is an outcast and the international order is a fiction. From that pointy of view, the cooperation between all the BRICs, namely -between Brazil and Russia, seems to us indispensable.

Table In this table we try to foresee some possible directions of such cooperation

Spheres of security	Position of Brazil	Perspectives of cooperation with Russia
1. Constitutional	High. Long-term positive tendency	Strategic partnership
2. Economy	Upper middle. Positive tendency	Active economic cooperation
3. Energy	Upper middle. Long-term positive tendency	Joint projects, cooperation in the international markets
4. Science and technology	Middle. Positive tendency	Joint projects and investigations
5. Natural resources	High	Realization of common policies
6. Ecology	High	Realization of common policies
7. Agriculture and foodstuffs	High	Cooperation in the international markets. Realization of common policies
8. Information security	Lower middle. Positive tendencies	Realization of common policies
9. Social security	Lower middle. Positive tendencies	Common aims and values. Realization of common policies
10.Military security	Lower middle. Positive tendencies	Arms sales. Military and technical cooperation

Continue Table

Spheres of security	Position of Brazil	Perspectives of cooperation with Russia
11. "Civilization" and cultural security	Middle. Positive tendencies	Realization of common policies
12. Humanitarian security	Middle. Positive tendencies	Establishment of common links
13. Regional and global	Middle. Positive tendencies	Cooperation in the wide range of the most actual problems

Clearly, this table doesn't pretend to be any exhaustive, but some things can draw attention. First of all, as we see, many things in the security positioning of Russia and Brazil do coincide, and this opens a wide specter of cooperation between the two countries. Besides, the position of Brazil in 10 points from the main 13, which are usually included in the notion of "wide" or "complex" security, can already be qualified as "high" or "upper middle". Mindful of the results of the development of this country during the last 10 years and the policies of its leaders, based on the broad national basis, one can expect in the period from 5 to 15 years, the sharp upraise in the significance of the rest of the security points. And in this case the coincidence of its security needs with Russia's will become even deeper.

The most important, on our point of view, is the use of common approaches to such problems of the global policy as multilateral diplomacy and the role of the international law, restructuring of the international organizations, including the ONU, struggle against terrorism, illegal drugs and piracy, nuclear nonproliferation, human rights, non-discrimination in the international trade and many other things. On such issues we always mark the "proximity or coincidence" of our positions in all our diplomatic documents.

But, sooner or later, the closest attention, on our point of view, must be paid to the new directions of the security strategy. We mean the natural resources, ecological and energetic security, which is directly connected with the problem of climatic changes. And, consequently, soon there will appear a new necessity to cooperate in the sphere of the information security.

One should pay attention to the passage of the newest Russian document "The Strategy of the national security of Russian Federation until 2020".

It says: "The pivotal point of the world policy for the long-term period will be concentrated around the possession of the world sources of energy. The "information wars" will become more current together with the aggravation of the world demographic and ecological situations. In such situations one can't exclude the use of military force." This passage is in complete coherence with the "Document on the National Defense policy of Brazil" of 2005, where the risks in the ecological and the environmental security are understood in the terms of "future disputes for the world stocks of fresh water, vast ocean areas, energy sources and the cosmic space". Among the most vulnerable areas Brazilian Amazonia (almost 52% of the territory) is specially mentioned as a region, possessing the unique bio-diversity, mineral and hydro-energy richness, but, at the same time, having the smallest human density for 1 km^2. Seven Amazonian states have the density of their population up to 3.35 persons, among them the biggest – Amazonas, only 1.79 persons for a km^2.

"Brazil will be watchful to the unconditional reaffirmation of its sovereignty upon the Brazilian Amazon region. It will repudiate, by means of actions of development and defense, any attempt of external imposition on its decisions regarding the preservation, development and defense of the Amazon region. It will not allow organizations or individuals to serve as instruments for alien interests political or economic – willing to weaken the Brazilian sovereignty. It is Brazil that takes care of the Brazilian Amazon region, at the service of mankind and at its own service" – such is the position contained in the newest document, dated by December 2008. And later: "This will require – especially from the Ground Force – that the conventional force develop some of the attributes assigned to non-conventional forces. The Armed Forces with such attributes will be the only ones capable of operating in the vast spectrum of circumstances that the future might bring".

The concretization of the threat, contained in the Brazilian document, helps to understand the significance of the depopulation also for the vast regions of Russia in Siberia, the Polar regions and the Far East. There Russia possesses about 98% of its general known reserves of oil, 68% of coal, 95% of gas and 89% of fresh water (in the lake Baikal and the Siberian rivers). Here one should mention the fact, that namely Brazil and Russia occupy the 1st and the 2nd places in the world as for the deposits of the fresh water, which, according to some scientists, will soon become even the greater deficit that oil and gas. The population density in those Russian Regions of Siberia oscillates from 1 to 10 and in many cases it's not more than 1 person for a km^2, which approximates them with the most depopulated areas of Brazilian Amazonia.

To illustrate a possible threat, which soon can await both our countries, we could cite the book by the American authors F. Hill and K. Gaddy ("Siberian Curse" Brookings, 2003), whose advice, given to Russia, "to tighten up", though not yet geographically, but in the sense of its "economical limits", is characteristic enough. The authors advocate there for a greater share of economic sovereignty for the transnational corporations, leaving for Russia a vague right of a political "supervision" over those regions. Though it's quite clear to anybody that no political sovereignty can subsist without an economic one.

On our point of view, the character of the global positioning of such countries as Russia, Brazil, China, India and some others in the coming century will depend not so much on the level of their democratic development or even their marked success in the process of liquidation of social and economic inequalities, but on their capability or incapability to effectively control its own territory. Much will depend on the elaboration by them of their proper long-term strategies of national development in the energy and the ecological spheres.

Other area of cooperation between the four countries, already mentioned in their basic national security documents, is the security of the outer space. One shouldn't forget, that the control over the outer space nowadays simultaneously means the control over climate, territories, natural resources, energy reserves, oceanic areas and fresh water. So one could agree with some authors who foresee the possibility of renovation of the inter-state conflicts of the past with a view to enhance or "redistribute" the control over cosmic, oceanic and polar territories in the present times. Same can be said about the enhancement of the future struggles for the control of information.

International practice shows, that any potential threat to the international order acquires its sinister parameters only when ignored for a long time by the international community. This is fully adaptable to the problem of the international terrorism, drastically aggravated nowadays. One of the most principal tasks for the BRIC countries, taking into account their possibility of renovated perception of the international realities, will be, accordingly, to prevent the "maturing" of the new generation of global threats, which could throw the mankind back to the period of inter-state wars, capable of complete annihilation of it.

BRICs: Significance, Basis for Partnership and Their Role in Shaping the Global Order

Xu Wenhong[*]

The Significance of the Rising of the BRICs

Ever since the Age of Discovery, the world had been gradually taken control of by western countries' influences. "Every talk begins with Greece and Rome" was a trend of time, and "westernization" or "Americanization" has become the byword for "modernization" and "globalization". However, when it comes to the new millennium, a series of issues has demonstrated that the non-western world has become more and more important, especially after the "9.11" and the global financial crisis which started from 2008. It shows that the western style of development which is represented by America is just one of the modes for development, and is inevitably problematic in some degree, and it is not and should not become the only way of development; at the same time, the international structure which is led by America and western countries is transforming gradually and quietly in a subtle way. The best illustration of this change is the summit conference of BRICs and even the mechanism of it in Yekaterinburg in June in place of the former genius speculation on BRICs by Jame O'Neill who is an the American economist.

The reason of why the BRICs have taken the attention of the world is that their scale and track record of development are remarkably significant:

— China, Russia and Brazil are countries with vast territory.

* Xu Wenhong, research associate fellow, the Institute of Russia, East Europe and Central Asia, Chinese Academy of Social Sciences.

— China and India are countries with the biggest population in the world, and Brazil ranks the fifth in population worldwide.

— Russia has proved the most incredible huge resources.

— Brazil is rich in resources, big in the potential of arable land, adequate in water resource, and is the largest developing country in the southern hemisphere.

BRICs take 26% of the total land area of the world, 42.9% of the world population, and 15.5% of the world GDP. In some way, the development of the BRICs is the development of half the people in the world. According to the statistics of economic development in recent years, the increment speed of the BRICs is even faster than the most optimistic predication made by Goldman Sachs Group led by Jame O'Neill:

— Based on the statistics show by IMF, the average economic growth rate of the four countries from 2006 to 2008 is 10.7%. The contribution rate of BRICs to the world economic growth from 2000 to 2008 is over 30%, and this rate is even raised to 45% from 2007 to 2009 during the period of financial crisis which tortured the western countries greatly.

— In Goldman Sachs 2001 annual report, Jim O' Neill claimed the GDP of "BRICs" would account for over 10% of world's total. In fact, at the end of 2007, the four countries' proportion was over 15%[①].

— The trade volume of the "BRICs" has been growing during recent years, specifically, in the year of 2008, the volume increased by 2%, accounting for 13% of world's total. Roberto Jaguaribe, the Secretary for Political Affairs, Ministry of Foreign Affairs of Brazil, predicted that between 2008-2014, the "BRICs" would constitute 61.3% of global economic growth rate[②].

— The foreign exchange reserves of the four countries are nearly $3 trillion.

— 31st.July.2010, Yi gang, the Vice-President of the People's Bank of China, announced China has substituted Japan, becoming the second-largest economy in the world[③].

Apart from that, when America and other European countries have been severely conflicted by economic crisis, the banking and economic systems of the BRICs were

① "The BRICs and the N-11",published in 18th Dec.2007,see http://www.21cbh.com/HTML/2007-12-31/HTML_SUHPF14KRII4.html.

② "BRICs Summit to Focus on Economic, Financial Issues", Xinhua, 9th Apr.2010,see http://www.china.org.cn/business/2010-04/09/content_19779476.htm.

③ "The Best Choice of China's Exchange-rate", Yi Gang, Hu Shuli, 30th July 2010,see http://www.safe.gov.cn/model_safe/news/new_detail.jsp?ID=90000000000000000,814&id=2.

running smoothly and present strong capacity on resisting the financial crisis, with the exception of Russia. The stable economic growth provides an access for the "BRICs" to unprecedentedly boost their influence and expectation of the world. In a certain sense, the development of the BRICs is a main driving force behind the global economic growth. In addition, the four countries have exerted positive influence upon eliminating the effect of financial crisis and promoting the global economic recovery. Overcoming this financial crisis proves the BRICs are indispensable part of stimulating economic growth and keeping this world stable and prosperous.

Meanwhile, the development patterns of the BRICs are different from typical western ones as they are not traditional western countries. To be exact, China is exploring the way to build socialism with Chinese characteristics and Russia is striving for rejuvenation through modernization depending on system innovation and economic innovation, leading by Putin's team, as well as India and Brazil are also developing their own way of development, although India has been greatly influenced by the western world. The sound and steady growth of the BRICs has not only proved the capacity of non-Western economy, but also is a landmark on the exploration of non-Western development pattern whist the western pattern has encountered serious problems during the financial crisis.

Additionally, with the strengthening cooperation and coordination among the BRICs, the discourse power on many global issues such as climate change, energy demand and prices of energy, and food, environmental issues etc, has been enhanced. As an apt illusion, in the Iranian nuclear issue, Brazil, uniting with Turkey, has actively mediated in this issue, and finally reached an agreement on Tehran research reactor fuel supply problem in 2010. Undeniably, the four countries' influence has been growing and will continue to grow.

Goldman Sachs also proposed the concept of "N-11"① which stands for the 11 countries whose importance and status are just below the BRICs. When the recovery of the global economy is still in a dilemma and the countries across this world are still facing enormous complex problems, it is not feasible to let only several developed countries shoulder the responsibility of leading the whole world; hence, the ideal pattern of solving global issues should be bestowing the emerging non-Western countries, especially the BRICs, equality and discourse power and strengthen the communication and cooperation between developed and developing countries; thereby solving global issues with joint forces, reaching and complementing agreement on the global issues, dedicating to address economic and financial problems and subsequently introducing a more balanced,

① Next Eleven, N-11:South Korea, Indonesia, Vietnam, Philippines, Pakistan, Bangladesh in Asia, Nigeria, Egypt, Mexico, Latin America in Africa , Iran in the Middle East, and Turkey in Europe.

unbiased, sustainable and beneficial international economic, financial and trade order, which will benefit the global economic recovery as a whole.

The basis for cooperation of the "BRICs"

The BRICs has developed from a visionary concept proposed by the economists from Goldman Sachs into a platform for international cooperation and international dialogue; furthermore, it has been growing into an international economic organization; Nevertheless, after two leader's summit, as well as several times' communication and cooperation, the functionality, statues and development in prospect of the BRICs still have not been impartially reflected by the contemporary international economic and political configuration.

On the one hand, Goldman Sachs holds the opinion that the BRICs has infinite potential on development, on the other hand, some claim that instead of forming long-term cooperation alliance, there are obvious and stiff competitions among these countries, even on some objectives sharing interests such as free trade, energy pricing and how to reform in current policies, these countries have fundamental divergences since the four countries have different cultures, development patterns, religions, social and political systems and different status of economic development; hence, some prophet instead of being an "economy club "like"G8"or "G20" which has the discourse power to exert influence upon the global economic configuration and economic order, the BRICs may only be and will be an organization like "Shanghai Cooperation Organization (SCO)" which is a "quasi political organization" and has limited influence upon this world. We think only when the four countries coordinate tightly and voice out their own opinions on the solving of global issues, the vitality can be instilled in and the influence can be enhanced. Not until we get a fully understanding of what is the upcoming tasks of the "BRICs", the basis for cooperation and the expectations and objectives of the four countries for this organization, can we get a clear perspective of the four countries' development in the future.

The naming of the BRICs was highly connected with the situation of the four countries economic and financial circumstances, therefore, to strengthen the cooperation on economy and finance such as forming new international financial order, promoting the recovery and development of global economy and preventing the trade protectionism are the basis and starting point for the cooperation of the BRICs, meanwhile, energy security, climate change and other global issues are priorities for the four countries to coordinate and cooperate.

The establishment of new international financial order

The global economy has been severely damaged by this financial crisis and the cost of this financial crisis is several times as world wars', subsequently made a serious effect upon the global economy and the people's life of every country. The four countries claim that international community should take necessary anti-crisis measures and advance the establishment of a new international financial order and set up an effective long-term mechanism for the development of global economy. Therefore, the four countries will reach agreements on the following issues:

Improving international finance supervision system

Finance is the core of modern economy and economic globalization is inevitably attached by financial globalization. With the process of financial liberalization, financial innovation and global financial integration, financial liberalization will also expand financial risks all around the world. The scale and influence of the current financial crisis indicated that on the one hand, with the process of globalization developing countries are accelerating the pace of financial reform, promoting the domestic convertibility, opening the financial market and loosening the management of international capital flows. Thus the scope of capital flow is expanding; on the other hand, the flowing speed of international capital is increasing in different markets. Therefore, the risks are increasing as well. The influence of this international financial crisis made international society have a new understanding of the international financial supervision.

The reform of international financial supervision system, as the important content for rebuilding the international financial order have a great influence on the countries finance, economic and social development. The financial supervision system involves the basic interests of the countries'. Every country must re-examine financial supervision system which is to prevent the possible risks effectively. What's more, nowadays under the economic globalization background, the necessity of strengthening international cooperation on financial markets, the supervision of mechanism and tool aspect becomes more and more important.

The BRICs have different views from the United States and Europe on this issue. Through communication and negotiations, the BRICs commonly recon those new consensuses of international financial order needs "the solid foundation of law. The activities of national supervision would not conflict with the international standards organization"[①]. So the basic principle of new international financial order should strengthen the mutual management of risks and supervision practice. The BRICs committed that "they will strengthen domestic supervision, promoting the reform of international financial supervision system and getting close cooperation with international

---

① "The leaders joint statement of the BRICs in Yekaterinburg, Russia" see http://www.fmprc.gov.cn/.

standard organization including financial stability forum"[①]. On the joint efforts of the BRICs and together with other countries, the declaration getting through in the G20 summit meeting in Washington, London and Pittsburgh announce that each country would take joint action honoring the commitment of reforming financial department, including the four pillars according to the schedule or acceleration of the process and reform the financial supervision.

The cooperation in the reform of financial supervision will make each countries have more sound development environment and a more favorable economic operation mechanism, effectively avoid the impact of financial crisis in the area of economic globalization. The sound environment and a more favorable economic operation mechanism are the important premise of the cooperation in every area among the BRICs.

Changing of the U.S. dollar's international hegemony and promoting the diversity of international monetary system

In current international financial order, BRICs takes large foreign exchange reserves (China, $245 trillion dollars, at the first place; Russia, $4693 billion, the third; India and Brazil respectively at fourth and seventh). U.S. dollar takes a large proportion of foreign exchange (for example, 70% of China's foreign exchange reserves is U.S. dollars). On the one hand this situation made the BRICs have to face the current America‘s account deficit and fiscal deficit since the breaking up of financial crisis , on the other hand, BRICs need to pay a huge sums of seigniorage revenue. Therefore, the BRICs' assets at foreign exchange reserves are reducing gradually.

In addition, in the financial crisis, U.S. dollar and its instability financial system impact world economy through a spreading way which made many countries in the world take the current financial order and the international currency system into consideration: the current monetary system is unreasonable. And global economy depends overly on U.A. dollars which inherently has systemic risks. What's more, there are conflicts between America interest and other countries taking us dollar as an international exchange reserve.

Therefore, the revival world economy cannot rely on America itself circumventing the risks. In order to prevent the global financial crisis and the collapse of dollar appearing again, the reform of the current international monetary system becomes emergence. Not only the emerging marketing countries but other developed countries also have this desire of reforming the international monetary system. The BRICs has the common appeal on this issue: Russia openly expressed many times that they hope rubles become an international exchange of reserve. O'Neil the economists who firstly put forward the BRICs said that rubles would join in IMF as a currency evaluation and would be taken

① "The Joint Statement of BRICs' Leaders in the Second Joint Meeting," see http://www.fmprc.gov.cn/.

into the basket of currencies by the year of 2015. Although it is a long way for Brazil and India to develop their currency into an international currency, they take on optimistic attitude to change the hegemony of U.S. dollars.

China has made great effort to realize the internationalization of RBM. The bank of China signed the agreement about 65million RMB exchange respectively with Argentina, South Korea, issued bonds in Hong Kong and expanded cross-border trade settlement by using RMB. Despite of the prospect of RMB internationalization is unclear, there are several conceive for this, such as: creating the surplus sovereignty SDR①; forging Asian currency with other countries or eventually becoming the core of an international exchange reserve like dollar and euro.

But the internationalization of RMB is irreversible due to the increasing of China' s economy. Although RMB would not replace the dominance of dollar in short-term, its international status is raising because of the development of China's economy, subsequently, the people in the world have more expectation of RMB. More and more countries hope that RMB would be the international exchange reserve. China is aware of the position that the internationalization of RMB cannot be fulfilled overnight. During this period, Chinese government suggested that world relevant organizations should be completed in the distribution and regulation mechanism of reserving currency, and also keeping the stability of the main reserve currency so as to promote the diversity and reasonability of the international monetary system. In international society, decreasing the dependence of U.S. dollars would reduce the risks brought by financial crisis and also reduce the impact of the risk of dollar to world economy.

Improving the reform of international financial institutions and promoting the developing countries' discourse power in international financial organizations

The key to reconstruct the international financial order is the reform of international financial organizations and the core of the reform is international monetary fund (IMF). In Brettos woods system, IMF is the core of global economy. And IMF has the following three basic functions:

1) Maintaining the system of the fixed exchange rate;

2) Providing short-term financial arrangements to those countries out of payments

3) Monitoring the economy of the members.

However, IMF is out of the rapid development of world economy and is also out tend of globalization because of that IMF lacks funds of dealing with crisis. Its available resources for loan are only $250 billion which cannot effectively huddle large scale of

① Zhou Xiaochuan, the president of the People's Bank of China, published three articles with a week in March 2009. The three articles are : "Thoughts about the Transformation of International Currency System" on 23rd March, "Thoughts about Saving ratio" on 24th March and "To further probe into changes of macro and micro procyclical period".

crisis; the decision-making mechanism and operation mechanism is neither fair nor transparent. When providing loans to the members, IMF is seriously influenced by western countries. There is not any warning before the crisis and are no effective botches after crisis. The sharing of voting right is seriously not confirmed to emerging economies' economic proportion and its contribution to the world economy; poor countries voices cannot be reflected.

The four countries have common views on the reform for IMF. Therefore, on 14th March 2009, Yekaterinburg joint statement during G20 financial minister meeting the BRICs appeal that IMF should get rid of the attachment to some great countries and restore its independence. The BRICs appeals IMF members increasing capital to enhance the function of IMF, combining the amount of distribution to the adding fund of emerging marketing countries, and finally reach the goal of sharing equal voting right between developing countries developed countries; increase resources to international financial institutions and add the sums of fund for developing countries. Hereby in 2009 IMF initially issued 1.1 trillion bonds in aid of poor countries impacted by crisis.

China has intended to purchase $50 billion bonds. Russia and Brazil will buy $10 billion bonds respectively. The cooperation of the BRICs on this issue, on the one hand, supplements the IMF which enhanced the function of IMF when dealing with financial problems; on the other hand promoting the diversification reserve currency, reducing the risk of buying American bonds.

Besides, the BRICs also requests the reform of bank of China and other international financial reorganizations, increasing dialogues among emerging economic system, enhancing cooperation on restructure and trade field, adding capital support to those countries impacted by crisis among international financial institutions.

The common position and joint announcement among the BRICs in the reform of IMF and other international institutions indicate that the BRICs will enhance cooperation of establishing new international financial order. This also the cooperate foundation to members of the BRICs.

The coordination of BRICs stands and making contribution to promote the sustainable and balanced growth of the world economy

The global financial crisis highlights the interactions between countries. As a result, it is more important to strengthen international conversation and cooperation. "When the world economy swooned in a low point situation the BRICs jointly send out a signal of booting the world economy as soon as possible"①. And through making great effort in

① President Hu: "Cooperation, Opening Up, Mutual Benefit and Win-Win Situation — the Speech at the BRICs Leaders Meeting," see http://www.fmprc.gov.cn/.

protecting their domestic economy, the BRICs leadingly realize its economic increasing which give great confidence for countries achieving the survival of its economy. For the united efforts in 2009, to some extent, world economy started to be restored. However, the severe challenges still exist. To ensure the overall recovery of world economy as a sustainable and balanced situation, strengthening cooperation and coordination among the BRICs become more and more important. This was particularly critical when the BRICs connected with America respectively.

America is not only the main engine driving force to develop the world economy but also the main cooperator of other countries in funds, newly high technology, and developing trade market but also has the most powerful military force, which mains the biggest economy in the world. Therefore, developing relationship with the United States for each member of the BRICs is prior to each of the BRICs. Fighting for equilibrium is the best choice of the BRICs. As a result, the BRICs should set goals for improving the survival of world economy.

Trade protectionism

Being against protectionism and trade barriers preventing the impeding of protectionism and trade barriers becomes one of the main topics in the third G20 summit meeting. This is the common choice of international society. The BRICs commonly emphasized that international trade and the direct investment play an important role in economic recovery around the worldwide. The BRICs appeal all sides to taking any effort to improve the international trade and investing the environment. Urge all parties maintaining a stable and multilateral trading system, curbing trade protectionism and promote the negotiation of world trade organization. Doha round meeting have gained a comprehensive and balanced succeeds[①]. But in fact the specific circumstance is different.

At first the difference is relevant to different economic system and development mode. The four countries take a large proportion of domestic demand, so they strongly insist to protect their domestic market. But china highly relate to on the external market.

China is sensitive to international market's demand. Therefore China is against protectionism while Russia, Brazil and India do not show a determined attitude to protectionism.

Secondly, the difference is relevant to the resources endowment. China and India have larger demand in Russia's energy resources, and Brazil's mineral resources. To some extent, the BRICs formed a supplement and demand relationship among the biggest trade partner. Russia is at the second place. But the position of Brazil, India, and Russia would not be noticeable.

---

① "The Leaders Joint Statement of the BRICs in Yekaterinburg, Russia," see http://www.fmprc.gov.cn/.

Therefore, on the trade protection issue, the BRICs against protectionism and stimulate global economy while protecting the interests of their own side because of the special condition of their own. But, the BRICs emphasize that "WTO as a multilateral trading system plays an important role in keeping an open, stable, fair and non-discriminatory international environment. Besides, they committed to resist various forms of trade protectionism, and stroked the visible trade restrictions. And finally on the basis of respecting authorization and keeping the achievements including negotiation mode, the BRICs should promote Doha round to achieve a comprehensive and balanced succeed as soon as possible"[①].

Energy Cooperation

Since the third technological revolution, the dependence of world economy on energy had been gradually strengthened. Energy is the lifeblood of the modern economy. Countries have a clear understanding of how energy impact on the economic. During the period of 2000-2008, the influence of the fluctuation of international energy prices on the world economy is memorable.

In the field of energy cooperation, on the one hand, the standpoint of the four countries is not entirely consistent. Russia is a big energy producing country in the world, they hope that long-term continued rising of world energy prices stimulate their own economies; while China, Brazil, and India are energy consuming countries, in the next few decades, China, India and Brazil, respectively, will be the world's leading energy consumer, and thus the three countries want to stabilize energy prices at a relatively low level; on the other hand, China's and India's dependence on foreign oil increased year by year, Brazil's and Russia's massive oil reserves has become the foundation of strengthening the cooperation of the four countries.

Hence, the BRICs has a consensus on to ensure the stability and sustainability of energy supply through cooperation in the energy sector, such as: China and Russia reached a broad consensus and signed a number of important documents on the crude oil pipeline, a long-term crude oil trade, loans, package of cooperation project in February 2009. During the financial crisis, to strengthen energy cooperation between China and Russia has great significance on deepening bilateral relations, stabilizing international energy prices, and coping with the international financial crisis; Petrobras and Sinopec will cooperate on development of energy, China should be involved in the energy development in Brazil, and will becoming important members. In the new international environment, the four countries will address energy security challenges into opportunities to strengthen cooperation.

---

① "The Joint Statement of BRICs' Leaders in the Second Joint Meeting," see http://www.fmprc.gov.cn/.

Meanwhile, the BRICs Energy companies are also constantly enhancing their strength, according to Goldman Sachs statistics, including PetroChina, Gazprom, Petrobras, Sinopec, Rosneft and Lukoil, CNOOC and Oil and Natural Gas Corporation from the BRICs energy companies, is rapidly catching up the U.S. and Western energy companies①.

Furthermore, China and India are also actively developing new energy technologies independently. Cooperation and exchanges between the four countries in the development of wind energy, solar energy and other new energy sources and energy efficiency aspects also been further enhanced. Diversification of energy structure will be promoted through the enhancement of the appropriate share of renewable energy. The use of cleaner, more efficient fossil energy and other energy will be encouraged. Cooperation will also be launched in aspects of training in the energy sector, R&D, consulting, technology transfer etc②.

Environmental issues and climate change

The "BRICs", as an outlook of the future of world economic, means that human beings will have more healthy and sustainable living environment and a more ideal model of development. For this reason, protecting the present earth and taking good care of our homes today have become the consensus of the world. Copenhagen recently witnessed the endeavor of countries in the world endeavor with regards to environmental protection. The BRICs described a common position on this issue of the four countries in two summit meetings and a joint statement after the meeting.

According to statistics, in the 2008 ranking of global greenhouse gas emissions, China ranked second, Russia ranked third, Brazil ranked eighth, India ranked seventeenth. This is not only the objective statement of the four countries, under certain conditions, and in the existing international economic order and the status of the international division of labor, but also showed that the four countries still have a long way to go to reduce emissions and to protect our environment. Thus, the four countries face similar tasks and have similar demands on the issue of energy conservation and environment protecting in the development of the economy. Among these, there are not only their own needs of changing in the mode of production, but also the historic mission of protecting the environment.

---

① "Goldman Sachs Report BRICs Has Been Outpacing the U.S. Dominance of Global Energy," see *Financial Times* Website, http: //www.financialnews.com.cn/cj/txt/2007-06/27/content_32209.htm.

② See the 8th article of "Joint Declaration of BRICs summit in Yekaterinburg"; the 19th, 20th and 21st articles of "Joint Declaration of the second official meeting of the BRICs leaders". See The website of the People's Republic of China Ministry of Foreign Affairs.

The four countries have expressed the will of reducing emissions and protecting the environment: by 2020, Russian carbon emissions will lower by 20% -25% compared with 1990's level, before 2020, India carbon emissions will lower by 20% -30% compared with 2005's level, Brazil plans to reduce greenhouse gas emissions by 36.1% -38.9% based on the expected reduction. Over the past three decades, China's economic achievements have attracted worldwide attention, at the same time, China have long-term unremitting efforts on the environment protecting to cope with the climate change. Through these actions, China make its due efforts on energy saving and environmental protection. Base on this, China has proposed that they will cut down 40% -45% carbon dioxide emissions per unit of GDP than in 2005 by 2020, in this period, arduous efforts will be taken to realize such a large scale reduction of carbon dioxide emissions.

Thanks to the typical sense of the economic size and development pattern of the four countries, it can be said that without the actively participation of the four countries, any relevant environmental protection proposal is nothing but a dead letter; Without the effective implementation of the four countries, any results of in greenhouse gas reduction will be subject to a certain extent. As representatives of emerging economies and leaders of developing countries, the four countries have more reason to put forward their views and advocate on the sustainable way of the future world and development model base on their 42% of the world's population and more than 50% of the contribution on global economic growth rate.

As we all know, the "Kyoto Protocol" specifies emissions reduction targets in the first commitment period to 2012 for the developed countries. But the actual implementation is that emissions of many developed countries go upwards. The international community has to make effective institutional arrangements under the framework of the Convention to promote the developed countries to fulfill their commitments and continue to provide adequate financial support the developing countries, accelerate the transfer of climate friendly technologies, tackle climate change, and protect the environment by the teamwork of the international community. In short, among the BRICs there will be very broad space for cooperation on the protection of the earth and protection of environment.

In addition to the wide range of common in cooperation in the above five areas, of in the BRICs also have similar or common positions in the other global involved issues. This is the foundation to strengthen further cooperation between the four countries. Brazilian President Lula made highly of the cooperation between the BRICs in the second Summit: to further cooperation between "BRIC countries" is good for multi-polar world and the development of international democratic. "The four countries will continue to strengthen cooperation with the economic crisis, call for a change an unjust situation and prepare for future transform.

Self-awareness of the BRICs and their role in world

From the first meeting to regular meeting, from the formation of economic cooperation mechanism to the formal establishment of Summit mechanism, the BRICs traversed an extraordinary path. In order to have more room and more influence in international political and economic life in the future, the BRICs must have not only a clear understanding of themselves (including the self-awareness of their own and the understanding of the relationship between member countries), but also a clear judgments on the pattern of their own role in the future world (the subjective role and objective role).

In the decision-making process of today's international affairs, the BRICs member countries have played an essential role: China and Russia play an important role as permanent members of UN Security Council, Brazil and India are also playing an important international role in political life (such as on May 17, 2010, Brazil and Turkey reach the Iranian nuclear fuel exchange agreements, highlights Brazil's role in the international arena).

In the regard of the strategic consideration of the future international political and economic role and impact of the BRICs, by contrast, Brazil and Russia are more positive than China and India. Brazil has the minimal global influence compared with the other three countries, Brazil expect to have more "voice" in the international community, while have no conflict of interest with the other three countries, so Brazil can coordinate well between the interests of all countries; Russia strongly want to integrate into the West but cannot get due recognition, at the same time due to suffering more serious from financial crisis, Russia's status in the "Group of Eight" is not secure and can only participate in part of the dialogue, thence, Russia hopes to develop the BRICs into a stronger political and economic union in order to have weight in dialogue with the West. China is happy to see the consolidation of the tripartite dialogue between China, Russia and India, and the establishment of the more close quartet dialogue mechanism between China, Russia, India and Brazil, however, China's strategic consideration for the BRICs is limited to the development of a closer economic cooperation; on cooperation in the field involved in politics, China will analyze specific issues; China's expectations on the military cooperation between the BRICs is not high, at most limited to symbolic courtesy visits.

Therefore, on the whole, is a four-nation international dialogue and cooperation platform, when necessary, there will be a strong collaboration, but in the foreseeable future BRICs will not become a military alliance.

When dealing with cooperation with States or international organizations, its economic achievements, overall national strength and international status make China must consider from all aspects like their own long-term interests, core interests of the other side, and world theme of the times of peace and development: China is a member of the United Nations permanent, is one of the five nuclear states, China has become the world's second largest economy, is also proposed so-called "G2" or "Chimerica" [①] by American scholars, which means the U.S. global potential partners. To some extent, there is no doubt that China is a big country.

However, because of its large population and weak base, China's per capita GDP just exceed over 3000 dollars, economic development, improving people's livelihood is still a formidable task, thus, during the period of development opportunity in the two decades at the beginning of this century, many of the characteristics of China's economic development and China's current special situation doomed that China is still a developing country. Therefore, in this period, maintaining world peace and promoting world economic recovery and development, strengthening positive interaction between the world's major countries, creating a peaceful and stable external environment for China's reform and opening up are the fundamental task of China's foreign policy.

In addition, the rapid development of China and China's peaceful rise caused many of the suspicions and doubts in the world, while the "China threat theory" spread in many countries[②]. From this argument, we can see that China's peaceful rise face numerous resistances. With regards to this, in order to create a good surrounding and global environment for China's peaceful rise, it is necessary to consider the establishment of China's multi-level diplomacy. The author believes that: based on the Shanghai Cooperation Organization and the BRICs, establishing multi-level diplomacy in which China play as the key member.

As an important member of the BRICs, in a number of issues involved interest of China and the developing countries, China can combine together these countries to make their voices heard. China always adheres to an independent, non-aligned and peaceful foreign policy, but this does not impede China and other countries have one voice with some issues on which they have common interests, strengthen coordination within the framework in the "Group of 20", and safeguard their own and the general developing countries' interest. China and some developing countries and emerging countries have similar colonial history, common urgent desire of economic development and common interests on many issues, on most issues they held the same or similar position, and this

① "G2"is proposed by famous American economist Fred Bergsten in 2008, he suggested a conception that forming a group by China and the U.S to replace the old "G8", in order to solve the world economic problem together. The conception of "chimerica" is proposed by Professor Neil Ferguson of Harvard University in 2007.

② The author use "China threat" for key words, search onwww.google.com, results about 9,790,000 Articles.(searched on 2010.08.02).

is the basic need for China to actively cooperate with developing countries and emerging countries. At the same time, it also became a solid foundation for China to further develop good relations with emerging countries and developing countries represented by the BRICs.

Although not bordering with Brazil, but China's demand for Brazil's resources has made Brazil a close neighbor of China's economy. China and Brazil had established a "strategic partnership", China and Brazil summit and the "China-Brazil High-level Coordination and Cooperation Committee" have maintained good relations, the bilateral trade is increasing, the mutual investment is growing gradually, the economic interdependence between China and Brazil is rising. Brazil is China's largest trading partner in Latin America and 11th largest trading partner in the world, China has become Brazil's largest trading partner, largest export target country and the second largest source of imports.

Russia is China's largest neighbors, it has the longest border with China, in history, there have been many problems between the two countries, but thanks to the long-term version of the leaders of the two countries, the Sino-Russian relations have move forward a couple of steps in two decades, resolved the border issue between the two countries by treaty, established a " the twenty-first century strategic partnership", signed the "Sino-Russian Good-Neighborly Friendship and Cooperation Treaty", formulated "The People's Republic of China Northeast regional and the Russian Federation Far East and East Siberia regional cooperation Plan ", all these actions have laid a solid foundation for the Sino-Russian Friendship and Cooperation.

India has the largest population among our neighboring countries, in the border disputes have been occurred between China and India in the history, and India gave an excuse of China's factors for their nuclear tests[①], to some extent, China's rapid development has also made India feel under pressure. The West countries have also been interested in comparing China's development with India's. Currently China and India have established a "peace and prosperity for the strategic cooperative partnership", "ten strategies" have been established to deepen the strategic partnership between the two countries; China is India's second largest trading partner, India is China's ninth largest trading partner, in addition to the BRICs close ties and cooperation, India and China maintain close communication and cooperation ,also in China, India and Russia tripartite cooperation, the five developing countries, "the basis four countries", the Doha Round

① India had conducted three nuclear tests in May 1998, statement of the India's Ministry of Foreign Affairs on May 11, 1998 has been implied, it claimed that India's nuclear test was due to "serious concerns on India's surrounding nuclear environment". Indian Defense Minister George Fernandes openly declared when interviewed with the media in the May 3, "China is the number one threat", claimed that its nuclear tests is a response to China's "threat".

negotiations.

Based on the major differences of value, the BRICs (Brazil, Russia, India and China) are seeking ways of development which are radically different from the development mode of the western countries (lead by the U.S.) yet can fulfill the very needs of themselves. Because the lack of independent strength to develop alone on the global configuration of economy and politics, uniting each other to gain a better leverage on the affairs of decision-making and the right to express distinct opinions about the way of development to the western countries seems to be the interior momentum of cooperation between the BRICs. "Different social systems can be tolerated, different development modes can cooperate, different histories can draw on the experiences of each others, and different cultures can communicate." Today the BRICs are all facing the same challenges of maintaining the growth of economy along with improving the living standards of their own citizens. Thus, they hold same or similar stands on some of the global affairs. Strengthening and deepening the mutual beneficial cooperation between each other becomes the inclination of their foreign affairs. Those similarities are the solid foundations of their collaborations.

We hold a view that in the forming new international political and economic order, the roles of the BRICs will be as follows:

The representatives of developing countries

In a western oriented international political and economic order, the BRICs will stand out and speak as the voice of developing countries and emerging powers, to try to make their own voices to be heard by the west and ensure their own interests unharmed.

Playing the role of "BRICsK" in the global economy

According to a research conducted by Goldman Sachs, the BRICs will definitely become the main engine of global economy within a couple of decades, and the fraction of global economic growth which can be attributed to the contribution of theirs will grow steadily. During the time when most of the rich nations were struggling with the overwhelming impact of economic recession, the BRICs were still able to maintain their stable economic growth due to the structural reformation of global economy which had made the emerging powers benefited from the constant increase in their domestic demands. With 26% of land area and 42% of global population at their own hands, at least to some degree the development of the BRICs also means the big leap forward of almost half of the global population. Hence the continuous increase of global economy will gain a more concrete foundation once the "BRICsK" of the global economy— the BRICs thrive.

The coordinator between the nations who have different interests

Several international summits during the aftermath of the economic recession have reflected a variety of voices and demands between nations. Having been the influential regional powers of their own continents (including Asia, Europe and Latin America), the

BRICs were able to muster enough strength and leverage to coordinate between different countries. Therefore the success of those international summits could not have achieved if there weren't for the exceptional coordination of the BRICs. The BRICs have become the coordinator between different economic entities.

The active advocates of the new international financial order

The BRICs have already declared their stands over the issues of global economic, currency and financial supervision systems that they are the determined proposers of new international financial order. And that have earned unmatched endorsement and reputation among the Third World nations which cover the majority of the world population and land area. The BRICs have become the proposer of the new international economic order.

The pushers of global multi-polarization

As burgeoning economic entities, the BRICs are becoming more and more essential powers in the global community as well. Having significant impacts on the international political configuration, the very existence of theirs are about to accelerate the formation of global multi-polarization. During the Yekaterinburg Summit the president of Russia, Dmitry Medvedev had called on the BRICs to help creating a fairer and multi-polarized world together. There were western media said that the BRICs are not merely significant economic entities but the main challengers of the existed international power configuration.

Besides, the role of China has its own characteristics which can be easily distinguished from other BRICs nations due to its unique development mode:

The engine of global economic recovery and development

The recovery from the devastating economic recession is bound to be a slow process. Yet as the country with the largest population and second largest economy, China have managed to maintain a relatively fast economic growth in a relatively long period which merely itself is enough to be a significant contribution to the stability and recovery of the global economy. In the current situation where other economic entities in the world are still struggling for survival during the aftermath of the recession, the awakening and thriving of a market that has a population of 1.3 billion means there is still hope for the recovery and even further expansion of the global economy. China is becoming one of the deciding powers of the development of global economy without self-awareness.

A China mode

As one of the typical non-western nations, China's 30-year-long "economic miracle" has drawn countless spotlights from all over the world. Despite still facing some problems such as adjusting the economic structure and altering the pattern of economic growth, the accomplishments of China have numerous impacts not only inside China but also on the whole world. The living standard of the 1.3 billion people has been increased by a large margin. And China itself has become the paragon of non-western development mode. An invaluable example has also been set for the developing countries who are still seeking ways of development which fit their own needs.

The representative of the creditor nations of us dollar assets

Most of the nations in the world have reserve assets that are in the forms of us dollars due to the supremacy of us dollar. Because of its largest us dollar foreign currency reserve and bond in held, China has become the representative of the benefits of us dollar creditor nations. Paying special attention to the maintenance of value of its dollar assets, China has repeatedly requested America to maintain the value of other countries' dollar assets. These are the actions of responsibility not only for the benefits of China itself but also for the interests of other countries who have dollar assets in held.

Conclusion

It is a historic event that the BRICs hold the summit meeting –which means nearly half people of the world get together in order to get a greener and more stable development of the economic and political. After the institutionalization of the BRICs, the summit meeting suggests that with the emerging of the organization, which will leads to a series of positive phenomenon to the politics and economy of the world.

Although the meeting may not bring out some specific measures, but the most critical significance is to put the linkage mechanism between the four countries into operation. Through political and diplomatic efforts of the four countries, the second summit meeting shows the desire of the four countries to strengthen international cooperation and develop closer relations. Promoting the international political and economic diversification of configuration, maintaining the rapid recovery of the world economy to against the trade protectionism, Concerning for the environment and the other global problems are the foundation of the corporation of four countries, and they are also the bond to strengthen the cooperation. Especially in the background of current international financial crisis, cooperation is particularly important to the four countries. This will not only benefit the four countries, but also in line with the international community's common expectations and interests and contribute to the early recovery of world economy. Conversation and cooperation between the BRICs not only meets the common interests of the emerging economies and the developing countries, but also to build a lasting peace, co-prosperity and harmonious world.

We are convinced that through the cooperation of the four countries, the BRICs will become a real "BRICsK" of the world economy and make a greater contribution to the better development of the world.

The Institutionalization of BRICs and China's Role

— Multilateral Cooperation with Orientation

Wang Junsheng *

After the end of the Cold War, international structure has experienced enormous changes, which include a group of emerging economies rise rapidly and simultaneously, and so called BRICs countries, namely, Brazil, Russia, India and China, are the best representatives. Nearly 60 percent of the total increase in world output in 2000–2008 took place in developing and transitional countries, half of which occurred in the BRICs①. The BRICs' rising promoted the position of the whole developing world. Comparing with the indifferent attitude in past, developed countries have to make some adjustments and concessions in global issues, particularly in some areas related to the core interests of developing countries. The impact of BRICs on international situation and even the whole post-Cold-War international relations is still ongoing. However, most of the current available researches mainly started from economic or financial perspectives, but rarely viewed from the perspective of international relations. Thus, this paper will explore BRICs' mechanism and China's role, and try to use the concept of "multilateral cooperation with orientation" to draw a conclusion. The following part will elaborate this concept through specific cases.

Core topics and background analyzing

In order to better understanding BRICs' future and China's role, it is necessary to review

---

* Wang Junsheng, assistant research fellow, the Institute of Latin American Studies, Chinese Academy of Social Sciences.

① As for this, many western scholars were shocked and describe it as 'the rise of the rest'. See Fareed Zakaria, *The Post-American World* (New York: W.W. Norton & Co., 2009). Parag Khanna, *The Second World: Empires and Influence in the New Global Order* (New York: Random House, 2008).

and summarize the characteristics of the four-country cooperation. There are so many clear differences among BRICs, the driving forces for their closer multilateral cooperation are numerous and complicated. Only give a simply list cannot grasp the essence. Therefore, this paper presents the concept of "orientation", mainly refers to the primary driving forces of multilateral cooperation, which reflect the prior option in foreign policy making.

It is impossible to have a deep analysis of BRICs' cooperation without considering the background of post-Cold War, when huge transformation happened. Firstly, the collapse of Soviet Union made the superpower status of United States step forward deeply. In spite of some adjustments, the essence of relations between Europe and United States remains the same. Led by the US, NATO continued to implement its global strategy while EU tried every means to push forward eastward expansion. During the Cold War, Soviet Union can effectively limit the action of the US-led Western camp to some extent. However, a prominent feature of the international relations in the post-cold war era is, the action of western camp dominated by US can hardly be effectively restricted. Under this background, the United States and its NATO allies always ignored the authority of UN and launched Kosovo war, Iraqi war, and Afghanistan war. As for the relationship between US and China, some unpleasant connections have been taken place successively, such as the Yinhe incident, the bombing of the Chinese Embassy in Belgrade, and the South China Sea incident. Among which, America's behavior violated the international law, but haven't been punished, because it always in dominating place.

Secondly, globalization is going forward deeply and comprehensively. Comparing with the two separate camps during the Cold War, the world after cold war is undergoing an all-round globalization. One reason is the political barrier made by the two camps has been removed because of the collapse of Soviet Union, and another is the development of technology. Since then, things happened in United States, Europe, Asia, Latin American, and Africa, are totally be involved into the globalization process. The global village characterized by interdependent was formed in human history at the first time. On the one hand, domestic politics "internationalized", international politics "nationalized", a more mature and enduring international civil society initially formed; on the other hand, regional and global issues began to transcend countries' border, and the destiny of humankind is more interlinked. "Co-management" has become a more rational option. Even the superpower United States sometimes has to co-manage with other small countries while facing the global environmental degradation, preventing the proliferation of nuclear arms, striving against poverty, so on and so forth.

Finally, the end of the cold war catered to the general interests of mankind, and most of countries enhanced their independence as well as improved their international status. Despite many unfair areas still existed in current international system, such as in the international financial system and the international energy distribution system, etc. However, the future for developing countries is still promising as long as they improve international status through economic development and make international system fairer through gradual reform. Therefore, they generally don't follow antagonistic, but cooperative model to connect with Europe and the United States.

The closer cooperation among BRICs happened in this context. The four countries hold 26 percent of world territory, 25 percent of the world population, and 15 percent of the gross world product. Among the world top 20 energy companies, 35 percent from the BRIC countries, and among the world 20 largest mining companies, the BRIC countries accounted for 20 percent[①]. As for foreign exchange reserves, the BRIC countries possessed 3 trillion US dollars, accounted for more than 40 percent of the world reserves. They are the four largest economies outside the OECD. Excepted Russia, they achieved sustainable growth contrasting with other countries during the great recession. Because of this, the BRICs attracted much attention from the world when they tried to unite together. Thanks to the collective efforts of the four countries on September 2009, the Group of Twenty (G20) summit in Pittsburgh closed with a great advancement, namely, 3 percent of the voting rights of the IMF and 5 percent voting rights of the World Bank were redistributed to emerging and developing economies. In fact, although each country plays an important role in the international community, they are not strong enough to win while competing with United States respectively. Therefore, BRICs, as one of the most eye-catching coalition, the institutionalization is crucial for their rights fighting, as well as for the evolution of the international structure.

Review on the institutionalization of BRICs

The institutionalization of BRICs is a process of gradual development. The term "institutionalization" means to make certain dialogue pattern in advance, and to negotiate a series of norms, regulations, and standards, etc, namely, to form a pattern of solving problems. Dealing with international relations as same as that of domestic issues, the better way is to create a mechanism arrangement. On the one hand, this daily mechanism is essential for the prevention of crisis out of control which may cause complicated issues. On the other hand, we can use this mechanism to promote a better understanding of the intentions, principles, and information of other members through discussions, debates, and talks in every regular meeting. Also in this process, intentions and principles of each member coordinate together, and bring the possibility

---

① Yan Wang, "Whether the BRICs Countries Can Impulse the World Economic Structure under the Background of Financial Crisis?," *Manager*, Volume 16, 2009, p.58.

for substantive cooperation.

The coalition of BRICs constructed a general identity from international society, the perception of the outside world, in turn, strengthened the collective identity of the four countries. In 2005, G7 finance ministers meeting in London invited the BRICs to attend for the first time. In 2006, as BRICsks mania gathered momentum, the four governments, at the initiative of former Russian President Vladimir Putin, collectively lifted themselves from the pages of investment reports to hold their first foreign ministers' meeting on the sidelines of the annual UN General Assembly session. After a second meeting of the four foreign ministers in New York in September 2007, the BRICsks launched a consultative process at the level of deputy foreign ministers to foster regular contacts and multilateral diplomacy. By 2008 the four BRICsks foreign ministers, and on a different track the finance ministers, hold meetings in Russia Yekaterinburg, to discuss common approaches to international problems, including the global financial crisis, which is also the first time BRICsk countries hold meeting outside the framework of the UN. Again at Russia's initiative, the four BRICs heads of state met in July on the sidelines of the G8 (the G7 plus Russia) summit in Japan and issued a joint statement, and plans were laid for a formal summit to be held in the Yekaterinburg, Russia in June 2009①.

So, on June 16, 2009, BRICsks' head held an inaugural summit in Yekaterinburg, which includes four activities: small-scale talks, a wide range of talks, joint press conferences and working dinner. This summit issued "Joint Statement of the BRICsk Countries' leaders Yekaterinburg, Russia", which mainly covers the following items. (1) We stress the central role played by the G20 Summits in dealing with the financial crisis. (2) We are committed to advance the reform of international financial institutions, so as to reflect changes in the world economy. We also believe that there is a strong need for a stable, predictable and more diversified international monetary system. (3) We call upon all parties to work together to improve the international trade and investment environment. We urge the international community to keep the multilateral trading system stable, curb trade protectionism, and push for comprehensive and balanced results of the WTO's Doha Development Agenda.(4)The implementation of the concept of sustainable development, and we stand ready for a constructive dialogue on how to deal with climate change.(5)We stand for strengthening coordination and cooperation among states in the energy field, in an effort to decreasing uncertainty and ensuring stability and sustainability.(6)we reaffirm the need for a comprehensive reform of the UN with a view to making it more efficient so that it can deal with today's global

① Cynthia Roberts, "Challengers or Stakeholders? BRICs and the Liberal World Order," *Polity (2010)* 42,pp. 1–13. See http://www.palgrave-journals.com/polity/journal/v42/n1/full/pol200920a.html.

challenges more effectively.(7)We reaffirm to advance cooperation among our countries in science and education.(8)Russia, India and China welcome the kind invitation of Brazil to host the next BRICs summit in 2010①.

The discussion sphere is quite wide. Due to the background of this summit taking place is US dollar's position seriously questioned and developing countries collectively seek to more say, so this summit has attracted more attentions. One paper in Singapore's "Lianhe Zaobao" says this summit represents these four countries are designing the world new order in the post crisis era. Russia president Dmitry Medvedev himself called this meeting as "the epicenter of world politics".

Although these remarks somewhat exaggerated, and more rhetoric than substance②, people really come to realize the possibility that co-manage international challenges through four countries cooperation from this summit. Among these, there are two points particularly deserve more attention. (1) The first summit issued "joint statement" by four state head, which indicates BRICsk countries have "common orientation" in political level, since joint statement reflects the consensus of all parties and can give some restriction to practical action. (2) Joint Statement confirmed next summit will be held in Brazil, which means BRICsks develop toward the direction of the summit institutionalize.

According to the arrangement in advance, the second BRICsk countries' head summit was held in Brazil capital Brazilian on the April 15, 2010, and issued "The Joint Statement of BRICs Group Summit Brasilia". The sphere that items covered in this joint statement is almost as same as Yekaterinburg summit, such as world economic and financial situation, the Group of Twenty affairs, international financial institutions reform, climate change, trade and economic cooperation, and etc. But the following items should be given more attention. In the interest of promoting international economic stability, we have asked our Finance Ministers and Central Bank Governors to look into regional monetary arrangements and discuss modalities of cooperation between our countries in this area. In order to facilitate trade and investment, we will study feasibilities of monetary cooperation, including local currency trade settlement arrangement between our countries. We express our satisfaction with the Meeting of Ministers of Agriculture and Agrarian Development in Moscow, where they discussed ways of promoting quadripartite cooperation, with particular attention to family farming. We are convinced that this will contribute towards global food production and food security. We welcome their decision to create an agricultural information base system of the BRICs countries, to develop a strategy for ensuring access to food for vulnerable population, to reduce

① Joint Statement of the BRICs Countries' leaders Ekaterinburg, Russia, 16 June 2009, see http://www2.mre.gov.br/dibas/BRICs_Joint_Statement_I_Summit.pdf.

② "BRICs, Emerging Markets and the World Economy," Jun 18th 2009, From *The Economist* print edition. See http://www.absolutbrazil.info/article-BRICs-emerging-markets-and-the-world-economy/.

the negative impact of climate change on food security, and to enhance agriculture technology cooperation and innovation.We welcome the following sector initiatives aimed at strengthening cooperation among our countries: (1) the first Meeting of Ministers of Agriculture and Agrarian Development; (2) the Meetings of Ministers of Finance and Governors of Central Banks; (3) the Meetings of High Representatives for Security Issues; (4) the I Exchange Program for Magistrates and Judges, of BRICs countries, held in March 2010 in Brazil following the signature in 2009 of the Protocol of Intent among the BRICs countries' Supreme Courts; (5) the first Meeting of Development Banks; (6) the first Meeting of the Heads of the National Statistical Institutions; (7) the Conference of Competition Authorities; (8) the first Meeting of Cooperatives; (9) the first Business Forum; (10) the Conference of think tanks. Brazil, Russia and India appreciate the offer of China to host the III BRICs Summit in 2011①.

From the agenda discussed in the second summit, we really can see the cooperation among BRICsk countries is closer with the substantial issues, the field of cooperation is further deepening and progressive refinement, and the foundation of cooperation is gradually tamped②. For instance, the summit in Yekaterinburg put forward abstractly that "we should build more stable and more diversified international monetary system", but Brasilia' summit put forward that "we will study feasibilities of monetary cooperation, including local currency trade settlement arrangement between our countries", which is more specific. For another example, the cooperative memos signed in the second summit by Russia foreign economic bank, China state development bank, Brazil national social and economic development bank, and India export and import bank, will gradually drive BRICsk countries build real inter-bank system, which also took the first step for providing financial support for BRICsk countries' investment with each other. Just like Chairman Hu Jintao said in Brasilia summit speech, "our four countries' dialogue and cooperation contents gradually enrich, cooperation level gradually expends, and achievements consistently emerge" ③. At the same time, this Joint Statement confirmed next summit will be held in Beijing on 2011, which makes the summit more predictable, and constant

---

① "The Joint Statement of BRICs Group Summit Brasilia," April 16, 2010, see http://www.indonesia.mid.ru/press/155_e.html.

② Comparing to the period before Brasilia summit, the international society has stronger anticipation in BRICs' challenge to the existing international financial order before the Yekaterinburg summit, such as the Big Four Cooperate to challenge US dollar, or set up ultra-sovereign currency, etc. To some extent, the reaction of international society reflected the four countries' increasingly pragmatic attitude on the institutionalization of BRICs.

③ "Cooperation and Openness for Mutual Benefit and Win-Win Progress,"remarks at the BRICs Summit, by Hu Jintao, President of the People's Republic of China, Brasilia, 16 April 2010, See http://www.fmprc.gov.cn/chn/pds/ziliao/zyjh/t682096.htm.

meeting and dialogue more possible①. Basing on this summit, all parties' understanding of their own identity, preference and interest will be gradually influenced, and thus be propitious to mold group identity and mutual consciousness. Finally, Substantial Cooperation will be realized.

To sum up, the development of four countries cooperation from invited collectively by G7 to initially held head summit, in which every step not only promoted this cooperation more substantial, but also more institutionalized. If we take BRICsk group like an arranged marriage by international public opinion and organizations (such as Goldman Sachs, etc) before Yekaterinburg summit held, then Yekaterinburg summit made this concept more visualized and practical, and Brasilia summit push it more institutionalized. As for the driving forces that push BRICsk countries into multilateral cooperation and institutionalized direction, is also called orientation in this paper, just like Robert Keohane and Henry Kissinger said, for example, all countries must have national interests which overlap, creating mutual benefits in exchange for cooperative effort②. Kenneth Waltz and John Mearsheimer both also establish that while overlapping national interests may assist in the establishment of cooperation, without strong incentives to continue, divergent or competing interests among members will probably cause countries to break off cooperation③.

Multilateral cooperation with orientation

If analyze the orientation of four countries multilateral cooperation, we must explore the primary agenda in four countries foreign policy making. As for Brazil, since 90s of 20th century, economy developed very rapid, the relation with neighbor countries such as Argentina improved, and the dependence on the US economy is also declined. Therefore, Brazil began to pursue more diversified diplomacy with the aim to reflect the influence and play the role as a regional power, while constantly developed the stable traditional relations with United States and European countries. Brazil former president Cardoso said, "In this multi-polar world, Brazil should be one polar", "Brazil is one of the world major powers, we will implement a more aggressive foreign policy, and Brazil

① In fact, the G20 head summit has already institutionalized, so it is hard to please all. The developed countries often coordinated points in advance, however, this action forced the emerging economies to stand together to protect their common interests, which also indirectly promote the normalization of the BRICs head summit.

② See Robert Keohane, *International Institutions and State Power* (Boulder, Colo.: Westview Press, 1989), p. 138, and Henry Kissinger, *Does America Need a Foreign Policy?* (New York: Touchstone, 2001), pp. 152-53.

③ See Kenneth Waltz, *Theory of International Politics* (Reading, Mass.: Addison-Wesley Publishing Company, 1979), p. 106, and John Mearsheimer, *The Tragedy of Great Power Politics* (New York: W. W. Norton, 2001), p. 373.

shouldn't be ignored when major international decision be made". Lula administration extended and developed this diplomatic strategy, but gave more emphasis on establishing ties with developing countries, even to build potential bloc①. To this end, Lula actively participated in "G8 +5" dialogue, proposed the establishment of "India - Brazil - South Africa Forum", and actively promoted coordination and cooperation among developing countries. Generally speaking, Brazil has two priorities for pursuing the strategy of major power diplomacy. One priority is to develop friendly, good-neighborly relations with South American countries. The other priority is to develop the relations with new emerging developing powers. The former one is foundation and starting point of this strategy, Brazil want play the leader role, while the latter one is the main political strength Brazil need to rely on in pursuing major power status②.

As for India, big power identity deeply rooted in its history. Becoming a major power with full of sound and color was put forward by India first Prime Minister Nehru, which faithfully expressed Indian political elite's political ideology and political aspiration. This goal didn't change for party politics, and became "India's national consciousness" ③. In recent years, India's manufacture achievement is becoming the focus of world attention, and information technology industry is also taking off. In the diplomatic arena, the relations with neighbor countries entered in the best era, and the other foreign relations also have been greatly improved. India becomes more and more confident for being a critical factor to build a new future international order, and thinks it is much visible for being a major power④.Generally speaking, there are three priorities for India foreign policy making. Firstly, India foreign policy tends to emphasize balance of power, actively moves in different countries, in order to create favorable external environment for domestic development⑤. Secondly, India gave more attention to practical diplomacy, not only valued hooking in and stabilizing neighbor countries through using regional cooperation association in South Asia, but also actively involved in the cooperation among developing countries, so as to enhancing trust, gaining resource, and win support. Meanwhile, India emphasized to obtain the support from major powers in pursuing process of great power renaissance. Thirdly, India gave more and more emphasis on playing big role in international affairs, establishing confident and independent international image, and expanding international influence consciously.

---

① Zhihua Wu, "Brazil's Regional Power Diplomacy," *Journal of Latin America Studies*, Volume 4, 2005, pp. 9, 11, 15.

② Zhihua Wu, "Brazil's Regional Power Diplomacy," *Journal of Latin America Studies*, Volume 4, 2005, pp. 9.

③ Shihai Sun, "Indian Diplomacy will be more Solid," *Global Times*,17 May 2004.

④ Jiali Ma, "the Foreign Policy of India," *Peace and Development*, Volume 2, 2006, pp.34-35.

⑤ Xiangyu Zeng, "On the Duality of Indian Foreign Policy," *South Asian Studies Quarterly*, Volume 2, 2005, p. 94.

In modern times, Russia has been played a major role on the international stage, even became one superpower (with United States) as long as half of century since the end of Second World War. After the collapse of Soviet Union, just as Russia former president Vladimir Putin said, "Russia is in the most difficult period. It even can be said that Russia for the first time may become the second or third level country in international stage in recent 200-300 years" ①. Therefore, while inherited the idea of world should be multi-polar put forward by Boris Yeltsin, Putin administration gave more emphasis on pursuing major power position, and against the monopole hegemony of US②. Medvedev is continually executing Putin's roadmap of foreign policy, emphasized that "it is totally illusion if one country want to be the world government", and "currently world management system are not suitable to face current challenges, which should be changed"③.In order to regain major power status, Russia foreign policy has three priorities. The first priority is to develop relations with neighbor countries, and CIS (Commonwealth of Independent States) is the first priority. The second priority is to take all-round and multi-polar balance foreign policy, which based on pragmatism as core factor. Thirdly, domestic goals are given more priority than international goals unconditionally④.

Let's look at china's situation lastly. China has been a major power since ancient times, but came to decline for more than one century with the development of industrial Revolution in which China didn't catch up. Since the establishment of PRC in 1949, particularly the reform and open policy executed in 1978, China's many development indexes rapidly increased. Take financial sector as example, in five years ago, the top 10 largest banks in market value mainly belong to United States and European countries, but now two China's banks are top 5, which include Industrial and Commercial Bank of China (the market value is 250.2 billion U.S. dollars) and China Construction Bank (the market value is 190.9 billion U.S. dollars) ⑤. In fact, these two banks were still facing the crisis of survival, so we can imagine how rapid China developed. China currently is now the world's largest suppliers of financial capital, the savings available for investment reach 2 trillion U.S. dollars, but in recent 150 years, United States is the world's largest suppliers of financial

---

① Hongye Bi, "A Review on Russian Diplomacy in the Period of Post Cold War," *Northeast Asian Forum,* Volume 7, 2009, p.199.

② Zhao Qu, "A Review on Reinspire *Russia: Putin's Foreign Strategy and Diplomatic Policy,*" *Studies of Russia, Middle Asia and Eastern Europe,* Volume 1, 2009, p.90.

③ Yujun Feng, "Rising Strongly, Financial Crisis and the Adjustment of Russian Foreign Policy," *Contemporary World,* Volume 3, 2009, p.17.

④ See Wei Wang, "The Diplomatic Decision of Medvedev," *Contemporary World,* Volume 6, 2008, p.16; "A Review on Russian Diplomacy in the Period of Post Cold War," *Northeast Asian Forum,* Volume 7, 2009, p.199; Guilin Liu, "The Diplomatic Trend after the Russia Election and the Sino-Russia Relation, " *International Information,* Volume 2, 2008, p.39.

⑤ [Russia] Aleksandar. ·Koksharov, "Hegemony without Enthusiasm," *Experts* (Russia), 29 March 2010.

capital. The GDP of US and Japan are 15 times and 8 times respectively that of China in 1990.But in 2009, the former number is no more than 3 times, and is very close with Japan's. The military spending of US and Russia are 35 times and 13 times respectively that of China in 1990. But in 2008, this US military spending is 8 times that of China. In contrary, China's military spending has surpassed Russia, as same as 2 times, and ranks the second in the world. If take the index such as world trade, foreign direct investment and etc as example, we still can get the same result. Meanwhile, from the perspective of soft power to see, such as the psychology of citizen and international recognition, we also can find this rising trend①. Therefore, to realize the great rejuvenation of Chinese nation, and develop a world power, is no longer a dream or a slogan, but is the goal Chinese people are striving for step by step. To sum up, China has two priorities in foreign policy making. One is to create favorable international environment for domestic economy development, namely use or construct the opportunities in this important strategic period in support of domestic development. The other one is to build more responsible major power image in international community with the strength increase and status rise, such as six-party talks in resolving North Korea nuclear issue.

Thus it can be seen BRICsk countries foreign policy priorities which overlap is to strengthen or consolidate the regional or international status, and strive for more say and more dominant right in international affairs. In order to fulfill this priority, BRICsk countries have two common orientations. (1) Due to every single country is not strong enough to overthrow the current international system, so these four countries tend to reform it through joint efforts②. For example, BRICsk countries all consider the root that the current financial crisis happened lie in the current unfair international economical and financial system and it should be reformed, but none is likely to match this goal, at last cooperate with each other becomes the best choice. As for this, Brazil President Lula said in 2008, Brazil should keep close cooperation, even establish united front, with Russia, India and China which have more foreign exchange reserves, so that exert greater influence③. In fact, the strongest area of convergence among the BRICsks in two summits is their common aspiration for greater representation and leadership positions in international economic and financial institutions.(2) Four countries all tend to create favorable situation for domestic economic development trough jointly cooperation,

① See Junsheng Wang, "World Power and Strategic Environment: New Subject of China's International Role," *Modern International Relation*, Volume 4, 2010, p.38-45.

② Relative Theoretical Analysis see John Mearsheimer, *The Tragedy of Great Power Politics* (New York: W. W. Norton, 2001): 41. Wohlforth, "The Stability of a Unipolar World." See also Amitav Acharya, "The Emerging Regional Architecture of World Politics," *World Politics* 59 (July 2007),pp.629–52.

③ Yunpeng Wang, "The Direction of the BRICs under the Financial Crisis," *Science and Technology Innovation Herald*, Volume 11, 2009, P.175.

so that build the stable foundation for playing big role in international stage. For these "orientations" BRICsk countries made closer cooperation, even with characteristics that institutionalized. Through jointly cooperation, BRICsk countries really have objective conditions to realize these orientations. On the one hand, four countries have similar standpoints on many international and regional issues, for instance, on the reform of current international economic and financial system, as well as on reducing the instabilities of U.S. dollar. On the other hand, four countries also have close relations on international trade. In past 9 years, the trade among BRICsk countries has increased 9 times, but only 1 time increased in global international trade. Meanwhile, four countries didn't simply copy "Washington Consensus" or other Consensus, but insist on their own national traditions and national characteristics.

For these reasons bilateral cooperation among BRICsk countries is not only very active such as Sino-Russia, Russia-India, Sino-Brazil, but trilateral cooperation among three Asia region countries China, Russia, and India also already initiated. As early as the middle of 1990s, the then-premier of Russia Yevgeny Primakov proposed the concept of "strategic triangle" construction among Beijing, New Delhi, and Moscow for the first time①. In 2002, these three countries' foreign ministers began to hold informal meeting in UN. In 2006, three foreign ministers hold meeting in Vladivostok of Russia, the first time in the occasion out of UN. Meanwhile, three state heads hold meeting when they participated in G8 summit, which confirmed the idea and will for enhancing three countries cooperation at the highest level of state leaders. This also laid the foundation for BRICsk countries cooperation.

It must be given notice, although the noun of BRICsks created and sensationalized in 10 years, these four countries summit inaugurated in 2009 also from the need that facing financial crisis. The reason BRICsks summit can happen because the growing insecurity related to the current crisis, and the BRICsks are a product of the great recession, said Masha Lipman, a political analyst at the Carnegie Center in Moscow②. Then, under the background that global economic situation are improved and gradually get out of recession, if these "orientations" that making four countries cooperation institutionalized will disappear? What prospects it will be?

The prospect and route of further institutionalization

The BRICsk countries multilateral cooperation resulted in these "orientations" is not

① China worry this act will be mistook by America to form anti-US alliance, therefore, the attitude is negative. See Xuetong Ya, "International Environment and Diplomatic Thinking," *Contemporary International Relations*, Volume 8, 1999, p. 11.

② Lyubov Pronina and Alex Nicholson, "BRICs May Buy Each Other's Bonds in Shift From Dollar," see http://www.bloomberg.com/apps/news?pid=20601086&sid=aSdhVkf.e1RY.

only the consequence of interaction between four countries practical diplomacy and international situation, and it also can be used to analyze the prospect and route of further cooperation institutionalized. From historic practice to see, the mechanism of international cooperation platform has two models: EU model and APEC model. EU model has strong restriction on member states activity through different treaties, and also has standing body, with the destination of internal integration and external one voice. But APEC model has no restricted treaty and no standing body, let alone internal integration and external one voice. Its function mainly promoting member states take according responsibility in economic or moral fields through jointly promises and statements, based on the principles of volunteer and consensus, then expend the new cooperation fields through constant dialogue①. Former model also includes ASEAN and other many regional integration mechanisms, while latter model includes G8 and triangle dialogue among China, Japan, and South Korea, etc. It must be noted that, EU model is more practical, while APEC model usually just discuss principles. But the former model have some necessary preconditions, including member states should have consensus political vision, powerful driving forces, high homogeneity(such as historical and cultural factors, etc) , and they usually from the same region.

As for BRICsk countries, in addition to the common orientations mentioned above, the homogeneity is quite low. They are very different in national conditions, history, political and economic system, and culture. Two of them located in Asia, one straddles Europe and Asia, and the other one in South America. Moreover, Europe Model also needs member states have similar perception or definition towards friends and enemies, as well as have good bilateral relations. The BRICsk countries also don't match these. They are not facing a common security threat, as Europe. Russia take US as a strategic rival, but India take US as a potential ally. Although China's relation with Brazil getting closer, it has been complicated by security tensions with India②, even with Russia③. Beijing and Moscow are not enthusiastic about Brazil and India's push to broaden the United Nations Security Council. Besides these, there are also many differences on climate, trade,

---

① "BRICs Summit End Quickly, Leaders Reassemble in China the Next Year," Guangzhou Daily, 04/17/2010. See http://shandong.chinadaily.com.cn/hqcj/zgjj/2010-04-17/content_171426_3.html.

② Jing-dong Yuan, "The Dragon and the Elephant: Chinese-Indian Relations in the 21st Century," *Washington Quarterly* 30 (Summer 2007), pp.131-44; and John W. Garver, "China's Influence in Central and South Asia: Is It Increasing?" in *Power Shift: China and Asia's New Dynamics*, David Shambaugh, ed., (Berkeley: University of California Press, 2005), pp.205-227.

③ Although the head dialogue regularly held, but the cognition of taking opposite party as counterworkers reappeared at times, especially at the military level. Actually, there are many problems left between china and Russia need to be solved. For instance, Russia reduced the weapon sales to China; Chinese emigration to Far East area; the competition of Central Asia region's influence; the opinion divergence in Shanghai Cooperation Organization, and the Russian people's negative impression of China.

currency issues, even the attitude towards US dollars. As the largest creditor, China still approves (even supports) dollar dominance. But as for Russia and Brazil foreign exchange reserves, US dollars just accounted for 30%, so they are very active to promote reducing dependence on the US dollar.

Meanwhile, due to BRICsks' mechanism represents the trend that developing countries pursuing more say, which essence is to surpass the dominant position in international financial affairs by western countries, then whether these diplomacy "orientations" that drive four countries into cooperation exceed their dependence with western countries, particularly with US. The answer is no. Since China took reform and open policy and integrated comprehensively into current international system, highly interdependent relations built between China and US, such as US dollar stability[①], cross Taiwan strait issues, Korea peninsular issues, and etc. Honeymoon period between India and US just began, "in India's strategic adjustment with major power relations, US is the first priority"[②]. Therefore, to build high level institutionalized alliance at the expense of the mutual trust with US doesn't match New Delhi's foreign strategy. Meanwhile, considering the close economic and geopolitical connection between Latin America and US, Brazil obviously will not to build alliance with other BRICsk three countries at the expense of deteriorating relations with US. On April 12, just three days before the Brasilia BRICsk summit held, Brazil and the United States signed a bilateral defense agreement in Washington[③], DC, the first between both countries since 1977, which is the best footnote for Brazil's diplomatic strategy. As for Russia's foreign policy, the majority of Russians think Russia can't realize its core interest just through opposing US, and instead, they think these interests just can be realized effectively at the active support of US[④]. Medvedev pointed out before the first BRICs summit held, "to create a super-sovereign reserve currency will not shake the position of US dollar's reserve currency", through this declaration to appease US, the unrelated part of BRICsk, also represents Moscow is very prudent on building the new mechanism which may challenge US. In short, four countries cooperation also has another orientation, each of the BRICsks tends to avoid using their collaboration as a means to challenge the United States or overthrow the Western order.

In fact, United States also has the ability to set up effective barriers for BRICsks further

① Taking the foreign exchange reserve as an example, only Chinese leaders dare to undertake the pressure of the wealth accumulated by hard work shrinking continuously because of the depreciation of US dollars. Even under this tough circumstance, China still willing to invest 500 billion dollars to purchase the bond of IMF to maintain the stability of US dollars.

② Yongnian Wu, "On the Adjustment of Indian Diplomatic Strategy in the Beginning of 21th Century," *Studies of South Asian*, Volume 2, 2004, P.19.

③ M auricio Cárdenas,"Brazil and the United States: A New Beginning?" See http://www.brookings.edu/opinions/2010/0419_us_brazil_cardenas.aspx.

④ Wei Wang, "The Diplomatic Decision of Medvedev," *Contemporary World*, Volume 6, 2008, p.19.

institutionalized. Nowadays, the combined total GDP of BRICsk countries is just as same as about 60% that of US, and per capital GDP is just 8% that of US①. It seems that BRICsk countries are very clear for this. For instance, in two summits joint statement, they both stressed BRICsk countries cooperation should be made under the framework of G20, in which US and European countries still take the leading role②. This shows these orientations that driving four countries into cooperation are not enough to build EU model mechanism. "Don't expect the BRICsks to make bombastic or revolutionary proposals because it's not going to happen", BRICsk is not the mechanism that has to make execution, it just provides the platform four countries can exchange viewpoints, said April 1 2010 by Roberto Jaguaribe, undersecretary of political affairs at Brazil's foreign ministry③.

It is because of these barriers mentioned above, the pessimistic arguments that BRICsk Platform finally collapsed are also very welcomed, think BRICsk countries are simply too diverse to achieve meaningful cooperation.They have little in common besides being large, fast-growing economies with massive domestic markets. ④ Why is BRICsk ignoring Mexico, Turkey and Indonesia? It's a selection based on the fact that it is a cool acronym⑤. This paper advocates the analysis of BRICsk mechanism's prospect should be given still from these orientations' perspective. As for the US factor, although each of the BRICsk nations recognizes that in a unipolar world, its relations with the U.S. are most important, but all of the BRIC countries are deeply concerned that America's dominant power position will allow it to behave as it pleases and damage their fundamental interests⑥. Therefore, each also wants to limit its excessive dependence on the U.S. by developing important relations with other countries to try to increase its options and freedom⑦. As for one-off need that facing financial crisis, we must notice that under the current situation that world gradually recovers, the driving forces of western countries to

① Yueqin Lin, "Diplomatic Impact and the Sustainable Development of New Economies: Basing on the Analysis of BRICs," *Studies of Economy and Management*, Volume 7, 2009, p.114.

② As for the further analysis of relationship between BRICs and America, see Roya Wolverson, "Building a BRICs Foundation," April 15, 2010, see http://www.cfr.org/publication/21910/building_a_BRICs_foundation.html; Harsh V. Pant, "Feasibility of the Russia-China-India 'Strategic Triangle:' Assessment of Theoretical and Empirical Issues," *International Studies* 43 (2006),pp. 51-72.

③ [Russia] Igor·Naumov , "BRICs No Longer Taking US Dollars as their Currency of Settlement," *Independence*(Russia), April 2,2010.

④ Raymond Colitt, "ANALYSIS-BRICs Divided on Global Agenda, Look to Mutual Trade," April 14, 2010, see http://www.alertnet.org/thenews/newsdesk/N14156241.htm.

⑤ "BRICs: Acronym or Coherent Strategy?" See http://www.ftchinese.com/story/001014611/en.

⑥ Hurrell, "Hegemony, Liberalism and Global Order: What Space for Would-be Great Powers," *International Affairs* 82 (January 2006),p.18.

⑦ Evan S. Medeiros, "China's International Behavior: Activism, Opportunism, and Diversification," *Joint Forces Quarterly* 47 (4th quarter 2007),p.33.

seek help from developing countries will be further weakened, and exert much pressure to developing countries like before may happen again, so it is much more necessary for developing countries work together. At the worst, no one need sacrifice anything currently, so, however tiny the potential gains, they are worth pursuing①. So, four countries will still drive this platform into the direction of more institutionalized, "they' ve only just started to pull together"②. Jim O'Neill, head of global economic research at Goldman, who coined the BRICs term, is more optimistic, until they can shake up or wake up the leaders of the developed world to stop treating them as guests for coffee, then the meetings of the BRICsk leaders will become a feature of the global landscape and indeed possibly one that interests global financial markets and the media more than the G8③.

In short, the BRICsk divisions will not paralyze the group, and the general direction of four countries cooperation will continue, so the problem is the model. If APEC model taken to develop BRICsk, it is very possible to become one dialogue platform that very loose and even attempt and accomplish nothing, which may be disorganization at any moment. One important function of multilateral mechanism is to regulate member states activities, and punish the activities that violated the regulation by multilateral strength, in which process mechanism construction can be realized. As for APEC model, in addition to held regular dialogue, there are no regulations arranged in advance. Therefore, from the long run, considering characteristics of these "orientations" that four countries cooperation, we should make mechanism arrangement between EU model and APEC model.

Firstly, BRICsk countries should start further institutionalized from the orientation of creating favorable international situation four domestic economic developments, and set building a win-win Economic Community as the primary goal. The starting period of institutionalized is also the period that identity construction, in which clear goal is most important④. This just like chairman Hu Jintao said, "We should set a clear goal for further cooperation, and give emphasis from the strategic level". Due to the mechanism just starts and the expansion of agendas may dilute member states' core attentions,

---

① Some scholars take it as the basic barrier of the further institutionalization of BRICs. See The trillion-dollar club, April 15 2010, From The Economist print edition, see http://www.economist.com/world/international/displaystory.cfm?story_id=15912964.

② Cynthia Roberts, "Challengers or Stakeholders? BRICs and the Liberal World Order," *Polity* (2010) 42,pp.1–13. See: http://www.palgrave-journals.com/polity/journal/v42/n1/full/pol200920a.html; Roya Wolverson, "Building a BRICs Foundation," April 15, 2010, See http://www.cfr.org/publication/21910/building_a_BRICs_foundation.htm.

③ Jim O'Neill, "We need BRICs to build the world economy, "*The Times*, June 23, 2009.

④ In fact, the mechanism construction of the BRICs just encounter this problem, See Andrew S. Weiss, "BRICs-a-Brac," *Foreign Policy* (on-line), June 2009.

therefore, the goal of this period should be conservative and limited, and try to avoid the agendas too many to bear its capacity. Meanwhile, too many agendas also make more difficulties for realization, and in turn it will weaken members' confidence. As for BRICsk, through the goal set in this way also can avoid containment from US in this period. More grand and ambitious goal can be set after the level of institutionalize gradually higher[①].

As mentioned above, the reaction to financial crisis is very important background that BRICsk summit can happen, and the clearest expression of a coherent BRICs agenda is for reform of the international financial system. Under the current situation that world still doesn't recover thoroughly from crisis and even enter the post-crisis era, how to reform the unfair international financial system and even to deal with beggar-my-neighbor trade policy of western countries is still the task that BRICsk countries have to give more attention. Take trade protectionism as example, if US implement a wide range of trade sanctions to China, even restrict export, China's export not only will be decreased significantly, but also will affect the interest of other three BRICsk countries. As for India, Brazil, and Russia, it is the same meaning. Meanwhile, the excessively dependent on developed countries' fictitious economy is the main reason that BRICsk countries be sensitive and fragile to this crisis[②]. Through building regional economic cooperation community would help members' inter-communication among four material economies. Moreover, there are many new areas, "the virgin land", can be open up. For instance, there almost no trade intercourse between Brazil and Russia, and just very small size between Brazil and India, as well as China is just the seven trade partnership to Russia, etc. In fact, the mutual complementarities among BRICsk countries are quite high. Brazil and Russia are commodities exporters, specializing, respectively, in agriculture and natural resources. By comparison, India specializes in services and China in manufactures; China and India are big consumers of commodities and building materials, while Russia is a leading oil producer and Brazil is rich in natural resources. So from the logical way to predict, BRICsk countries have good conditions to launch comprehensive cooperation and build high level institutionalized economic community.

Secondly, BRICsk should deal with US factor tactfully. Just as mentioned above, if practical breakthrough wants to be achieved during the process of BRICsk institutionalized, as for external relations with other countries, the most important one is US. Despite the current US attitude is still "wait and see", but as noted above, if BRICsk

---

① Siddharth Varadarajan, "From IBSA to CHIBSA? BRICs to BRICs? Not yet," Online edition of *India's National Newspaper*, Saturday, April 17, 2010. See http://www.thehindu.com/2010/04/17/stories/2010041754991400.htm.

② Yueqin Lin, "Diplomatic Impact and the Sustainable Development of New Economies: Basing on the Analysis of BRICs," *Studies of Economy and Management,* Volume 7, 2009, p.110; Martin Wolf, "The West No Longer Holds all the Cards," *Financial Times*, 23 September 2009.

cooperation institutionalized process continue, particularly has some breakthrough achievement, it's predictable that US will involve it. What shall BRICsk do? First of all, making use of the international situation in post era, four countries should promote US to better understand BRICsks' positive significance in world governance through dialogue and cooperation with US. From which, decrease the containment willing from US, and actively shape the common interest and consensus between BRICsk and US. Secondly, the institutionalized process should be accomplished step by step, and the starting step should be from regional economy community building. When comes to the issues related to international crisis management and world governance, particularly in fields as foreign diplomacy and security, BRICsk can introduce and welcome US involved through the arrangement like "Grand power co-management", from which the interest and willing of US also can be represented. Finally, it must set some restrictions for US's involvement, with the aim to avoid the negative influence caused by US's excess of involvement, particularly regular and arbitrary involvement. As for US, in turn, also should notice the change and trend of international structure in post cold war era, and understand the justifiability of institutionalized cooperation among four countries which share the similar development stage and has strong economic complementarities, then change the cold war perception and achieve a good interaction between BRICsk and US[①]. Robert Hormats, America's under-secretary of state for economic affairs, compared the 2010s to the late 1940s and said: "Our big challenge is to work out how large emerging economies integral to the financial and trading system take some responsibility for maintaining it."[②]

Thirdly, in order to change these diplomatic orientations into substantial activities, BRICsk should construct necessary carrier in which daily cooperation can be available. Just as Robert Keohane and Stephen Krasner state, must be established to act as vehicles to facilitate regular co-management among major powers[③]. As for BRICsk, although it is not possible to establish standing body in member states from the short term, it still can build some working groups, and consolidate foundation and yield practical achievements, enable them have the function like standing body. For instance, Russia can lead "Four countries energy cooperation group", India can lead "Four countries IT cooperation group", Brazil can lead "Four countries agricultural products cooperation group", while China can lead "International monetary reform group". Every group should have regular meeting, and in which each of BRICsk countries should send relative stable representative and has responsible department. The consensus of dialogue should be arranged with

---

① See [Ameirca]Walter S.Carpente, *A World of Regions: Asia and Europe in the American Imperium*, translated by Yaqing Qin, Peking University Publishing House, 2007, p.253.

② See http://www.economist.com/node/15912964?story_id=15912964.

③ See Robert Keohane, *After Hegemony* (Princeton, N.J.: Princeton University Press, 1984), p. 244, and Stephen Krasner, *Problematic Sovereignty* (New York: Columbia University Press, 2001), p. 182.

restriction treaty in order to execute, which should be given special attention, and set supervisory agency is a good way. In fact, only the consistency and frequency of substantial policy coordination is quite high, and also accompanied with practical activity, then the construction of mechanism can get breakthrough.

The fourth, BRICsk should further expand these common orientations, in order to increase the driving forces of cooperation. In order to better institutionalize, Beijing, Moscow, Brasilia, and New Delhi should maintain and enlarge the driving forces that four countries cooperate, through multi-layer connection. It requires BRICsk countries not only hold meetings in official level, but also emphasize public diplomacy. Fortunately, four countries have begun this kind of cooperation. As mentioned above, in Brasilia summit, in addition to state head meeting, Meeting of Development Banks, the first Meeting of Cooperatives, the first Business Forum, and the Conference of think tanks, etc, is also held. From long run, it will have very positive influence for tamping cooperation foundation, enhancing mutual trust and understanding. In fact, public diplomacy is very important. The orientations of cooperation after expanding should be beyond simple strategic and political issues, such as seek "leverage" strength to play major power role, and also should be beyond just "crisis facing", such as facing financial crisis. In contrary, the involvement of business circles and civil corporations should be given more attention to, such as four countries' cooperation in technology and education field. In fact, only cooperation orientations have the foundation of public trust and civil understanding, then it can lay the stable foundation for much higher level and continual institutionalized, such as EU. There many means can strengthen mutual trust and understanding, public education and young people exchange are good way. The former one can be available through building "BRICsk research center" in four countries' think tank, while the latter one can be through exchange students, and etc.

The fifth and finally, the direction of institutionalized can start from the orientation of seeking "leverage strength", further expand the representative of BRICsk, gradually absorb more emerging developing countries such as South Africa, Mexico, Saudi Arabia, and etc[①]. Nowadays, Mexico, Indonesia, Turkey has expressed the interest that join in. Through expansion, on the one hand, it can increase the validity of this mechanism, while strengthening its influence. On the other hand, it also represents the trend of co-management in international affairs. In fact, global issues are the main contents that

---

① Scholars possess different opinions on how to expand members, *CHAPTER ELEVEN, THE N-11: MORE THAN AN ACRONYM,* March 2007, http://www2.goldmansachs.com/ideas/BRICs/book/BRICs-Chapter11.pdf. Michael Schuman, "Should BRICs Become BRIICs?," March 3, 2010, http://curiouscapitalist.blogs.time.com/2010/03/03/should-BRICs-become-briics/; William Pesek Jr., "South Korea, Another 'BRICs' in Global Wall," December 8, 2005, http://www.bloomberg.com/apps/news?pid=newsarchive&sid=aoJ4WG5LSf1s&refer=market_insight-redirectoldpage.

BRICsk summit discussed. Take Brasilia think tank summit as example, two agendas in all four agendas are related to this, the one is how to deal with global climate change, the other one is what role that new emerging developing countries can play in global governance. As we know, due to developing countries have more common interests in these issues, they give more common attention is obviously valid and necessary. But we should remember, according to the laws of institutionalized, during the process of expansion, Beijing, Moscow, New Delhi, Brasilia should take the leading role. From the major of administration to see, one important factor for whether one loosely organized dialogue platform can be effectively institutionalized, lies in whether they have the leaders to look forward to the future and to spread blueprint. Their functions are not only set goals, but also as a "steersman", drive institutionalized process into the arranged direction. Moreover, from the theory to see, in this anarchic international community, if we manage international affairs with highly mechanism, which also needs leaders to actively organize, initially enact rules, and constrain member states activities if necessary.

The Choice of China's role in BRICs

During the post-cold war period, Chinese elite from all levels reach a common ground on the multilateral cooperation and international mechanism after a fairly long consideration and reflection, which is the orientation of china's way to deal with BRICs' cooperation. Namely, construct a sound international environment through actively participate in domestic development, and then promote international status. Therefore, analyzing China's role in the institutionalized process of BRICs must base on the orientation.

In fact, the international community has been given high expectation on China's role in BRICs. From their point of view, in the "economic, financial and political field, China has and will continue to overshadow the other three countries. Because the GDP of China is larger than them in all, the export volume and the foreign exchange reserves of China are two times than them in all". Meanwhile, China is the biggest potential market, and also are the U.S. partner in the G2. "Without China, the BRICs are just the BRI, a bland, soft cheese"; "China is the muscle of the group, without China, who cares BRICs really?" ① Therefore, "the BRIs' need for China surpass China's need for BRI", China have effective veto power over any BRICs initiatives, "So long as Beijing sees value in conducting some

① David Rothkopf , "The BRICs and what the BRICs would be without China," Monday, June 15, 2009, http://rothkopf.foreignpolicy.com/posts/2009/06/15/the_BRICs_and_what_the_BRICs_would_be_without_china ; Bobo Lo, *Axis of Convenience: Moscow, Beijing and the New Geopolitics* (Washington, D.C.: Brookings Institution Press, 2008, pp.43, 46, 177.

of its diplomacy in the BRICs format, this unusual but successful coalition is likely to endure"[①]. These judgments may with some bias, but, as an essential member of the BRICs, the choice and performance of China obviously play an importance role in its further institutionalization which also will affect China deeply.

First, the cooperation of BRICs can diffuse the energy of US, and thus reduce its containment and restraint to China, which will also optimize the international environment. Moving toward into the new century, many symbolic events happened in China have already arisen scholars' intense discussion on China's international status[②]. For example, the success holding of Olympic Games, the splendid National Day parade to commemorate the 60th anniversary of the founding of New China, the high efficient policy to deal with financial crisis, the great Shanghai World Expo, and the tremendous rise in GDP ranking. Under this situation, the recognition of China as great power spread universally. Basing on the theory of realism and the historical experience, the existing great power would take the certain rising power, which has the potentiality to become the future world power, as its opponent and try every means to contain them because of the limit of international resources. After the Cold War, China was gradually regarded as a world power. But faithfully speaking, China at present is still a latent power, which is also the basis of the raise of '20 year period of strategic opportunity'. Certainly, the revival of China will continue. So, after the strategic time, China's comprehensive power may as strong as America. How will china manage while America's overall restraints become inevitable? Face to face seems unreasonable. According to the history, almost all the rising power, such as German and Japan, finally defeat when they challenge against the world power. Especially, as the countries with most nuclear weapons, the conflict between China and US will definitely cause human disaster. In this case, the wise choice of China is to carry out a more feasible foreign policy[③]. By teaming up with Brazil, Russia and India, China can avoid to be the target of public criticism. Hence, US has to contain not only China, but Russia, India, Brazil

① Cynthia Roberts, "Challengers or Stakeholders? BRICs and the Liberal World Order," *Polity* (2010) 42, pp.1-13. http://www.palgrave-journals.com/polity/journal/v42/n1/full/pol200920a.html, Raymond Colitt, ANALYSIS-BRICs divided on global agenda, look to mutual trade, 14 Apr 2010, http://www.alertnet.org/thenews/newsdesk/N14156241.htm.

② For example, taking 'China's role' as keyword to search in 'google.com', there will be 124,000,000 results. http://www.google.cn/search?hl=zh-CN&source=hp&q=China%27s+role&aq=f&oq=.

③ China itself has already carry out some measures. For instance, on March 4, 2010, China announced that the year defense budget only increase 7.5%, viz. 78 billion US dollars. (Since the reform of military modernization in 1989, china keeps the increasing pace at 10% for nearly 20 years.) This decision has two purposes: one for coping with the global financial crisis, the other for indicating the firm determination of disarmament. The India's military expenditure, however, increased 8% in the same period. Therefore, China wants to convey an explicit information: we Chinese love peace.

at the same time, the cost is really huge[1]!

During the financial crisis period, Russia and Brazil criticized US government more directly than China did, plus, they also actively urged to reform financial system[2]. Particularly, concerning the vital international issues about Balkan Peninsula, Kosovo, Iraq War, Iranian nuclear project, Russia's criticism on America are more incisive. As for India and Brazil, they challenged the western countries many times in the WTO negotiations. The most famous event is Cancun conference in 2003[3]. Therefore, it is practical for China to support BRICs diplomacy as a mean to hide its growing capabilities and avoid some negative comments from western countries, although the BRICs may unite together to exert pressure on the appreciation of RMB, or their criticism on US may indirectly implicate china.

Second, China could play actively in co-managing international affairs through taking advantage of other powers. If China is unable to provide 'good public products' to other countries in the process of growing up, how can it build the status of great power? As we analyzed in the beginning, a prominent character of international relation after Cold War, is the highlight of global issues. Any single country has no enough ability to solve them, in that the interdependence of human destiny. Co-management was put forward just under this historical moment, and a lot of international cooperation already reflected this new trend, such as the joint management of China and US, G8, G20, BRICs, the integrating of Europe, East Asia, North America, Latin America and Africa, etc. Nowadays, China gained much more attention because of its far speed development. So, it is impossible for china to keep silent while they were gradually endowed with more international responsibility.

In international relations, to establish great power status mostly rely on the identification of other counties or organizations, but not 'self-sensation'. In this sense, the breakthrough of improving china's international image is to participate in and to lead the construction of multilateral cooperation mechanism positively. Only with this kind of energetic action, can china co-manage the international affairs, and meanwhile protect the most nations' (especially the developing countries) common interests, and finally enhance the reliability among people and countries. This idea also reflected in the President Hu Jintao's address in Brasilia Summit: "First, China's development is a

① The Copenhagen climate summit in 2009 is a good example. When US president Obama intended to have conversation only with China, yet, found the leader of South African, Russia, and Brazil with Chinese Premier Wen Jaibao in the same room. Unfortunately, the planed negotiation with China became the negotiation with developing coutries. By this way, China not only successfully avoided the possibility of undertaking risk alone, but also ehanced the nation's soft power.

② "BRICs Nations Say No IMF Cash without Representation," *Reuters*, March 13, 2009.

③ Andrew Hurrell and Amrita Narlikar, "A New Politics of Confrontation? Brazil and India in Multilateral Trade Negotiations," *Global Society* 20 (2006),pp.415-33.

long and arduous task. Second, peaceful development is China's only and logical Choice. Third, China's development is an inclusive, win-win process. Fourth, China follows a responsible approach in pursuing development"①. Considering today's international system still largely controlled by Western Countries, China also needs to spare no effort to strengthen its own discourse while coordinate with other big powers. It is inadvisable to be marginalized in international community, such as Russia's status in G8.

Third, China's economic development will benefit from a closer BRICs format. Taking oil trade as an example, about 4.3 percent of oil production was in China, but its oil consumption reached 8.8 percent, ranked second in the world. So, half of China's oil needs depend on importing. From 2003, the rate of Brazil's crude oil export to China increased 89.5 percent per year②; Russia planed to occupy 15 percent shares of Chinese oil market in 2015. At the same time, India's ironstone export to china hold 65 percent of the gross of Sino-India trade exchange③, while China was the world largest ironstone importing country. Therefore, constructing a relative high-institutionalized free trade community among BRICs will greatly stabilized the energy supply of China.

In addition, China's relation with BRIs, especially with India and Russia, are not always harmonious because of some sensitive bilateral issues, the further institutionalization of BRICs and developing BRICs forum just provide an excellent opportunity for China to bolster links with the three countries, which may create three good results. First, it may well express rising China's willing to follow win-win cooperation model, but reluctant to threaten or challenge other nation's interests. In the other words, it may reduce, or even avoid, to some extent, the possibilities of Russia, or India joins "anti-China" ally led by US. Second, it is convenient for China to learn advanced experience from the three countries. Third, it is more available for China to shape a sound role of developing country, while some nations pushed to treat China as a developed country④.

Obviously, the role that China played in the institutionalization of BRICs is to be an active guider, but not a leader. First, China should be very cautious to act as a leader. On one hand, "China also risks being perceived as participating in a political bloc whose

① "Cooperation and Openness for Mutual Benefit and Win-Win Progress,"remarks at the BRICs Summit, by Hu Jintao, President of the People's Republic of China, Brasilia, April 16 2010. http://www.fmprc.gov.cn/chn/pds/ziliao/zyjh/t682096.htm.

② Kang Zhang, "Looking the Direction of BRICs' Cooperation from their Status in World Oil Trade," *Petroleum & Petrochemical Today*, Volume 8, 2009, p.9.

③ Xiong Deng, "Analyzing the Economic Prospect of BRICs," *Teaching and Studies of Finance*, Volume 5, 2008, p.52.

④ Gregory T. Chin, "China's Evolving G8 Engagement: Complex Interests and Multiple identity in Global Governance Reform," in *Emerging Powers in Global Governance: Lessons from the Heiligendamm Process*, Andrew F. Cooper and Agata Antkiewicz eds. (Waterloo, Ontario: Wilfrid Laurier University Press, 2008), pp.83-114.

aim is to challenge and undermine the U.S. and the western liberal order"[①]. In any case, America is still the biggest influential factor to China's role building in a relatively long period. So, China should never be mistaken as a leader of any anti-US alliance. On the other hand, objectively speaking, China's comprehensive power, at present, is insufficient to dominate the institutionalization of BRICs. Second, the wise choice for China is to guide the institutionalization positively by taking more discourse of every important section, which includes the target programming, the raise of the prior topic, the construction of mechanism, etc.

Conclusion

In fact, every mechanism of international dialogue and multilateral cooperation has a certain "orientation", which is a key point to force them to discuss relative issues and achieve the anticipated goals. Furthermore, two additional reasons caused the writer to study the institutionalization of BRICs and the related China's role through the "orientation". First, BRICs was lumped together as a group by the chief economist of Goldman Sachs. "How to deep the ties can be between the BRICs is a matter of debate"[②], the writer's research method can well answer these debate. Second, the international structure has being adjusted after the Cold War, in which financial crisis became a new variable[③]. In this process, the improvement of china's status was concerned considerably by international society. So, China needs to partly change the diplomatic policy to adapt to the new situation, one of the most important adjustments is accepting multilateral cooperation. When integrated into the international system, China itself also created some multilateral mechanism, such as the six-party talks, the SCO, etc. Then, as an essential member of the BRICs, Chinese scholars should undoubtedly have a close study on the "orientation" of China in the further institutionalization of BRICs.

The global independence caused a gradually vague boundary between international

---

① Michael A. Glosny, "China and the BRICs: A Real (but Limited) Partnership in a Unipolar World," p.11. http://web.mit.edu/polisci/research/gradresearch/Glosny-China%20and%20the%20BRICs-Clean%20Sept%2011%20version%20ISA%20paper.doc.

② Roya Wolverson, "Building a BRICs Foundation," April 15, 2010, http://www.cfr.org/publication/21910/building_a_BRICs_foundation.html; Andrew Hurrell, "Hegemony, Liberalism and Global Order: What Space for Would-be Great Powers," *International Affairs* 82 (January 2006),pp. 1–19.

③ There many papers discussing the shift of power, some Indian Scholars even put forward the Conception of PIGS (Portugal, Italy or Ireland, Greece, Spain), which reflected the international structure after the Cold War always in transforming. Christopher Layne, "The Waning of U.S. Hegemony: Myth or Realty," *International Security* 34 (Summer 2009): 147-72.David Shambaugh,ed.,*Power Shift: China and Asia's New Dynamics*(Barkeley and Los Angeles: University of California Press,2005);Andrew Zvirzdin, "Of BRICs and PIGS," *International Economics* on Monday, February 8. 2010.

politics and domestic politics. Under this situation, diplomatic operation played an important role in the process of nations' growing up. As we can see, BRICs is a good union of four emerging countries for achieving their strategic goals. Therefore, boosting the construction of BRICs institutionalization should to move from economic field to political field, and to solve difficulties basing on the "orientation" of the four countries. Horizontally, each country need to consolidated and expand their own orientation; vertically, they can take advantage of other counties' orientation, namely, absorb new members into the union, to enhance influence and validity. Of course, American factor must be taken into consideration. If all these approaches carry out effectively, the BRICs will become the core of the interest coordination in the non-western world, which will force the international mechanism mainly led by developed countries to adopt a fairer method to dispose their relationship with developing countries.

So, China should not deviate from the "Orientation" without enough reason at current juncture. As the fast developing country with strong power and big concerns, China has to take advantage of other emerging powers as well as benefit them, by keeping pace with the time, facing challenge with objective judgment. In this sense, the "orientation" is an available approach to realized solid cooperation among BRICs, which, if flexible used, may benefit China more and meanwhile serve the general goal of peaceful development and mutual benefit. On one hand, China could protect and expand national interest through actively constructing multilateral mechanism of coordination. On the other hand, china could weaken the developed countries' defense to China through mild treatment of international system.

In brief, the special orientation of BRICs' cooperation depends on their pragmatic diplomacy by analyzing the international situation after the Cold War, which will certainly affect their further institutionalization. Namely, each of the BRICs will possess different orientation in the union. Hence, an in-depth study of the BRICs' institutionalization and the related China's role must pay attention to this orientation.

China & India: How to Lead Asia's Self-sustained Growth?

Liu Xiaoxue[*]

Although both lack of appropriate supervision and over-leveraged financial markets seem to be the immediate causes of the sub-prime crisis, it is global unbalance lying deep inside. To achieve sustained growth, both the industrial countries and the newly emerging economies have to transform themselves so as to adapt into the changing international economic context.

Asia's self-sustained growth and role of China and India in it

With rebalancing effort between saving and consumption by the American consumers, the global demand will consequently slow down in the long run

After the crisis, the western countries began to rebalance their economies at various levels. The patterns of America's saving and consuming have shown some changes, for example, people are trying to rebuild their wealth on the basis of saving. The unemployment rate is still as high as 10 percent, which may result in the vicious circle between jobs and consumption. Therefore, due to shrinking wealth and weak job market, American consumption cannot return to the pre-crisis level in a few years.

---

* Liu Xiaoxue, research associate fellow, the Institute of Asia-Pacific Studies, Chinese Academy of Social Sciences.

Challenged by the new situations, Asian export–oriented economies will pay more attention to interregional market.

Asian economies only have two alternatives in response to the declining Euro-US Market demands, one is to look for the new export markets beyond the industrial western world, and the other is to expand the domestic markets. With their respective huge market scales and the highest growth rates, China and India will be most possible ones to replace Euro –US markets as the largest destinations of export products of the rest of Asian economies. As for expanding the domestic demands, only the major economies in the region can take advantage of their domestic markets to maintain the catching up and surpassing growth momentum, while the rest of Asia's economies with small domestic market would still hold export as their growth engine. Thus, we see rising importance of China and India in leading Asia' s self-sustained growth in the future,

The road to self-determined and self-sustained growth by China and India

The global financial crisis brought great changes upon the external development environments for China and India. At the same time, for having grown at relatively high rates for a long time, both China and India are also facing domestic challenges economically as well as socially. In the future in order to maintain a considerably high growth rate, both countries need to make necessary transitions: China will make a transition from manufacturing-led, export-oriented growth strategy to a more balanced between export markets and domestic ones, and environment-friendly growth pattern, while India as no longer content with so-called "Indian Pattern", which is characterized with service-led, domestic-oriented growth, will to some extent draw close to East Asian Model. A successful transition will definitely take China and India on to the road of self-determined and self-sustained growth.

China's transition

Three bottlenecks

Today, as the world manufacturing factory, China is increasingly strangled by the three bottlenecks: resource bottleneck, environment bottleneck, and market bottleneck. Most of the time resource bottleneck and environment bottleneck are two sides of the same coin. Compared with its huge population and economic scale, it is undeniable that China's resources are relatively limited. In terms of using resources, China neither uses them intensively nor manages their discards carefully, which consequently exacerbates the effects of bottleneck of resources and environments as well. The market bottleneck does not come from saturation of the destination market, instead, it is a result of a deliberative trade policy aiming to protect local jobs and reduce trade deficit by a country. The market bottleneck poses the immediate threat to China's growth in a short run.

Ways of breaking the bottlenecks

In a short run, China must find ways to break the market bottleneck so as to recover its growth momentum. To do so, China has to raise its domestic private consumption and transfer its outdated or losing-competitiveness industries to the less-developed region. In the past decade, share of China's private consumption to GDP kept declining, from 45% in 2000 down to 36.1% in 2008, the lowest one in the developing Asian economies. There are two reasons accounting for it: unjustifiable income distribution mix and lack of effective social security network. In China, we have seen the government revenues and enterprises profits rising more quickly than the resident incomes. Lack of social security network raised uncertainty of the residents for the future life, which forced them to over save for the future. For realizing importance of private consumption in economic sustainable growth, China's government should take forward big reforms: to reform the current income distribution mix, to build up social security network with wide coverage. The East Asian Flying-Geese Model is characterized with transfer of industry among East Asian economies at various development levels. If some losing- competitiveness industries due to rising producing costs in China could be shifted to Vietnam or Cambodia or South Asian countries, China will not only reduce its costs of updating industries, but also promote the industrial development in those receiving countries. More importantly, by doing so, China could avoid trade barriers for its export products. However, the steps of Chinese firms to go overseas are still hesitating. The main reason for it is that, to secure local jobs, the local governments used to distort resource prices or deliberately neglect environmental costs.

In a long run, to achieve sustainable development, China should also overcome both resource bottleneck and environment bottleneck. Hence, China must reduce its over reliance on processing trade, promote industrial upgrading and creativity, and transform itself from a big trading country to a strong trading nation. Besides, China also needs to develop its service industry especially those productive service sectors as quickly as possible, which as the new growing points, not only could accelerate manufacturing development toward more intensive production at more advanced stage, but also could help China's economy turn to more environment- friendly.

India's reindustrialization

Limitations of Indian Growth Pattern

There are two service sectors with the highest growth rates: one is IT-enabled outsourcing service, the other is modern service sectors including banking and communication services, which benefit most from widespread use of information technology. While IT-enabled outsourcing service is subject to influence of business cycle as well as interference of protective trade policy of the foreign countries, the modern service sectors cannot keep independent from the development of industry and agriculture. According to the economies successfully going through economic take-off stage, no one could skip over industrialization stage to join the rank of developed economies. For an economy like India with huge population, it is especially hard to be exception. In the next four decades, India will have 13 million additional labors every year. To provide jobs to them is not only a big economic challenge, but also a serious threat to the political stability. Therefore, India must develop its manufacturing industry to absorb its large number of the low-skilled labor.

In the first decade of 21st century, Indian economy seemed riding on the same business cycle as the world economy did, which brought a consensus to India people that India needs foreign capital and market to achieve a much higher and sustainable growth rate. However, due to its relatively backward manufacturing industry, India's export products are less competitive than some its counterparts like China, as a result its trade growth targets are often missed. Many an obstacles for investment remain untouched, which holds back FDI inflow in a much larger volume.

Making great efforts in developing manufacturing

To develop Indian manufacturing industry, India needs develop its infrastructure at first. However, with huge fiscal deficit, Indian governments at various levels have very little resources to carry out large-scale infrastructural construction. Thus, India is eager to see private capital flowing into this field. As we know, as one of public or quasi-public goods, its production and supply needs much more supportive public policy, which is not yet in place. Secondly, India's higher tariff rates prevent its small and medium enterprises (SMEs) from participating global production network, which has been proved to be a shortcut of growth for SMEs in other developing economies.

Expending Spill–over Effects to the Neighboring Economies through Much Tighter Regional Cooperation

By promoting a much more opened and flexible regional trading and investment framework, China and India could expend spill-over effects of their growth to the neighboring economies.

At present, most of Asian trade arrangements are bilateral or sub-regional ones, instead of a unified market like EU or NAFTA. According to ADB, there are 92 FTA among the Asian economies. As one party of negotiation, such "Noodle Bowl" free trade arrangements are much easier to reach a conclusion. However, for the enterprises as the potential beneficiary of the FTA, more FTAs mean more complexity and more costs to use them. In addition, current trade co operations within the region mostly are led by the relatively small countries, while the big regional powers just make their response. Therefore, pulling force is not enough.

Table 1 Main indicators of China and India in 2008

		Account for the world (%)	Account for Asia (%)
Chinese population	1.3 billion	20	33
Indian population	1.1billion	17	28
China's GDP	4.3 trillion $	7	25
India's GDP	1.2 trillion $	2	7
China's total trade	2.56 trillion$	8.3	11.7*
India's total trade	496.7billion $	1.5	—

* Share of China in Developing Asia (What ADB calls DMCs).

Table 2 2000-2008 trade with China in their total foreign trade

Unit: %

	2000	2005	2008	Countries	2000	2005	2008
India	2.4	7.0	11.5	Philippine	2.0	8.0	17.9
Indonesia	5.0	8.7	10.1	Singapore	4.6	9.4	9.8
Hong Kong, China	38.8	45.0	47.5	Taiwan, China	3.6	16.4	22.7
Korea	9.4	18.4	22.3	Thailand	4.7	8.9	10.2
Malaysia	3.5	8.8	12.6	Vietnam	9.8	13.2	15.2
New Zealand	4.7	8.2	9.7				

Table 3 Consumption in selected countries in 2004(in percent of GDP)

	Labor income	Disposable income	Personal consumption	Government provided health and education	Adjusted consumption
USA	57	74	70	10	80
Britain	56	66	65	12	77
France	52	62	56	6	62
Germany	51	66	57	6	63
Japan	51	59	57	5	62
Korea	44	54	51	5	56
India	—	84	67	4	70
China	56	60	41	3	44

Source: Jahangir Aziz (2006).

Think-Tank Forum Initiates New Dialogues Channel for the BRICs Countries

Zhou Zhiwei[*]

The Institute for Applied Economic Research (IPEA) affiliated to the Secretariat of Strategic Affairs (SAE) of the Presidency of Brazil held BRICs Countries Think-Tank Forum titled BRICs Countries' Role in Post-Crisis Global Restructure on April 14-15, 2010. Scholars from China, Brazil, India and Russia exchanged their views on important topics that concern the four countries currently. The forum has accumulated abundant experiences for deepening dialogues among think-tanks. The main ideas are as below:

The international status of the BRICs has upgraded rapidly. The scholars from the four countries generally believed that US will remain as a super power for quite a long period to come. But multi-polarization has already become the direction of world pattern which is now speeded up by financial crisis. The BRICs' international status has upgraded rapidly by showing economic vitality and their importance has been recognized by the developed countries. To promote the establishment of a new international order, it is necessary for the four countries to interact and cooperate frequently and participate in international affairs with a common position. According to Antonio Patriota, Brazilian Deputy Foreign Minister, the involvement of the BRICs in international affairs is still not enough, and it is possible for the four countries to be in the UN Security Council simultaneously in 2011 which will be helpful for them to express the common wishes of the developing countries. Guimarães, the head of SAE claimed that the BRICs can play an important role in the democratization of international order. Emerging powers should reinforce the solidarity and integration among them, strive for a bigger say and change the

* Zhou Zhiwei, research associate fellow, the Institute of Latin American Studies, Chinese Academy of Social Sciences.

situation that minority powers dominate global affairs. The BRICs share common identity, demands and pursuit of interest. The deepening of mutual beneficial cooperation among the four countries facilitates not only their respective economic and social development, but also the establishment of a new international order.

The BRICs should participate in global governance actively. The experts at the Forum agreed that as the international status of the BRICs rises, the highest priority for their participation in global governance should be enhancing coordination and cooperation, and increasing emerging economic powers' say in global affairs. However, some experts believed that there's great difference in the influence of the four countries in the global affairs: G2 has already become the de facto pattern of global governance; Brazil's international involvement is limited by many weaknesses, which makes it difficult for Brazil to be an axis of South America, let alone an international power; Russia is actually marginalized in the global governance for its economic frangibility and lack of soft power. Some experts even took the difference in political system and democratic institution as the obstacle of the cooperation among the four countries and the reason why the institutionalization of the BRICs can hardly be realized. Some experts pointed out that promoting the establishment of a new international order is the junction of major interests for the four countries. The four countries should try their best to seek common ground while put aside differences. The cooperation among the four countries should not be linked up with political and democratic system. They should further strengthen their strategic common view, work out detailed common action plan, and enrich the channels for dialogues and communication among them.

The BRICs should strengthen their cooperation in coping with financial crisis. The scholars fully elaborated the reason and the channel of dissemination of the crisis, and the measures taken by the major economies, analyzed the reason why the BRICs have taken the lead in coming out of the crisis, and predicted the future trend of the four countries' economies. According to some experts, although China, India and Brazil have gained some achievements in coping with the crisis, they all face some problems such as economic overheat and the rising pressure of inflation. The four countries should enhance their coordination on the policy of exit strategy and ensure the safety of their own foreign reserves. In addition, there are also some experts who believed that the four countries should extend their cooperation, coordinate their positions, participate in negotiations as a group and strive for a bigger say in the course of rebalancing global economy and rebuilding global economic order.

The BRICs should work together to boost intra-trade. The scholars from the four countries came to a consensus that the intra-trade of the BRICs has become a new growth area of the four countries' foreign trade, among which China-India trade has accelerated at the most prominent speed. As to how to further develop the intra-trade potential, some experts emphasized the importance of government's involvement and regarded extending staple trade as an effective way to promote intra-trade among the four countries. The Indian scholars believed that each country should endeavor to exploit the potential of each others' market, coordinate each others position in the agricultural negotiations in WTO and urge the developed countries to open their markets. The Brazilian scholars claimed that China-Brazil trade is more like the trade relations between northern and southern countries. Single export product is the same problem that Brazil, India and Russia are facing in trading with China. Efforts should be made by the three countries to change the situation. As a response, the Russian scholars said that the problems in bilateral trade should be solved by both sides instead of blaming one side. The Indian scholars mentioned that the exchange rate of RMB has causal relations with trade gap. Chinese scholars argued that these two issues don't have necessary connections. China pursues a market-based, managed floating rate system. Since rate system is a matter of national interest, the time and margin of rate adjustment should be determined by China depending on its macro-economic situation.

The BRICs will become important sources of global foreign direct investment. The experts believed that the BRICs are attractive to foreign direct investment due to their market size, labor cost, infrastructure plan, currency devaluation, expectation of economic development and open trade. In this respect, China's experiences in economic restructuring and strategy of infrastructure are worth learning for reference for the other three countries. China grows rapidly in external investment which is mainly driven by enterprises' international strategy and need of upgrading international competitiveness, service for macroeconomic development, economic restructuring (transfer labor-intensive industries to other countries) and high demand for resources and raw materials. Some experts asserted that the BRICs will become important sources of global foreign direct investment because of their high speed of economic growth, enlarging economic scale, implementation of global economic strategy and increase of surplus in balance of payments. In order to boost the increase of investment among the four countries, the experts suggested they make common developing strategy, improve mechanism of investment policy coordination, financial cooperation and investment promotion, and give full play to the role of their governments in guiding investments.

The BRICs should coordinate and work together in coping with climate change. The experts from the four countries introduced the policies and measures taken by their own countries in coping with climate change. China's policy of increasing energy efficiency and popularizing clean resources is appreciated by the experts from the other three countries. In terms of climate negotiations, the majority of the experts claimed that the four countries should adhere to the principle of common but differentiated responsibility, and the developed countries should fulfill their commitments of transferring technique and capital to the developing countries. However, some experts believed that the BRICs play different roles in climate negotiations. China is a climate super power who possesses veto power along with US and EU. India, Russia and Brazil are climate potential powers along with Japan, Indonesia, Mexico, Korea and South Africa. Therefore, some experts requested that the four countries should play more active roles, change their defensive positions on climate as Brazil is doing, and ask other emerging powers to establish their own goals of emission reduction. Moreover, some experts had the impression that the BRICs are out of step in coping with climate change. Brazil and China attach more importance to international cooperation. China's low carbon technology leads the other three. China and Brazil have some comparative advantages in wind energy technology and bio-energy technology respectively. The four countries could complement each other' s advantages in these areas. There are also several experts asserted that there's no feasible common action plan and the climate negotiations are still at the bargaining stage.

The BRICs should reinforce cooperation in technical renovation area. The BRICs have strengthened their policies of supporting technical innovation in recent years. Brazil and Russia have made laws on technical innovation. But the four countries share the same problem of attaching importance to science while belittling technology. In addition, in terms of input in research and development, China has some characteristics differentiated from the other three countries. First, the speed of acceleration of China's input in research and development leads the other three. Second, China has already stepped into the stage that enterprises lead the research and development. Third, China has explored a research pattern that enterprises and universities cooperate with each other. In the post-crisis era, the four countries should share their experiences in technical innovation and work together for the establishment of new international patent system.

Communication among the think-tanks is an important complementation to the high-level dialogs among the four countries in the following aspects: First, the four countries all lack in-depth research of the other three countries and overall knowledge of their related strategic blueprint. Conversations among the think-tanks provide a platform for the four countries to increase understandings with each other. The scholars from the four countries may use this platform expressing their concern and seeking the junction of interest. Second, through the exchanges among the think-tanks, the scholars from the four countries could discuss related topics, explore new method for deepening cooperation and ensure smooth and efficient cooperation among the four countries. The think-tank forum among the BRICs should be long-term and institutionalized, and give full play to the active role of second-track diplomacy in promoting the cooperation among the four countries.

Media Reports

“金砖四国”智库为深化四国合作献计献策

新华网巴西利亚4月14日电（记者 杨立民 毕玉明）在“金砖四国”领导人第二次正式会晤即将举行之际，由四国主要学术机构发起的首届“金砖四国”智库峰会14日在这里开幕。

这次会议的主题是“‘金砖四国’在后危机时期全球变革中的作用”。在为期两天的会议中，来自中国、巴西、俄罗斯和印度的专家学者和官员将就当前的世界经济形势和后危机时期四国面临的共同挑战和发展机遇进行交流，为各国政府拓展和深化四国之间的合作献计献策。

巴西应用经济研究所所长马尔西奥 · 波切曼在开幕式上说，四国在后危机时期既面临着严峻的挑战，也迎来难得的历史机遇。作为新兴大国，四国应该进一步开展建设性的对话，推动南南合作，维护发展中国家的权益，促进可持续性发展。为此，四国学术机构之间应该建立一个共同的工作日程，协助各国领导人制定长远的发展规划。

中国社会科学院副院长李扬表示，希望通过此次对话，增加四国智库学者之间的了解和互信，共同为四国在后危机时期的经济和社会持续与和谐发展、相互合作出谋划策，为全球经济的完全复苏贡献一份力量。

印度与俄罗斯的学者在开幕式的发言中也表示，“金砖四国”的学术机构应该积极发挥智库作用，为四国扩大合作，更好地应对后危机时期和全球化的挑战作出贡献。

根据会议日程，本届智库峰会将就“金砖四国”如何应对国际金融危机、国际贸易、全球气候挑战、外国直接投资、技术创新等议题进行深入探讨。

(Source: http://news. xinhuanet. com/world/2010-04/15/c_1233914. htm.)

李扬率学者代表团参加“金砖四国”智库峰会

周志伟

近日，中国社会科学院副院长李扬率领以中国社科院学者为主的中国学者代表团受邀参加了在巴西举行的“金砖四国”智库峰会，此次峰会系“金砖四国”首脑峰会的“二轨”会议，其主题为“后危机全球转型中‘金砖四国’的角色”。

在“金砖四国”智库峰会开幕式上，李扬与巴西总统府战略事务部部长吉马良斯、巴西外交部常务副部长帕特里奥塔、应用经济研究所所长波克曼、印度驻巴西大使普拉卡什、俄罗斯科学院拉美所所长达维多夫一道为峰会致辞。李扬在讲话中指出，“金砖四国”拥有共同身份、共同需求和相似的利益诉求，深化四国互利合作不仅有利于各自经济社会发展，而且有助于国际新秩序的建立。巴西总统府战略事务部部长吉马良斯指出，“金砖四国”在国际秩序民主化中扮演重要角色，新兴大国应加强团结，实现力量整合，谋求更大发言权，改变由少数大国主宰全球事务的局面。开幕式结束后，组委会特别安排了一个记者招待会，四国智库代表团团长共同回答了各国记者提出的有关“金砖四国”合作、金融危机未来走势、国际格局转型、国际储备货币改革等问题。

在峰会的专题讨论环节，中国社科院亚太所所长李向阳、世经政所所长张宇燕、俄罗斯东欧和中亚研究所所长吴恩远、中国国际问题研究所副所长刘友法、拉美所所长郑秉文、上海国际问题研究院全球治理所副所长叶青分别就金融危机、国际贸易、气候变化、外国直接投资、技术创新、全球治理等专题作了发言并参加了讨论。通过与其他三国学者的直接交流，中方代表团与上述国家学术界在相关问题上达成共识，同时也为深化智库对话积累了丰富经验。

除参加“金砖四国”智库峰会外，李扬还率中国学者代表团部分学者专程拜访了巴西总统府战略事务部部长吉马良斯并举行了工作会谈，吉马良斯感谢中国社会科学院为推动中巴学术交流作出的贡献，并表示愿意将自己的著作《大国时代巴西的挑战》交付中国社会科学院拉美研究所巴西研究中心翻译并出版。中国学者代表团还访问了巴西劳工党圣保罗总部。劳工党向代表团详细介绍了巴西国内政治、经济现状以及该党对中国的政策并赠送了该党中文版党章，并宴请了代表团部分成员。另外，代表团还与里约热内卢天主教大学“金砖四国”研究中心举行了座谈，就“金砖四国”机制化和未来合作研究等问题坦诚交换了意见，双方都表达了进一步加强中巴智库学术交流的愿望。

“金砖四国”智库峰会的创意最初由中国社会科学院“金砖四国”课题组提出，其目的是为第二届“金砖四国”首脑峰会提出对策建议。为确定合适的巴西智库机构，拉美所所长郑秉文曾于 2009 年 12 月利用出访瑞典的机会转道巴西考察应用经济研究所和巴西国际关系研究中心，经过与其反复协商后，应用经济研究所表示愿意承办此次“金砖四国”智库峰会。此次峰会由巴西总统府战略事务部下属的应用经济研究所主办，受邀参会的中、印、俄三国学者代表团人数分别为 17 人、6 人和 4 人，参与的四国主要智库有中国社会科学院、中国当代世界研究中心、中国国际问题研究所、上海国际问题研究院、里约热内卢天主教大学、巴西利亚大学、巴西国际关系研究中心、拉美经委会、俄罗斯科学院、俄罗斯 Russkiy Mir 基金会、印度尼赫鲁大学、印度国际经济关系研究委员会、印度发展中国家资讯系统研究中心、印度观察家研究基金会、印度艾哈默德巴德管理学院等。

(Source: *Cinese Social Sciences Today*, May 20, 2010)

BRIC–Think Tank Summit Starts in Brasilia

April 15, 2010

The BRIC-Think Tank Summit started on Wednesday in the Brazilian capital Brasilia with a call for more cooperation among the participants of the group.

At the event's opening ceremony, representatives of the main research institutes of Brazil, Russia, India and China said that although trade among the four countries has improved significantly in the past few years, it can increase even more.

They said that the international financial crisis offered an opportunity for the BRIC countries to help build a more inclusive world, in which the needs of all countries are addressed. The representatives also stressed that the BRIC countries have managed to minimize the crisis' effects on their economies by applying stimulus plans.

"The proportion of BRIC economic aggregate in the global GDP increased from 13 percent in 2007 to 15 percent in 2009," said Li Yang, vice president of the Chinese Academy of Social Sciences. " What is most important is that the combined contribution of BRIC countries to the world economic growth exceeded 50 percent over the past five years."

Meanwhile, the representatives criticized the concentration of political, economic and military power in the hands of a few countries, and called for more participation of the BRIC members in the global governance organizations, in order to reflect the new multipolar reality of the world.

Secretary-general of Brazil's Ministry of Foreign Affairs Antonio Patriota also stressed that the BRIC countries won't ignore the needs of other countries in the world. He said that the BRIC countries will not repeat the mistakes of the past and will pay attention to the needs of the so-called "G172," or the countries that do not belong to the G20, as well.

Later in the day, the four countries' representatives will discuss the BRIC's role in the international financial crisis and their stance on the climate change issue. The BRIC-Think Tank Summit closes on Thursday, after discussions on foreign direct investment, technology and global governance organizations.

(Source: Xinhua http://news.xinhuanet. com/english2010/China/2010-04/15/c_13251637. htm.)

BRIC Countries' Think Tanks to Strengthen Cooperation

April 15, 2010

Major research institutions from the BRIC countries—Brazil, Russia, India and China—intend to tighten their cooperation to achieve joint views on issues of common interest and help the work of the BRIC governments, it was announced on Wednesday.

A two-day seminar gathering think tanks of the BRIC countries to examine the global economic situation and the role of those countries in the post-crisis global transformation, was opened in Brasilia on Wednesday morning, preceding the second BRICs summit scheduled for Friday in the Brazilian capital.

The most important aspects of the current relations between the four countries was presented in a press conference by Marcio Pochmann, from Brazil's Institute of Applied Economic Research (IPEA), Li Yang, vice-president of China Academy of Social Sciences, Indian Rathin Roy, from the United Nations Development Programme (UNDP), and Vladimir Davydov, from the Russian Academy of Sciences.

The objective of the seminar is to establish a working agenda between BRIC research institutions, and even play the role of being a supplement to the second summit, to define common tasks beyond the immediate interest of the heads of state, Pochmann said.

He stressed that these institutions could provide joint responses to errors in assessment, which happens frequently in international institutions, for example on the evolution of poverty rate in developing countries, because there is "no dialogue with researchers from the countries (themselves)."

Li Yang noted that China's intellectuals are a very important source for the government, which should be extended to the relationship between countries. "I think that an active and dynamic interaction between us would promote the formation of consensus among the heads of state. It is very important for us to have made contact with several research institutes in Brazil," he said.

Roy said that there is a long tradition of exchange between institutions of the four countries, while Davydov stressed the importance that policy is linked to the academic world to better adapt to the new historical realities.

Pochmann anticipated that the BRIC research institutions will organize this year a seminar on water resource management and environmental quality.

(Source: Xinhua http://news.xinhuanet. com/english2010/China/2010-04/15/c_13251653. htm.)

Para pesquisadores, Bric deve discutir moeda

15 de Abril,2010

Brasil, Rússia, China e Índia devem coordenar-se para influir no modelo para o sistema financeiro internacional que emergirá da crise mundial, defenderam, ontem, dirigentes de alguns dos principais centros de estudo desses países, em seminário que antecedeu o início da cúpula de chefes de Estado dos chamados Bric, que começa hoje em Brasília. Os pesquisadores também defenderam as discussões entre os governantes para a criação de mecanismos monetários que dispensem o uso do dólar nas transações internacionais e preparem para uma eventual substituição da moeda americana como referência internacional.

"Não pensamos que o sistema monetário dominado pelo dólar seja moldado no futuro próximo, mas iniciativas como diversificação das reservas internacionais podem coexistir com esse regime", comentou o vice-presidente da Academia de Ciências da China, Li Yang, que defendeu, porém, a construção gradual de alternativas ao dólar. "Não acreditamos em alterações significativas agora. Observamos com interesse acordos de comércio com trocas diretas de moedas locais."

"Estamos num processo de rearticulação do sistema político econômico internacional, e, nesse processo ou as regras continuarão a privilegiar alguns países ou teremos uma situação de acordo com a dimensão de nossas sociedades", disse o ministro de Assuntos Estratégicos, Samuel Pinheiro Guimarães, defendendo aliança entre os Bric para influir nas novas regras financeiras internacionais.

No discurso mais enfático do seminário, Pinheiro Guimarães acusou os países desenvolvidos de pressionarem para evitar a emergência de novos atores nas esferas mundiais de decisão. "A crise ambiental passa pelas fontes renováveis de energia, pela energia nuclear, e precisamos saber que controlará o processo nuclear", disse. "No fundo há uma disputa tecnológica e científica entre países", disse. "Isso está em foco: saber se algumas nações continuarão a se achar superiores, e, portanto, com mais direitos, ou não", insistiu, reivindicando apoio para a reforma do Conselho de Segurança da ONU, onde Índia e Brasil ambicionam um assento permanente.

Li Yang previu que mudar o sistema monetário mundial será "árduo e de longo prazo" e sugeriu maior cooperação em termos de administração de reservas internacionais, diversificando o uso de moedas. O diretor do Instituto de América Latina da Academia de Ciências da Rússia, Vladimir Davidov, previu a criação de alternativas "por regiões geográficas", como a criação de um Fundo Monetário Europeu, à parte do Fundo Monetário Internacional (FMI).

Intelectuais dos quatro países concordaram que será necessário cooperar para garantir a reforma do FMI e das regras que regem as finanças. Reconheceram, porém, que apesar do grande aumento na presença desses países no cenário internacional, eles são incapazes de compensar, com investimentos e importações, o peso do declínio americano na economia mundial.

O título do seminário, "Cúpula Bric de Think Tanks" era um atestado da resistência dos conceitos anglo-saxões nas relações entre os Bric-uma sigla, aliás, criada por um economista de financeira sediada nos EUA. Na entrevista que se seguiu às apresentações, nas quais inglês e português foram alternados como língua oficial, a falta de uma língua comum aos participantes teve um exemplo prosaico, quando o pesquisador da China teve de usar dois tradutores, um que vertia suas respostas para o inglês e outro que as traduzia do inglês ao português.

As propostas para as diversas discussões internacionais também têm pontos de conflito, como reconheceram os debatedores (a Rússia, por exemplo, está satisfeita com o peso que tem no FMI; o Brasil, não). Mas, como explicou o presidente do Instituto de Pesquisa Econômica Aplicada (Ipea), Márcio Pochmann, que preparou o seminário, com a Academia de Ciências da China, a primeira reunião de centros de estudos dos quatro paises abre possibilidade de pesquisas conjuntas, com pontos de vista mais úteis para a tomada de decisão dos chefes de Estado. "Precisamos ver a nós mesmos com nossos próprios olhos", definiu Pinheiro Guimarães.

Como mostrou o diretor do Instituto de Estudos da Ásia e Pacífico, Li Xiangyang, pelo menos um ponto aproxima os quatro países e os diferencia das nações desenvolvidas: enquanto Europa, Japão e Estados Unidos ainda se debatem com as consequências da crise financeira, o problema, nos Bric é evitar superaquecimento da economia, entrada de capital especulativo e pressões inflacionárias.

"A cooperação entre nós pode nos trazer benefícios mútuos", defendeu Li Yang. "O atual sistema monetário internacional é desfavorável aos países em desenvolvimento", comentou Li, defendendo mudanças na estrutura do FMI. Foi apoiado por Pochmann, que defendeu uma aliança entre os Bric para "um novo padrão de consumo e produção" e a formação de um sistema monetário que não se baseie na moeda de um só país.

(Fonte: Valor Econômico http://www. sae. gov. br/site/?p=3242)

Ipea discute papel do Bric depois da crise econômica mundial

O Instituto de Pesquisa Econômica Aplicada (Ipea) realiza hoje (14) e amanhã em Brasília a Cúpula Bric: O Papel do Bric após a Crise Econômica. O encontro começa às 8h30 no Hotel Mercure. O Bric é o grupo que inclui o Brasil, a Rússia, a Índia e a China.

O encontro reúne representantes dos governos e pesquisadores de centros de estudos dos quatro países. Logo após a abertura, haverá entrevista coletiva com o presidente do Ipea, Marcio Pochmann, e representantes dos demais países. Às 10h, a coordenadora de Estudos de Relações Econômicas Internacionais do Ipea, Luciana Acioly, apresenta o comunicado Rússia, Índia e China: Comércio Exterior e Investimento Direto Externo.

O estudo apresenta os diferenciais de cada país do Bric no comércio internacional, seus pontos fortes e desafios. Durante os dois dias da Cúpula, será discutido o novo papel desses países no cenário mundial, com destaque para os impactos da crise financeira internacional, a dinâmica do comércio exterior, a mudança climática global e o papel dos investimentos estrangeiros diretos, entre outros.

Participam da solenidade de abertura o ministro-chefe da Secretaria de Assuntos Estratégicos, Samuel Pinheiro Guimarães, o secretário-geral do Ministério das Relações Exteriores, Antônio Patriota, o diretor do Centro Internacional de Políticas para o Crescimento Inclusivo, Rathin Roy, o vice-presidente da Academia Chinesa de Ciências Sociais, Li Yang, e os embaixadores da Índia, B. S. Prakash, da China, Qiu Xiaoqi, e da Rússia, Sergey Pogosovich Akopov.

(Fonte: Agência Brasil http://www. ipea. gov. br/003/00301009.jsp?uCD_CHAVE=14076.)

Postscript

On the June 30th 2009 meeting about the management reform of international division of Chinese Academy of Social Sciences (CASS) chaired by Wang Weiguang, the executive vice president of the Academy, I proposed to set up a cross-institute project – International Network of BRIC Think Tank Summit, which aimed to do some policy research for the forthcoming second BRIC leadership summit. Wang Weiguang approved my proposal immediately, and soon the Bureau of Scientific Research Management of CASS approved this project and appropriated the start-up fund, and I was appointed the coordinator of this project. Then Yang Yang the director of the Bureau of International Cooperation of CASS convened the director generals of the institutes from international division several times to discuss the preparation arrangement, including Zhang Yuyan the director general of the Institute of World Economics and Politics (IWEP), Wu Enyuan of the Institute of Russia, Eastern European & Central Asian Studies (IREECAS), Li Xiangyang of the Institute of Asia-Pacific Studies (IAPS) and Zheng Bingwen of the Institute of Latin American Studies (ILAS). In December 2009, with the help of Brazilian Ambassador Clodoaldo Hugueney to China, I went on a special trip to Brazil to visit Ambassador José Botafogo Gonçalves, the president of the Brazilian Center for International Relations (CPRI) and Marcio Pochmann, the president of the Institute for Applied Economic Research (IPEA), to discusse the arrangement of BRIC think tank summit before the BRIC Leadership Summit. Though we met for the very first time, Mr. Marcio Pochmann gladly agreed to bear the duty of host to take charge of the think tank summit.

After intense preparing work of several months, a Chinese delegation group of 16 members headed by Li Yang, the vice president of CASS, and Wang Hua, the director of

International Exchange Center at the International Department of Central Committee of CPC, finally made a trip to Brasília to attend the BRIC think tank summit titled "the role of BRIC in post-crisis gloal transition", which was hosted by IPEA of the Secretariat for Strategic Affairs of the Presidency of the Republic of Brazil. The delegation group was composed of experts and scholars from Chinese Academy of Social Sciences, International Department of Central Committee of CPC, Institute of International Studies of the Ministry of Foreign Affairs and Shanghai Institute of International Studies. The Institute of Latin American Studies of Russian Academy of Sciences and the Observer Research Foundation (India) also delegated dozen scholars to attend the summit.

Prof.Li Yang the vice president of CASS made a keynote address to the summit. Scholars of Chinese delegation exchanged views on some important issues with those from the other three countries of BRIC, identified both the consensus and differences among the academic communities of BRIC. During the summit, Chinese delegation group also visited Ambassador Samuel Pinheiro Guimarães the then Minister of the Secretariat for Strategic Affairs, as well as other academic agencies of Brazil.

Prof.Li Yang paid high attention to the fruit of this summit and emphasized the sustainability of the research of BRIC. He directed that the papers submitted on the summit be compiled and published. Thus we got this proceeding of the BRIC think tank summit.

As the coordinator of this project, I'm grateful to the above-mentioned agencies and leaders for their support. I should thank Chinese Social Sciences Documentation Publishing House for its support. I should also thank Chen Duqin the director of the Center of Brazilian Studies of ILAS and former ambassador to Brazil, Wu Baiyi the vice director of ILAS, Yang Xi and Zhou Zhiwei the research associate. I'm especially grateful to Wu Zhihua the director and chief journalist of People's Daily stationed in Brasília, without whom the cumbersome communication task for this international summit cannot have carried out so smoothly. Finally, I should thank Feng Yumin of IREECAS and Ye Hailin the research fellow of IAPS.

The publication of this proceeding marks an end of this project. As an experience of BRIC studies, this postscript aims to present the origin and context of the first BRIC think tank summit to readers, and also to promote the BRIC studies to move forward.

Prof. Zheng Bingwen, ILAS at CASS
Feb 17th, 2011

“金砖四国”与国际转型

BRICs智库巴西峰会的思考

BRICs & THE GLOBAL TRANSFORMATION

李扬／主编

社会科学文献出版社
SOCIAL SCIENCES ACADEMIC PRESS (CHINA)

目　录

“金砖四国”与环境

技术创新与“金砖四国”合作展望

中外媒体报道

序言

当前，我们正处于后危机时期。这个时期的问题是：一方面，造成此次金融危机的各种因素，如全球经济结构失衡、南北经济失衡、金融发展对实体经济的“疏远化”、货币政策效力递减、金融市场杠杆率过高、金融机构公司治理结构扭曲等，尚未消除；另一方面，危机中各国采取的非常规措施，如货币信贷供应增长过快、财政赤字骤增、市场秩序崩坏等，又在严重阻碍经济的复苏。这些问题若得不到有效解决，全球经济很难真正走上复苏之路。这意味着，尽管我们可能已经渡过了危机冲击最为严重的时期，但是，全球经济重回正常的增长之路，依然充满了困难和不确定性。

然而我们看到，在应对此次百年不遇的金融危机的过程中，“金砖四国”（中国、印度、俄罗斯、巴西）发挥了令世人瞩目的独特作用。危机爆发后，四国政府根据各自的国情采取了相应的经济刺激计划，并且收到了明显的效果，“金砖四国”的经济总和占全球 GDP 的比重由 2007 年的 13% 上升为 2009 年的 15%。最重要的是，过去 5 年中，“金砖四国”对世界经济增长的贡献率达到 50%。这些变化，不仅缓解了危机对四国经济的冲击，加速了南北经济格局的变化，也对全球经济的复苏作出了不可忽视的贡献。正是因为如此，世界普遍认为，“金砖四国”的发展正进入一个新的历史阶段，同时，“金砖四国”的合作也面临一个难得的历史机遇。

四国之所以应该，而且能够推进和拓宽相互间的合作，是因为我们都是发展中国家，有着相同的历史任务和共同的利益诉求。

作为发展中国家，四国都希望能改变现行的国际经济格局和政治秩序；都希望发展中国家能获得更为宽松的发展条件；都反对各种形式的贸易保护主义；都谋求增大发展中国家在国际事务和国际标准制定过程中的发言权；都要求改变作为此次全球危机重要根源的不合理的国际金融秩序；都致力于推动各类国际组织的改革，使之更充分地反映发展中国家的利益。更为重要的是，四国都希望以协商、合作、互利、共赢的方式，来解决现有国际体系中的问题，应对全球共同面临的挑战。

作为发展中国家，“金砖四国”之间存在着广阔的合作空间。

第一，四国在资源禀赋和经济结构方面存在较强的互补性，已经形成较好的经贸合作基础。在危机爆发之前的世界经济增长周期中，“金砖四国”之间的贸易增长迅速，从 2003 年的 359 亿美元增至 2008 年的 1685 亿美元，年均增长率高达 73.8%，增幅超过了同期世界贸易年均增长率的 3 倍。2009 年受全球金融危机的影响，四国间的贸易额减少了 15%，但与全球贸易形势相比，四国间的贸易仍显示出一定的活力。中国取代美国成为巴西第一大贸易伙伴，巴西和印度的双边贸易继续保持增长。这些发展使我们看到，尽管四国之间在局部贸易领域存在竞争，但是，金融危机事实上已经为四国提供了挖掘贸易潜力、调整贸易结构的机遇。

第二，四国在跨国直接投资方面存在广阔的合作空间。作为外国直接投资（FDI）的接受国，近年来“金砖四国”受到了全球投资者的青睐。2008 年四国当年吸收的 FDI 总量达到 2652 亿美元，占全球 FDI 总额的比重从 2005 年的 10% 增至 16%。金融危机进一步加速了这种趋势性变化，流入新兴市场和发展中国家的 FDI 已经超过了发达国家，2009 年中国吸收的 FDI 达到 900 亿美元，跃居世界第二位，俄罗斯的世界排名也升至了第四位。联合国贸发会议发布的《2009～2011 世界投资前景调查》报告指出，“金砖四国”将成为 FDI 的重点市场。尽管目前“金砖四国”之间的 FDI 依然极为有限，但是，通过改善国内投资环境、加大四国间相互引资的力度，并提供相应有利的条件，四国间的投资合作可以大有作为。

第三，四国在技术创新方面的合作同样具有较大的潜力。国际金融危机爆发后，四国都在寻找科技创新的突破口，并将此作为产业升级、拉动经济增长、走出危机的积极而有效的对策。中国政府在这次应对危机的过程中，在推出 4 万亿元投资政策的同时，加快了16项科技专项的实施，最近又提出了大力发展战略性新兴产业的目标。我们看到，“金砖四国”中的其他三国也都在根据自己的优势寻找科技创新的突破口。比如，俄罗斯发展纳米技术与核能技术，巴西发展乙醇和生物柴油等清洁能源技术，印度将信息业置于技术创新的优先产业等。我们相信，四国在科技创新，并以此引领经济长期持续增长方面，拥有加强合作、优势互补、共同发展的巨大潜力。

第四，气候变化及其带来的一系列问题是当今人类社会面临的严重问题之一，这不仅给我们四国提出了新的研究课题，同时也将为四国开辟又一个合作的平台。在这方面，巴西已经积累了很好的经验，并且具有国际领先的优势。在中国方面，大力发展绿色经济，研发和推广气候友好技术，实现经济与自然资源和环境的和谐发展，已经被确定为战略方针。所以，“金砖四国”在应对气候变化方面，除了在重大问题上协调各自的立场之外，还可以通过清洁能源、森林保护、提高能源使用效率等具体技术交流，进一步拓宽合作的领域。

全球金融危机对“金砖四国”的挑战是严峻的，但同时也让我们看到了扩大和深化四国合作的巨大潜力和机遇。尽管四国的国情存在较大差异，但在当前的形势下，我们共同面临着促使全球经济全面复苏并步入可持续发展的正常轨道，使我们的人民安居乐业的任务。这些就是实现“金砖四国”更密切合作的基础所在，同时也是四国合作的努力方向。求同存异、加强团结合作、维护发展中国家的共同利益、谋求发展中国家利益的最大化，应是推进“金砖四国”合作的方针和原则。

自20世纪末开始，中国就提出了经济发展方式转型的新战略。这一新战略追求的是科学发展和和谐发展的目标。中国所说的科学发展，指的是中国的经济发展要以满足广大人民的多方面需求和促进人的全面发展为出发点和落脚点，要以全球经济的均衡发展为出发点和落脚点；中国所说的和谐发展，指的是中国的经济发展追求的是人与自然之间、人与人之间、国家与国家之间的和谐共处。正是基于这一战略思维，中国高度重视发展与巴西、俄罗斯和印度的合作关系，高度重视发展与世界各国的合作关系。

在探索后危机时期有利于“金砖四国”深化合作的机制过程中，四国的智库可以发挥独特的作用。专家学者们可以通过各自的研究和努力，对于本国的经济社会发展，对于四国间的协调发展，对于全球经济的恢复，发挥重要的作用。

我认为，四国智库间的对话应该而且可以成为四国合作的重要渠道、平台和支持体系。我想，随着四国合作的不断深入，四国智库将肩负更重大的责任，这自然也就向四国的专家学者们提出了更高的要求。今后，各方需要进一步密切相互间日常性的学术交流，并开展更具针对性的合作研究。作为亚洲乃至世界的重要智库之一，中国社会科学院愿意为加强与巴西、俄罗斯和印度智库之间的联系与合作做出努力。

本书是参加 2010 年 4 月 14 ~ 15 日于巴西召开的“金砖四国”智库峰会的部分中外学者的论文汇编，为公众认识“金砖四国”，了解“金砖四国”合作现状和前景提供了一个窗口。

李　扬

中国社会科学院副院长

“金砖四国”与金融危机

“金砖四国”面临的危机考验

弗拉基米尔　M. 达维多夫　吴孝芹（译）*

“金砖四国”作为世界经济和国际政治合作新中心是历史新现象。但是在过去的四年里，从外交部层次的定期政治磋商发展到年度首脑会议经历了艰难的过程。“四方对话”涉及对待四个成员国国家利益和国际利益的广泛议题。

同时，人们对“金砖四国”现象的分析和科学性认知存在争议。一方面，其具备预测能力（高盛投资公司）；另一方面，它又通常滞后于实践。考虑到四国各自的特定市场和生产潜力，一些人认为不存在国家利益合作的广泛基础，它们也没有看到四个成员国之间为合作互动提供平台的商业和经济联系的大幅增加。该观点可能出于以下两点原因：当代全球发展观的西方中心主义倾向；传统全球经济和政治中心的某些集团致力于阻碍四国的友好关系并企图在四国间播下怀疑的种子。

学术界对于“金砖四国”现象的研究迄今仍主要为个人行为，基于国家的研究主要集中在国际比较方面。但是考虑到四个成员国之间的合作实践及发展前景，研究者的目标将决定四国合作潜力实现的可能性、四国之间的相互影响及对全球发展进程的总体影响。从这个角度而言，很难估算与第二次“金砖四国”

---

* 弗拉基米尔　M. 达维多夫，俄罗斯社会科学院（RAC）社会科学办公室成员、RAC 拉丁美洲研究所所长、俄罗斯联邦外交部研究委员会成员；吴孝芹，太原工业学院管理工程系讲师。

首脑会议同步举行的学术论坛的重要性。

考虑到以上所提任务的相关性，我们不得不就当前全球经济危机的影响进行探讨。当前存在的经济危机带来了全球发展的质量问题并突出了“金砖四国”的作用。这是一块试金石也是一个艰难的考验。当前危机需要我们对全球发展规律、“金砖四国”对变革环境的应对和战略选择，以及全球共同行动的内在逻辑进行新的理解。

一 当前危机的特性

当前的危机有着显著的特性。20 世纪后半期经济周期明显平缓（见图 1 和图 2）。

在过去的 30 年里，作为当代资本主义大本营的美国第一次成为经济危机中心。当前危机在对全球经济衰退的影响、传播速度及覆盖范围方面均为前所未有。

对于本次危机特性的讨论主要通过与 20 世纪 30 年代的大萧条比较进行。通过对两次危机进行比较，我们可以认为当前危机与大萧条相比在衰退程度及持久性上（2009 年下半年开始出现缓步增长）或有不及。但很明显，它在传播速度及覆盖范围上打破了纪录。

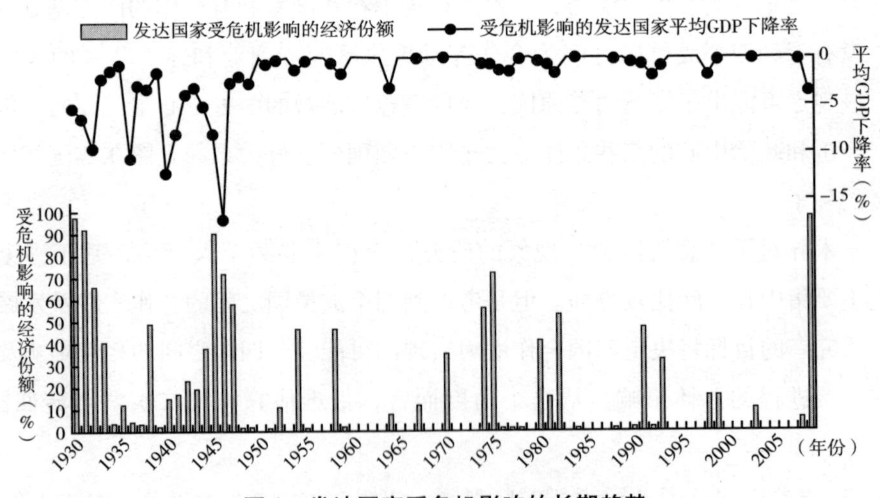

图 1 发达国家受危机影响的长期趋势

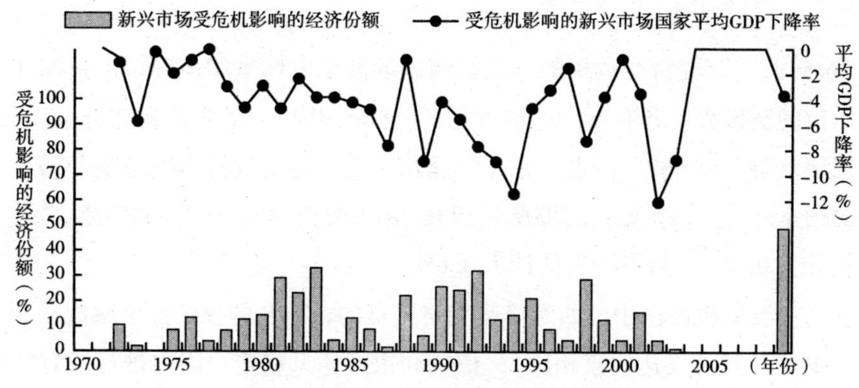

图 2 新兴市场受危机影响的长期趋势

这一事实引导我们对全球经济及国内经济的再生产机制变革的全球效应进行深思。基于"前全球化"（pre-globalization）标准对国内和国际市场进行监管可能会带来破坏市场力量的新风险。

这一环境决定了当前危机的特性。这场全球化时代的第一场危机揭露了基于微电子革命的技术进步带来的全球化进程所积累的矛盾和风险。

危机前新自由主义放松监管及国家背离其经济社会责任无疑加剧了这一情况的严重性。

当前国内和国际当局无法控制金融工具不断增加（尤其是衍生品）及传统全球经济中心（大量家庭、企业及独立国家）过度负债的势头。海外商业巨头越来越不受控制。毋庸置疑，全球化体系内部有一个环节出现问题（如美国抵押市场）将会导致整个国际金融环境的不稳定，进而影响国际贸易及处于行业生产关键领域的实体部门。因此此次危机不能仅仅被界定为金融危机，而应被称为全球经济危机。

二 "金砖四国"应对危机的情况

"金砖四国"如何应对当前危机？各国采取的反衰退措施效果如何？笔者相信来自巴西、俄罗斯、印度及中国的同行们均会根据各自国家的具体情况提出相应观点。

在此，笔者将对"金砖四国"的应对措施进行简要比较，总结各国应对危机的教训、采取的经济政策规律及"金砖四国"的合作前景，请各位同行批评指正。

"金砖四国"经济受危机的不良影响远远低于全球平均情况，但各国在危机中显示出的坚挺程度各有不同。以下笔者将按"BRIC"的顺序依次进行介绍。

巴西 《经济学家》杂志（伦敦）指出，巴西是受危机影响最晚并最早开始恢复的国家之一。[①] 事实上，2009 年巴西 GDP 增长率没有超过最低警戒线（一些人估计为 0.3%，另一些人估计为 0.6%）。

在第一波危机冲击中巴西经济是相对坚挺的，涉及的投机性金融流动和实体经济较少（与其他发达国家相比），信贷和银行体系稳定，国内进行了有效的监管控制。

巴西充分利用了危机前的牛市。首先，将外部债务纳入监管渠道，并将大量流动性储备纳入净债权类。其次，致力于消除巴西经济赤字，实现原料碳氢化合物的自给自足。再次，巴西在国际贸易多元化方面取得长足进展，与最具活力的市场进行了广泛合作（包括"金砖四国"）。最后，致力于减贫的多项社会计划取得可喜成绩，巩固了国内市场。

需要特别关注的是，2007～2010 年间致力于基础设施现代化目标的 PAC（促进经济增长计划）的实现。金融资源流入该计划（2.8 亿美元）使交通、能源系统管理、通信及扩大住房建设均取得了显著进展。对于各种商业活动的支持保证了危机期间国内各市场的正常运行。

在信贷和银行系统占据较大份额的国有银行对于巴西从危机中恢复起到了积极作用。国有银行信贷占总信贷活动的比重从 2008 年 6 月的 34%（占 GDP 的 12%）增至 2009 年 9 月的 41%（占 GDP 的 18.5%）。[②] 国有银行的活动刺激了 2009 年底民间借贷的复苏。

笔者预计 2010 年巴西 GDP 增长率为 3%～5%，经济将持续复苏，对巴西经济的外国和国内直接投资以及有价证券投资将增加。

当然，巴西的情形亦非理想情形。巴西的经济发展依然存在诸多障碍，例如，社会两极分化、大量贫困地区的存在。优化投资环境还受到高犯罪率的影

① 巴西腾飞："2010 年经济学家"，伦敦，14－20，11.2009，p.5。

② CEPAL（拉丁美洲经济委员会）：《2009 年拉丁美洲和加勒比经济概览》，智利圣地亚哥，2009 年 12 月 12 日，巴西——P.1。

响。研发（R&D）成本增加，但其水平还不足以采用创新发展模式。为了确保其作为全球经济新领头羊之一的地位，巴西还需扩大对生产性投资的积累以增强经济增长的总体活力。

俄罗斯 该国对此次危机的应对并不成功，尽管危机前期俄罗斯有较高经济增长率及大量的外汇储备。该经济增长率主要得益于世界市场能源产品价格的上涨及过去十年国内政治局势的稳定。

由于其出口主要局限在石油和天然气方面，以及在尽量减少对外公共债务的同时伴随着企业对外负债的大量增加，世界主要经济中心的严重衰退对俄罗斯产生了极大冲击。企业对外负债的增加可能源于长期信贷货币供给较少、成本较高（否则，他们将在外国市场提供过剩资金）及国家监管机构对企业部门从外国贷款缺少适当控制。

危机前期的资源积累为克服流动性短缺提供了大量资源。正如俄罗斯前总统普京所言，截至2009年春已有占GDP12%的资源用于复苏。值得注意的是，政府选择扶持大量弱势群体。2009～2010年调整政府预算后，社会支出依然维持该数额，甚至有所增加。自然，从短期看，这制约了其他领域的恢复。

俄政府有部分项目用于支持那些拥有不良资产但具有战略意义的公司及经济专业化程度极为狭窄的城市，以防止失业出现毁灭性的蔓延。2009年政府采取了一些措施，用于支持中小企业（如税收豁免和信贷支持）。自2009年中期开始，该措施呈现出显著效果，部分行业生产不再下降。2009年底，失业率停止上升，并于2010年初逐渐下降。

与此同时，反衰退措施的批评者们发现，这些措施存在明显迟滞效应并产生了大量成本。银行部门在注入流动性的过程中，没有严格规定信贷资金的特定用途，这意味着该资金是由政府提供的。结果资金被用于金融和外汇交易，导致资本外逃。反衰退行政措施的实施则滞后了好几个月。

虽然如此，当前复苏呈积极态势。政府可以从严重衰退中汲取教训，在制定政策时应致力于实现经济现代化、出口多元化并逐步转向创新发展。这是绝对必要的战略变革。

印度 该国经济政策（尼赫鲁创立）致力于自给自足的传统导向在此次反危机政策中得到充分体现。来自银行系统的国家支持领域非常狭窄，但小额贷款数量增加。新税法促进了国内消费。大量投资投向基础设施领域，而该领域

（包括交通和能源）在印度经济中处于弱势地位。可以预期 2010 年 GNP 增长率将达到之前水平，尽管没有现代化的基础设施保持长期活力是不可能的。

近期的中等教育免费决策是积累“人力资本”的重大举措。尽管国家预算会比较艰难，但从长期来看该决策将改善劳动力市场。但是短期内该决策会恶化预算赤字，该国预算赤字在“金砖四国”中最高（占 2010 年 GNP 的 6.4%）。

中国 该国在危机期间将保持收入稳定，约为高位收入的 86%。2009 年的情况证实了这一点。的确，超过 2 万亿美元的巨额外汇储备及国内市场的发展使得中国能够平稳渡过危机，但对于中国而言这一指标仍不尽如人意。人口和社会责任需要较高的发展活力。毫无疑问，发展减缓将加剧中国经济与社会的内部矛盾和不平衡。

同时，中国作为当代经济火车头的形象在不断强化。巴西人毫无理由地认为，向中国出口是其反危机的最有效措施。事实上，2009 年中国超过美国成为巴西产品的最大进口国。同时，巴西对向其他区域的出口进行了严格限制。

中国的反危机政策主要体现为如下行动：对具有战略地位的企业进行直接财政支持；从“硬性”金融信贷政策转化为“软性”政策；从人民币汇率渐进式升值转为与美元挂钩（以维持出口）；启动内部消费，包括对耐用品实行优惠价格；拓宽社保覆盖面（国内居民）；通过税收政策刺激出口。

中国允许从危机初期积累的巨额财政储备中拿出 5 亿美元用于维持实体经济部门，主要投放于基础设施项目，推动交通和能源体系的现代化。简言之，2009 年初中国用于反危机的金额约占 GNP 的 13%。

现有的政治体制有助于中国政府对地方决策的实施提供有效指导。中国的“垂管力”（“Power Vertical”）使得决议不仅可以传达给中高层政府，还可以传达给经济部门。政府实际上对所有大中型企业均有约束。当然，人们不应该对中国的“垂管”过度评价，但应注意到，在全球经济危机中，中国政府在强化经济方面做了很多，如调用内部市场储备，优先发展十七大决议计划通过的项目。

三　从危机中汲取的教训及“金砖四国”之间的合作

根据危机反映出来的积极或消极特征，我们可以说“金砖四国”作为世界经济的一部分，将推动世界经济发展。2008 年“金砖四国”对全球 GDP 增长的贡献高达 52%（见表 1）。

表 1 对全球经济增长贡献比较

单位：%

国家 \ 份额	占全球 GDP 的份额	对全球 GDP 增长的贡献份额	国家 \ 份额	占全球 GDP 的份额	对全球 GDP 增长的贡献份额
美　国	20.7	2.7	巴　西	2.8	4.6
日　本	6.2	-1.5	俄罗斯	3.3	5.8
欧　洲	15.6	3.9	印　度	4.9	11
欧盟(27 国)	21.9	7.6	中　国	11.3	31.1
“金砖四国”	22.3	52.5			

资料来源：根据 IMF 和世界银行统计资料估算而成。Год планеты. Ежегодник. Выпуск 2009. Гл. ред. В. Г. Барановский. М., 2009, с. 302.

若将全球各经济中心的 GDP 预测值进行比较，我们可以发现，在危机“高峰期”的 2009 年及之后（2010 ~ 2011 年）“金砖四国”对全球经济增长的贡献将进一步提高（见表 2）。

表 2 GDP 增长率/下降率估算*

单位：%

国家 \ 年份	2009	2010	2011
美　国	-2.4	3.1	2.9
日　本	-5.7	1.7	1.6
欧　洲	-3.8	1.2	1.4
巴　西	0.3	5.0	4.5
俄罗斯	-7	3.5(5.0*)	4.3
印　度	5.5	7.7	8
中　国	8.2	9.6	8.2

* 世界银行估算。

资料来源：The Economist Intelligence Unit, *The Economist*, London, 28.11.2009, p.97; 27.03.2010, p.97。

可见，在当前及未来，中国经济将是（全球经济增长的）主要动力，其次为印度。俄罗斯经济在危机“高峰”期所反映出来的脆弱性需要正确评价以便进行矫正，但也无需对其过度夸张。自 2009 年下半年起俄罗斯经济活动已开始恢复并继续保持恢复势头，通胀率、失业率开始下降，国内市场增长，信贷成本下降，外国投资进入该国。

尤为重要的是，鉴于俄罗斯当时的情况，该国政府领导人决定在经济发展上进行创新型经济模式的战略转型。

俄罗斯不仅具有重要的地缘政治地位，还是“金砖四国”实现战略和创新互动的重要纽带。由于中国和印度面临不断增长的资源和生态制约，拥有丰富自然资源的巴西可从中国和印度获得大量收益。同样，俄罗斯在空间和能源（包括核能）技术及其他关键领域的科技潜力也使得它与其他“金砖四国”成员存在广泛合作的可能性（见表3）。

表3 “金砖四国”相互贸易额

项目＼年份	2007	2008	2009
巴西			
向其他三国出口(10亿美元)	15.4	22.2	26.5
占其总出口的比重(%)	7.8	11.2	17.3
印度			
向其他三国出口(10亿美元)	12.4	14.5	13.0
占其总出口的比重(%)	8.5	8.0	7.0
中国			
向其他三国出口(10亿美元)	64.0	83.5	71.1
占其总出口的比重(%)	5.2	5.8	5.8
俄罗斯			
向其他三国出口(10亿美元)	19.3	28.4	23.7
占其总出口的比重(%)	5.5	6.0	7.9

资料来源：WTO（http://stats.wto.org）；联合国（http://unstats.un.org）；俄罗斯联邦海关局（http://www.customs.ru）。

2009年“金砖四国”之间的相互贸易证明四国需要进行合作。在过去的十年里（1999～2008年），“金砖四国”之间的相互贸易增长率高于世界平均水平，也高于其与传统世界经济中心的贸易增长率。

此外，2009年“金砖四国”的相互贸易与全球经济形势相比显示出一定的稳定性。可以说在危机这一大背景下，这部分贸易是整个世界贸易中最为坚挺的。

2009年，“金砖四国”之间的商品贸易总额下降20.4%，全球商品贸易总额平均下降23%，欧盟（27个国家）商品贸易总额下降21.3%，日本商品贸易总额下降25.7%。

巴西对“金砖四国”其他成员的出口额上升，从2008年的222亿美元上升为2009年的265亿美元。“金砖四国”其他成员占巴西出口份额的比重从11.2%上升到17.3%。

俄罗斯的总出口明显下降（主要原因为价值贬值），但增加了对“金砖四国”其他成员的销售份额（从2008年的6.0%增加为2009年的7.9%）。“金砖四国”其他成员占俄罗斯贸易额的比重从9.5%上升为11%。

印度的这一指标下降，从8.0%降为7.0%。其与俄罗斯的贸易情形恰好相反，2009年俄罗斯对印度的出口上升约13.5%，而印度对俄罗斯的出口仍保持在2008年的水平。

2009年中国的情形有所不同。经历了危机前期（截至2008年）对“金砖四国”其他成员的贸易稳步上升后，出现了显著下跌（约下跌26.5%）。但是，根据2010年1月份的数据显示，其与“金砖四国”其他成员的贸易活动呈现恢复势头。

可以肯定，“金砖四国”均会从危机中汲取教训。我们将从以下三个共性层面逐步展开分析：第一，各国处理国家发展问题的方式；第二，“金砖四国”之间的联系；第三，四国在重建世界经济国际监管制度中所处的地位。

危机强化了国家在经济发展、工业现代化及创新进程中进行系统组织的重要性，要求国家具有发展的战略视角并在其影响较大的领域为企业活动提供有利条件。所有“金砖四国”成员均在经济政策和社会心理方面具有这样的传统。

当前形势要求实施经济保障机制和预防性反周期行为。解决这一问题不在于积累充足的国际储备，而在于以合理的生产方式使用该储备的能力。

此外，应对危机还取决于控制国内经济和金融部门进行跨国投机的能力。此次危机中这一教训是惨重的。发展无法保证未来不再发生波动。长期统计信息可以反映历史规律，可能下个十年里经济还会出现周期性下滑。经济政策和政府监管机制的修正依然无法使我们相信，这能阻止下一次普通危机转化成非同一般的危机。

“金砖四国”的所有成员，面临的首要问题是无法在长期内维持高速经济增长以逐步实现现代化。“金砖四国”基础设施的落后成为实现长期经济高速增长的严重瓶颈。

当前的一大紧迫任务就是，努力降低贫困和收入不均衡（社会和地区）程度。否则，“金砖四国”将无法在长期内发挥内部市场大量资源的潜力从而提升其在下一个经济周期（尤其是恶性周期）中的稳定性。

“金砖四国”进入创新阶段各有不同的历史和渊源。俄罗斯的目标是：防止研发（R&D）领域腐败（有大量传承）、重建各领域的内部联系（将基础科学与生产领域对接）、建立企业的有效激励机制。

其他"金砖四国"成员的任务又有所不同。中国正处于创新周期的模仿阶段，采取了大量措施试图"迈入"更高阶段。但是，这显然还需要长期的努力。印度和巴西在某些前沿领域已经形成了开展创新的微观环境，但资源、高素质人才及制度激励的缺乏依然限制了其进一步发展。因此，我们有必要对所有创新环节予以关注，尤其是 R&D 的高端环节。

自从发起"金砖四国"外交磋商机制以来，政治上的"四方对话"已经开始，经济合作越来越密切，业已实现了双边合作。

四国近期已就某些经济问题（金融、能源、农业）进行了四方磋商。在本次巴西利亚举行的首脑会议期间，首次举行了企业家会议。但是，很明显，未来四国需要进行更广泛的合作（比如"三边合作"）。合作领域可包含航空、传统或非传统能源、食品等。

"金砖四国"之间的贸易已经彰显了其重要性。四国贸易不断增加的可能性成为四国经济稳定的重要保障（即便在面临危机时）。这应获得"金砖四国"贸易和经济政策决策层的高度重视，但四国仍未就相关合作项目进行讨论。似乎这一问题目前还不够紧迫，但我们不应忽视各领域四边合作项目的重要性。

"金砖四国"的合作弥补了 20 国集团匹兹堡峰会通过的世界经济及金融机制的缺陷。这一机制对世界金融制度的发言权及资本权进行了首次重新分配，尽管这仅仅是开始。全世界及 20 国集团（作为世界经济最强组合）依然对世界机制的重新分配缺乏充分的理解和接纳。尽管对此进行了大量讨论，但仍缺乏进行变革的政治意愿，主要国家似乎也未作好技术上的准备。

可能现在还不是讨论采用更多比例代表制的"世界经济政府"的合适时机，但现有体制在方法和建构新制度上取得了一定进展。区域层面的重构进程已经开始。欧洲委员会（EC）已就欧洲 IMF 进行了讨论，拉丁美洲这方面的区域合作也已开展。"金砖四国"已通过金融活动多元化及使用国内货币进行部分交易结算等预防措施保障各国免受美元波动的影响。

为了适应 21 世纪的要求，"金砖四国"作为新兴经济体之间的一种合作，不仅有利于世界经济稳定，还在推动世界经济转向全球监管制度、最小化转型期风险及拟定世界经济稳定发展的灵活模式方面扮演着不可或缺的历史角色。

后危机时代“金砖四国”合作空间加大

李向阳*

作为新兴市场经济体的代表，在国际金融危机之前，“金砖四国”的崛起就已经引起国际社会的广泛关注。在这场国际金融危机及其复苏进程中，“金砖四国”经济的抗危机能力得到了充分体现。它们不仅受到危机的打击较小，而且早于发达国家走出衰退，实现了强劲的复苏。进入后危机时代，由于世界经济的发展模式、格局及治理结构都将发生重大调整和变化，“金砖四国”无论是在短期经济政策协调还是长期发展战略方面，无论是推动全球经济可持续发展还是参与全球治理都将面临新的机遇和挑战。因而，四国拓展其合作空间既是维护自身利益的共同诉求，也是对全球经济的贡献。

一 经济刺激政策退出的协调机制

目前，国际金融危机已经进入复苏阶段，但仍然存在诸多风险，其中最为突出的要属经济刺激政策的退出。危机爆发之后，在20国集团内部，无论是发达国家还是新兴市场经济体均为遏制危机采取了大规模刺激政策。实践证明，这种政策协调是非常有效的。从2009年第二季度开始，伴随经济复苏，主要发达国家与新兴市场经济体的经济走势呈现出愈来愈大的差异：美日欧三大经济体复苏

---

* 李向阳，中国社会科学院亚洲和太平洋研究所所长、研究员。

进程迟缓，而以“金砖四国”为代表的新兴市场经济体则出现了强劲的复苏态势（见图1）。因此，尽管有20国集团峰会的协调，发达国家之间、发达国家成员与新兴市场经济体成员之间的政策导向已经出现巨大的分歧。这在2010年的多伦多峰会上表现得非常明显。甚至不同国际经济组织之间的政策建议也大相径庭：国际货币基金组织担心大国经济刺激政策同时退出引发“二次探底”，而经合组织则坚持尽快实施退出政策。

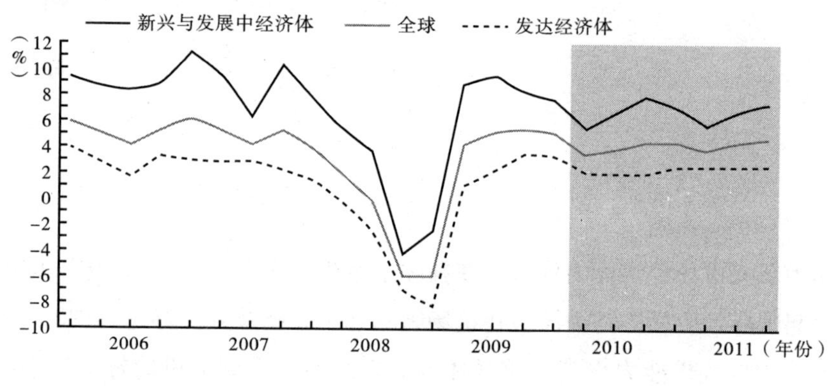

图1　全球经济增长率

资料来源：IMF（2010）World Economic Outlook：Update，July 2010。

对“金砖四国”而言，围绕经济刺激政策的退出时机和方式不仅需要与发达国家之间进行协调——这是维护全球经济稳定复苏的必要条件，而且还需要相互之间进行协调，以维护自身的经济稳定。

这场国际金融危机对“金砖四国”经济是一次纯粹的外部冲击。除俄罗斯之外，与发达国家相比，其他三国经济受到的冲击较轻。进入复苏阶段之后，“金砖四国”经济增长率要远高于发达国家。与此相对应，目前“金砖四国”经济已经明显进入过热状态：国内通货膨胀压力显现，资产价格涨幅过大（一定程度上源于危机阶段调整幅度不足）。

另外，2010年上半年的欧洲债务危机为全球经济复苏的进程投下了阴影。进入2010年下半年，美国、日本第二季度经济增长数据低于预期导致对全球经济“二次探底”的担忧再次盛行；主要国际经济组织对2011年全球经济增长率的预测（低于2010年）也加剧了对经济复苏可持续性的担忧。由于这些隐患均来自发达国家，国际资本（尤其是热钱）正在大规模地流向以“金砖四国"为代表的新兴市场经济体，从而加剧了后者的货币汇率升值。对此，"金砖四国"政府管理部门在退出经济刺激政策上正在面临两难困境：国内经济过热迫切实施紧缩性财政货币政策；外部风险又限制了包括提高利率在内的政策退出。如果提高利率，外资的流入会进一步加剧汇率升值与国内资产泡沫的压力。

目前，主要发达国家与"金砖四国"在刺激经济政策退出问题上客观上形成了两大阵营：由于财政赤字压力巨大，多数发达国家已经宣布实施紧缩财政政策的退出战略（同时继续保持低利率）；而"金砖四国"总体上财政赤字压力不大，退出战略的重点只能放在紧缩货币政策上。在时机的选择上，发达国家希望"金砖四国"能够延后政策的退出，继续引领全球经济的复苏。而"金砖四国"则面临进退两难的困境，尽管印度和巴西已经步入了加息轨道，中国也有选择地退出了刺激政策。

短期内，如何协调各自的退出战略及其与发达国家政策相匹配的退出战略是"金砖四国"合作的一个新领域。

二　全球"再平衡"压力与经济增长模式的调整

在国际金融危机之前，"金砖四国"经济高速增长的一个重要来源是外需。作为大国经济，尽管四国经济的对外依存度存在差异，但总体来看四国经济的对外依存度水平较高（见图2）。这种格局的背后是以美国为首的发达国家负债消

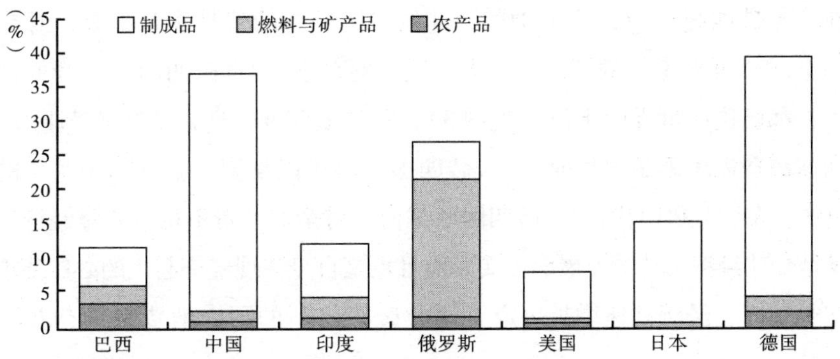

图2　"金砖四国"与美国、日本、德国的对外依存度（商品出口/GDP，2007年）

资料来源：WTO。

费模式。

国际金融危机已经证明，负债消费模式不仅对危机负有不可推卸的责任，而且也是不可持续的。因此，“再平衡”将是全球经济可持续增长的一个必要条件。作为“再平衡”的一方，美国已经开始调整其储蓄—消费格局，试图改变多年来的负债消费模式。这种调整主要来自两种机制：一是提高私人储蓄率，二是降低负债/个人可支配收入比率。如果以1990年代的水平为调整目标，这种调整对全球总需求的影响将是十分巨大的。在1990年代，美国家庭的储蓄率维持在7%~8%，负债/个人可支配收入比率为100%。截至2010年7月的最新统计数据显示，美国的私人储蓄率已经从危机前的不足1%上升到6.4%。① 负债/个人可支配收入比率目前为130%左右。按照麦肯锡全球研究所（McKinsey Global Institute）估计，在其他条件不变的情况下，美国私人储蓄率每上升1个百分点，消费将减少1000亿美元左右；在收入不变的条件下，负债/个人可支配收入比率每下降1个百分点，消费也将下降1000亿美元左右。② 此外，考虑到日本经济和欧洲经济短期内难以找到国内消费需求新的增长点，整个发达国家消费需求增速放慢将是一个必然趋势。

作为“再平衡”的另一方，亚洲经济理应作出相应的调整，原因是亚洲经济是一直拥有巨大的贸易顺差。但就目前来看，一方面亚洲自身的经济规模和消费需求规模不足以弥补美国所留下的消费需求缺口；另一方面，多数亚洲经济体尚未作好调整出口导向型模式的准备。因而，后危机时代全球经济将面临一个巨大的挑战：消费需求不足。

在“金砖四国”中，除了中国，其他三国经济的贸易顺差不大，看起来直接受到全球“再平衡”的压力也不大。但问题在于，“金砖四国”本身的经济规模庞大，都已位居世界前十位（见图3），对外依存度较高，且有继续上升之势。面对全球消费需求不足的局面，“金砖四国”将难以复制“亚洲四小龙”的经济起飞模式。在后危机时代，“金砖四国”如何应对全球消费不足与调整经济发展模式不仅是全球经济可持续发展的需要，而且也是自身实现经济起飞的必然要求。

在长期内，经济高速增长决定了“金砖四国”的国内消费需求有着巨大的

---

① Federal Reserve Bank of New York，U. S. Economy and Financial Markets，Aug. 15，2010.

② 《美国消费者怎么了》，2009年4月16日英国《金融时报》Lex专栏。

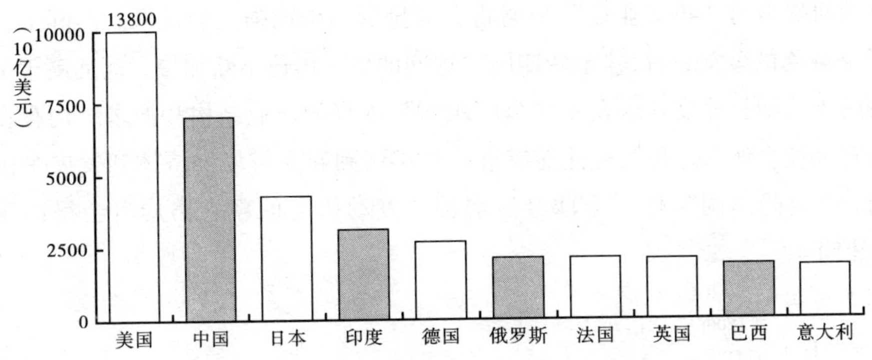

图3 金砖四国与主要发达国家经济规模比较
（按购买力平价，2007年）

资料来源：IMF。

潜力。以中国为例，中国政府已经明确提出转变经济发展方式，其中一项重要内容就是扩大国内消费需求，改变过去以投资和出口为主的经济增长模式。为此，在即将于2011年实施的“十二五”规划中会把扩大国内消费需求作为核心战略目标。由于中国人均GDP已经跨越了3000美元的关口，中国城市居民对汽车、住房的需求增速加快。2009年中国已经成为世界第一大汽车生产国和消费国（见图4）。同时，中国政府也在积极推进城市化的进程，进入城市的农民将成为新的消费需求来源。再以印度为例，连续多年的高速经济增长已经使印度形成了一支庞大的中产阶级队伍，他们的消费需求将为进一步的增长奠定基础。同时，

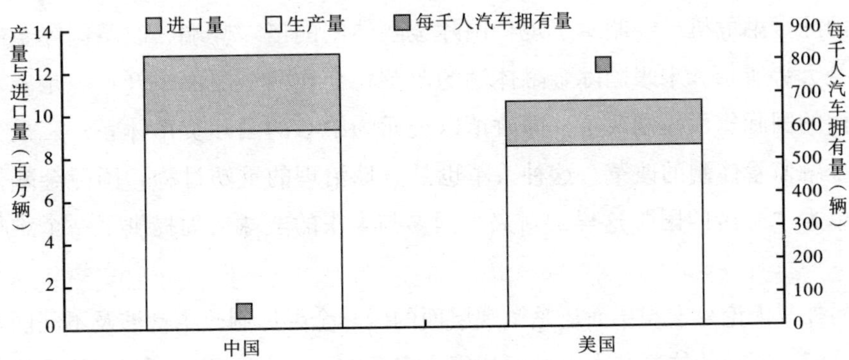

图4 中国超过美国成为世界最大的汽车生产与进口国

资料来源：IMF。

印度政府提出的“再工业化”战略将会对投资品构成强大的需求。实际上，自国际金融危机爆发之后，“金砖四国”之间的贸易增速不断加快，远远高于全球贸易的平均增长速度。这表明“金砖四国”本身的产业结构和需求结构存在巨大的互补性。如果这种互补性能够进一步扩展到新兴市场经济体和发展中国家之间，“金砖四国”作为全球经济增长“发动机”的现有格局将会得以延续（见图5）。

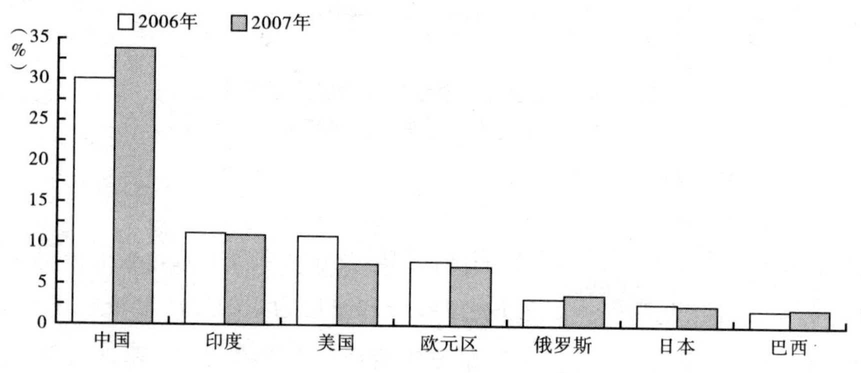

图5　金砖四国对全球经济增长的贡献（以PPP为基础）

资料来源：IMF，World Economic Outlook，2008。

三　国际金融体制改革与全球治理参与

国际金融危机已经昭示了现行国际金融体制的诸多弊端，改革国际金融体制将是大势所趋。未来国际金融体制的改革将会在两个层面展开：一是宏观经济层面的国际货币体制改革，即改革以美元为中心的国际货币体系；二是微观层面金融监管体制的改革。这种改革也是全球治理的重塑过程，国际金融体系的改革为“金砖四国”这样的新兴大国参与未来的全球治理提供了一个难得的机遇。

另外，无论是宏观层面还是微观层面的国际金融体制改革都涉及不同国家的利益分配，原有的体制基本上是发达国家主导的。对发达国家而言，目前的改革是一种不得已的选择。一是国际社会对美国次贷危机引发国际金融危机普遍持批评立场，要求美国承担责任的呼声加大，而美国客观上又需要国际社会共同应对危机。这就迫使它在金融改革问题上不得不做出让步。二是来自国内政治压力：金融纾困计划本质上是纳税人为金融家不负责任的冒险行为埋单，等于是私人债务的国家化（或全民化）。更有甚者，得到纾困的华尔街金融机构仍然继续发放巨额的奖金。对金融界的民愤开始影响到政党的选举，这是一种比外部国际压力更大的改革动力。迄今为止，各方对改革的方向提出了多种方案。问题的关键在于，改革的力度将会有多大。这将取决于发达国家的意愿。具体地说，未来国际金融体制改革的进程将不能损害发达国家在全球金融业中的主导地位。在这种意义上，"金砖四国"要想利用国际金融体制改革扩大对全球治理的参与度将会面临巨大的挑战。

以"金砖四国"为代表的新兴市场经济体要求参与国际金融体制的改革是大势所趋。以美元为中心的国际货币体系是战后初期布雷顿森林体系的产物，是美国经济霸权利益的体现。经过 1970 年代的危机和改革，欧洲与日本的利益开始在一定程度上有所体现，但广大发展中国家的利益总体上是被忽略的。以这场国际金融危机为标志，新兴市场经济体的诉求已经到了不可忽视的地步。例如，在全球经济中，"金砖四国"的经济规模份额已经超过了 15%（这还是以市场汇率计算的），外汇储备份额达到了 40%，进出口贸易和吸收的外国直接投资份额也都超过了 15%，至于四国近年来对全球经济增长的贡献度则更是无与伦比（见图 6）。20 国集团取代八国集团讨论国际金融危机的应对措施和出路就是最明显的标志。目前可以这么说，没有"金砖四国"参与的国际金融体制改革已

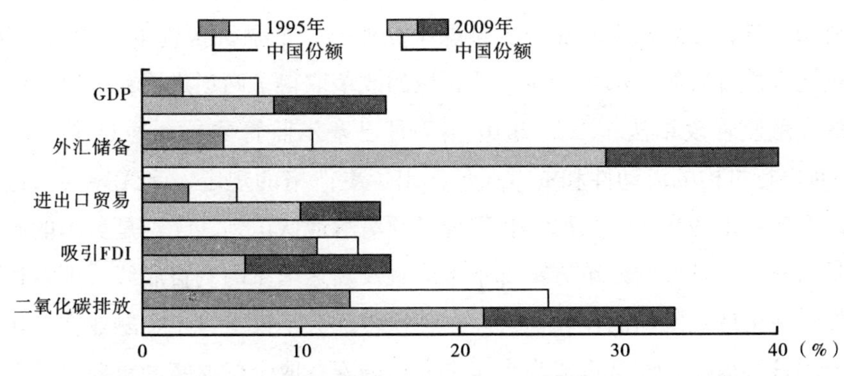

图 6　金砖四国在全球经济中的地位

资料来源：IMF；WTO；UNCTAD；EIA。

经失去了其合法性。然而，需要强调的是，要求“金砖四国”参与国际金融体制改革并不意味着“金砖四国”的利益诉求能够自动得到体现。在这一点上，“金砖四国”存在巨大的合作空间。

在宏观层面，对美元国际货币体系的改革迄今为止还只是局部的。国际金融危机已经证明，建立在民族国家货币基础之上的世界货币体系存在固有的缺陷，即货币发行者的不负责任行为。改革的方向应该是扩大国际货币基金的特别提款权在未来国际货币体系中的地位。然而，如果美国在国际货币基金组织中的主导地位不改变，这种改革不可能取得实质性的进展。目前，特别提款权的基础是发达国家的货币：美元占44%，欧元占34%，日元和英镑各占11%。如果不改变发达国家主导国际货币基金组织的格局，即使未来世界货币从美元转向特别提款权，世界货币的基础也难以有根本性变化。国际金融危机爆发以来，我们看到相对于美元，欧元、日元、英镑的地位不是上升，而是呈现衰落之势。因而，至少在中期内，以美元为核心的国际货币体系不会发生根本性变化。此外，国际货币体系的稳定性还面临着一个新的风险，那就是发达国家沉重的财政赤字负担（见表1）。这一问题如果得不到妥善解决，所有的改革措施都将会化为泡影。例如，倘若某些大国最终选择通货膨胀方式解决政府债务危机（这在发达国家历史上是屡见不鲜的），国际货币体系的稳定性将不复存在。

在微观层面，对金融监管的改革同样存在巨大的阻力。加强对金融业的监管涉及广泛的领域，原因是每个环节的监管缺失都对这场金融危机的发生负有不可推卸的责任，如金融监管机构的设置与职责，金融机构的内部激励机制，非银行金融机构业务，金融衍生品业务，金融中介业务，金融机构资本金比例与构成，金融机构规模过大等。迄今为止，该领域的改革取得了两项进展：一是美国通过了新的金融监管改革法；二是2010年7月巴塞尔监管委员会通过了“巴塞尔Ⅲ”，对银行机构的流动性和资本充足作出了更严格的规定。毫无疑问，这是朝正确的方向迈出的步伐。然而，我们也必须清醒地认识到，无论是美国的改革方案还是巴塞尔委员会的改革方案都不可能触及发达国家的利益底线，即发达国家金融体系在全球范围内的比较优势。这种比较优势不仅支撑了金融业在发达国家经济中的核心地位，而且也成为多年来发达国家获取全球财富的重要来源。以美国金融监管改革法为例，此前被舆论认定为最重要的内容（也是“沃克尔规则”的核心之一）——金融机构“大而不能倒”的问题并没有得到解决。至于“巴塞尔Ⅲ"更是发达国家之间相互妥协的结果。目前，我们虽然还无法确切地评估这些改革举措对发展中国家的影响，但在推进这些改革过程中要提防一种可能的风险，即发达国家"生病"，发展中国家"吃药"。

表1 国家排序*：按债务的可持续程度

	占 GDP 的百分比(%),2010 年预测数		减去融资成本的 GDP 增速(%)♀	主权债务，到期的时间(年)♂
	基本预算差额,经过周期性调整§	净债务§		
希腊	-4.6	94.6	-3.2	7.7
爱尔兰	-7.0	38.0	-5.1	6.8
英国	-6.7	59.0	-1.5	13.7
日本	-5.9	104.6	0.1	5.4
葡萄牙	-2.7	62.6	-2.3	6.5
西班牙	-4.3	41.6	-3.0	6.7
法国	-3.8	60.7	-0.7	6.9
美国	-7.0	65.2	1.4	4.8
波兰	-5.3	32.4	-0.7	5.2
意大利	2.2	100.8	-1.0	7.2
匈牙利	4.2	62.1	-3.5	3.3
比利时	1.3	85.4	-0.6	5.6
荷兰	-1.4	36.5	-0.6	5.4
奥地利	-0.9	42.9	-0.6	7.0
德国	-1.2	54.7	-0.5	5.8
捷克	-1.9	5.3	0.0	6.4
挪威	-7.8	-143.6	2.4	4.9
加拿大	-2.7	32.6	2.0	5.2
丹麦	-1.4	1.6	0.1	7.9
澳大利亚	-0.7	-1.3	0.2	5.0
瑞士	0.4	11.0	0.5	6.7
芬兰	-0.9	-46.4	0.9	4.3
瑞典	-0.3	-13.1	1.5	6.4

注：* 排序基于一国前三种债务指标的总额。

§ 指中央政府。

♀ 对 2010～2011 年名义 GDP 平均增长率的预测数（扣除最新到期国债收益）。

♂ 加权平均。

资料来源：Blooberg；EIU；OECD；*The Economist*。

四 贸易保护主义抬头与推动多哈回合谈判

受国际金融危机的冲击，2009 年全球贸易出现了战后最严重的下滑。与此同时，危机阶段各国政府所推出的一揽子刺激经济政策包含了许多新型保护主义措施。这些措施之所以被称为新型保护主义措施是因为它们并不违反现有的多边贸易规则，但其造成的后果客观上阻碍了自由贸易。其一，购买本国货条款。为了拉动国内需求，为本国企业创造商机，在危机阶段推出的财政刺激方案中，很多国家政府明文规定，政府支出项目优先或只购买本国供应商的产品。理由是，用纳税人的钱刺激经济，如果购买外国产品，那就丧失了刺激本国经济的目的。2009 年初美国奥巴马政府在其经济刺激方案中就明确附加了“购买美国货”条款。按照该条款的要求，只有和美国签订自由贸易区协定或者签署世界贸易组织《政府采购协定》的国家和地区才有可能获得美国政府经济刺激计划中的采购合同。此外，像英国布朗政府提出的“把英国的就业机会留给英国人”的口号实际上和“购买美国货”条款有同样的效果。这些做法虽不违背 WTO 相关条款，但明显与 WTO 的非歧视原则相悖。其二，加大对本国陷入困境企业的补贴与救助力度。在国际金融危机期间，欧美发达国家对本国企业的救助力度是前所未有的，尤其是对金融机构的救助。名义上看，这种救助是为了维护金融体系的安全，保护出资人的利益。但如果考虑到发达国家企业的全球经营网络特征，这种补贴或救助实际上与对制造业企业出口进行补贴并无二致。其三，金融保护主义成为这次危机中的一种新型保护主义。与以往经济危机阶段盛行的贸易保护主义不同，此次危机还增加了金融保护主义。原因是，受国际金融危机打击最重的是欧美发达国家的金融业，金融机构的流动性短缺极为严重，对企业的惜贷成为经济复苏的最大障碍。为此，各国政府向金融机构注入大量流动性，以遏制信贷市场的枯竭。然而，为了防止金融机构获得流动性以后向外国企业贷款，许多发达国家政府附加了只能向本国企业贷款的条款。这在本质上同样违背 WTO 的非歧视原则。同时，金融保护主义还表现为一些国家采取税收优惠等措施，诱使本国金融机构把海外的资金抽回，缓解国内流动性短缺的压力。危机阶段流动性短缺是各国面临的共同难题，这种以邻为壑的政策无疑是一种保护主义。

受20 国集团的委托，2010 年 2 月 WTO、OECD 和联合国贸发会议（UNCTAD）共同提交了一份研究报告，对全球保护主义进行了评估，结论是国际金融危机并没有使反倾销、反补贴措施增加（见图 7）。对此，许多经济学家认为，该报告忽略了危机阶段出现的许多新型保护主义措施。这些措施必须纳入未来的多边贸易谈判议程之内。

进入后危机时代，面对全球需求不足的格局，各国都把经济复苏的希望建立在增加出口之上。比如，奥巴马政府提出，未来五年内要把美国的出口额在现有基础上增加一倍；长期内美国的经常项目赤字/GDP 比例要降低到 1990 年代中期的水平，即 1% ~2%。为实现这一目标，美国将不得不求助于美元汇率贬值。果真如此的话，全球贸易流向和格局将会发生重大变化，全球贸易保护主义的压力也将相应增大。

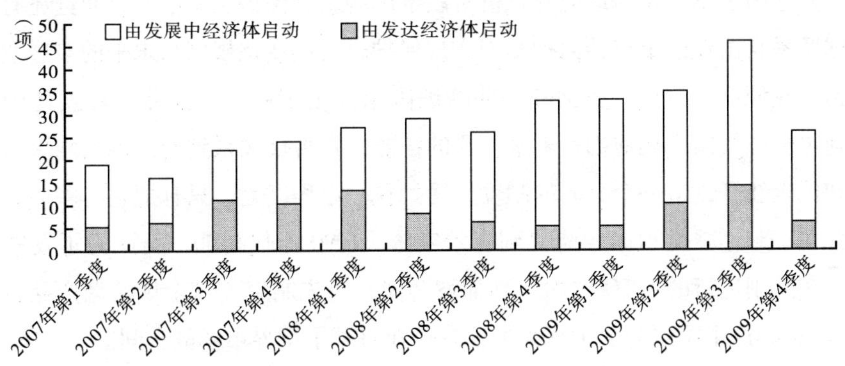

图 7 新启动的贸易补偿调查（2007 年第 1 季度至 2009 年第 4 季度）

资料来源：Global Antidumping Database。

受上述因素的影响，后危机时代国际贸易领域最急迫的任务、最大的挑战将是重启新一轮多边贸易谈判，制定出适应未来发展格局的多边贸易规则。2009 年的 20 国集团匹兹堡峰会已经就重启多哈回合谈判达成了共识。但我们认为，在 WTO 层面达成全面的贸易投资自由化规则并不容易。其障碍主要来自两个方面：一是对市场经济理念，尤其是对英美模式的认知分歧加大；二是发达国家与发展中国家对自由贸易的认知分歧加大。

针对市场原教旨主义与国际金融危机的因果关系已经得到了广泛的认同，英美模式对发展中国家的示范效应明显削弱。与此同时，危机阶段，各国政府干预范围之广、力度之大都是过去三十年来所罕见的。对政府干预的合理性和边界（包括危机阶段实施的新型保护主义措施）都在重新认识过程之中。即便是原先最积极倡导市场自由化的国际货币基金组织，其立场也在改变。不久前国际货币基金组织首席经济学家布兰查德所领导的研究团队发表文章，反思以往主流的宏观经济政策理念。[①] 其中，对政府管制资本流动的做法给予了肯定。对自由放任与政府干预的这种认知变化将成为未来多边贸易规则谈判的首要障碍。

由于重新启动的多哈回合谈判面临既有旧账又有新债的双重障碍，2010 年上半年的谈判在其初始阶段就因发达国家与发展中国家之间的严重分歧而宣告终结。未来的谈判难度将进一步加大。即使原有的分歧得以化解，发达国家与发展中国家还是有可能面临新的分歧。面对后危机时代“再平衡”与新型保护主义的压力，发展中国家更倾向于推进以降低贸易壁垒、提高市场准入门槛为核心的贸易自由化。而发达国家不会轻易地放弃危机阶段推出的新型保护主义措施，而且还有可能把全球贸易自由化的重点转向把知识产权保护、气候变化规则与未来的多边贸易规则挂钩。我们已经看到，美国和一些欧洲国家提出了碳关税主张。对发达国家来说，制定全球气候变化规则是未来首要的任务，它直接关系到发达国家能否为清洁能源和低碳经济创造一个必需的制度环境。在一定程度上，只有把它与多边贸易规则结合在一起，减排承诺才能得到有效实施。1990 年代初期，美国为了发展信息产业，在刚刚运行的 WTO 之内（新加坡会议）首先制定了《全球信息产品自由化协定》。正是这个协定为美国新兴的信息产业打开了世界市场的空间。

未来发达国家与发展中国家有可能都打着推进全球贸易自由化的大旗，但各自所要达成的多边贸易规则却是不同的。因而，未来多边贸易谈判的难度在加大。后危机时代全球贸易的发展空间与制度环境都不容乐观。

“金砖四国”作为发展中国家的代表在多边贸易谈判中发挥着不可替代的作用：一方面对内协调发展中国家的立场；另一方面对外与发达国家讨价还价，维护发展中国家的利益，维护多边贸易体制的健康发展。

五　全球气候变化规则的制定与工业化发展模式

200 年前现在的发达国家在没有受到环境因素的任何制约条件下完成了其工业化的进程。今日当众多发展中国家步入工业化进程时却面临着一个新的障碍：

---

① Olivier Blanchard, Giovanni Dell'Ariccia, and Paolo Mauro, "Rethinking Macroeconomic Policy," IMF Staff Position Note, February 11, 2010. Jonathan D. Ostry, Atish R. Ghosh, Karl Habermeier, Marcos Chamon, Mahvash S. Qureshi, and Dennis B. S. Reinhardt, "Capital Inflows: The Role of Controls," IMF Staff Position Note, February 19, 2010.

全球气候变暖。为遏制气候变暖，实现温室气体减排，国际社会正在制定从减排额度、补偿机制到各种实施机制的规则，我们把这些统称为全球气候变化规则。围绕全球气候变暖问题，尽管在科学上还有争论，但全球范围内的规则制定已经开始。一旦建立起有约束力的规则，它将会对全球经济的结构和发展方式产生前所未有的影响。表面看来，为遏制全球气候变暖而制定的规则是一个科学问题，符合全人类的共同利益，但它对不同国家的经济影响却有很大的差别。围绕全球气候变化规则争议的核心是经济利益的分配与成本的分担。未来气候变化规则不仅将重塑全球产业结构的形态和布局，而且将为清洁能源和低碳经济的发展创造制度环境。这在一定程度上将决定各国在未来国际分工中的地位。总体而言，发达国家将成为全球气候变化规则的净受益者。[①] 尽管“金砖四国”的国内自然环境存在很大的差异，如森林、人口、能源等，但有一点是共通的，即它们都是全球工业化进程的后来者，未来将面临工业化与全球气候变化规则之间的矛盾。这就是2009年哥本哈根会议上发达国家与发展中国家分歧的根本原因所在。

目前，全球气候变化规则正在多层面形成之中。在联合国层面，联合国气候变化框架公约（UNFCCC）将就减排的额度、分配及补偿作出规定。这是全球气候变化规则的核心内容。哥本哈根会议上各国的巨大分歧都集中于这些领域。一旦在这些领域达成共识，下一阶段的重点将会转向实施机制。在民族国家层面，为落实减排可供选择的制度安排主要包括碳税（carbon tax）和碳交易机制（cap-and-trade，或者 emission-trading system，ETS）。为了落实全球温室气体减排规则的实施，发达国家还有可能在双边和多边层面推出新规则。在双边层面，美国关于征收碳关税（或边境税，BTA）的提案已经引起了国际社会的广泛关注。这种提案的基础是所谓的碳泄露机制。碳泄露也称竞争力损失，是指一组国家碳排放减少被其他国家排放增加所抵消。由于现有的检测手段无法准确衡量每种产品的碳含量，征收碳关税无疑将为贸易保护主义打开方便之门。这一提案遭到了广大发展中国家的激烈反对。鉴于未来全球温室气体减排规则的实施过程非常复杂，部分发达国家有可能打着推进减排规则有效实施的旗号，单方面推出碳关税措施。除了双边层面的碳关税之外，多边层面的谈判，尤其是WTO的未来新规

① 李向阳：《全球气候变化规则与世界经济的发展趋势》，《国际经济评论》2010年第1期。

则谈判有可能与减排挂钩（或者与广义的环境保护挂钩）。

制度非中性原理决定了全球气候变化规则对发达国家和发展中国家的影响是有差别的。气候变化规则会因减排而提高所有国家的能源成本，但这并不等于所有国家所分摊的成本是一致的。同样，气候变化规则收益的分配在不同类型国家之间也是不均等的。

从成本分摊的角度来看，发展中国家分摊的成本要远高于发达国家。OECD 最近的一项研究显示：假定全球碳密度稳定在 550ppm 水平上，碳排放到 2025 年达到峰值，全球碳价格要从 2008 年的不足 30 美元/吨上升到 2050 年的 280 美元/吨。到 2050 年 GDP 与趋势水平相比：石油输出国、非欧盟的东欧国家、俄罗斯会低 15%，中国低 10%，而欧盟、美国、日本下降幅度不足 2%。[①] 世界银行的另一项研究表明，减排成本的规模与分配是和全球气候变化规则的安排密切相关的。[②] 在多数情景约束下，发展中国家的福利损失都远高于发达国家。在发展中国家内部，能源密集度高的经济体福利损失最大。这种差距的大小取决于减排规则的具体安排。其中，主要影响因素包括以下几个方面。首先，同时减排。这将最大限度地降低"碳泄露"的可能性。其次，排放权是否可交换。排放权可交换意味着形成了一个全球统一的碳价格。这对发展中国家有很大的损害，因为统一碳价格等于变相剥夺了发展中国家所享有的"差别待遇"权利。最后，转移支付，也就是发达国家给予发展中国家的减排补偿。这种补偿是发达国家对全球碳排放存量不均衡所应尽的道义和责任。从这三个领域我们可以看出发达国家与发展中国家之间在全球气候变化规则制定过程中的分歧所在。

从减排的收益分配来看，在发达国家与发展中国家之间，谁将是全球气候变化规则的净受益者同样取决于他们的相对竞争地位。在气候变化规则的约束下，对单个国家而言，碳排放既可能是一种债务（成本），也可能是一种资产（收益）。究竟是债务还是资产将取决于该国在全球碳排放市场上的竞争地位。处于竞争优势的国家，碳排放就成为一种资产（在碳交易市场上可以作为商品来出售）；反之，碳排放就是一种债务（额外投资来减排，或者向其他国家购买排放权）。

---

① OECD, *The Economics of Climate Change Mitigation*, 2009.

② Mattoo, A. et al., "Can Global De-Carbonization Inhibit Developing Country Industrialization?" *Policy Research Working Paper*, No. 5121, 2009.

首先，发达国家经济属于"轻型化"的产业结构，其能源密集度和碳密度远低于发展中国家（见表2）。这种格局并不意味着在减排问题上发达国家对发展中国家具有道德优势。这是发达国家率先完成工业化进程（也是率先完成碳排放进程）的结果。而发展中国家的工业化进程才刚刚起步，产业结构的"重型化"在短期内是一个难以改变的事实。其次，发达国家在低碳技术领域具有领先优势。这是多年来全球产业分工的结果。技术作为一种特殊商品，能否像发达国家所承诺的那样，为促进减排而向发展中国家转移还存有很大疑问。如果只是通过正常的市场渠道转移技术，那么这种承诺是没有意义的。其结果将是增加发展中国家对发达国家的技术依赖程度。再次，以气候变化规则作为突破口发展清洁能源和低碳经济，除了有助于发达国家摆脱金融危机，还有一个额外的收益，那就是提高发达国家在世界能源市场上的博弈能力。最后，发展清洁能源有助于拉动发达国家的相关产业发展。以生物能源为例，因为发达国家是目前全球粮食的主要出口国，对粮食原料的需求使发达国家的农业获得了新的发展机遇。显然，发达国家将是气候变化规则的净收益者。

表2 不同产业的碳密度（2004年）（直接和间接合计）

单位：吨/百万美元

项目＼国家	EU27 + EFTA	美国	日本	巴西	中国	印度	俄罗斯	世界
农业	74	141	76	129	350	301	307	168
所有能源业	541	1096	433	186	2800	1749	1333	928
所有制造业	62	159	79	168	681	518	848	187
能源密集型	107	272	140	286	1163	888	1193	330
其他	42	111	51	107	459	354	568	122
服务业	46	94	40	101	340	231	409	92
总计	74	153	70	149	772	535	767	187

注：EU27指欧盟27国；EFTA指欧洲自由贸易联盟。

资料来源：Mattoo, A. et al, "Reconciling Climate Change and Trade Policy," *Policy Research Working Paper*, No. 5123, 2009。

对"金砖四国"为代表的发展中国家而言，目前正在形成中的全球气候变化规则在一定程度上将决定着它们未来的工业化发展模式。虽然"金砖四国"在气候变化规则谈判中也存在一定的分歧，但在决定工业化路径选择这一基本问题上，其成本—收益模式是相同的。

“金砖四国”的汇率变动与汇率制度安排

——共性与个性

黄　薇*

2001 年 11 月，高盛在《全球需要更好的经济之砖》（*Building Better Global Economic BRICs*）一文中首次提出了由巴西（Brazil）、俄罗斯（Russia）、印度（India）和中国（China）构成的“金砖四国”（BRICs）的概念。其后它又在 2003 年 10 月发布的《“金砖四国”之梦：通向 2050 年之路》（*Dreaming with BRICs*：*The Path to* 2050）中预言，2025 年“金砖四国”的产出将达到并超过 G6 的一半，在今后不到 50 年的时间中，“金砖四国”将与美国和日本一起成为世界新的六大经济体，英国、德国、法国和意大利则将被超越。从学术层面而言，2003 年的高盛报告并不十分严谨，但其合理的逻辑分析框架（人口预测、资本积累以及生产率增长模型）与大胆的研究结论，引发了从实业界到学术界的广泛兴趣。该文作者吉姆·奥尼尔（Jim O'Neill）特别指出，该预测仅仅是对“金砖四国”发展潜力的估计，是以四国经济平衡能力不变、国内外宏观经济环境的稳定（包含价格稳定）、四国经济发展相关制度的顺利配套建设等众多假设为前提，并非是对现实发展的预测。然而，由于广袤的地幅和庞大的人口规模，加上快速增长的国内生产总值，谁也无法轻视这四个国家对于未来世界经济的影响。

高盛在其预测中特别提到，“金砖四国”的汇率将出现显著的升值趋势。报告认为，未来这四个国家的 GDP（美元计价）增长中，约 1/3 将来自货币升值

* 黄薇，中国社会科学院世界经济与政治研究所副研究员。

（每年约2.5%的平均升值速度）的贡献。其中，中国的货币可能在未来十年中升值一倍。然而，2007年以来，全球金融环境发生了很大变化。对于新兴发展中国家而言，金融系统遭受的痛苦远小于主要的发达国家。但是由于经济全球化带来的影响，"金砖四国"也被迫面临和经历一段相对痛苦的时间。

尽管"金砖四国"是世界上最大的新兴经济体，但大部分国家都曾经遭受过金融危机的侵扰（见表1）。从表1可见，印度似乎并未受危机困扰，但事实上该国在20世纪90年代初也曾经遭受"卢比危机"的影响。国际收支平衡表危机严重影响了国家的国际清偿能力，并临近违约的边缘。外汇储备岌岌可危，[①] 同时卢比大幅贬值，从1991年的17.5卢比兑1美元贬为1992年的45卢比兑1美元。这些金融危机的发生一方面与国情有关，另一方面在很大程度上也与各国对于价格的管理水平以及资本管控能力有很大关系。

表1 BRICs金融危机一览

国　别	危机次数	持续时间(年)	危机时间(年份)
巴　西	3	16	1983～1995,1998～2000,2001～2002
中　国	0	0	
印　度	0	0	
俄罗斯	1	3	1998～2001

资料来源：标准普尔，IMF，世界银行及笔者统计。债务危机判定标准：标准普尔定级为违约（being in default），或者该国得到IMF的优惠性贷款超过其配额的100%。

一　全球金融危机前变动趋势

在危机前的二十年中，这四个国家拥有一个共同的特征，即相对于美元的名义汇率均经历了一个相对较长时期的先贬值再升值过程，其分水岭为2002年（见图1）。汇率作为两个国家货币之比，这一变化过程背后除了受到各国不同的制度安排影响外，美元币值本身的变动趋势也起到了非常重要的作用。2002年2

① 1991年1～6月，印度的外汇储备已动用过半。货币当局不得不向IMF申请22亿美元的紧急贷款。作为抵押，印度储备银行分别向英国银行和瑞士联合银行运输47吨和20吨黄金。

月是强势美元和弱势美元的分水岭。如图2所示，美元指数从2002年2月开始下跌，这一跌势一直持续到2008年3月。

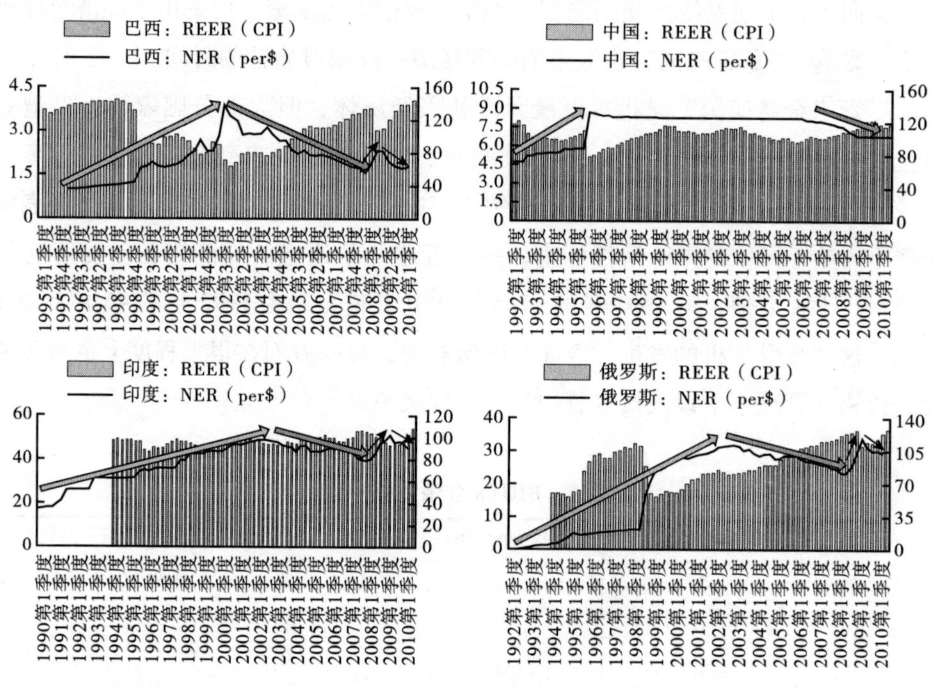

图1 "金砖四国"汇率变动情况

注：①上图中NER指名义汇率，REER（CPI）指基于CPI的实际有效汇率。
②左侧箭头代表贬值趋势，右侧箭头代表升值趋势。
资料来源：IMF，BIS。

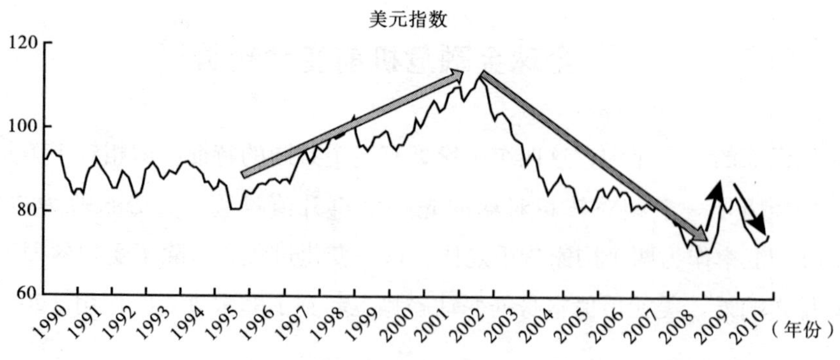

图2 美元指数变动情况

资料来源：美国联邦储备委员会。

由于国情与开放程度的差异，每个国家经历的拐点时间、升值（贬值）的时期以及幅度均有所不同。20 世纪 90 年代初，中国和印度最早驶入贬值通道，随后是俄罗斯和巴西。20 世纪初，由于新兴市场经济的蓬勃发展，四国开始远离贬值通道，呈现升值趋势。尽管"金砖四国"均为典型的高增长新兴市场经济体代表，但由于过去各国在历史、社会因素方面的差异性较大，个案分析可能是最好的分析方式。关于各国汇率波动趋势背后的制度安排与推动力量，详见本文第三部分的分析。

尽管名义汇率存在较为一致的波动，但由于各国国内价格水平变动差异较大，可以看到各国实际汇率的变化趋势差异明显。相较而言，中国和印度的实际汇率以及国内通货膨胀的表现相对平稳，没有出现持续显著的大起大落。

进入 21 世纪以来，巴西国内价格水平的管控能力得到极大提高，价格的波动幅度显著缩小。与名义汇率的变动几乎同步，巴西的实际汇率水平在 2002 年降到谷底，2010 年已经重新恢复到 20 世纪末的水平。

相对于其他三国而言，俄罗斯国内价格水平的波动更大，通胀速度常年保持在两位数，如图 3 所示。1998 年第 3 季度俄罗斯金融危机爆发。卢布汇率从 1998 年 6 月底的 6.2 卢布兑 1 美元，急剧贬值为当年年底的 20 卢布兑 1 美元。1999 年 3 月 24 卢布可以兑换 1 美元，而到 1999 年底则需要 28 卢布。名义汇率贬值超过 4 倍，而消费价格指数仅翻了一番。同期的世界价格水平仅仅只有负的变动，这导致俄罗斯的实际汇率水平在危机期间贬值将近一半。实际汇率的大幅贬值，提升了俄罗斯产品的国际竞争力。随着国内经济情况的逐步稳定，在 21 世纪的前 10 年，卢布的实际有效汇率一直保持着逐步升值的趋势。

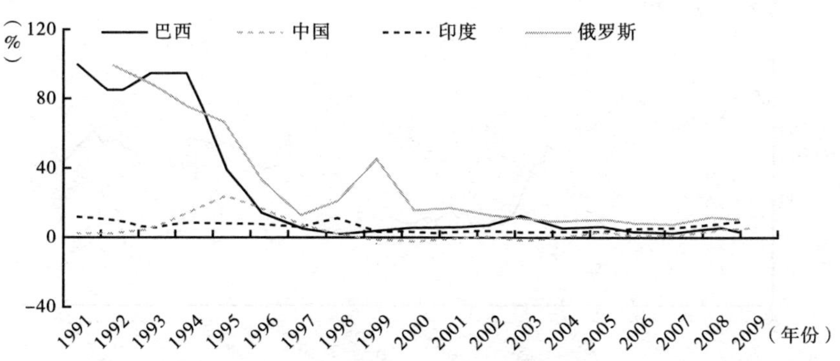

图 3 "金砖四国"消费价格指数的变动

资料来源：IMF。

二　危机后“金砖四国”的汇率表现

2007～2008年，当次贷危机在美国爆发，很多人相信“金砖四国”可能在全球金融海啸中独善其身。然而，随着大部分发达国家金融体系在2008年底陷入泥潭，外国投资者纷纷将资金撤出“金砖四国”。从图4和图5中可以看到，2008年四国的外汇储备以及代表四国股票市场表现的MSCI“金砖四国”指数均出现了急速的下跌。由于这次下跌如此不同寻常，俄罗斯和巴西当局甚至暂时关闭了它们的股票市场以避免进一步的损失。然而，由于强劲的国内消费需求、大规模的外汇储备和高额的贸易盈余，我们有理由相信“金砖四国”将比其他国家更快地从危机中恢复过来。

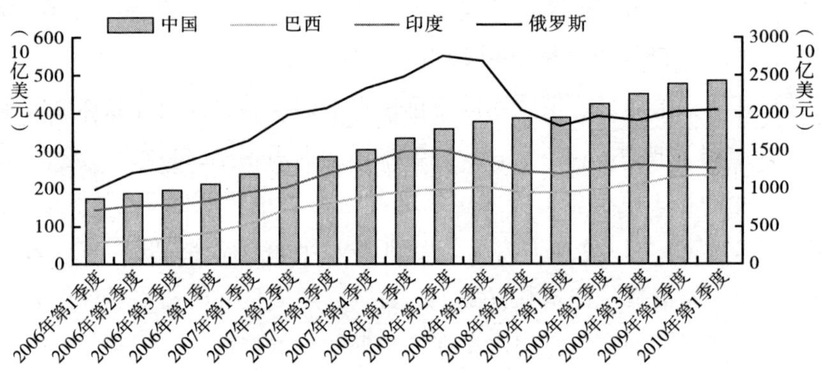

图4　“金砖四国”外汇储备的变动

注：中国参考右轴，其他国家参考左轴。

资料来源：IMF。

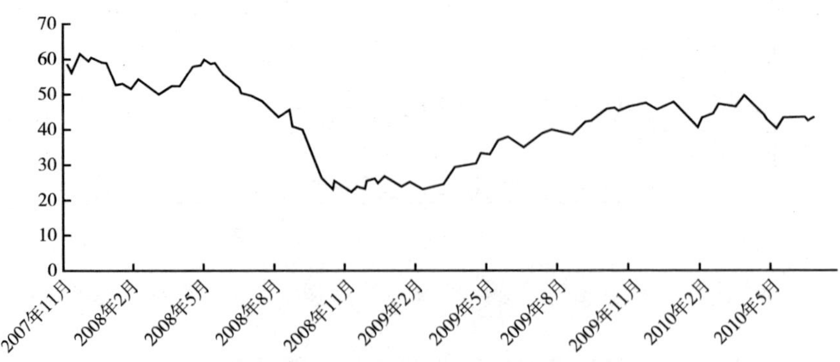

图5　MSCI“金砖四国”指数变动情况

资料来源：IMF。

全球金融危机爆发以来，除了中国以外，其他三个国家均呈现明显的第二轮先贬值再升值过程，其分水岭为2008年第4季度（见图1）。由于金融市场受到严重冲击，国际投资者风险偏好大幅降低，国际资本寻求避险资产。美元"安全天堂"功能再现。国际资本纷纷从发展中国家撤离，开始追逐美元资产。2008年3月开始，美元币值一改6年来的跌势，呈现上升势头。美元的强势，使得实行浮动或管理浮动汇率制度的国家汇率呈现不同程度的贬值，这一现象不仅出现在新兴国家中，在发达国家也同样存在。随着危机趋缓和经济逐步复苏，美元从2009年3月再次进入贬值轨道。危机爆发后，最先进入贬值通道的是印度，其次是俄罗斯和巴西，但这三个国家进入升值通道的时间点几乎一致，均在2009年第1季度。与其他国家不同的是，中国在危机期间采取的是钉住美元的做法，因此人民币对于美元的汇率表现相对平稳。

以上基本特征说明了一个不争的事实，即至少到目前为止，作为国际货币的美元，其兴衰在很大程度上决定了新兴国家的汇率变动趋势。如何在不伤及自身经济发展的前提下，逐步脱离未来可能出现的长期弱势美元影响，将成为摆在新兴发展中国家面前的一道难题。

三 "金砖四国"的汇率安排经验分析

1. 中国

20世纪80年代以来，人民币汇率的变动大致可以划分为以下几个阶段。

（1）1981～1984年：中国进入以经济建设为中心的时期。为解决外贸部门出口换汇成本过高以至于亏损的问题，原来的汇率被"双重汇率"取代。1981年1月，中国货币当局对外贸进出口商品实行带配额的内部结算汇率，1美元兑2.8元人民币，仅为官方牌价汇率（1美元=1.5元人民币）的一半。之后，官方汇率开始不断贬值并向内部结算汇率靠拢。

（2）1985～1993年：内部结算价取消，贸易和非贸易的外汇结算均采用统一汇率。为了改变1984年国际收支从顺差转为逆差的局面，中国政府开始实施出口导向政策。当局逐步将人民币贬值以增强出口商品的价格竞争力，同时抑制进口需求。人民币汇率从1985年初的2.8元人民币兑1美元大幅贬值为1994年的8.7元人民币兑1美元。

（3）1994~2004年：1994年，货币当局官方宣称采取的是管理浮动的汇率机制。然而，实际上在短期的名义汇率贬值后，从1995年起人民币实际采用的是钉住美元的汇率管理方式。这段时间里，中国的国民经济取得了快速稳定发展，贸易顺差逐年扩大。为了维持一个稳定的汇率，中国人民银行不得不大规模地干预市场，2004年外汇储备迅速飙升为GDP的30%。2003年开始人民币面临越来越大的升值压力。

（4）2005~2007年：2005年7月，中央银行宣布采用参考一篮子的汇率决定机制，重新开启了人民币升值的通道。人民币相对美元升值2.1%，并设定了±0.3%的浮动带。在短短不到三年时间里，人民币累计升值超过26%。然而，在一些学术研究中，这段时期的中国事实汇率制度依然被定义为钉住一个几乎所有权重都在美元身上的货币篮子。（Frankel和Wei，2007）

（5）2008~2009年：由于2007年开始的全球金融危机，考虑到中国以及世界的利益，2008~2009年间人民币的浮动带被主动缩小。危机期间，在其他货币对美元呈现明显波动的情况下，人民币兑美元的汇率被稳定在1美元兑6.83元人民币。稳定的汇率有助于中国更好地处理外部需求的变化，同时也减缓了金融危机带来的冲击。

20世纪80年代以来，中国汇率管理体系的主要事件如表2所示。

表2　中国汇率制度安排变迁

年份	汇率安排变化
1980	国务院下令禁止中国国内使用外汇作为支付手段
1981	①采用双重汇率结构。对于拥有外汇配额的贸易相关交易采用内部结算汇率(1美元=2.8元人民币)。其他交易结算仍使用官方汇率(1美元=1.5元人民币)。②试点性质的外汇交易体系在中国银行建立
1985	内部清算汇率被废除,双重汇率合并为单一官方汇率。中国居民被允许持有外汇和开设可以存取款的外汇账户
1986	人民币汇率在"可控浮动"的前提下根据收支状况以及竞争国汇率情况被频繁调整。上海国际信托投资公司被授权从事外汇业务
1991	汇率管理改为根据如国际外汇市场情况、相对价格表现以及出口成本变动趋势等一系列指标来做频繁的调整。1991年底,汇率为1美元兑5.43元人民币
1994	官方汇率与调剂市场汇率统一。货币调剂中心由上海的中国外汇交易系统(CFETS)取代。该系统是一个银行间外汇交易的电子平台。1994~1997年,汇率基本保持稳定,伴随4%的小幅缓慢升值。汇率从开始的8.7元人民币兑1美元,升值为8.28元人民币兑1美元
2005	2005年7月21日,人民币汇率机制改革基于供需的参考一篮子货币的有管理的浮动汇率制度。2005年底,汇率升值为8.07元人民币兑1美元,之后逐步升值至2008年中期的6.83元人民币兑1美元
2010	6月,中国人民银行宣布中国将进一步深化人民币汇率机制改革以增强人民币汇率的弹性

资料来源：中国人民银行，国际货币基金组织。

相比后面将要介绍的三个国家而言，中国的汇率制度改革还在进一步推进过程中。汇率制度安排与资本账户开放都将成为近期对外金融工作的重点工程。尽管从历史表现来看，中国经济的稳定性更高，但这并不意味着中国未来的道路也是一帆风顺的。

2. 印度

在1947年印度独立以后，由于历史上的天然联系，印度卢比采取了钉住英镑的汇率制度。由于20世纪70年代，布雷顿森林体系的瓦解，以及英国在印度对外贸易中地位的下降，卢比开始逐步放松与英镑之间的联系。1975～1979年，卢比的汇率由在一个±5%的名义带内波动的一篮子加权货币决定，印度储备银行采用主要的贸易伙伴国的货币作为篮子货币。正如C. Rangarajan博士在1993年所言，"这段时期的汇率制度可以被归纳为一个在浮动带内可调的名义钉住，名义汇率管理的目标在于维持实际有效汇率的中期均衡"。

在20世纪80年代后期，印度的经常账户急剧恶化，10年中经常账户赤字翻了3～4倍。1980～1984年印度经常账户赤字约20亿美元，之后一路上升为1988年和1990年的超过70亿美元。这种不断恶化的趋势逐步积累引发了1990～1991年印度的国际收支危机。印度带着高额的经常账户赤字步入20世纪最后十年，赤字规模约为1990年GDP的3.2%。

由于不断收紧的短期信贷，经常项目赤字难以为继。印度的外汇资产大幅锐减，从1990年的31亿美元，减少为1991年7月的9.75亿美元（甚至低于该国一个月的进口额）。1991年，由于持续增加的贸易赤字以及外债①，印度卢比面临极大贬值压力。迫于国民经济遭遇严重危机，同时国际债务急剧恶化，印度政府启动"自由化、私有化、国际化"的经济转型改革。1993年除了采取市场决定的统一汇率（见表3），印度储备银行还采取了一系列措施以扩宽和深化外汇市场改革，包括机制转变、放松运营限制以及减少政府对金融机构的干预等。

① 印度政府在20世纪80年代大量借款以缓解经常账户赤字。其对外债务（EDT）的未偿额从1980年的206亿美元上升为1991年的716亿美元，10年间外债上涨了248%，而同期其GDP的实际增长仅为71%。

表 3 印度的汇率制度安排变迁

年份	汇率安排变化
1931	实行事实钉住英镑的汇率制度,1 卢比 =1 先令 6 便士(1 英镑 =13.33 卢比)
1961	与英镑的经常项目可兑换重新恢复。但美元的重要性开始上升,削弱了与英镑间的联系
1966	6 月 6 日卢比相对英镑贬值 36.5%,从 1 英镑兑换 13.33 卢比变为兑换 21 卢比。相应的,卢比也对美元有所贬值,从 1 美元兑换 4.7619 卢比变为兑换 7.5 卢比
1967	11 月英镑相对美元贬值 14.3%(从 1 英镑兑换 2.8 美元,变成兑换 2.4 美元),同时卢比兑英镑的汇率变动为 18:1,而卢比兑美元以及黄金的比率维持不变
1971	8 月布雷顿森林体系解体。12 月,卢比兑美元汇率依然维持在 1 美元 =7.5 卢比,卢比兑英镑的汇率为 1 英镑 =18.9677 卢比,两个汇率均保留 2.25% 的浮动空间
1972	6 月 23 日英镑汇率自由浮动,26 日卢比与英镑汇率为 1 英镑 =18.95 卢比。因美元与黄金脱钩,6 月 24 日至 10 月 9 日期间印度联邦银行暂停购买美元。7 月 4 日由于英镑对美元贬值,卢比也相应对英镑有所升值(1 英镑 =18.8 卢比)
1975	9 月起开始采用钉住一篮子货币(货币组成不公开)的汇率制度,并保留 2.25% 的双向弹性。实际上,这段时期卢比兑英镑被固定在 1 英镑 =18.3084 卢比
1979	1 月底篮子的边际弹性被拓宽了 5%,整个篮子的浮动区间变为 10%
1991	7 月 1 日卢比相对英镑贬值 17% ~18%(1 英镑 =34.36 卢比变为 1 英镑 =37.19 卢比),到 7 月 3 日进一步贬值为 1 英镑兑换 41.56 卢比。同时,卢比相对于美元也在贬值(从 1 美元兑换 21.2 卢比,变为兑换 25.8 卢比)
1992	开始建立自由化的汇率管理体系(LERMS),出口外汇收入与汇入汇款的 40% 需通过中央储备银行用官方汇率换成本币,用作外汇储备。剩余外汇以及其他外汇收入可以通过市场汇率交易。资本账户下的许可收支也采用市场汇率进行交割(除非是与 IMF 等机构的官方往来)。3 月 4 日开始,使用美元作为汇率干涉货币
1993	3 月 1 日开始全面采用市场汇率,取消双重汇率,1 季度末汇率为 1 美元兑 31.2 卢布

资料来源：RBI Annual Reports, EXIM Bank, 1993。

1996 年，外汇市场改革专家组提出了印度外汇市场改革的路线图。印度储备银行决定将政府债务偿还支付通过市场完成，以保证卢比汇率能够全面反映市场的供求信息。同时，银行间借款的现金准备金要求被取消。为了提供更大的运营灵活性，银行被允许自由设定自身的外汇头寸限制。为了给居民在外汇交易中提供对冲工具，货币当局允许银行与授权交易商签订远期合约、外汇期权合同、外汇—卢比互换合同、利率掉期/货币掉期/票息掉期/外汇期权/远期利率合同等。

印度目前的汇率制度是没有固定目标汇率的波动管理，同时在一段时期内允许汇率运动有序地由市场供需状况决定。现在，印度汇率管理政策的三个主要目标分别是：①通过在必要的时候提供外汇来维持健康的外汇市场环境，同时防止出现投机活动；②帮助将国家的外汇储备维持在足够的水平上；③为了促进健康的外汇市场发展，帮助消除市场中存在的约束。在 IMF 对 20 个发展中工业国家的研究中，印度的外汇政策被描述为亚洲"理想的"汇率政策。

从印度的经验来看，慎重调整对外部门的改革开放的步伐和次序是非常必要的。我们必须要认识到自由化进程的任何一步都很难回退，因为市场会对这种改变做出非常负面的反应。在浮动汇率制度下，关于汇率的各种保证，无论是直接的还是间接的，都应该尽可能地避免。应该鼓励经济个体运用对冲工具来管理汇率波动中带来的风险。另外，也必须清醒地意识到国际资本流动偏好短期债务。因此，直接投资应该被给予高于间接投资（证券投资）的优先级。

3. 巴西

从 1980 年开始，巴西开始面临经济增长较低且有波动，同时通货膨胀水平较高（直到 1994 年 6 月）的局面。1991 ~ 2006 年巴西的经济增长仅为 2.1%，远远低于 20 世纪 40 ~ 80 年代实行进口替代工业化战略时 7.1% 的增长速度。由于该国外部金融相对脆弱，国内又采用相当高的实际利率水平，所以投资率长期处于较低的水平。

20 世纪 90 年代初以来，为应对恶化的国内经济形势，巴西政府采取了不同的货币战略：1990 ~ 1994 年主要采用爬行钉住的汇率制度，同时伴随一定的名义贬值，造成高的贸易盈余与资本流入，同时伴随高的通货膨胀。1994 ~ 1999 年，随着"雷亚尔计划"① （Real Plan）的推行，巴西开始以美元作为"名义锚"（1 Real = 1 MYM）。巴西开始走出恶性通货膨胀，CPI 的波动从 1993 年的 5000% 下降为 1998 年的 2.5%。

1994 ~ 1998 年，雷亚尔实际采用爬行钉住的汇率制度，以控制其对美元的逐步贬值。1996 ~ 1998 年，巴西央行动用外汇储备以避免本国货币出现急剧的贬值，这期间外汇储备减少了 240 亿美元，约占总储备的 40%。之后，由于国际收支严重失衡，加上国际市场上的不利传言，金融危机再次光临巴西。尽管 IMF 在 1998 年提供了 415 亿美元的贷款给巴西，但巴西央行仍决定在 1999 年 1

---

① "雷亚尔计划"，即用新的名为"雷亚尔"的货币代替过去的旧货币，新旧货币的兑换率在 1994 年 6 月 30 日为 1 雷亚尔 = 2750 克鲁扎多。

月将雷亚尔贬值8%，该月末雷亚尔相对于美元的贬值幅度高达66%。由于大量外资抽逃、持续的贸易逆差，外汇储备不断减少，最终巴西政府不得不宣布从实质上的固定汇率转变为浮动汇率制度。

实际上，早在1997年，巴西政府已经意识到雷亚尔面临的贬值压力，并动用了75亿美元的外汇储备来保护雷亚尔的爬行钉住汇率制度。经常账户赤字，停滞的GDP增长以及高涨的政府债务是贬值压力的主要源头。同年爆发的亚洲金融危机表明，即使是拥有稳健经济增长和良好财政状况的国家，也易于遭受投机性攻击。巴西政府有理由相信同样的情况可能会出现在雷亚尔身上。然而，钉住汇率制度和将近1000亿美元的政府债务，使得巴西央行几乎没有多少政策空间。自由国际资本流动下的钉住汇率制度意味着在一定程度上丧失了货币政策的有效性，同时高企的政府债务以及预算限制使得财政政策也难以施展拳脚。从这个角度而言，在接受IMF贷款后，1999年巴西央行公开承认雷亚尔被高估需要从两个方面理解。一方面，此举增强了市场对于央行行为遵循市场化的信心，但另一方面，随后的雷亚尔突然贬值也在一定程度上伤害了巴西的国际信誉。

4. 俄罗斯

1991年底，苏联瓦解为15个独立国家，俄罗斯独立。1992年1月，俄联邦中央银行、莫斯科市政府和俄罗斯银行协会共同创办了股份公司形式的"莫斯科银行间货币交易所"，这一交易所成为银行间进行外汇和其他金融工具交易的主要场所。从此，俄罗斯中央银行即根据该交易所提供的外汇交易情况来确定官方的卢布对美元汇率。

在美国经济学家Jeffrey Sachs的建议以及总理和改革经济学家盖达尔的主持下，俄罗斯开始向市场经济转型。1992年初，该国完全实行了定价的完全市场化，同时允许卢布内部可兑换，汇率由交易市场确定。然而，由于该国民用工业竞争力不足，价格自由化一开始，即导致俄罗斯的价格水平迅速上升。到1992年底消费价格上升了25倍，同时卢布的购买力迅速下降。卢布汇率从1992年1月份的100卢布兑1美元贬值为同年底的415卢布兑1美元。相较于俄罗斯国内价格的高涨，卢布汇率的变化要温和许多，因此使得国外商品相对更加便宜。将卢布汇率稳定在一个比较高的水平的最大好处是稳定了不断膨胀的国内价格水平。然而，高估的卢布政策也带来了一系列负面影响：出口部门的国际竞争力下降，同时低的进口商品价格也伤害了国内同类商品生产者。激进改革后引发的经济衰退和恶性通货膨胀，大大刺激了本国企业和居民对美元的需求。汇率大幅下跌伴随着资本外逃，到 1995 年 7 月卢布汇率变为 4553 卢布兑 1 美元。

为了稳定卢布汇率，1995 年 7 月，俄罗斯中央银行和联邦政府共同确定"外汇走廊"制度。不再完全由市场供求决定汇率，中央银行对外汇交易所和银行间外汇市场上卢布对美元的比价预先规定一个上下浮动的范围。① "外汇走廊"制度一直延续到 1998 年初。

1998 年金融危机爆发，提升利率的操作已达到极限。然而，俄罗斯政府与货币当局采用了更为严格的稳定汇率的政策。1998 年初，俄罗斯货币当局将卢布汇率锚定在 6.2 卢布兑 1 美元（1999 年中心汇率为 6.1 卢布兑 1 美元）加上 15% 的双向波动空间，以稳定国内价格水平。该方案与"货币走廊"类似，但由于给出了中心汇率，相较而言属于更加严格的钉住。同时，政府宣布更换货币单位，卢布计价单位缩小 1000 倍，即 1000 单位的旧卢布等值于 1 单位的新卢布。

由于 1998 年油价的大幅下跌，以及亚洲金融危机的影响，俄罗斯卢布承受了更大的压力。1998 年 8 月卢布的不断卖出导致了一场货币危机。由于卖出卢布的量非常巨大，政府无力继续稳定汇率。当年 9 月 9 日，俄罗斯政府不得不宣布放弃目标区间。从那一天起，卢布转变为浮动汇率制度（实际为管理浮动）。

考虑到"金砖四国"的货币体系发展历史，显然固定汇率并不是巴西和俄罗斯陷入麻烦的唯一原因。即使采取了浮动汇率制度，也无法修正所有遭遇的问题。事实上，对国内通货膨胀管理的考量，可能是巴西和俄罗斯一开始采用爬行钉住（或者"外汇走廊"）制度的首要原因。

四 结语

2002～2007 年，中国的年实际平均 GDP 增长率为 10.4%，印度为 7.9%，俄罗斯为 6.9%，巴西为 3.7%。快速发展的经济，稳定的经济基本面以及庞大

① 该系统下，卢布的浮动范围从开始的 4300～4900 卢布 :1 美元放宽到 1996 年 1 月 4550～5100 卢布 :1 美元。

的人口，使得“金砖四国”成为世界上最有希望的市场。尽管“金砖四国”也受到了全球金融危机的影响，然而高额贸易盈余和高额外汇储备使得这些国家更容易从危机中恢复过来。

“金砖四国”的汇率与汇率制度方面既有共性也有个性。“金砖四国”历史上接连不断的金融危机，则表明了这些新兴发展中国家过去并未完全处理好开放与发展之间的节奏和关系。中国和印度的例子说明了采取渐进的、谨慎的、以减少外部波动为政策导向的管理方式的正确性。由于历史上的货币危机的影响，四国里面的巴西、印度和俄罗斯均已开放金融市场并转向浮动汇率制度。目前仅中国还在向浮动汇率的方向演进。中国相较于其他三国而言，在金融市场开放程度上要更落后一些。当然，正是这种落后使得我们在一定程度上避免了外部冲击以及货币比价的非意愿大幅波动。历史是一本教科书，由于中国与其他金砖三国的经济发展阶段、模式、规模较为接近，这些国家在汇率管理中的经验和教训值得借鉴。

“金砖四国”与贸易

世界经济体系中的“金砖四国”

——基于国际贸易视角的分析

张宇燕　田　丰*

近数十年来，BRICs（Brazil，China，India and Russia）在世界舞台上扮演着越来越重要的角色。在世界货物贸易领域，巴西、中国、印度和俄罗斯四个BRICs组成国均具有举足轻重的地位（见表1、表2和图1）。2009年，BRICs合计出口1.8万亿美元，占世界出口总额的14.4%；合计进口1.6万亿美元，占世界进口总额的12.7%。从国别来看，中国出口1.2万亿美元，占世界出口总额的9.9%，进口1万亿美元，占世界进口总额的8.1%，是世界第一大货物出口国和第二大货物进口国，其进出口额分别相当于巴西、印度和俄罗斯进出口额之和的两倍。BRICs其余三国——巴西、印度和俄罗斯也都是排名世界前30位的贸易大国。全球金融危机爆发后，BRICs相对快速的复苏与发展更是备受瞩目，在全球经济治理中的地位相应提升。2009年6月16日，巴西、中国、印度和俄罗斯等国领导人在俄罗斯叶卡捷琳堡举行了首次正式会晤。然而，目前与BRICs发展紧密相关的一些重大问题还没有得到圆满的回答，这些问题包括：BRICs在世界经济体系中的贸易联系处于什么状态，与过去相比发生了什么重要变化，这些变化可能对上述国家经济增长的前景产生什么影响，BRICs内部贸易的未来发展趋势如何。

* 张宇燕，中国社会科学院世界经济与政治研究所所长、研究员；田丰，中国社会科学院世界经济与政治研究所副研究员。

表 1　BRICs：商品贸易（出口）（2009）

单位：10 亿美元，%

	金额	年度变化率				排名	份额
	2009 年	2005～2009 年	2007 年	2008 年	2009 年	2009 年	2009 年
巴　西	153	7	17	23	-23	24	1.2
中　国	1202	12	26	17	-16	1	9.6
印　度	155	12	23	30	-20	22	1.2
俄罗斯	304	6	17	33	-36	13	2.4
世　界	12147	4	16	15	-23		

注：①在"金额"中的"世界"未排除欧盟内部贸易。

②计算"份额"时，为与 WTO 数据保持一致，使用的世界贸易总额是纳入了主要转出口或为了转出口的进口贸易的总量，即 124610 亿美元。

③在排名时，欧盟未作为一个整体统计。

资料来源：WTO 网站。

表 2　BRICs：商品贸易（进口）（2009）

单位：10 亿美元，%

	金额	年度变化率				排名	份额
	2009 年	2005～2009 年	2007 年	2008 年	2009 年	2009 年	2009 年
巴　西	134	15	32	44	-25	26	1.1
中　国	1006	11	21	18	-11	2	8
印　度	244	14	29	40	-24	15	1.9
俄罗斯	192	11	36	31	-34	17	1.5
世　界	12385	4	15	16	-24		

注：①在"金额"中的"世界"未排除欧盟内部贸易。

②计算"份额"时，为与 WTO 数据保持一致，使用的世界贸易总额是纳入了主要转出口或为了转出口的进口贸易的总量，即 124610 亿美元。

③在排名时，欧盟未作为一个整体统计。

资料来源：WTO 网站。

针对上述问题，本文尝试着做了一些初步的工作。首先，我们分析了全球金融危机经由国际贸易渠道影响 BRICs 经济增长的具体途径与方式并在此基础上对"脱钩论"（即不管发达国家情况如何，包括 BRICs 在内的新兴市场大国都可实现自身的长期增长）提出了自己的看法。其次，我们在 HS96 六位码的基础上考察了 BRICs 对不同市场出口商品数量的变化情况，并进而探究了这些情况对于 BRICs 各组成国经济增长可能具有的意义。在第三部分里，我们对 BRICs 各组成国对世界、代表性国家和代表性国家组的贸易平衡状况进行了系统的分析，揭示出贸易平衡状况变化背后的比较优势变化情况及其对经济增长的影响。为了更全

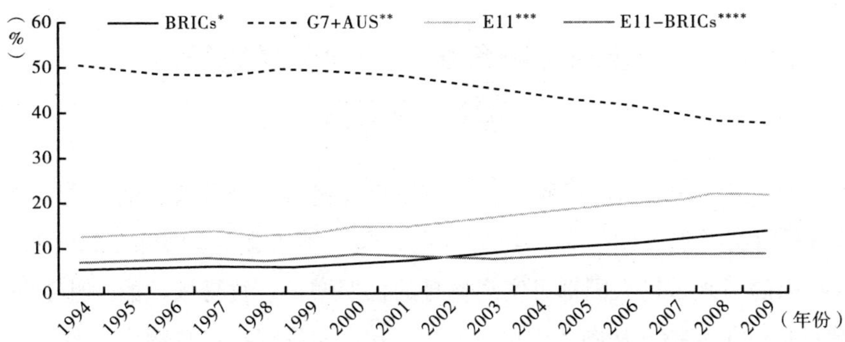

图1 BRICs商品贸易/世界商品贸易总额（1994~2009）

注：* BRICs代表BRICs内部交易；** G7 + AUS代表BRICs与主要发达国的贸易；*** E11代表BRICs与新兴经济体的贸易，其中E11是指20国集团中的11个发展中国家；**** E11 - BRICs代表E11中除BRICs以外的国家。

资料来源：WTO网站。

面分析BRICs在世界经济体系中的贸易联系对这些国家的影响，我们在本文第四部分里基于HS96六位码计算了BRICs与特定国家或国家集团的竞争互补指数与竞争压力指数。最后是本文的结语。

为了便于研究与比较，本文在分析BRICs在世界经济体系中的贸易联系时，侧重于BRICs与三个代表性国家组的贸易联系。这三个代表性国家组分别是BRICs内部贸易联系，在文中以BRICs代表；BRICs与新兴经济体的贸易联系，在文中以“E11”代表；BRICs与主要发达国家的贸易联系，在文中以“G7 + AUS”代表。其中，“E11”指20国集团（G20）中的11个发展中国家，“G7 + AUS”指G20中除欧盟以外的发达国家。① 此外，我们还分析了BRICs各国与美国、日本和德国等世界主要进出口大国间的贸易联系，以使读者得到更为清晰全面的信息。为了反映最新的情况，在没有特别说明的情况下，本文使用的国别贸易数据均为2009年的数据。因数据可获得性原因，印度的分类贸易数据为2008年的数据，总量贸易数据仍然为2009年的数据。

① “E11”具体包括阿根廷、巴西、中国、印度、印尼、韩国、墨西哥、俄罗斯、沙特阿拉伯、南非和土耳其。“G7 + AUS”具体包括美国、日本、德国、英国、法国、意大利、加拿大（即七国集团，G7）和澳大利亚。关于“E11”和“G7 + AUS”两个概念的更详细讨论参见张宇燕、田丰《新兴经济体的界定及其在世界经济格局中的地位》，《国际经济评论》2010年第4期（总第88期），第7~26页。

一　全球金融危机传导的贸易途径与 BRICs 的贸易联系

在全球金融危机以前，“脱钩”一直是世界经济领域热议的话题之一。所谓“脱钩”是对某类观点的统称，其基本主张是，不管发达国家情况如何，包括 BRICs 在内的新兴市场大国都可实现自身的长期增长。贸易领域的一些数据也为这种观点提供了支持。从图 2 中可以看出，BRICs 各国出口总额中，对主要发达国家（G7 + AUS）的份额直到美国次贷危机演变成全球金融危机前（2007 年）基本呈下降趋势，仅俄罗斯对 G7 + AUS 出口的份额基本维持在与 2000 年大致相当的水平。与对发达国家市场依赖程度下降形成鲜明对照的是，BRICs 各国对新兴经济体（BRICs，E11，E11 – BRICs）出口的份额均显著上升。对巴西而言，新兴市场的重要性甚至已经提升至与发达国家市场大致相当的水平。

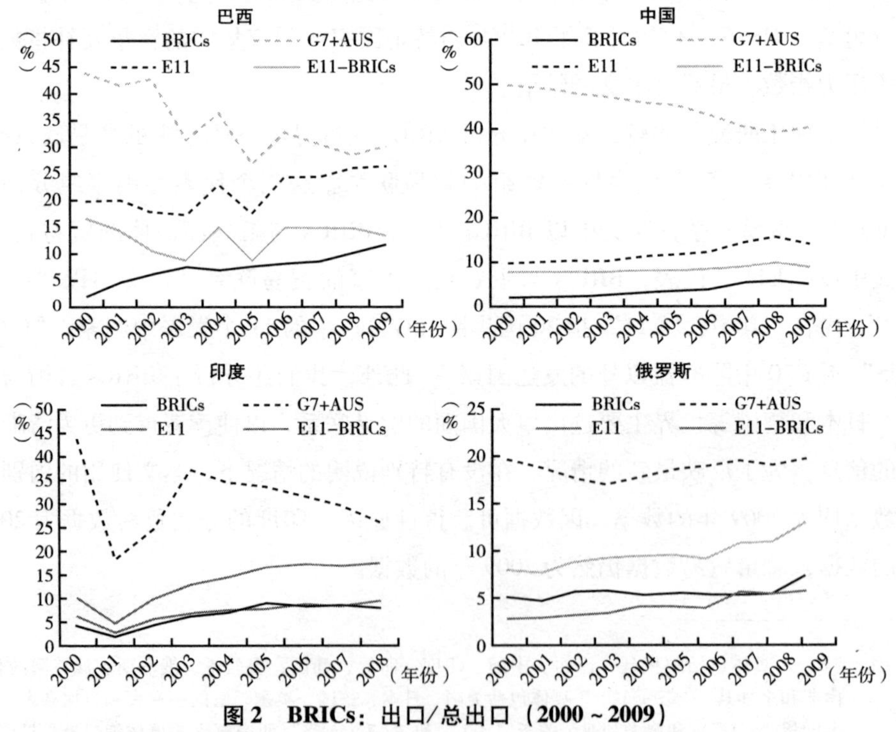

图 2　BRICs：出口/总出口（2000 ~ 2009）

注：因数据可获得性原因，在分析印度出口总额时我们使用的是 2000 ~ 2008 年的数据。

资料来源：作者根据联合国 COMTRADE 数据库数据计算。

但是全球金融危机的爆发使我们在某种程度上对“脱钩”的看法产生了怀疑。一系列经验研究已经表明，国际贸易是危机跨国蔓延的主要途径之一（Eichengreen and Rose，1999；Glick and Rose，1999；Forbes and Chinn，2003）。[①] 2009 年，巴西、中国、印度和俄罗斯的出口金额相对于 2008 年分别大幅下挫 23%、16%、20%和36%（见表1）。显然，发达国家的经济衰退和进口缩减严重影响了 BRICs 的出口。那么这一切是怎么发生的呢?

事实上，尽管主要发达国家市场对 BRICs 出口的重要性（按照出口/总出口衡量）在下降，G7 + AUS 仍是 BRICs 最主要的出口市场（见图2）。2007 年，巴西 31.8% 的出口、中国 40.5% 的出口、印度 29.4% 的出口、俄罗斯 20.6% 的出口面向 G7 + AUS。另外，BRICs 的内部贸易只占巴西出口的 10%，中国出口的 5%，印度出口的 8%，俄罗斯出口的 5%。即使是面向 E11 的出口，也只占巴西出口的 25%，中国出口的 14%，印度出口的 17%，俄罗斯出口的 11%。并且，如果我们按照出口/GDP 的方法来衡量发达国家对 BRICs 出口的重要性，从图 3 可以看出，2000～2007 年，巴西、中国和印度的这一比例基本维持在大体相当的水平，仅俄罗斯略有下降。

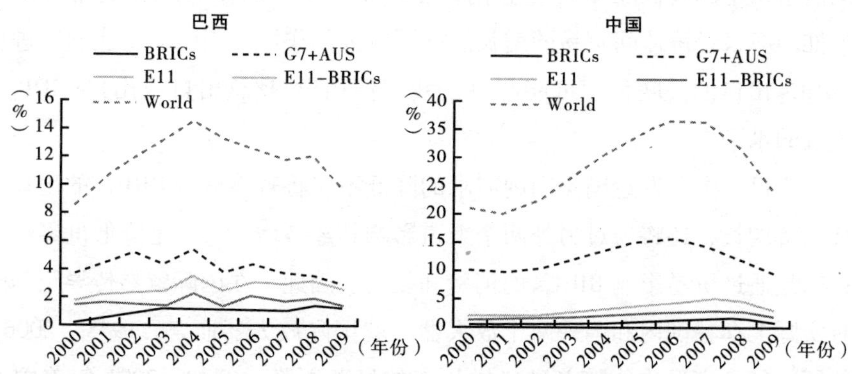

① Eichengreen, Barry and Andrew Rose, 1999, “Contagious Currency Crises: Channels of Conveyance,” in Takatoshi Ito and Anne Krueger (eds.), *Changes in Exchange Rates in Rapidly Developing Economies*, University of Chicago Press, Chicago. Glick, Reuven and Andrew Rose, 1999, “Contagion and Trade: Why Are Currency Crises Regional?” *Journal of International Money and Finance*, Vol. 18, August, pp. 603 - 617. Forbes, Kristin and Menzie Chinn, 2003, “A Decomposition of Global Linkages in Financial Markets Over Time,” *NBER Working Paper No. 9555*, NBER, Cambridge, MA, March.

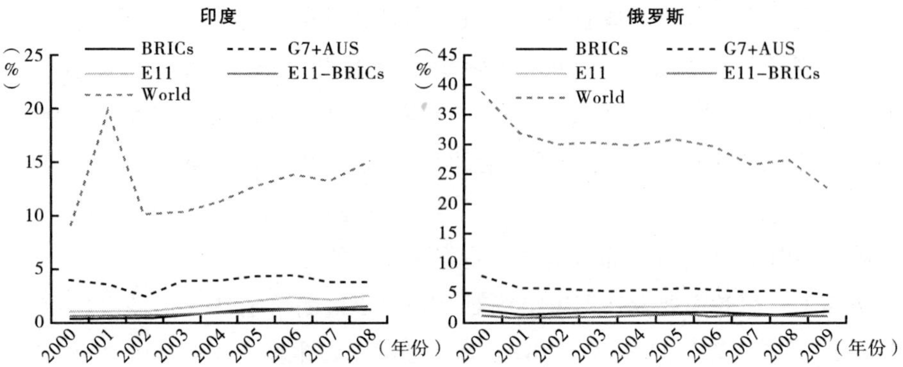

图3 BRICs：出口/GDP（2000～2009）

资料来源：作者根据联合国 COMTRADE 数据库数据计算。

危机的传导也与贸易结构紧密相关。虽然同一时间序列的数据显示，BRICs 各国与 G7 + AUS 的贸易，BRICs 内部贸易，以及 BRICs 各国与 E11 的贸易在金额上都显著增长，然而增长的动力可能存在较大差别。前者主要反映了 G7 + AUS 在巨大的国内市场背景下对产品多样化的需求，后两者反映的是企业在全球范围内组织生产提高了垂直专业化程度。尤其是中国作为组装枢纽与出口平台，为推动新兴经济体间贸易的增长发挥了巨大的作用。因此，发达国家进口增长与 BRICs 出口的关联程度可能超过了我们使用出口/总出口或出口/GDP 衡量所能体现的水平。

进一步讲，主要发达国家国内需求的降低不仅将直接减少 BRICs 的出口进而影响其经济增长，还将通过另外两个渠道影响其经济增长：一是降低世界经济增长率；二是通过贸易影响 BRICs 的消费和投资。因此，在国际贸易传导全球金融危机时实际上存在国内和国外两个放大器。就国际放大器而言，1948～2006 年，美国的历次经济衰退均伴随着进口增长率的显著下降。例如，2001 年美国 GDP 增长率下降了 2.9 个百分点，同时其进口增长率下降了 14.6 个百分点，同时世界 130 个经济体中有 74 个当年 GDP 增长率和向美国的出口增长率同时下降了。而且总体来看，向美国的出口增长率下降得越多，其 GDP 增长率也下降得越快。这就意味着，美国经济衰退在导致其进口下降的同时，也确实会导致出口国的 GDP 增长率下降。美国进口下降会导致一些出口国的 GDP 下降，出口国的收入下降会进一步引起这些出口国的进口下降。进一步的传导会放大美国进口下降对世界贸易总额和世界经济增长率的影响，最终放大全球金融危机对 BRICs 贸易和经济增长的影响。

二 出口多样性与 BRICs 的贸易联系

我们前面的分析已经显示，2000～2009 年，BRICs 对有代表性的三大国家组和世界的出口金额都出现了显著增长。而在国际贸易理论研究中，出口的增长可分为广度边际（extensive margin）和深度边际（intensive margin）。广度边际意味着对现有或新地理市场出口了种类更多的商品，深度边际则指现有产品对现有市场出口量的增长。在该部分，我们尝试着从研究者相对较少涉及的广度边际入手，[①] 考察 BRICs 在世界经济体系中贸易联系的变化。具体做法是，在 HS96 六位码的基础上，我们对 1999 年和 2009 年 BRICs 出口商品数量情况及其变化进行了分析。[②]

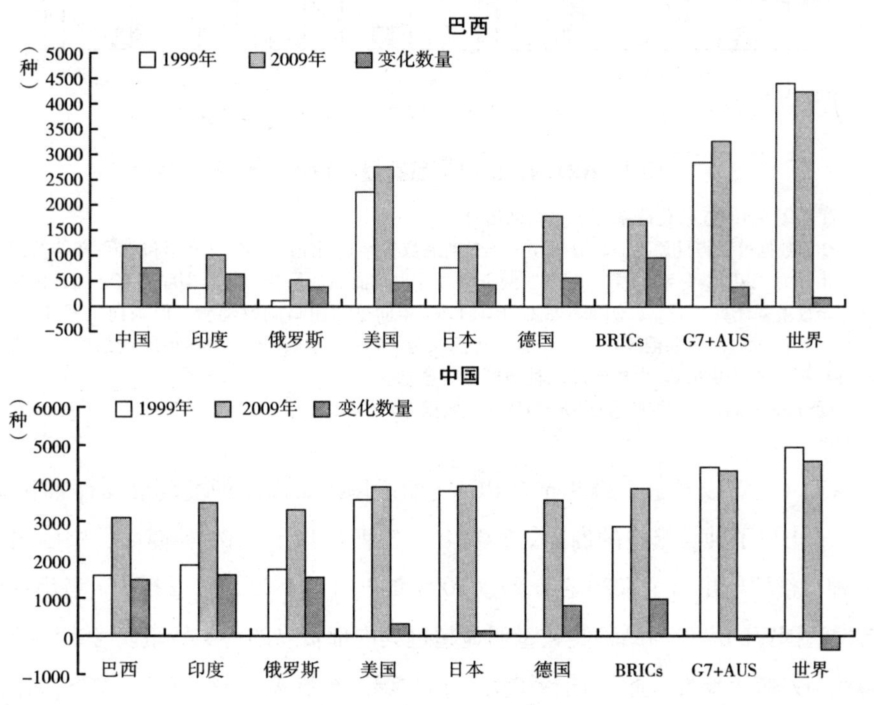

① 值得一提的是，在该领域，仍然有不少研究者做了重要的工作。对此，我们将在后文中有所涉及。

② 因数据可获得性原因，在分析印度出口商品数量时我们使用的是 1999 年和 2008 年的数据。

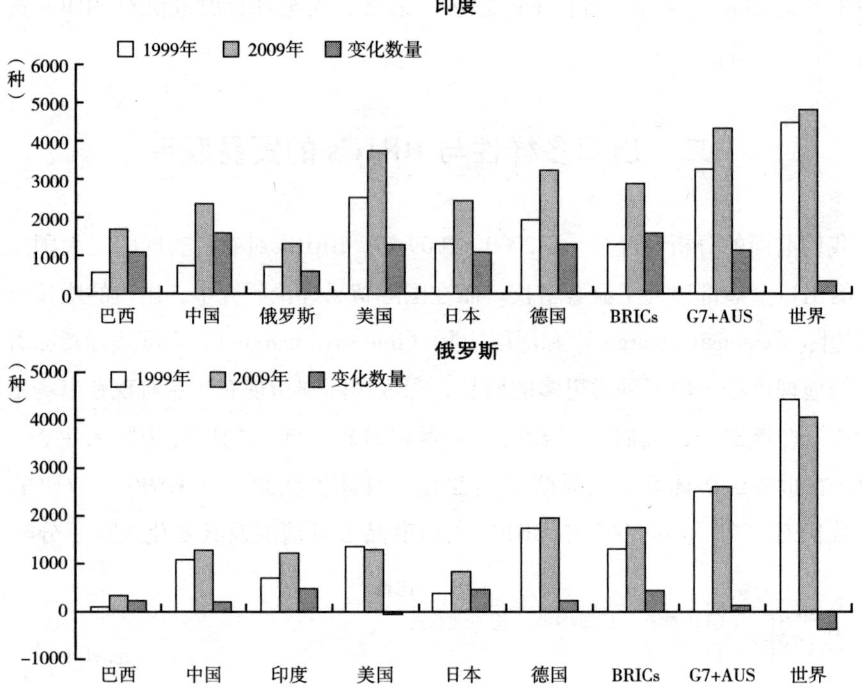

图 4　BRICs：出口商品数量（1999～2009）

注：①在 HS96 六位码基础上进行的统计。

②因数据可获得性原因，在分析印度出口商品数量时我们使用的是 1999 年和 2008 年的数据。

③分为“BRICs”和“G7 + AUS”两个组统计出口商品数量变化时，剔除了可能因各组内部贸易导致重复计算的商品。例如，如果中国 1999 年向巴西出口动物油脂，但未向俄罗斯出口，2009 年则同时向巴西和俄罗斯出口，那么我们认为，1999～2009 年中国向俄罗斯出口商品数量增加 1 种，向“BRICs”出口的商品种类则没有增加。

资料来源：作者根据联合国 COMTRADE 数据库数据计算。

从图 4 中可以看出，2009 年 BRICs 各组成国出口商品种类数量具有如下特点：①BRICs 出口了种类繁多的商品。2009 年，巴西出口了 4209 种商品，中国出口了 4569 种，俄罗斯出口了 4036 种，印度 2008 年出口了 4829 种。②BRICs 各组成国对主要发达国家的出口商品种类数量明显超过其内部贸易的种类数量。考虑到数据可获得性与系统重要性，我们选择了美、日、德三个国家以及“G7 + AUS”作为整体，计算了 BRICs 各组成国对其出口种类数量的情况。我们发现，无论是分国别的比较还是对 BRICs 和 G7 + AUS 两个组的比较，我们都可以得出上述结论。唯一稍显特殊的可能是中国。2009 年中国对巴西、印度、俄罗斯、美国、日本和德国出口了大致相当种类数量的商品，并且对 BRICs 和 G7 + AUS 两个组出口的商品种类数在 HS96 六位码基础上仅相差 458 种。

而在 1999 ~ 2009 年，BRICs 各组成国对不同贸易伙伴出口商品种类数量的变动情况如下。①BRICs 各组成国对世界出口的商品种类仅有少量增长，甚至有所下降。造成这一现象的原因可能有以下两点：一是 1999 年这四个国家就已经出口了种类繁多的商品，因而一定程度上限制了出口种类未来增长的空间；二是全球金融危机可能影响了这些国家出口的种类数量。[①] ②BRICs 中任何一国对其他三国的出口商品数量具有显著增长，其中中国出口数量的增长以及其他三国对中国出口数量的增长最为显著。巴西对中国出口商品数量增长 750 种，对印度出口商品数量增长 637 种，对俄罗斯出口商品数量增长 385 种；中国对巴西出口商品数量增长 1470 种，对印度出口商品数量增长 1615 种，对俄罗斯出口商品数量增长 1555 种；印度对巴西出口商品数量增长 1117 种，对中国出口商品数量增长 1611 种，对俄罗斯出口商品数量增长 558 种；俄罗斯对巴西出口商品数量增长 193 种，对中国出口商品数量增长 186 种，对印度出口商品数量增长 481 种。③BRICs 中任一国对美、日、德等主要发达国家的出口商品数量也有所增长，但幅度基本小于对其他三国出口数量的增长。在这一点上，中国表现得尤为明显。④如果对比分析巴西、中国、印度和俄罗斯对 BRICs、G7 + AUS 和世界出口商品数量变化的情况，这四个国家对 BRICs 出口商品数量增加最多，对 G7 + AUS 的出口商品数量次之，对世界出口商品数量增长最少，甚至还有所减少。

从定义上看，BRICs 组成国对特定市场出口商品数量的增长应视为广度边际。虽然我们的分析仅是初步的，只进行了两个年度间的比较，但已经可以非常清楚地看出，广度边际是 BRICs 组成国出口增长，尤其是 BRICs 内部贸易增长的重要动力。相关理论研究还发现，发展中国家主要是通过边界内创新（inside-the-frontier）[②] 实现出口多样性。在人均 GDP 10000 美元（1995 年，PPP）左右，边界上创新（on-the-frontier）的作用开始显现。[③] 根据 IMF2010 年 4 月发布的

---

① 即使考虑到这一缺陷，为了反映最新的情况，我们仍然选用了 2009 年的数据。

② 即技术扩散。

③ 即创造发明。参见 Klinger, B., and D. Lederman, “Diversification, Innovation, and Imitation inside the Global Technological Frontier,” *Research Policy Working Paper 3872*, World Bank, Washington, D.C. 2006。

《世界经济展望》数据，2009年按照现价美元计算，巴西的人均GDP是8220美元，中国是3678美元，印度是1031美元，俄罗斯是8694美元。这样，在今后相当长一段时间内，通过边界内创新，对现有市场出口种类更多的商品仍将是BRICs出口增长的重要方式。从这一点看，相对于主要发达国家，BRICs的内部贸易显然更具增长潜力。

与出口多样性研究密切相关的一个重要问题是，出口商品种类数量的增长是否有利于出口国的经济增长。一些研究表明①，出口多样性的增长将对一国出口产生类似于金融领域证券投资综合效应（portfolio effect）的作用，降低出口的不确定性，在长期内实现出口收入的稳步增长。出口不确定性的危害在于，它将减少风险厌恶型企业（risk-averse firms）的投资，提高宏观不确定性，损害长期经济增长。此外，出口多样性的增长还将带来知识（生产技术、管理和营销等）外溢，从而有益于其他产业的发展。② Al-Marhubi（2000）、Agosin（2007）和Lederman and Maloney（2007）所作的实证研究也证明了这一点。③ 所以，BRICs内部贸易中出口商品种类数量的增长对于各组成国的经济增长均具有积极意义。

三 贸易平衡、比较优势变化与BRICs的贸易联系

在全球经济衰退阴影有所消散的后危机时代，人们关注的焦点开始转向如何实现世界经济的可持续、平衡增长。在国家间的双边贸易往来中，贸易平衡状况不仅是受关注的焦点之一，也日益成为一个具有高度政治敏感性的话题。在本节

① Hesse, Heiko, "Export Diversification and Economic Growth", *Working Paper* No. 21, World Bank, Washington, D. C, 2008. Ghosh, A. R., and J. Ostry, "Export Instability and the External Balance in Developing Countries." *IMF Staff Papers* 41: 214 – 35. 1994. Bleaney, M., and D. Greenaway, "The Impact of Terms of Trade and Real Exchange Volatility on Investment and Growth in Sub-Saharan Africa." *Journal of Development Economics* 65: 491 – 500, 2001.

② Amin Guitierrez de Pineres, S., and M. J. Ferrantino, *Export Dynamics and Economic Growth in Latin America*, Burlington, Vermont: Ashgate Publishing Ltd. 2000.

③ Al-Marhubi, F., "Export Diversification And Growth: An Empirical Investigation," *Applied Economics Letters* 7: 559 – 62, 2000. Agosin, M. R., "Export Diversification and Growth in Emerging Economies," *Working Paper* No. 233, 2007. Departamento de Economía, Universidad de Chile. Lederman, D. and W. F. Maloney eds., "Trade Structure and Growth," in *Natural Resources: Neither Curse Nor Destiny*, Palo Alto: Stanford University Press, 2007.

中，我们对BRICs各组成国对世界、代表性国家和代表性国家组的贸易平衡状况进行了系统的分析，揭示出贸易平衡状况变化背后的比较优势变化情况，并进而探讨了这些变化对于BIRCs各组成国经济增长可能具有的意义。

表3 BRICs：贸易平衡（2009）

单位：百万美元

	巴西	中国	印度	俄罗斯
BRICs				
巴　西	0.0	-14162.5	2080.8	-2515.6
中　国	4279.7	0.0	-18346.1	-6760.1
印　度	1224.1	15952.3	0.0	3294.1
俄罗斯	1456.5	-3769.2	-3236.9	0.0
E11 - BRICs				
阿根廷	1503.8	-823.1	-211.0	-953.5
印度尼西亚	163.1	1056.8	-3786.2	-357.5
墨西哥	-107.5	8417.1	-1083.4	88.0
韩　国	-2196.2	-48871.8	-4103.7	609.0
沙特阿拉伯	355.4	-14642.4	-17647.3	305.1
南　非	826.5	-1327.7	-3073.7	-124.6
土耳其	210.5	6588.0	-276.8	7045.2
G7 + AUS				
澳大利亚	-351.5	-18793.2	-8243.6	-530.8
加拿大	110.8	5648.9	-903.5	-604.4
法　国	-676.0	8580.6	-3026.0	-1169.0
德　国	-3690.7	-5844.5	-4844.6	-9273.6
意大利	-647.4	9223.3	-400.7	12434.1
日　本	-1097.9	-33026.6	-3734.4	-246.2
英　国	1318.5	23400.0	398.4	3346.7
美　国	-4469.2	143539.9	-2179.3	-1019.4
GROUPS				
BRICs	6960.3	-1979.4	-19502.2	-5981.6
E11	7715.9	-51582.6	-49684.3	630.0
E11 - BRICs	755.6	-49603.2	-30182.1	6611.6
G7 + AUS	-9503.4	132728.4	-22933.7	2937.4
世　界	25347.4	196091.5	-133851.2	124357.1

注：①制作本表的基础数据——国别进出口数据均来自联合国COMTRADE数据库，但是因为各个报告方统计上的差异，导致计算出的贸易差额有所不一致。例如，当巴西为报告方时，巴西对中国有贸易顺差42.8亿美元；而当中国为报告方时，中国对巴西有贸易逆差141.6亿美元。

②因数据的可获得性，印度使用的是2008年的数据。

资料来源：作者根据联合国COMTRADE数据库数据计算。

从表3可以看出，除印度外，BRICs其余三国均为全球贸易的顺差国。2009年，巴西贸易顺差总额为253.5亿美元，其中大约1/3来自BRICs的内部贸易（69.6亿美元），对中国的贸易顺差为42.8亿美元，对印度的贸易顺差为12.2亿美元，对俄罗斯的贸易顺差为14.6亿美元。中国的贸易顺差总量虽然高达1960.9亿美元，但约2/3的顺差来自与主要发达国家的贸易（G7 + AUS），对E11和BRICs均为逆差。特别是，E11中除BRICs以外的国家（例如韩国）是中国贸易逆差的重要来源地。俄罗斯的贸易顺差在2009年也达到了令人瞩目的1243.6亿美元，其中29.4亿美元来自G7 + AUS，66.1亿美元来自E11中除BRICs以外的国家，与BRICs其余三国的贸易给俄罗斯带来了59.8亿美元的逆差。印度是BRICs中唯一处于全球逆差地位的国家。2008年其逆差总额为1338.5亿美元，其中195亿美元来自BRICs其余三国，301.8亿美元来自E11中除BRICs以外的国家，229.3亿美元来自G7 + AUS。

我们对2009年BRICs各国贸易平衡状况的分析虽然有助于掌握最新的动态，但如前所述，受金融危机的影响，2009年可能是一个较为特殊的年份，因为BRICs的进出口受到内外部宏观环境变动的冲击，进而对其贸易平衡状况产生较大影响。为了展望未来，我们更需要知道导致BIRCs四国贸易平衡变化的结构性因素。为了达到这一目的，我们在HS96两位码的基础上，结合2000年的情况进行了更为细致的分析。

我们首先假定，如果一国的比较优势没有发生变化，那么其所有贸易品的顺差或逆差状况应该随着该国总体贸易平衡状况同比例变化。否则，我们可以大致认定该国在某种产品上的比较优势发生了变化。例如，如果2009年中国的贸易顺差是2000年的3倍，而同期中国来自服装业的贸易顺差是2000年的4倍，那么我们就可以大致认为中国在服装业上的比较优势有所强化。在该假定基础上，我们先分别计算出2000年和2009年BIRCs各国对全球（world）贸易和其内部贸易（BRICs）的顺逆差情况，之后通过散点图的方式画出一国2000年和2009年贸易平衡状况变化的趋势线。那些较为偏离趋势线的产品，我们即认为其比较优势发生了变化。具体计算结果见图5。

根据计算结果，我们在HS96两位码的基础上整理出了BRICs 2000 ~ 2009年比较优势变化的情况（见表4）。可以看出，在这10年中，巴西、印度和俄罗斯比较优势强化的商品基本上排列在HS编码表的前列，而比较优势削弱或比较劣

巴西（世界）

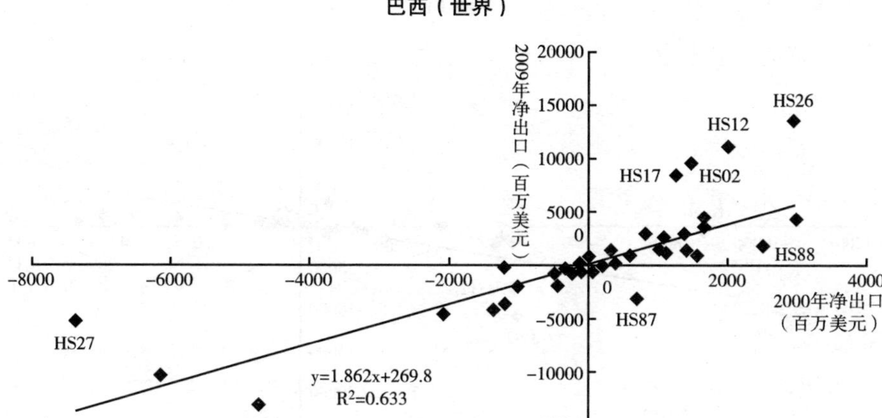

巴西（BRICs）

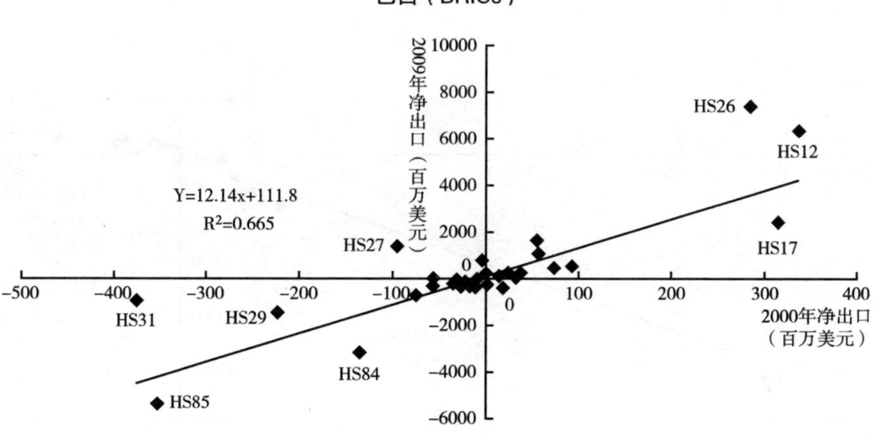

中国（世界）

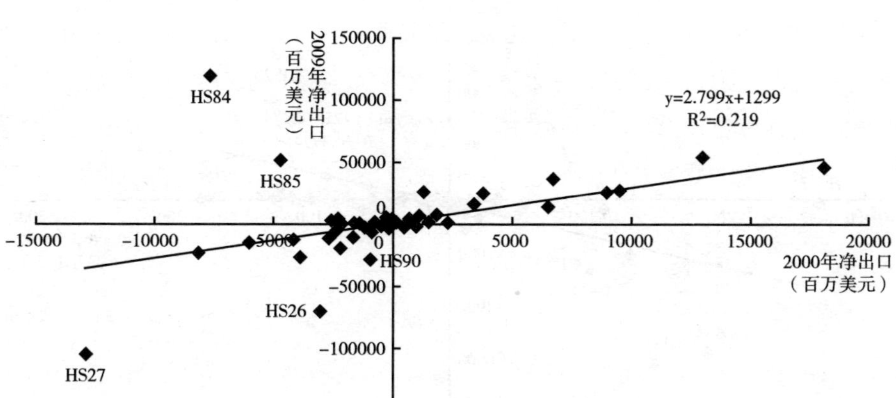

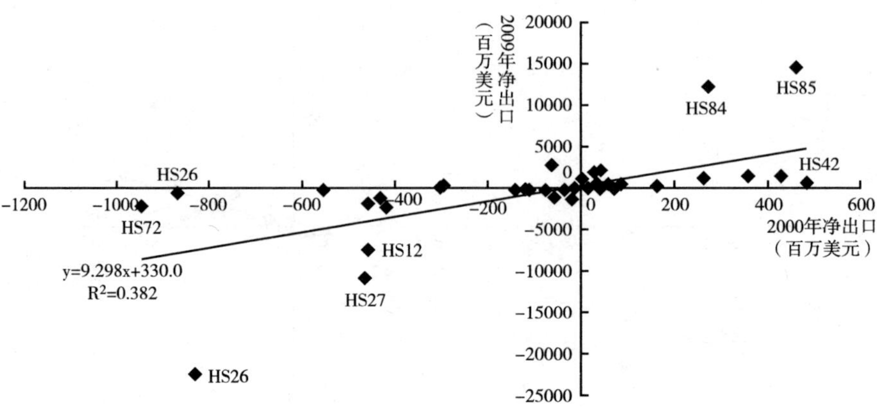
中国（BRICs）
2009年净出口（百万美元）
2000年净出口（百万美元）
HS85
HS84
HS42
HS26
HS72
HS12
HS27
HS26
y=9.298x+330.0
R^2=0.382

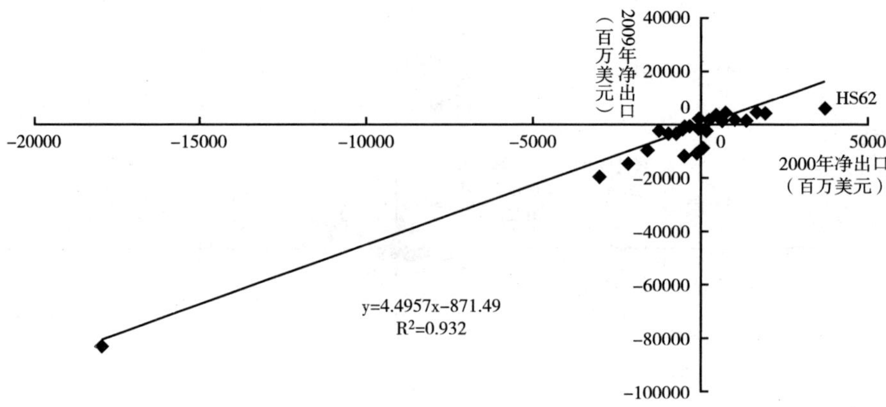
印度（世界）
2009年净出口（百万美元）
2000年净出口（百万美元）
HS62
y=4.4957x−871.49
R^2=0.932

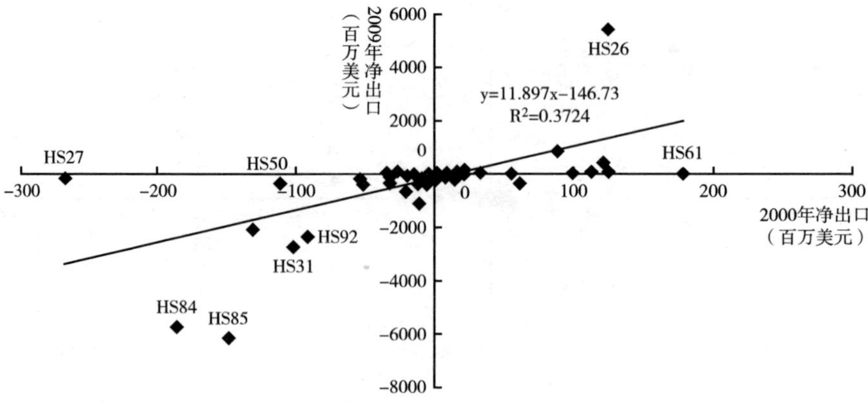
印度（BRICs）
2009年净出口（百万美元）
2000年净出口（百万美元）
HS26
y=11.897x−146.73
R^2=0.3724
HS27
HS50
HS61
HS92
HS31
HS84
HS85

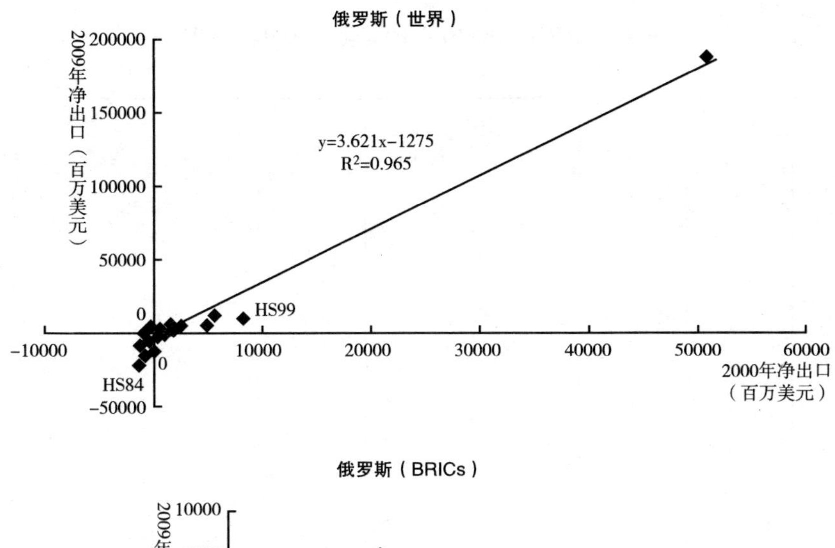

图 5　BRICs：贸易平衡状况的结构性变动（2000～2009）

注：HS02 肉及食用杂碎；HS12 含油子仁及果实，杂项子仁及果实，工业用或药用植物，稻草、秸秆及饲料；HS17 糖及糖食；HS26 矿砂、矿渣及矿灰；HS27 矿物燃料、矿物油及其蒸馏产品，沥青物质，矿物蜡；HS29 有机化学品；HS31 肥料；HS42 皮革制品，鞍具及挽具，旅行用品、手提包及类似容器，动物肠线（蚕胶丝除外）制品；HS44 木及木制品，木炭；HS50 蚕丝；HS61 针织或钩编的服装及衣着附件；HS62 非针织或非钩编的服装及衣着附件；HS72 钢铁；HS76 铝及其制品；HS84 核反应堆、锅炉、机器、机械器具及其零件；HS85 电机、电气设备及其零件，录音机及放声机、电视图像、声音的录制和重放设备及其零件、附件；HS87 车辆及其零件、附件，但铁道及电车道车辆除外；HS88 航空器、航天器及其零件；HS90 光学、照相、电影、计量、检验、医疗或外科用仪器及设备、精密仪器及设备，上述物品的零件、附件；HS92 乐器及其零件、附件；HS99 其他。

资料来源：作者根据联合国 COMTRADE 数据库数据计算。

势加强的商品则大多位于 HS 编码表的后列。而中国正好相反，比较优势强化的商品基本上排列在HS 编码表的后列，而比较优势削弱或比较劣势加强的商品则

表 4　BRICs：比较优势的变化（2000~2009）

单位：百万美元

	巴西		中国		印度		俄罗斯	
	世界	BRICs	世界	BRICs	世界	BRICs	世界	BRICs
HS02	+							−
HS12	+	+	−					
HS17	+	−						
HS26	+	+	−	−		+		
HS27	+	+	−	−		+		+
HS29		+						
HS31		+				−		+
HS42			−					
HS44								+
HS50						+		
HS61						−		
HS62					−			
HS72			+					−
HS76			+					−
HS84	−	−	+	+		−	−	−
HS85		−	+	+		−		−
HS87	−							
HS88	−							
HS90				−				
HS92						−		
HS99							−	

注：HS02 肉及食用杂碎；HS12 含油子仁及果实，杂项子仁及果实，工业用或药用植物，稻草、秸秆及饲料；HS17 糖及糖食；HS26 矿砂、矿渣及矿灰；HS27 矿物燃料、矿物油及其蒸馏产品，沥青物质，矿物蜡；HS29 有机化学品；HS31 肥料；HS42 皮革制品，鞍具及挽具，旅行用品、手提包及类似容器，动物肠线（蚕胶丝除外）制品；HS44 木及木制品，木炭；HS50 蚕丝；HS61 针织或钩编的服装及衣着附件；HS62 非针织或非钩编的服装及衣着附件；HS72 钢铁；HS76 铝及其制品；HS84 核反应堆、锅炉、机器、机械器具及其零件；HS85 电机、电气设备及其零件，录音机及放声机、电视图像、声音的录制和重放设备及其零件、附件；HS87 车辆及其零件、附件，但铁道及电车道车辆除外；HS88 航空器、航天器及其零件；HS90 光学、照相、电影、计量、检验、医疗或外科用仪器及设备、精密仪器及设备，上述物品的零件、附件；HS92 乐器及其零件、附件；HS99 其他。

资料来源：作者根据联合国 COMTRADE 数据库数据计算。

大多位于HS编码表的前列。一般而言，HS的分类原则是按商品的原料来源，结合其加工程度、用途以及所在的工业部门编排商品。在原料相差不大的情况下，加工程度越复杂的商品越往后排。例如，活动物排在第1章，鲜肉排在第2章，肉类的保藏则排在第16章。活树排在第6章，木材排在第44章，木制玩具排在第95章，木制工艺品排在第97章。因此我们可以形成的一个基本判断是，中国在加工程度较复杂商品上的比较优势在强化，其余国家在特定动植物产品和矿产品上的比较优势在强化。这样，中国与其余三国的互补性应该在提高，而其余三国间的竞争性应该更为凸显。

尤为值得注意的是，巴西、俄罗斯和印度三国在第26章和第27章的比较优势都在加强。这两章涉及的均为矿产品，其中第26章是矿砂、矿渣及矿灰，第27章是矿物燃料、矿物油及其蒸馏产品。并且，巴西、印度和俄罗斯三国在这两章比较优势的强化主要体现在BRICs内部贸易上。由此引发的一个问题是，在初级产品上比较优势的强化是否会危及这些国家的长期增长。

"资源的诅咒"（Resource Curse）和"荷兰病"（Dutch Disease）是我们耳熟能详的两个词。前者指丰富的自然资源对经济增长具有抑制作用，认为相对于自然资源贫乏的经济体，自然资源较丰富的经济体反而呈现出较差的经济发展绩效。荷兰病一词来自于20世纪60年代的荷兰。在这一时期荷兰发现了大量天然气，此后因资源行业高速畸形发展，反而抑制了荷兰农业部门、其他工业部门以及出口行业的发展。之后"荷兰病"一词特指一国经济的某一初级产品部门异常繁荣而导致其他部门衰落的现象。

然而，最近的研究发现，所谓资源的诅咒不一定具有合理性。Lederman and Maloney（2007）① 指出了相关实证研究的缺陷。世界银行（2002）的研究认为，丰富的资源能促进技术进步，带来新知识。② 澳大利亚和加拿大的经验也说明，自然资源丰富的国家也能成功实现工业化和经济的多样化。所以，我们更需要做的是深入分析与研究资源行业发展促进经济增长的机制和前提条件，从而为BRICs的共同发展和进一步合作奠定基础。

---

① Lederman, D., and W. F. Maloney, eds., "Trade Structure and Growth," in *Natural Resources: Neither Curse Nor Destiny*, Palo Alto: Stanford University Press, 2007.

② World Bank, *From Natural Resources to the Knowledge Economy: Trade and Job Quality*, *Latin American and Caribbean Studies*, Washington D. C, 2002.

四 竞争互补、竞争压力与 BRICs 的贸易联系

为了全面了解 BRICs 在世界经济体系中的贸易联系对这些国家的影响，我们需要对这些国家的贸易结构进行更深入分析。一些研究者已经采用了不同的方法对国家间贸易竞争效应和互补性效应的大小进行测算，其中包括 Jorge 等（2006）所构造的专业化系数 CS（coefficient of specialization）和一致性系数 CC（coefficient of conformity）[①]，Weiss 与 Gao（2003）等采用的恒定市场份额法（constant market share analysis）。[②] 在本节中，我们采用的计算方法是樊纲、关志雄和姚枝仲（2006）所构造的竞争互补指数（CCI）和竞争压力指数（CSI）。[③]其中竞争互补指数衡量的是特定国或国家组间竞争性较大还是互补性较大的指标。该指数取值在（0～1）之间，数值越大，两国竞争性越强。竞争压力指数则衡量一国对贸易伙伴的竞争压力，取值也在（0～1）之间，数值越大，贸易伙伴感受的来自该国的竞争压力越大。竞争互补指数的具体计算方法是，考察一国与其贸易伙伴对特定市场出口总额中，重叠部分所占比例。竞争压力指数的具体计算方法是，一国与其贸易伙伴对特定市场出口的重叠部分占该国出口额的比重。基于本文的需要，我们在 HS 六位码的基础上分别计算了 2000 年与 2009 年 BRICs 各国对其余三国、E11 和主要发达国家（G7 + AUS）在世界市场上总体的竞争压力和竞争互补情况。

总体上看，BRICs 各国与新兴经济体的竞争性大于与主要发达国家的竞争性（见图6）。具体表现为，巴西、中国、印度和俄罗斯等国对 BRICs 或 E11 贸易竞争互补指数的值，基本上都大于与 G7 + AUS 该指标的值。仅中国稍有例外。2009 年，中国与 G7 + AUS 的竞争互补指数为 0. 286，高于与 BRICs-China 的竞争互补指数（0. 178），但仍然低于与 E11-China 的竞争互补指数

① Jorge, Blàzquez - Lidoy; Javier, Rodr guez and Javier, Santiso, "Angel or Devil? China's Trade Impact on Latin American Emerging Markets," OECD Development Centre Working Paper 252, 2006.

② Weiss, J. and Gao, S., "Peop le's Republic of China's Export Threat to ASEAN: Competition in the US and Japanese Markets," ADB Institute Discussion Paper No. 13, 2003.

③ 樊纲、关志雄、姚枝仲：《国际贸易结构分析：贸易品的技术分布》，《经济研究》2006 年第 8 期。

(0.367)。然而从发展趋势看，BRICs 各国与主要发达国家竞争性提升的速度远远超过与新兴经济体竞争性的提高。尤其是中国，2009 年与主要发达国家的竞争性已经明显超过与 BRICs 其余国家。另外，巴西、印度和俄罗斯等国在与 BRICs 其余国家以及主要发达国家竞争性显著提升的同时，与中国的竞争性都有不同程度的下降。

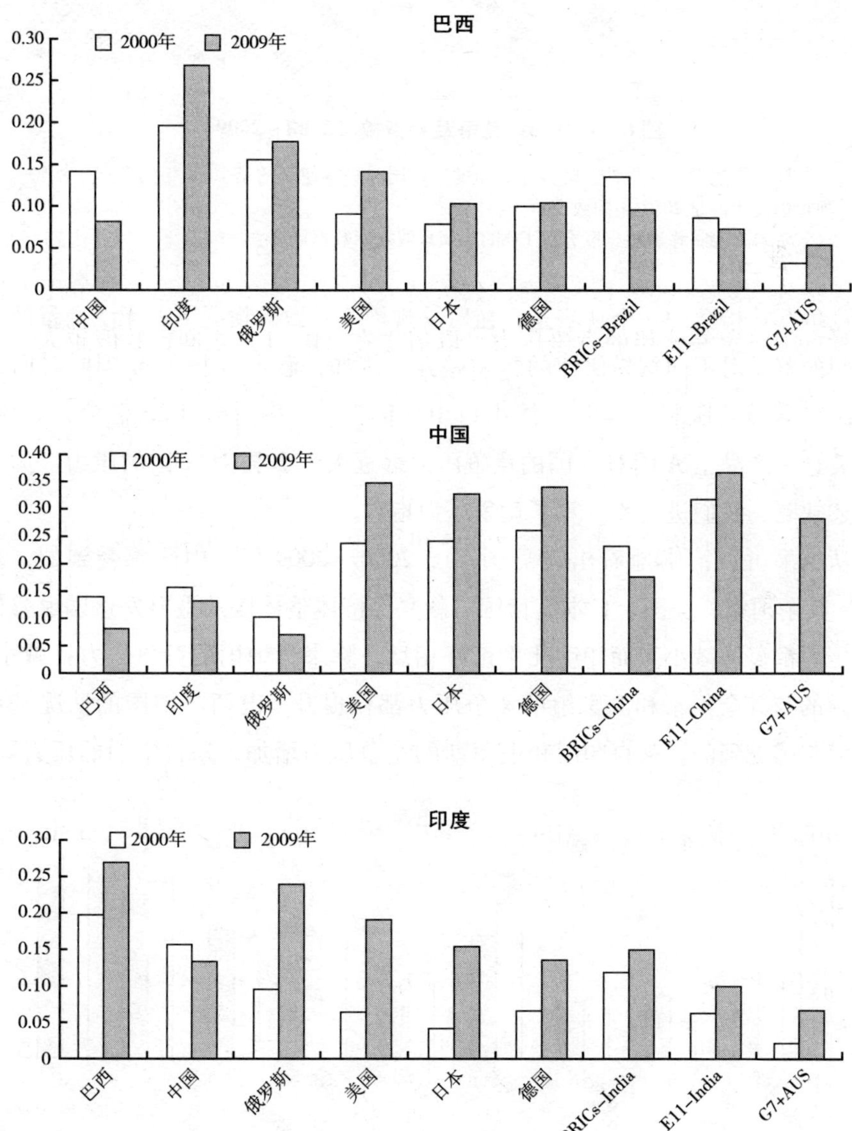

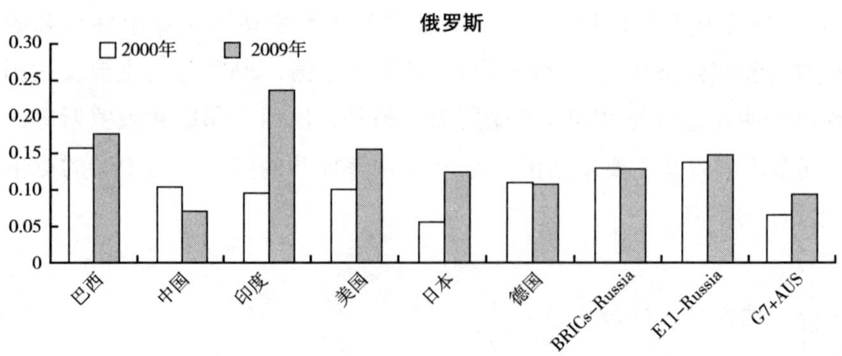

图 6　BRICs：竞争互补指数（2000～2009）

注：因数据可获得性，阿根廷、印度、韩国和日本使用的是 2008 年的数据，沙特阿拉伯使用的是 2007 年的数据。

资料来源：作者根据联合国 COMTRADE 数据库数据计算。

竞争互补指数的一个缺陷是，在贸易规模不一致的情况下，无法衡量两个经济体间的贸易对不同贸易伙伴的影响差异。例如，假定 A 国与 B 国同时向世界市场出口同质的服装，其中 A 国出口 100 亿美元，B 国出口 20 亿美元。显然，在服装这一产品上 A 国对 B 国的竞争压力远远大于 B 国对 A 国的压力。为了弥补上述缺陷，我们进一步计算了竞争压力指数。

从结果可以清晰地看出（见图 7），2000～2009 年，中国感受到的，来自 BRICs 其余国家、美国、日本、德国、新兴经济体整体以及主要发达国家整体的竞争压力都显著减小。而印度几乎正好相反，除来自中国的竞争压力在减小外，感受到的与其余国家和国家组的竞争压力都在提升。巴西与中国的情况基本类似，但它感受到的，来自印度和俄罗斯的竞争压力增加，来自中国的压力降低。

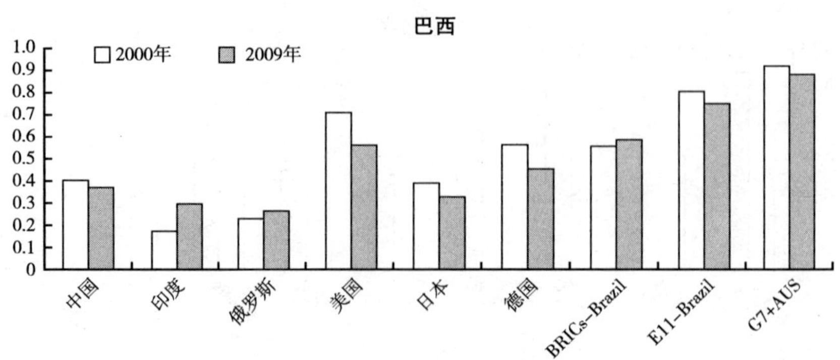

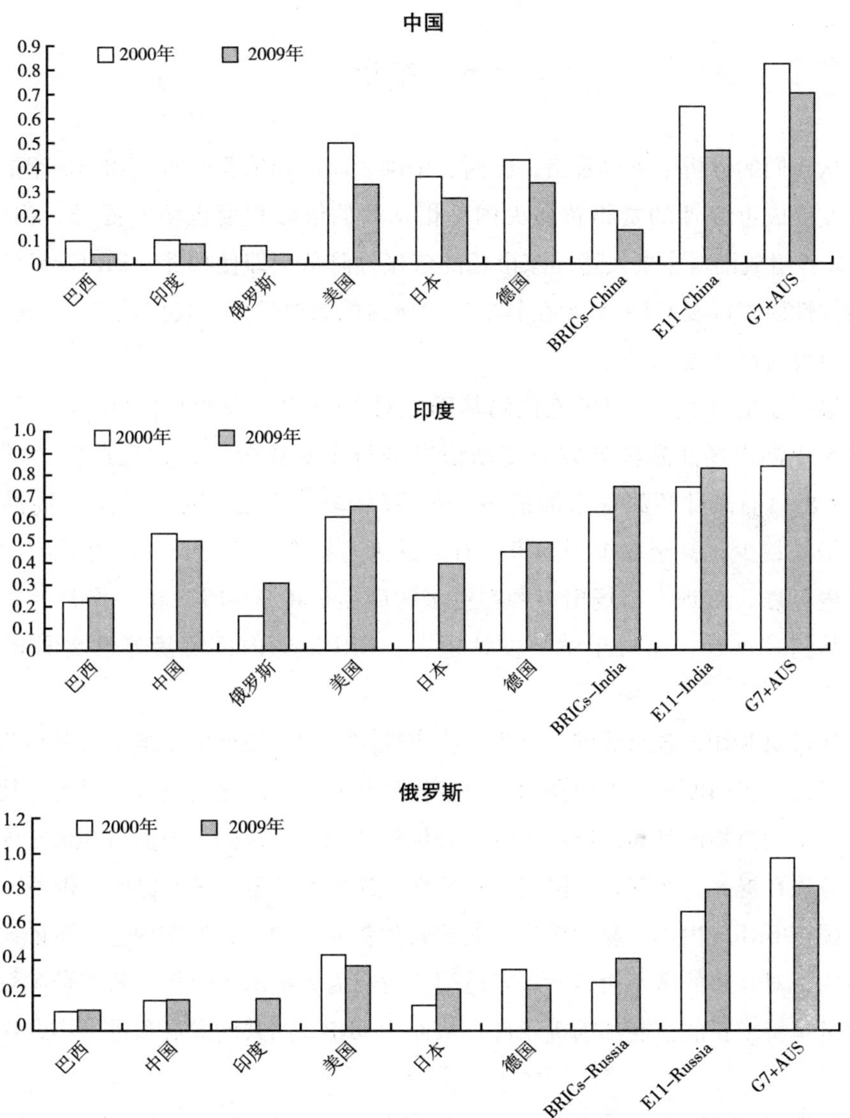

图 7　BRICs：竞争压力指数（2000～2009）

注：因数据可获得性，阿根廷、印度、韩国和日本使用的是 2008 年的数据，沙特阿拉伯使用的是 2007 年的数据。

资料来源：作者根据联合国 COMTRADE 数据库数据计算。

俄罗斯感受到的来自新兴经济体（无论是单个国家还是整体）的压力都在增长，而来自美国、德国和 G7 + AUS 的压力降低。

五　结语

从我们的分析中可以看出，巴西、中国、印度和俄罗斯四个BRICs组成国均已经发展成世界性的货物贸易大国，相互间的依赖程度也明显提升。相应的，BRICs各组成国对主要发达国家市场的依赖性降低。即使如此，BRICs对外贸易的结构性因素以及G7 + AUS在其出口中所占的重要份额使我们认定，“脱钩论”尚有值得商榷之处。

进一步的，我们在HS六位码基础上对1999年和2009年BRICs各组成国出口至不同市场商品种类数量变动情况进行了对比分析，发现这四个国家对BRICs出口商品种类数量增加最多，对G7 + AUS次之，对世界出口商品种类数量增长最少，甚至在个别国家还有所减少。在今后相当长一段时间内，通过边界内创新，对现有市场出口种类更多的商品仍将是BRICs出口增长的重要方式。从这一点看，相对于主要发达国家，BRICs的内部贸易显然更具增长潜力。

通过对BRICs各组成国对世界、代表性国家和代表性国家组贸易平衡状况的系统考察，我们发现，中国在加工程度较复杂商品上的比较优势在强化，其余国家在特定动植物产品和矿产品上的比较优势在强化。这样，中国与其余三国的互补性应该在提高，而其余三国间的竞争性应该更为凸显。虽然巴西、俄罗斯和印度三国在BRICs内部贸易中矿产品的比较优势显著增强，但是理论与实证研究均已表明，对具体的国家而言不一定适用。我们需要更深入分析与研究资源行业发展促进经济增长的机制和前提条件，从而为BRICs的共同发展和进一步合作奠定基础。

我们对BRICs各组成国与其主要贸易伙伴相互间的竞争互补情况和竞争压力情况进行的研究显示，总体上BRICs各国与新兴经济体的竞争性大于其与主要发达国家的竞争性。但是从发展趋势看，BRICs各国与主要发达国家竞争性提升的速度远远超过它与新兴经济体竞争性的提升速度。并且，BRICs各国感受到的来自内部贸易的竞争压力远小于来自外部世界的同一压力。

综合以上因素，我们有理由对BRICs内部贸易的未来前景持乐观态度，并且我们认为相互间贸易的发展有利于这些国家的经济增长。值得一提的是，欠佳的世界经济增长前景、停滞不前的多哈回合谈判、全球范围内有所抬头的贸易保护主义倾向、有效性尚待提高的相互间政策协调以及尚未形成的对全球经济治理格局的共识，这些都给 BRICs 内部贸易的进一步发展带来了不确定性。总体上，BRICs 在贸易领域的合作宜循序渐进，依托 G20 这个全球经济治理的主要平台，加强重大问题上的协调一致。

巴西对外贸易的地理导向：正确的选择？

雷纳托·鲍曼　吴孝芹（译）*

一　导言

单词有时具有无法估量的作用。五个首字母简写单词 BRICs（“金砖四国”）提升了一组特定国家的关注度。尤其，巴西受到了不同于以往的关注：对于某些分析家而言，巴西不只是“发展中国家”，而是将对未来国际局势产生影响的重要国家。

这种变化不只体现在符号上。近年来这些国家的经济绩效和宏观经济指标吸引了对其潜力的大量关注。巨大的国内市场使其更易实现“增长带动出口”而非“出口带动增长”，这意味着这些国家将在国际关系中扮演积极角色。

近年来巴西受邀参加最发达国家集团会议（尽管作用较小）、世界贸易组织多边磋商会议，以及巴西前高层领导经常参加应对国际金融体系改革的专家会议，并非偶然。巴西代表在多边机构讨论中扮演积极角色，致力于改变这些机构在决策过程中的“政治经济”。

以上活动使得该国成为最重要多边机构的创始成员之一，并按照这些组织商定的规则和纪律进行外交活动。

---

* 雷纳托·鲍曼，联合国拉丁美洲和加勒比经济委员会驻巴西代表；吴孝芹，太原工业学院管理工程系讲师。

这些行动强化了巴西成为联合国安理会固定成员以及以更积极的姿态参加7国集团会议（并进而使7国集团扩为10国集团）的愿望。

可以预期，作为“金砖四国”的成功国家应有与其经济潜力、相对稳定的经济形势及在国际局势中的鲜明形象相匹配的生产能力。这是这些国家有资格参与高峰论坛的条件。

巴西经济的活力（80%）主要来自国内需求（尤其是消费，投资占GDP的比重仅为20%）。近年来，外部需求比重上升，贸易政策侧重于进行高附加值和高技术含量产品出口的区域贸易。

这一重心招致了尖锐的批评。第一，拉丁美洲和加勒比账户仅占全球GDP的6%。[①] 因此，其吸纳巴西产品的能力是有限的。

第二，该区域市场应对贸易变动的能力相当脆弱：近期商品价格下降（主要是区域出口）已经严重影响了巴西制造业向该区域的出口。[②] 出口收入的下降促使该区域部分国家设置贸易壁垒。一些分析家预期，若国际形势没有发生积极变化，这种行动在未来的一段时间将大行其道。[③]

巴西一半工业产品出口总量来自跨国公司的分公司。这意味着当局在重新设计贸易流的地理导向时受制于这些企业的内部决策及其对销售渠道的控制。这就限制了该国在工业化国家开发高附加值和高技术含量产品出口市场的能力。因此，该区域市场能为改进出口结构提供一定空间。

深化区域贸易的支持者认为区域贸易对该国在国际峰会[④]上的谈判能力及对贸易流的质量（允许大量高技术含量工业品出口）有显著贡献。批评者认为，区域出口重点应转向更大、更有潜力的市场，而该市场的激烈竞争将使得出口结构趋于成熟。

这种讨论将贸易流的地理导向和激励行业集中出口融合在一起。20世纪80年代，部分关注亚洲国家竞争的美国经济学家[⑤]开发了分析“战略出口政策”基本原理的几个模型。其基本观点是对一些行业的国内企业提供激励使其获得相对

① 见世界银行发展指数在线数据库。

② 2008年第四季度巴西向拉丁美洲的制造业产品出口增长额仅为2007年相应数据的1/3。

③ 包括巴西采取在周边国家更积极开展经济活动的政策。

④ 见外交部长阿莫里姆的声明（2008）。

⑤ 见赫尔普曼、克鲁格曼（1989）和克鲁格曼（1990）。

于国外竞争者的竞争优势。

以下分析将有别于不偏向特定行业的贸易政策，相反，主要讨论如何识别来自邻国的贸易收益。假定区域一体化政策有助于克服近期贸易保护主义倾向，认为应关注区域贸易，但也面临大量障碍。

本文首先对近期经济指标的主要特征进行简要介绍（第二部分），然后展示巴西和主要国际机构的关系（多边方式），反映巴西的多边视角（第三部分）。第四部分对巴西将区域选择作为提升出口技术含量的工具进行讨论，提出在现有地理因素和面临其他区域的若干区域集团前提下，区域选择是不可避免的，但面临许多困难（第五部分）。最后进行总结。

二　近期贸易趋势

对于巴西经济所呈现的贸易绩效，难有发展中国家能与之抗衡。过去 30 年里它的出口远远超过进口。1974～2008 年的共 34 年里，仅有 12 年（1974～1979 年和 1995～2000 年）出现贸易赤字。

国外价格是主要解释因子。1974～1980 年巴西经济主要依靠石油进口，而当时石油价格攀升至历史最高纪录。这（加上进口紧缩）解释了当时出口量增速远大于进口却出现贸易赤字的原因。1995～2000 年情况类似（见表 1）。事实上只有 1991～1995 年和 2005 年之后，进口量增速超过出口量增速。

表 1　巴西贸易量增长速度：1975～2007（年平均增速）

单位：%

年份 \ 项目	出口	进口	年份 \ 项目	出口	进口
1975～1980	7.3	0.0	1996～2000	8.1	3.7
1981～1985	6.1	-0.1	2001～2005	13.1	1.3
1986～1990	5.9	2.2	2006～2007	1.4	19.8
1991～1995	6.9	28.9	1975～2007 合计	6.6	5.3

资料来源：FUNCEX（巴西外贸研究中心基金会）。

随着与其他拉美和加勒比国家贸易关系日趋紧密，1990～2007 年出口额增长 5 倍以上（从 310 亿美元上升至 1600 亿美元）。1990～2006 年，巴西对该区域出口所占权重翻番，且随着出口总额的不断提高，近几年该权重保持稳定（见表2）。

表2　巴西对拉丁美洲和加勒比地区出口的相对权重（1985～2006）（占总出口额的百分比）

单位：%

年　份	1985	1990	1995	2000	2006
拉丁美洲和加勒比地区	9.2	11.4	22.5	24.6	25.5
南美	7.8	8.6	20.4	20.1	19.4

资料来源：ECLAC/BADECEL（拉丁美洲和加勒比经济委员会/拉丁美洲和加勒比对外贸易数据库）。

努力促进区域贸易通常体现为区域市场满足了如下条件：①动态发展相对优势，大部分出口为工业化产品；②相对竞争优势不仅来自高附加值，还来自精密技术产品的低市场准入；③出口活动的“学习过程”，允许国内厂商通过开发不成熟市场获得专业知识，以便在未来能够应对工业化国家消费者的更多需求；④地缘政治观点，相邻国家的共同立场可以增强国际谈判能力。

如表3所示，在向拉丁美洲和加勒比地区的出口中工业品所占份额高于其他区域。比如，1990年巴西向其他拉美和加勒比国家的出口品中大部分[①]为工业品。16年以后，情况依然如此。众所周知，拉美国家工业品出口一向集中于美国和其他拉美国家。向拉丁美洲和加勒比地区出口的中高技术产品较其他市场更为密集。区域贸易中这些产品所占份额约为其总出口份额的2倍。

这迥异于其在欧亚地区以初级产品出口为主的模式。

从表3可见，巴西生产商和贸易商通过相对较高的工业化程度和密集的研发（R&D）活动开拓区域市场和邻国市场。大量贸易得益于优惠的市场准入条件。[②]

自20世纪80年代中期至2000年，许多因素影响了巴西出口的活力。高国内通胀（至1995年）、出口激励减少、国企份额降低引致的投资下降、进口竞争力增加、实际汇率下降及其他因素均导致巴西的国际市场地位急剧下降：巴西占世界出口的份额从1984年的1.49%降为1999年的0.85%（见图1）。

① 其中14.0%为低技术产品，48.3%为中技术产品，8.5%为高技术产品。

② 见CEPAL（2006）：2005年有2/3的区域贸易根据优惠协定进行。

表3 巴西向特定市场出口的不同产品比重（1990～2006）

单位：%

工业品——低技术

国家及地区 / 年份	拉丁美洲和加勒比*（33）	美国	欧盟**（27）	亚太***（16）	中国	日本	其他	全球
1990	14.0	20.6	10.7	23.5	17.3	5.3	14.0	14.7
2000	16.8	16.2	9.0	11.6	4.5	3.3	5.7	12.1
2006	11.6	13.9	8.6	9.6	5.5	2.4	3.9	9.2

工业品——中等技术

国家及地区 / 年份	拉丁美洲和加勒比*（33）	美国	欧盟**（27）	亚太***（16）	中国	日本	其他	全球
1990	48.3	28.7	16.1	39.3	28.9	18.1	19.6	25.7
2000	44.9	26.6	14.8	26.8	9.0	8.0	12.8	25.1
2006	46.9	32.0	17.5	18.9	7.8	10.1	14.5	26.4

工业品——高技术

国家及地区 / 年份	拉丁美洲和加勒比*（33）	美国	欧盟**（27）	亚太***（16）	中国	日本	其他	全球
1990	8.5	7.7	2.9	1.8	0.3	0.9	1.7	4.3
2000	12.6	22.3	9.2	2.6	5.1	10.6	5.4	12.5
2006	12.3	11.0	5.0	4.0	1.4	0.4	5.5	7.7

注：*安提瓜和巴布达、阿根廷、巴哈马、巴巴多斯、伯利兹、玻利维亚、智利、哥伦比亚、哥斯达黎加、古巴、多米尼克、厄瓜多尔、萨尔瓦多、格林纳达、危地马拉、圭亚那、海地、洪都拉斯、牙买加、墨西哥、尼加拉瓜、巴拿马、巴拉圭、秘鲁、委内瑞拉、多米尼加共和国、圣基茨和尼维斯、圣文森特和格林纳丁斯、圣卢西亚、苏里南、特立尼达和多巴哥、巴西、乌拉圭。

**德国、奥地利、比利时、塞浦路斯、丹麦、斯洛伐克、斯洛文尼亚、西班牙、爱沙尼亚、保加利亚、芬兰、法国、希腊、匈牙利、爱尔兰、意大利、拉脱维亚、立陶宛、卢森堡、马耳他、荷兰、波兰、葡萄牙、英国、捷克共和国、罗马尼亚、瑞典。

***澳大利亚、文莱、柬埔寨、菲律宾、中国香港、印度、印度尼西亚、老挝、马来西亚、孟买、新西兰、韩国、新加坡、中国台湾、越南、泰国。

资料来源：CEPAL（拉美经委会），2008。

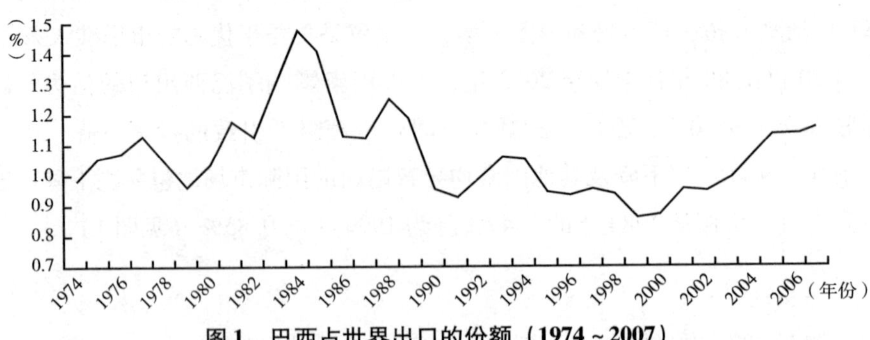

图1 巴西占世界出口的份额（1974～2007）

资料来源：Ipeadata。

2000年汇率制度变革带来的本币贬值、积极贸易政策降低了外部冲击的消极影响（20世纪90年代后期）以及较高的商品价格均推动巴西采取更积极的贸易政策并提升了该国在国际贸易中的地位，但巴西产品出口占世界总出口的份额依然不到1.2%。

这意味着有98.8%的国际市场潜力可供巴西提升出口份额，最近的一系列贸易措施也反映了这一认知。进口方面，近年来也恢复了产品流入，尤其是亚洲原产地产品的流入。

两方面的活动（更多的出口和进口）增强了巴西在国际谈判中的地位。这有利于该国寻找坚持WTO基本规则的新市场，不致遭遇新壁垒。与此同时，进口的增加使巴西启动了应对倾销行为指控的法律程序。

近年来巴西在促进区域市场出口和在亚洲、非洲和东欧开发新的非传统市场方面进行了大量努力。出口目的地多元化成为巴西贸易政策的一个中心议题：2000年10个主要贸易伙伴国占其总出口的份额为70.4%，2006年降至59.2%。

美国占巴西出口的份额从2000年的24%降为2007年的15%。[①] 这并非说明巴西撤出了美国市场，因为从数额上看，巴西对美国的出口量呈现如下指数[②]：1990~1995年平均为43.0，1991~2000年平均为54.8，2001~2007年平均为94.0。[③]

对欧盟出口情况类似。欧盟占巴西总出口份额从2000年的28%降为2007年的24%。其数量指数如下：1990~1995年平均为43.8，1996~2000年平均为53.7，2001~2007年平均为89.1。

与此同时，亚洲占巴西出口份额从20世纪90年代的15%上升为2007年的约18%。巴西对东欧的出口份额也相应从3%上升到4%。三个非洲贸易伙伴（安哥拉、南非和尼日利亚）占其总出口的份额不到3%。[④]

由此可见该出口绩效不只得益于这段期间出口价格的上涨[⑤]，还应归功于市场的多元化。

---

① CEPAL（2008）。

② 2006=100。数据来源于FUNCEX。

③ 数据来源于FUNCEX。

④ 对其他金砖国家的出口占总出口的份额也是有限的：2007年俄罗斯占2.3%、中国占6.7%。

⑤ 1990~1995年出口价格上涨2.3%，1996~2000年下降3.1%，2001~2007年年均上涨6.1%。

巴西经济与国际市场的紧密联系还与资本流有关。1980～1995 年每年外国直接投资总流入量为 10 亿～30 亿美元。随后，外国直接投资额迅速上升，达到 2000 年的 400 亿美元和 2007 年的 500 亿美元的相对较高水平。近几年，新兴经济体中巴西在吸引 FDI 方面排名第二，仅次于中国。

1994 年之前，巴西对他国进行的外国直接投资很少（每年平均约为 8 亿美元）。近几年数额大增，尽管每年变化幅度较大。

有价证券投资总流入也很显著。1993 年前平均流入额不到 250 亿美元（包括投资于股票市场、固定利率债券的境外资源及其他投资），受对境外投资者法律限制的较大制约。近年来，平均流入额大幅上涨，2001 年达到 2100 亿美元。

这些数据表明，巴西经济在商品、服务和资本方面越来越开放。变革力度与流入额的相关性较大。相应，传统方法更多地运用于多边机构，它集中在：①运用机构规则；②对新兴经济体区别对待。关于这点我们将在下一部分进行简要讨论。

三 多边方法

巴西是 1947 年关税及贸易总协定（GATT）的 23 个发起国之一。作为一个发展中国家能够加入所谓的"富人俱乐部"有其本身的原因。这反映了巴西外交政策的一大特征：与其他 9 个国家相邻却无明显冲突，巴西的外交活动长期集中于经济领域。作为国际市场的弱者，保持存在和规则与监管的有效性十分重要。在所有发起国中，巴西是 WTO 向发展中国家提供"特殊和差别"待遇的积极拥护者之一。①

这部分解释了巴西在 GATT 以及最近在 WTO 扮演的积极角色。自 1994 年 WTO 建立以来，巴西在许多争端案件中是备受瞩目的：24 个案件中担任仲裁、14 个案件中为被告、49 个案件中为第三方。争端案件的总体结果对该国是积极的，大部分是对巴西有利的。

在以前的谈判回合中，巴西和其他新兴经济体主要表现为低姿态，受惠于其

① GATT 自创立之日起就接受新兴经济体出现的特定经济问题。GATT 第 18 条即为对经济发展的援助。关贸总协定第四部分——贸易和发展——更是发展中国家取得的政治成就。后来，授权条款进一步强化了普惠制。巴西在推动这些条款方面发挥了积极作用。

他成员在各回合谈判中达成的最惠国条款。但自从乌拉圭回合以来，尤其在多哈回合的筹备期间，毫无疑问，巴西扮演着积极角色，参加了凯恩斯集团及多个多国集团（G77、G20、G4 等）。

贸易中的高披露及不同峰会发起的相关行动刺激了巴西政策制定者，使其尝试成为决定国际事务的最重要国家集团的一员。这导致巴西不断申请成为联合国安理会的固定成员以及频繁表示希望获得 G7 集团会议的邀请。

经济条件的不断改善、对国际资本市场的不断融入以及投资重点的变化导致巴西与负责提供外汇流动性（IMF）和长期资本（世界银行）的多边机构的关系也发生了变化。

巴西是 1944 年布雷顿森林协定的缔约国之一，同样也是 IMF（国际货币基金）和世界银行初始运作时的缔约国之一。1954 年 IMF 首次通过美国的进出口银行（Eximbank）向巴西提供了一笔贷款，该贷款于 1958 年到期。

巴西与 IMF 的关系并非一直友好，两者在 1959 年出现了双边冲突。20 世纪 80 年代，巴西与 IMF 签署了 6 个意向合同，但大部分承诺后者未予实现。因此，两者在此之后的 10 年关系都比较紧张。1994 年考虑到巴西财政调整不适合维持低通胀水平及对其汇率政策的怀疑，IMF 决定不对雷亚尔计划提供支持。

国际冲击使巴西经济在 20 世纪 90 年代后期陷入困境。为了稳定公共债券占 GDP 的比重，1998 年 11 月，巴西与 IMF、世界银行、泛美开发银行（IDB）以及一些国家签订了协议。2001、2002 及 2003 年又签订了新的协议。2005 年巴西决定对 IMF 停止续展信贷，并偿还了从以上几个协议中获得的尚未使用的信贷。

按规定，成员国可按该国在 IMF 存款份额的一定比例获得资源。但是 1992、1998、2001 和 2002 年该基金对巴西的贷款均超过该份额（依次为 103%、600%、400%和 902%）。从未有其他拉美国家获得如巴西 2002 年取得的相对其份额如此之高比例的贷款。

巴西与世界银行的关系同样源远流长。1949 年世界银行对巴西发放了 7500 万美元的第一笔贷款（用于能源），从那以后世界银行在该国基础设施融资方面扮演着重要角色。20 世纪 50 年代世界银行向巴西的贷款主要集中用于基础设施项目，尤其是用于能源和交通建设。20 世纪 60 年代，贷款依然主要用于能源，农业和制造业也开始占用了一部分资源。20 世纪 70 年代，这种分化更为明显。

20 世纪 80 年代初期情况发生了显著变化，世界银行改变了战略，不再投资于上述项目，开始重点促进监管和金融政策，越来越关注贫穷、环境和性别等问题。与此同时，巴西政府削减了在基础设施和生产活动方面的公共投资。

不管该变化是源于世界银行、巴西政府或其他因素，事实表明，在后来的多年内从世界银行和 IMF 流入巴西的资源相当少。

与这些多边机构关系的变化及 20 世纪 90 年代和 21 世纪初不断进军国际主权债券和私人债券市场促使巴西变得更加谨慎。事实上，巴西当局经常讨论 IMF 要求附加信用额度和积极预防来应对流动性危机的作用。巴西也经常强调应提升新兴国家在决策过程中的作用。

进入国际资本市场可能性的增加使巴西调整监管和规范，以使国内企业能从不断完善的信贷条件中获益。大量巴西企业通过发行 ADRs（美国存托凭证）来增加流动性：2004 年交易额达 4.34 亿美元，2008 年交易额翻了近 5 倍，高达 19 亿美元。[①]

巴西还是美洲开发银行（InterAmerican Development Bank，IDB）发起国之一。巴西通常通过美洲开发银行进行基础设施项目的融资，自 20 世纪 90 年代中期以后还进行社会领域、环境和公共部门监管方面项目的融资。与 IMF 和世界银行的情况相似，近年来，来自于 IDB 的资源净流入越来越少。

巴西近期提高了在安第斯开发银行（Corporación Andina de Fomento，CAF）的资本份额，该行主要将国际市场资源转至拉美，向官方和私人机构提供多种银行服务。CAF 支持的多数项目旨在促进区域一体化。这也是巴西成为其股东的原因。

另外，巴西的对外政策转向支持其他新兴国家，即所谓的南南合作。[②] 这是一个不断摸索的过程。总体来说，合作存在两种主要模式：①与近邻合作［南方共同市场（MERCOSUR）除外］，在卫生政策、技术标准、制度强化、消费者权利及其他方面采取联合行动，共同努力克服一体化进程中存在的困难；②与第三国进行大范围项目的合作。

与非南方共同市场国家的合作包括劳动力培训、基本教育、预防艾滋病、农业技术转移、饥饿和贫困斗争经验交流以及其他项目。与巴西进行项目合作

① 见 www.cvm.gov.br。

② 详细信息见 www.abc.gov.br。

的国家包括非洲的葡萄牙语国家、东帝汶、其他南美国家、海地等。这不仅是对依赖南南合作外部帮助的人口进行实际支持，也是提升国际形象的一种手段。

巴西的对外政策在国际环境中扮演积极角色的同时，还致力于深化区域联系。当然，这与它对区域市场的收益预期有关，以下将对此进行讨论。

四　区域选择孰是孰非

尽管外部政治认同，但从巴西经济角度考虑，不得不关注以下问题：区域市场能否为国内生产商和出口商提供足够动力，能否提升国内产品的技术含量。

初级产品的区域贸易主要取决于由其他因素决定的商品价格。谈判的重点在于双边贸易能否以比国际市场更低的成本提供这类产品。

服务贸易的范围和重要性还比较有限，区域市场讨论的焦点依然集中在制造业产品上。因此，问题是区域选择能否持续维持制造业产品出口并为高技术产品提供市场。拉美和加勒比地区账户总额占全球 GDP 的 6%。[①] 集中于一个相对潜力有限的市场似乎是一种短视选择。

巴西做出该选择的原因有三：①该区域其他国家的收入水平和需求模式；②巴西产品相对该区域其他国家的国内产品及其从其他市场进口的第三国产品有优势；③当地消费者偏好巴西产品。

近年来允许巴西产品出口至其他拉美国家的需求模式主要得益于由贸易效应[②]引发的财富效应、劳动力市场的发展（正式就业增加及较高工资[③]）及社会政策。这有助于增加该区域的中产阶级人数，相应增加了该区域对制造业产品，尤其是汽车及其他耐用消费品的需求。

出口价格下降可能影响收入进而减少区域贸易。这是影响该区域对巴西制造产品需求的一大威胁（贸易保护主义除外）。对巴西传统品牌的接受和优先进入市场有助于将出口活动维持在一定水平。当国外通货的流动性受限时，可以采取

① 固定美元（从 2000 年为基准）。数据来自于世界银行（世界发展指数在线数据库）。

② 10 年内拉美国家整体从贸易中获益约占 GDP 的 1% [CEPAL（2008）]。

③ CEPAL（2008）。

特定机制来维持区域贸易，后文将对此进行讨论。

同样，代理机构很重要。跨国公司占据了一半工业品的出口份额和大部分中高技术产品的出口份额。它们将巴西作为向区域市场出口的平台（Baumann; Galrao，2002）。这一方面取决于这些跨国公司的内部政策，同时也反映了巴西产品竞争力的局限性。尚无迹象表明这些公司计划将工厂向该区域其他国家转移,[①] 且近年来投资越来越向巴西集中。

此外，区域市场对中小企业非常重要：区域贸易流所占比重更高。因此，从国内分配效应角度来看，区域选择更有利可图。

该区域大部分 R&D 活动发生在巴西。其国内市场能够容纳大规模生产。巴西相较该区域其他国家而言采取了更为多样化的行业政策。

这些特点反映了巴西生产商较其邻国的本土竞争者更能从规模和技术产品中获益。大量产品能在相当长时期内保持比较优势。

维持或提升巴西产品的市场份额至少取决于以下三点：①巴西品牌的竞争力；②成本差异和贸易偏好导致的市场进入差异；③基于政治原因对巴西产品的依赖。特定品牌的竞争力取决于各生产商的微观经营绩效。所以相关讨论主要集中于后两点。

大部分区域贸易均根据优惠贸易协定进行。但该区域的优惠额依然有限，离真正的区域贸易自由化还有一定距离。为了应对从第三国进口的竞争压力[②]，为了完全受惠于区域一体化及保护区域贸易以防其他拉美国家和一些工业化竞争者签订各种优惠协定而导致贸易转移，迫切需要实现区域贸易真正自由化。

当然，这是个非常敏感的话题。考虑到各国规模和潜在竞争力的差异，只有各经济体能明确从该过程中获得利益，才可能出现进一步的妥协。贸易的制度性不平衡、投资转移使规模较大的贸易伙伴受益以及工作创造步伐较慢等因素均使得区域一体化进程受阻。至少在南方共同市场很少有成员有动力去推动改革。[③]

---

① 从智利与美国、欧盟或一些亚洲国家签订的双边优惠协定获利的部分（智利投资者除外）。

② 例如，近年来巴西产品在阿根廷的市场份额从 2005 年的 36% 下降到 2008 年的 31%，与此同时中国产品的市场份额上升了 3 倍，从 4% 提高到 12% ［CNI（2008）］。

③ 鲍曼和穆西（2006）提供的一些指数显示南方共同市场的 4 个发起国之间的利益分配亦不均衡。

维纳波尔（2008）指出，当缺少价格均衡因子时，贸易转移会惩罚规模较小的经济体并在企业间进行重新分配，从而使国家间的收入差距“在经济一体化进程中进一步扩大和加深”。这就需要积极措施来缩小差距。

这种观点并未考虑巴西正在成为“区域霸主”的现实。相反，其认为要想继续区域一体化进程必须允许所有参与方均能从各自所作的让步中获得利益。

开发区域市场取代工业化国家会对出口产品的技术密集度产生怎样的影响？

总的来说，制造动力、吸收规模收益能力及提升巴西产品技术含量的动力均来自国内市场。各行业的出口总额约占总产出的1/5。

要了解实际出口份额，就需对向区域市场和OECD国家出口的产品差异进行实证分析。只有在与向高收入国家出口的成熟产品相比区域市场存在显著差异时，才能说明关注区域市场会妨碍技术融合。无论如何，要改变该状况不能仅取决于国内政策，因为大部分中高技术产品的贸易取决于跨国公司的市场战略。

总之，区域市场将会带来潜在收益，这一点政策制定者不应忽视。吸收这些收益（且实现长期收益）绝非区区小事。深化区域贸易存在诸多障碍，下一部分将具体讨论这一问题。

五　区域选择面临的挑战

关注与其他拉美国家及南美国家的经济政治关系是近期巴西对外政策的重点。自20世纪80年代中期以来，巴西与邻国的交往日渐紧密，并呈加速趋势。

由于该区域贸易与其他区域贸易相比份额较小，不少人对该选择持怀疑态度。亚洲国家区域内贸易占总出口的35%，而在西欧该数字超过60%。拉丁美洲整体区域内出口占总出口的份额约为20%。

在现有经济及其他决定因素条件下，区域贸易的重要性到底有多大？区域贸易占总出口的20%是否为合理水平？有没有一个理想的数字？这些问题可能无法立即回答，并且也超出了本文讨论的范围。本文主要讨论区域市场能否为巴西制造部门在增加生产和缩小技术差距方面提供足够的动力。

尽管地理接近且存在潜在收益，区域选择也绝非一帆风顺，仍需要大量努力。深化区域联系面临如下五方面挑战。

1. 与不同成员打交道

巴西经济政治外交的一个基本特征是保持其在国际事务中的全球角色。“全球角色”不仅是指该国关注与世界大多数国家维持和发展贸易——无论在商品结构还是在出口区域方面均采取多样化策略——还指该国与每个国家保持积极外交关系，不干预双边关系。

很明显，美国和西欧在经济政治事务上是传统伙伴。长期贸易关系、投资流动、市场的重要性及各自的国际地位等均使得大多数经济政治关系与这些国家密不可分。

由于亚洲最大经济体发展动力强劲且亚洲各国联系紧密，亚洲是其新的经济动力。

由于西非绝大多数国家与巴西关系源远流长，巴西人口中非洲裔人口比重较大（这在理论上有助于形成特定的经济联系），且部分非洲国家，如南非的经济潜力很大。但是在该区域市场巴西产品份额很低，可以说非洲是重要的潜在合作对象。

东欧是个潜在市场，目前在该市场巴西产品所占份额很小。与转型经济体的贸易在增加，尽管水平较低。

但是，巴西目前在寻求深化与其他拉美国家及南美国家的联系。近年来，巴西在该区域进行了大量外交努力。

巴西与其他南美伙伴的系统、持续联系面临较大挑战。深化经济联系不仅存在自然壁垒，如亚马逊丛林和安第斯山脉，需要大量基础设施建设才能实现交通便利，此外，在文化、制度、社会特征方面与巴西和西班牙语国家也存在较大差异。不管怎样，一个多世纪的友好相处确实是巴西与邻国培养紧密关系的重要财富。

与不同经济体的经济联系和地理距离同样很关键。巴西有1.9亿居民，南美洲第二大人口国哥伦比亚有4600万居民，第三大人口国阿根廷有3900万居民，其他国家人数更少。

关于是否需要深化区域联系的讨论在前几部分已经有所涉及，但仍需关注这一事实，即南美洲的自然资源极为丰富（巴西的铁、大豆和糖，阿根廷的小麦和牛肉，委内瑞拉的油，玻利维亚的天然气，智利的铜，苏里南的铝土矿等），通过系统开发将能获得大量潜在收益。并且，南美还拥有具备全球生物最为多样的最大热带雨林和最大的淡水储量。

对南美的持续关注表现为1995～2000年巴西对该区域出口上升了17%，2000～2006年上升了140%，约占总出口的19%。

巴西经济产值约占南美生产总值的一半（占制造业总产值的60%，占农业总产值的一半）。这些差别体现在多方面。从较好的供给条件（巴西与邻国贸易一再呈现贸易盈余），到密集的R&D活动（巴西的R&D活动是南美总额的80%），这使得巴西相对该区域其他国家具有长期竞争力。

在过去10年内，该区域的贸易平衡被打破，逐渐向有利于巴西的技术密集型产品集中。因此，巴西的中高技术产品在区域内贸易比在区域外贸易更具活力（见表3）。

区域资本流动依然有限，但来自巴西企业的FDI在收购邻国企业方面扮演着重要角色，涉及部门包括水泥、金融服务、钢铁、食品、汽车零配件、汽油、纺织以及鞋类。

通过联合项目和联合研发活动可以增强国家间生产的互补性，从而减少差异。近年来这方面取得了一定进展，南方共同市场的南共市统一基金即为一例，但还需继续努力。

南美基础设施计划项目正在努力解决南美各国基础设施问题，以克服能源供给、交通及通信方面的瓶颈。

物理环境依然是影响南美国家实现一体化的主要障碍。除了交通和通信方面的基础设施不足外，部分国家还面临能源供给困难。亚马逊地区——包括9个国家及巴西的9个州——相对该地区的版图而言，巴西占了其中的60%，在许多领域具备非常明显的相对优势，但对该地区进行有效、持续、系统开发的潜力依然无法确定。

基础设施不足及供给潜力差异只是拉丁美洲区域贸易存在的困难之一。邻国之间有限的贸易优惠、该区域国家之间及与其他区域国家签订的贸易协定的多元化更是加剧了贸易的复杂性。

2. 全球优惠贸易协定的区域主义

西雅图会议失败后，在WTO多哈回合谈判准备过程中，随着对多边谈判的了解——近年来出现了大量的双边和诸边谈判，我们发现，它们确定贸易优惠条件，但经常是制定处理争端的原则而非解决某一具体贸易问题，通常就产权、政府采购政策、竞争政策、环境问题、劳工政策等问题签署协定。

拉美和加勒比国家均积极加入这一谈判浪潮。越来越多的国家与邻国及其他区域国家同步进行谈判。多种一体化方式的同步进行及大量的区域外协定均可能对区域一体化计划产生影响。表4反映了拉美和加勒比地区的情况。

除了多元协定可能带来的风险外，同时签订多种协定还可能带来成本问题。海关对任何同类产品均需根据其原产地不同按不同的关税税率征税。同步进行的多元化协定会增加风险，可能会采取比WTO规则激进的规则，若谈判发生在经济规模差异悬殊的国家之间，这种风险会进一步增加，因为发展中国家比工业化国家的利益集团要弱势得多。激增的优惠协定还可能会弱化WTO在国际贸易中作为规则制定者的角色，进而对WTO的存在意义及运作能力产生消极影响。

不同协定可能形成不同的“壁垒”。毫无疑问，各种协定规定的关税削减日程将可能减缓关税减让的步伐。在未来若干年内大量壁垒将依然存在。

这里至少有两个理由要求约束多元化协定的签订：①关税优惠在拉美和加勒比国家中占据较大份额（拉美和加勒比国家超过2/3的贸易是基于各种区域内或区域外的优惠市场准入条件进行的）；②区域一体化项目有助于高附加值产品的出口。

总之，深化区域联系在所难免。但是，缺乏对拉美区域贸易的明确预期通常会导致该目标无法实现。从而，试图降低现存壁垒的谈判进程将会变得更为复杂。

若数十年前就将深化区域联系作为实现工业化的工具，根据巴西现有经济特征，该进程可能更难预期。拉美国家规模和生产潜力差异将使得区域一体化目标更难明确并进一步影响整个谈判进程。

3. 何去何从

建立共同市场实现区域工业化——扩大国内市场实现规模收益——20世纪40年代以来拉丁美洲和加勒比经济委员会（ECLAC）等智囊机构就将之作为推进区域一体化的理由。

20世纪50、60年代，贸易周期性平衡和减少资本品进口、优先发展工业化的观点进一步强化了区域一体化的需求。为了不影响对资本品市场准入的限制，贸易优惠应逐步进行。此外，该优惠应给予该区域规模较大的国家，对于较小的经济体应区别对待。

表 4　拉丁美洲和加勒比区域贸易协定分布情况（2006）

	签署协定	当前谈判
区域内	LAIA、MERCOSUR、ANCOM、CACM、CARICOM、NAFTA、ALBA、UNASUR、SACN、ACS MERCOSUR－智利；MERCOSUR－玻利维亚；MERCOSUR－秘鲁；MERCOSUR－哥伦比亚、厄瓜多尔、委内瑞拉； 委内瑞拉－CARICOM；智利－玻利维亚；哥伦比亚－CARICOM；智利－哥伦比亚；玻利维亚－墨西哥；智利－厄瓜多尔； 哥伦比亚－委内瑞拉；智利－秘鲁 哥斯达黎加－墨西哥；CACM－多米尼加共和国；CACM－智利；哥斯达黎加－特立尼达和多巴哥；哥斯达黎加－CARICOM； 尼加拉瓜－墨西哥；墨西哥－危地马拉、萨尔瓦多、洪都拉斯 CARICOM－多米尼加共和国 智利－玻利维亚；智利－委内瑞拉；智利－哥伦比亚；智利－墨西哥；智利－中美洲；智利－古巴 墨西哥－委内瑞拉、哥伦比亚；墨西哥－哥斯达黎加；墨西哥－乌拉圭；墨西哥－巴拿马	CARICOM-MERCOSUR CAN－危地马拉、萨尔瓦多、洪都拉斯 墨西哥－MERCOSUR
区域外	智利－加拿大、美国、欧盟、EFTA 墨西哥－美国、加拿大、EFTA、欧盟、日本 CAFTA－多米尼加共和国－CACM；多米尼加共和国－美国； 厄瓜多尔－美国 哥斯达黎加－加拿大 智利－韩国；智利－新西兰、新加坡、文莱 MERCOSUR－印度；MERCOSUR－以色列；MERCOSUR-SACU 秘鲁－加拿大；秘鲁－美国 哥伦比亚－美国	厄瓜多尔－美国 MERCOSUR－欧盟 CACM－欧盟 CARICOM－欧盟； CARICOM－加拿大 智利－中国 秘鲁－中国台湾 MERCOSUR－波斯湾国家 巴西－摩洛哥；巴西－埃及

注：表中 LAIA 为拉丁美洲一体化协会；MERCOSUR 为南美共同市场；ANCOM 为安第斯共同市场；CACM 为中美洲共同市场；CARICOM 为加勒比共同市场；NAFTA 为北美自由贸易协定；ALBA 为美洲玻利瓦尔联盟；UNASUR 为南美国家联盟；SACN 为南美国家共同体；ACS 为加勒比海国家协会；EFTA 为欧洲自由贸易区；SACU 为南非关税同盟；CAN 为安第斯国家共同体。

资料来源：ECLAC（2006）。

20 世纪 70 年代是拉丁美洲最不热衷于区域一体化的时期。困难包括：第一次石油冲击引起的支付约束、拉丁美洲自由贸易协会（LAFTA）决策制约以及该区域一些国家通过政府武装捍卫民族主权。

第二次石油危机和债务危机使得大部分拉美国家面临外汇短缺。贸易绩效下降，部分国家需求停顿与一些国家需求过旺并存，20 世纪 80 年代中期区域一体化被逐渐提上政治日程。

此时，区域一体化不仅是扩大国内市场实现规模收益的手段，而且有助于走出危机：短期内区域贸易能够充分利用生产能力，并通过中央银行使得区域贸易无需使用稀缺的外汇。从长期来看，区域一体化持续的基础不是完全消除贸易壁垒，而是能够实现生产结构互补，因此，一体化被视为创造经济共同体的工具。最近，随着对经济一体化兴趣的复苏，大部分经济体采取了更自由的贸易政策应对通胀，不仅一体化进程需与多边开放相协调，向邻国出口产品也应被视为"学习过程"，生产商通过出口可以获得经验并进而开发更广阔的市场（ECLAC 1984；CEPAL 1985）。

20 世纪 90 年代是拉美"改革的 10 年"，在强调多边开放的同时提升竞争力。区域一体化可以通过减少竞争来降低非生产性租金、影响国内和国外投资者的预期、降低交易成本、提高生产效率，从而实现物价稳定并通过减少垂直生产过程、小型企业分包及雇用熟练工人促进技术进步的吸收。因区域内贸易的产品较向其他区域出口的产品更趋技术密集型，区域贸易自由化应为行业内专业化分工提供支持。通过积极影响经济和制度环境——联合建设基础设施及共同开发教育和资本市场，经济一体化将带来深远影响，将取得进一步收益。（ECLAC 1994）。

因此，在 20 世纪 50、60、80 及 90 年代地区各国均支持促进区域一体化。但进入 21 世纪后，新的局势对区域一体化观点提出了新的挑战。

贸易特许受国际资本流动的影响，贸易自由化并非独立于资本账户政策。这尤其适用于宏观经济合作较少的拉丁美洲。

区域谈判内容远超贸易范畴，各国日益需要就能源、环境政策及水供给等基础设施资助项目进行谈判，而就促进金融合作方面的具体措施谈及甚少。当经济条件不同的国家签订区域协定时，这将成为主要制约因素。

2000 年以来拉美区域一体化进程较其他区域进展缓慢。一方面是由于该区域一体化与大量区域外优惠协定同步进行。另一方面是部分国家的国内政治环境与促进区域一体化进程所需要进行的让步不兼容。

由于多数国家开放了贸易和资本账户使得国际资本高度流动，极大影响了双边汇率，进而决定了贸易流及生产的增长，并进一步影响潜在投资者的预期。

随着双边和多边协定的不断增加，WTO 被弱化，贸易转移的可能性增加，对区域贸易产生了消极影响，从而降低了区域贸易通过生产结构变革推动经济发展的潜力。

随着国际局势中新兴成员的加入（如部分亚洲国家），一些工业化国家被弱化，国际经济政治关系呈现“多元中心”的态势。这增加了拉美国家签订双边协定伙伴时的“自然候选人”。近期协定包含的内容远超单纯的贸易领域，同时与不同伙伴签订相似协定可能会破坏该区域原有参与国的收益。

最后，各国分别与第三方谈判签订协定可能导致以不同方式处理同一问题，出现规则多样化。

因此，相对于以前，最近10年各国或国家集团更难明确预期区域优惠协定的作用。

此外，各国应对资本流的波动予以关注。很明显，金融中心监管效果不佳，随着新工具（如主权基金）作用的提升，新兴经济体的宏观经济政策面临新挑战，并引发货币合作及建立共同基金应对危机的讨论。

4. 货币合作的必要性

该区域货币和金融合作呈现两个基本特征。即受推动区域一体化方式影响，该领域合作的重点为：大量计划或致力于资助大型、必需基础设施项目，或旨在建构外汇短缺应对机制或建立区域资本市场。

这些目标本身均是宏伟目标，但同时进行时，会使得实际方向（无论是措施还是优惠关系）变得越来越不明朗。

过去25年里在遇到流动性危机时，拉美国家从IMF获得比亚洲发展中国家更多的支持，无论是所获支持次数（1984～2007年，拉丁美洲共获得84次支持，亚洲国家获35次支持）还是所获支持金额（1984～2007年亚洲国家共获得260亿DES,[①] 而拉丁美洲获得660亿DES）。亚洲国家致力于建构区域机制（如储备库、区域债券市场、共同监督机制及其他计划）以应对外部冲击，而拉丁美洲国家则旨在识别可能延缓区域应对危机方案决策行为的“道德风险”（鲍曼和穆西，2008）。

尽管拉丁美洲并未实现完全一体化，但事实上，在培育区域贸易机制和流动

① DES为“特别提款权”的葡萄牙文缩写。它是国际货币基金组织创设的一种储备资产和记账单位。

性保障方面至少有两条积极经验可以借鉴。

1965 年拉美一体化协会（LAIA）成员国中央银行签署了互惠结算和信贷协定。1989 年前至少 90% 的区域贸易使用该机制。1966 ~ 2004 年（随着环境的变化，该机制实际已不复存在）该工具使得近 1/4 的区域贸易无须中央银行之间进行外汇转移。这种外汇“互换”方式远远早于亚洲的“清迈倡议”（2000 年通过）。

1978 年安第斯山脉国家建立了拉丁美洲储备基金。该基金旨在面临外部债务危机时向成员国提供外汇兑换。这较“清迈倡议”早 22 年。

即便如此，拉丁美洲依然认为货币和金融合作应在区域一体化的最后阶段进行。这种认知遭到了不断的质疑，因为合作可以在不同阶段促进一体化进程。当各国均以贬值来应对外部冲击时，缺少合作会阻碍一体化进程。

近期巴西和阿根廷允许双边贸易以当地通货结算。了解这种机制的实际结果可能还为时尚早，但可以预期交易成本的潜在下降将会促进双边贸易，对于中小企业而言尤为如此。

理论上，与邻国贸易所占权重越大，双边贸易不均衡情况越明显，促进宏观经济融合就越有利可图。拉丁美洲区域贸易只占总出口贸易的有限份额。其原因之一是生产潜力的差异，关于这一点前文已有论及。

为了应对这些差异，巴西和其他南美国家已尝试开发互补生产项目，改善小型经济体的供给条件使其能够享受大规模生产的利益，进而提升竞争能力。这就要求建立一些机制——如建立区域资本市场或促进外部金融资源进入的举措——为投资项目提供低成本的长期资本。

同时，若外部冲击引致波动并在区域蔓延将产生破坏性影响。因此，有必要建立某种外汇提供机制应对非预期冲击。近年来，由于良好的外部环境及 20 世纪 90 年代中期危机的教训，拉美国家（及大部分新兴经济体）均建立了大量外汇储备。既然没有广泛有效的机制，大部分国家均寻求某种“自我保障”。

但是，高额储备意味着高额成本。亚洲和安第斯山脉国家的经验表明，若存在储备库机制，则可以较低成本获得适当储备。

因此，区域议程应包括恢复需求导向机制、促进区域贸易（如互惠信贷协定和优先在拉美国家间进行贸易）及提供应对外部冲击的工具，如联合流动性保障（兑换机制及储备库）。

5. 危机的影响

当前经济低迷和流动性不足给区域贸易带来了新的挑战。前文已对多元优惠贸易协定引致的贸易转移及 WTO 弱化所带来的风险进行了讨论。经济活动低迷可能会降低进行新的优惠谈判的动机。即便有新的谈判，为了保障国内就业，政治压力也会抵制作出任何让步。

由于多边谈判效果难以预测，将谈判作为开发出口市场的手段就面临压力。但可能也有例外——至少在某些时候——若国内生产商有富余生产能力，则致力于减少优惠的行动将持续抵制恢复多哈回合谈判。

期望在生产紧缩、大量失业及在 WTO 没有恢复多边谈判的话语权时不出现贸易扭曲（以开放或变相壁垒或对特定行业进行补贴等名义）是不现实的。

类似环境均可能带来对深化区域经济联系的争议。20 世纪 80 年代初期的经验很有启发性：当拉美国家缺乏硬通货时，他们通过加强区域贸易保持正常的经济活动和贸易流。拉美国家政府将区域市场作为弥补外部需求不足的机制就不足为怪了。

近年来亚洲此类情况也很突出：相对较高的区域贸易占总出口的份额反映了对主要面向欧美市场的产品生产结构的补充。这些市场的衰退导致亚洲生产活动显著减少。这与拉美区域贸易中大量最终产品供国内消费的情况正好相反。通过互补生产共同开发第三方市场是克服国家差异深化区域一体化的必要条件，但这不能取代降低贸易壁垒改善开发区域市场特色环境的需求。

总之，区域选择不是充分条件，可以将之视为“全球贸易”的补充措施。与邻国发展贸易关系将会促进经济活力，即便各国经济存在差异。克服差异可使区域贸易进入良性循环。

六 结语

国内市场潜力较大的国家的经济政策制定者很难选择是面向国内市场还是国际市场。而小型国家作出完全依附于国际市场的选择则要容易得多。

巴西已逐渐增加了商品、服务和资本的国际流动。本文讨论了这一进程的几个基本特征，无论其开放的深度、速度及结果如何，深化区域联系依然是巴西国际议程的重要议题。无论是近期危机的特征还是寻求扩大和深化与邻国生产联系的结构化趋势，都不太可能让这一议题退回到20世纪70年代的状态。

区域一体化进程取决于政府和私人部门的联合行动。这些机构的参与程度取决于对未来成就的积极预期。

然而，对于未来很难作出明确预期。相对于总出口而言，区域贸易的相对重要性或其可能取得的成就到底有多大？与其他区域贸易相比，该区域贸易在激励中高技术产品方面的效果如何？与其他市场相比，区域市场对经济周期的敏感性如何？区域贸易在多大程度上依赖于与邻国的贸易收益？近期是否会实行较低的商品价格？什么样的制度安排有助于深化区域贸易？区域贸易带来多大的共同利益才会有助于国际谈判？对区域市场重视到何种程度将会影响与其他富裕伙伴贸易的潜在收益？

根据其他区域的经验，深化区域贸易联系是合理的、不可避免的选择，但是实际区域环境带来的一系列问题还需进一步评估，可能的成就预期还应进一步识别。本文认为要在区域贸易上取得显著发展很难一帆风顺，需要经济机构的明确选择、强烈的政治意愿及大量特定措施，但是一旦取得发展将会带来积极效应。

通过以上分析，可以得出如下政策建议。第一，扩大区域贸易优惠。第二，采取联合开发第三方市场的措施，例如互补投资计划。考虑到区域一体化的收益及维持区域一体化的先决条件，这两项措施均有助于获得邻国的积极认可。第三，开发在巴西境内实行跨国补贴的激励机制，提升出口清单的技术含量而改善基础设施及提高人员素质均为提升技术含量的必要条件。第四，过去的经验已经证明在外汇供给不足时允许对区域贸易提供金融支持非常重要。当资源紧缺时，开发相应机制将为发起方带来极大收益。

“金砖四国”与投资

“金砖四国”相互投资前景广阔

刘友法*

一 “金砖四国”开展相互投资前景分析

在国际金融危机催化下，“金砖四国”已由一个纯学术概念逐步演变成新兴大国之间的新型合作机制，成为不同地域、不同制度、不同模式、不同文明携手合作的范例。巴西、俄罗斯、印度和中国均系重要的新兴大国，经济与社会发展各具特色，各国均具有本国特色的产业或技术优势，均处在经济快速增长的阶段。金融危机以来，上述四国在国际事务中，均发挥着日益重要的作用。更为重要的是，共同的国际关切使之演变为政治集团，共同的经济发展阶段催生了相似的发展理念，共同的发展战略引发了诸多领域的合作，尤其是投资领域。在后金融危机时代，“金砖四国”加强合作有利于增强四国整体经济实力，有利于扩大四国集体影响，有利于四国经济整体推进，有利于把不断增长的经济力量转换为地缘政治影响力，从而为世界和平、安全和发展作出应有的贡献。

1. 共同的国际战略地位使“金砖四国”构成独特的政治俱乐部

回眸近代国际关系历史，没有任何其他国际因素能像2008年国际金融危机那样，将“金砖四国”径直推向国际事务的中央舞台，并使之成为解决重大国

---

* 刘友法，中国国际问题研究所副所长。

际事务不可或缺的决策者和推动者，成为构建国际新秩序的主要推动力。与此同时，金融危机也为四国加深经济合作提供了政治和经济基础，尤其是投资领域的合作。原因很简单：几乎所有的发达国家都受到了国际金融危机的冲击，进而成为需要救助的对象。与之相对应，上述四国，除俄罗斯外，成功地抵御了金融危机的冲击并尽快实现了经济复苏或保持了经济快速增长态势。据世界银行统计，2009 年，“金砖四国”对世界经济增量的贡献额超过 50%，因而构成危机年份世界经济发展少有的亮点。

危机期间，“金砖四国”作为新的政治力量，积极参与并推动国际救助和国际管理活动。一方面，四国领导人积极协调反危机政策，避免相互贸易大起大落，通过相互投资拉动相互经贸关系平稳发展。另一方面，四国领导人利用历次国际峰会，联手推动重大国际问题的决策。来自“金砖四国”的声音愈益受到国际社会和有关各国的关注和重视。在多边外交领域，四国领导人协调政策立场，推出改革现行国际规则的建议和政策主张，以便为广大的发展中国家，尤其是为“金砖四国”谋求公平的商业竞争舞台。

展望未来，在经济全球化条件下，投资是确保相互贸易可持续发展的重要手段，是推动深化相互经贸关系的必由之路，也是各国充分发挥各自资源禀赋优势，实现国际经济合作“溢出效应”的重要途径。后危机时代，“金砖四国”欲保持经济发展势头，欲谋求低碳经济发展比较优势，必须继续携手推动国际社会改革存在问题的国际金融游戏规则，继续推动国际社会改革脆弱的国际金融机制。更为重要的是，四国必须把握时代脉搏，充分利用“金砖四国”的政治优势，携手推动建立新的国际秩序，推进共同主张，提出共同议程，维护和促进共同利益，进一步提升四国在国际事务中的地位与作用。

从全球范围现行各类合作机制看，四国需要进一步加强经贸合作，尤其是投资合作，以期为良好的政治合作奠定经济基础。事实上，此次金融危机已经为四国进一步拓展合作关系奠定了坚实的政治和经济基础，尤其是投资领域的合作。理由无须赘述。“金砖四国”进一步深化合作有助于提升集团影响力，有助于促进各国经济增长，有助于将各自经济力量转换成地缘政治影响力，有助于促进全球和平、安全与发展。

2. 共同面临的挑战使“金砖四国”成为新的利益共同体

从微观经济领域看，在金融危机的尘埃纷纷落定之际，国际金融领域存在问题的交易方式仍在实行，有毒金融创新产品仍以更大的规模在更大范围内交易。那些一手造成此次国际金融危机的人员仍逍遥法外。美欧等发达国家已推进的关于金融体制的改革尚无助于从根本上解决金融风险防范问题。其结果是，导致上述金融危机的问题机制事实上仍在继续运行，好像什么都没有发生一样。有鉴于上述情况，"金砖四国"在后危机时期欲实现经济腾飞，既需要面临金融危机诱发的后续冲击波威胁，也需要应对金融危机导致的新的国际形势和新问题。从国际"游戏规则"领域看，"金砖四国"作为工业化的后来者，在参与国际分工与合作进程中，普遍面临传统大国的防范、国际经济体制的障碍、国际规则的挑战。因此，加强四国合作，充分发挥各自比较优势，谋求协作发展的综合优势，成为四国领导人的必然选择。

从宏观经济领域看，"金砖四国"均主张国际关系格局多元化，尊重发展模式多样化，主张发展平等的伙伴关系，推行合作共赢经贸关系。后危机时期，四国在国际事务中有着广泛而共同的利益和关切。一是协调立场，加强合作，率先摆脱金融危机的影响，率先实现"金砖四国"的经济复苏，进而谋划后危机时期经济先发优势。二是如何平衡四国与发达国家及与发展中国家的经济关系问题。"金砖四国"在与发达国家展开经济合作和竞争的同时，必须注意加强与其他发展中国家的合作，努力寻求新的发展机遇。三是如何在推进国际经济机制改革和创新进程中协调战略和政策问题。四国必须尽快确立科学的路线图，既有助于有效推动国际政治和经济体制改革，又有利于稳步推进国际新秩序的建设。四是如何防止国际贸易保护主义回潮问题。四国政府必须尽快筹谋应对投资和贸易保护主义的"工具箱"，谋划共同发展必须依赖的国际贸易环境。五是如何协调领域外交政策问题。后危机时期，世界经济发展势将面临诸多新问题和新挑战。其间，各国必须协调立场，共同应对气候变化、环境保护、核扩散等重大挑战，共同提出政治主张，维护共同利益。

3. 共同的发展阶段促使"金砖四国"成为互利合作伙伴

纵观全球范围现行经贸合作机制，国家之间的经贸关系始于贸易，紧跟贸易合作的是投资合作机制，而后是技术合作。

从发展阶段层面考察，"金砖四国"通过工业化、经济转轨或改革开放，均已建立了具有本国特色的经济结构，均已形成了基于本国资源禀赋的产业优势。

例如，四国在能源、天然资源、资本三大领域各自扮演着重要的角色，在投资领域存在极大的优势互补性，互利合作蕴含着巨大商机。更为重要的是，后金融危机时代，"金砖四国"均面临进一步提高经济发展水平、改善民生的艰巨任务，在全球性问题上有相同或相近立场，均十分重视加强和深化互利合作。上述为四国进一步开展相关领域的合作，尤其是投资合作提供了强有力的政治基础。

毋庸置疑，"金砖四国"作为新型大国的代表，其经济结构仍存在下列阶段性特征。其一，生产力水平相对低下。四国虽然拥有各自产业、自然资源和人力资源等比较优势，但生产效率却普遍低于发达国家。四国无一例外需要从发达国家进口中高档工业制成品。其二，经济结构呈现二元化。这种经济结构的二元化，不仅体现在不同经济部门之间、城乡之间，还体现在一国内部不同地区之间。历史经验证明，上述差距继续扩大，将导致国家发展最终失去原动力，并将导致社会动荡乃至政权易手。其三，产业结构相对落后。"金砖四国"的产业结构中，农业和初级产品产业所占比重较大，而制造业尤其是服务业所占比重较小。这是区别发达国家与发展中国家的重要经济指标。其四，在国际经济关系中处于劣势地位。因此，相关国家在国际贸易和投资领域往往被迫做出次佳选择。其结果是，相关国家可望轻易扩张涉外经济规模，而发展利益则不然。

从发展战略层面考察，进入21世纪，"金砖四国"纷纷加快了民族复兴或国家振兴的步伐。随着"金砖四国"逐步机制化，四国间合作领域势将不断拓宽，合作程度势将不断加深，以期充分发挥各自比较优势，实现协作发展的综合效应。然而，"金砖四国"作为工业化和全球化的后来者，尚缺乏强有力的跨国公司群体来承担相互投资的主体。四国企业遵循不同的市场规则，崇尚不同的企业文化，对其他三国的投资环境普遍缺乏了解，普遍缺乏实际市场进入的实践经验。正因为如此，有效推进四国投资合作的关键在于相关国家领导人的政治意愿，在于政府的政策和经济扶持，以期通过扩大相互投资形成经济发展合力，谋求经济发展的"溢出效应"。

从贸易合作层面考察，随着"金砖四国"不断推进经贸合作，四国间的经济互补性和相互依存度均有所提高。据联合国有关机构统计，上述四国中任何一国对集团其他三国的出口占自身出口总额的比重均有所增长。2000年，巴西为3.1%，俄罗斯为6.4%，印度为4.2%，中国为2.0%。到2008年，上述四国的相应数字分别提高到11.2%，6.1%，7.9%和5.8%。另据世界贸易组织统计，

2003～2008 年，四国出口年平均增长率都在 20% 以上。2008 年，四国出口占全球出口总额的 14.5%，四国进口则占全球进口总额的 11.9%。其中，中国出口增长最快，从 2003 年占全球出口总额的 5.9% 增长到 2008 年的 9.1%。

从投资合作层面考察，"金砖四国"拥有的土地面积占世界总面积 40%，人口占世界总人口的 42%，对全球 GDP 的贡献总量超过 14%，外汇储备占世界外汇储备总量约 3/4。据相关权威机构估算，"金砖四国"正形成日益强大的中产阶级，其中产阶级的数量未来甚至有可能超过欧美日等发达国家中产阶级的总和。因而，"金砖四国"将成为全世界最为重要的消费市场。这些国家富裕阶层的崛起，将为相关国家相互吸引投资、提升产业结构和转变经济增长方式提供强有力的市场支持。

从科学技术领域考察，科学技术是国家经济实现可持续发展的灵魂。后金融危机时代，世界各国迎来的低碳经济是以高科技为特色的后工业化经济新的发展阶段。各国能否抓住机遇，谋求应有的地位并获得应有的利益，在很大程度上取决于本国的科技研发与应用能力。从全球范围的经济一体化机制看，加大科技创新投入和推进科技创新体系建设是相关国家实现可持续发展的有效途径，是成员国提升国际竞争力的有效手段，是相关经济一体化机制形成和增强整体经济实力的重要途径。

后金融危机时期，世界经济发展将以新一轮产业结构调整为先导，以产业振兴为特点，以低碳经济为主导，以替代能源和清洁能源技术研发为国际竞争的主要领域。其间，发达国家已建立起本国（集团）竞争优势，并已处于有利的竞争地位。因此，"金砖四国"想要实施赶超计划，必须组建以产业技术为主导的科技攻关机制，以集团力量谋划国际竞争比较优势。其他别无选择。

二 "金砖四国"加强相互投资对策思考

2008 年发生的国际金融危机给"金砖四国"的最大教训是，在全球化条件下，任何可持续的经济发展，既需要市场这只"看不见的手"，也需要政府这只"看得见的手"。上述原则同样适用于"金砖四国"的相互投机活动，以期实现经济发展综合效应。后危机时代，低碳经济正向我们走来。有鉴于此，"金砖四国"作为新兴大国，理应以各国综合国力为基础，在平等、互惠、互利原则基础上，积极协调发展战略和政策，尤其是投资政策，描绘集体实施可持续发展的蓝图。

1. 积极发挥政府引导作用，促进相互投资

概而言之，推进“金砖四国”相互投资离不开政府引导，离不开政策扶持，离不开强有力的信息服务，离不开行业监督。

其一，推动四国领导人会晤机制化。四国领导人应通过定期高层会晤达成共识，进行政治决策，解决重大问题，以期促进四国一体化进程。其二，加快部长会议机制化。四国应通过部长年会贯彻落实峰会政治决策精神，评估相互投资与贸易领域的合作进展情况，协调产业相互开放政策，加快相互投资进程，以期不断拓展各自优势产业链的国际空间，谋求集团经济发展的“扩大效应”。其三，积极推动签署相互贸易与投资促进协定，并为各国企业开拓对方市场奠定政策和法律基础。其四，建立四国投资促进机制，鼓励和引导各国企业综合开拓四国市场。其五，建立四国投资合作信息服务体系。该体系应具有下列功能：收集、加工和发布关于四国经济与社会发展状况的信息以及关于四国经济结构、产业政策、市场准入、商业机会和项目招标等领域的信息。

2. 建立合作科技研发机制，为四国经济发展谋划后劲

科学技术是任何国家实现经济可持续发展的关键，并与国际直接投资密切相关。在低碳经济大背景下，“金砖四国”必须引领世界经济发展潮流，充分利用各自优势，组建四国科技联合攻关联盟。具体而言，需要遵循下列原则：信息共享；资源配套；联合攻关；合作开发；国际交易；互利共赢。

其一，建立四国一体化研究机制。尽快成立由四国专家和智囊成员构成的四国机制化研究机构，研究全球一体化进程及其经验与教训，探索“金砖四国”机制化存在的问题和发展方向，研讨对策思路，进而为四国首脑峰会和部长会议提供相关信息和对策建议。其二，建立科技研发基金，以期为各国相关企业和科研机构联合技术攻关提供资金支持。其三，建立科技交易机制，以期有效发挥科技研发的经济与社会效益。其四，建立和完善四国科学技术国际转让机制，以期有效延长相关产业技术的生命周期，并为广大发展中国家实现经济可持续发展提供外部技术支撑。其五，创造条件建立四国科研人员交流和互换机制，为各国加快本国科技创新能力提供人力资源支撑。

3. 建立和完善集团金融机制，促进相互投资

金融是当代经济发展的命门产业，是实现经济与社会可持续发展的核心产业。因此，金融合作是“金砖四国”促进相互投资的重要保障。

其一，加强各国中央银行间金融政策协调，互换金融信息，防范共同风险，以期为四国投资合作提供政策和金融支撑。其二，加强各国银行间大型项目共同融资机制，发挥金融机构对促进相互投资和联合对外融资的能力。其三，创造条件建立银行联合体，为成员国企业开展相互投资及相关国家地方政府开展双边合作提供融资服务。其四，有计划地推出集团成员国之间的大项目合作，以期发挥各自产业比较优势，推动相互投资，优化促进相互投资必备的基础设施。其五，建立有效的货币互换机制。四国应进一步强化四国货币互换机制，以期有效抵御四国内外经济风险，降低企业在四国进行投资的汇率风险。

4. 相互开放市场，实现贸易与投资互动

国际贸易是世界经济发展的主要动力，也是促进国际投资的前提条件。后危机时代，“金砖四国”想要充分发挥各自产业比较优势，保持经济可持续发展势头，必须在相互贸易方面下工夫，进而为相互投资奠定市场基础。

其一，建立有效的政策协调机制。四国应通过峰会机制和部长会议机制商定进一步拓展集团内部贸易的原则，进而为推动相互贸易提供政策引导。其二，建立和完善行业协会或商会机制。四国政府应帮助本国企业在投资东道国建立和完善行业协会或商会，使之成为自我管理与监督的工具，以期有效监管行业企业的商业行为，推行统一的行业标准，提升行业企业的产品和服务质量，提升本国在东道国的商业形象。其三，建立和完善“金砖四国”展览会机制。四国应建立和完善相关技术和商品展览会，以期使新项目获得更多的竞争者，新产品获得更多的展示舞台，新技术获得更多的潜在客户。其四，建立和完善经贸纠纷仲裁机制。四国应通过政府协商和谈判妥善解决相关国家之间产生的贸易和投资纠纷，为集团内部贸易健康发展营造良好的经济和社会氛围。其五，创造条件建立有助于对方企业拓展贸易的出口加工区或高新技术开发区，以期吸引集团内部更多的企业前往投资兴业。

中国企业的国际化

卢西亚娜·阿西奥丽　玛利亚·阿巴蒂亚·S. 阿尔维斯
罗德里格·皮门特尔·F. 莱昂　周志伟（译）*

本文旨在概述中国企业国际化的近期发展进程、国际化特点和推动国际化进程的主要政策措施。同时，文章也将涉及巴西应用经济研究所（IPEA）合作与发展部（DICOD）正在开展的“巴西企业国际化”研究项目的初期研究结论。

有关生产国际化的经典理论已不能完全阐释中国企业国际化的进程（Moraes et. all. 2007）。在中国，企业国际化是由国家强力主导的，因此，只有通过近期政策和体制的变化才能较好地理解这一现象。从2002年“走出去”政策制定以来，中国政府除了从行政程序上为企业实施投资提供便利外，还开始为国际化的企业提供了一系列刺激政策。中国海外投资的主要特点也表明，中国企业国际化的动机除了纯粹的贸易考虑外，也有着维护国际收支平衡和地缘政治上的考虑。

一　外国直接投资的国际趋势

从20世纪80年代到2000年，世界经济经历了多次转型，这一点可以从多个

---

* 卢西亚娜·阿西奥丽，巴西应用经济研究所合作与发展部研究人员；玛利亚·阿巴蒂亚·S. 阿尔维斯，巴西瓦加斯基金会公共政策和管理学博士后、巴西应用经济研究所合作与发展部奖学金获得者；罗德里格·皮门特尔·F. 莱昂，巴西UNICAMP大学经济发展专业硕士，巴西应用经济研究所合作与发展部奖学金获得者；周志伟，中国社会科学院拉丁美洲研究所副研究员。

不同国家的经济增长率波动中得到体现（见表1）。在这期间的头十年（1980～1989），世界经济以年均3%的速度增长，尤其以亚洲国家和美国最为显著。接下来的十年，亚洲发展中国家属经济增长最快的行列，中国是典型代表（年均增长率为10%）。在发达国家中，只有美国实现了相对快的GDP增长（年均增长率为3.1%），而日本和欧盟实际上处于停滞状态，尤其日本更是如此。最后，在最近的十年间，除亚洲以外，拉美和加勒比也成了引领世界经济增长的地区，而亚洲地区更是扮演着绝对的主角。

表1 主要国家、地区及世界经济增长率（1980～2007）

单位：%

国家或地区 \ 时期	1980～1989	1990～1999	2000～2007
世界	3.02	2.72	3.19
欧盟	2.28	2.18	2.09
美国	3.10	3.13	2.52
日本	3.71	1.50	1.74
中国	9.75	9.99	10.11
南亚地区	5.55	5.32	6.79
东亚及太平洋地区	7.71	8.21	8.82
拉美和加勒比地区	1.80	2.94	3.52

资料来源：世界银行数据库。

这也就意味着，从2007年之前的十年开始，世界经济的增长主要由发展中国家驱动。比如，2007年前，南亚地区年均增长6.8%，东亚和太平洋地区年均增长8.8%，拉美和加勒比地区年均增长3.5%。伴随着这一过程，发展中国家在外国直接投资的流入与流出中所占的分量越来越重，同时也发挥着越来越重要的角色。

具体而言，我们可以看到，通过外国直接投资带动的生产国际化从20世纪80年代中期以来有了显著增长，只有1991～1993年和2001～2003年世界经济萧条时曾出现两个萎缩期。外国直接投资从1990年的2300亿美元增至2007年的1.8万亿美元。① 与第二次世界大战后至20世纪80年代初相比，国际化进程中

① UNCTAD年报（2008年）。

跨国公司的对外投资表现出不同特征，比如外国直接投资改投服务行业，以及新投资项目（绿地投资）中企业并购的盛行（包括企业间超过10亿美元的大型协议）。从地域来看，20世纪80年代的外国直接投资的流动几乎全部集中在美国、日本和欧共体。1991～1992年的经济萧条后，外国投资转向发展中国家，并且自2000年开始，发展中国家日益成为外国直接投资的执行者。

世界五大经济体的持续增长，亚洲增长极的涌现，资本账户自由化的扩大，与证券市场发展相联系的汇率和利率的波动等因素，改变了资本国际流动的方向和形式，进而改变了跨国大公司的投资和定位战略。国际金融的变动使得投资以利润资本的形式交叉流动，如果不是这样，就很难解释整个时期通过跨国并购（外国直接投资增长的引擎）所带动的外资流量。① 为全球提供信贷基金的新融资工具保障了企业间的大运作。另外，亚洲作为制造业中心的崛起以及经济的高增长率使得全球生产开始重构，并显示了在近几十年来的全球化过程中，采取不同参与战略的发展中国家所取得的成果。

二　发展中国家的直接投资：亚洲的崛起

在最近三年中，跨国公司的海外资产、海外销售和海外就业年均分别增长了10%、16%和12%，这也赋予了跨国公司在世界经济重构中的关键角色。尽管这些跨国公司中的绝大部分来自发达国家，但是在最近，发展中国家的一些公司也出现在世界非金融类跨国公司的100强行列中（根据联合国贸发会议的统计方法，以海外资产额占总资产比重来排序）。

根据联合国贸发会议的统计数据，在2006年发展中国家10大跨国企业中（以海外资产衡量），9个来自亚洲，中国和韩国占5席，它们分别是和记黄埔有限公司、三星电子公司、现代汽车公司、中国国际信托投资（集团）有限公司、怡和洋行。与亚洲相比，拉丁美洲的情况就要逊色一些，该地区只有6家企业进入发展中国家跨国企业30强行列，尤其以巴西和墨西哥为主，两国共占了5席：墨西哥水泥公司、淡水河谷公司、巴西石油公司、美洲电信公司和墨西哥电信。在这份排

① Acioly, L., “Brasil, China e índia: O Investimento Direto Externo nos anos 90”, *Tese de Doutoramento*, IE: UNICAMP, Campinas, São Paulo, 2004.

名中，我们可以看到，10 强企业中存在部门多样化的特点，或者说，没有被某一特殊部门所垄断。但是值得注意的是，韩国的两家企业都是来自电气设备行业。

如果从海外销售角度来看，我们分析的这些企业之间便呈现较大差异。在发展中国家跨国公司海外销售 10 强中，亚洲占了 7 家（全部来自中国和韩国），其余 3 家来自拉丁美洲（2 家巴西公司和 1 家墨西哥公司），并且 10 强企业几乎全部集中在电子电气设备、非金属矿产和石油等行业。

根据以上所述及表 2 中所列的情况，可以明显发现，中国、韩国和巴西、墨西哥分别是亚洲和拉丁美洲在企业国际化过程中的领先国家。

表 2　2006 年主要发展中国家的大型跨国企业（海外资产）

单位：万美元

企业名称	所属国家	行　业	海外资产	总资产
三星电子公司	韩　国	电子电气设备	2701.0	8711.1
现代汽车公司	韩　国	电子电气设备	1958.1	7606.4
和记黄埔有限公司	中　国	多 样 化	7067.9	8714.6
中国国际信托投资(集团)有限公司	中　国	多 样 化	1762.3	11735.5
墨西哥水泥公司	墨西哥	非金属矿产	2441.1	2974.9
墨西哥电信	墨西哥	电　信	870.1	2947.3
淡水河谷公司	巴　西	矿　产	1497.4	6095.4
巴西石油公司	巴　西	石　油	1045.4	9868.0

资料来源：联合国贸发会议，2008。

通过对外直接投资推进的发展中国家企业的国际化进程可以从三个对外直接投资“浪潮”来加以理解。①

1. 20 世纪 60 年代至 80 年代

该时期的亮点是拉丁美洲企业（阿根廷、墨西哥、哥伦比亚和委内瑞拉）和一些亚洲企业（新加坡、马来西亚、菲律宾、中国香港、韩国和印度）。国际化的主要动机是克服商业壁垒的需要，国际化活动主要与采矿业、民用工程和民

① GAMMELTOFT, P., Emerging Multinationals: Outward FDI from the BRICS Countries Copenhagen Business School, Disponível em http://www.inderscience.com/research/index.php?action=record&rec_id=16184&prevQuery=&ps=10&m=or (acesso em 01-04-2009), 2007, http://www.fmprc.gov.cn/zflt/eng/zyzl/hywj/t280369.htm.

用建筑有关，邻国成为投资的主要目的地。

2. 20世纪80年代中期至90年代

亚洲企业处在国际化的领先位置，其主要动机是开发新市场，大部分投资集中在高科技行业（信息技术、电子技术和汽车行业），着眼于出口，不仅仅是针对投资接受国的出口。

3. 当前时期

随着拉丁美洲的复兴，俄罗斯和南非的兴起，该时期的企业国际化呈现更强的地理多元性。主要的投资者是：中国香港、中国台湾、新加坡、巴西、南非、中国内地、韩国、马来西亚、阿根廷、俄罗斯、智利和墨西哥。尽管（该阶段）投资目的地仍以地区性为主，但已经是全球性的，甚至包括发达国家。投资的主要意图与增强市场权力（尤其在自然资源方面）和提高资本价格相联系。

三　中国直接投资：特性

作为对外直接投资的重要实施者，中国内地的地位巩固发生在上述的第三波。1990~2007年，中国在世界的直接投资增长了近30倍。1982年，中国内地的对外直接投资额为4400万美元，1990年为8.3亿美元，到2007年则增至225亿美元（见表3）。这一阶段的加速增长尤其以2003年和2004年以来的这段时间最为明显，当时实施了一系列鼓励国际化和程序简化的政策。① 从那时开始，

表3　最近25年中国内地对外直接投资情况

单位：亿美元，%

项目＼时间	1982~1989（年均）	1990~2000（年均）	2001	2002	2003	2004	2005	2006	2007
总量	4.53	21.95	68.85	25.18	28.55	54.98	122.61	211.60	224.69
占亚洲发展中国家FDI比重	9.5	8.1	13.9	6.8	12.7	6.1	15.4	15	11.5
占发展中国家FDI比重	7.2	5.9	8.3	5.1	6.3	4.6	10.4	10	8.9

资料来源：UNCTAD，2008。

① UNCTAD年报（2008）。

中国内地的投资超过了其他亚洲发展中国家的海外投资，比如韩国和新加坡。根据联合国贸发会议公布的数据，2007 年中国内地已成为第二大对外直接投资的国家和地区，仅次于中国香港。从存量来看，中国内地在 2006 年只占世界总存量的 0.6%（750 亿美元）。

从对外直接投资增量来看，与其他“金砖四国”和南非相比，2000～2007 年，中国排名第二位，仅次于俄罗斯。在 20 世纪 90 年代，中国的领先位置是无可争议的。

中国的表现与其企业国际化的决心相联系，而企业的决心则由政策鼓励支撑。表 4 中列出了 2006 年海外资产排名前五位的中国企业（不包括中国香港企业），它们在企业国际化中处于核心位置。值得指出的是，这些公司都属于国有企业。从部门来看，存在某种多样化特征：2 家石油公司，1 家在金融行业处于显要地位，1 家来自运输行业，1 家来自民用建筑业。

表 4　中国主要跨国企业及其在发展中国家跨国公司中排名情况（2006）

企业名称/排名	资产(百万美元)		销售(百万美元)		就业		附属公司	
	海外	占比(%)	海外	占比(%)	海外(人)	占比(%)	海外(个)	占比(%)
中国中信集团公司/7	17623	15.02	2482	24.54	18305	17.05	12	10.71
中国海运(集团)总公司/13	10397	55.57	8777	55.77	4432	6.37	245	25.87
中国建筑工程总公司/19	6998	43.78	4483	24.17	25000	21.01	23	32.86
中国石油天然气集团公司/21	6374	3.56	3036	2.65	22000	1.88	5	7.69
中国中化集团公司/26	5326	59.86	19374	82.11	220	1.05	31	19.25

资料来源：UNCTAD，2008。

在表 4 涉及的企业中，最具国际化的企业是 1979 年成立的中国中信集团公司，它已发展成中国规模最大的跨国企业。目前，该集团公司已拥有 44 家海外金融附属公司，公司业务的主要市场是中国香港、美国、加拿大、澳大利亚和新西兰。该公司在东京、法兰克福和纽约也设有办事处，公司业务主要涉及金融领域，为工业和服务业的发展提供资金支持。

根据联合国贸发会议的统计，中国中信集团公司 2006 年的海外资产额达 170 亿美元（占公司总资产的 15%）。在国际销售方面，中信集团为五家公司中最少的一家，为 20 亿美元，约占公司总销售额的 25%，海外创造的就业数同样可观，约为 1.8 万人（占公司总就业数的 17%）。

在 2006 年海外资产排行中排第二位的是中国海运（集团）总公司，该公司主要经营海洋运输及相关业务。创立于 1993 年 2 月 16 日的中国海运（集团）总公司兼并了中国外轮代理公司、中国船舶燃料供应公司、中国汽车运输总公司等 3 家大公司。除此之外，该公司下属的 8 家分公司在 150 个国家的 1100 个港口拥有 600 多条商船，其主要市场为亚洲和欧洲，尤其以德国、新加坡和泰国为主。

联合国贸发会议的同一份统计数据显示，中远集团在 2006 年的海外资产额为 100 亿美元，约占资产总量的 55%；海外销售额为 80 亿美元，占总销售额的 55%；海外员工数约为 4000 人，只占公司总员工的 6%。这也就是说，尽管中远集团的业务集中在海外，但仍以国内员工为主。

比中远集团排名低一位的是中国建筑工程总公司。公司成立于 1982 年，主要从事工程规划和施工、民用建筑设计与管理。据《工程新闻记录》（*Engineering News-Record*）杂志统计，该公司排在 2002 年世界跨国大企业的第 16 位。其海外市场集中在亚洲和非洲，主要为新加坡、韩国、纳米比亚、菲律宾、泰国、博茨瓦纳、阿尔及利亚和中国香港。

尽管排名低于中信集团和中远集团，中国建筑工程总公司的海外资产额超过了 60 亿美元，占公司总资产额的 43%；海外销售额和海外员工占公司总销售额和总员工数的比重较低（与海外资产占比相比），但依然非常可观，两者占比分别为 24%（海外销售额为 40 亿美元）和 21%（海外员工为 2.5 万人）。

在联合国贸发会议的同一份排名中，国际化程度排第四位的是中国石油天然气集团公司。该国有石油公司成立于 1988 年，1993 年开始其海外业务，从事石油、天然气勘探和开采，以及燃料运输。作为世界上石油、工程和施工的主要提供者，中国石油天然气集团公司在勘探、开采、炼化、化工、地球物理、钻孔、生产测试和工程等该行业的所有领域都实现了专业化。因此，该公司的海外分公司主要集中在石油生产大国较为集中的中东、非洲和亚洲。在表 4 所列的企业中，中国石油天然气集团公司的海外资产、海外销售、海外员工占公司总比重最小。在所有类别中，海外部分所占比重都没有超过 5%，也就是说，公司的业务和员工还是集中在国内。尽管如此，中国石油天然气集团公司的海外资产达到了 60 亿美元，海外员工数量也有 2.2 万人。

排名第五也是表 4 中最后一位的是中国中化集团公司。这家国有企业的业务主要是在石油和化工领域，2006 年的海外资产为 50 亿美元，约占公司总资产的 60%；海外销售额为 190 亿美元，占销售总额的 82%；在海外市场创造的就业数量则很不起眼，不到该公司总员工数量的 1%。

总而言之，我们可以从中国企业国际化进程中总结出以下趋势。第一，这些企业在海外所雇用的员工较少，也就是说，公司的员工大多数集中在中国国内。第二，海外销售额占公司总收入的比重显著上升，公司销售额的至少 1/4 来自海外市场（中国石油天然气集团公司除外）。第三，中国大企业的业务主要集中在基础设施和石油领域，这一现状证明了中国大企业在中国经济发展和中国在国际市场地位方面所发挥的战略作用。比如，在石油领域，中国的高投资是与国家为维持当前发展速度对自然资源和能源的需求密切相关的。

因此，从部门特征的视角来看，就像上面所分析的，中国境内自然资源的相对匮乏使得资源投资成为一种当然选择。最近几年，中国已实施了一种活跃的海外投资政策，像“寻找资源”（resource seeking），它们由各行业中的国有大企业所引领。方框 1 列出了这些行业中的中国企业所开展的主要投资，除此之外，也展示了中国对外直接投资的主要行业。

方框 1　中国在自然资源领域的投资实例

1. 中国石油天然气集团总公司、中国石油化工股份有限公司、中国海洋石油总公司和其他中国公司在 30 个国家投资了 139 个项目，投资额超过 70 亿美元。

2. 中国五矿集团公司购买了智利国家铜业公司新开发的 GABY 铜矿 25% 股份。初始投资额为 5.5 亿美元，总投资额有望达到 20 亿美元。中国五矿集团公司还在巴西和澳大利亚分别投资铁矿和铀矿。

3. 20 世纪 90 年代初，中国首钢集团购买了秘鲁铁矿石公司 98.4% 的股份；宝钢集团在 2001 年与淡水河谷公司签署在巴西合建钢厂的协议；2002 年与澳大利亚哈默斯利铁矿石公司（力拓矿业集团的附属公司）签署合作协议；武钢、唐钢、马钢和沙钢与澳大利亚的 Brokenhill-Biliton 公司决定建立合资企业。这些投资的目的在于保障铁矿石的供应。中国钢铁企业在 2006 年的钢产量达 4 亿吨，超过世界消费量的 30%。

资料来源：Yang e Teng，2007。

在中国开展海外投资的主要领域中，服务业（尤其是金融服务）是投资的主要目标，约占 2006 年投资总额的 45.4%（见表 5）。制造业是中国投资较少的行业，2006 年仅占 5%。方框 2 列出了中国在制造业中的一些重要投资。

表5　2003～2006年中国对外直接投资的部门分布情况

单位：百万美元，%

产业 \ 年份	2003	2004	2005	2006
第一产业	1460(51.1)	2089(38.0)	1781(14.6)	8725(49.5)
农业、林业、畜牧业、渔业	80(2.8)	289(5.3)	105(0.9)	185(1.0)
矿业和石油	1380(48.3)	1800(32.7)	1675(13.7)	8540(48.4)
第二产业	620(21.7)	756(13.7)	2280(18.6)	907(5.0)
第三产业	775(27.1)	2654(48.3)	8200(66.9)	8003(45.4)
金融和信贷服务	280(9.8)	749(13.6)	4942(40.3)	4522(25.6)
批发与零售	360(12.6)	800(14.5)	2260(18.4)	1114(6.3)
运输与储存	80(2.8)	829(15.1)	577(4.7)	1377(7.8)
其他	55(1.9)	276(5.0)	422(3.4)	991(5.6)
合　计	2854(100)	5498(100)	12261(100)	17634(100)

资料来源：OECD，2008。

方框2　中国在第二产业的投资实例

1. 俄罗斯边境城市乌苏里斯科(Ussuriysk)的贸易区接受了60家从事皮革和电气材料制造的中国企业。

2. 2004年11月，上海汽车集团股份有限公司以5000万美元购买了韩国第四大汽车公司双龙汽车公司(SAG)股份的48.9%，这是中国汽车企业的首次海外收购。2005年，上海汽车集团股份有限公司以6700万英镑购买了Rover两个汽车品牌的生产权。

3. 2003～2004年，TCL以4.5亿美元兼并Thomson公司；为进入欧洲市场。TCL还与法国的阿尔卡特公司建立一个合资企业。2004～2005年，联想集团以17.5亿欧元收购IBM的PC业务。

4. 2005年，另一家中国电气企业海尔兼并American Metec未果。

5. 最近几年，中国最大的通信设备制造商华为在发展中国家中的业务迅速扩展。

资料来源：Yang e Teng，2007。

关于进入海外市场的方式，中国企业海外投资最常用的方式是建立海外分公司和合资企业。但是最近，兼并和收购作为进入其他国家的途径的运用逐渐增多。通过兼并和收购，中国对外直接投资从1990年的6000万美元增至2006年的150亿美元，到2007年减至45亿美元。① 与“金砖四国”其他

① 具体分析请参阅OECD年报（2008）。

国家和南非相比，通过这种形式的中国海外投资呈上升趋势，但仍未占主导。

兼并和收购在技术、通信和自然资源行业常被运用，作为获取技术、销售网络、品牌的一种选择途径，可被定性为“战略资产寻求型”（以寻找海外资产为取向）和“市场寻找型”（以开拓海外市场为取向）为动机的投资。

从2006年中国对外直接投资的地域分布来看，超过5000家中国公司在170个国家和地区投资了将近1万个项目。虽然国家数量似乎反映了中国投资地域的多元化，但对外投资却高度集中在部分国家和地区。2003～2006年，超过80%的对外直接投资集中在中国香港和维尔京群岛、开曼群岛等税收天堂，并用来成立控股公司，以开展金融投资。通过具体分析，我们可以看出中国投资的一些趋势和特点。①

（1）亚洲和中东是中国投资的主要目的地，约占中国海外投资总额的60%。这源于与这些国家已建立起的历史关系，以及中东和亚洲地区充足的石油储备。

（2）在亚洲，中国投资的很大一部分流向东盟成员国（20%～30%）。中国在这些国家投资初级产品和自然资源行业，比如在泰国、柬埔寨、马来西亚、印度尼西亚、菲律宾、越南和新加坡等国的橡胶、棕榈油、石油、天然气、农工产品部门。

（3）中国是海湾地区的最大投资国，投资集中在石油和天然气行业。

（4）在南亚，中国投资集中在巴基斯坦。中国80%的投资（2.5亿欧元）和技术用于在深海区域的第三大港口建设。另外，中国还在海尔经济区开展投资，用于电气产品的组装。同样，铁路建设项目也正在开展，以替代马六甲航线。

（5）在拉丁美洲，除了增加中国产品的市场份额外，最基本的利益在于获取资源（石油、铜、铁矿石）。当前的确存在实现中国和拉美经济关系增长的空间，但事实上中拉经济关系发展较慢，原因在于中国企业在海外惯用的模式

---

① 具体分析请参阅 YANG，M. E TENG，S.，“China Overseas Direct Investment，” *EAI Background Brief no. 340*，Singapore：East Asian Institute，National University of Singapore，2007。

（尤其是在建筑行业）使得这种经济关系停滞不前。比如在非洲，中国企业习惯带着本国员工开展工程施工，而这种方法却很难在拉美地区运用。中国产品在拉美国家市场份额的增加给当地企业带来巨大压力，针对中国的大量反倾销行为便一定程度上反映了这种敌对情绪。①

（6）近些年中国在非洲的投资增长显著，在接下来的分析中我们能看到这一点（见方框3）。非洲超过美国成为中国投资的第三大接受者。在非洲大陆，中国投资集中在石油勘探、矿业和基础设施等领域（在下文中，我们将探讨中非关系的一些细节问题）。

中国在非洲的直接投资值得进一步探讨，因为这种投资在近些年呈现出迅速增长的势头。根据经合组织的统计数据，在20世纪90年代的后半期，中国在非洲的投资年均约为1.07亿美元。2003～2006年，年均投资额超过了以前的3倍，达到了26亿美元。

尽管投资增长显著，但中国仍只是非洲大陆的小投资者之一。2006年其投资额占非洲大陆外国投资总量的比重还不到1%。根据联合国贸发会议的统计，非洲的主要外国直接投资国是英国、美国和法国，三国分别占外国投资总量的16.6%、9.2%和7.7%。

尽管参与度较低，但存在一个预期：中国投资在未来几年中增幅会更大。除此之外，中国是在非洲投资最多的发展中国家。并且在亚洲国家中，中国在非洲的投资也超过了日本和韩国。

中国在非洲的投资特点显示，参与投资的800家公司中，100家是国有企业，它们是主要投资项目的参与者，尤其是在自然资源勘探领域。总的来说，私有企业的投资主要集中在服务业和制造业，且投资额较小。②

大型的基础设施项目同样由中国公司负责建造，这些项目的目的在于为中国公司的业务提供便利。这些公司要么是在非洲大陆的分公司，要么是在中国国内但向非洲出口的公司。从地域来说，中国投资遍布整个非洲大陆，总共分布在48个国家。投资额居前五位的是阿尔及利亚、尼日利亚、南非、苏丹和赞比亚。

① http://noticias.uol.com.br/midiaglobal/fintimes/2007/12/21/ult579u2329.jhtm.

② 请参阅OECD年报（2008）。

方框 3　中国与非洲的战略关系

中国在非洲开展生产投资的兴趣与中国对战略和自然资源需求的上升密切相关，而非洲大陆的资源禀赋一定程度上也能解释中国在非洲大陆的投资兴趣。然而，地缘政治秩序的考虑同样也应该加以分析，这也是中国海外投资新动机的例证。正如以上所论及的，这种可能性同样有助于理解中国在拉美地区的投资扩张。

20 世纪 50 年代，在第二次世界大战后建立的两极格局下，中国的指导原则是扩大自己盟友的数量。20 世纪 60 年代，中苏关系发生变故，当中国宣布反对“超级大国霸权”，这种战略变得更加明确。在那个时期，中国政府在非洲许多国家支持一系列解放运动，而一些协议和会议巩固了中国和非洲大陆很多国家的关系。1950 年，中国只与 5 个非洲国家保持外交关系，到 60 年代末，这一数字增至 19 个。

据阿毛里・波尔多・德・奥利维拉（Amauri Porto de Oliveira）认为，中国大陆密切与非洲的关系，目的非常明确：阻止非洲国家与中国台湾建立外交关系，争取非洲国家在联合国大会上的支持。1971 年，联合国大会取消了台北在联合国的代表权，恢复了北京的合法席位，而 1/3 的支持票就来自非洲国家。

20 世纪 70 年代，中非关系面临矛盾：一方面，中国继续支持非洲民族解放武装运动，比如在葡萄牙殖民地国家；另一方面，为抵消和阻止苏联在非洲的渗透，公开帮助法国或美国在非洲的行动。尽管如此，中国继续扩大了自己在非洲的外交存在，44 个国家与中国保持正式外交关系。

20 世纪 80～90 年代，非洲脱离中国外交政策的中心。直到最近，尤其是从 2000 年开始，中国与非洲大陆的政治关系重新得到强调。2000 年的象征意义主要由于首届“中非合作论坛”的举办，这也建立了当前中非合作的基础。2006 年 11 月，第三届“中非论坛”出台了中国对非洲的一揽子援助措施，并设定了用以指导《北京行动计划（2007～2009）》的一系列目标。

提出的行动方案*包括：提供 50 亿美元的优惠贷款，设立一个 50 亿美元的基金，支持在非洲的中国投资，承诺向非洲出口开放市场，签署一系列基础设施项目，免除非洲一些国家的政府债务，在非洲建立 3～5 个合作区。

注：* 完整的协议请参阅 http://www.fmprc.gov.cn/zflt/eng/zyzl/hywj/t280369.htm。

资料来源：Oliveira，2007。

中国在非洲建立起来的关系证明，在商业利益以外，还存在其他的诉求。充足的自然资源、基础设施建设的巨大空间、非洲消费市场的机遇也与中国的地缘政治利益紧密相关。尽管非洲不是中国外交的优先地区，但除了政治因素外，作为原材料来源地和出口市场的非洲大陆自始至终对中国有着巨大吸引力。①

四　中国企业国际化进程及主要政策措施

中国企业的国际化进程包含 5 个阶段。最初阶段是 1979～1983 年，当时主要是为制造业保障原材料的供应，这也是中国政府鼓励企业的主要意图。

① OLIVEIRA，A. P.，A Política Africana da China，（Disponível em http://www.casadasafricas.org.br/site/img/upload/674760.pdf），Acesso em 25－03－2009，2007.

在这个阶段，还没有关于中国企业国际化的法律法规。国有企业实际成为海外投资的唯一主体，每项投资计划都需在国务院进行逐一论证，而国务院也是负责审批投资项目的唯一机构。

从20世纪80年代中期到90年代初，中国政府开始允许私有企业申请在其他国家设立附属公司，同时，为统一授权程序，出台了一些关于海外投资的法规，以及致力于海外投资的公司必须遵循的申请程序。在这个时期，部分中国企业的国际化实际上是一种“回流”（round-tripping）行为——一些公司在美国或者维尔京群岛注册后，以外企身份回到中国，以此得到诸如低利率等优惠政策待遇。①

1993～1998年，中国的海外投资出现相对萎缩，这是香港房地产业泡沫破裂和证券市场投资等因素的综合结果。为此，中国政府采取措施保证生产性投资的优先性，而非投机性投资。为此，成立的专门机构可以在提交至对外贸易经济合作部（MOFTEC）对超过100万美元的投资项目进行审核。对外贸易经济合作部也为那些有志于开展海外投资的企业出台了新规章和要求。

20世纪90年代末至2002年，随着“关于鼓励企业开展境外带料加工装配业务的意见”文件的出台，生产性投资被明确确定为优先目标，中国进入了一个更为有效地鼓励企业国际化的阶段。国务院也开始为企业的原材料和机械工业生产国际化提供技术和资金援助。诸如纺织、机械、电气材料等行业的国际化尤其受到鼓励。

此后，通过中国共产党第16次全国代表大会的决定，以及以增加中国海外投资为目标的“走出去”战略，有关中国企业国际化的条例得以制定。在这方面，最具里程碑意义的文件是2004年出台的《国务院关于投资体制改革的决定》，② 它表明了中国政府在对外投资方面的立场。这份文件提出了诸如改革项目审查和审批制度以保障企业投资自主权，拓宽国际化项目融资渠道，简化和调整投资项目审查和审批程序等目标。

对该文件中提出的一些目标（如上所述）的简单回顾，可以清晰地表明中国政府对本国企业国际化的新立场。关于该文件的指导方针，将在下文中展开论述。

---

① 参阅 YANG, M. E TENG, S.,“China Overseas Direct Investment,” *EAI Background Brief no. 340*, Singapore: East Asian Institute. National University of Singapore, 2007。

② 完整文件见 http://en.edrc.gov.cn/policyrelease/t20060207_58851.htm。

（一）资本管制、主权基金的建立和中国企业国际化

需要强调的是，20 世纪 90 年代末之前，中国海外投资受到国家外汇管理局（SAFE）的严格限制，目的在于为国家储备外汇。但是，国家外汇管理局的资本管制在近些年中发生了重要改变，尤其是从中国外汇储备飞速上升的那个时期开始。

随着外汇储备的增加，1999 年中国在产品的海外加工和装配方面进行了首次项目放开的尝试。在这个尝试中，投资应以货物和设备，而不是以资金的方式来实施，同时允许在不使用保证金的情况下使用信用证来开展投资。但必要前提是将利润直接汇回中国。2002 年，国家外汇管理局在 14 个省市开始解除对外国投资的限制。也就是从这一年开始，这 14 个省市的公司有关利润直接汇回国内的限制被取缔。这样，投资者可以将其利润重新投资于海外。2005 年，国家外汇管理局下级单位（省一级分局）也具备了对 1000 万美元以下的投资审批权。同年，这种只限于 14 个省市的优惠政策被推广到了全国。

为细化与资本管制有关的事项，国家外汇管理局于 2006 年公布了“关于调整部分境外投资外汇管理政策的通知”。

中国外汇储备的增加也允许一个对中国海外投资产生重要影响的国家主权基金的设立。这种基金是用国家外汇储备建立起来的，但这些储备是分开来管理的。这是在多数时候被采用的投资模式，以获得外资企业的参与。这些投资是一种高风险和高回报的投资。根据联合国贸发会议的统计，迪拜、挪威、卡塔尔、新加坡、中国的主权基金规模较大。目前世界上存在 40 多个主权基金，资金总额超过了 3 万亿美元。

主权基金并不是世界范围内的一种新现象，而是从 20 世纪 50 年代开始就已存在，主要存在于资源（尤其是石油）出口国。但是，此前的这些基金仅限于获取发达国家的债券，如今基金的大部分被投在有利可图的领域，比如不动产、黄金和大公司股票的购买。

中国的主权基金成立于 2007 年，注册资本达 2000 亿美元，并在各种资产收购中表现得非常积极。比如，2007 年，该基金中的 30 亿美元被用来收购黑石集团私募股权基金 10% 的股份。该集团是美国非常活跃的公司，是希尔顿酒店连锁网络、德国电信等公司的母公司。在分析家看来，这笔来自主权基金的大投资

不仅有金融方面的考虑，同时也提出了一个增加在西方企业中的中国参与的战略方针。

（二）鼓励国际化的政策和程序简化

从鼓励海外投资的目的出发，中国政府为方便国内投资者"走出去"采取了一系列措施，推动行政程序的改变，为投资者提供融资或引导。除此之外，中国政府还从投资接受国层面去影响海外投资，或者为投资提供便利。其方式主要有两种：通过签署双边协定，尽力明确投资接受国的某种承诺或政策调整；通过加强与其他国家的外交关系。

关于项目评估和审批程序的简化，中国对外直接投资的规定仍处在形成和调整阶段。除国务院外，还有三家机构履行着中国企业国际化管理的职能，它们分别是国家发展和改革委员会、中国商务部和国家外汇管理局。但是，"为保持和扩大自身在中国对外直接投资监管体制建立中的影响力，这三家机构陷入无休止的斗争中"。①

尽管存在这种斗争，这三个机构在近几年中还是在为中国海外投资审批及程序简化寻找解决办法。2004 年 10 月以来，中国相继出台了两个文件，目的在于简化相关程序。第一个是由国家发展与改革委员会制定的《境外投资项目核准暂行管理办法》，第二个是由中国商务部制定的《关于境外投资开办企业核准事项的规定》。

在已发生的那些变化中，有两点变化是最重要的。其一是审批程序的权力下放。自这些文件公布以后，地方政府能够审批 3000 万美元以下的投资项目（以前的上限仅为 100 万美元）。其二是官僚程序也得到了简化。此前，投资项目（在报批过程中）应配有一个技术和经济金融可行性报告，而现在获取海外投资授权只需要从互联网上提交申请。其他文件和规定也通过互联网公布。

1. 财政和金融刺激政策

中国海外投资项目可根据投资优先目的进行划分，在一些有投资偏好的投资项目中，以下几类值得强调。

---

① MULCAHY, N., "Chinese Regulation of Outwards Direct Investment," *Memorandum*, Arnall Golden Gregory LLP, 18 September, National of Statistics of China, 2007, p. 3.

（1）弥补国内资源不足的项目；

（2）能促进国内出口、带动就业、促进技术发展的工业和基础设施项目；

（3）研发项目；

（4）能提高中国企业在海外市场的竞争力，并有助于其国际市场拓展的兼并和收购项目。

通过低息贷款政策，这些项目从中国政府获得了充足的资金支持。虽然其他一些国有银行也为海外投资提供贷款，但国家开发银行和中国进出口银行是提供资金支持最主要的两家国有银行。

在这两家银行中，中国进出口银行发挥着更重要的作用。从 2004 年开始，国家发展与改革委员会与该银行就海外投资项目达成协议：除在融资方面提供其他便利外，协议利率应比市场通行利率优惠 2%，市场利率与优惠利率之间的差额由中国财政部补齐。

除优惠的公共融资外，OECD2008 年报告也提到了特殊基金的存在。这些基金的成立宗旨是鼓励中国海外投资。这些基金向投资者提供优惠贷款和直接补贴。

2. 信息和指导及其他支持方式的提供

中国商务部也努力指导投资者。2004 年，商务部面向有意开展海外投资的企业发布了包含 67 个国家的投资指南，列出了这些国家一些有投资潜力的行业，尤其强调农业、矿业、工业和服务业。除此之外，中国政府还建立了多个国家投资环境的数据库，以供企业家咨询。这些信息涉及内容从商业环境到文化、政治问题。

中国政府也越来越担心国内企业在海外市场的竞争力。根据 2005 年的一个报告显示，在中国企业参与的兼并中，70% 出现股票价格下跌的结果。其他数据也显示，30% 的海外投资出现亏损，40% 遭遇破产，只有 30% 实现了盈利。

中国政府还鼓励企业在一些工业园和出口加工区开展集体投资，以此在越南、柬埔寨、巴基斯坦和俄罗斯等国建立自己的空间。

3. 国际协定

最后，我们应该强调国际协定（国际投资协定）在中国企业国际化过程中的作用。一般而言，这些协定列出了一些与投资促进、投资和外国投资者司法保护等条款。

虽然，总的来说这些协定对新投资的作用有限，但越来越多地被中国政府采用，并作为鼓励其企业国际化发展的另一工具。在下文中，我们挑选了中国作为协议方的一些协议条款，以佐证中国处理这些事务的方式。

中国与科威特双边协定确定了两国优惠的投资领域：

第二条　投资促进和保护

缔约国应定期就各自领土和海域内各经济领域的投资机会进行磋商，以确定对缔约两国最为有利的投资领域，并根据缔约两国随时商定的范围、条款和条件，给此种投资以适当的便利、激励和其它形式的鼓励。

这个协议，也涉及了两国在对方的投资有关税收减免的可能性。

关于第二条：缔约任何一国的投资者在东道国应有权根据东道国的法律和法规或缔约两国间的协定随时规定的范围、条款和条件，向东道国有关当局申请适当的便利、激励或其他形式的鼓励（特别包括税收的减免）。

中国与韩国的协定提出了两国定期举行会谈，以确定针对两国接收对方国家投资的具体建议：

第14条

一、为便于执行本协定，缔约双方同意设立由双方代表组成的联合委员会。

二、联合委员会的职责主要包括：

（一）审查协定的执行情况及两国间有关投资的事宜；

（二）结合一方或双方国家关于接受外国投资的法律制度或政策的发展，就本协定的适用及与本协定的适用有关的事项进行磋商；

（三）必要时向两国政府提出适当的建议。

三、联合委员会根据缔约任何一方的要求在北京和汉城轮流举行。

中国与科特迪瓦的双边协定确定，两国都应推动双边会晤，以探讨投资促进：

第 13 条　磋商

一、缔约双方为下列目的应定期进行会谈：

（一）审查本协定的执行情况；

（二）交流法律信息和投资机会；

（三）解决投资产生的争议；

（四）提出促进投资的建议；

（五）研究与投资有关的其他事宜。

正如联合国贸发会议所指出的，我们应该注意这样的一个事实，即在中国签署的 14 个双边国际协定中，其中 9 个是与非洲国家签订的，它们是贝宁、吉布提、赤道几内亚、几内亚、马达加斯加、纳米比亚、塞舌尔、突尼斯和乌干达。这反映了中非之间的良好关系。或许非洲大陆不太稳定的政治环境能解释签订更加正式的、明确中国投资者最低保障的协议的必要性。

五　结语

关于中国企业国际化的结论可以总结为以下几点。

（1）存在着一个这样的共识：根据国际化给经济（产量、竞争力、海外汇款、上缴国家的红利）所带来的乘数效应和连锁效应，企业有必要实现国际化。

（2）存在着一个根据国家工业政策目标而定的产量扩大战略，与此同时也存在对国际收支平衡的担心。如果不推进企业国际化，货币的不可兑换的政策就很难实现。

（3）政府支持国际化政策的重要性。这种政策以一种协调的方式（并非意味着没有争端）出现。在这方面，最关键的是已设立的机构给予的支持。

（4）银行（主要是提供融资的银行）的作用。它不仅体现在融资数量上，而且也体现在投资部门和投资目的地的引导方面。

（5）由于认识到这是一场全球性的财富游戏，企业国际化在世界生产的重构、国家在世界格局中的政治定位中有着重要的作用。

更具体地讲，它还体现在：

（6）虽然开展海外投资的主要中国企业在海外资产和销售方面取得了显著

成效，但在海外创造就业方面并未呈现同步发展。也就是说，这些企业的劳动力仍然集中在中国本土。

（7）从地理分布来看，中国投资的大部分流向亚洲和中东这些最具活力的地区。

（8）在国际化政策支持方面，针对企业的融资政策、财政和金融鼓励、信息提供与指导、优先领域的国际协议签订等政策呈互补关系。

三 “金砖四国”与环境

为了世界更美好的未来：环境问题与“金砖四国”

吴恩远[*]

人类生存环境问题的变化甚至进一步恶化的趋势是21世纪人类社会面临的最严峻挑战之一。早在20世纪70年代，国际社会就开始注意到人类社会生存环境越来越恶化，注意到由于环境特别是气候的变化对社会发展造成的灾难性后果。诸如全球气候变化、臭氧层破坏、生物多样性减少、酸雨蔓延、土地荒漠化、水环境污染、大气污染、森林植被破坏、持久性有机污染物的污染等一系列问题严重威胁人类生存环境。如在资源破坏方面，由于过度消耗各种矿产资源，按照传统的消耗量计算，世界石油仅够维持50年，煤、天然气仅够开采200~300年。在生态破坏方面，20世纪50年代以来，全球森林资源已失去了一半。据联合国粮农组织统计，地球上每分钟有2000平方米森林被毁掉；世界沙漠化土地已经达3600万平方公里，几乎是中国、美国和俄罗斯国土面积的总和；地球上平均每天就有一个物种消灭，预计在未来的30~40年中，将有6000种植物在地球上消灭……而这一切的直接后果是，人类生活环境恶化。1973年非洲萨赫勒地区大旱，导致数百万人失去生命。

为了使未来的天更蓝，水更清，环境更优美，人们的生活更幸福——为了这个目标，保护现在的地球，爱护我们今天的家园事关人类生存和各国发展，需要国际社会，包括“金砖四国”民众携手努力、合作应对。

* 吴恩远，中国社会科学院俄罗斯东欧中亚研究所所长。

一 国际社会关于环境问题治理的沿革和重要发展阶段

1.《联合国气候变化框架公约》

早在1974年，联合国大会第六届特别会议就要求世界气象组织展开气候变化研究，由此揭开人类社会探寻环境问题解决的序幕。1992年巴西里约热内卢联合国环境与发展大会上通过了《联合国气候变化框架公约》，这是世界上第一个为全面控制二氧化碳等温室气体排放，应对全球气候变化给人类经济和社会带来不利影响的国际条约，也是国际社会在应对全球气候变化，进而影响环境变化问题上进行国际合作的一个基本框架。截至2009年12月缔约方第15次会议在丹麦首都哥本哈根举行，目前加入该公约的缔约国增加至192个。这是国际组织第一个关于环境治理的文件，因而具有里程碑似的意义。

2.《京都议定书》

1997年12月，在日本京都召开的《联合国气候变化框架公约》缔约方第三次会议通过了旨在限制发达国家温室气体排放量以抑制全球变暖的《京都议定书》(全称《联合国气候变化框架公约京都议定书》)。

《京都议定书》有若干条款，其目标是“将大气中的温室气体含量稳定在一个适当的水平，进而防止剧烈的气候改变对人类造成伤害”。

《京都议定书》需要占全球温室气体排放量55%以上的至少55个国家批准，才能成为具有法律约束力的国际公约。中国于1998年5月签署并于2002年9月3日决定通过该议定书。截至2005年8月13日，全球已有142个国家和地区签署该议定书，其中包括30个工业化国家，批准国家的人口数量占全世界总人口的80%。2005年2月16日，《京都议定书》正式生效。它是《联合国气候变化框架公约》的补充条款，也是人类历史上首次以法规的形式限制温室气体排放，同样具有里程碑的意义。

但《京都议定书》的贯彻却并不顺利。许多人认为京都议定书是一个险恶的计划，它或者会延缓世界的工业化民主进程，或者会把财富以“全球社会主义”向第三世界国家转移；某些批评家则认为《京都议定书》会阻碍经济增长。其中反对声最大的是美国。美国曾于1998年签署了《京都议定书》。但2001年3月，布什政府以“减少温室气体排放将会影响美国经济发展”和“发展中国家也应该承担减排和限排温室气体的义务”为借口，宣布拒绝批准《京都议定书》。前总统布什已经说他不会把条约提交国会批准。他表示原则上他并不反对《京都议定书》的思想，但是他认为议定书规定的要求太高会损害美国的经济。

3. “巴厘路线图”

2007年12月联合国气候变化大会在印度尼西亚巴厘岛举行。由于2012年的临近，《京都议定书》第一承诺期即将到期。因此，联合国气候变化大会通过了“巴厘路线图”，启动了加强《联合国气候变化框架公约》和《京都议定书》全面实施的谈判进程。

巴厘路线图确认了加强公约和议定书全面、有效和持续实施的授权，一是为确保公约全面、有效和持续实施，就减缓、适应、技术转让、资金支持等做出相应安排；二是确定发达国家在《京都议定书》第二承诺期进一步量化减排指标。

作为2007年联合国气候大会最重要的决议，“巴厘路线图”确定了世界各国今后加强落实《联合国气候变化框架公约》的具体领域，强调了国际合作，突出了“共同但有区别的责任”原则。另外，该路线图把美国纳入进来。

由于拒签《京都议定书》，美国如何履行发达国家应尽义务一直存在疑问。“巴厘路线图”明确规定，《联合国气候变化框架公约》的所有发达国家缔约方都要履行可测量、可报告、可核实的温室气体减排责任，美国也不例外。

4. 《哥本哈根协议》

2009年12月19日，联合国气候变化大会在丹麦哥本哈根达成不具法律约束力的《哥本哈根协议》。《哥本哈根协议》维护了《联合国气候变化框架公约》及其《京都议定书》确立的“共同但有区别的责任”原则，就发达国家实行强制减排和发展中国家采取自主减排行动作出了安排，并就全球长期目标、资金和技术支持、透明度等焦点问题达成广泛共识。

正如中国总理温家宝所说，《哥本哈根协议》体现了各方积极应对气候变化的政治意愿，重申了“共同但有区别的责任”原则，坚持了“巴厘路线图”关于《联合国气候变化框架公约》和《京都议定书》的双轨谈判进程，确认公约和议定书工作组主席案文为下一步谈判的基础，锁定了各方达成的共识。该协议是推动“巴厘路线图”取得成果的政治基础，为推进应对气候变化国际合作奠定了基础，为今后谈判指明了方向。

二　发达国家是否真正承认其历史责任，是协调各国共同采取保护环境立场的关键

根据上述对国际社会治理环境沿革的分析，我们可以得出两点结论：第一，世界各国在治理人类生存环境这一点上认识一致，而且持之以恒地探索这个问题的解决，这使我们对人类社会发展的前景还能够抱以希望；第二，但在具体解决的方式上，各国态度不一，有时甚至难以达成协议，这又使我们忧心忡忡。

那么，这个矛盾的症结在什么地方？解决这个问题的关键、突破口在什么地方？

从历史承担的责任方面看，发达国家认为，在当今世界，最大的温室气体排放者中有很多新兴经济国家，如中国、印度和巴西。新兴国家污染物排放总量大，应该承担更大责任，这些国家需要大量减排。新兴国家则认为，人类大量排放温室气体，已有近两百年历史，其中主要是西方国家排放的，它们负有重大责任。发达国家人均排放量大，能源资源消耗多，而且新兴国家的相当一部分排放量是为了生产发达国家居民消费品而产生的，发达国家应该承担更大的责任。

在减排目标上，发达国家认为，不止它们，新兴国家也应该制定具体的减排目标；新兴国家则认为，《京都议定书》中仅仅规定了发达国家要有具体减排、限排目标，而对发展中国家暂时没有要求。这个“区别责任”原则应该坚持。至于新兴国家，可以根据本国情况自愿提出减排的具体目标。

在资金问题上，欧洲国家提出3年72亿欧元的承诺，这和发展中国家的要求相差甚远。工业发达国家承诺在2010～2012年为发展中国家提供300亿美元，到2020年每年提供1000亿美元的财政援助，以帮助发展中国家实现减排目标。但实际上，欧美国家至今才到位100亿美元的援助。美国不作具体数字承诺，并对资金提出很多限制性的要求。

此外，在落实发达国家减排行动和指标、提供资金和技术上实行三可原则（即可报告、可监测、可核实），而发展中国家自主采取的减排行动不接受三可原则以及任何变相的三可原则问题上双方也存在分歧。

如何理智看待和处理这些分歧，是当前国际社会治理环境向前走一步的关键。

由于世界各国发展程度不一，对造成人类环境变化的责任不一，因此在治理

环境恶化方面承担的责任应当有所不同。正如《京都议定书》中所明确指出的，参与国达成了以下共识：无论从历史上还是现在来看，发达国家都是主要的温室气体排放国；发展中国家的人均排放量还是很低的；发展中国家的排放控制应该和他们的社会发展水平相适应。这就提出了世界各国在环境治理方面的一个十分重要的原则——“共同但有区别的责任”。

中国有句古话，“冰冻三尺，非一日之寒”。这句话形象地说明了造成当今人类环境变化的根源。相关研究表明，当前的气候环境变化等问题主要是过去 150 年间发达国家在其工业化过程中所造成的。从人类历史上看，发达国家在实现工业化、现代化的过程中，无约束地、大量地排放了温室气体，主要是二氧化碳。

从工业革命开始到 1950 年，在化石燃料燃烧释放的二氧化碳总量中发达国家占了 95%。1950～2000 年的 50 年中，发达国家的排放量仍然占到总排放量的 77%。

以美国为例，美国人口仅占全球人口的 3%～4%，而它排放的二氧化碳却占全球排放总量的 25% 以上，为全球温室气体排放量最大的国家。

到目前为止，在污染大气的二氧化碳等气体中，80% 是由只占 20% 的人口造成的，如果这 20% 的人不为此作出努力，不为此作出补偿是不公平的。

因此，发达国家理应为改善世界环境承担有法律约束力的义务。可以说，发达国家是否真正承认其历史责任，是协调各国共同采取保护环境立场的关键。

国际社会要在公约框架下做出切实有效的制度安排，促使发达国家兑现承诺，向发展中国家持续提供充足的资金支持，加快转让气候友好技术，并通过国际社会的通力合作，共同应对气候变化，保护环境。

“共同但有区别的责任”原则是国际合作应对气候变化的核心和基石，应当始终坚持。正如在叶卡捷琳娜堡“金砖四国”外长会议上所阐明的那样：只有在一个公正的全球经济体系内，充分考虑各国利益，才能实现世界各国经济的长期可持续发展。

三 “金砖四国”节能减排、保护环境的真诚意愿

近年来，新兴发展中国家工业发展迅猛，如巴西被称为“世界原料基地”，

俄罗斯被称为“世界加油站”，印度被称为“世界办公室”，中国被称为“世界工厂”。在发展经济的同时节能减排，保护环境。在这一问题上四国有着类似的任务，相近的诉求。其中既有转变生产方式的自身需求，又有保护环境的历史使命，四国应该为使全球环境变好承担相应的责任和义务。

在当今世界，可以说，没有“金砖四国”的积极参与，任何有关环境保护的建议都是一纸空文，任何有关削减温室气体行动的效果都会受到一定程度的影响。四国作为新兴经济体的代表和发展中国家的领头羊，拥有世界42%的人口，全球国内生产总值的15%，四国更有理由为世界未来的生存方式和发展模式提出自己的意见和主张。

我们高兴地注意到，“金砖四国”都表达了减低排放量，保护环境的真诚意愿。

俄罗斯近年来有100多个城市和工业区的大气污染指数超标。其中冶金、化工、石化、建筑、动力等企业废气排放以及汽车尾气超标排放是大气污染的主要原因。有害废物除从本地排放外，还从其他遥远的地方和国外排入森林、湖泊和农田。俄罗斯欧洲部分的领土每年从边界排入超过1万吨含硫氧化物废物，比俄罗斯本土产生的还要多。由于约40%的污水排放到饮用水水源和鱼塘，俄罗斯大多数饮用水和鱼塘水质不符合卫生和渔业标准。土壤植被也有日益退化的趋势。据统计，俄罗斯1990年的温室气体排放量占世界总量的17.4%，因此治理俄罗斯的环境污染也成为历届政府的大事。

早在2004年9月，时任俄罗斯总统普京曾经口头表示过支持《京都议定书》中与俄罗斯相关的内容。俄罗斯政府经过反复权衡批准议定书的利弊之后，于2004年9月30日通过了有关批准《京都议定书》的法律草案，并提交俄罗斯议会批准。俄罗斯国家杜马（议会下院）和联邦委员会（议会上院）分别于10月22日和27日通过议定书，俄罗斯总统普京随后在议定书上签字。按照俄法律程序，俄罗斯总统在议定书上签字后，该议定书已经成为俄罗斯的法律文本。

现任俄罗斯总统梅德韦杰夫对俄罗斯应承担的国际减排义务作了阐述，主要包括两方面：一是俄罗斯计划在2020年前将温室气体排放量降低300亿吨；二是俄罗斯计划在2020年前使排放量比1990年减少20%～30%。俄罗斯完全有实力成为国际减排的领先国家，当然这需要俄罗斯在节能、提高能效及植树造林方面付出努力。

作为南半球最大的发展中国家，巴西在气候变化问题上态度鲜明。第一，巴西政府对此高度重视。总统卢拉多次要求发达国家充分意识到所承担的历史责任，在减排问题上作出更强有力的承诺。2009 年 11 月 13 日，巴西总统卢拉在圣保罗召集民事办公室、环境部和科技部等相关部门负责人会议，就减排目标问题达成一致。巴西民事办公室主任迪尔玛·罗塞芙在新闻发布会上说，希望这一“自愿做出”的减排承诺能向全世界表明巴西政府在应对气候变化问题上的明确立场。第二，巴西具有巨大减排潜力。由巴西科技部组织编写的一份初步报告指出，巴西目前的林场总面积为 36 万平方公里。在巴西的能源结构中水电和生物质能源比重大，温室气体排放主要来自毁林。只要巴西缩减毁林面积 80% 的目标，就相当于少排放 1.21 亿吨二氧化碳。巴西又是生物燃料研发大国，如果进一步推广生物燃料应用，每年还可以少排放 5000 万吨二氧化碳。此外，如果政府部门资助农业领域退耕还林，将可以恢复 1100 万公顷用于放牧的草地。

所以巴西政府宣布，计划到 2020 年将温室气体排放量在预期基础上减少 36.1% ~38.9%。罗塞芙对此解释道，最乐观的估计是到 2020 年实现减排 38.9%的目标，其中农牧业减排 6.1%，能源业减排 7.7%，钢铁企业减排 0.4%。有分析说，如果能够实现这一目标，那么巴西的温室气体排放量在 2020 年时将接近其 1994 年的排放水平，相当于在 2005 年的基础上减少 20%。巴西将于 2009 年 12 月向哥本哈根联合国气候变化大会提交这一减排计划。

2002 年 8 月印度签署了《京都议定书》。由于印度是《联合国气候变化框架公约》控制框架以外的国家，所以也不受温室气体排放限制。印度强调需要发展经济以解决贫困问题，并将采取有效措施提高能源效率和发展可再生能源。印度还宣布，其人均温室气体排放量在任何时候都不会超过发达国家的水平。

据《印度快报》网 2009 年 2 日晚报道，经讨论印度政府将公布减排目标，到 2020 年，使废气排放比 2005 年减少 24%，到 2030 年，减少 37%。

四 中国为应对气候变化和保护环境付出的努力

中国政府一贯重视环境问题对人类社会发展的影响，充分认识到环境、气候变化问题的严重性和紧迫性，一向本着对人类长远发展高度负责的精神，坚定不移地走可持续发展道路。中国作为发展中国家，虽然不承担量化的温室气体减排的指标，但这不等于中国不承担应尽的国际义务和责任。

过去的三十年间，中国为应对气候变化，保护环境付出的努力是众所周知的。中国政府通过制定一系列法律法规，完善相关的税收、价格等制度，为保护环境建立了系统的体系。一方面大力节能减排，另一方面大力推广可再生性能源。在利用清洁能源风能、太阳能方面，中国是世界上发展速度最快的国家。此外，2005～2008年，中国已经使可再生能源增长了51%，年均增长达14.7%。仅2008年，中国可再生能源利用量就达到2.5亿吨标准煤，农村有3050万户用上沼气，相当于少排放二氧化碳4900多万吨。中国在水电装机容量、核电在建规模、太阳能热水器集热面积和光伏发电容量方面均居世界第一位。中国还是世界上人工造林面积最大的国家，人工造林面积达5400万公顷。通过这些实际行动，中国为节能减排，保护环境做出了自己应有的努力。

目前，中国还处于工业化、城镇化、现代化快速发展的关键阶段，而且中国的能源结构以煤为主，短时间大幅度降低排放存在着实际的特殊困难。但是，中国始终把应对气候变化，保护环境作为重要战略任务。1990～2005年，单位国内生产总值二氧化碳排放强度下降46%。在此基础上，中国又提出，到2020年单位国内生产总值二氧化碳排放比2005年下降40%～45%。在此期间，这样大规模地降低二氧化碳排放，需要付出艰苦卓绝的努力。

正如中国总理温家宝强调的，中国将采取积极措施，努力实现提出的国内自主行动目标：到2020年单位国内生产总值二氧化碳排放比2005年下降40%～45%，非化石能源占一次能源消费的比重达到15%左右，森林面积比2005年增加4000万公顷，森林蓄积量比2005年增加13亿立方米。

目前，"金砖四国"之间双边关系彼此巩固，政治互信逐步加强，合作机制正在不断完善，特别是相互间的经贸关系日益密切，这为加强相互之间的合作创造了有利条件。我们坚信，在保护地球、保护环境的合作方面，"金砖四国"之间具有非常广阔的合作空间。

“金砖四国”的环境问题

——人文维度

尼古拉·米哈伊洛夫　吴孝芹（译）*

“地球可以满足每个人的需要，但是，不能满足每个人的贪婪。”

——圣雄甘地

想象一下，一只青蛙坐在一个正在加热的装满水的锅里。水正慢慢变热，快要沸腾。青蛙也在慢慢变热，但未觉得任何不适。问题是：“将会发生什么？或在一切还来得及之前什么能使青蛙跳出该水面?”让我给出提示：该青蛙将难以逃脱，除非面临外部严重威胁或上级命令其撤离。这正如我们没有将全球变暖当成一个如同某行星将在给定时间点撞上地球一样的决定性威胁，仅仅由于无人告知我们准确的截止日期及没有全球政府会对我们发出指令，只能一切寄希望于外星人了。

换句话说，我们并不相信有什么真正不好的事情发生，我们不相信我们（可能）将灭亡。现在将青蛙换成人类，假定我们比青蛙更敏感，在全球危机到来之际我们能做什么，应做什么。

面对环境变化，我们只有三种选择：迁徙或移民、适应或退化（degenerate）和灭亡。面对诸如干旱、饥荒、传染病及其他自然灾害的干扰，动物（包括人

* 尼古拉·米哈伊洛夫，俄罗斯 Russkiy Mir 基金会研究人员；吴孝芹，太原工业学院管理工程系讲师。

类）总是习惯于作出其中一种选择。前两项选择提供生存的机会，没有这两项选择，个体、部落及人类将面临死亡和灭绝。按照目前的资源使用、污染排放和人口膨胀速度，地球很难按照这种状态持续存在较长时间。

面对资源枯竭或污染等长期干扰，人类通常会迁移到条件较好的栖息地。首先是在国内迁移，如果国内不起作用，人们将跨国迁移，离开被污染地区，选择较好的生存环境。很清楚，因环境引起的移民将增加，大规模环境移民引起的紧张也将相应增加。当世界人口在未来短短 40 年增加到 90 亿 ~ 100 亿时，将没有几个地方可以避难，并且接收移民的地区也将无法提供配套的生活条件。

人类的生物学特征使其有可能适应大幅度的环境变化，但这种适应是有限度的。如果超出这一限度，人类将失去生物意义上的可持续性，面临灭绝。那些没有能力或不愿意迁徙的人别无选择，只能选择适应、变弱和最终退化。有人争辩说，人类几个世纪以来不断通过迁移适应新环境。适应自然环境变化与适应诸如土壤、水和空气污染等非自然条件不可同日而语。在技术文明创造的当前环境下，能够适应新的不友好环境的资源日趋下降。

当代世界环境问题的本质在于人类生产活动和全球环境与生态系统稳定性之间的矛盾日益增加。人类财富基本来自农业、制造业和矿产资源。复杂的现代社会的一切均建立在矿物资源及能源、汽车、食物、农药或塑料袋的不断消耗之上。但是，最近我们才意识到，实际上所有经济活动都对环境产生破坏性影响。

致命的疾病、干旱、洪水、高热、风暴及海平面上升对城市和农村的危害以及对农业的不利影响等首先会引起社会争端，接着就是政治和军事争端。一旦灾难出现，无论是突然出现还是慢慢出现，全球人类合作的可能性都不大。人类本能将会占据上风，导致分裂，将引发战争而非合作。

一　挑战

对环境的密集伤害始于 19 世纪的最后 25 年，但是，直到最近我们才开始明白这种发展将会影响人类生存。我们才意识到当代世界的所有问题，无论是能源、食品还是人口问题归根结底是影响所有人类的环境问题。

我们还有什么其他重要发现呢？我们还意识到肯定存在增长限制，并且这些限制主要源于自然资源的耗尽。结果是，发达国家转而掠夺其他国家的资源，从而引发了持续不断的"资源战争"。这一切战争始于殖民征服并持续至 20 世纪后半叶，共发生 73 次战争和军事冲突，大部分源于对石油、钻石、铜矿、可可、古柯（coca）甚至橡胶等资源的控制。若发生新的更大型的资源战争也无需惊奇。

然而，到目前为止最重要也最具戏剧性的发现是，人们开始认识到有事物会影响人类的生存。从二战结束起，我们用了 20 多年才意识到人类不再永恒。

直到最近我们才意识到，如果维持目前的经济增长速度，全球环境可能做出这样的反应：250 年后，人类可能将无法延续。

谁造成了过度消费和污染？是人口占世界总人口 23%、资源消耗却占 66% 的较发达国家，还是未来 30 年内人口将翻一番、导致食物和水将耗尽及由于燃烧煤炭、缺乏排放控制、滥用农药和管理宽松引起的有毒废物排放而导致污染进一步恶化的较不发达国家？

毋庸置疑，人口达到 60 亿是不可持续的。过去 40 年世界人口已翻了一番。现在全球人口已经超出维持目前生活水平的地球生态承载能力的 30%，但是，人口增长仍未趋稳定，预计 2050 年世界人口将达到 100 亿。动物的数量也是不可持续的——每年由于丧失栖息地而永久灭绝的动物种类达 7 万种。随着人口增长，动物的灭绝数量还会增加。人口可能在达到 120 亿时稳定下来，但是，这并不意味着人类居住区将稳定下来。

如果要求发达国家适应自然的生态友好的循环，他们的总消费必须减少 10 倍，美国必须降低 50 倍。但是，很明显发达国家不会迅速作出回应。世界需要减少一半的二氧化碳排放，然而，联合国成员只同意到 2012 年减少 5%。

相当长时期内，我们曾努力创造这样一种经济，即其产出通过耗费地球自然资源而增加。在全球经济泡沫危害全球之前缩小该泡沫是一大挑战。必须采取紧急行动减少能源和水消耗，将排放稳定在可持续水平，保持人口规模稳定（尤其是发展中国家）。

这大概是"诺亚洪水"（Noah Flood）以来人类首次遇到的真正的全球威胁。从那时以来，人类历史上还没有遇到像今天存在的如此众多紧迫的威胁。整个世界已经进入历史关键阶段，是时候拷问到底是什么导致了这种情形。

二 人类中心主义还是生态中心主义

现代经济发展是建立在人类支配自然的人类中心主义理念基础上的，该理念宣称人是这个星球的推动力量和主人。这一切始于所谓的文艺复兴时期，新生的"人本主义者"（humanists）将人类置于宇宙的中心地位，宣称人类是取代上帝的创造者。关键问题就是人和自然如何发生联系。与这一时期科学的爆发式发展一致，弗兰西斯·培根提倡用科学方法控制自然为人类谋福利。16世纪勒内·笛卡尔（Rene Descartes）的机械哲学进一步强化这一实验方法，笛卡尔认为通过实验方法人类可以"使自己成为自然的主人和所有者"。自此，自然被降格，沦为人类的服务者。这种理念创造了技术统治论思维的基础，并最终导致了控制自然并以各种可能方式改造自然的技术统治的意识形态。工业革命事实上是对关于人类在世界的地位和角色的传统理念进行革新并最终转变的媒介。

最近的两次科学革命——19世纪的进化论和20世纪生物技术的产生，使传统的世界观，特别是关于人在自然中的地位遭到质疑。进化论通过证明所有生物包括人类都是长期进化而来，对物种不变的传统观念提出了挑战。

经济利益蒙蔽了道德和伦理准则。事实上人类已经完全拥有为追逐经济利益而为所欲为的权力。同时，这一观念使人们在社会和环境活动中忽略了传统道德理念和方向。宇宙和生物得到一个过分简单的解释，经过大幅改造的进化论占据了中心地位。

仍处于统治地位的经典科学已经发展成二元论范式。在这样的范式中，观察者与她或他观察的事物是割裂的且有显著区别。这促成了这样一种观念：世界由相互独立的物质对象组成，每个对象都有独立的特性，其整体表现可通过各个组成部分的表现进行解释。经典科学代表着绝对真理的源泉，经常作为决策的基础且常被当作最值得尊敬的探索自然的方法。

自然界被看作是与人类分离的，像机器一样可以分解成基本组成部分进行客观研究和预测。自然界还被当作应由人类按照自己的意志进行处理的各种资源及半成品的无生命的载体。人类对自然的塑造仅取决于人类的塑造能力。鉴于此，关于人类不再是固定和永恒的真相则不再可信。自由使人类不像其他生物一样以世界某一角色展现自己，而是按照自己的选择来塑造和展现自己。

大多数人都认为人类是价值的中心。相应的，人类中心主义者主张既然所有价值源于人类，那么其他非人类实体或对象只有与人类联系时才有价值。人类中心主义者进一步将价值定义为满足人类的偏好。这类掠夺性的人类中心主义学说是环境危机产生的基本原因。

不断增长的人口、能源危机和滥用及污染地球自然系统是引起环境危机的三个最重要和最紧迫的因素。这三个及其他引起环境危机的因素都与科学的、人类中心主义世界观有联系。价值存在并源于人类的观念，导致了认为人类优于其他生物、人类生命才是终极价值的认识。保护人类生命的努力推动了医药创新和医疗物质条件的不断提高，而这种提高又导致人类人口更多、寿命更长。实现人类生命价值目标，间接地促进了人口的增长。优越性与科技的不断发展导致了无休止满足人类基本需要的社会情景。更多的医疗和社会救助、更多的娱乐和舒适生活需求转化为改善生活水平的需求。不断增长的人口和对现代社会的物质需求带来了对能源供给的需求增加。尽管希望更好的生活不是坏事，但是，考虑到人口激增，当前能源危机不可避免，这使一切环境问题都卷入其中。

我们通常把科学作为拯救地球及其自然价值的工具。每年数十亿的资金投向生物科技、化学、军事、农业产业化及类似的应用研究上。每天都能听到“资源大规模流向发展技术创新、支持部署和应用最好的技术与工艺”的呼吁。

人类中心主义战略转变了环境因素，但没有考虑到环境系统的复杂性。环境系统是对多个因素的变化作出整体反应，这些因素的变化使得系统的整体质量下降，需要额外的努力以及能源和资源来中和这些负面因素的影响。目前许多企图保护和维持人类进步、满足人类需求、实现人类抱负的努力是不可持续的——无论穷国还是富国。实际上我们的成就往往带来矛盾的结果：在追求短期目标的同时通常带来不期望的副作用。这些后果与我们努力的目标背道而驰，并可能轻易地抹掉我们的积极成果。

人类中心的研究增加了短期利润和竞争，促进了工业产出、国防、卫生、舒适生活及食品生产的能力。同时，我们每天都听到渔业崩溃，水土流失，地下水、淡水和土壤污染，湖泊枯竭，臭氧层破坏，研究产生的化学污染对风景的慢性毒害，森林消退，大量物种灭绝，地球变暖，赤贫国家贫困加剧，急剧增加的生态难民等消息。

随着对政府和企业的影响力的充分了解，地球上生存了几十亿年的数以百万计的物种和生态系统正在退化或消失。诸如荷尔蒙杀虫剂等新型的化学物质在公众不知晓的情况下被有意识地应用在人类食品中。简言之，尽管地球及其栖息者处于困境之中，我们的政府和产业领导却继续资助那些会加深环境危机的研究。

因此，将环境问题交予科学去解决将导致对该问题狭隘的理解，并产生短视的解决方法。从这一角度看，科学不应该被视为未来的最终希望，显然也不应完全承担解决环境危机的责任。这就是为什么当代经济科学创造的可持续发展的概念只被视为一种技术变革而非全面解决问题的方法。

需要的新的科学模式应是生态的，而不是以经济和开发为目的的。处于危险境地的不仅仅是地球上大量美丽的复杂的生命形态和生态系统，还包括生活在这个美丽星球上的人类的生存质量。当前科学发展的优先顺序应该如下：应提供一个更和谐的对自然界的基本价值的解释；应该使人们明白从细菌到人类都负有稳定地球生态圈的责任。

我们还面临哪些其他威胁呢？现代科学技术对自然界的理性主义和破坏性倾向产生了另一个影响：当我们削弱自然和环境时，也削弱了自己的本性从而直接导致人类被奴役。这绝非夸张。奴役自然界后，人就开始奴役其他人，最后奴役自己。实际上，技术统治论的宣传首先将我们从自然界分离，同时将我们与更强的创造新需求捆绑起来，直至培养出需要通过技术满足每一个需求的巨大需求。

当人类沉浸在好斗的、人造的环境中就失去了他们的自然属性。随着体力劳动的减少和脑力劳动的增加，人变得更脆弱，新的疾病、出生缺陷、毒瘾和恐惧症就出现了。我们的感官和免疫系统开始变坏，压力、失眠、抑郁和各种过敏症使我们受不了。看看发达国家中不断增长的长期离不开药物生活的人数，我们只能称这种生活为人造生活了。换言之，我们将自己变成一种奇怪的生物，由于总有机器围绕身边，人类不再需要活动能力了。

人类不能停止自己置身其中的大自然的改变，但是必须停止那种不考虑自然法则的不负责任的改变方式。这就是将通过环境政策、立法和监管来约束环境污染、改善环境质量作为应对环境危机的方法被广泛接受的原因。不幸的是，各国政府大多不愿意制定这样的政策。将这样的政策建议包含在政纲中无异于政治自杀，因为这些政策最终与致力于 GDP 增长和增加选民个人财富的竞争性政治程式相抵触。显然，只要激励我们行动的价值观不改变，将责任赋予科学或政府来校正当前形势都很难有用。

既然我们对目前的危机都负有责任，那么我们就应承担责任。不仅需承认我们的个人行为导致了环境危机，还应对我们的行为负责。

如果要避免气候变化引致的风险，我们必须立即在资源配置、经济、人类和制度上作根本性改变，在心态和行为上进行根本性改变。当代最大的挑战是重构文明，因此环境危机具有了人文维度。这表明，我们需要对我们的文化和社会模式进行重新评估，摆脱消费和占有为基础的文化。环境迫切要求我们对什么是恰当的个人和集体行为进行重新界定。

技术创新与“金砖四国”合作展望

“金砖四国”在“国家创新体系”(NIS)中政府作用的比较

——趋同性与根植性的分析角度

钟惠波　郑秉文*

20世纪90年代以来，国家创新体系（NIS，National Innovation System）逐渐受到全球关注。一般认为所谓国家创新体系，指的是一国境内在私营企业、公共企业、大学和政府机构之间对科学技术的应用与发展所产生的一种相互反应的机制网络；这些机构在机制网络下的反应，目的在于促进技术创新的发生、扩散和持续；其反应方式可以是技术的、商业的、法律的、社会的和财政的。① 在一国国家创新体系中，由于创新及其过程的高度不确定性、高度风险性、高度互补性以及准公共产品等特性，② 仅依靠市场机制远不能将用于创新的社会资源配置自动调节到最优水平，③ 必须发挥政府的领导作用来解决“市场失灵”问题。④ 就“金砖四国”而言，由于同属发展中国家，通过政府主导的强制性和诱导性制度与技术移植变迁，有意识地实现赶超战略是最为关键的战略举措。由此，政府干预就成为推动国家创新系统演化的

* 钟惠波，北京理工大学人文学院副教授、博士后；郑秉文，中国社会科学院拉丁美洲研究所所长、研究员。

① 郑秉文：《知识经济与国家创新体系》，经济管理出版社，1998。

② 钟惠波、连建辉：《当代创业企业：创新知识的综合定价机制》，《科学学研究》2005年第6期。

③ 当然，政府的重要功能并不拘囿于优化资源配置，而更体现为推动学习与创造这个国家创新体系的内核上，即政府的主要功能体现为资源（特别是知识）创造而不仅仅是资源配置问题。见贾根良《创新体系与东亚模式的精髓》，《南开学报》2001年第5期。

④ 郑秉文：《知识经济与国家创新体系》，经济管理出版社，1998。

第一推动力。

国家创新系统的演化受一国的科技与经济发展规模和水平、产业结构特征、技术路径依赖等多种因素的影响，具有鲜明的地域根植性特征。政府在国家创新系统的功能取决于自己的政策体系、经济体系及社会经济发展阶段，不同国家政府在创新系统中的角色是不一样的。

本文试图从三个方面对“金砖四国”政府在国家创新系统中的作用进行比较分析：其一，四国政府直接投资于国家创新系统建设的情况比较；其二，四国政府国家创新体系建设中采取的政策措施比较；其三，四国政府各自与国家创新体系关系中存在的问题及改进的方向比较。

一 “金砖四国”政府国家创新体系投资机制比较

政府的直接投资可以为技术创新提供资金储备和人才与公共硬件支撑条件，引导产业技术创新的方向，刺激企业技术创新投入的增长。可以说，投资机制是政府影响国家创新体系的一个最直接的途径。通常政府的投资包括提供科技创新的研发经费特别是对基础科学研究以及源头创新的支持，投资建立创新所需的公共硬件条件，以及培养创新人才的教育投资等。由于不同的发展历程及社会经济基础，“金砖四国”政府对国家创新系统的直接投资有着各自的特点。

从政府研发经费支出的角度看，2002 年与 2007 年的对比表明（见表 1），在政府研发经费支出总额方面，按照美元购买力平价计算，中国政府的研发经费支出居四国之首，2007 年达到 201.4 亿美元。其次是印度，同年达到 187.5 亿美元。俄罗斯和巴西与中、印的差距较大，同年分别仅为 68.9 亿美元和 36.8 亿美元；在政府研发经费支出增长率方面，2002 ~ 2007 年五年的年均增长率印度最高，达到 18.5%，中国次之，为 15.6%，俄罗斯与中国接近，为 15.2%，巴西最低，仅为 9.5%；在政府研发经费占总支出的比重方面，中国呈明显的下降趋势，2002 年为 28.7%，2007 年则降到 19.2%。俄罗斯则相反，呈上升的态势，2002 年为 24.5%，2007 年则上升到 29.3%。而巴西和印度基本没有变化，分别为 21.3% 和 75.3%。这些数据的变动情况从一个侧面说明了以下几个问题。第一，中、印两国政府都在大力加大研发经费投入，特别是印度政府，虽然其研发经费支出总额不及中国，但年均增长率则比中国高约3个百分点。考虑到同期印度年均GDP增长率及财政总收入都远不如中国，其2007年的政府研发经费支出总额与中国相差不到14亿美元，这说明印度政府在研发经费上加大了投入力度。巴西和俄罗斯两国也在加大政府研发经费投入，但力度远不如印度和中国。第二，中国的研发经费支出结构已经日趋合理。企业研发经费支出的快速增长，使得中国政府即使以年均15.6%的增长率增加研发经费支出，政府研发经费占总支出的比重5年间还是下降了接近10个百分点。第三，印度除政府外，其他创新主体创新的努力尚未被有效激发，研发经费基本呈政府单边支出的状态。第四，在巴西，无论是政府，还是企业、高校等，他们的创新主体的创新努力在"金砖四国"中均处于较弱状态，表现为政府研发经费支出增长率较低以及研发支出结构基本没有变化。第五，俄罗斯政府研发经费支出力度的加大并未激发企业、高校等主体的创新积极性，使得政府研发经费占总支出的比重在2002~2007年五年间增长了近5个百分点。

表1 2002年与2007年"金砖四国"政府研发经费支出比较

单位：亿美元，%

国家	研发经费支出总额		政府研发支出占比		政府研发经费总额		研发经费GDP占比	
	2002年	2007年	2002年	2007年	2002年	2007年	2002年	2007年
巴西	121	173	20.6	21.3	24.9	36.8	0.9	1.0
中国	394	1049	28.7	19.2	113.1	201.4	1.1	1.5
印度	129	248	75.6	75.3	97.5	187.5	0.7	0.8
俄罗斯	160	235	24.5	29.3	39.2	68.9	1.2	1.1

资料来源：GERD, researchers data and related indicators: UNESCO Institute for Statistics (UIS) estimations, May, 2009。

从创新人才培养的角度看，2002年与2007年的对比表明（见表2）：在研究人员总数方面，中国的优势极其明显，2007年达到142万人，占全世界研究人员总数的1/5，是俄罗斯的3倍多、印度的9倍多和巴西的12倍多，而巴西的研究人员数量最少，2007年仅为11.83万人，占全世界研究人员总数的1.7%；在研究人员数量增长方面，2002~2007年的年均增长率中国最高，达到15.12%，其次是巴西，为12.95%，印度的年均增长率为8.8%，俄罗斯则以年均1%的比例负增长；在占世界研究人员总数的比重方面，中国从2002年的14%增长到

2007年的20.1%，五年间增长了6.1%，巴西也略有增长，印度基本维持不变，而俄罗斯则处于倒退的状态，从2002年的8.5%降到2007年的6.6%，下降了近2个百分点；在每百万人口拥有研究人员的数量方面，俄罗斯最高，2007年为3291.8人，人口基数最大的中国的该项指标在"金砖四国"中仍居第二位，2007年为1071.3人，是同年印度的7.9倍、巴西的1.7倍；在研发人员人均拥有科研经费方面，按照美元购买力平价计算，印度和巴西较高，2007年都为15万美元左右，为同年中国的2倍左右、俄罗斯的3倍左右；在人均科研经费增长率方面，2002～2007年间，巴西研发人员的经费处于年均2.6%的负增长状态，俄罗斯、中国和印度则分别以年均10.8%、10.3%和8.8%的速度增长。总体而言，我们可以得出以下结论。第一，中国政府在创新人才培养方面成效显著，其研究人员数量、增长率及每百万人口拥有研究人员数量等指标都表现良好。第二，印度和巴西两国政府在创新人才培养方面取得一定进步，但成效并不显著。第三，俄罗斯政府在创新人才培养方面基本上处于倒退状态，2007年研究人员总数、占世界研究人员比例、每百万人口拥有研究人员数量等指标都比2002年低。

表2 2002年与2007年"金砖四国"研究人员数量及经费比较

国家	研究人员总数（万人）		占世界研究人员总数比例（%）		每百万人口拥有研究人员数量（人）		每个研发人员经费（万美元）	
	2002年	2007年	2002年	2007年	2002年	2007年	2002年	2007年
巴西	7.18	11.83	1.2	1.7	400.7	624.8	16.85	14.62
中国	81.05	142.34	14	20.1	629.1	1071.3	4.87	7.37
印度	11.59	15.48	2.3	2.2	110.8	136.5	11.13	16.02
俄罗斯	49.19	46.91	8.5	6.6	3365.8	3291.8	3.25	5.01

资料来源：UNESCO，*Human Development Report 2009*。

从政府发展教育的情况看（见表3）：在基础教育方面，中国政府进行了大量的投入并在1986年推行9年义务教育政策。作为人口最多的国家，中国的成年识字率已经达到90.9%，在"金砖四国"中只略低于俄罗斯，但比成年识字率为61%的印度高约30%。在高等教育方面，俄罗斯的高等教育入学率具有显著的优势，2004年达到68.2%，比中国、印度、巴西三个国家的总和还高，为俄罗斯提供源源不断的高素质研究人才。这也是俄罗斯每百万人口拥有研究人员

表3 "金砖四国"政府发展教育相关数据比较

指　　标	巴西	俄罗斯	印度	中国
识字率(%,15岁以上人口,2006年)	88.60	99.40	61.00	90.90
平均受教育年龄(2000年)	4.88	10.03	5.06	6.35
中学教育入学率(%,2004年)	102.00	92.90	53.50	72.50
高等教育入学率(%,2004年)	22.30	68.20	11.80	19.10
学校互联网接入情况(1~7分,2006年)	3.60	3.80	3.80	4.00
财政性教育经费支出占GDP比重(%,2005年)	4.00	3.80	3.20	2.20
科学及数学教育质量(1~7分,2006年)	2.90	4.50	5.70	4.10
人员培训强度(1~7分,2006年)	4.20	2.90	4.80	3.40
商学院质量(1~7分,2006)	4.10	3.60	6.00	3.40
人才流失情况(1~7分,2006)	3.90	3.50	3.70	3.80

资料来源：世界银行网站，www.worldbank.org，相关指标得分按照"最好"和"最差"以7分制的形式打分汇总而得。

数量远高于其他三个国家的主要原因。中国政府自20世纪90年代中期开始扩大对高等教育的投入，到2004年中国高等教育入学率已经达到19.1%，其中工科学生占40%。印度自20世纪50年代开始设立理工类及管理类大学，为本国软件业和通信技术产业发展提供了大量人才。虽然印度政府也致力于发展高等教育，但到2004年高等教育入学率与中国仍有7%的差距，仅为11.8%。显然，相对较低的高等教育入学率将是印度知识密集型服务业持续快速发展的一个障碍。巴西在高等教育方面的发展虽然迟缓，但其高等教育入学率仍然略高于中国和印度。在教育硬件基础设施投入及教育质量方面，根据世界银行2006年的调研数据：在学校互联网设施方面，中国做得最好，其得分是4；在科学及数学教育质量方面，印度是最好的，其得分是5.7，接近巴西的2倍；在人员培训强度方面，俄罗斯的得分最低，只有2.9，另外三个国家的得分都在4左右；在商学院教育质量方面，印度的得分是6，比居第二位的巴西还高2分，这可能与英语作为印度官方语言的背景有关。一个值得关注的现象是，在2005年财政性教育经费支出占GDP比重方面，中国为2.2%，比3.2%的印度少了1%，俄罗斯和巴西则分别为3.8%和4%。考虑到长期缺少政府的教育投资会影响一个国家人力资源的国际竞争优势，过去几年中国加大了政府在教育领域的投资力度。据统计，2009年中国财政性教育经费支出已经占当年GDP比例的3.59%，比2008年的3.33%增加了0.26个百分点。①

从政府发展公共硬件设施的角度看，鉴于知识的传播、扩散和使用是国家创新系统的核心功能，信息和通信基础设施平台是政府投资国家创新体系硬件设施建设的主要方面之一。与其他三个国家比较（见表4），中国的信息和通信基础设施建设是最有效率和最现代化的。与同样人口规模的印度比较，除了信息和通信支出占GDP的比重及人均互联网使用支出等少数指标外，其余指标印度均不足中国的1/3。俄罗斯的总体情况比巴西略好，但2005年其信息和通信支出占GDP的比重是四个国家中最低的，不到居首位的巴西的一半。需要提及的是，支持国家创新系统硬件基础设施建设的另外一个重大举措是，“金砖四国”政府都大力推进技术孵化中心与高科技园区的发展。中国在1988年设立了北京高科技产业试验区，并为该试验区提供了诸如税收减免等18项优惠政策。到1999年，中国在全国范围已经建立了54个国家级高科技产业园区。② 印度政府则在1991年耗资60亿卢比在班加罗尔设立了该国第一个软件科技园区，该科技园区

表4 “金砖四国”信息和通信基础设施比较

指　标	巴西	俄罗斯	印度	中国
千人拥有电话数量(部,2004年)	587.10	773.10	84.50	499.40
千人拥有电话线路数量(条,2004年)	230.40	255.80	40.70	241.10
千人拥有手机数量(部,2004年)	356.70	517.30	43.80	258.30
千人拥有电脑数量(台,2004年)	105.20	132.20	12.10	40.90
家庭拥有电视比例(%,2004年)	90.00	98.00	37.00	91.00
千人拥有报纸数量(份,2000年)	46.00	—	60.00	59.00
网络带宽(字节/人,2004年)	149.30	99.90	11.40	57.40
千人使用互联网数量(2004年)	119.60	111.20	32.40	72.50
人均互联网使用支出(美元/月,2003年)	28.00	10.00	8.70	10.10
信息和通信支出占GDP比重(%,2005年)	7.82	3.58	5.91	5.28

资料来源：世界银行网站，www.worldbank.org。

① 教育部、国家统计局、财政部：《2009年全国教育经费执行情况统计公告》，2010年12月7日《中国教育报》。

② Lv Ping, “The Role of The State In National System of Innovation-China Case Study,” IDRC Seminer: *Comparative Study of the National Innovation Systems of BRIC Countries*, Rio de Janeiro, Brazil, 2010.

2008年的出口额已达到150亿美元，印度的软件出口额占全球软件出口市场份额的20%。① 俄罗斯的第一个科技园是1990年在托姆斯克创办的，到2005年底该国的科技园已达近百家。② 巴西的科技园区多数设立在高校附近，圣保罗大学设立的科技园区目前已经是拉丁美洲最大的"硅谷"园区。③

二 "金砖四国"政府国家创新体系政策措施比较

(一)"金砖四国"政府国家创新体系政策措施的共同之处

1. 采取激励措施提升主体创新努力

"金砖四国"政府都采取了一系列鼓励企业和研究机构开展创新活动的政策措施，包括对技术导向型企业给予税收优惠、利息补贴和融资支持，对与国家未来密切相关的研究项目给予资金资助，对创新成果商业化给予财税支持，通过政府采购支持创新导向性产品等。如印度政府于1996年成立技术开发委员会，负责筹集资金，重点扶持研发项目的商业化，并制定了如税收减免、海关关税免除、财政支持与补贴、政府奖励等诸多支持企业科技活动的优惠政策；俄罗斯于1994年成立"促进科技型小企业发展基金会"作为小企业科技支持机构，通过预算外资金资助小企业的技术开发；巴西则早在1984年就颁布《科技进步法》规定，如果企业5%的产值用于科技投资，可减免50%的所得税，从1990年起，巴西政府又出台了一系列鼓励企业技术创新的法令；④ 中国政府在1996年和1999年分别颁布《促进科技成果转化法》、《国家科学技术奖励条例》，用于鼓励主体的创新活动，2007年13个部委联合下发了《关于支持中小企业创新的若干政策》，专门提出针对中小企业创新发展的财政、税收和金融等相关配套政策和措施。

2. 致力于改进和完善创新环境

其一，四国政府都致力于建立和维护市场环境，保护创新收益的活动。为了

① 周楚兴等：《印度软件产业考察的启示与建议》，《嘉兴市对外经济贸易合作局简报》2009年第9期。

② 龚惠平：《俄罗斯国家创新体系的新发展》，《全球科技经济瞭望》2006年第12期。

③ 于兆兴、楚汉：《巴西科学技术进步原因探析》，《拉丁美洲研究》2006年第3期。

④ 于兆兴、楚汉：《巴西科学技术进步原因探析》，《拉丁美洲研究》2006年第3期

激励和保护知识创新，1997 年巴西引入了专利法，并颁布了新《工业产权法典》，1998 年又制定了《应用研究和知识转让法》。2000 年巴西推出了"新千年研究所计划"和"技术中心：创新与推广"计划，旨在跟踪国际前沿，促进国际交流和合作，促进科技成果转化，培养科技人才，营造良好的技术创新环境；为适应市场环境变化，改善支持创新的市场环境，20 世纪 90 年代以来印度对《专利法》进行了数次修订，并出台了《版权法》、《商标法》、《外观设计法》等系列的法律和规章；20 世纪 90 年代中后期以来，俄罗斯着力不断修改有关知识产权的法律，并加强了知识产权转让的法律保护。1995 年俄罗斯提出著作权法修订案，1997 年修改国家秘密法，1998 年提出专利法修改案，2000 年提出了专利法、商标法、计算机软件和数据库保护法、集成电路拓扑图保护法以及著作权法的修改草案，2009 年实施《共有技术转让法》；而中国则在 1982 年制定了第一部与保护知识产权相关的法律《商标法》，之后又陆续出台了《专利法》（1984 年）、《技术合同法》（1987 年）、《著作权法》（1990 年）、《计算机软件保护条例》（1991 年）、《科技进步法》（1993 年）、《促进科技成果转化法》（1996 年）等。

其二，四国政府都致力于鼓励产学研有机结合，促进创新成果转化的创新环境建设。俄罗斯现有创新体系改革的特征就是确立在工业和研究机构密集的、持续的交互关系，改革的方向是鼓励产业和科技建立更好的合作关系，支持研究者的流动，以及公共和私有部门结成伙伴关系；[①] 在 20 世纪 90 年代以后，印度政府日益重视增强产学研的合作，1992 年政府资助印度理工大学成立"创新与技术转让基金会"，致力于在高等院校和企业间建立联系。印度科技部还直接成立了名为"印度国家研究开发公司"（NRDC）的国有企业，致力于将国家研究开发实验室的技术成果向工业部门转让。印度政府的《2003 科技政策》提出成立自治的技术转移组织作为大学和国家实验室的辅助组织，由它们促进知识向产业的转移，并鼓励科学家和技术专家将他们产生的知识向产业转移，成为接受经济回报的一方；2004 年巴西政府颁布了科技《创新法》，旨在鼓励产学研有机结合，并建立起一种和谐的战略伙伴关系，使科研机构和高校参与创新的全过程，以培育企业的自主创新能力，增强发展原创力，提高竞争能力，改变技术成果转

① 柳卸林、段小华：《转型中的俄罗斯国家创新体系》，《科学学研究》2003 年第 3 期。

化滞后的被动局面，促进社会经济可持续发展；1996年，中国政府颁布了《促进科技成果转化法》，成为推动创新主体间合作的代表性法律，对成果转化的组织实施及相关各方的权责益作出了明确规定。此外，中国还大力发展科技企业孵化器、科技咨询机构及生产力促进中心等促进技术成果转化的技术服务中介机构，使之成为转移、扩散科技成果和有效配置科技资源的重要渠道。

其三，四国政府都积极探索发展科技金融，为创新体系提供金融支撑子系统。1986年，印度政府决定每年划拨1亿卢比，建立印度第一家风险投资基金。据统计，2006年印度风险资本共投资94个项目，涉投金额已达505亿卢比，占同年印度私募股权市场份额的7.06%。[①] 巴西早在20世纪70年代就提出建立风险投资基金的构想，但由于受同时期经济产出反复波动的影响，到1986年才正式设立风险投资基金，此后在政府的扶持下发展迅猛，2005年巴西风险投资的规模已达6.5亿美元。[②] 受财政预算限制，投资高风险项目动力不足，俄罗斯到2000年才设立第一家风险投资基金。2006年8月，俄罗斯政府决定拨出150亿卢布（约5亿多美元）正式建立国家风险投资基金，其主要投资领域恰恰是非政府风险投资基金所不愿涉足的高技术项目和中小企业创新。[③] 需要提及的是，虽然俄罗斯政府自2000年开始非常重视风险融资平台建设，到2009年俄罗斯也已经有40多家风险基金投资创新项目，然而俄罗斯风险基金直接投资于高科技项目的投资额不足其投资总额的1%。[④] 中国政府在发展科技金融服务方面出台一系列政策文件，1985年《中共中央关于科技体制改革的决定》首次提出以风险投资的方式支持高科技产业的开发，之后陆续出台了《建立我国风险投资机制的若干意见》（1999年）、《外商投资创业投资企业的若干规定》（2001年）、《关于推进资本市场改革开放和稳定发展的若干意见》（2004年）、《创业投资管

① Sunil Mani, “Financing of Industrial Innovations in India, How Effective are Tax Incentives for R&D?” IDRC Seminer: *Comparative Study of the National Innovation Systems of BRIC Countries*, Rio de Janeiro, Brazil, 2010.

② Luiz Martins de Melo and Márcia Siqueira Rapini, “Innovation, Finance and Funding The National System of Innovation: The Brazilian Case,” IDRC Seminer: *Comparative Study of the National Innovation Systems of BRIC Countries*, Rio de Janeiro, Brazil, 2010.

③ 龚惠平：《俄罗斯国家创新体系的新发展》，《全球科技经济瞭望》2006年第12期。

④ Preliminary, “Innovation, Finance and Funding The National System of Innovation,” IDRC Seminer: *Comparative Study of the National Innovation Systems of BRIC Countries*, Rio de Janeiro, Brazil, 2010.

理暂行办法》(2005 年) 等支持风险资本投资于高新技术产业的科技金融政策性文件。与政府的大力扶持相对应，中国风险投资产业发展迅猛，2006～2009 年其资产规模年均增长 48%。截至 2010 年 9 月份，全国备案的创业投资企业已有 571 家，资本规模达 1074 亿元人民币①。

3. 在国家战略层面引导技术发展方向

巴西 2000 年推出了“新千年研究所计划”和“技术中心：创新与推广”计划，旨在跟踪国际前沿，促进国际交流和合作，营造良好的技术创新环境。2001 年科技部发布了科技创新绿皮书，同年召开了全国科技创新大会，确定了未来 10 年巴西科技发展的指导方针和战略规划。2002 年发布的《科技创新白皮书》明确提出要推动生物技术、航天、卫生等重点领域的技术创新，这为巴西制定技术创新政策奠定了基础。2005 年又召开了全国第三次科技大会，制定了巴西科技创新 10 年战略计划以及制定全国科技创新总体规划，旨在巩固和扩大全国科技创新体系，以技术创新促进社会协调发展。2007 年巴西政府公布了“2007～2010 年科学技术和创新行动计划”，提出要巩固和扩大全国科技创新体系，促进能源、生物、航天、国防、公共安全等战略领域的创新。通过制定科技发展计划，引导创新方向，整合科技资源，巴西已初步形成了技术创新政策体系。②

俄罗斯政府非常重视技术创新方向的引导与规划，2005 年批准了《2010 年俄罗斯联邦发展创新体系政策基本方向》，对国家创新体系的建设进行了中期规划。2008 年，俄罗斯政府出台了“2020 年前经济社会发展战略”，明确提出优先发展科技，实现社会经济发展方式由严重依赖自然资源出口向创新推动型转变的国家战略。2009 年，俄罗斯教科部和科学院先后推出了三个版本的“长期科技发展预测”报告，对 2030 年前科技发展进行预测。另外，俄罗斯政府还着力发挥技术优势，积极主导重大科研攻关项目的国际合作，如倡议建立国际灾害预警航空航天系统，呼吁制定太空“交通规则”，参与欧洲新一代激光研究项目等。

印度政府在国家技术发展方向预测方面也投入大量的人力物力，2003 年印

① 国家发改委财政金融司、中国投资协会创业投资专业委员会：《中国创业投资行业发展报告》，财政金融出版社，2010。

② 卢立峰、李兆友：《巴西技术创新政策演化及启示》，《技术与创新管理》2010 年第 3 期。

度政府成立由 20 个政府部门共同组成的国家技术信息预测评估委员会，出版《2020 年的印度——新千年的愿景》，对印度在技术领域的优势与弱势进行全面评估，就 2020 年印度成为全球四大经济体之一所应依赖的技术能力及技术创新方向进行评价与界定，并对纳入范畴的技术领域进行重点扶持，对国家整体技术创新的方向有着深远的影响。

中国政府一直持续推进国家科技发展战略规划的制定，20 世纪 80 年代，科学技术部先后组织实施《技术创新工程》、国家星火计划、火炬计划、国家重点科技攻关项目、高技术研究发展计划（863 计划）等科技发展计划。90 年代，科技部等政府部门先后推出科教兴国发展战略、第十个五年计划“人才、专利、技术标准”三个战略、知识创新计划等。进入 21 世纪，代表性的事件是 2006 年国家科技大会上明确把提高自主创新作为国家战略，并发布了《国家中长期科学和技术发展规划纲要（2006 ~ 2020）》，对中长期国家科学与技术发展的重点领域及其优先主题、重大专项、前沿技术等进行明确界定。

总体而言，“金砖四国”政府都是从激励机制、环境机制及引导机制三个层面建构其国家创新系统的政策体系，因此四国国家创新系统政策结构具有相似性。但是，虽然同属发展中国家，“金砖四国”各自在经济发展阶段、经济结构、资源禀赋、政治体制、技术基础、市场化程度以及历史文化背景等方面都有较大的差异。因此，四国各自政策的目标、模式、途径与方向都各有侧重，同时同一政策在不同国家的实施效果也可能存在较大的差别。

（二）“金砖四国”政府国家创新体系政策措施的相异点

1. 政策侧重点不同

巴西国家创新体系的一个重要特征就是社会经济结构的不平衡性，① 并且这一特征显著反映在收入分配结构上。据统计，2003 ~ 2006 年，巴西每年的基尼系数都在 0.55 以上，② 处于收入差距悬殊的边缘。这种收入高度集中的分配结构

---

① Rodrigue, O. , *Furtado e a Renovação da Agenda do Desenvolvimento*, In Celso Furtado e o Século XXI. Sabóia, J. ; Carvalho, F. (org.) . Barueri, SP: Manole; Rio de Janeiro: Instituto de Economia da Universidade Federal do Rio de Janeiro, 2007.

② IBGE, *Estatística do Cadastro Central de Empresas 2006*, Fundação Instituto Brasileiro de Geografia e Estatística (IBGE), Rio de Janeiro, 2008.

影响了需求和消费的模式，进而影响生产结构以及对创新的需求。[①] 由此，改变社会经济结构的相关政策也就构成了巴西国家创新体系政策措施的重要组成部分。

印度国家创新体系的显著特点是，政府在国家创新体系建设中居于绝对主导的地位。政府承担了绝大部分的研发经费支出，如上述2007年印度政府提供的经费占该国当年研发经费支出的75.3%。与此同时，研发活动也大部分集中于政府设置的研究机构。以2005年为例，在总数23万的全国研究人员中，1.59万人（69%）来自政府研究机构。[②] 由此，改变政府单边主导的局面，激励企业等主体参与创新活动，促进产学研之间的交流与互动，就成为近期印度创新政策的重点。[③]

俄罗斯的特点则在于继承了苏联时期的科技基础与科技管理体制。由此，改变国家创新体系中的计划经济形式，实现国家研发体系由中央集权的管控结构向自由市场经济环境下运行的柔性体系结构转变，就成了俄罗斯政府国家创新体系政策措施的重中之重。

中国国家创新体系政策的重心则与其经济建设为中心的国家战略紧密相关。伴随改革开放以来持续经济增长而带来的资源与环境约束，目前中国正处在转变经济增长方式的关键时期，提高企业创新能力特别是自主创新能力，依靠科技实现民族复兴与建设创新型国家成为现阶段中国国家创新体系政策措施的重点。

2. 技术基础与政策目标不一

“金砖四国”在技术基础和政策目标上特点各异：俄罗斯从“拥有”出发，以实现技术的财富效应；[④] 中国从“重点突破”开始，以实现创新型国家战略；印度从“自力更生”出发，以提高其全球竞争力；巴西则从“技术引进”开始，以实现自主创新。

俄罗斯继承了苏联先进的科学技术基础条件，这一基础即使到目前也是许多

① Cassiolato, J.; Lastres, H., “Discussing innovation and development: Converging points between the Latin American school and the Innovation Systems perspective?” GLOBELICS Working Paper Series No. 08-02, The Global Network for Economics of Learning, Innovation, and Competence Building System, 2008.

② 张俊芳：《印度国家创新系统的历史演进》，《中国青年科技》2007年第7期。

③ V. V. Krishna, “Role of The State In The Evolution of The National Innovation System In India,” IDRC Seminer: *Comparative Study of the National Innovation Systems of BRIC Countries*, Rio de Janeiro, Brazil, 2010.

④ 阿尔巴金：《俄罗斯发展前景预测——2015年最佳方案》，社会科学文献出版社，2001。

技术领域世界的领导。与此同时，俄罗斯每百万人口研发人员比例在今天仍是全世界最高的国家之一。但是俄罗斯却没能有效地将它的世界级科学能力转化为社会财富。2007 年俄罗斯高技术产品出口仅占全球出口贸易总额的 0.3%，创新产品的产值仅占本国 GDP 的 5.5%。[①] 由此，将科学能力有效转化为财富一直是 20 世纪 90 年代以来俄罗斯国家创新体系改革的目标。

中国在科技资源相对稀缺的情况下，采取计划的科技体制，集中有限的科技资源投入于对经济社会长远发展有重要意义的科研项目上，在中国科技力量的显著突破方面发挥了重要作用。1998 年，中国提出依靠科技实现民族复兴的国策，2005 年提出建设创新型国家的重大战略，2006 年进一步提出了自主创新的国家战略。

印度政府一直强调工业发展与产业技术基础，重视基础研发，并推行以政府为主导进行研发投入的自力更生的科技政策，取得了一定成效，并形成了一个完整的科技体系。1991 年经济体制改革以后，印度虽未放弃其自力更生的科技政策，但随着自身经济日益融入全球经济体系，印度更加注重全球的科技合作以及提升经济及企业的全球竞争力。2003 年印度 20 个政府部门共同出台的《2020 年的印度——新千年的愿景》文件对 2020 年印度成为全球四大经济体之一所应依赖的技术能力及技术创新方向进行评价与界定，并成为印度国家创新体系的政策目标。

巴西曾靠引进外资和技术实现了工业化，创造了"巴西奇迹"。但在这个过程中，本国企业的技术能力依然落后，缺乏国际竞争力。20 世纪 90 年代，巴西政府开始重视自主创新，并出台一系列技术创新政策，其短期的政策目标是减少本国对外部的技术依赖，中长期目标则是在关键领域实现技术突破，提升巴西的国际竞争力。[②]

3. 政策路径不同

从支持研发的侧重点看，巴西、印度和俄罗斯更侧重于基础研究，而中国则

① Tatiana Kuznetsova, "The Role of The State In National System of Innovation In Russia," IDRC Seminer: *Comparative Study of the National Innovation Systems of BRIC Countries*, Rio de Janeiro, Brazil, 2010.

② Priscila Koeller and José Luis Gordon, "The Role of The State In National System of Innovation In Brazil," IDRC Seminer: *Comparative Study of the National Innovation Systems of BRIC Countries*, Rio de Janeiro, Brazil, 2010.

侧重于应用研究。据统计，巴西政府研发经费的75%～80%用于基础研究，[①] 印度的这一比例是18%[②]，俄罗斯是13.1%[③]，而中国基础研究经费在全国研发经费支出总额中的比重仅为5.2%。[④] 从政策传导机制看，巴西、印度和俄罗斯侧重于通过对研发项目和高新技术企业提供资金资助与财税激励的方式推动国家创新体系建设，着力点在直接的创新供给；中国也非常注重通过直接的资助与财税激励的方式促进主体的创新努力，但与此同时还致力于多渠道增加创新供给，包括通过大力发展基础教育和高等教育来提高国民素质及吸收创新知识的能力，同时增加研究人员数量提升研发能力，以及积极融入全球化进程分享国际贸易及国际投资的技术溢出。

三 "金砖四国"政府与国家创新体系关系存在的问题

（一）"金砖四国"存在的共性问题

1. 过分偏重于创新的研发和技术因素

诚然，没有基于科技体系与技术积累的创新体系是不可能创造出令人满意的创新能力的。但是，创新能力不仅在于技术水平的提升，更在于新技术在生产部门的转移、扩散和应用，后者才是一个经济体获得持续高速的经济增长与国际竞争力的关键。"金砖四国"政府都在不同程度上存在过分强调创新的研发和技术因素，忽视创新成果商业化的社会、制度和市场因素问题，并由此阻碍了国家创新体系的全面协调演进。

以巴西为例，20世纪90年代以来，巴西国家创新体系政策的落脚点可以归结为三个方面：激励企业和研究机构开展创新活动、资助基础研究以及促进企业和研究机构的合作。这些聚焦于研发的创新政策带来的问题就是：第一，偏重于技术创新与优先支持研发的政策忽略了决定创新活动的其他重要因素，特别是忽

① 李明德：《巴西科技体制的发展和研发体系》，《拉丁美洲研究》2004年第3期。

② 张瑞山：《印度的科研机构布局及对中国的启示》，《南亚研究季刊》2006年第3期。

③ 科技部科技统计分析中心：《我国R&D经费支出特征的国际比较》，《科技统计报告》2008年第22期。

④ 科技部科技统计分析中心：《我国R&D经费支出特征的国际比较》，《科技统计报告》2008年第22期。

视了巴西经济社会发展的不平衡性，而后者正是巴西国家创新体系矛盾性和脆弱性的根源;[①] 第二，聚焦于建立企业和研究机构间的直接伙伴关系使得中介服务机构等其他主体参与创新过程变得更为困难;[②] 第三，技术主导型的创新政策把创新视为一个简单线性过程，而技术研发正是这个过程的源头，即"技术研发—制造—营销—用户"过程。[③] 这种过分关注技术供给的创新体系既忽视了消费者、企业等利益相关者对技术发展的影响，也因为忽视市场需求而大大降低了创新的商业转化率。

再以印度为例，直到20世纪90年代，在长达50年的时间里，印度科技政策都着眼于技术供给，其结果是建立了一个庞大的科技体系，包括一系列的"大科学"部门和多个领域的高技术积累，但这些技术能力并未能被有效利用。诚如罗森博格所言，印度代表一个低工资与发达的科技基础设施并存的现象……通往创新过程中各种公共部门和私营机构之间的联系尚有大量的工作有待开展。[④] 90年代中期以后，印度政府开始逐步关注创新的需求方，但收效甚微。印度现行创新体系的一个主要的问题仍然是缺少促进公共研究成果转移和商业化的风险资本以及中介机制的创新的生态系统。

与巴西和印度相比，俄罗斯政府单方面主导创新供给的倾向更为明显，其研发经费的61.9%由政府提供，73%的研究机构隶属于政府，78%的研究人员在政府研究机构工作，86%的研发固定资产属于公有资产。[⑤] 缺乏有效监督机制的政府主导下的技术创新导向型创新政策与依赖自然资源出口推动型经济增长方式相结合的结果是，研发部门资源使用效率低下与商业部门创新需求不足并存。这也是当下俄罗斯国家创新体系迫切需要解决的关键问题。

---

① 宋霞:《影响巴西竞争力的深层原因：国家创新体系的矛盾性和脆弱性》,《拉丁美洲研究》2008年第6期。

② Priscila Koeller and José Luis Gordon, "The Role of The State In National System of Innovation In Brazil," IDRC Seminer: *Comparative Study of the National Innovation Systems of BRIC Countries*, Rio de Janeiro, Brazil, 2010.

③ 保罗·特罗特:《创新管理和新产品开发》，中国人民大学出版社，2005。

④ Rosenberg, N, *Inside the Black Box: Technology and Economics*, Cambridge: Cambridge University Press, 1990.

⑤ V. V. Krishna, "Role of The State In The Evolution of The National Innovation System In India," IDRC Seminer: *Comparative Study of the National Innovation Systems of BRIC Countries*, Rio de Janeiro, Brazil, 2010.

中国同样存在过度关注创新供给的问题，1998 年至今大量的创新政策都集中于科研机构改组和改进工业企业创新能力上，① 长期存在的经济、科技、教育和工业部门相互脱节的状态依然未能得到有效解决。

2. 各种政策缺乏有效融合

毫无疑问，政府制定创新体系政策时必须基于整个国家的全面发展来考量。由此，创新体系的设计就不能不考虑本国特定的历史、经济与社会发展环境问题，不能不考虑创新支撑及环境子系统中的教育政策、宏观经济政策及社会发展政策等相关政策之间的有效融合问题。

以巴西为例，其创新政策与教育政策明显脱节。在技术供给主导型的创新政策推动下，巴西拥有先进的高等教育人才培养体系和研究体系。但其中小学教育滞后，国民整体素质偏低，致使企业严重缺乏合格的、熟练的、能够吸收创新知识的人力资源。② 据调查，44.9% 的工业企业缺乏合格的劳动力，服务业企业更为严重，60.3% 的电信企业、67.6% 的信息服务业缺乏合格的劳动力。③ 其结果是，企业不得不花大量精力和财力弥补大部分员工基础教育的不足，无力培训高技能人才，无力开展创新活动。科技政策与教育政策缺乏有效的融合意味着，巴西创新体系丧失了诸多发展与演进的机会。④

俄罗斯创新政策缺乏有效融合，从而导致政府研发部门的改革严重滞后于其他经济部门。肇始于 20 世纪 90 年代的市场化改革虽然涉及俄罗斯经济体系的各个方面，但科研体系领域的市场化改革却收效甚微。2007 年的俄罗斯经济中只有 3.3% 的组织和企业是公有的，但在研究机构中这一比例却高达 70% 以上。⑤

---

① Lv Ping, "The Role of The State In National System of Innovation-China Case Study," IDRC Seminer: *Comparative Study of the National Innovation Systems of BRIC Countries*, Rio de Janeiro, Brazil, 2010.

② 宋霞：《影响巴西竞争力的深层原因：国家创新体系的矛盾性和脆弱性》，《拉丁美洲研究》2008 年第 6 期。

③ PINTEC, *Pesquisa Industrial de Inovação Tecnológica 2003 – 2005.* Instituto Brasileiro de Geografia e Estatística - IBGE. Rio de Janeiro, 2007.

④ Priscila Koeller and José Luis Gordon, "The Role of The State In National System of Innovation In Brazil," IDRC Seminer: *Comparative Study of the National Innovation Systems of BRIC Countries*, Rio de Janeiro, Brazil, 2010.

⑤ V. V. Krishna, "Role of The State In The Evolution of The National Innovation System In India," IDRC Seminer: *Comparative Study of the National Innovation Systems of BRIC Countries*, Rio de Janeiro, Brazil, 2010.

绝大部分研究机构的经费体系与监管规则依然保留计划经济的形式，其结果是，俄罗斯的科技体系存在一种政府研发投入持续增长与科技部门发展明显停滞并存的相互矛盾的趋势，大量科技资源低效使用。

印度这方面的问题表现为缺少一个由风险投资和各类中介组织共同参与的能够促进技术转移和商业化的创新生态系统，加上国家实验室和大学研究机构掌握了大部分科研经费，科技能力得不到有效利用。与此同时，印度至今尚未对国家创新体系政策作系统化的安排，其科技与创新政策是按照部门（如航空、原子能、生物制药、计算机软件等）和问题导向（如气候变化、灾害管理等）来设计的，各种政策和创新主体之间缺乏协调和网络化交互的机制，远非一个完整的体系。①

就中国而言，由于每个政府部门的职责与目标各不一样，不同部门在创新管理过程中各自分立，缺乏有效的协调机制，这也极大限制了中国创新能力的提升。②

（二）“金砖四国”存在的个性问题

1. 巴西

20 世纪 80 年代中期以来，巴西政府就国家创新体系的建立和完善出台了一系列的政策措施，但从执行效果看，其结果并不令人满意。根据世界经济论坛的评价，巴西的综合竞争力排名一直处于中等偏下的地位。尽管近几年巴西经济持续增长，但排名仍不尽如人意。2006 年巴西的国际竞争力全球排名第 62 位，2007 年跌至第 72 位，2008 年第 64 位，2009 年第 56 位。③

上述问题的根源在于，巴西国家创新体系的矛盾性和脆弱性，使得巴西先进的科学技术资源未能有效转化为现实的生产力和竞争力。④ 具体表现如下。

---

① V. V. Krishna, “Role of The State In The Evolution of The National Innovation System In India,” IDRC Seminer: *Comparative Study of the National Innovation Systems of BRIC Countries*, Rio de Janeiro, Brazil, 2010.

② Lv Ping, “The Role of The State In National System of Innovation-China Case Study,” IDRC Seminer: *Comparative Study of the National Innovation Systems of BRIC Countries*, Rio de Janeiro, Brazil, 2010.

③ 世界经济论坛网站，http://www.weforum.org。

④ 宋霞：《影响巴西竞争力的深层原因：国家创新体系的矛盾性和脆弱性》，《拉丁美洲研究》2008 年第 6 期。

其一，经济的持续增长和严重的贫富两极分化并存，使知识和创新的发展与分配严重失衡，造成巴西的知识创新呈现精英科学和满足穷人就业需求的“适当技术”并存的特征，创造出来的新知识因有效需求不足而难以进入生产应用阶段。

其二，巴西的科技进步迅猛，但创新能力发展很不平衡，创新行为只局限在少数领域，技术开发战略在很大程度上没有惠及多数产业。第一，巴西缺乏一种知识产权保护、注册和申请专利的文化，如同圣保罗州研究基金会主席卡洛斯·沃格特所言，巴西创新体系中存在“文化障碍”。据世界知识产权组织的报告称，世界各国2005年共注册专利60万项左右，比2004年增长6.6%。而巴西的知识产权部门2005年一共仅收到1.61万份专利申请，注册专利2349项，注册专利数量比2004年减少13.8%，而且注册专利的90%均来自外国企业。[①] 第二，历史上形成的独立的科学研究模式使巴西缺乏一种将科学技术成果应用于经济和社会领域的创新机制。2004年新出台的巴西《创新法》鼓励大学和企业联合创新的做法就引来科学团体的极大反对，他们认为将大学置于市场压力之下会破坏知识发展的平衡。这种创新只是为了产业的利益而不顾及与民众有关的社会发展的需求，还容易导致公共资源的私有化。第三，巴西重视高等教育而忽视基础教育的教育体制，导致难以找到具有足够教育水平的技术工人，进而影响本土企业掌握先进生产技术的能力，给创新带来长期危害。

其三，知识和创新过度集中于大学和公共研究机构的“理论”研究，占经济主体的民族中小企业（其中小型和微型企业占巴西企业的90%）缺乏创新动力和创新资金。巴西应用经济研究所2007年的统计数据表明，全国企业科技投入不到其全部收入的0.6%，利用政府创新扶持基金的企业不到19%。[②]

当然，这些问题多数是历史沉淀的结果，绝非一朝一夕可以解决的。进入21世纪以来，巴西政府已意识到并开始着手解决这些问题，如2004年制定的《创新法》、2007年的“创新行动计划”等，都旨在鼓励企业创新，促进产学研结合，扩展和巩固国家创新体系。有一点是明确的，除了现有的做法之外，如果

① 世界知识产权组织网站，http：//www.wipo.int/portal。

② Priscila Koeller and José Luis Gordon，“The Role of The State In National System of Innovation In Brazil，” IDRC Seminer：*Comparative Study of the National Innovation Systems of BRIC Countries*，Rio de Janeiro，Brazil，2010.

不彻底改革不平等的分配制度、不合理的教育体制及传统的创新“文化障碍”，巴西国家创新体系的矛盾性和脆弱性很难得到根本的解决。换言之，宏观经济政策、教育政策、社会发展政策与创新政策之间相互脱节，是巴西国家创新体系取得成效的主要障碍。

2. 俄罗斯

俄罗斯政府在构建和完善国家创新体系方面做了大量工作。从俄罗斯最新的创新政策文件可知，俄罗斯正逐渐向国际惯例靠近。[①] 但从执行的效果看，收效甚微。一方面，俄罗斯自然资源出口依赖型经济增长模式并没有得到根本改变。据统计，过去几年俄罗斯燃料类产品出口在总出口中的比重一直居高不下，2004年这一指标为59.9%，2005年达到61%，2006年进一步升高至67.8%，2007年与2006年基本持平，为67.7%，而2008年则上升到73%。[②] 目前，俄罗斯GDP的30%、国家预算收入的50%～60%和外汇收入的60%均来自资源性产品的出口。[③] 另一方面，企业创新需求不足的局面没有得到根本改观。2007年，在俄罗斯研发项目中企业负责的仅占10.6%，只有5.5%的创新成果来自企业。[④] 其深层次原因主要有三。

其一，濒于“资源诅咒”怪圈的循环。丰富的自然资源使俄罗斯企业投资于研发创新比投资于采矿业的风险更高，而利润更少，企业对创新活动兴趣索然。换言之，在拥有大量自然资源且出口自然资源的收益远高于创新收益的条件下，鼓励创新的政策自然犹如石沉大海。可以说，单一依靠油气与自然资源驱动的经济增长方式既是俄罗斯国家创新体系要解决的关键问题，也是俄罗斯国家创新体系收效甚微的症结所在。因此，只有宏观经济结构得到改变，企业才有望在研发和创新中扮演一个中心的角色，商业部门创新需求不足的问题才有望得到根本解决。

其二，市场调节机制缺失。在经济转型过程中，俄罗斯尚未建立完备或基本的

---

① Tatiana Kuznetsova, “The Role of The State In National System of Innovation In Russia,” IDRC Seminer: *Comparative Study of the National Innovation Systems of BRIC Countries*, Rio de Janeiro, Brazil, 2010.

② 郑新立：《国际经济分析与展望》，社会科学文献出版社，2010。

③ 国务院发展研究中心欧亚社会发展研究所主编《欧亚形势与展望（2009）》。

④ Tatiana Kuznetsova, “The Role of The State In National System of Innovation In Russia,” IDRC Seminer: *Comparative Study of the National Innovation Systems of BRIC Countries*, Rio de Janeiro, Brazil, 2010.

市场机制。这样，市场体制下的企业的内生和外生调节功能就难以形成。典型的案例是，以私有化为核心的所有制改革使俄罗斯的企业和科技组织已具有明晰的产权关系，但由于大部分俄罗斯工业企业没有强大的研发能力，而具有强大研发能力的科研组织原来又不是企业，在要素市场和资本市场不具备或作用微弱的情况下，两个系统的组织仍然没有进行组织间的紧密联合的渠道。换言之，在市场机制不完备的情况下，所有制的变革可能并没有促进企业的创新能力，反而成为提升创新能力的短期障碍。因而，俄罗斯工业企业仍然没有成为创新中应有的重要力量。①

其三，行政管理协调不力。俄罗斯科技管理体系层次复杂，部门条块分割，缺乏有效协调的机制，大大降低了研发资源的使用效率。俄罗斯科技管理体系纵向上分为立法机构、管理部门和活动主体三个层级；层级内部又有分工，如国家杜马中设教育及科学委员会，该委员会下分设教育和科学两个分委员会。横向上，同一层次又有相互制约的机构，如国家杜马和联邦委员会各设管辖范围包括科学及科技问题的委员会。科技体系设计的繁复，导致跨部门协调机构的增加，如“跨部门科技政策协调委员会”既有民口又有军口各部的代表，也有联邦机关、地方和学术界与科学管理有关部门的代表。这种部门众多、条块分割的格局，既影响了决策效率，也给新技术的开发和利用造成极大的障碍。2009 年 5 月，俄罗斯总统梅德韦杰夫主持召开的“经济现代化和科技创新委员会”会议，就曾严厉批评科技主管部门工作不得力，导致经济结构调整举步维艰，企业创新积极性停滞不前，科研经费屡遭挪用。②

最后，缺乏企业家精神。除上述经济环境和制度方面的问题外，缺少企业家精神的文化因素也制约了俄罗斯国家创新体系的演进。

综上分析，俄罗斯国家创新体系除在现有的微观层次方面存在一定问题外，在更为宏观的体制层面也存在较多问题。在某种程度上看，后者才是解决问题的根本。

3. 印度

印度国家创新体系的特征可概括为政府主导、技术主导与自力更生主导。这种模式的优势在于可以集中资源实现关键领域的技术突破以及特定的国家战略目标，对国家科技体系及创新能力的建构意义重大，但也存在自身的问题。

---

① 张寅生、鲍鸥：《俄罗斯科技创新体系改革进展》，《经济社会体制比较》2005 年第 3 期。

② 董悦：《未来科技：俄印巴西新兴之路》，2010 年 6 月 2 日《经济参考报》。

其一，过分强调政府主导及其集中化。印度的创新决策由于过分强调政府的主导，抑制了众多企业满足市场需求的"草根创新"，既不利于形成创造力迸发的创新社会局面，又因为对政府资助缺乏有效的监管手段而造成创新资源的浪费。

其二，过分偏重国防技术。众多政府研究机构主导研究的项目偏重于国防技术、空间技术和原子能技术，忽视了与经济发展和人们生活关系密切的民用科学技术；科学技术进步和经济发展的关联不够紧密；技术能力提升与工业需求脱节，大量技术成果被束之高阁。

其三，过分强调自力更生。由于过分强调自力更生，创新政策往往出现导致忽视吸收全球知识的倾向。正如世界银行 2006 年印度企业观察报告的调研结果所言，对于大多数印度企业来说，获得全球新知识比在国内创造知识更有利于提高劳动生产率。

除上述问题外，印度国家创新体系还面临其他一些挑战。比如，研发支出占 GDP 的比重偏低，2007 年不足 1%，在"金砖四国"中是最低的；高等教育入学率低，研究型大学少且缺乏创新的文化；缺少提高科技部门执行创新政策效率的监管机制等。

4. 中国

改革开放以来，中国政府在各个层次上采取了一系列措施推动国家创新体系的建设，如制定政策、实施科技规划、直接投资或资助研发、税收激励、公共采购、科技奖励以及包括管理要素在内的科技资源配置等。这些举措在创造一个良好的科技进步与创新环境体系方面发挥了极其重要的作用，但总体而言，国家创新体系所取得的进步与中国经济社会发展需求间的缺口依然存在，仍有不少问题与困难有待解决。

其一，主体创新能力仍然较弱。首先，企业还不完全是科技成果商业化的主力，多数企业缺乏技术创新能力，参与市场竞争主要依靠成本优势，通常注重设备引进，忽视消化、吸收和创新。虽然联想、华为等中国高科技企业在国际市场上引人关注，但不到 1% 的中国企业申请 1 个及以上专利，只有 0.03% 的企业拥有自主知识产权。① 其次，中国科研机构缺乏原始创新的能力、科技发展的支撑

① Liu Weiling, "High Tide," *China Daily*, 12/12/2005, p. 9, http://www.chinadaily.com.cn/english/doc/2005-12/12/content_502577.htm.

条件，科技资源整合与利用的效率都还比较低。再次，大学作为人才培养与创新的重要平台，其潜力尚未被充分发挥，大学科技资源利用的机制与体系都还有待完善。最后，服务于创新的中介机构力量薄弱，无法满足创新要素的整合与扩散以及充分发挥创新网络功能的需要。

其二，科技成果商业化的环境条件有待改善。目前支持自主创新成果产业化的市场环境仍有许多缺陷。首先，促进科技成果产业化的法律法规还不完善。其次，知识产权缺乏保护，侵犯知识产权的情况还比较严重，加大了企业从自主创新中获得高额回报的难度。再次，缺乏扶持科技创新成果产业化的融资体系。最后，自主创新成果在市场化早期阶段缺少引导和培养，低效的政府采购措施无法为自主创新成果的产业化提供足够的支持。

其三，创新机制还不完善。首先，开放、交互、竞争、协作的机制尚未形成，创新要素彼此分离，缺乏协作，知识和信息流动效率低。其次，产学研交互机制有待改进，大学、研究机构与企业间缺少联系和协作。再次，科技投资机制未能满足创新的需要，近年来政府科研经费支出虽然持续增长，但低于同期财政经费总支出的增长幅度，政府科研经费使用也缺乏有效的监督机制。同时，缺少引导和鼓励各种社会资源投资于创新的有效机制。最后，市场机制在引导和促进创新方面的主导作用尚未充分发挥。

其四，创新文化未能满足发展的需要。首先，部分高校和科研机构还保留行政管理的方式，学术民主不够充分。其次，协作精神不足，阻碍了创新主体间的交流和协作，增加了创新的难度。再次，急功近利的现象还比较严重。最后，竞争意识和创新精神还有待加强。受长期计划经济体制下的科研体系和激励机制的影响，研究人员缺乏竞争的动力，缺少企业家精神与勇气。

四 趋同性与根植性：两个简要结论

前文从投资、政策及存在的问题三个方面对“金砖四国”政府在国家创新体系中的作用作了梳理与比较，我们可以得出如下两点结论。

（一）“金砖四国”构建国家创新体系具有趋同性的倾向

政府作用和政策协调在国家创新体系建构及国家创新能力演进方面具有关键

性的作用，但四国政府制定的政策与采取的措施却日益趋同。尽管"金砖四国"的历史、制度与经济社会环境有较大差异，针对各自国家创新体系的建构与完善，四国政府制定政策和采取举措的力度、方向、目标、路径等也都各有侧重，但采取的政策措施却大同小异，例如，加大政府研发投入、完善法律制度环境、制定国家创新战略规划、支持创新基础平台建设、鼓励企业成为创新主体、培养技术创新人才、促进产学研协作等。四国政府在国家创新体系建设中扮演的角色大多集中于为创新活动创造良好的环境和合适的机制、解决市场失灵、引导创新资源的有效配置、促进和激励各种创新要素的相互作用、监控和评价国家创新体系建构过程等方面。

总体而言，"金砖四国"建设国家创新体系的政策正日益趋同，并与最佳的国际实践日益接近。当然，衡量政府在国家创新体系中的作用不在于出台了多少政策文件，也不在于促进了多少技术成果的产生，而在于最终对本国经济社会发展所产生的作用与效果。

（二）"金砖四国"构建国家创新体系缺乏根植性的现状

创新具有地域根植性，国家创新体系的建构具有深刻的经济社会与历史文化背景特征。正如迪肯所言，创新是社会性和制度性深植的社会过程，技术供给的增加并不必然自动带来经济社会的发展。① 虽然国家创新系统的目的在于促进技术创新的发生、扩散和持续，但除了从技术供给（直接作用于创新，如研发政策等）层面考虑外，还必须从更为宏观的社会经济条件及历史文化背景的视角（间接作用于创新，如发展政策等）来考虑政府构建国家创新体系的着力点，考虑社会发展政策与创新政策的融合，考虑如何打破诸如"资源诅咒"怪圈以解决特定的发展问题。

换言之，创新政策要作用于经济社会发展，就必须考虑本国的现实，而不仅仅是照搬发达国家的现成药方。只有从经济社会全面发展的视角，从系统性和根植性的角度考虑本国的创新政策，才有可能构建一个高效的国家创新体系。与此同时，一国国家创新体系建构的过程也是本国社会经济结构变迁和差异化战略及国家竞争优势建构的过程。

---

① Dicken, P. *Global Shift*, 3rd edition, New York: The Guilford Press, 1998.

“金砖四国”：国际安全领域合作视角

鲍里斯·F. 马丁诺夫　吴孝芹（译）*

“金砖四国”在国家、区域和全球安全领域的合作，全方位显示了现代国际安全合作的理念，展现出自己的特色。“金砖四国”对国际法持有特有的尊重态度，对当前国际问题有特定的“文明”观念。很明显，在“实力均衡”（balances of forces）时代处理国际问题的方法已不适用于当前的国际问题。现代世界缺乏创新，（仅有的）创新来自于国家的文明，并与所谓的“大”政策脱离，且在20世纪声名扫地。

但是，即便新兴的行为体能对世界秩序产生积极影响，同样会存在安全问题，它们的崛起可能会遭受质疑。它们面临的安全威胁既有内部的，如经济快速增长引发的固有问题，也有外部的，如他国的恶意（ill will of others）。因此，“金砖四国”重申它们在当前发展阶段的经济、政治、文化、环境及信息事务上的基本安全权利是很自然的。

“金砖四国”面临的安全威胁各有不同。中国和俄罗斯既是核大国又是安理会常任理事国，印度也是有核武器的国家，这三个国家似乎可以保障自己的安全。但是，事实并非如此。目前，安全威胁大多数是非军事性的，并且主要集中在国家领土范围之内。核超级大国苏联的垮台就是证明。

---

* 鲍里斯·F. 马丁诺夫，俄罗斯莫斯科国际关系学院教授；吴孝芹，太原工业学院管理工程系讲师。

"金砖四国"中的俄罗斯与多民族的中国和印度面临相似的安全问题：激进民族主义、仇外主义（xenophobia）、分离主义、政治极端主义、恐怖主义、腐败和毒品交易（narcotraffic）。为应对这些问题，俄罗斯、中国、哈萨克斯坦、乌兹别克斯坦、塔吉克斯坦、吉尔吉斯斯坦在2001年建立了"上海合作组织"。印度显示了对该组织的兴趣，成为该组织的观察员。同年，上海合作组织成员签署了反恐怖主义、反分裂主义的专门公约。随后上海合作组织成立了反恐怖主义专门委员会，指导集体措施（如情报交换、经验交流）、联合演习、金融控制措施等。

人们经常会听到这样的观点，即从安全角度看，巴西与俄罗斯距离遥远，因此，对俄罗斯而言巴西不如临近的同属"金砖四国"的中国和印度重要。这是一种短视的观点，与一些重要的当代趋势相矛盾。第一，我们不能忽略那些业已存在、目前尚不突出，但在21世纪20年代可能会迅速恶化的问题。第二，我们决不可忽视全球化的影响。全球化不仅加速了人员、产品和信息的流动，而且使貌似距离遥远的国家之间产生了相似的问题。第三，有足够证据表明，当国际法律被遗弃和国际秩序形同虚设时，任何国际安全领域缔结的条约和协议均不应因循守旧。按照这一观点，所有金砖国家，包括俄罗斯与巴西的合作似乎是不可或缺的。

表1是对巴西和俄罗斯合作走向所作的预测。

表1　巴西和俄罗斯合作走向

安全领域	巴西的意愿和立场	与俄罗斯合作的前景
宪　法	高/长期积极倾向	战略伙伴关系
经　济	中高/积极倾向	积极经济合作
能　源	中高/长期积极倾向	联合项目、国际市场合作
科学与技术	中等/积极倾向	联合项目与研究
自然资源	高/	实现共同政策
生　态	高/	实现共同政策
农业与食品	高/	国际市场合作，实现共同政策
信息安全	中低/积极倾向	实现共同政策
社会保障	中低/积极倾向	共同目标和价值标准，实现共同政策
军事安全	中低/积极倾向	武器销售，军事与技术合作
"文明"与文化安全	中等/积极倾向	实现共同政策
人权保障	中等/积极倾向	建立共同联系
区域与全球问题	中等/积极倾向	在大多实际问题上进行广泛合作

虽然表1并不详尽，但我们仍可从中看出如下特征。首先，在安全领域，俄罗斯与巴西在很多问题上立场相一致，这为两国合作开启了广泛的合作空间。其次，在上述13个可归类的领域中，巴西在6个（原文为10个，实为6个。——编者注）领域中的立场可用"高"或"中高"表示。由于该国过去十年的发展及领导人的决策均有广泛的民众基础，可以预期其他几个安全领域的重要性在未来5~10年将急剧上升。因此，巴西与俄罗斯的安全合作将进一步深化。

我们认为共同应对全球问题是最重要的，如多边外交政策、国际法的作用、重构国际组织（包括联合国组织）、反恐怖主义、毒品交易和盗版、核不扩散、人权、国际贸易及其他事务的反歧视等。在外交文件中，我们经常将这些立场描述为"接近"或"一致"。

但是，我们迟早应将关注重点置于安全战略的最新方向，如与气候变化有直接关联的自然资源、生态和能源安全等问题。而且，不久我们将有必要在信息安全领域进行合作。

我们需要注意最新通过的一个文件——《2020俄罗斯联邦国家安全战略》（The Strategy of the National Security of Russian Federation until 2020）。该文件称，长期世界政策中心将围绕能源资源的拥有情况。"信息战"将与世界人口、生态状况恶化一起盛行。在这种状况下，不排除使用武力的可能。这与巴西2005年的国防政策文件完全一致。该文件把生态和环境安全风险用"世界淡水储藏、广袤的海洋区域、能源资源和宇宙空间的争端"表述。文件提出，巴西亚马逊地区（约占巴西领土的52%）是最脆弱的区域，拥有独一无二的生物多样性、丰富的矿产和水利资源，同时这里也是人口密度最小的区域——每平方公里1人。亚马逊地区有7个州的人口密度超过每平方公里3.35人，而面积最大的亚马孙州的人口密度仅为每平方公里1.79人。

"巴西将保持高度戒备，重申其对巴西亚马逊地区的绝对主权。巴西将采取措施发展和保护该地区，反对任何外部力量对其保护、发展和防卫亚马逊地区决策的不合理要求。不允许任何组织或个人作为企图削弱巴西主权的国外政治和经济利益集团的工具。照料亚马逊地区使之服务人类、服务巴西是巴西人的事。"上述立场包含在2008年12月的最新文件中。之后的文件又指出，"这就要求传统军事力量发展出一些非传统军事力量的特点，特别是地面军事力量。拥有这种特点的武装力量应是能在未来可能出现的多种环境下运转的军队"。

巴西文件中提到的具体威胁，有助于我们理解俄罗斯广袤的西伯利亚、北极地区和远东地区同样面临的人口减少问题。那里蕴藏着俄罗斯98%的石油、68%的煤炭、95%的天然气和89%的淡水资源（在贝加尔湖和西伯利亚河）。需要指出的是，巴西和俄罗斯在淡水资源储量上分别排世界第一位和第二位。据一些科学家研究，淡水很快将变成比石油和天然气更紧缺的资源。俄罗斯西伯利亚地区的人口密度在每平方公里1~10人之间波动，很多地方不足1人，与巴西亚马逊地区人口最稀少的地方接近。

为了阐明两国即将面临的可能威胁，我们引用美国作家F. 希尔和K. 加迪（《西伯利亚诅咒》，布鲁金斯，2003）对俄罗斯的建议，即不是在地理上，而是在"经济"上"加紧联系"。作者还建议给跨国公司让渡更多的经济主权，让俄罗斯保留对这些区域进行政治监管的模糊权力。尽管任何人都清楚没有经济主权就不可能有政治主权。

我们认为，诸如俄罗斯、巴西、中国、印度以及其他一些国家在全球的地位特征并不取决于其民主发展水平或在消除社会经济不平等方面取得的成就，而在于这些国家是否有能力有效控制自己的领土，在于能源和生态长期发展战略的正确实施。

四国在基本国家安全文件中提及的其他合作领域为外太空安全。不要忘记，在当代控制了外太空就意味着同时控制了气候、领土、自然资源、能源储藏、海洋和淡水资源。曾有作家预见，过去国家间的冲突在当前将变为对宇宙、海洋、极地的控制权进行强化或"重新分配"。未来对信息控制的斗争也将进一步增强。

国际实践表明，任何对国际秩序的潜在威胁只有在国际社会长期忽视的情况下才会演变为真正的危险。这完全适用于目前日益加剧的恐怖主义问题。根据当前的国际形势，"金砖四国"的一个主要任务是阻止产生新的可能导致国际战争并毁灭全人类的全球威胁。

“金砖四国”的意义、合作基础及在世界格局中的角色

许文鸿*

全球性金融危机背景下的世界经济仍处于变化之中，谋求和平、可持续发展和促进平等合作已成为时代的要求，开展广泛而积极的国际合作是应对新威胁和新挑战、克服国际金融危机等全球性问题的重要而有效的途径。

“金砖四国”（BRICs）由一个经济学家的构想变为一种国际合作的机制和国际对话的平台，已成为带动全球经济成长的重要动能之一，未来只要能有效地加强成员国之间的合作，就将有助于强化“金砖四国”在世界经济体系中的地位，给四国乃至世界都带来更多的发展机会，从而成为推动全球经济复苏、发展乃至繁荣的积极因素。本文试从“金砖四国”兴起的意义、四国加强合作的共同基础、“金砖四国”的未来以及中国与“金砖四国”在国际格局中的角色等方面进行阐述。

一 “金砖四国”兴起的意义

自从地理大发现以来，西方国家的影响力逐渐控制了世界，“言必称希腊”[①]曾经是一个时代的潮流，“西化”或“美国化”一度成为“现代化”和“全球化”的代名词。进入新千年以来，一系列事件的发生表明，非西方世界开始变

---

* 许文鸿，中国社会科学院俄罗斯东欧中亚所助理研究员。

① “言必称希腊”一语，出自毛泽东《改造我们的学习》，《毛泽东选集》第3卷，人民出版社，1991。

得日益重要，尤其是"9·11"事件和2008年开始的全球性金融危机表明：以美国为代表的西方发展模式只是世界发展过程中的众多模式之一，这一模式也存在一定的问题，它不是也不应该是唯一的模式；同时，以美国和西方国家为主导的国际格局也正在悄然发生着渐进式的变化。"金砖四国"从美国经济学家吉姆·奥尼尔的天才构想变为2009年6月的叶卡捷琳堡的"金砖四国"首脑会议的召开乃至机制化就是这一系列变化的最好例证。

"金砖四国"之所以引起世人瞩目，主要是因为它们的规模和发展轨迹具有标志性意义：

——中国、俄罗斯、巴西都是幅员辽阔的大国。

——中国、印度是世界上人口最多的两个大国，巴西是世界第五大人口大国。

——俄罗斯拥有不可思议的巨大的已探明的资源。

——巴西资源丰富、耕地潜力巨大、水热资源充足，是南半球最大的发展中国家。

"金砖四国"的领土总面积占世界陆地总面积的26%，人口占全球总人口的42.9%，国内生产总值占世界总量的15.5%。"金砖四国"的发展在某种意义上讲就是世界上将近2/3人口的发展。从近年的经济增长速度来看，"金砖四国"的增长速度比吉姆·奥尼尔为首的高盛团队的最乐观的预测还要快：

——根据国际货币基金组织的统计，2006~2008年，四国经济平均增长率为10.7%。2000~2008年，"金砖四国"对全球经济增长贡献率超过30%。而在金融危机重挫西方发达国家的2007~2009年，这一比例更上升至45%。

——在高盛2001年的报告中，奥尼尔提出"金砖四国"的经济在2010年将超过全球GDP的10%。实际上，当2007年临近结束的时候，他们在全球经济中的分量已经达到15%。①

① 《金砖四国与金钻十一国》，2007年12月18日，详见http：//www.21cbh.com/HTML/2007-12-31/HTML_ SUHPF14KRII4.html。

——“金砖四国”贸易量在全球的比例近年也持续上升，仅2008～2009年期间，就提高了约两个百分点，达到约13%。巴西外交部政治事务秘书贾古里波（Roberto Jaguaribe）表示，“2008～2014年，‘金砖四国’将贡献61.3%的全球经济增长”。①

——四国外汇储备总和有近三万亿美元。

——2010年7月31日，中国人民银行副行长易纲宣布，中国已经超越日本，成为世界第二大经济体。②

不仅如此，在美国金融机构深受重创，欧洲各国饱受债务危机困扰之际，“金砖四国”的银行体系完好无损，经济体系稳定运行。除了俄罗斯受影响比较深之外，其余三国都在此次危机中显示了抵御危机的超强能力。经济增长的活力成为“金砖四国”影响力及期望值空前提升的重要背景。从某种意义上来说，“金砖四国”的发展代表着世界经济增长的主要推动力量和未来发展的潜力。“金砖四国”为消除本次国际金融危机的影响，促进全球经济的复苏发挥了积极的作用。经过本次金融经济危机的考验，“金砖四国”被证明是维护世界经济发展，保持世界稳定繁荣的“砖”。

同时，“金砖四国”不是传统意义上的西方国家，它们的发展模式都同典型的西方发展模式有所不同：中国在探索中国特色的社会主义发展道路；俄罗斯在普京团队的治理下，依靠制度创新和经济创新实现俄罗斯的现代化，寻找俄罗斯的复兴之路；印度虽然深受西方的影响，但印度的发展模式显然同西方的发展模式有所不同；而巴西的“再次崛起”所依靠的也是与西方不同的拉美发展模式。在以美国为代表的西方模式遭遇危机、发展乏力的背景下，“金砖四国”的发展意味着非西方经济发展模式的新潜力和可能。“金砖四国”的发展，标志着世界对非西方发展模式的探索。

此外，“金砖四国”之间的国际合作与协调，增强了它们在全球所有领域的

① “BRIC summit to focus on economic, financial issues”，2010年4月9日，详见http：//www.china.org.cn/business/2010－04/09/content_19779476.htm。

② 易纲、胡舒立：《人民币汇率制度的最佳选择》，2010年7月30日，详见中国国家外汇管理局网站，http：//www.safe.gov.cn/model_safe/news/new_detail.jsp？ID＝90000000000000000，814&id＝2。

话语权，不论是气候变暖、能源需求及价格、粮食、环境等全球性问题，还是部分区域性问题（如在伊朗核问题中，巴西联合土耳其积极参与斡旋并于2010年最终达成就德黑兰研究堆燃料供应问题签署的协议就是一个很好的例证）。"金砖四国"的影响力在显著增强。

除了"金砖四国"，高盛还提出了"金钻十一国"（N-11），即仅次于"金砖四国"的十一个国家。[①] 当前，全球经济复苏预期尚不明朗，全球仍面临诸多复杂的问题，由少数几个发达国家单独承担领导全球使命的时代已经不复存在。因此，最理想的解决全球问题的方案就是给予"金砖四国"为代表的非西方新兴力量以平等的地位和应有的话语权，在发展中国家和发达国家之间加强对话与合作，各国共同应对全球问题并达成一些有执行力的协议，如共同致力于解决经济、金融等方面的全球课题，建立更加平衡、公平、长效、利于世界经济全面复兴的新的国际经济、金融、贸易秩序。

二 "金砖四国"合作的基础

"金砖四国"由高盛经济学家描绘的未来世界发展状况的一种愿景发展为一个国际对话的平台，并成为一个正在形成中的国际性经济团体。尽管已经经历过两次首脑峰会和多次各级别的对话与合作，但它的地位和作用以及未来的发展方向在当前的国际经济、政治格局中还没有得到客观的反映，它的影响和地位或被有意无意把放大和拔高，或被贬得毫无价值。一方面，高盛认为"金砖四国"有无限的发展潜力；另一方面，也有人认为，"金砖四国"在文化背景、发展方式、宗教信仰、社会政治制度和经济发展状况上很不相同，彼此间没有长期的合作同盟关系，相互还存在着明显的比较竞争关系，即使在有共同利益的目标，如自由贸易、能源定价以及如何改革现行制度方面也存在根本性的分歧。因此，有人预言，"金砖四国"可能将只是一个类似于影响力有限的"上海合作组织"那样的国际"准政治组织"，它不可能成为像"G8"或"G20"那样能对全球经济格局和经济秩序产生"话语权影响"的"经济俱乐部"，其未来所能起到的影响

① Next Eleven，N-11："金钻十一国"是指亚洲的韩国、印尼、越南、菲律宾、巴基斯坦、孟加拉，非洲的尼日利亚、埃及，拉丁美洲的墨西哥，中东的伊朗以及欧洲的土耳其。

力也是微乎其微的。我们认为，“金砖四国”作为一个国际经济政治对话平台，其生命力和影响力在于成员国之间紧密地相互配合与相互协作。只有四国之间密切协作，在应对国际问题时发出共同声音，才能充分证明和拓展其影响力。正确认识“金砖四国”的潜力及其未来就要客观认识和了解该组织所面临的任务，合作的基础以及各成员国对该组织的期望和目标。只有这样，才能对“金砖四国”的未来发展有比较客观的认识。

“金砖四国”这一命名就是由四国的经济和金融状况产生的，因而在经济和金融领域内加强合作，如新的国际金融秩序的建立、促进世界经济的恢复和发展、反对贸易保护主义等是“金砖四国”合作的基础和起点。同时，能源安全、气候变化等全球性的重大问题也是四国协调与合作的重点。

（一）新的国际金融秩序的建立

此次金融危机使得全球经济遭受重创，一次金融危机的代价相当于进行了多次世界大战，给世界经济和各国人民的生活带来严重的影响。四国认为，除了在危机期间采取一切必要的反危机措施外，推动建立新的国际金融秩序，为世界经济的发展建立长效机制应该是国际社会共同努力的方向和目标。为此，四国将在以下几个问题上达成共同的认识。

1. 改进国际金融监管体制

金融是现代经济的核心，经济全球化的过程必然伴随着金融全球化的进程。随着金融自由化、金融创新和全球金融一体化的进程，金融全球化也将金融风险推向全球。本次金融危机的规模和影响表明，一方面，随着全球化的进程，发展中国家纷纷加快了金融改革步伐，推进本币自由兑换，开放金融市场，放松国际资本流动的管制，资本流动的范围和规模不断增加；另一方面，国际资本在不同国际金融市场的流动加快，风险也在不断增加。此次国际金融危机的影响，使得国际社会对国际金融监管有了新的认识：国际金融监管体制改革是国际金融新秩序重建的重要内容，对各国金融业影响巨大，并进而影响各国经济社会发展，涉及国家根本利益。各国必须重新审视金融监管体制，以便有效预防可能发生的风险。因此，在经济全球化的今天，针对金融市场监管体制方面的国际合作的必要性日益凸显。

“金砖四国”在此问题上与美国和欧洲有着不同的观点。经过沟通和磋商，四国一致认为，在新的国际金融秩序中"坚实的法律基础；各国监管机构和国际标准制定机构活动互不抵触；加强风险管理和监管实践"① 应该是基本原则。四国率先做出承诺："加强国内监管，推动国际金融监管体系改革，并同包括金融稳定论坛在内的国际标准制定机构开展密切合作。"② 经过四国及其他国家的共同努力，20 国集团多伦多峰会上通过的宣言中规定，各国"将采取共同行动，按期或加速兑现华盛顿、伦敦和匹兹堡峰会关于改革金融部门的承诺"，并将进行包括四个支柱在内的金融监管改革。

金融监管改革领域的合作将使得各国拥有更良好的发展环境和经济运行机制，有效避免全球化时代金融危机对本国经济的冲击。这是四国间各领域合作的重要前提。

2. 改变美元的国际霸权地位，推动国际货币体系多元化

在现行的国际金融秩序中，"金砖四国"作为外汇储备大国（中国 2.45 万亿美元，居第一位；俄罗斯 4693 亿美元，居世界第三位；印度和巴西分列第四位和第七位）。由于美元占"金砖四国"外汇储备的比例较大（如中国 2.45 万亿外汇储备中的 70% 为美元资产），"金砖四国"一方面直接面对金融危机以来美国迅速增加的经常账户逆差和财政赤字问题；另一方面向美国支付巨额的铸币税，四国的外汇储备资产不断被侵蚀。再加上在此次危机中，美元及其金融体系的不稳定性通过放大效应向全球扩散给世界经济带来的冲击，世界各国对现行的金融秩序和国际货币体系开始进行新的反思：当前国际货币体系不合理，存在着内在风险和系统性风险，全球过度依赖美元，而美国的本国利益与美元作为国际储备货币的利益有着天然的冲突，不能依靠美国自身来规避这种风险。为了防止全球性金融危机的再次发生和美元的崩溃，对现行的国际货币体系进行改革势在必行。不仅新兴市场国家要求改革当前的国际货币体系，其他发达国家也有这样的愿望。四国在此问题上有着共同的诉求：俄罗斯多次公开表示希望卢布成为国际储备货币。"金砖四国"的首倡者、经济学家奥尼尔说，到 2015 年，俄罗斯卢布或许有可能加入国际货币基金组织的计价范围，纳入特别提款权计价的一篮

---

① 《"金砖四国"领导人俄罗斯叶卡捷琳堡会晤联合声明》，详见中华人民共和国外交部网站，http://www.fmprc.gov.cn/。

② 《"金砖四国"领导人第二次正式会晤联合声明》，详见中华人民共和国外交部网站，http://www.fmprc.gov.cn/。

子货币。尽管巴西、印度的货币成为国际货币还有较长的路要走，但两国对改变美元霸权的局面也持积极态度。

中国在这方面作出了积极的努力，在金融危机的背景下开始探索实现人民币国际化的路径：中国人民银行先后同阿根廷、韩国等六国央行签署了6500亿人民币的货币互换协议；在香港发行了人民币债券；人民币跨境贸易结算的规模也在不断扩大等。尽管人民币国际化的前景尚未明确——是创造出超主权的SDR[①]，还是同亚洲其他国家联合打造“亚元”，抑或是最终成为和美元、欧元一样的核心国际储备货币，但是中国推动人民币走向国际化的道路已经随着中国经济实力的增强而变得不可逆转。虽然人民币在短期内还不足以取代美元的霸主地位，但它在国际上的地位正在不断提高，中国经济的表现让人们对人民币有了更多的期待，越来越多的国家希望人民币能够担当国际储备货币。俄罗斯等国已经表示对此予以积极支持。中国对人民币的国际化进程有着清醒的认识：人民币国际化不可能一蹴而就，而应该循序渐进。在此期间，中国政府主张健全储备货币的发行和调控机制，稳定主要储备货币汇率，促进国际货币体系的多元化和合理化，在国际金融机构中减少对美元的依赖，以降低今后可能发生的国际金融危机带来的风险，减少或降低美元独大给世界经济带来的冲击。

3. 推动国际金融机构改革，提高发展中国家在国际金融组织中的话语权

重建国际金融新秩序的关键是国际金融机构的改革，而国际金融机构改革的核心是国际货币基金组织（IMF）的改革。在布雷顿森林体系下，国际货币基金组织是全球经济的核心金融机构，其基本职能有三：一是维护固定汇率制度；二是向出现国际收支问题的国家提供短期融资安排；三是对成员国经济实施监测。但是，随着时代的发展和布雷顿森林体系的崩溃，国际货币基金组织日益跟不上世界经济的迅速发展和全球化发展的趋势：该组织可用于应对危机的资源有限，可供贷款资源仅有2500亿美元，不能有效应对较大规模的危机；决策机制不公平，运行机制不透明；在对成员国提供贷款方面严重地受到西方国家的影响，机械地反映西方国家的立场；在应对危机方面，危机前没有有效的预警机制，危机

① 2009年3月，中国人民银行行长周小川在一周内连续发表了三篇署名文章：3月23日《关于改革国际货币体系的思考》；3月24日《关于储蓄率问题的思考》；3月26日《关于改变宏观和微观顺周期性的进一步探讨》阐明自己的主张。

爆发后反应迟钝；新兴市场国家的份额投票权与新兴市场国家在世界经济中的比重和贡献严重不符；贫穷国家的声音在该组织得不到应有的反映等。

在国际货币基金组织的改革问题上，四国有着相似和共同的立场。为此，2009 年 3 月 14 日，"金砖四国"在 G20 财长会议期间发表了该"集团"的首份联合公报，呼吁重新评估国际货币基金组织的角色。四国主张，国际货币基金组织应该摆脱对某些大国的依附，恢复其独立性；为国际货币基金组织增加资本，扩大国际货币基金组织的职能，将国际货币基金组织的额度分配与新兴市场国家的增资相结合，扩大发展中国家的"话语权"，最终实现发达国家与发展中国家平等分享投票权的目标；增加国际金融机构的资源，提高对发展中国家的贷款规模。为此，国际货币基金组织于 2009 年计划首次发行 1.1 万亿美元的债券，以援助受金融危机重创的贫穷国家。中国已表示将购买 500 亿美元，俄罗斯和巴西也将各买 100 亿美元。四国在此问题上的合作，一方面给国际货币基金组织补充了实力，为解决世界金融问题贡献了力量；另一方面也将有利于推动储备货币多元化，降低单纯购买美国国债的风险。

四国还要求对世界银行等其他国际金融机构进行改革，增加新兴经济体及发展中国家的话语权，提高世界银行的监管效率和有效性；加强世界银行（WB）、多边开发银行（MDBs）、国际货币基金组织等国际金融机构之间的相互合作，在基础设施和贸易融资领域引入新的贷款机制，加强对危机冲击国的资金支持等。

四国在国际货币基金组织等国际金融机构的改革方面的共同立场和联合声明是四国在构建新的国际金融秩序方面加强合作的重要表现，也是四国在国际金融领域合作的重要基础。

（二）协调立场，共同为促进世界可持续与平衡增长作出贡献

此次全球金融危机凸显了国家间前所未有的国际关联性，加强国际对话与合作显得更为重要。"金砖四国""在世界经济一片低迷的气氛中，共同发出推动世界经济尽快复苏的强烈信号，并进行艰苦努力，率先实现经济恢复增长"，[①] 给世界经济的复苏增添了信心。经过"金砖四国"与世界各国的共同努力，

① 胡锦涛：《合作　开放　互利　共赢——在"金砖四国"领导人会晤时的讲话》，中华人民共和国外交部网站，http：//www.fmprc.gov.cn/。

2009年以来世界经济已经有所恢复，但严峻的挑战依然存在，发达国家的主权债务危机对世界经济复苏依旧构成威胁。为确保世界经济的全面复苏和高质量的就业增长，实现世界经济的可持续、平衡增长，四国加强合作与协调显得非常重要，尤其是当四国各自同美国进行联系的时候更是这样。

美国目前仍然是世界最大的经济体，是世界经济恢复和增长的主要引擎，同时也是各经济体发展自身经济所需的资金、高新技术、贸易市场的主要合作伙伴，美国还拥有世界上最强大的军事实力。因此，同美国的关系对“金砖四国”中任何一国来说都是优先发展和考虑的因素。同美国发展密切的关系在某种意义上讲，要比“金砖四国”成员国之间发展关系更为重要。“金砖四国”成员国之间的任何合作在争取正当利益时同美国相抗衡是最佳选择，而当这种合作有演变为挑战美国的霸权地位时将变得危险。

为此，四国在加强合作与对话时，要对美国的地位和影响力有充分的认识，将四国合作的目标和重心集中在促进世界经济的尽快复苏，以及实现可持续与平衡增长方面。

（三）反对贸易保护主义

反对和防止贸易保护主义和新的贸易壁垒对世界经济的复苏进程造成阻碍，是近三次20国集团峰会的主要议题之一，也是包括“金砖四国”在内的国际社会的共同呼声。在首次“金砖四国”首脑会晤之后发表的《叶卡捷琳堡会晤联合声明》中，四国一致强调国际贸易和外国直接投资对全球经济复苏的重要作用，呼吁各方共同努力改善国际贸易和投资环境，敦促各方保持多边贸易体系稳定，遏制贸易保护主义，并推动世界贸易组织多哈回合谈判取得全面、平衡的成果。① 尽管四国作出了上述声明，但实际上，四国的具体情况还是有所不同。

第一，四国的经济结构和增长方式有所不同。在俄、巴、印经济模式中，本国内需所占比重较大，因而对市场的保护性较强，而中国经济对外依存度比较高，对国际市场的需求比较敏感，因而中国对保护主义持反对态度，而俄、巴、印三国反对贸易保护主义的态度则不够坚决。

① 《“金砖四国”领导人俄罗斯叶卡捷琳堡会晤联合声明》，中华人民共和国外交部网站，http：//www.fmprc.gov.cn/。

第二，四国发展经济的自然资源禀赋和生产条件有所不同。中国、印度对俄罗斯的能源和巴西的矿产资源有比较大的需求，在一定程度上四国中的中国、印度和俄罗斯、巴西形成了供求关系的双方。中国是巴西、印度的第一大贸易伙伴，是俄罗斯的第二大贸易伙伴，但巴西、印度、俄罗斯在中国的贸易伙伴中所占据的位置并不引人注目。因此，双方的立场并不完全一致。

因此，在贸易保护问题上，四国既有着反对贸易保护主义、促进全球经济发展的一面，又有着因各国特殊条件而维护本国利益的一面。但是，四国强调"世界贸易组织作为多边贸易体制在维护开放、稳定、公平、非歧视性的国际贸易环境方面所发挥的重要作用"；承诺并敦促各国抵制各种形式的贸易保护主义，打击隐形贸易限制；在尊重授权、锁定包括谈判模式在内已有成果的基础上推动多哈回合谈判早日取得全面、均衡的结果，实现"发展回合"目标。①

（四）能源合作

自第三次科技革命以来，世界经济对能源的依赖逐步加强。能源是现代经济的血脉。对能源的经济影响，各国有着清醒的认识。它们都对2000～2008年国际能源价格的波动对世界经济的影响记忆犹新。在能源合作领域，一方面，四国的立场并不完全一致：俄罗斯是世界能源生产大国，对世界能源价格长期持续走高以拉动其本国经济抱有希望；而中国、巴西、印度都是能源消耗大国，未来几十年间，中国、印度、巴西将是世界最主要的能源消费国，因而三国希望将能源价格稳定在相对低的水平上。另一方面，中国和印度对外石油依存度逐年上升，巴西和俄罗斯的巨大石油储备又成为四国加强合作的基础。为此，"金砖四国"对通过在能源领域的合作确保能源供应的稳定性和可持续性有着共识。中俄两国2009年2月就原油管道、长期原油贸易、贷款等一揽子合作项目达成广泛共识，并签署了多项重要文件。中俄两国在金融危机期间加强能源领域的合作，对深化两国关系、保持国际能源价格稳定和应对国际金融危机具有重要意义。巴西国家石油公司将和中石油合作开发能源，中国不仅要参与巴西能源的开发，还将成为这一开发的重要成员。四国在新的国际环境下，亟须解决能源安全的挑战并将其

---

① 《"金砖四国"领导人第二次正式会晤联合声明》，中华人民共和国外交部网站，http://www.fmprc.gov.cn/。

转化为加强合作的机遇。

与此同时，“金砖四国”能源公司的实力也在不断增强。据高盛统计，包括中国石油、俄罗斯天然气公司、巴西国有石油公司、中国石化、俄罗斯石油公司和卢克石油公司、中海油以及印度国有石油和天然气公司等来自“金砖四国”的能源企业，正在飞速追赶美国和其他西方国家的能源公司。①

除此之外，中国和印度也都在积极自主研发新能源技术。在开发风能、太阳能等新能源和提高能效方面，四国之间的合作与交流也在不断加强。通过适当提升可再生能源比重，促进能源结构多样化，鼓励使用更清洁、更有效的能源。在能源领域的培训、研发、咨询、技术转让等方面开展合作。②

（五）环境问题和气候变化

“金砖四国”作为对未来世界经济前景的一种展望，意味着人类将会有更舒适的生活环境和更理想的发展模式。为此，保护现在的地球，爱护我们今天的家园已经成为全世界的共识。2009 年 12 月的哥本哈根会议见证了世界各国为此而付出的不懈努力，“金砖四国”也在两次首脑会晤和会后的联合声明中阐述了四国对这一问题的共同立场。

据统计，在 2008 年的全球温室气体排放排名中中国排第二位，俄罗斯排第三位，巴西列第八位，印度列第十七位。这既是在一定条件下四国在现有的国际经济秩序和国际分工中地位的客观体现，同时也表明，四国在降低排放，保护环境的问题上任重而道远。因而，在发展经济的同时节能减排，保护环境方面，四国有着类似的任务和相近的诉求。其中既有转变生产方式的自身需求，又承担着保护环境的历史使命。

四国都表达了降低排放量，保护环境的意愿。到 2020 年，俄罗斯碳排放量将较 1990 年的水平减少 20% ~30%，印度在 2020 年前将在 2005 年的基础上减少 20% ~25%，巴西计划到 2020 年将温室气体排放量在预期基础上减少

① 《高盛报告：金砖四国已赶超美国全球能源老大地位》，详见《金融时报》网站内容，http：//www. financialnews. com. cn/cj/txt/2007 －06/27/content_ 32209. htm。

② 详见《“金砖四国”领导人俄罗斯叶卡捷琳堡会晤联合声明》第八条；《“金砖四国”领导人第二次正式会晤联合声明》第十九、二十、二十一条。详见中华人民共和国外交部网站，http：//www. fmprc. gov. cn/。

36.1%～38.9%。过去的30年间，中国的经济建设成就举世瞩目，与此同时，中国在应对气候变化和保护环境方面也付出了长期不懈的努力。通过这些实际行动，中国为节能减排、保护环境作出了自己应有的努力。在此基础上，中国又提出，到2020年单位国内生产总值二氧化碳排放比2005年下降40%～45%。在此期间，这样大规模地降低二氧化碳排放，需要付出艰苦卓绝的努力。

由于四国的经济规模和发展模式的典型意义，可以说，没有四国的积极参与，任何有关环境保护的建议都是一纸空文；没有四国的切实履行，任何有关削减温室气体行动的效果都会受到一定程度的影响。四国作为新兴经济体的代表和发展中国家的领头羊，以世界42%的人口，对全球经济增长超过50%的贡献率，更有理由为世界未来的生存方式和发展模式提出自己的意见和主张。

众所周知，《京都议定书》明确规定了发达国家至2012年第一承诺期的减排指标。但从实际执行情况看，不少发达国家的排放不减反增。国际社会要在公约框架下作出切实有效的制度安排，促使发达国家兑现承诺，向发展中国家持续提供充足的资金支持，加快转让气候友好技术，并通过国际社会的通力合作，共同应对气候变化，保护环境。总之，在保护地球和环境的问题上，“金砖四国”之间将有非常广阔的合作空间。

除了在上述五个领域的合作中“金砖四国”有着广泛的共同点外，在其他涉及全球性的问题上四周也有着相近或共同的立场。这是四国加强进一步合作的基础。巴西总统卢拉在第二次首脑会议之后对“金砖四国”的合作作出高度评价：“‘金砖四国’的进一步合作，有利于世界多极化、国际民主化的发展。”四国将继续加强合作，借助经济危机呼吁改变不公平的现状，为未来的变革做好准备。

三 “金砖四国”的自我认识及在世界格局中的角色

“金砖四国”从开始会晤到定期会晤，从形成经济合作机制到正式建立元首会晤机制走过了不平凡的道路。“金砖四国”要想在未来国际政治经济生活中有更大的发展空间和更大的影响力，就必须对自我有清醒的认识（包括成员国对自身的认识以及对成员国相互间关系的自我认识），对在未来世界格局中自己所扮演的角色（主观的角色和客观的角色）有明确的判断。

在当今国际事务的决策过程中，“金砖四国”都扮演着必不可少的角色：中国和俄罗斯作为联合国安理会常任理事国发挥着重要的作用，巴西和印度也是国际政治生活中重要的角色（如2010年5月17日，巴西和土耳其达成了伊朗核燃料交换协议，凸显了巴西在国际舞台上的作用）。在对“金砖四国”在未来国际政治经济中的作用和影响的战略考虑方面，相比较而言，巴西和俄罗斯比中国和印度更积极。巴西同其他三国比较，全球影响力最小，期望在国际社会有更多的“话语权”，同时与其他三国没有利益冲突，因此可以很好地协调各国之间的利益。俄罗斯极力想融入西方但得不到应有的承认，同时由于受金融危机打击比较严重，在“八国集团”中的地位不稳固，只能参与部分对话，因而希望把“金砖四国”建成一个政治性比较强的经济联盟，以便增加其在同西方对话时的分量。中国对巩固同俄罗斯和印度的三方对话，以及建立同俄、印、巴之间更紧密的四方对话机制乐观其成，但是，对于“金砖四国”的战略考虑仅限于发展更紧密的经济合作；对涉及政治领域中的合作要具体问题具体分析；对“金砖四国”之间的军事领域的合作期望不高，最多只限于象征性的礼节互访。因此，总体上来说，“金砖四国”是一个四国间开展国际对话与合作的平台，在必要的时候，会有较紧密地协作，但在可预见的未来不会成为一个军事同盟。

中国的经济成就、综合国力以及国际地位使得中国在处理与国家或国际组织的合作时必须从本国自身的长远利益，合作方的核心利益以及世界的和平与发展这个时代的主题来考虑。中国是联合国常任理事国，是五个有核国家之一，目前已成为世界第二大经济体，同时又是美国学者提出的所谓的“G2”或“中美国”[①] 中的美国的全球潜在合作伙伴。在一定程度上，中国毫无疑问是一个大国。但由于中国人口众多，底子较薄，人均国内生产总值刚刚超过3000美元，发展经济、改善民生的任务十分繁重。在21世纪初的20年发展机遇期内，中国经济发展的许多特点和目前中国的特殊国情决定了中国仍然属于发展中国家。因此，在此期间，维护世界和平，促进世界经济的恢复和发展，加强同世界主要国家之间的良性互动，为中国的改革开放创造和平、稳定的外部环境是中国外交政

① “G2”是2008年由美国著名经济学家弗雷德·伯格斯滕提出来的，建议由中、美两国组成一个Group（集团）来代替旧有的“G8”（八国集团），以携手合作解决世界经济问题的一个概念。“中美国”的概念是由哈佛大学教授尼尔·弗格森于2007年提出的。

策的基本任务。

此外，中国的迅速发展和中国的和平崛起已经在世界上引起了众多的猜忌和疑虑，同时"中国威胁论"在许多国家泛滥。[①] 鉴于此，我们可以看到中国的和平崛起的面临重重阻力。为此，从为中国的和平崛起创造良好的周边及世界环境角度出发，有必要考虑建立中国的多层次外交。笔者认为，中国应该以上海合作组织和"金砖四国"为基础，建立以中国为主要成员国的多层次外交。中国作为"金砖四国"的重要成员，在一些涉及中国以及发展中国家利益的问题上，可以联合这些国家共同发出自己的声音。中国一贯坚持独立自主、不结盟的和平外交政策，但这不妨碍中国同一些国家就某些具有共同利益的问题发出同一个声音，在"二十国集团"框架内加强协调，维护自身和广大发展中国家的利益。中国与发展中国家和新兴国家有相似的历史背景，有着共同发展经济的迫切愿望，在许多问题上享有共同的利益，在绝大多数问题上都持相同或相近的立场。这是中国积极同发展中国家、新兴国家展开合作的基本需求。同时，这也成为中国同"金砖四国"为代表的新兴国家、发展中国家进一步发展良好关系的坚实基础。

尽管同巴西不接壤，但中国对巴西资源的需求已经使得巴西成为中国经济上的近邻。中国同巴西建立了"战略伙伴关系"，中巴元首会晤和"中巴高层协调与合作委员会"都保持着良好的关系，双边贸易关系不断加强，互相投资逐渐增长，经济依存度在日益增加。巴西是中国在拉美地区最大贸易伙伴和全球第十一大贸易伙伴，中国成为巴西第一大贸易伙伴、第一大出口对象国和第二大进口来源国。

俄罗斯是全世界面积最大、与中国边境线最长的邻国，两国在历史上也曾存在过许多问题，但两国领导人从长远角度出发，在二十年间，使中俄关系连上几个台阶。两国通过条约解决了边界问题，建立了"面向二十一世纪的战略协作伙伴关系"，签署了《中俄睦邻友好合作条约》，制定了《中华人民共和国东北地区与俄罗斯联邦远东及东西伯利亚地区合作规划纲要（2009～2018 年）》，为中俄友好合作奠定了坚实的基础。

印度是中国众多邻国中人口最多的国家。历史上，中国同印度发生过边界纠

① 笔者以"China threat"为关键词在 www. google. com 搜索，获得约 9790000 条结果（2010 年 8 月 2 日查询）。

纷，并且印度曾借口中国因素进行核试验，[①] 中国的迅速发展也使得印度在一定程度上感受到压力，西方国家也一直有意把中国同印度的发展放在一起比较。目前中国同印度建立了“面向和平与繁荣的战略合作伙伴关系”，制定了深化两国战略合作伙伴关系的“十项战略”。与此同时，中国是印度的第二大贸易伙伴，印度是中国的第九大贸易伙伴。除了在“金砖四国”框架下的密切联系和合作外，两国还在中印俄三方合作、发展中五国、“基础四国”、多哈回合谈判中保持密切沟通与合作。

四国具有不同的价值观，四国都在探索与以美国为代表的西方发展模式不同、符合自己实际国情的道路，但在国际政治经济格局中各自缺乏独立抗争的实力。联合起来争取更多的话语权，表达不同于西方的对未来国际政治经济发展的看法是四国合作的内在动力。为此，“不同社会制度可以相互包容，不同发展模式可以相互合作，不同历史文明可以相互借鉴，不同文化传统可以相互交流”，四国都面临着进一步提高经济发展水平和改善民生的艰巨任务，在全球性问题上有着相同或近似的立场，都十分重视加强和深化成员国之间的互利合作。这是“金砖四国”合作的坚实基础。

我们认为，在正在形成中的新的国际政治经济新秩序中，“金砖四国”将具有以下角色定位。

1. 发展中国家的代表

作为新兴国家和发展中国家的代表，在同西方主导的国际政治经济秩序的构建中代表新兴国家和发展中国家的利益和声音，为发展中国家争取相应的权益和话语权。

2. 世界经济发展的基石

按照高盛集团的研究，在未来的几十年内，“金砖四国”毫无疑问将是世界经济发展的主力，对世界经济的贡献将会逐步增加。当多数富裕国家都陷入了经济衰退，“金砖四国”（仅俄罗斯受金融危机影响较深，增速有限）仍将强劲增长，因为全球经济发生了结构性转变，最大的新兴国家将从国内消费的持续增长

① 印度于1998年5月先后进行了三次核试验，印度外交部在1998年5月11日发表的声明中已经有所暗示，声称印度核试验是出于“对印度周边核环境的严重关切”。印度国防部长费尔南德斯在5月3日接受媒体采访时公开宣称，“中国是头号威胁”，声称其进行核试验是为应对来自中国的“威胁”。

中获益。"金砖四国"的领土总面积占世界陆地总面积的26%，人口占全球总人口的42%，"金砖四国"的发展在某种意义上讲就是世界上1/4的面积和近1/2人口的发展。只有"基石"——"金砖四国"发展了，世界经济的发展才有更稳固的基础。

3. 不同利益国家间的协调者

金融危机后的几次国际会议反映了各国不同的声音和多样的需求，"金砖四国"分别作为亚洲、欧洲、拉丁美洲三个不同大洲的代表，在会议过程中积极协调，保证了会议的成功举行，成为不同利益经济体的协调者。

4. 全球金融新秩序的积极倡导者

"金砖四国"在全球经济体系、国际货币体系与金融监管体系等全球性问题上表明了自己的立场，作为改革和建立新的国际经济金融新秩序的倡议，赢得了广泛的支持与拥护，成为世界经济新秩序的倡导者。

5. 世界多极化格局的推动者

"金砖四国"作为一个新兴的国际经济组合，成为国际社会一支重要的力量，它的出现，必然对国际政治格局产生重大的影响，推动世界格局多极化的形成。俄罗斯总统梅德韦杰夫在叶卡捷琳堡峰会上呼吁四国联手创造一个"更加公平的世界"和"多极化的世界"。西方有媒体称，"金砖四国"不仅是一个重要的经济体，更是现有全球权力格局的挑战者。

除此之外，由于中国发展的特点与其他三国不同，中国还自觉不自觉地承担了以下角色。

1. 世界经济复苏和发展的引擎

金融危机过后，世界经济的复苏将是一场缓慢的过程，中国积极采取措施，恢复和保持了本国经济在较长时间内较快增长的势头。作为世界第一人口大国和第二大经济体，中国经济的复苏与发展本身就是对世界经济的稳定和复苏所做的最大贡献。在世界其他经济体复苏乏力的背景下，中国内需的扩大将意味着13亿人口的巨大潜力市场的苏醒，意味着中国经济发展的潜力和世界经济的拓展空间。中国不自觉地成为世界经济发展的引擎。

2. 非西方发展模式的典范

作为典型的非西方国家，中国近30年的"经济奇迹"举世瞩目。尽管中国经济目前也面临着调整经济结构、改变增长方式等问题，但中国经济的成就使

13 亿人口的大国的生活水平得到了大幅度提高，成为非西方发展模式的典范，为其他发展中国家探索符合自己本国国情的道路提供了借鉴。

3. 美元资产债权国利益的代表

由于美元的霸权地位，世界各国都储备了一定的美元或美元资产。作为最大的美元资产储备国和债权国，中国成为美元资产权益国利益的代表，对美元资产的保值给予了特殊的关心。中国政府曾多次直接要求美国对美元资产进行保值，这既是对中国自身美元资产利益负责的做法，同时，也是对世界其他有美元资产国家利益的支持和保护。

四 结论

“金砖四国”举行首脑峰会本身就是一个具有历史意义的事件——意味着世界上近一半的人为了更健康、更持续稳定的世界经济政治的发展而聚合在一起。而当“金砖四国”首脑会晤机制化以后，随着“金砖四国”这一组织的兴起，世界政治经济由此将产生一系列积极的现象。

虽然会晤可能不会产生非常具体的措施，但其最关键的意义是让这四个国家之间联动的机制开始运行。经过四国政治外交的努力，第二次首脑会晤更加显示了四国加强国际合作，发展密切关系的意愿。推动国际政治经济格局的多元化、促进世界经济的迅速复苏、反对贸易保护主义、关注环境等具有全球性的问题既是四国共谋合作的基础，也是加强四国间密切合作的纽带。尤其是在当前国际金融危机尚未见底的大背景下，四国合作尤其重要。这种合作不仅对四国有利，也符合国际社会的共同期待与利益，有助于世界经济的早日复苏。“金砖四国”的对话与合作不仅符合新兴市场国家和发展中国家的共同利益，而且有利于建设一个持久和平、共同繁荣的和谐世界。

相信通过四国的通力合作，“金砖四国”将会成为世界经济真正的“砖”，对世界更美好的发展作出更大的贡献。

“金砖四国”机制化与中国角色

——带倾向性的多边合作

王俊生[*]

冷战结束后，国际格局发生了重大变化，其中最大的变化之一就是同属新兴经济体的一批发展中国家同时迅速崛起，其中被称为“金砖四国”的中国、俄罗斯、印度、巴西最具有代表性。“2000~2008年世界产值的60%来自于发展中国家与转型国家，其中的一半来自‘金砖四国’。”① 四国的崛起也整体上提升了发展中国家的地位，西方发达国家也从开始的忽视到今天不得不在一些事关全球问题特别是发展中国家利益的重大问题上作出调整与让步。四国的崛起对国际格局乃至整个冷战后的国际关系的影响仍在持续。但是目前已有的研究，绝大部分是从经济或金融角度入手，很少从国际关系角度对其进行分析。有鉴于此，本文就以“金砖四国”的机制化与其中的中国角色为考察对象，并尝试以“带倾向性的多边合作”这一基本概念对其加以总结概括。下面将结合具体案例对这一概念加以详细阐述。

一　中心议题与分析背景

为了更好地理解“金砖四国”机制化的前景以及其中的中国角色，梳理和

---

* 王俊生，中国社会科学院拉丁美洲研究所助理研究员。

① 对此，以至于西方学者惊呼，“西方外的崛起”。参见 Fareed Zakaria，*The Post-American World*，New York：W. W. Norton & Co.，2009；Parag Khanna，*The Second World*：*Empires and Influence in the New Global Order*，New York：Random House，2008。

总结四国合作的特点是很有必要的。作为差异明显而且又是近年来国际社会中蓬勃发展的四个新兴发展中大国，它们走向更紧密的多边合作的动因也较为复杂。如果我们只是简单地罗列这些动因，就无法抓住本质。因此，本文提出“带倾向性”的课题。所谓“带倾向性”，指的是四国在走向合作时的主要动力，反映的是外交优先选项。

要分析四国的合作，就不能不考虑时代背景。冷战后的国际格局发生了巨大变化。首先，苏联的解体使得美国的超级大国地位相对进一步上升。欧美关系尽管作了部分调整，但是本质并没有改变。北约组织继续在美国的主导下执行其全球战略，欧盟的东扩也在美国的助推下继续进行。如果说冷战期间还有苏联可以有效制约美国主导的西方阵营的话，那么冷战后国际关系的一个突出特点就是西方阵营在国际体系中的主导地位很难得到有效制约。正是在这一背景下，美国及其北约盟友绕开联合国相继发动了科索沃战争、伊拉克战争、阿富汗战争。在对华关系上，相继发生了银河号事件、轰炸中国驻南联盟大使馆事件、南海撞机事件。在这些事件发生后，美国的蛮横无理不仅得不到应有的国际制约，反而是事态的后续发展也往往在其主导下推进。

其次，全球化的深入发展。如果说冷战期间国际社会还是一个分裂的世界的话，那么冷战后的世界确实进入了整体的全球化时代。这种格局的形成不仅因为科技的发展，也由于苏联解体后美欧所主导的全球化因为没有了政治上的人为设障而“攻城略地”。美国、欧洲、亚洲、拉丁美洲、非洲等都成了这个整体全球化的一部分，以相互依赖为特点的地球村在人类历史上首次形成。这样一来，一方面，国内政治“国际化”，国际政治“国内化”，一个较为成熟有韧性的国际市民社会初步形成；另一方面，超越一国国境的地区和全球性问题凸显，人类命运更为休戚相关。“共同管理”世界成了人类不得不面对的选择。在诸如应对全球环境恶化、防止核武器扩散、减轻贫穷与饥饿等问题上，即便是超级大国美国也不得不与其他中小国家共同管理。

最后，冷战结束顺应了人类的普遍利益，除少数国家的地位出现下降外，绝大多数国家在国际社会中的自主性增强，地位上升。因此，尽管现有国际体系对于发展中国家来说仍然存在诸多不合理之处，比如在国际金融体系、国际能源分配体系等方面，但是各国也都看到了以经济发展提升国际地位，透过渐进改革逐渐实现国际体系更为公平正义的前景。因而在与欧美国家关系的处理上，其他各国普遍采取了避免正面对抗，在相关议题上积极合作的态度。

正是在这一背景下，作为发展势头最好的新兴发展中大国——“金砖四国”走向了更为紧密的合作。四国领土面积占世界总领土面积的26%、人口占全球人口的42%、四国GDP总值占世界GDP总值的15%。世界前20名的能源公司中有35%来自“金砖四国”，全球20大矿产企业中，“金砖四国”占到了20%。① 而在全球外汇存底中，“金砖四国”持有3万多亿美元，超过世界的40%。正因为这种“大块头”，四国联合一经出现就令国际社会侧目。2009年9月，得益于四国的集体亮相，20国集团（G20）匹兹堡峰会取得了突破性进展，即把国际货币基金组织3%的投票权和世界银行5%的投票权重新分配给新兴和发展中经济体。事实上，尽管四国中每个国家的经济规模在国际社会中都举足轻重，但每个国家都不拥有单独与西方国家进行博弈取胜的实力。那么，作为后冷战时代国家间最为醒目的联合之一，“金砖四国”能否机制化，不仅对于四国争取权益至关重要，而且对于国际格局的演变也意义深远。

二 “金砖四国”的机制化回顾

冷战后，“金砖四国”的机制化是一个逐渐发展的过程。所谓机制化，也就是预设某种对话模式，以及商定一系列规范、规定、标准等。换句话说，就是处理或管理问题模式化。处理国际关系如同处理国内关系一样，比较好的办法就是形成一种机制化安排。一方面，对于较为棘手的问题，在其演变过程中，爆发危机乃至失控的危险始终存在，这种常态化的机制对于预防危机失控至关重要；另一方面，对于需要日常管理的问题，四周正是依托这种机制，使得各方实现定期会晤，在讨论、辩论、谈判的过程中促进各方对其他参与国的信念、意图和信息的更多了解，实现观念和偏好的逐渐趋同，从而为实质性合作带来可能。

“金砖四国”的联合，建构了国际社会对其作为一个整体的认同，而外界的认知又反过来强化了四国的集体身份。2005年，G7财长伦敦会议首度邀请“金砖四国”列席。2006年，在俄罗斯时任总统普京的建议下，四国外长在联合国大会外举行会晤。在2007年四国外长于纽约再次会晤后，为了加强实质性接触，

① 王艳：《金融危机下金砖四国能否冲击世界经济格局?》，《经营管理者》2009年第16期，第58页。

四国在副部长级层面上进行了定期工作会晤（consultative process）。2008 年，四国外长在俄罗斯叶卡捷琳堡市举行联合国框架外的首次会晤，并决定将这种会晤定期化。同期，四国财长也举行了会晤。2008 年，在日本北海道的八国集团峰会后，四国元首进行了单独会晤并发表了联合声明，标志着“金砖四国”合作受到了四国最高领导人的关注与肯定。2009 年 3 月在 20 国集团（G20）伦敦峰会上，四国首次单独发表了联合公报。同年 5 月四国外长会晤后又发表了联合公报。① 四国最高领导人专门举办首脑峰会的机会渐渐成熟。

于是，2009 年 6 月 16 日，“金砖四国”首脑在俄罗斯叶卡捷琳堡举行首次正式峰会，峰会举行四场活动——小范围会谈、大范围会谈、联合记者会和工作晚宴，发表了《“金砖四国”领导人俄罗斯叶卡捷琳堡会晤联合声明》。该“声明”涵盖以下几方面的内容。①加强和 20 国集团的合作，应对金融危机。②推动国际金融机构改革，建立稳定和多样化的国际货币体系，使其体现世界经济形势的变化。③改善国际贸易和投资环境，维护多边贸易体系稳定，遏制贸易保护主义。④强调可持续发展理念的环境因素，改变经济发展模式，在应对气候变化问题上开展建设性对话。⑤在能源领域加强协调与合作，以降低不确定性，确保能源稳定性与可持续性。⑥联合国改革。⑦加强科技和教育合作。⑧下次峰会在巴西召开。②

由上可见，四国讨论的议程相当广泛。由于峰会的召开正值美元地位备受质疑、发展中国家集体要求扩大话语权的背景下，格外引人注目。新加坡《联合早报》认为，“金砖四国”此举正在“谋划‘后危机时代’的世界新秩序”。俄罗斯政治基金会主席尼科诺夫甚至预言，这个夏天之后，“金砖四国”将成为一个“能够决定 21 世纪面貌的机构”。③ 尽管这些言论多少有点言过其实，而且此次峰会“花言巧语（rhetoric）超过实质性（substance）合作”④，但透过本次首

---

① Cynthia Roberts, “Challengers or Stakeholders? BRICs and the Liberal World Order,” *Polity*, No. 42, 2010, pp. 1 - 13, http://www.palgrave-journals.com/polity/journal/v42/n1/full/pol200920a.html（2010 年 5 月 8 日查看）。

② 《“金砖四国”领导人俄罗斯叶卡捷琳堡会晤联合声明》，中华人民共和国外交部网站。资料来源，http://www.fmprc.gov.cn/chn/pds/ziliao/1179/t568224.htm（2010 年 5 月 8 日查看）。

③ 王俊生：《关于“金砖四国”机制的猜想》，《领导科学》2009 年 8 月，第 13 页。

④ “BRICs, Emerging Markets and the World Economy,” June 18 2009, from *The Economist* print edition, http://www.absolutbrazil.info/article-brics-emerging-markets-and-the-world-economy/（2010 年 5 月 8 日查看）。

脑峰会人们切实地看到了四国合作管理国际挑战的前景。这其中有两点尤其值得关注。其一，四国首脑在首次峰会上就发表了"共同声明"——共同声明体现了各方共识，并对各方行动具有一定约束力——表明四国对于联手合作具有政治上的"共同倾向性"。其二，联合声明确定了下一次峰会将在巴西召开，表明峰会朝着机制化的方向发展。

按照既定安排，"金砖四国"领导人第二次峰会于2010年4月15日在巴西首都巴西利亚举行，并共同发表了《"金砖四国"领导人第二次正式会晤联合声明》。声明所涵盖的议程仍然为：世界经济金融形势、20国集团事务、国际金融机构改革、气候变化、经贸合作等。但是以下条款值得注意："第12条：……我们要求四国财长和央行行长对有关区域货币机制进行研究。我们将研究货币合作的可行性，包括四国本币贸易结算"；"第17条：会议讨论了推进四国在农业领域，特别是家庭农场方面的合作方式。……我们欢迎会议决定设立四国农业信息库系统，制定确保脆弱群体粮食供给的战略，减少气候变化对粮食安全的负面影响，以及加强农技合作和创新"；"第27条：加强四国专业领域合作的倡议：a. 农业部长首次会议；b. 财长和央行行长会议；c. 安全事务高级代表会议；d. 2010年3月举行第一届'金砖四国'地方法官交流项目；e. 发展银行首次会议；f. 国家统计局长首次会议；g. 国际竞争力大会；h. 首次合作社会议；i. 首次商业论坛；j. 智库研讨会"。此外，四国将研究编纂"金砖四国"大百科全书的可行性；① 声明决定下次峰会在中国召开。

由上可见，第二次声明虽然在议程设置上没有新的东西，但是我们的确可以看到四国合作触及了更多的实质问题，② 合作领域进一步深化与细化，合作根基在逐渐夯实。比如，2009年的声明提出要建立"稳定和多样化的国际货币体系"，采用了比较抽象的提法。2010年的声明则提到要研究和推进使用本国货币进行贸易结算的问题，更为实质化。再如，俄罗斯对外经济银行、中国国家开发

---

① 《"金砖四国"领导人第二次正式会晤联合声明》，中华人民共和国外交部网站。资料来源，http://www.fmprc.gov.cn/chn/pds/ziliao/1179/t688360.htm（2010年5月8日查看）。

② 这种实质性和务实性还表现在，在叶卡捷琳堡峰会前，国际社会对于四国将要挑战现有国际金融秩序的预期相当强烈，有关四国合作挑战美元、设立超主权货币的猜想也比较活跃。相比之下，巴西利亚峰会前国际社会在此方面的预期与猜想显然弱了许多。国际社会的预期，在一定程度上反映了四国对"金砖四国"这一机制的态度更趋务实。

银行、巴西国家社会经济开发银行和印度进出口银行签署了合作备忘录，这将逐步推动建立真正的银行间系统，也为四国投资项目建设提供金融保障迈出了实质性第一步。正如胡锦涛主席在发言中所指出的那样："我们四国对话和合作内涵不断丰富、层次不断拓展、成果不断涌现。"① 同时，声明再次提前把下次峰会召开的地点公布，增强了可预期性，使持续的会晤与对话成为可能，② 而只要各方依托这一平台将会晤与对话持续开展下去，就能逐渐影响相关行为体对自己身份、偏好和利益的定义，从而有利于塑造集体身份与共同意识。在此基础上实质性的合作就有可能实现。

综上可见，四国从被 G7 集体邀请到四国首脑主动举行单独的峰会，每一步前进不仅推动了四国合作的实质化，而且合作的机制化也得到了加强。至此，如果说在俄罗斯叶卡捷琳堡首次峰会召开前，"金砖四国"更多是"被四国"（arranged marriage）的话，那么叶卡捷琳堡峰会则首次将国际舆论所创造出的"金砖"概念形象化；到了巴西利亚峰会，这种形象化的概念则开始固化，四国合作的机制化进一步发展。而对于四国走向多边合作与机制化的动力，也即背后的"倾向性"，正如罗伯特·基欧汉和亨利·基辛格所强调的那样：这些国家必须存在利益的交集，各方通过共同努力都能预期从中受益。③ 肯尼思·沃尔兹和约翰·米尔斯海默也都曾强调，国家间合作若缺乏强烈的动力去维持，那么这些国家间的利益分歧和竞争因素很可能使其合作最终中断。

三　带倾向性的多边合作

要分析四国走向多边合作的倾向性，就必须考察四国外交的优先议程。就巴西来说，20 世纪 90 年代以来，经济快速发展，与阿根廷等拉美邻国的关系得到

① 《合作　开放　互利　共赢——在"金砖四国"领导人会晤时的讲话》，中华人民共和国外交部网站，http：//www. fmprc. gov. cn/chn/pds/ziliao/zyjh/t682096. htm（2010 年 5 月 8 日查看）。

② 事实上，由于 G20 首脑峰会已经机制化，而 G20 峰会往往"众口难调"，发达国家往往事先协调立场，也就迫使新兴经济体的代表不得不协调彼此立场，推动 G20 更好地传达发展中国家的声音，这也会间接推动"金砖四国"首脑峰会的常态化。

③ 参见 Robert Keohane，*International Institutions and State Power*，Boulder，Colo.：Westview Press，1989，p. 138；Henry Kissinger，*Does America Need a Foreign Policy?*，New York：Touchstone，2001，pp. 152 - 153。

了改善，对美国的经济依存度也在下降。因此，在继续稳定与美国和欧洲国家传统关系的基础上，巴西推行更加多元化的外交路线，以体现和发挥一个地区大国的政治作用和影响力为目标。卡多佐总统认为，“在这个多极的世界里，巴西应当是其中的一极”，“巴西是世界大国之一，希望今后能实行一种更有进取性的外交政策。……不应该在作重大国际决策时被排除在外”。卢拉政府延伸和发展了这种外交战略，不过更加强调与发展中国家建立和发展关系，甚至建立具有集团性质的关系。[①] 为此，卢拉积极参与“G8 + 5”对话会，倡导成立“印度—巴西—南非三国论坛”，积极推动发展中国家间的协调与合作。总的来说，巴西推行“大国外交”战略有两个重点：第一，强调发展同南美国家的“睦邻友好关系”；第二，重点发展同世界上其他发展中大国的“新兴大国关系”。前者是巴西“大国外交”的基础和出发点，巴西在这一领域所要发挥的是“领导者”作用；后者是巴西“大国外交”所要依靠的政治力量。[②]

印度的大国意识根深蒂固，由来已久。做“有声有色”的大国，是印度开国元首尼赫鲁提出来的，它忠实地表达了印度政治精英的政治思想和政治抱负。这个奋斗目标，没有因为政党的轮换而改变，也没有因为政府的更迭而中断，成了“印度的国家意识”。[③] 近年来，印度制造业的成就举世瞩目，信息技术产业开始腾飞。在外交舞台上，它与周边国家的关系处于历史最好状态，其他对外关系也大幅改善。印度越来越相信自己是构建未来国际新秩序的一支重要力量，对成为世界大国的憧憬日益清晰。[④] 总的来说，第一，印度外交更加讲究平衡与均势，积极周旋于世界各国之间，营造有利于国内经济发展的外部环境。[⑤] 第二，更加重视通过务实外交来获取利益，不仅重视利用南亚区域合作联盟拉拢和稳定南亚诸国，而且注意融入发展中国家中，以此增强信任、获取资源、赢得支持。同时，印度也借助发达国家的力量实现自己的大国复兴之梦。第三，印度越来越强调发挥其大国的作用，树立起自信和独立的国际形象，有意识地扩大国际影响力。

---

① 吴志华：《巴西的“大国外交”战略》，《拉丁美洲研究》2005 年第 4 期，第 9、11、15 页。

② 吴志华：《巴西的“大国外交”战略》，《拉丁美洲研究》2005 年第 4 期，第 9 页。

③ 孙士海：《印度外交将更为稳健》，2004 年 5 月 17 日《环球时报》。

④ 马加力：《印度的外交战略》，《和平与发展》2006 年第 2 期，第 34 ~ 35 页。

⑤ 曾祥裕：《略论印度外交成熟与不成熟的两重性》，《南亚研究季刊》2005 年第 2 期，第 94 页。

近现代以来，俄罗斯一直是世界舞台上的主要角色，二战后的半个多世纪里甚至和美国一道成为超级大国。苏联解体后，正如普京所言，“俄罗斯正处于最困难的一个时期。可以说，最近200~300年以来，俄罗斯第一次面临处于第二、三流国家的实际危险”。[①] 因此，普京在继承叶利钦后期所提出的多极化构想的同时，在外交战略上更加强调追求大国地位，反对美国的单极霸权。[②] 梅德韦杰夫继承了普京的外交路线，强调“关于一个国家可以扮演全球政府角色的见解完全是幻想”，“现在的全球管理制度体系不适应当前的挑战”，应该改变。[③] 为恢复大国地位：第一，俄罗斯外交政策强调优先发展同邻国的关系，独联体是最优先方向；第二，坚持独特的以实用主义为核心的全方位、多极平衡的外交构想；第三，国内目标无条件地高于外部目标。[④]

最后再来看中国的情况。中国自古以来就是一个大国，只是到了工业革命后由于没有赶上世界步伐而衰落了一个多世纪。1949 年特别是改革开放以来，中国各项指标迅速提升。比如在金融领域，5 年前全球市值最大的 10 家银行主要属于美国和欧洲，而现在，世界 5 大银行中已包括中国工商银行（市值 2502 亿美元）和中国建设银行（1909 亿美元）。[⑤] 而 10 年前这两家中国银行还面临着生存危机，中国发展速度之快由此可见一斑。中国是目前全世界最大的金融资本供应者，可用于投资的储蓄达到 2 万亿美元，而此前 150 年，是美国充当了世界最大的金融资本供应者的角色。1990 年，美国和日本的 GDP 分别相当于中国的 15 倍和 8 倍。到 2009 年，美国的 GDP 已不到中国的 3 倍，而中国与日本已非常接近。再比如军费开支，1990 年时，美国和俄罗斯分别相当于中国的 35 倍和 13 倍，而到 2008 年时，美中的比例已缩小到了 8 倍。中国反而超过俄罗斯，接近俄罗斯的 2 倍，世界排名第二。从世界贸易、吸收外国直接投资等情况中，都可

---

① 毕洪业：《后冷战时期俄罗斯的外交构想及评价》，《东北亚论坛》2009 年第 7 期，第 199 页。

② 屈昭：《博采众长　独辟蹊径——读〈重振俄罗斯——普京的对外战略与外交政策〉》，《俄罗斯中亚东欧研究》2009 年第 1 期，第 90 页。

③ 冯玉军：《强势崛起、金融危机与俄罗斯对外政策的调整》，《当代世界》2009 年第 3 期，第 17 页。

④ 相关分析可以参见王伟《梅德韦杰夫的外交选择》，《当代世界》2008 年第 6 期，第 16 页；毕洪业《后冷战时期俄罗斯的外交构想及评价》，《东北亚论坛》2009 年第 7 期，第 199 页；刘桂玲等《俄大选后外交走向及中俄关系》，《国际资料信息》2008 年第 2 期，第 39 页。

⑤ 〔俄〕亚历山大·科克沙罗夫：《不狂热的霸权》，2010 年 3 月 29 日《专家》（俄罗斯）。

以看到中国相关指标的迅速上升。在国民心态、国际认知等层面也都可以看到这种上升的态势。[①] 因此，实现中华民族的伟大复兴，成为一个世界大国，已经不再是一个梦想或口号，而是中华儿女正在脚踏实地努力达到的目标。为此，中国重点在两个方面的外交优先议程上着力。第一，为国内经济发展创造良好的国际环境，即利用与建构一个战略机遇期以便实现国内发展；第二，随着实力提升与地位上升，在国际社会中树立更为负责任的大国形象，比如在朝核问题六方会谈上。

由此可见，四国外交的优先目标都是为了加强或巩固各自的地区和世界大国地位，在国际事务中争取更多的话语权与更多的主导权。因此，四国在外交上有两个共同"倾向性"。其一，在目前单个国家力量稍嫌欠缺的情况下，四国都倾向于通过联手合作，以便发挥超过每个国家单独发挥的影响力，共同推进国际政治经济环境向着有利于它们发挥大国影响的方向发展。[②] 比如，此次金融危机，四国均看到危机爆发的根本原因在于不合理的国际经济与金融体系，需要对其改革。但是，尽管四国中每个国家的经济规模都举足轻重，但每一个国家都不拥有单独与西方国家进行博弈取胜的实力。通过合作"互相借力"就成了必然的选择。巴西总统卢拉2008年表示，巴西应该与拥有较多外汇储备的俄罗斯、印度和中国等新兴国家联合起来，成立统一战线，以便施加更大影响力。[③] 其二，四国都倾向于通过联手合作优化内部经济发展的环境，为各自在国际舞台上扮演大国角色奠定经济基础。

正是这些共同的"倾向性"促使四国走向了更为紧密的合作，以至让人看到了进一步机制化的前景。而四国的这种"倾向性"透过联手合作确实也具备了实现的客观条件。一方面，四国在许多国际与地区问题上的看法接近，比如，在对现行国际经济和金融秩序进行改革，以及减少美元带来的不稳定性等方面。另一方面，四国间的贸易关系也较为紧密。在过去9年，"金砖四国"间的贸易

---

① 详见王俊生《世界大国与战略环境：中国国际角色的新课题》，《现代国际关系》2010年第4期，第38～45页；王俊生《中国当前的国际角色评估——实力·定位·认知》，《中国与世界观察》2010年春季号。

② 相关理论分析也可见 John Mearsheimer, *The Tragedy of Great Power Politics* , New York: W. W. Norton, 2001, p. 41; Wohlforth, "The Stability of a Unipolar World"; Amitav Acharya, "The Emerging Regional Architecture of World Politics," *World Politics* , No. 59 , July 2007, pp. 629 - 52。

③ 王云鹏：《金融危机下"金砖四国"何去何从》，《科技创新导报》2009年第11期，第175页。

额增长了9倍，而同期全球的贸易总量仅增加了1倍。同时，四个国家都坚持自己的民族传统和国家特性，自主选择发展模式，没有简单地接受什么“华盛顿共识”或者其他什么“共识”。

正因为如此，四国内部不仅早已开展了紧密的双边合作，比如中俄、俄印、中巴等双边合作，而且同属亚洲的中俄印三国之间也早已经开始联手合作。早在20世纪90年代中期，俄罗斯时任总理普里马科夫就首先提出了建立俄中印“战略三角”的构想。① 2002年，三国外长开始在联合国举行非正式会晤。2006年，三国外长首次在俄罗斯符拉迪沃斯托克单独会晤。同期，三国领导人在俄罗斯圣彼得堡参加G8峰会期间，单独举行了会晤，在最高领导人层面上确认了加强三国合作的意愿和决心。这也为“金砖四国”的合作打下了基础。

我们也必须看到，“金砖四国”被舆论炒了10多年，但是四国外长峰会，特别是首脑峰会能在2009年登场，也源于应对金融危机的需要。这正如俄罗斯学者所言，“四国峰会是伴随着金融危机导致四国在国际金融领域越来越缺乏安全感而召开的”。② 那么，在目前全球经济趋向好转并逐步走出衰退的情况下，四国进一步机制化的这些“倾向性”是否会消失，机制化的前景如何呢？

四　进一步机制化的前景与路径

源于这种“倾向性”的四国多边合作既可以看做是四国务实外交与国际环境的碰撞，又可被用来分析进一步机制化的前景与路径。从经验上看，国际合作平台的机制化主要有两种模式：欧盟模式和亚太经合组织（APEC）模式。欧盟模式通过各种条约约束成员国的行为，有常设机构，最终目标是对内一体化，对外一个声音。而APEC模式没有约束性条约，也没有常设性机构，内部

① 中国担心此举会被美国误认为在结成“反美”联盟，所以态度消极。参见阎学通《国际环境与外交思考》，《现代国际关系》1999年第8期，第11页。

② Lyubov Pronina and Alex Nicholson，“BRICs May Buy Each Other's Bonds in Shift From Dollar，” http：//www. bloomberg. com/apps/news？ pid = 20601086&sid = aSdhVkf. e1RY（2010年5月7日查看）。

一体化与对外用同一个声音发言都谈不上。APEC 模式主要采取自主自愿、协商一致的原则，以共同承诺或共同声明，促使成员在经济或道义上担负起相应责任，同时，通过对话不断拓展合作的新领域。① 前者包括东盟等区域一体化机制，后者还包括八国集团与中日韩对话机制等。必须看到，欧盟模式比较务实，而 APEC 模式比较务虚。但是前者需要成员国拥有一致的政治远景、强大的动力因素，以及较高的同质性（历史与文化因素等），而且成员国往往同属一个地域。

而反观“金砖四国”，除了上述提到的两大共同“倾向性”外，同质性却很低：各自在国情、历史、政治经济制度和文化理念等方面差异也很大。况且，从经验上看，欧盟模式机制的形成也需要成员国对朋友和敌人有着大致相近的认知，以及成员国之间存在着良好的双边关系。对此，四国也不尽满意。俄罗斯在战略上视美国为对头，但印度却视美国为一个潜在的盟友；中国尽管与巴西和俄罗斯的战略关系相交日深，但和印度的关系总是不太和谐。② 即使在中俄之间，也存在诸多问题。③ 而中俄对于印度和巴西争取成为安理会常任理事国的努力也并不怎么真心支持。四国之间的分歧即使在对待美元的态度上也相当明显。中国是美国最大的债主，仍然认可美元的主导地位。而俄罗斯和巴西由于其国家外汇储备中美元仅占 30%，积极地推动减少对美元的依赖。

同时，由于“金砖四国”机制代表了新兴发展中国家要求更多话语权的事实，其本质在挑战西方发达国家在国际金融事务中的主导地位。那么四国合作的这种“倾向性”是否超过了其与西方大国间的相互依赖？答案是否定的。自从中国实行改革开放以来，中美之间在很多问题上形成了高度相互依存的关系，比

---

① 《金砖四国峰会闪电落幕　首脑明年在中国再聚》，2010 年 4 月 17 日《广州日报》。http：//shandong. chinadaily. com. cn/hqcj/zgjj/2010 - 04 - 17/content_ 171426_ 3. html（2010 年 5 月 7 日查看）。

② Jing-dong Yuan，“The Dragon and the Elephant：Chinese-Indian Relations in the 21st Century，” *Washington Quarterly*，No. 30，Summer 2007，pp. 131 - 44；John W. Garver，“China's Influence in Central and South Asia：Is It Increasing?” in *Power Shift*：*China and Asia's New Dynamics*，David Shambaugh，ed.，Berkeley：University of California Press，2005，pp. 205 - 227.

③ 尽管存在首脑定期对话，但是两国视对方为对手的认知仍不时浮现，特别是在军方之间。俄罗斯大量减少了出售给中国的武器，在中国向远东地区移民、中亚地区的影响力竞争、上海合作组织中的意见分歧以及俄罗斯公共舆论对中国的消极印象等问题上，中俄之间还有诸多问题需要解决。

如美元稳定性①等。印美蜜月期刚开始，"在印度大国关系战略的调整中，美国在印度大国外交中的地位属于重中之重"，② 印与中、俄、巴形成高度机制化的联盟可能破坏其与美国的互信，因此未必合新德里的心意。而考虑到拉美地区与美国紧密的经贸与地缘联系，巴西也不会甘冒与美国关系恶化的危险而与地理上相距遥远的中、俄、印三国形成联盟。巴西利亚峰会召开的前夕，卢拉与奥巴马在华盛顿签署了两国自 1977 年以来的第一份双边防御协定（a bilateral defense agreement）也许最能说明巴西的态度。③ 对于俄罗斯目前的对美政策，其国内普遍认为脆弱的俄罗斯不可以通过反对美国实现自己迫切而重要的利益，这些利益只有得到美国的积极支持才能更有效地实现。④ 梅德韦杰夫在首次峰会召开前指出，"创建超主权储备货币并不会动摇美元的储备货币地位"。在峰会还未召开就安抚理论上的"无关者"，也显示出莫斯科对构建潜在与美分庭抗礼新机制的态度小心谨慎。由此可见，四国合作还具备另外一个共同倾向性——倾向于避免与美国对抗。

事实上，美国也有能力对四国进一步的机制化设置有效障碍。目前四国 GDP 总量加起来仅是美国的60%左右，四国人均 GDP 水平只有美国的8%。⑤ 四国对此也十分清楚，比如在两次首脑峰会的联合声明中，都再三强调四国合作要在20 国集团框架下进行。由于20 国集团仍以欧美国家为主导，四国对可能挑战西方领导地位举措的小心翼翼可见一斑。⑥ 因此，四国合作的这种"倾向性"还不足以形成欧盟式的机制。正如巴西副外长罗伯托·雅瓜里贝在巴西利亚首脑峰

① 以当前中国外汇储备中的两万亿美元为例，没有哪个中国领导人敢于承担美元不断贬值甚至崩溃导致中国辛勤积累的财富不断缩水的压力。而这一点显然是中国与"金砖四国"其他三国间的关系中所不存在的。这也是为什么就在四国峰会召开的前几天，中国还出资 500 亿美元购买国际货币基金组织债券维持美元稳定的原因所在。

② 吴永年：《论 21 世纪初印度外交战略的调整》，《南亚研究》2004 年第 2 期，第 19 页。

③ Mauricio Cárdenas, Brazil and the United States: A New Beginning? http://www.brookings.edu/opinions/2010/0419_us_brazil_cardenas.aspx（2010 年 5 月 7 日查看）。

④ 王伟：《梅德韦杰夫的外交选择》，《当代世界》2008 年第 6 期，第 19 页。

⑤ 林跃勤，《外部冲击与新兴经济稳定持续发展——基于"金砖四国"的分析》，《经济与管理研究》2009 年第 7 期，第 114 页。

⑥ 对于四国与美国关系的进一步分析可参见 Roya Wolverson, "Building a BRIC Foundation," April 15, 2010, http://www.cfr.org/publication/21910/building_a_bric_foundation.html（2010 年 5 月 7 日查看）；Harsh V. Pant, "Feasibility of the Russia-China-India 'Strategic Triangle': Assessment of Theoretical and Empirical Issues," *International Studies*, No. 43, 2006, pp. 51-72。

会前所表示的那样，"金砖四国不是做出必须执行的决定的机构，而是使占世界GDP40%的四国立场靠拢的平台"。①

也正是由于以上障碍，认为"金砖四国"平台最后将走向分崩离析的悲观论点一直存在。例如，"四国除了都具备规模巨大与发展迅速的特点外，其他极少有共同之处"；②"为什么不是土耳其、印尼，而是这四个国家？是因为要组建一个词语 BRIC"，"让'金砖四国'联系起来的只是每个国家的首个字母而已，除此以外，没有任何意义"，四国合作毫无前景。③ 笔者认为，对此还必须从四国走向合作的"倾向性"上进行分析。对于美国因素，四个国家尽管都把发展与美国的关系作为重中之重，但是"四国也深深担心美国的超级霸权会影响各国的根本利益"，④ 都倾向于通过发展、深化与其他大国的合作减少对美国的过度依赖，以便保持行动的更大自由并拥有外交上的更多选择。⑤ 至于应对金融危机的一时之需，四国也必须看到，在当前世界逐渐走出危机的情况下，由于欧美国家需要发展中大国协助的动力会进一步减弱，因此可能对其施加更大的压力，发展中大国联合自强的必要性反而更为紧迫。退一步讲，由于四国合作在目前"没有任何国家要牺牲任何东西，但是却存在潜在的巨大收益"，⑥ 因此，"四国仍然会继续向前推动这一机制"，"目前仅仅是刚刚开始齐心协力（pull together）而已"。⑦ 奥

① 〔俄〕伊戈尔·瑙莫夫：《"金砖四国"不再将美元作为结算货币》，2010年4月2日《独立报》（俄罗斯）。

② Raymond Colitt, "ANALYSIS-BRICs Divided on Global Agenda, Look to Mutual Trade," 14 Apr, 2010, http://www.alertnet.org/thenews/newsdesk/N14156241.htm（2010年5月9日查看）。

③ "Brics: Acronym or Coherent Strategy?" http://www.ftchinese.com/story/001014611/en FT.com / FTfm - Emerging Markets: Brics sceptics have their backs to the wall（2010年5月8日查看）。

④ Hurrell, "Hegemony, Liberalism and Global Order: What Space for Would-be Great Powers," *International Affairs*, No. 82, January 2006, p. 18.

⑤ Evan S. Medeiros, "China's International Behavior: Activism, Opportunism, and Diversification," *Joint Forces Quarterly*, No. 47, 4th quarter, 2007, p. 33.

⑥ 也有学者认为这是四国合作能否进一步机制化的根本障碍，见"The Trillion-dollar Club," April 15, 2010, from *The Economist* print edition, http://www.economist.com/world/international/displaystory.cfm?story_id=15912964（2010年5月10日查看）。

⑦ Cynthia Roberts, "Challengers or Stakeholders? BRICs and the Liberal World Order," *Polity*, *No. 42*, 2010, pp. 1-13. 参见 http://www.palgrave-journals.com/polity/journal/v42/n1/full/pol200920a.html（2010年5月9日查看）；Roya Wolverson, "Building a BRIC Foundation," April 15, 2010, http://www.cfr.org/publication/21910/building_a_bric_foundation.htm（2010年5月9日查看）。

尼尔更为乐观，"直到西方发达国家真正平等对待'金砖四国'之前，四国领导人的会晤将成为未来国际社会的一道风景线，这完全有可能对全球金融市场和世界媒体都有利"。[①]

由此可见，四国联手合作的总体方向会继续下去，问题在于合作的模式。如果采取 APEC 模式，很可能仅仅是一个十分松散甚至无所作为，且随时都可以走向解体的对话平台而已。多边机制的重要作用之一在于规范成员国行为，用多边力量对违规的成员国进行惩罚，在此过程中对机制本身进行制度建构。而 APEC 模式除了定期的对话外，本身就无"规"可言。因此，从长远来看，根据四国合作的倾向性特点，可以考虑一种介于两者之间的机制化模式。

第一，继续从"优化四国内部经济发展的国际环境"这一倾向性入手，中短期内应以构建一个多赢的经济利益共同体为首要目标。机制化的起步阶段也是机制的身份建构阶段，清晰的目标至关重要。[②] 正如胡锦涛主席在巴西利亚峰会上所表示的那样，"我们应该为进一步的合作设定清晰的目标，并从战略高度给予重视"。而这一阶段的目标应当是保守型的、有限的，避免议题过多而超过机制的承载量，同时避免由于议题过多而无法兑现减弱各方的信心。对于"金砖四国"而言，此举也能避免引起美国过早的防范。更为宏大的雄心与目标可以等机制化程度较高后逐渐开展。而在目前，应该着重从经济领域入手。[③]

如上所述，应对金融危机的经济考虑因素本身就是四国首脑峰会召开的重要背景。在全球仍然没有彻底走出金融危机的今天乃至接下来的"后危机"时代，如何逐渐改革不合理的国际金融体系，应对欧美国家"以邻为壑"的贸易政策，仍然是四国必须关注的课题。以贸易保护主义为例，假如美国对华实施大范围的贸易制裁，限制出口，不仅会使中国的出口下降，也必将导致世界贸易大幅度下滑，危害到其他三国的利益。对印度、巴西、俄罗斯而言，同样是如此。而且，"对发达

---

① Jim O'Neill, "We Need Brics to Build the World Economy," *The Times*, June 23, 2009.

② 事实上，当前四国机制化建设就面临这样一个问题，参见 Andrew S. Weiss, "BRIC-a-Brac," *Foreign Policy* (on-line), June 2009。

③ Siddharth Varadarajan, "From IBSA to CHIBSA? BRIC to BRICS? Not yet," online edition of *India's National Newspaper*, Saturday, April 17, 2010, http://www.thehindu.com/2010/04/17/stories/2010041754991400.htm（2010 年 5 月 14 日查看）。

国家虚体经济的多重依赖是'金砖'国家金融危机过敏症的主要因素"。[①] 四国建立区域经济合作组织，也有利于四个实体经济增强内部经济交流。更何况，四国经济交流还有很多处女地可以开垦。比如，巴西与俄罗斯几乎没有贸易往来，与印度的贸易也少得可怜，中国仅仅是俄罗斯的第七大贸易伙伴等。四国间的互补性也很强。巴西盛产大豆和铁矿石，被称为"世界原料基地"。俄罗斯拥有极为丰富的石油和天然气资源，石油蕴藏量居全球第七位，天然气蕴藏量和生产量均居世界首位，被称为"世界加油站"。而印度和中国则分别被称为"世界办公室"和"世界工厂"。因此，巴西和俄罗斯可以为中国和印度提供发展所需的原材料，而后者可以为前者提供加工制作与信息服务。合乎逻辑的预测表明，"金砖四国"之间具备广泛开展合作、形成固定经济集团的条件。

第二，四国合作机制化的处理与美国的关系。如上所述，四国合作机制化要想取得实质性进展，就外部关系而言，最重要的莫过于处理好与美国因素的关系。尽管目前美国的态度仍然以观望为主，但如上所述，如果四国在迈向机制化的道路上继续前进，特别是要取得突破性进展，美国必然会以某种方式介入。四国怎么办？首先，应利用后冷战时代的国际环境，通过对话与合作诱导，耐心地推动美国加深理解四国合作之于全球治理的积极意义，减弱防范心理，积极塑造和推进美国与四国的共同利益和国际共识。其次，从建立区域经济体入手，分层次进行机制化。而在危机管理、全球治理等事务中，可以尝试在如"大国共同管理"这样的国际合作方式下充分引入美国因素，使四国合作中的重大事务（特别是外交与安全）也能体现美国的利益和意愿。最后，四国也必须为美国的参与设定限制，审慎对待美国因素，避免过于制度化的、专断的美国参与，防止美国因素的过度参与对四国合作机制化的破坏性影响。而美国也应当看到后冷战时代国际格局发生的变化与趋势，理解发展阶段相近、经济互补的四国开展机制化合作的正当性，改变旧有的冷战思维，实现二者良好的互动。[②]

---

① 林跃勤：《外部冲击与新兴经济稳定持续发展——基于"金砖四国"的分析》，《经济与管理研究》2009 年第 7 期，第 110 页。Martin Wolf, "The West No Longer Holds all the Cards," *Financial Times*, 23 September 2009.

② "如果忽视了地区的动态发展，美国外交政策就会处于危险之中，美国帝权在改变着地区，反过来地区也在改变着帝权"，参见〔美〕彼得·卡赞斯坦《地区构成的世界：美国帝权中的亚洲和欧洲》，秦亚青等译，北京大学出版社，2007，第253 页。

第三，为了使四国合作的倾向性转化为实质性的行动，应构建日常化合作得以进行的必要载体。正如罗伯特·基欧汉（Robert O. Keohane）和斯蒂芬·克莱斯纳（Stephen Krasner）所论述的那样，必须建立有效的机制和制度作为一个载体，从而在国家间进行日常的共同管理，这也是机制化建设必不可少的关键一环。① 对于“金砖四国”，尽管短期内不太可能在某一个成员国内设置常设机构，但是四国可以建立一些工作组，并将其工作夯实，赋予其类似常设机构的功效。比如，俄罗斯可以牵头领导“四国能源合作小组”，印度可以牵头领导“四国 IT 合作小组”，“以农立国”、“以农富国”的巴西可以牵头领导“农产品合作领导小组”，而拥有最大外汇储备的中国，可以牵头领导“国际货币改革领导小组”。针对每一个小组，应有定期的会晤，各国有固定的会谈代表与领导机构。其会谈成果应在四国首脑峰会上达成有约束力的协议，并设立监督机构，特别要注意实施问题。事实上，只有实质性政策协调的密度和频率上去了，并有后续具体行动配套，机制化建设才能取得质的成效。

第四，进一步扩大四国合作的共同倾向性，以便增强合作的动力。为了更好地推动机制化，北京、莫斯科、巴西利亚、新德里需要通过多层面接触以维持和扩大四国合作的动力。这就要求不仅要在官方层面举行会议，而且也需要在公众之间进行交流。可喜的是，四国在这方面的合作已经开始。如上所述，本次巴西利亚峰会期间，除了领导人的高端会晤之外，还同时举行了企业家论坛、发展银行会议、合作社会议、智库研讨会等一系列平行的活动。从长远来说，这对夯实四国的合作基础、增进四国的相互信任和理解将发挥积极的影响。事实上，公众外交非常必要。扩大后的合作倾向性应该超越纯粹的战略与政治议题，比如目前“借力”推进大国影响和为国内经济发展创造环境，应该超越纯粹的“危机应对”；比如应对金融危机，应当加强工商界和民间社团的参与；比如四国间应开展科技与教育的交流。事实上，只有合作的倾向性具有民间信任与理解的基础，才能为较高和可持续的机制化打下基础，比如欧盟。有许多途径可以加强彼此信任与理解，公众教育与推动青年人的交流就是很好的办法。对于前者，可以在四国智库中分别建立“金砖四国”研究中心为政府提供对策服务并进行大众教育，

① 参见 Robert Keohane, *After Hegemony*, Princeton, N. J.: Princeton University Press, 1984, p. 244; Stephen Krasner, *Problematic Sovereignty*, New York: Columbia University Press, 2001, p. 182。

而至于后者，则可以开展诸如互派留学等更多的交流活动。

第五，从联合借力的倾向性入手，可以进一步扩大"金砖四国"的代表性，逐渐吸收南非、墨西哥、沙特等更多具有地区影响力的新兴国家加入。[①] 目前，墨西哥、印尼、土耳其已经表示了加入的兴趣。通过扩员，一方面，在进一步增强该机制影响力的同时，也会进一步提升机制本身的合法性；另一方面，体现了国际社会中的共同管理。事实上，全球性问题也是四国峰会讨论的重要内容。以巴西利亚峰会的智库研讨会为例，在总共四个议程中，有两个与之有关，一是新兴大国如何应对全球气候变化，二是新兴大国在全球治理中应该发挥怎样的作用。而由于发展中国家在这些问题上拥有共同利益，共同关注也具有正当性与必要性。但在这一过程中，根据机制化的规律，北京、莫斯科、新德里、巴西利亚应该切实担负起领导责任。从行政学本身来讲，一个松散的对话平台能否有效机制化的重要因素之一就在于是否拥有最先展望未来和最先绘制蓝图的领导者。他们的作用不仅是确立目标，而且作为舵手，推动机制化进程朝着既定的目标前进。从理论上讲，在一个无政府的国际社会里，对相关事务引入并进行高度组织化的管理，也需要领导者积极组织，牵头制定规则，必要时规约相关成员的行为。

五　中国角色的选择

经过后冷战时期相当长时间的酝酿与思辨，中国的各界精英在对待多边合作与国际机制的态度上基本上达成了一种共识，这就是上述中国走向"金砖四国"合作的"倾向性"：通过积极参与为国内发展建构一个有利的国际环境，"借力"提高国际地位。那么，分析中国在"金砖四国"进一步机制化进程中的角色，还必须从这种"倾向性"入手。

事实上，关于中国在"金砖四国"中的角色，国际社会一直给予很高期待，

① 关于如何扩员，学者也有不同意见。对此可参考 CHAPTER ELEVEN，THE N－11：MORE THAN AN ACRONYM，March 2007，http：//www2. goldmansachs. com/ideas/brics/book/BRICs-Chapter11. pdf（2010 年 5 月 19 日查看）。Michael Schuman，"Should BRICs Become BRIICs?，" March 3，2010，http：//curiouscapitalist. blogs. time. com/2010/03/03/should-brics-become-briics/（2010 年 5 月 19 日查看）；William Pesek Jr.，"South Korea，Another BRIC in Global Wall，" December 8，2005，http：//www. bloomberg. com/apps/news? pid = newsarchive&sid = aoJ4WG5LSf1 s&refer = market_ insight-redirectoldpage（2010 年 5 月 19 日查看）。

认为在“经济、金融和政治领域，中国已经并将继续使其他三国黯然失色。中国的GDP比其他三国加起来的还大，中国的出口总量与外汇储备比另外三国加起来的两倍还要大”，中国有最大的潜在市场、在G2中是美国的伙伴，“没有中国，‘金砖四国’就成了BRI——一种柔和的、软质的干酪”，“中国是这个组织的肌肉（muscle）所在，没有了中国，谁还真正在乎‘金砖四国’”?[①] 因此，“其他三方对中国的需要超过中国对其他三方的需要”，中国在这一机制的发展上具有实质性的否决权，“只要中国认为有必要，并能在‘金砖四国’机制化过程中继续进行外交努力，那么这个不同寻常但终将成功的合作机制将会继续下去”。[②] 尽管这些判断的客观性值得推敲，但是作为四国中的重要一员，中国的角色选择与角色表现对于机制化的进一步建设显然举足轻重。而反过来，四国的进一步机制化对于中国也意义深远。

第一，四国合作可以稀释美国的防范，从而减轻美国对中国的遏制与打压，有利于优化国际环境。进入21世纪以来，特别是随着中国近几年发生的几件标志性事件——奥运会的成功举办；建国60周年阅兵仪式；迄今应对金融危机的快速、成功、有效；正在召开的上海世界博览会；GDP位居世界第三等——国内外学者对中国国际角色的讨论突然热烈起来，[③] 对中国的世界大国角色有了更为普遍的认知。从现实主义理论与历史经验上看。一旦某个新兴大国被广泛视为世界大国，往往也会被既有世界大国视为挑战者。由于国际资源的有限性，前者必将遭到后者的围堵与遏制。从冷战后的中美关系来看，尽管中国被视为一个世界大国，但那是“潜在”的，并非当的前事实。这也是中国提出“20年的战略机遇期”的根

① David Rothkopf，“The BRICs and What the BRICs Would Be without China,” Monday, June 15, 2009, http：//rothkopf. foreignpolicy. com/posts/2009/06/15/the_ brics_ and_ what_ the_ brics_ would_ be_ without_ china（2010年5月15日查看）；Bobo Lo, *Axis of Convenience*：*Moscow, Beijing and the New Geopolitics* Washington D. C.：Brookings Institution Press, 2008, pp. 43, 46, 177。

② Cynthia Roberts, “Challengers or Stakeholders? BRICs and the Liberal World Order,” *Polity*, No. 42, 2010 pp. 1 - 13, http：//www. palgrave-journals. com/polity/journal/v42/n1/full/pol2009 20a. html; Raymond Colitt, “ANALYSIS-BRICs Divided on Global Agenda, Look to Mutual Trade,” 14 Apr 2010, http：//www. alertnet. org/thenews/newsdesk/N14156241. htm（2010年5月20日查看）。

③ 比如，笔者以“中国角色”（China's role）作为关键词在“google. com”里进行搜索，有124000000条结果，见http：//www. google. cn/search? hl = zh - CN&source = hp&q = China% 27s + role&aq = f&oq =（2010年3月31日查看）。

本依据所在。但是，中国复兴的步伐不会停止。20年战略机遇期后中国怎么办？也就是说，中美权力转移很可能会发展到两国接近平起平坐，而美国会竭力围堵与遏制中国的时候。正面挑战？从历史上看，所有新兴大国对既有大国的正面挑战要么被后者击败，要么两败俱伤，无一成功。德国如此，日本也是如此，更何况对于中美两个核大国来说爆发战争将是全人类的灾难。那么，中国的选择就在对外战略运作上。[①] 四国的联合行动，避免了中国单独出头而成为“众矢之的”。美国可以遏制中国，但是如果让它同时遏制中国、俄罗斯、印度、巴西，它就不得不考虑成本问题。[②]

事实上，在本次金融危机爆发后，俄罗斯与巴西对美国的批评远较中国更为直接，改革金融秩序的呼声也高于中国。[③] 而在整个冷战后的许多重大国际问题上，尤其是在巴尔干半岛、科索沃、伊拉克战争、伊朗核项目等问题上，俄罗斯对美国的批评都远较中国尖锐。尽管没有俄罗斯尖锐，但印度与巴西在多轮WTO谈判中就自由贸易等问题也多次直接挑战西方国家，最为著名的事例发生在2003年的坎昆会议上。[④] 因此，尽管其他三个国家在诸如人民币升值等有关问题上有可能联手向中国施压，而且三国对美国的直接批评也有可能“牵连”中国，但是作为目前最受西方瞩目的发展中大国的中国，通过四国合作“稀释”西方国家的负面关注，以及“隐藏”自身力量对其仍具有现实意义。

第二，中国可以通过“借力”为共同管理国际事务扮演积极角色。如果中国无法在崛起的过程中尝试向其他国家提供“良好的公共产品”，我们又如何能够真正确立大国地位？正如开头所分析的那样，冷战后国际关系的一个突出特点，就是全球问题凸显，人类命运空前互相依赖，解决的办法也超出了某个国家

---

① 中国本身也做了很多姿态。比如，中国2010年3月4日宣布当年度的防务预算仅增加7.5%，而不是以往的每年增加10%（自1989年中国宣布大规模军队现代化改革以来，近20年一直保持该速度）。目前降低防务预算幅度一是为了应对目前的全球经济危机；二是为了向世界其他国家表明，中国正在裁军。而同期印度军费增加了8%。中国向世界传递的信息相当明确：中国爱好和平。

② 2009年哥本哈根气候峰会可以说就是一个例子。当美国总统原本想找温家宝总理谈判时，却发现屋子里还有南非、俄罗斯、巴西三个国家的首脑。这样一来，美国发现，原本想和中国进行的谈判却成了美国与发展中国家的谈判。中国不仅借此规避了单独承担风险的可能性，也增强了其软实力。

③ “BRIC Nations Say No IMF Cash without Representation,” *Reuters*, March 13, 2009.

④ Andrew Hurrell and Amrita Narlikar, “A New Politics of Confrontation? Brazil and India in Multilateral Trade Negotiations,” *Global Society*, No. 20, 2006, pp. 415 – 33.

的能力，于是“共同管理”应运而生。“中美共治”、“八国集团”、“金砖四国”、“20 国集团”，以及方兴未艾的欧盟一体化、东盟一体化、东亚一体化、北美一体化、非洲与拉美地区的一体化等，实质上都反映了这样一个态势。在中国越来越被视为国际社会中的主要角色时，在共同管理人类共同事务上其也越来越被赋予更大的国际责任。中国不可能在全世界的关注中选择沉默，甚至逃避。在国际关系中，大国地位和大国豪情不是“自我感觉”，最重要的是“他人”的知觉。通过积极参与并主导多边机制建设，在此基础上对国际事务进行共同管理，维护多数国家（特别是发展中国家）的共同利益，放大其他国家和人民眼中中国的可靠性，就是中国改善国际形象、树立更为负责任大国形象的重要切入点。这也正是胡锦涛主席在巴西利亚峰会上对于中国角色进行说明的主要内容：“首先，中国的发展任重道远。其次，中国的发展只能也必然是和平发展。再者，中国的发展是开放共赢的发展。最后，中国的发展是负责任的发展。”① 但与此同时，由于欧美国家仍然主导当今国际体系，中国对相关国际事务的管理要想积极有效，同其他大国进行联合从而“借力”增加自己的话语权也是一个很好的选择。相反的例子是俄罗斯在西方八国集团中的边缘化角色。

第三，除了战略上的收益外，四国建立更紧密的机制化，对中国的经济发展也有着现实意义。中国是世界第二大石油消费国、第八大石油进口国，石油生产量约占世界的 4.3%，消费量却占世界的 8.8%。从 2003 年起，巴西每年都向中国出口原油，年均增长率为 89.5%。② 而俄罗斯预计 2015 年前在中国市场所占的份额将占 15%。同时，中国还是全球最大的铁矿石进口国，自 2003 年其进口比例就超过了 50%，铁矿石消耗量已占世界的 47%。从进口来源来看，从巴西进口的铁矿石已占中国进口总量的 25%，而从印度进口铁矿石占中印贸易合作的 65%。③ 如果四国间能逐渐形成较高机制化的自由贸易体，对于中国的能源供给与稳定也大有助益。

除此之外，由于中国在与其他三个国家的双边关系上，特别是与印度和俄罗斯

---

① 《合作 开放 互利 共赢——在“金砖四国”领导人会晤时的讲话》，中华人民共和国外交部网站，http://www.fmprc.gov.cn/chn/pds/ziliao/zyjh/t682096.htm（2010 年 5 月 15 日查看）。

② 张抗：《从金砖四国在世界石油中的地位看其合作发展方向》，《当代石油石化》2009 年第 8 期，第 9 页。

③ 邓雄：《“金砖四国”的经济形势分析》，《金融教学与研究》2008 年第 5 期，第 52 页。

的双边关系上，一直都存在不和谐声音，更为紧密的机制化也可以为中国解决相关双边问题提供一个机制化的平台。中国通过与俄罗斯和印度更为紧密的合作，可以向这两个国家显示中国即使崛起也不会威胁或挑战他们的利益，而是追求合作共赢。中国此举也可以在某种程度上减弱甚至避免印度或俄罗斯加入美国可能领导的“‘反华’或‘围华’联盟”。同时，中国和这三个同为发展中大国的国家结为更为紧密的合作关系，也为中国学习与借鉴其他国家的经验提供了一个非常好的机会。此外，由于近年来的迅速发展，中国越来越多地被视为一个发达国家，通过与发展中大国的紧密合作乃至进一步让其他中小发展中国家加入“金砖四国”，在塑造“金砖四国”发展中国家俱乐部集体身份的同时，也有利于塑造中国的发展中国家身份。①

综上所述，中国在“金砖四国”机制化进程中的角色选择的倾向性就相当清晰了，即不应该当“老大”，但要积极而为，起到主导作用。第一，中国对于任何担当“老大”角色的尝试应当慎之又慎。一方面，“作为四国中最强大的中国最容易被美国认为想领导一个‘政治组织’挑战和破坏美国和西方的自由秩序”。② 无论如何，从中长期来看，对中国角色影响最大的还是美国因素。被美国视为要挑头组建反美联盟仍然是中国应竭力避免的事情。另一方面，客观上讲，中国的国家实力还不足以支持其在“金砖四国”机制化建设中担当“老大”角色，担当“老大”对于中国外交而言是“力不足”。③ 第二，尽管不应担当

① 参见 Gregory T. Chin，“China's Evolving G8 Engagement：Complex Interests and Multiple Identity in Global Governance Reform，” in *Emerging Powers in Global Governance：Lessons from the Heiligendamm Process*，eds.，Andrew F. Cooper and Agata Antkiewicz，Waterloo，Ontario：Wilfrid Laurier University Press，2008，pp. 83 - 114。

② Michael A. Glosny，“China and the BRICs：A Real（but Limited）Partnership in a Unipolar World，” 11，http：//web. mit. edu/polisci/research/gradresearch/Glosny-China% 20and% 20the% 20BRICs-Clean%20Sept%2011%20version%20ISA%20paper. doc（2010 年 5 月 20 日查看）。

③ 从以上“金砖四国”机制化的回顾中可以看到，对于机制化目前最积极的国家要数俄罗斯。俄虽然是 G8 成员，但是和其他七个国家相比，在会议上受到不同的待遇。G20 中起主导作用的国家仍然是欧美，新兴发展中国家要数中国。因此，从俄罗斯的角度看，确实想在“金砖四国”中扮演主要角色。尽管俄罗斯的 GDP 仅仅相当于中国的 1/3，而四国中俄罗斯受到金融危机的打击最大，但是俄罗斯人均 GDP 超过一万美元，相当于中国的三倍。根据高盛公司的估计，到 2050 年，俄罗斯也是唯一一个人均 GDP 能赶上欧盟的国家。2/3 的年轻人有机会接受大学教育，而中国的这一数字仅仅是 1/5。在引领世界发展的前 50 项技术中，俄罗斯占 12 ~ 17 项。在军事能力方面，俄罗斯也是唯一能与美国抗衡的军事大国。同时，俄罗斯也是世界上唯一资源能自给自足的国家。“俄罗斯不仅远远较巴西发达，而且在许多层面也远远发达于印度与中国”。参见 Anders Aslund，“Does Russia belong in the Brics?，” *Financial Times*，January 20，2010。

"老大"角色，但这也并不意味着中国无论怎样都能坐享收益最大化的效果。如果我们在"金砖四国"的机制化建设进程中，在目标规划、谈判议题优先项的设置、制度架构的建设等方面不能取得较大的话语权，就不能很好地维护中国的国家利益。因此，应创造条件使自己起到积极的主导作用。

六　结论

事实上，任何国际对话平台与多边机制都有一定的倾向性，这也是此类平台与机制形成的根本性动力所在，因此这个倾向性也就成了考察类似问题的重要切入点。而本文之所以以"倾向性"来考察"金砖四国"的机制化以及其中的中国角色，原因还包括以下两点。其一，"金砖四国"这样一个由经济学家创造的词语走向了首脑峰会以至逐步机制化，关于其动因、现状、前景，存在诸多争议，"如何深化四国的联系是一个具有争议性的问题"。① 而以各国走向合作的"倾向性"作为切入点进行考察可以很好地回答这些争议。其二，冷战后的国际格局一直处于调整当中，金融危机可以说是最新的一个变量，② 而这个过程中中国角色的上升始终是国际社会最为关注的课题。为了适应新的国际背景，中国外交也确实处于相应的调整当中，从过去拒绝多边到逐步走向多边是其中最重要的调整之一。中国不仅融入了许多多边国际体系，而且也创设了相应的多边对话平台与机制，比如朝核问题六方会谈、上海合作组织等。那么，作为"金砖四国"中的最受关注的一方，中国在四国合作与进一步机制化中的"倾向性"是什么，如何实现这种"倾向性"。作为中国学者当然应该当仁不让地对其进行考察。

① Roya Wolverson, "Building a BRIC Foundation," April 15, 2010, http://www.cfr.org/publication/21910/building_a_bric_foundation.html（2010年5月17日查看）；Andrew Hurrell, "Hegemony, Liberalism and Global Order: What Space for Would-be Great Powers," *International Affairs*, No. 82, January 2006, pp. 1－19.（2010年3月31日查看）。

② 同时讨论权力转移的文章也非常多，甚至有印度学者最近提出了"笨猪四国"（PIGS）（Portugal, Italy or Ireland, Greece, Spain）的概念。本质上讲，这些讨论都从一个侧面反映了冷战后的国际格局还未定型，一直处于变化过程当中。可参见 Christopher Layne, "The Waning of U.S. Hegemony: Myth or Realty," *International Security*, No. 34, Summer 2009, pp. 147－72. David Shambaugh, ed., *Power Shift: China and Asia's New Dynamics*, Barkeley and Los Angeles: University of California Press, 2005；Andrew Zvirzdin, "Of BRICs and PIGS," *International Economics* on Monday, February 8, 2010。

本质上讲，四国的这种"倾向性"代表了冷战后一批新兴国家正在努力利用变化了的国际背景与世界格局实现崛起的现实。必须看到，这种超越发展是个持之以恒的艰苦过程。在全球化相互依赖的情况下，国内政治与国际政治界限逐渐模糊，外交运作也成了其能否成功实现崛起的至关重要的一环。而"金砖四国"就是四个新兴国家为实现崛起而在外交上的最新联合。透过本文的分析可见，这四个国家的联合确实有利于四国战略目标的实现。因此，应该根据四国走向合作的"倾向性"因素，因势利导，从先经济后政治，先难后易入手，积极推动机制化建设。在这一过程中，横向上巩固与扩大"倾向性"，纵向上利用其他发展中国家的"倾向性"，通过吸收新成员扩大影响并增强合法性，同时要注意处理美国因素。这样一来，"金砖四国"不仅能成为多极世界中的主要的非西方中心利益协调的核心，而且四国的联合发声也有助于西方为主的国际机制采取更为公平的方法来处理与发展中国家的关系。

在这样一个重要的历史时期，新兴国家中经济发展速度最快、实力最强，以及国际关注度最高的中国，也应顺应形势，积极而为，但同时应注意自身的角色定位，冷静客观，牢记自身的发展中国家身份，既注意向其他发展中大国"借力"，也要顾及发达国家的利益。同时，不要轻易偏离这种"倾向性"。如果从"金砖四国"机制上进一步延伸，中国角色的这种"倾向性"的指导意义仍然适用。一方面，为了实现这种"倾向性"，应该积极主动地创设各种多边协调机制、合作机制，维护和拓展国家利益；另一方面，以渐进而非变革的手段对待现有国际体系，减弱西方发达国家对中国的防范。这样一来，不仅有利于实现中国的这种"倾向性"，而且也有利于和平发展与"合作共赢"的世界大局。由此可见，四国机制化建设的战略意义不仅仅体现在处理四国关系上，而且也可服务于全球和平和发展的总体目标。

总之，四国走向合作的这些"倾向性"的形成可以说是四国朝野在冷战后根据变化了的国际形势进行务实外交的产物。它将对四国接下来的合作及其机制化产生重大影响。也就是说，尽管四国合作已经成为共识，但不同的国家在合作时却有着不同的"倾向性"。所以，我们在研究"金砖四国"进一步的机制化建设以及其中的中国角色时应该特别注意这个"倾向性"问题。这也是分析研究四国关系及其发展变化的基础。

中印两国如何引领亚洲的自主增长

刘小雪*

美国的次贷危机在全球引发了一波深 V 字形的经济震荡。即使在两年后的今天，全球经济也依然未能完全回到危机前的增长轨道上。危机还加强了经济走势的不稳定性和不确定性，困扰着各方。于是，学界开始从危机之初连篇累牍地解释和夸大这场危机，转向探讨各国乃至世界在后危机时代何去何从。迄今，所能形成的共识就是，缺乏监管且过度杠杆化金融市场，虽是危机的最直接源头，但更深层次的原因却在于全球经济的不平衡。无论是以美国为首的工业化国家，还是以中国为代表的新兴市场国家，要实现可持续的经济增长，就必须做出相应的转变。

一　亚洲的自主增长与中印两国在亚洲的地位

（一）亚洲自主增长的必要性

美国消费增长持续走低，将影响全球总需求。尽管美国人口仅占世界总人口的 4.5%，但 2007 年其消费支出大约为 9.7 万亿美元，占世界 GDP 的 19%。相比之下，人口占世界 1/5 的中国，其消费总额仅 1 万亿美元。在 1996 ~ 2006 年

* 刘小雪，中国社会科学院亚洲太平洋研究所副研究员。

的十年间，美国消费的年增长率达到4%，消费支出已占GDP的72%。而这一时期也正是亚洲新兴国家对美出口不断扩大、贸易盈余不断上升的时期。居民消费的增长一般源于两个因素：收入增加和财富累积。而自20世纪90年代中期以来，美国的个人收入为经济增长提供的动力逐渐减弱，同时财富效应作为一股越来越重要的力量成功地推动着美国消费的增长。① 收入不增加，但又希望通过增加消费来实现经济增长，那就只能鼓励中产阶级增加负债消费了。美国家庭的负债占美国GDP的比例也从1979年的46%上升到2007年12月的98%，户均负债额创纪录地达到个人可支配收入的133%。英国也一样，家庭负债占GDP的比重30年间从20%上升到了80%。法国、德国都不例外。此次金融危机证明，高负债推动下的消费主导型发展模式蕴含巨大风险，危机之时被迫实行的“去杠杆化”过程使国民财富短时间内大幅缩水，恐慌由此出现，并最终使整个经济深陷“流动性陷阱”之中。所以这种模式更像是饮鸩止渴，难以持续。

目前，以美国为代表的西方发达国家正在进行不同程度的经济“再平衡”。美国的消费和储蓄模式已开始发生变化，美国家庭开始重建以个人储蓄为基础的财富积累。2009年12月份，美国的国民储蓄率不断上升，目前国内居民储蓄净额占GDP的比重已由危机初期的-1.2%提高到6.5%，而且仍在继续上升。美国个人消费虽较危机之初有所恢复，但很难再回到危机前的增长水平。目前美国的失业率依然高达10%。国际货币基金组织（IMF）最新的报告将美国近期的经济复苏称为“没有就业的复苏”。② 预计其高失业率还将持续若干年。失业率上升对美国家庭造成了灾难性的影响，有可能引发与消费间的恶性循环。因此，鉴于危机过后财富萎缩，就业前景黯淡，美国消费在未来几年中很难回到危机前的增长水平。

亚洲新兴经济体的出口导向型战略面临挑战，区内市场将受重视。亚洲各新兴经济体，借着西方发达国家主要是美国的繁荣的消费市场，不断提高产能、扩大出口，最终实现了自身的高速增长。而现在，随着美国房市泡沫的破灭，美国经济陷入了自20世纪30年代以来最严重的一次萧条。亚洲国家也不幸被卷入其

① 〔美〕史蒂芬·罗奇：《对全球经济的展望》，《未来的亚洲：新全球化时代的机遇与挑战》，中信出版社，2009，第5页。

② 参见IMF发布的《2010年世界经济前景》。

中。2007 年亚洲新兴经济体的平均增长率为 10.6%，2008 年就降至 7.9%，2009 年更进一步降至 6.5%。其中，东盟的降速最明显，2009 年它的增长率只有 1.3%。这场全球性的经济危机，归根结底是由全球失衡造成的。作为解决失衡的一种途径，“亚洲脱钩”也因此受到了更大的关注。“亚洲脱钩”，简单地说，就是亚洲新兴经济体不再依赖西方市场，从而也不再受西方经济波动的影响。

对于亚洲出口导向型国家而言，“脱钩”不外乎两个选择，即寻找西方发达国家以外的市场，或者扩大内需。而这两项选择无一不与中印两国有关。因为选择前者时，放眼世界，只有中印两国凭借其庞大的市场规模和领先的经济增速，有能力吸收更多的进口产品；而扩大内需，也主要是对区内大国而言，小国或地区通过扩大内需来实现赶超型经济增长会非常困难，甚至不现实（如新加坡、中国香港和中国台湾）。为此，我们可以说，“与西方脱钩”也就意味着亚洲自主增长的开始。然而，在全球化时代，不同地区之间完全拒绝相互影响是不可能的，准确地说，亚洲自主增长应该是一种既不过度依赖国际市场，也不完全受限于国内市场的相对稳定的增长。

目前全球性金融危机已经为亚洲脱钩提供了一个难得的时机。一方面，这场危机使“脱钩”成为亚洲国家不得不为之的选择。陷入萧条的西方发达国家原本市场就已萎缩，又因为失业率居高不下，基于政治利益考虑纷纷开始采取贸易保护措施。未来亚洲新兴经济体要恢复危机前的出口增长水平将更为困难。另一方面，危机之后亚洲发展中经济体通过自身政策的调整，更早地实现了强劲的经济复苏。其中，中国、印度的回升最为明显，这在一定程度上得益于它们国内消费支出和投资支出的猛增。同时，区内贸易和区内成员间的相互投资也都较危机前有所增加。这些都加强了亚洲新兴经济体对“脱钩”的信心。

（二）在亚洲经济格局中中印两国地位举足轻重

作为世界上最大的两个发展中国家，中印两国都曾有过辉煌的古代、屈辱的近代历史，在现代化的发展道路上，又都走过不少弯路。中国自从改革开放以来，已经连续 20 多年保持经济高速增长，人民的生活水平有了极大的提高。中国的成功，在很大程度上刺激了印度的经济改革并且成为印度改革进程中的参照系。20 世纪 90 年代印度经济增长平均增速达到 6%，比过去 40 年中备受世人嘲笑的3%的“印度速度”快了一倍。进入21世纪，印度经济连续五年保持近8%的增速，使之成为除中国外世界经济的又一个亮点。受次贷危机的影响，两国的出口都大幅下滑：2008年中印两国的出口增速分别为17.6%和13.7%（中印两国2008年的主要经济指标见表1），2009年就分别降至-16%和-15%。为了应对危机，两国都力图通过扩张型财政政策和货币政策，刺激内需，最终成效明显。2009年中国的增速达到8.7%，而印度也达到了6.7%。

表1　中印两国2008年主要经济指标

项　目	数　额	占世界比(%)	占亚洲比(%)
中国人口(人)	13亿	20	33
印度人口(人)	11亿	17	28
中国GDP(美元)	4.3万亿	7	25
印度GDP(美元)	1.2万亿	2	7
中国对外贸易(美元)	25616.3亿	8.3	11.7*
印度对外贸易(美元)	4966.5亿	1.5	—

* 这里指的是中国的对外贸易占发展中亚洲经济体的份额。

中印两国对亚洲经济增长的带动作用，如果从统计角度来看，表现为占有重要权数的中印经济，通过自身的高增长提升了加权平均后得出的亚洲增速（见表2）。以东亚为例，2009年东亚各经济体除韩国经济略有增长外，中国香港、中国台湾、蒙古都为负增长，但因为该地区中国内地的优异表现，东亚当年平均增长率达到5.2%。如果从经济增长实际发生的溢出效应来看，中印两国扩大内需的努力也在一定程度上带动了周边国家对它们的出口，从而加快了这些国家的经济复苏。这种情况从中国与东亚、东南亚经济体之间的贸易中看得最清楚。中国作为东亚生产网络的一个环节，从周边国家进口零部件和原材料，经过加工和组装，将最终成品出口欧美市场。受危机冲击，中国对欧美出口锐减，相应的，中国从周边国家的进口也迅速下滑。但在2009年1月降至最低点之后，随着刺激政策的到位，中国从周边国家的进口开始反弹，到7月就已基本恢复到危机前的水平。而这一复苏是在中国对欧美国家出口没有相应复苏的条件下发生的。这说明中国吸纳了相当一部分进口并在国内市场上予以消化。中国在危机之后实现的高速增长，也增强了亚洲其他出口导向型国家的市场信心。

表2　2000～2008年中国的双边贸易占亚洲主要发展中经济体对外贸易的比重

单位：%

经济体＼年份	2000	2005	2008	经济体＼年份	2000	2005	2008
印　　度	2.4	7.0	11.5	菲 律 宾	2.0	8.0	17.9
印　　尼	5.0	8.7	10.1	新 加 坡	4.6	9.4	9.8
中国香港	38.8	45.0	47.5	中国台湾	3.6	16.4	22.7
韩　　国	9.4	18.4	22.3	泰　　国	4.7	8.9	10.2
马来西亚	3.5	8.8	12.6	越　　南	9.8	13.2	15.2
新 西 兰	4.7	8.2	9.7				

资料来源：ADB 网站。

二　中印两国迈向自主、可持续增长之路

全球金融危机使中印两国发展的外部环境发生了一定的变化，而它们自身在经历了一定时期的高增长之后，内部也出现了经济、社会的变化。未来中印经济要继续保持高速增长就必须做出相应的转变：中国将从目前以制造业为主的出口导向型增长模式向出口—内需更加平衡、产业结构向绿色和轻型化转变；印度则不再沾沾自喜于服务业带动的、以内需为主的“印度模式”，而会在一定程度上向“东亚模式”靠拢。可以说，成功的经济转型将引领两国走上自主的、可持续增长之路。

（一）中国的经济转型

1. 中国所追求的“世界工厂”遇到了增长瓶颈，中国转型势在必行

东亚经济体包括日本以及“四小龙”、“四小虎”，都经历过政府主导、制造业驱动，并伴有明显出口导向型特征的经济快速增长阶段，中国内地在1979年改革开放之后，也选择了这样的发展路径。基于国内廉价的劳动力和良好的基础设施，加上海外华人的投资和技术，中国很快就成了劳动密集型产品的出口基地，制造业的比重也从20世纪80年代初的36%上升到目前的55%，上升速度之快以及幅度之大，在全球各国中都少见。出口的收入又被投入基础设施建设中，政府鼓励竞争和劳动力的流动，使中国拥有了较好的基础设施和廉价的劳动

力，出口竞争力进一步加强。中国自身的优势加上政府对外国直接投资的积极吸纳使中国逐步成为“世界工厂”。然而，现在“世界工厂”却遇到了三个瓶颈：资源瓶颈、环境瓶颈和市场瓶颈。

资源瓶颈 现阶段中国面临的资源瓶颈，从国内资源的供给来看，主要表现为原材料价格、土地价格以及劳动力价格的上涨，直接损害了中国产品的国际竞争力；从国外资源的供给来看，则体现在由中国无止境的需求膨胀造成的国际基础物资价格的长期看涨趋势。据国际能源署（International Energy Agency）的最新数据，中国已超过美国，成为全球最大的能源消费国（这里的能源包括原油、核电、煤炭、天然气以及水力发电等再生资源）。多年来中国总体能源消费呈两位数的年率增长，这使中国消费的每样能源，从石油到铀再到其他自然资源的价格居高不下。再加上国际投机者的介入，既降低了中国厂家的资源可获得性，又导致价格剧烈波动，损害了厂商合理的定价能力。

环境瓶颈 与所有的工业化国家一样，中国的环境污染问题是与工业化相伴而生的。从20世纪80年代开始，随着改革开放和经济的高速发展，中国的环境污染渐呈加剧之势，特别是乡镇企业的异军突起，使环境污染向农村急剧蔓延。同时，生态破坏的范围也在扩大。在世界10大空气污染最严重的城市中，中国就占了5个；中国7大水系中近50%的河段污染严重，86%的城市河段水质普遍超标；中国还是世界上土地沙漠化严重的国家之一，近10年来土地沙漠化急剧发展。此外，物种灭绝、植被破坏等问题也非常严重。

资源瓶颈与环境瓶颈在很多时候像是一个硬币的两面无法分开。以中国为例，在资源有限的条件下，既没有实现资源的集约使用，又不能对废弃物、排放物进行必要的治理，其结果就是同时加剧了资源与环境瓶颈效应。

市场瓶颈 一个经济体对他国商品的长驱直入必定要设一个限度。设定这个限度的最常见理由就是要保护本国就业或是实现贸易平衡。出口市场瓶颈很少是因为市场完全饱和造成的。2009年中国的GDP总量已经超过4万亿美元，出口占GDP的比重达到了37%。在世界10大经济体当中，只有德国在这方面与中国大致相当，而其他的国家都远远低于中国：美国只有8.4%，日本为16.3%，英国为15.7%，法国为21.6%，意大利为23.4%，西班牙为7.4%，加拿大为29.2%，巴西为12.2%。中国与德国出口和进口的规模也大致相当，占世界出口和进口总额的比重相差无几，但两国在国际受到的待遇截然不同。关键的一点就在于两国出口的产品结构不同，德国的产品属于高精尖的居多，并享有一定的品牌效应，而中国的产品大都属于劳动密集型或资本密集型的产品，缺乏品牌影响，因而替代性强。实际上，中国目前的状况更接近于20世纪80年代初“广场协议”之前的日本。回想当年巨额的日美贸易逆差，最后是以日本让步、日元大幅升值而结束的，那么我们就可以推知，即使没有这场使欧美国家大伤元气的金融危机，未来中国的出口产品在欧美市场上的增长空间也已经非常有限了，而这场危机只会使问题变得更加严峻。根据 WTO 的数据，2008 年世界上34%的反倾销案是针对中国发起的。而到2009 年，随着各国出现了经济困难，对中国产品的反倾销调查变得更为密集。而恰在这一年中国超过德国成为世界第一出口国，结果自然是更多的中国产品成了发达国家和发展中国家推行贸易保护主义的靶子。

2. 突破瓶颈的举措

短期内，对中国经济增长威胁最大也最迫切需要解决的是市场瓶颈问题。有两种最基本的应对办法：一是促进经济平衡增长，从过度依赖投资和出口转向扩大内需，特别是提升消费需求对经济增长的带动作用；二是通过海外直接投资转移过剩产能，规避贸易壁垒。

私人消费在经济增长中的作用已得到重视。消费首先是收入的函数。在边际消费倾向一定的情况下，收入增加，消费相应的也将增加。中国是世界经济增长最快的地区，因此理论上看，中国的消费也应该是增长最快的。同时，从社会结构上看，中国正在完成从农业社会向工业社会的转变，伴随着迅速推进的城市化进程，城市中产阶级的队伍越来越庞大，社会的边际消费倾向将会因为这样新兴消费阶级的出现而上升。目前他们对汽车、房产不断膨胀的需求，正成为长期保持国内需求强劲增长的一个最主要动力。但事实是，中国的居民消费在过去10年中一直在下降，到2008 年只占 GDP 的 36.1%，比 2000 年低了近 10 个百分点，是东亚、东南亚和南亚的发展中国家中最低的。

中国居民消费水平下降的原因可以归结为两点。第一，居民劳动收入增长低于 GDP 的增速，中国居民可支配收入在国民可支配收入中的比重从 1997 年的66%降为 2007 年的 58%，而同期政府收入的比重却从 17%上升到 20%，企业收入比重也从 17%升至 22%。不合理的分配结构抑制了私人消费的增长潜力。第二，排除中国人口年龄较轻、储蓄的边际倾向较高的因素，对未来预期的不确定性也是中国人过度储蓄的一个重要原因。从表 3 中可以看出，中国居民可支配收入占 GDP 的比重高过韩国、日本，可是个人消费却远远低于它们。而这正是政府可以大有作为的地方：通过提供更广泛的社会保障和更高质量的公共教育服务，降低居民对未来支出的预期，缓解他们对未来的过度焦虑，使他们对待储蓄和消费能更为理性。

表 3　2004 年个别国家消费状况（占 GDP 比）

单位：%

国家 \ 项目	劳动收入	可支配收入	个人消费	政府提供的健康和教育服务	调整后的消费
美国	57	74	70	10	80
英国	56	66	65	12	77
法国	52	62	56	6	62
德国	51	66	57	6	63
日本	51	59	57	5	62
韩国	44	54	51	5	56
印度	—	84	67	4	70
中国	56	60	41	3	44

资料来源：Jahangir Aziz，2006。

在危机发生后中国政府为了刺激消费，采取了“家电下乡”、“汽车消费补贴”等政策。但这些都是治标不治本的政策。中国政府也意识到了这个问题。2009 年 3 月，分配给基础设施领域的投资份额由先前的 45% 下调到 38%，而用于民生项目（诸如卫生和教育等）的资金比例则从 1% 上调到 4% 左右。此外，中国政府正在考虑进行户籍制度改革。现有户籍制度将人口划分为农村和城市居民，这使进城务工的农民不能享受教育、医疗、住房和养老等领域的财政补贴。这种制度已经阻碍了劳动力的流动，减少了农民工的可支配收入，扩大了城乡收入差距。2009 年底，中国政府已经在部分地区放宽了户籍限制，但仅限于一些中小城市。总之，有利于提高居民收入和促进私人消费的改革已经开始，但实现私人消费的可持续增长尚需时日。

通过海外直接投资转移过剩产能进展缓慢。东亚雁形模式的一个核心特点就是产业在不同发展阶段的经济体之间传递。中国幅员辽阔，地区之间经济发展存在着很大的差异，如果不考虑市场因素，那么东部地区一些劳动密集型产业完全可以向中西部地区转移。但在目前阶段，市场瓶颈带来的压力如此之大，根本无法回避。如果中国能够将一些因为国内成本上升而渐失国际竞争力的产业果断地转移到越南、柬埔寨或者是南亚的国家，那么在实现国内产业升级的同时，势必也会带动这些国家的工业化的发展，而且也规避了一些国家专为中国产品高筑的贸易壁垒。但迄今为止中国制造型企业走出去的步伐依然缓慢。究其原因，在于地方政府出于对本地区就业的考虑，为挽留企业人为地扭曲资源价格和忽视环境成本，而企业又很少能以全局的眼光来看待产业的发展周期，面对市场困境，更多的是被动地期待市场景气的重新到来。

从长期的发展来看，中国还必须克服资源瓶颈和环境瓶颈，才有可能实现可持续的增长。因此，中国除了改变两头在外的加工贸易方式，通过产业升级和产业创新，变贸易大国为贸易强国外，还要大力发展服务业，特别是生产型服务业，在为经济寻找到新的增长点的同时，既推动制造业集约化、高端化发展，又促进产业结构“轻型化”，使经济发展更加绿色。

（二）印度的再工业化

1. 印度模式的局限性

印度的增长模式一直以来更像是中国模式矫枉过正后的结果，二者形成鲜明对比。而现在两国为了实现更为均衡的发展，开始从相反的两极向中间靠拢：中国要发展服务业，而印度要追求再工业化；中国要减少对外贸、外资的依赖，而印度则要扩大对外贸和外资的开放。如果说中国的经济增长主要是由制造业驱动，那么印度则是以服务业为主。在中国，外资和外贸发挥了重要的作用。在过去十年中，印度服务业的产值占 GDP 的比重迅速增加，已经占到 GDP 的 50%，比处在同等发展水平上的其他国家平均高出近 10 个百分点。印度服务业的快速增长有两个重要的原因，一个是信息技术的普及，提高了从银行到通信等现代服务部门的劳动生产率；二是信息技术带动了外包服务的发展。前者发展空间的大小最终取决于国内生产部门（农业和工业）的发展，而后者则受他国经济景气周期的影响，并且也会时常受到贸易保护主义的干扰。从已经实现了经济起飞的国家的经验来看，还没有一个国家可以绕过工业化道路直接进入发达国家的行列。对于印度这样拥有庞大农业人口的大国，更难以例外。未来 40 年，印度每年新增劳动力将达到 1300 万，解决他们的就业不仅仅是经济问题，更有着重要的政治意义。考虑到这些新增劳动力中，至少有 40% 的文盲，受过高等教育的只占 1/10 左右，因此，印度必须发展制造业，以缓解就业压力。

进入 21 世纪以来的这 10 年，印度经济运行轨迹已经越来越显现出与世界经济同步的特征。2003 ~ 2004 年到 2008 ~ 2009 年印度经历的这一轮经济高增长，就与全球以及发达国家经历的这一轮景气相同步。2008 年全球遭遇金融危机，印度经济增速也下降了近 3 个百分点。这正说明在过去的 10 年中，印度经济的开放程度有了很大的提高，已经越来越深地融入国际经济体系之中。印度政府也日益认识到，只有超越国内资本和国内市场的限制，才可能长期实现并保持一个更高的增速。

然而，由于制造业发展相对滞后，印度贸易产品普遍缺乏国际竞争力，这影响了印度实现贸易目标。早在 2004 年公布的印度中期（2004 ~ 2009 年）进出口政策中，印度政府就设定了两个目标，一是在五年内提升印度在世界贸易中的比重，二是以贸易为手段促进经济增长和就业。而 2005 ~ 2008 年的三年间，印度出口占世界出口的比重仅提升了 0.1 个百分点。对于外资，印度政府虽然持更加开放的态度，允许外资进入很多行业，并且不断提高外资的持股比例，但影响投资的结构性障碍还远未消除。这些障碍包括：过于严厉的《劳工法》，这一法律使得企业难以解雇工人；基础设施严重不足，影响了投资的效率；复杂的土地交易法规；繁琐而冗长的司法程序以及腐败的官僚体系，无谓地耗费了投资者大量的时间和金钱。

2. 大力发展制造业①

从目前印度制造业的发展状况看，无论是它在 GDP 中所占的份额，还是在就业中所占的比例，抑或是它的全要素生产率，都远远低于中国。特别是在消费品工业领域，印度国内中小企业在价格上几乎无法与中国的企业相抗衡。仅劳动生产率方面（以单位时间生产的产品数量为标准），中国工人就要比印度工人高出 10% ~300%。② 为了保护本国的企业，印度政府最后不得不利用 WTO 的反倾销法案，限制中国商品的进入。但正如印度工商部长马兰自己所承认的，反倾销税并不是控制中国商品涌入印度市场的永久良策，唯一的办法只能是印度大力发展制造业，提高本土企业竞争能力。

要发展印度制造业，首先必须改变印度落后的基础设施条件。因为从世界各

---

① Triveni Gandhi, *Indian Journal of Economics and Business*, Dec. , 2009.

② Amadeo Di Lodovico, "India: From Emerging to Surging," *The Mckinsey Quarterly*, No. 4, 2001.

国的经验来看，工业的发展离不开高效的基础设施支持，特别是便捷的交通运输、稳定的电力供应等。过去印度中央和地方政府的赤字总和一直占 GDP 的 10%左右，政府公债占 GDP 的 80%。庞大的财政赤字使政府无暇顾及基础设施建设，造成包括农业灌溉、道路交通以及电力供应等在内的基础设施投入严重不足。危机前两年政府的财政赤字比例本来已有所下降，危机中实行的刺激政策再度使赤字接近 10%。因此，印度现在越来越将发展基础设施的希望寄托在引入更多的私人投资上面。但由于基础设施作为公共物品或准公共物品，又与一般的商品不同，需要更多的公共政策扶持。目前阶段，由于政策不到位，私人投资对参与基础设施建设还持观望态度。其次，印度在发展中国家中依然维持着较高的关税水平，这不利于印度企业参与国际分工。东亚经济体的经验已经证明，中小企业如果能够加入全球供应链，就会在更激烈的竞争中和更大的市场上实现更快的成长。印度过去一直通过高筑壁垒的方法来保护中小企业的发展，结果适得其反。

三 促进地区合作、扩大两国经济增长对周边国家的溢出效应

中印两国凭借着它们所具有的人口优势、技术后发优势以及制度变革可能释放的增长潜力，如果政策得当，有理由相信它们在未来相当长的时期内能够保持较快的增长速度。危机后两国都迅速摆脱了经济下滑的趋势，增速稳步攀升，就证明了这一点。虽然这两个国家 2007 年的国内消费加起来还不足美国的 1/6，但它们巨大的消费潜力是不容置疑的。特别是中国，其 2008 年的居民消费只占 GDP 的 36.1%，是东亚、东南亚和南亚的发展中国家中最低的，如果能够进行有效的政策调整，那么它的消费比重至少可以上升 10～20 个百分点。鉴于中国的经济总量仅排在美国和日本之后，已超过 4 万亿美元，这意味着中国每年新增消费需求相当于整个韩国的产值。印度的中产阶级队伍也在不断扩大。如果保持目前7%～8%的增速，据估计到 2025 年印度的中产阶级将从 2005 年的 5000 万扩大到 5 亿。[①] 增长过程中需要更多的投入品，而增长之后随着收入的提高，居民也会需要更多高质量的消费品。一个国家的进口边际倾向会随着收入的提高而

① World Bank, *India Economy Update 2010*.

提高，这已成为一个普遍的规律。如何能够让周边国家或经济体从中印两国的经济增长中获得更大的溢出效应呢？那就是通过更加开放和灵活的地区贸易和投资安排，为贸易和投资自由化、便利化构筑一个友好的制度空间。

亚洲的贸易安排多以双边和次区域为主，尚未形成如欧盟和北美自由贸易区一般的统一的大市场。据亚洲开发银行统计，在2010年亚洲的221个自由贸易协定（FTA）中，双边协定达到170个，多边协定为51个。扣除跨区域的129个FTA，那么区域内经济体之间的FTA有92个之多。这种“轮辐式”的贸易安排，对于谈判双方而言，因其简单而灵活更易于达成FTA。但对一国的企业而言，面对几十个，甚至几百个FTA安排，会因为规则的复杂性而导致熟悉规则、利用规则的成本上升，从而降低了它们利用FTA的积极性。另外，亚洲经济体之间的贸易安排多为小国主导，大国参与，类似于“小马拉大车”，如东盟10国加上中日韩（10+3），动力不足则是很自然的事。

截至2010年5月底，中国与亚洲经济体签订的自由贸易区协议包括内地与港澳更紧密经贸关系安排、中国—东盟、中国—巴基斯坦、中国—新西兰、中国—新加坡、亚太贸易协定①等已生效的FTA；此外，还包括中国—海合会、中国—澳大利亚等正在谈判中的自由贸易区；以及中国—印度、中国—日本、中国—韩国、中国—日本—韩国等4个正在进行可行性研究的自由贸易区。印度目前也正在与东盟展开自由贸易区的谈判。它已经与韩国、新加坡和泰国以及南亚的斯里兰卡等国分别签署了双边的FTA。

目前来看，中国—东盟自由贸易区是一个很好的尝试。自由贸易区对双方的经贸往来的促进作用主要体现在三个方面。一是自贸区建成后，中国和东盟国家90%的贸易产品将实现零关税，贸易成本大大降低，必将扩大东盟与中国的进出口规模。二是双向投资前景广阔，潜力巨大。自由贸易区建成后，中国和东盟国家的投资政策环境将更加规范和透明，区域内资源配置将进一步优化，企业可以获得更优惠的投资待遇。三是加快双方服务贸易的发展。自由贸易区建成后，中国和东盟国家将实质性地开放服务贸易市场，为其提供优惠的待遇和条件。

---

① 《亚太贸易协定》前身为《曼谷协定》。《曼谷协定》签订于1975年，是在联合国亚太经济社会委员会（简称亚太经社会）主持下，在发展中国家之间达成的一项优惠贸易安排，现有成员国为中国、孟加拉、印度、老挝、韩国和斯里兰卡。

智库峰会开辟“金砖四国”对话新渠道

周志伟*

2010年4月14～15日，巴西总统府战略事务部下属的应用经济研究所在巴西利亚召开了题为“后危机全球转型中‘金砖四国’的角色”的“金砖四国”智库峰会。中国、巴西、印度和俄罗斯四国与会学者就当前四国关注的重要议题交流了看法，为深化智库对话积累了丰富经验。主要观点如下。

“金砖四国”的国际地位提升迅速。四国学者普遍认为，美国的超级大国地位在长时期内仍将延续，但“多极化”已成世界格局的发展方向，金融危机则加速了该趋势的推进。随着经济活力的显现，“金砖四国”的国际地位提升迅速，其重要性已得到发达国家的认可。为推动国际新秩序的建立，四国有必要实现频繁互动与合作，以共同立场参与国际事务。巴西常务副外长帕特里奥塔认为，“金砖四国”的国际参与仍然不够。2011年，四国很可能同时出现在联合国安理会中，这有助于四国表达发展中国家的共同愿望。巴西战略事务部部长吉马良斯指出，“金砖四国”在国际秩序民主化中扮演着重要角色，新兴大国应加强团结，实现力量整合，谋求更大话语权，改变由少数大国主宰全球事务的局面。“金砖四国”拥有共同身份、共同需求和相似的利益诉求，深化四国互利合作不仅有利于各自的经济社会发展，而且有助于国际新秩序的建立。

“金砖四国”应积极参与全球治理。与会专家均认同“金砖四国”的国际地

* 周志伟，中国社会科学院拉丁美洲研究所副研究员。

位呈上升趋势，加强四国协调合作，提高新兴经济体在全球事务中的话语权是“金砖四国”参与全球治理的当务之急。但有的专家则认为，四国在全球事务上的作用存在较大差异：“中美共治”（G2）已成事实上的全球治理模式；巴西的诸多弱点限制其国际参与，它不仅难以成为南美的轴心，更不是全球性大国；由于经济脆弱性和软实力欠缺，俄罗斯在全球治理方面实际处于边缘化状态。甚至有专家指出，四国政治体制和民主制度的差异是制约四国合作的障碍，因此“金砖四国”机制化很难实现。有专家则指出，推动国际新秩序的建立是四国的重大利益汇合点，四国应该尽可能地求同存异，四国合作不应与政治和民主体制挂钩，四国应进一步深化战略共识，制订具体的共同行动计划，丰富四国对话交流渠道。

“金砖四国”应加强合作共同应对金融危机。参会学者充分阐述了金融危机的爆发原因、危机传播的渠道和主要经济体应对危机的措施，分析了“金砖四国”率先走出危机的原因所在，并对四国未来的经济走势作出了预测。有专家提出，虽然中、印、巴三国应对危机取得了不错的效果，但三国都面临经济过热和通胀压力增大等问题。四国在“退出战略”上应加强政策协调，确保各自外汇储备的安全。另外，也有学者认为，在全球经济再平衡和全球经济秩序重建过程中，四国应扩大合作并协调立场，以集体的形式参与谈判，谋求更大的话语权。

“金砖四国”应共促贸易发展。四国专家一致认为“金砖四国”的内部贸易已成为四国外贸的新增长点，其中，中印贸易的增速最为显著。关于如何进一步开发四国贸易潜力的问题，有专家强调政府参与对贸易促进的重要性，而扩大大宗产品贸易是提升四国贸易的有效途径。印度学者则指出，各国应努力开发对方市场的潜力，并协调在WTO农业谈判中的立场，促使发达国家开放市场。巴西学者认为，中巴贸易关系更像南北贸易关系。巴、印、俄三国对华贸易均面临出口产品单一的局面，三国应努力改变这种状况。俄罗斯学者则回应，双边贸易问题不应归咎于其中一方，而应由贸易双方共同解决。针对印度学者提出的“人民币汇率与贸易失衡存在因果关系”的提法，中国学者表示人民币汇率与贸易失衡不存在必然联系，中国坚持以市场供求为基础，有管理的浮动汇率制，汇率制度关系国家利益，汇率调整时间和调整幅度应视中国的宏观经济形势而定。

“金砖四国”将成为全球外国直接投资的重要来源。与会专家认为“金砖四国”对外国直接投资的吸引力体现在市场规模、劳动力成本、基础设施规划、货币贬值、经济发展预期、贸易开放等方面。其中，中国在经济结构转型和基础设施战略方面积累的经验值得三国借鉴。在对外投资方面，中国增速显著，其投资动因主要为企业国际化战略、企业提升国际竞争力的需要、服务宏观经济发展、经济结构转型（劳动密集型产业转至他国）、对能源和原材料的高需求。有专家指出，由于四国的经济高增速、经济规模的扩大、经济全球战略的实施、国际收支盈余增加等因素，“金砖四国”将成为全球外国直接投资的重要来源。为推动四国间相互投资的增长，专家建议四国应制定共同发展战略，完善投资政策协调机制、金融合作机制、投资促进机制，充分发挥政府的投资引导功能。

“金砖四国”应协调共同应对气候变化问题。四国专家都介绍了各国在应对气候变化方面所采取的政策行动，中国提高能效、推广清洁能源等政策受到其他三国专家的肯定。在气候谈判方面，多数专家主张四国应坚持“共同但有区别的责任”原则，发达国家应履行向发展中国家转移技术和资金的承诺。但有学者认为“金砖四国”在气候谈判中的角色存在区别，中国与美国、欧盟可称为“气候超级大国”，它们在气候问题上拥有“否决权”。印度、俄罗斯、巴西与日本、印度尼西亚、墨西哥、韩国和南非等国可称为“气候潜在大国”。为此，有专家提出四国应发挥更主动的角色，改变防御性的气候立场，而巴西的气候立场正发生这种转变，并要求其他新兴大国制定各自的减排目标。此外，有专家认为“金砖四国”应对气候变化的步调并不一致，巴西和中国较印度和俄罗斯更重视国际合作，中国的低碳技术进步领先于其他三国，中国的风能技术和巴西的生物能源技术具有一定的比较优势，四国在这些领域可实现优势互补。有个别专家则认为，目前尚不存在可行的共同行动方案，气候谈判仍处在各国讨价还价的阶段。

“金砖四国”应加强技术创新领域的合作。“金砖四国”在近几年都加大了技术创新的政策扶持力度，巴西和俄罗斯已经制定了技术创新法律法规，但四国均存在“重科学、轻技术”的问题。此外，在研发投入方面，中国具有与其他三国不同的特点：第一，中国的研发投入增速超过其他三国；第二，中国已进入企业研发为主导的阶段；第三，中国已探索出企业与大学的合作研究模式。在“后危机”时代，四国应加强在技术创新领域的经验互享，共同推动新的国际专利制度的建立。

智库交流是四国高层对话的重要补充，其重要性体现在以下两方面。首先，四国都存在对其他三国研究不够深入的问题，缺乏对其他三国相关战略构想的全局把握，智库对话为四国增进了解提供了平台，四国学者可通过这一平台表达各自的利益关切，并寻求四国的利益汇合点；其次，通过智库对话，四国学者可就相关议题展开专业研讨，为四国深化合作探索新思路，并保障四国合作的顺畅和效率。“金砖四国”之间的智库对话应长期化、机制化，充分发挥“二轨外交”对四国合作的积极推动作用。

中外媒体报道

“金砖四国”智库为深化四国合作献计献策

新华网巴西利亚2010年4月14日电（记者杨立民　毕玉明）在“金砖四国”领导人第二次正式会晤即将举行之际，由四国主要学术机构发起的首届“金砖四国”智库峰会14日在这里开幕。

这次会议的主题是“‘金砖四国’在后危机时期全球变革中的作用”。在为期两天的会议中，来自中国、巴西、俄罗斯和印度的专家学者和官员将就当前的世界经济形势和后危机时期四国面临的共同挑战和发展机遇进行交流，为各国政府拓展和深化四国之间的合作献计献策。

巴西应用经济研究所所长马尔西奥·波切曼在开幕式上说，四国在后危机时期既面临着严峻的挑战，也迎来难得的历史机遇。作为新兴大国，四国应该进一步开展建设性的对话，推动南南合作，维护发展中国家的权益，促进可持续性发展。为此，四国学术机构之间应该建立一个共同的工作日程，协助各国领导人制定长远的发展规划。

中国社会科学院副院长李扬表示，希望通过此次对话，增加四国智库学者之间的了解和互信，共同为四国在后危机时期的经济和社会持续与和谐发展、相互合作出谋划策，为全球经济的完全复苏贡献一份力量。

印度与俄罗斯的学者在开幕式的发言中也表示，“金砖四国”的学术机构应该积极发挥智库作用，为四国扩大合作，更好地应对后危机时期和全球化的挑战作出贡献。

根据会议日程，本届智库峰会将就“金砖四国”如何应对国际金融危机、国际贸易、全球气候挑战、外国直接投资、技术创新等议题进行深入探讨。

（来源：新华网，http：//news. xinhuanet. com/world/2010 －04/15/c_ 1233914. htm。）

李扬率学者代表团参加“金砖四国”智库峰会

周志伟

近日，中国社会科学院副院长李扬率领以中国社会科学院（以下简称中国社科院）学者为主的中国学者代表团受邀参加了在巴西举行的“金砖四国”智库峰会，此次峰会系“金砖四国”首脑峰会的“二轨”会议，其主题为“后危机全球转型中‘金砖四国’的角色”。

在“金砖四国”智库峰会开幕式上，李扬与巴西总统府战略事务部部长吉马良斯、巴西外交部常务副部长帕特里奥塔、巴西应用经济研究所所长波克曼、印度驻巴西大使普拉卡什、俄罗斯科学院拉美所所长达维多夫一道为峰会致辞。李扬在讲话中指出，“金砖四国”拥有共同身份、共同需求和相似的利益诉求，深化四国互利合作不仅有利于各自经济社会发展，而且有助于国际新秩序的建立。巴西总统府战略事务部部长吉马良斯指出，“金砖四国”在国际秩序民主化中扮演重要角色，新兴大国应加强团结，实现力量整合，谋求更大发言权，改变由少数大国主宰全球事务的局面。开幕式结束后，组委会特别安排了一个记者招待会，四国智库代表团团长共同回答了各国记者提出的有关“金砖四国”合作、金融危机未来走势、国际格局转型、国际储备货币改革等问题。

在峰会的专题讨论环节，中国社科院亚太所所长李向阳、中国社科院世经政所所长张宇燕、中国社科院俄罗斯东欧和中亚研究所所长吴恩远、中国国际问题研究所副所长刘友法、中国社科院拉美所所长郑秉文、上海国际问题研究院全球治理所副所长叶青分别就金融危机、国际贸易、气候变化、外国直接投资、技术创新、全球治理等专题作了发言并参加了讨论。通过与其他三国学者的直接交流，中方代表团与上述国家学术界在相关问题上达成共识，同时也为深化智库对话积累了丰富经验。

除参加“金砖四国”智库峰会外，李扬还率中国学者代表团部分学者专程拜访了巴西总统府战略事务部部长吉马良斯并举行了工作会谈，吉马良斯感谢中国社会科学院为推动中巴学术交流作出的贡献，并表示愿意将自己的著作《大国时代巴西的挑战》交付中国社会科学院拉美研究所巴西研究中心翻译并出版。中国学者代表团还访问了巴西劳工党圣保罗总部。劳工党向代表团详细介绍了巴西国内政治、经济现状以及该党对中国的政策并赠送了该党中文版党章，并宴请了代表团部分成员。另外，代表团还与里约热内卢天主教大学“金砖四国”研究中心举行了座谈，就“金砖四国”机制化和未来合作研究等问题坦诚交换了意见，双方都表达了进一步加强中巴智库学术交流的愿望。

“金砖四国”智库峰会的创意最初由中国社会科学院“金砖四国”课题组提出，其目的是为第二届“金砖四国”首脑峰会提出对策建议。为确定合适的巴西智库机构，拉美所所长郑秉文曾于2009年12月利用出访瑞典的机会转道巴西考察应用经济研究所和巴西国际关系研究中心，经过与其反复协商后，应用经济研究所表示愿意承办此次“金砖四国”智库峰会。

此次峰会由巴西总统府战略事务部下属的应用经济研究所主办，受邀参会的中、印、俄三国学者代表团人数分别为17人、6人和4人，参与的四国主要智库有中国社会科学院、中国当代世界研究中心、中国国际问题研究所、上海国际问题研究院、里约热内卢天主教大学、巴西利亚大学、巴西国际关系研究中心、拉美经委会、俄罗斯科学院、俄罗斯 Russkiy Mir 基金会、印度尼赫鲁大学、印度国际经济关系研究委员会、印度发展中国家资讯系统研究中心、印度观察家研究基金会、印度艾哈默德巴德管理学院等。

（来源：2010年5月20日《中国社会科学报》）

BRIC-Think Tank Summit Starts in Brasilia

April 15, 2010

The BRIC-Think Tank Summit started on Wednesday in the Brazilian capital Brasilia with a call for more cooperation among the participants of the group.

At the event's opening ceremony, representatives of the main research institutes of Brazil, Russia, India and China said that although trade among the four countries has improved significantly in the past few years, it can increase even more.

They said that the international financial crisis offered an opportunity for the BRIC countries to help build a more inclusive world, in which the needs of all countries are addressed. The representatives also stressed that the BRIC countries have managed to minimize the crisis' effects on their economies by applying stimulus plans.

"The proportion of BRIC economic aggregate in the global GDP increased from 13 percent in 2007 to 15 percent in 2009," said Li Yang, vice president of the Chinese Academy of Social Sciences. "What is most important is that the combined contribution of BRIC countries to the world economic growth exceeded 50 percent over the past five years."

Meanwhile, the representatives criticized the concentration of political, economic and military power in the hands of a few countries, and called for more participation of the BRIC members in the global governance organizations, in order to reflect the new multipolar reality of the world.

Secretary-general of Brazil's Ministry of Foreign Affairs Antonio Patriota also stressed that the BRIC countries won't ignore the needs of other countries in the world. He said that the BRIC countries will not repeat the mistakes of the past and will pay attention to the needs of the so-called "G172," or the countries that do not belong to the G20, as well.

Later in the day, the four countries' representatives will discuss the BRIC's role in the international financial crisis and their stance on the climate change issue. The BRIC-Think Tank Summit closes on Thursday, after discussions on foreign direct investment, technology and global governance organizations.

(*Source*: http: //news. xinhuanet. com/english2010/china/ 2010 -04/15/c_ 13251637. htm.)

BRIC countries' think tanks to strengthen cooperation

April 15, 2010

Major research institutions from the BRIC countries-Brazil, Russia, India and China-intend to tighten their cooperation to achieve joint views on issues of common interest and help the work of the BRIC governments, it was announced on Wednesday.

A two-day seminar gathering think tanks of the BRIC countries to examine the global economic situation and the role of those countries in the post-crisis global transformation, was opened in Brasilia on Wednesday morning, preceding the second BRICs summit scheduled for Friday in the Brazilian capital.

The most important aspects of the current relations between the four countries was presented in a press conference by Marcio Pochmann, from Brazil's Institute of Applied Economic Research (IPEA), Li Yang, vice-president of China Academy of Social Sciences, Indian Rathin Roy, from the United Nations Development Programme (UNDP), and Vladimir Davydov, from the Russian Academy of Sciences.

The objective of the seminar is to establish a working agenda between BRIC research institutions, and even play the role of being a supplement to the second summit, to define common tasks beyond the immediate interest of the heads of state, Pochmann said.

He stressed that these institutions could provide joint responses to errors in assessment, which happens frequently in international institutions, for example on the evolution of poverty rate in developing countries, because there is "no dialogue with researchers from the countries (themselves)."

Li Yang noted that China's intellectuals are a very important source for the government, which should be extended to the relationship between countries. "I think that an active and dynamic interaction between us would promote the formation of consensus among the heads of state. It is very important for us to have made contact with several research institutes in Brazil," he said.

Roy said that there is a long tradition of exchange between institutions of the four countries, while Davydov stressed the importance that policy is linked to the academic world to better adapt to the new historical realities.

Pochmann anticipated that the BRIC research institutions will organize this year a seminar on water resource management and environmental quality.

(*Source*: http://news.xinhuanet.com/english2010/china/2010-04/15/c_13251653.htm.)

Para pesquisadores, Bric deve discutir moeda

15 de Abril, 2010

Brasil, Rússia, China e índia devem coordenar-se para influir no modelo para o sistema financeiro internacional que emergirá da crise mundial, defenderam, ontem, dirigentes de alguns dos principais centros de estudo desses países, em seminário que antecedeu o início da cúpula de chefes de Estado dos chamados Bric, que começa hoje em Brasília. Os pesquisadores também defenderam as discussões entre os governantes para a criação de mecanismos monetários que dispensem o uso do dólar nas transações internacionais e preparem para uma eventual substituição da moeda americana como referência internacional.

"Não pensamos que o sistema monetário dominado pelo dólar seja moldado no futuro próximo, mas iniciativas como diversificação das reservas internacionais podem coexistir com esse regime", comentou o vice-presidente da Academia de Ciências da China, Li Yang, que defendeu, porém, a construção gradual de alternativas ao dólar. "Não acreditamos em alterações significativas agora. Observamos com interesse acordos de comércio com trocas diretas de moedas locais."

"Estamos num processo de rearticulação do sistema político econômico internacional, e, nesse processo ou as regras continuarão a privilegiar alguns países ou teremos uma situação de acordo com a dimensão de nossas sociedades", disse o ministro de Assuntos Estratégicos, Samuel Pinheiro Guimarães, defendendo aliança entre os Bric para influir nas novas regras financeiras internacionais.

No discurso mais enfático do seminário, Pinheiro Guimarães acusou os países desenvolvidos de pressionarem para evitar a emergência de novos atores nas esferas mundiais de decisão. "A crise ambiental passa pelas fontes renováveis de energia, pela energia nuclear, e precisamos saber que controlará o processo nuclear", disse. "No fundo há uma disputa tecnológica e científica entre países", disse. "Isso está em foco: saber se algumas nações continuarão a se achar superiores, e, portanto, com mais direitos, ou não", insistiu, reivindicando apoio para a reforma do Conselho de Segurança da ONU, onde índia e Brasil ambicionam um assento permanente.

Li Yang previu que mudar o sistema monetário mundial será "árduo e de longo prazo" e sugeriu maior cooperação em termos de administração de reservas internacionais, diversificando o uso de moedas. O diretor do Instituto de América Latina da Academia de Ciências da Rússia, Vladimir Davidov, previu a criação de alternativas "por regiões geográficas", como a criação de um Fundo Monetário Europeu, à parte do Fundo Monetário Internacional (FMI).

Intelectuais dos quatro países concordaram que será necessário cooperar para garantir a reforma do FMI e das regras que regem as finanças. Reconheceram, porém, que apesar do grande aumento na presença desses países no cenário internacional, eles são incapazes de compensar, com investimentos e importações, o peso do declínio americano na economia mundial.

O título do seminário, "Cúpula Bric de Think Tanks" era um atestado da resistência dos conceitos anglo-saxões nas relações entre os Bric - uma sigla, aliás, criada por um economista de financeira sediada nos EUA. Na entrevista que se seguiu às apresentações, nas quais inglês e português foram alternados como língua oficial, a falta de uma língua comum aos participantes teve um exemplo prosaico, quando o pesquisador da China teve de usar dois tradutores, um que vertia suas respostas para o inglês e outro que as traduzia do inglês ao português.

As propostas para as diversas discussões internacionais também têm pontos de conflito, como reconheceram os debatedores (a Rússia, por exemplo, está satisfeita com o peso que tem no FMI; o Brasil, não). Mas, como explicou o presidente do

Instituto de Pesquisa Econômica Aplicada (Ipea), Márcio Pochmann, que preparou o seminário, com a Academia de Ciências da China, a primeira reunião de centros de estudos dos quatro paises abre possibilidade de pesquisas conjuntas, com pontos de vista mais úteis para a tomada de decisão dos chefes de Estado. "Precisamos ver a nós mesmos com nossos próprios olhos", definiu Pinheiro Guimarães.

Como mostrou o diretor do Instituto de Estudos da ásia e Pacífico, Li Xiangyang, pelo menos um ponto aproxima os quatro países e os diferencia das nações desenvolvidas: enquanto Europa, Japão e Estados Unidos ainda se debatem com as consequências da crise financeira, o problema, nos Bric é evitar superaquecimento da economia, entrada de capital especulativo e pressões inflacionárias.

"A cooperação entre nós pode nos trazer benefícios mútuos", defendeu Li Yang. "O atual sistema monetário internacional é desfavorável aos países em desenvolvimento", comentou Li, defendendo mudanças na estrutura do FMI. Foi apoiado por Pochmann, que defendeu uma aliança entre os Bric para "um novo padrço de consumo e produção" e a formação de um sistema monetário que não se baseie na moeda de um só país.

(*Fonte*: http://www.sae.gov.br/site/?p=3242.)

Ipea discute papel do Bric depois da crise econômica mundial

O Instituto de Pesquisa Econômica Aplicada (Ipea) realiza hoje (14) e amanhã em Brasília a Cúpula Bric: O Papel do Bric após a Crise Econômica. O encontro começa às 8h30 no Hotel Mercure. O Bric é o grupo que inclui o Brasil, a Rússia, a índia e a China.

O encontro reúne representantes dos governos e pesquisadores de centros de estudos dos quatro países. Logo após a abertura, haverá entrevista coletiva com o presidente do Ipea, Marcio Pochmann, e representantes dos demais países. às 10h, a coordenadora de Estudos de Relações Econômicas Internacionais do Ipea, Luciana Acioly, apresenta o comunicado Rússia, índia e China: Comércio Exterior e Investimento Direto Externo.

O estudo apresenta os diferenciais de cada país do Bric no comércio internacional, seus pontos fortes e desafios. Durante os dois dias da Cúpula, será discutido o novo papel desses países no cenário mundial, com destaque para os impactos da crise financeira internacional, a dinamica do comércio exterior, a mudança climática global e o papel dos investimentos estrangeiros diretos, entre outros.

Participam da solenidade de abertura o ministro-chefe da Secretaria de Assuntos Estratégicos, Samuel Pinheiro Guimarães, o secretário-geral do Ministério das Relações Exteriores, Antônio Patriota, o diretor do Centro Internacional de Políticas para o Crescimento Inclusivo, Rathin Roy, o vice-presidente da Academia Chinesa de Ciências Sociais, Li Yang, e os embaixadores da índia, B. S. Prakash, da China, Qiu Xiaoqi, e da Rússia, Sergey Pogosovich Akopov.

(*Fonte*: http: //www. ipea. gov. br/003/0030/009. jsp?u CD_ CHAVE = 14076.)

后记

2009 年 6 月 30 日，在中国社会科学院常务副院长王伟光教授主持召开的国际学部管理体制机制改革汇报会上，我代表拉美所提出设立跨所际的“‘金砖四国’智库峰会国际网络”项目的建议，旨在为即将召开的第二届“金砖四国”领导人峰会做些政策研究。伟光副院长当即表示支持，不久，科研局便批准立项并拨付启动经费。事后，院国际合作局时任局长杨扬先生多次召集中国社会科学院世界经济与政治所所长张宇燕研究员、俄罗斯东欧中亚研究所所长吴恩远研究员、亚洲太平洋研究所所长李向阳研究员和拉美所所长郑秉文研究员参加协调会，协商相关筹备事宜；在巴西驻华大使胡格内先生的支持下，我作为该项目的协调人于 2009 年 12 月专程赴巴西，拜见巴西的国际关系研究中心主任冈萨尔维斯大使和应用经济研究所所长波克曼先生，商谈将于 2010 年 4 月在巴西召开“金砖四国”领导人峰会前夕举行首次“‘金砖四国’智库峰会”的事宜。虽然是第一次见面，但波克曼先生欣然同意承担起会议东道主的责任和义务，负责主持召开首次“‘金砖四国’智库峰会”。

此后，经过几个月紧锣密鼓的筹备工作，在外交部的指导下和中联部的协调组织下，由中国社会科学院副院长李扬研究员为团长和中联部国际交流中心主任王华先生为秘书长，由中国社会科学院、中联部、外交部国际问题研究所和上海国际问题研究院的专家学者组成的中方代表团一行 17 人，终于启程奔赴巴西利亚，参加了 2010 年 4 月 14 ~ 15 日由巴西总统府战略事务部下属的应用经济研究所主持召开的“后危机全球转型中‘金砖四国’的角色”的“‘金砖四国’智库峰会”。俄罗斯科学院拉美所和经济所、印度观察基金会派出十几位专家学者参加了会议。

会上，中国社会科学院李扬副院长做了主题发言，中方代表团的专家学者与其他三国学者就一些重要议题交流了看法，明晰了四国学术界在相关问题上的共识与分歧。在巴西会议期间，中方代表团还拜见了时任巴西战略事务部部长吉马良斯先生和其他相关学术科研机构。

中国社会科学院李扬副院长十分重视此次会议的成果和“金砖四国”的研究工作的可持续性，指示将会议论文结集出版。于是，便有了这本文集。

作为该项目的协调人，我在这里十分感谢上述有关部门和各位领导的支持，十分感谢拉美所巴西研究中心主任、前驻巴西大使陈笃庆先生，还要感谢拉美所副所长吴白乙研究员、杨西副研究员和周志伟副研究员等同事的支持，感谢社会科学文献出版社的支持。特别要感谢的是人民日报社驻巴西分社社长兼首席记者吴志华先生，没有他的无私帮助，此次国际会议的诸多联络工作是不能如此顺利的。此外，还要感谢俄罗斯东欧中亚研究所的冯育民处长和亚洲太平洋研究所的叶海林研究员等同志作出的贡献。

这本文集的出版标志着该项目画上了一个句号。作为研究“金砖四国”的一段历史，对首次“‘金砖四国’智库峰会”的来龙去脉做个记述，是撰写这个后记的初衷，其目的也是为了使对“金砖四国”的研究在中国能够持续和深入地开展下去。

中国社会科学院拉丁美洲研究所　郑秉文

2011 年 2 月 17 日

图书在版编目（CIP）数据

"金砖四国"与国际转型：BRICs 智库巴西峰会的思考/李扬主编．—北京：社会科学文献出版社，2011.4

ISBN 978-7-5097-2191-9

Ⅰ.①金…　Ⅱ.①李…　Ⅲ.①世界经济-文集　Ⅳ.①F113-53

中国版本图书馆 CIP 数据核字（2011）第 034552 号

"金砖四国"与国际转型

——BRICs 智库巴西峰会的思考

主　　编／李　扬

出 版 人／谢寿光
总 编 辑／邹东涛
出 版 者／社会科学文献出版社
地　　址／北京市西城区北三环中路甲 29 号院 3 号楼华龙大厦
邮政编码／100029
网　　址／http://www.ssap.com.cn
网站支持／（010）59367077
责任部门／编译中心（010）59367139
电子信箱／bianyibu@ssap.cn
项目经理／祝得彬
责任编辑／李　博　段其刚
责任校对／高忠磊
责任印制／董　然

总 经 销／社会科学文献出版社发行部
（010）59367081　59367089
经　　销／各地书店
读者服务／读者服务中心（010）59367028
排　　版／北京中文天地文化艺术有限公司
印　　刷／北京季蜂印刷有限公司

开　　本／787mm×1092mm　1/16
印　　张／30.5　字数／601 千字
版　　次／2011 年 4 月第 1 版　印次／2011 年 4 月第 1 次印刷

书　　号／ISBN 978-7-5097-2191-9
定　　价／80.00 元